Dr Alan Garnham
Experimental Psychology
University of Sussex
Brighton
BN1 9QG

CW01072622

The Crosslinguistic Study of Sentence Processing

The Crosslinguistic Study of Sentence Processing

Edited by

BRIAN MACWHINNEY
Carnegie Mellon University

and

ELIZABETH BATES
University of California, San Diego

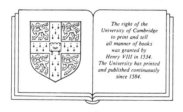

The right of the
University of Cambridge
to print and sell
all manner of books
was granted by
Henry VIII in 1534.
The University has printed
and published continuously
since 1584.

CAMBRIDGE UNIVERSITY PRESS

Cambridge
New York   Port Chester   Melbourne   Sydney

Published by the Press Syndicate of the University of Cambridge
The Pitt Building, Trumpington Street, Cambridge CB2 1RP
40 West 20th Street, New York, NY 10011, USA
10 Stamford Road, Oakleigh, Melbourne 3166, Australia

© Cambridge University Press 1989

First published 1989

Printed in the United States of America

Library of Congress Cataloging-in-Publication Data
The Crosslinguistic Study of Sentence Processing.
Includes index.
ISBN 0-521-26196-1

British Library Cataloguing in Publication Data
The Crosslinguistic study of sentence processing.
1. Languages. Sentences. Psycholinguistic aspects.
I. MacWhinney, Brian.   II. Bates, Elizabeth.
401'.9

ISBN 0-521-26196-1 hard covers

Contents

Foreword

Dan I. Slobin

This book takes us on a tour through a remarkable and exotic garden that has flowered from the seeds of a few simple sentences that were planted in the pages of the *Journal of Verbal Learning and Verbal Behavior* a quarter century ago. Because I tended and bred some of the early plants, and tried them out in foreign gardens, I have been kindly invited to say a few words at the beginning of the tour.

In 1962, Roger Brown, along with Colin Fraser and Ursula Bellugi, developed a new research method to study parents' age-old intuition that little children can understand more than they can say (Fraser, Bellugi, & Brown, 1963). Three-year-olds were shown pairs of pictures with minimal contrasts in order to test their control of ten different grammatical forms in English. The test included pairs of pictures contrasting only in direction of action, such as "a woman kissing a man" and "a man kissing a woman," in order to test imitation, comprehension, and production of simple active and passive sentences. For example, to test comprehension, the child was asked to point to the picture showing "The mommy kisses the daddy" / "The daddy kisses the mommy" or "The daddy is kissed by the mommy" / "The mommy is kissed by the daddy." This early study was not directly concerned with grammar, but rather with the relations between imitation, comprehension, and production. However, the investigators noted in passing that some of their children confidently pointed to the wrong picture when asked to comprehend passive sentences, apparently treating them as if they were subject-verb-object sentences "with odd appurtenances" on the verb. Fraser et al. were intrigued by this serendipitous finding, and suggested that it could lead to the development of a new research tool:

Processing the sentence in this way would enable [the child] to maintain the generality of the usual rule of English word order in which the subject precedes the object. With the Subject/Object contrast in the passive voice we turned up a revealing pattern of evidence by accident. If an investigator wanted to use the ... procedures to test hypotheses about particular aspects of grammatical operation, he could easily design problems that would be revealing by intention. (p. 133)

Roger Brown was kind enough to lend me these pictures for use in my dissertation research (Slobin, 1963, 1966), in which I was concerned with children's reaction times in verifying active and passive sentences. Noting that all of Brown's pictures were "reversible," since either noun could be construed as agent or patient of the action, I added a set of "nonreversible" pictures in which "a girl watered flowers," "a man ate a watermelon," and so on. This design allowed for anomalous NVN sequences, such as "The flowers watered the girl" and "The man was eaten by the watermelon." The seeds of the Bates and MacWhinney "Competition Model" had been planted, since it was now possible to pit "the usual rule of English word order" against the cues of passive verb morphology and the semantics of animate and inanimate nouns. It turned out that response time was slowed more for reversible than for nonreversible passives, suggesting that both syntax and semantics play a role in on-line sentence processing. My interest, however, was not in "competition," but "coalition." I suggested that correct assignment of agent-patient roles could be facilitated by semantic plausibility – or, to be more modern, that both lexical and morphosyntactic factors had to be considered simultaneously.

Later in the sixties, Tom Bever (1970) extended this technique to an acting-out task in which children were given small dolls and toys and were asked to show such actions as "The mother pats the dog" and "The dog pats the mother." Here there is a competition between word order and semantic plausibility (though not reversibility). Testing this out, Bever found that word order "won out in the competition" for 2-year-olds. (That is, children had the dog pat the mother in response to the second sentence.) With regard to reversible passives, he – like Fraser et al. – found a stage during which children tended to choose the first noun as actor. Bever introduced the influential notion of "strategy," proposing, in this instance:

Any *Noun-Verb-Noun* (NVN) sequence within a potential internal unit in the surface structure corresponds to *actor-action-object*. (p. 298)

He noted that, at some point in development, this strategy could be overriden by "specific semantic information." Bever suggested several strategies, again proposing a "coalition" model:

I have presented the strategies of segmentation, semantic labeling, and sequential labeling separately for purposes of exposition. It is obvious that the operation of one of the strategies can simultaneously aid the operation of another strategy. In actual perception the strategies combine simultaneously to isolate potential internal *actor-action-object... modifier* sentence units and to assign correctly the functional relations within those units. (pp. 301–2)

In the seventies, Bever and I and our co-workers extended this research design crosslinguistically, comparing children's sentence comprehension in English, Italian, Serbo-Croatian, and Turkish (Slobin, 1982; Slobin & Bever, 1982). We limited ourselves to simple, active sentences that were semantically reversible, since we wanted to focus on differences between word-order and inflectional cues in different types of languages. Again, we had the seed of a competition model, but we did not treat it as such. We found that inflectional cues (case marking on nouns) guided correct comprehension in Turkish at a younger age than word-order cues in English and Italian, and that Serbo-Croatian-speaking children at first required a coalition of word order and inflection for correct acting out of model sentences. We did note, however, that when word order and inflection were in competition in Serbo-Croatian (first noun marked as accusative), younger children tended to follow word order.

The rest of the story lies before you in the following pages, skillfully summarized in the editors' Preface. In a long series of studies, in a wide range of languages, Bates and MacWhinney have studied the competitive interaction of a number of cues to sentence interpretation: word order, inflection, animacy, stress, topicalization. They and their co-authors have developed a model that applies to child language acquisition, adult sentence processing, aphasia, second-language acquisition, and computer simulation. The seeds of the simple English sentence have blossomed into an exotic garden, including strange "semi-grammatical" plants and foreign flowers. The mapping of linguistic cues to categories of meaning has been systematized into an important set of six parameters: frequency, detectability, availability, reliability, conflict validity, and processability. The research program is flourishing, and promises to go far beyond the confines of this first overview. Many problems remain, of course. But we now know more about the assignment of actor-patient relations in simple sentences than we have ever known, and we have a model that is ready to face the challenges of more complex syntactic and semantic problems. The editors state that the Competition Model has no competitors. This collection certainly brings it into the marketplace!

Preface

Psycholinguistics is the study of human linguistic performance. A good psycholinguistic theory ought to account for many different aspects of natural language use, including comprehension and production of meaningful speech, first language acquisition, second language acquisition, the deterioration of language under pathological conditions, normal speech errors, error monitoring, and judgments of well-formedness. While accounting for this dazzling range of performance phenomena, a good psycholinguistic theory must also be so general that it will work equally well for any natural language. If the theory can explain facts about English but cannot account for sentence processing in Italian, Hungarian, or Warlpiri, then the theory ought to be rejected out of hand.

Thanks to pioneering research by Dan Slobin and his colleagues (Slobin, 1985), students of child language have come to terms with this crosslinguistic challenge. There are now published studies of language acquisition in several dozen languages and there are at least 12 languages that have been studied in some depth. Although there are some common themes in all these studies, the developmental variability evident across natural languages is impressive. Whether they consider themselves nativists, empiricists, Piagetians, Vygotskians, or Chomskians, few developmental psycholinguists are now willing to make sweeping generalizations about the Language Acquisition Device solely on the basis of evidence from English children. Unfortunately, a similar positive attitude toward the use of crosslinguistic data has not yet developed in areas of sentence processing that form the core of psycholinguistic theory and research. In this book, we seek to broaden the scope of psycholinguistics by drawing attention to the relevance of crosslinguistic data to the study of sentence processing.

In order to deepen the role of crosslinguistic data in psycholinguistics, we need to look both at the ways in which languages differ and the ways in which they are the same. Language differences are easy to illustrate. In English, a motorist may ask for directions to the park and one would tell him "You turn right after the school." In a morpheme by morpheme gloss, the Hungarian sentence for saying the same thing would be "Right-to turn-you the school after." If we were to look at how the same idea is expressed in Navajo, Spanish, or Tagalog we would find still further differences in word order and grammatical markings.

Where do these differences come from? Is one form of expression more natural than the other? Are there some forms of expression that are not used by any human language?

Language differences are most theoretically interesting when considered against the backdrop of crosslinguistic similarities. Functional linguists have found that, underlying between-language differences, there are a core set of communicative functions expressed in all languages. These functions include the roles of verb arguments, the identity of pronominalized or missing nominals, the antecedents of anaphoric references, and the relations between main and subordinate clauses. All languages assign a major role to these functions. However, languages differ greatly in regard to their construction of devices to mark these functions and the ways in which functions are mapped to devices. This is because, typically, a single linguistics device can express many different functions and a single function can be expressed by many different devices. So there is almost never a one-to-one mapping of devices to functions.

Linguists such as Joseph Greenberg, John Hawkins, Talmy Givón, and Joan Bybee and their colleagues have discovered many universal constraints on the shape of the phonology, morphology, syntax, and semantics of natural language. Some of these universals appear absolute. For instance, Behaghel's Law states that items that belong together mentally are grouped together syntactically. A consequence of this law is that universally articles are placed next to their nouns, so that no language can express an idea like "the boys like their dogs" with a sentence like "boys like their dogs the." Behaghel's Law appears to hold for all languages and does not depend on the presence of particular features. Other universals are implicational or conditional in nature. For example, Greenberg noted that, if a language has Subject–Object–Verb order in main clauses, statistically, it is also likely to use postpositions rather than prepositions and place adjectives after nouns, rather than before them.

The same sensitivity to typological insights that we find in child language research and functional linguistics is rarely evident in studies of language processing by adults. Current textbooks in psycholinguistics are filled with statements about "the speaker" and "the listener," followed by a description of some aspect of linguistic performance in an English-language experiment. This behavior then serves as the basis for broad generalizations about the Human Language Processor: the number and variety of modules contained therein, real-time constraints on the actions and interactions among component parts, and so on. Although we do find cautionary notes about the artificiality of psycholinguistic experiments, and the problem of generalizing from the laboratory to real life, we rarely find evidence of concern about the validity of generalizing from English to the other 1000+ languages that are subserved by the same Human Language Processor. Instead, we have forced the 19-year-old monolingual English-speaking college student to stand for the whole of mankind, carrying a White Man's Burden that was laid aside long ago in the other social sciences.

Like many of our collaborators in this volume, we entered into crosslinguistic research with adults from a developmental perspective. The techniques that we first selected were geared to work with very small children. They involved acting out simple sentences with animals and objects, and describing simple black and white pictures of concrete objects, actions, and events. But we made a critical detour in this developmental work that has taken us far afield; we added a group of adult controls in each of our target languages, and discovered that adult linguistic performance differed so radically from one language to another that it merited at least as much attention as we had devoted to children up to that point.

The research that followed challenged some widespread assumptions about sentence processing in the mature speaker/listener. For example, like many of our English-speaking colleagues, we had assumed that adults would always rely more on grammatical information than on event knowledge or lexical semantics in interpreting sentences like "The pencil kicks the cow." In fact, English adults confirmed these expectations in our first experiments by relying almost entirely on word order information to interpret simple sentences, even when word order and world knowledge were in conflict. But Italian adults – including sophisticated and literate adults with many years of university education – handled the linguistic problem that we had posed in a completely different way. Given the Italian equivalent of "The pencil kicks the cow," they pick the cow as the aggressor. In other words, when Italian adults are faced with a conflict between word order and semantics, semantic factors carry the day.

As we will outline in much more detail below, these crosslinguistic differences make perfect sense when we consider differences between English and Italian in the linguistic input that adults must interpret in everyday, informal situations. Even though Italian is not a case-inflected language (i.e., it has no markers on the noun phrase to tell the listener who did what to whom), it still permits a great deal of word order variation for pragmatic purposes. Italians can actually say things like "The spaghetti ate Giovanni" without invoking images of carnivorous pasta. As a result, word order is simply not a very trustworthy cue to meaning in Italian. Experiments in other languages have yielded similar results: the order of major constituents is often only a minor cue to basic sentence relations.

This point became clearer still when we began to manipulate other kinds of grammatical cues. For example, given a sentence like "The cow are kicking the pencils," our Italian subjects do not hesitate at all in assigning the actor role to a pair of inanimate objects. Given a conflict between word order and grammatical morphology, word order loses the "within grammar" struggle just as decisively as it lost the battle with lexical semantics and world knowledge. In the same situation, English subjects slavishly follow the dictates of Subject–Verb–Object ordering, ignoring Subject–Verb agreement (if they noticed it at all). Over the years, our own experiments and those of our international collaborators have shown that the Human Language Processor can be tuned in a variety of different ways. We have also found that the English pattern, with its heavy reliance on positional facts, represents an extreme that is unmatched in any other Indo-European or non-Indo-European language that we have studied to date. Think of the implications: 98% of the sentence processing studies in the literature to date have been carried out in an exotic language!

Leaving aside for the moment the appropriateness or inappropriateness of generalizations based on English, it did seem clear that our little experimental situation had produced a fact about processing with considerable potential for generalization across languages and across methodologies. Sentence processing in adults is attuned to meet the ecological demands of the speaker's native language. Speakers attend to and make use of cues to meaning according to their information value or cue validity.

This single insight has led us to the Competition Model, a detailed but flexible model of human language processing that can handle crosslinguistic differences in sentence comprehension and sentence production, in first and second language acquisition, in the study of language breakdown in aphasia, and (more recently) in on-line studies of word recognition and sentence interpretation in context. In its current form, the Competition Model reflects fourteen years of collaborative research in more than a dozen languages (including English, Italian, Spanish, French, German, Dutch and Serbo-Croatian as well as non-Indo-European languages like Hungarian, Turkish, Japanese, Chinese, Hebrew, and Warlpiri). Eleven of the papers in this volume represent explicit applications of the model; the other two by Sridhar and by Klein and Perdue were invited because the authors share our commitment to crosslinguistic research, within a coherent theoretical framework that is quite compatible with ours. As a result, this volume is considerably more than a collection of papers on sentence processing in different languages. It also represents the first comprehensive attempt to model linguistic performance across structurally and functionally different language types.

We begin the volume with an overview of the Competition Model. This overview outlines the model, discusses certain aspects of the model that have been difficult to understand, and then reviews the crosslinguistic evidence supporting the major claims of the model. Section I which follows presents four chapters on sentence comprehension, each illustrating some advantages of the model and some problems that it still has to face. These include a summary of research in French and Spanish by Kail, a survey of studies in Hungarian by Pléh, studies of sentence interpretation in Hebrew by Sokolov, and a paper by Bavin and Shopen on sentence interpretation by child and adult speakers of Warlpiri.

Section II contains two chapters on sentence production. First, Sridhar summarizes results from a massive crosslinguistic project initially undertaken in the 1970's by Charles Osgood. After this, Bates and Devescovi describe some applications of the Competition Model to aspects of sentence production in English and Italian.

Section III includes three chapters on "special" populations. Kilborn and Ito summarize a lengthy series of studies within the Competition Model on sentence comprehension in bilinguals. Klein and Perdue discuss sentence production and the problem of "inter-language" during second language acquisition by adults. Bates and Wulfeck summarize results to date from their crosslinguistic aphasia project, with an emphasis on lexical access within the Competition Model and the problem of "morphological vulnerability."

Finally, Section IV presents some new directions in the formalization of our processing model. McDonald provides a detailed exposition of the concept of cue validity, the major principle of the Competition Model and the source of our most important predictions for processing differences across languages. She shows how estimates of cue validity can be derived from texts and applied to data on first and second language acquisition in English, German, and Dutch. Next, McDonald and MacWhinney describe the application of maximum likelihood procedures to quantify complex profiles of performance in sentence interpretation. She shows how we can formalize our intuitions about the relative "distance" between two languages, and quantify in a precise way the degree to which a given group or individual deviates from ideal performance in a first or second language, during language acquisition and/or during language loss. In the final chapter, MacWhinney examines links between the Competition Model and the theory of Parallel Distributed Processing (PDP). He presents a series of PDP simulations of the acquisition of declension in German that illustrate basic principles of the Competition Model. He then presents the outline of a PDP-based account for the whole of language acquisition.

We are proud of the work described in this volume, but we are also aware of its limitations. Because time and energy are finite resources, we have had to make choices between depth and breadth. In contrast with the wide array of methods that have been applied in studies of English, our crosslinguistic database currently reflects the application of only two or three basic techniques, applied to only a subset of the structures and functions that characterize all natural languages. Our sampling of languages has been determined more by the availability of talented collaborators than by proper typological sampling techniques. Much more needs to be done before anyone can lay claim to a "universal" psycholinguistic theory. For example, a host of ingenious "on-line" techniques are now available to study the temporal microstructure of language processing, permitting us to ask many more detailed questions about cross-linguistic variation. We are also sorely in need of much more comprehensive studies of production, with an emphasis on the statistical as well as the structural properties of language use among adults and the language directed to children. In short, we have only scratched the surface. Nevertheless, we think that the chapters in this volume demonstrate the power and the importance of crosslinguistic research, encouraging investigators outside of the English-language academe to exploit the special properties of their own language and to challenge our thinking about the nature of the Human Language Processor.

Brian MacWhinney and Elizabeth Bates

Contributors

Elizabeth Bates
Department of Psychology
University of California
La Jolla, CA 92093, USA

Edith Bavin
Department of Linguistics
La Trobe University
Bundoora, Victoria 3083, Australia

Antonella Devescovi
CNR/Psicologia
Viale Marx, 15
Rome 00156, Italy

Takehiko Ito
Department of Educational Psychology
Tohoku University, Japan

Michèle Kail
CNRS Laboratoire de Psychologie Experimentale
28 rue Serpente
75006 Paris, France

Kerry Kilborn
Max-Planck-Institut für Psycholinguistik
Wundtlaan 1
Nijmegen, The Netherlands

Wolfgang Klein
Max-Planck-Institut für Psycholinguistik
Wundtlaan 1
Nijmegen, The Netherlands

Brian MacWhinney
Department of Psychology
Carnegie Mellon University
Pittsburgh, PA 15213, USA

Janet McDonald
Department of Psychology
Louisiana State University
Baton Rouge, LA 70803, USA

Csaba Pléh
Department of General Psychology
Loránd Eotvös University
P. O. Box 4
1378 Budapest, Hungary

Clive Perdue
Max-Planck-Institut für Psycholinguistik
Wundtlaan 1
Nijmegen, The Netherlands

Tim Shopen
Department of Linguistics
Australian National University
Canberra ACT 2600, Australia

Dan I. Slobin
Department of Psychology
University of California
Berkeley, CA 94720, USA

Jeffrey L. Sokolov
Department of Psychology
Carnegie Mellon University
Pittsburgh, PA 15213, USA

S. N. Sridhar
Department of Linguistics
SUNY Stony Brook
Stony Brook, NY 11794, USA

Beverly Wulfeck
Department of Pediatrics
University of California
La Jolla, CA 92093, USA

Introduction

1   Functionalism and the Competition Model

Elizabeth Bates and Brian MacWhinney

The Competition Model is a framework for the crosslinguistic study of language use. It is designed to capture facts about the comprehension, production, and acquisition of language by real human beings, across a variety of qualitatively and quantitatively distinct language types. Our own work on the Competition Model has been illuminated by the insights of a particular class of linguistic theories called "functional grammar." But the goals of linguistic and psycholinguistic research are often different, revolving around the now-classic distinction between competence and performance. Competence refers to the abstract knowledge of language possessed by an ideal speaker-listener, removed from the constraints and inconveniences of real-time language use. Performance refers to the actual process of language use by real people in real situations. As many linguists and psycholinguists have noted, there is no necessary and direct relation between competence and performance models (Fodor, Bever, & Garrett, 1974; cf. Bresnan, 1978). In principle, a given performance model may be compatible with a variety of competence models, and a given competence model may be compatible with many different characterizations of performance. The success of a performance model must be evaluated in its own terms. Can it predict when a speaker will use one form of expression and not another? Can it account for the use that listeners make of linguistic devices in comprehension? Can it account for the order of acquisition of grammatical devices in children? Can it relate language use to general aspects of human cognition and still account for specifically linguistic aspects of processing? Finally, and perhaps most importantly, can this model account for processing and acquisition in any given language no matter how much the structure of that language differs from that of English?

The particular performance model that we will offer here has grown out of a tradition in linguistics and psycholinguistics called functionalism. Linguistic functionalism is different in many ways from the functionalism of behaviorist psychology, and it is almost entirely in opposition intellectually to the functionalism of philosophy. Perhaps its closest relatives in other disciplines are in the "constructivism" of mathematics and psychology. Linguistic functionalism can be defined as the belief that "the forms of natural languages are created, governed, constrained, acquired and used in the service of communicative functions" (Bates & MacWhinney, 1982; MacWhinney, Bates, & Kliegl, 1984).

3

This approach is the natural alternative to theories of language that postulate a severe separation between structure and function, and/or theories that attempt to describe and explain structural facts *sui generis*, without reference to the constraints on form that are imposed by the goals of communication and the capabilities and limitations of human information processing.

A variety of competence models have been proposed within the functionalist tradition, including Eastern European functionalism (Dezső, 1972; Driven & Fried, 1987; Firbas, 1964, 1966; Firth, 1951; Mathesius, 1939), British functionalism (Halliday, 1966, 1967, 1968), generative semantics (Chafe, 1971; Fillmore, 1968), discourse analysis (Chafe, 1981; Givón, 1984; Li, 1975, 1976, 1977; Hopper & Thompson, 1980, 1984), Cognitive Grammar (Langacker, 1987; Lakoff, 1987), Construction Grammar (Fillmore, 1987), Role and Reference Grammar (Foley & Van Valin, 1984), and functionalist explanations couched within the formalisms of "standard theory" (Kuno, 1986). For the sake of simplicity, we will refer to these otherwise rather disparate linguistic approaches with the single term "functional grammar."

Although functional grammars are not designed to account for real-time processing, they are most compatible with highly interactive models of performance, that is, models in which different sources of information are integrated on equal footing, as rapidly as possible. They are less compatible with models of performance in which different linguistic data types (phonological, morphological, syntactic, semantic) are subserved by distinct and encapsulated processors that communicate only after they have completed their domain-specific analyses. Such "modular" approaches to performance are more compatible with "modular" theories of competence, that is, linguistic theories that emphasize the autonomy of various components and subcomponents of the grammar (cf. Berwick & Weinberg, 1984; Bresnan, 1982; Pinker, 1984).

The Competition Model is more compatible with functional/cognitive grammars. However, we have found over the years that functionalism means different things to different people. Much of this confusion arises from the different ways in which the term "functionalism" is used by philosophers, psychologists, and linguists. To dispel some of this confusion, we think that it would be useful to spell out in detail the particular functionalist assumptions that have motivated our work – with special emphasis on the role of processing constraints, and on the quantitative principles that separate our approach from many other functionalist theories. Then we will provide a more precise account of the model itself, together with some illustrations of the data that support our current claims.

What Is Functionalism?

The term "functionalism" appears repeatedly in Western intellectual history, but its uses from one field to another are often so divergent that it is difficult to find a single unifying theme. In philosophy, we find the term used to refer to a position which attempts to separate the form of human thought from the neuronal hardware. This brand of functionalism views concepts in terms of mathematical functions which, once defined, can be related to one another in terms of their pure conceptual form. This form of analysis can be used to defend the relevance of Artificial Intelligence to Cognitive Science. According to this viewpoint, although the hardware of a digital computer is quite different from that of the brain, the functions it computes can be combined into systems that may well operate in ways that are quite analogous (Pylyshyn, 1984). This type of philosophical functionalism goes directly against many of the assumptions of the Competition Model. When we characterize our position as "functionalist," we are certainly not thinking about this type of functionalism.

The term "functionalism" was also used to describe schools of empiricist psychology that were prominent in the first part of this century. Positivists like Dewey and Tolman and behaviorists like Skinner and Watson were all characterized as functionalists. Here the term "function" is being used to refer not to mathematical functions, but to the activities of the organism. These functionalists looked at ways in which the organism "functions" within either a real environment or a laboratory environment. The Competition Model also looks closely at relations between the environment and the functioning of the organism, but we are not using the word "function" in this way. Rather, we are using the word "function" to refer to "purpose" or "goal." When we view language as a functional system, we are not simply saying that it is a system of activities. Rather we are saying that it is a goal-directed system of activities. There is really no sharp line between these two senses of "function." Accordingly, our approach attempts to provide a unification of both the positivist emphasis on cue validity (Brunswik, 1956) and the cognitivist emphasis on goals and plans (Newell & Simon, 1972).

Within linguistics and psycholinguistics, both of these last two types of "functionalism" are clearly opposed to the doctrine of Chomskian generative grammar. Chomsky (1957) argues forcefully against attempts to relate sentence structure to aspects of the environment, and Chomsky (1975) argues for a kind of autonomy of syntax that would cut it off from the pressures of communicative functions. In the Chomskian vision, language is pure and autonomous, unconstrained and unshaped by purpose or function. Although the Competition Model does not posit the simple sorts of relations between communicative function and language proposed by Skinner (1957), neither does it accept the total divorce of language from communicative function embodied in Chomskian linguistics. Instead, it considers the relation between language form and language function as the major empirical phenomenon to be characterized by psycholinguistic theory.

Four major themes unify the particular functionalist approach to language that we will follow here: (1) cognition as the basis for language universals, (2) grammars as solutions to the mapping problem, (3) biology as providing the roots of function, and (4) quantitative analyses as ways of understanding qualitative variation. Let us first examine these four themes, and then move on to consider different levels and types of functional claims in linguistics and psycholinguistics.

Cognition, Language Universals, and Linguistic Relativism

We assume that the human biological apparatus is a constant across cultures. All normal adults have essentially the same apparatus for perception, articulation, learning, and memory, and we share a common set of social concerns. Human cognition and emotion provide the basic meanings and communicative intentions that any natural language must encode, together with a universal set of processing constraints that sharply delimit the way that meanings and intentions can be mapped onto a real-time stream of gestures and/or sounds. In other words, language universals derive from universal properties of the human mind.

The claim that there are cognitive universals underlying linguistic form does not mean that all human beings think alike. First, there are individual differences in the development of this basic apparatus; these differences exist within cultures, rather than across cultures. Second, cultures vary widely and the beliefs and practices of individuals vary accordingly. Culture-specific information is invariably reflected in the language spoken within a given community, and the rapid changes in culture arising from migration, cultural contact, or social change often result in rapid changes in vocabulary, idiomatic expressions, and sometimes even in changes in the more conservative morphosyntactic elements of the language. Nevertheless, there are certain basic categories of perception and thought that all natural languages must deal with at every point in their history: principles of motion, space and time, and principles of human action and intention. All natural languages have had to evolve some means of encoding distinctions among objects, qualities and events, modes of organizing events in time and space, human attitudes about those objects and events, and human attitudes toward one another. They have also necessarily evolved ways of encoding functions inherent in the communication process itself, that is, the identification of referents, the establishment of a given referent as a discourse topic, the process of making points or comments about particular topics, mechanisms for shifting and/or subordinating topics, and devices that help to create cohesion across the discourse as a whole. Every language is under constant pressure to develop and maintain ways of expressing these cognitive and communicative universals. It is not our goal in this paper to provide a complete account of those cognitive universals that are expressed in language. However, some useful accounts of parts of the universal system of cognitive representations are provided by Langacker (1987), Miller and Johnson-Laird (1976), Jackendoff (1983), Herskovits (1986), and Talmy (1977). Overviews of the universal perceptual-motor apparatus are given by Ladefoged (1980), Lenneberg (1967), and Lieberman (1975).

Note that we have stressed the roles of both cognitive content and cognitive processes in determining the possible forms that a language can take. This focus on process is crucial to our argument. Grammar is not a simple reflection of meaning. Content alone is not sufficient to explain why languages look the way they do, and the exigencies of real-time processing can ultimately result in forms that look relatively opaque (i.e., forms that have no obvious meaning or communicative goal). This, we think, is one of the major sources of misunderstanding in our field. A strong proponent of the autonomous grammar approach once asked us, "If you are right in your belief in the functional determination of grammar, why don't all natural languages look alike?" Other critics have, in all sincerity, accused us of not believing in grammar at all! Of course we believe in grammar, and in grammatical diversity. Indeed, we think that attention to grammatical diversity is long overdue in psycholinguistics. We are not trying to replace grammar with cognition; but we are trying to explain grammar in cognitive terms. We are convinced that Universal Grammar can ultimately be explained without recourse to a special "language organ" that takes up where cognition leaves off. Human cognition is the wellspring of language universals, setting limits on the form that any natural language can and must take. These are the same phenomena that some linguists have called "Universal Grammar," or UG. Certainly, a functionalist account will differ in detail from theories that are divorced from function, but the basic subject matter is the same: the universal properties of human language. Hopefully, this view will emerge more clearly as we elaborate on the interplay between content and form.

Nativists are not the only opponents of a functionalist approach to grammar. At the opposite empiricist extreme, we find followers of the Sapir-Whorf hypothesis (Bloom, 1981; Sapir, 1921; Whorf, 1967) who are willing to accept a strong form of linguistic relativism that questions the experiential basis of even the most fundamental segmentations of reality by the human mind. Whorfians argue that, insofar as languages can vary radically in their structure, human thought can also vary markedly. For these scholars, there are no "universal" principles of cognition or perception; rather, the categories of thought derive from the categories of language itself. Unlike the Chomskians, Whorfians recognize the importance of the relation between language form and language function. However, they see form as the determiner of function. For this reason, Whorfianism is often called "linguistic determinism." The Competition Model only rejects the most extreme forms of linguistic determinism. These extreme forms deny the possibility of universals of cognitive and communicative functioning. In our opinion, evidence for such universals is so overwhelming that the strongest forms of linguistic determinism cannot be accepted. Moreover, experimental tests of strong linguistic determinism have never been successful (Osgood & Sebeok, 1965).

Weaker forms of linguistic determinism, such as those discussed in Osgood and Sebeok (1965) or Bowerman (1985), are compatible with the Competition Model. As we will see later, the Competition Model assumes a mix of form-driven and function-driven learning. Linguistic forms are themselves a part of the world within which the organism functions and to which it must adapt. Forms may orient the organism to encode relations between cues that it already perceives. Forms may even induce the organism to piece together new concepts from universal primitives. However, it is unlikely that linguistic forms actually induce the learner to form new cognitive primitives. Cognitive primitives are too important to the organism to be left to the whims of social convention.

Grammars as Solutions to the Mapping Problem

Grammars can be viewed as a class of solutions to the problem of mapping nonlinear meanings onto a highly constrained linear medium whose only devices are word order, lexical marking, and suprasegmentals. The universal and culture-specific contents of cognition interact with universal constraints on human information processing, creating a complex multivectorial problem space (Bates & MacWhinney, 1982; Karmiloff-Smith, 1984). In fact, there may be no perfect and stable pathway through this problem space. As Slobin (1982) has pointed out, many processing constraints are in direct competition; hence stability in one area may create instability in another. The situation can be compared to the eternal competition for funds between federal agencies and programs. The charge to spend money for "guns" is in constant competition with the charge to spend money for "butter." Every fiscal budget is a compromise between these two charges and every new attempt to hammer out a budget requires a new resolution of these competing forces. Within language, the charge to be "quick and easy" is invariably opposed to the charge to be "clear." From the listener's point of view, a given linguistic marker will signal its meaning most efficiently if it is consistent, salient, and unique. For the listener, homonymy is a barrier to understanding and any deletion of phonological content can damage comprehension. The more detail the speaker provides, the easier the listener's job. From the speaker's point of view, homonymy facilitates retrieval and phonological weakenings and deletions cut down on articulatory effort. Composing utterances to meet the listener's needs requires both cognitive and articulatory effort. Hence, the clear and perceivable markers that evolve for comprehension are often subject to erosion in the service of rapid and efficient speech output.

There is a constant interplay between the forces of language erosion and language creation. Often a new marker will begin as a preposition or post-position. Over time, it will start to function as a prefix or a suffix and begin to undergo phonological erosion or leveling. At the same time, it may undergo functional reinterpretation (MacWhinney, in press; this volume). For example, the Hungarian accusative suffix developed out of a postposed element marking definiteness. As this element became identified with the marking of the role of the noun, a new way of marking definiteness emerged, this time as a preposed article. If a given marker were to express one and only one meaning, reinterpretations of this sort would be more puzzling. Why give up a marker of definiteness only to create another? But a central claim in the Competition Model is that forms often express a variety of correlated functions. This "peaceful coexistence" of functions helps both the listener and the hearer by allowing a small set of structures and markers to serve a myriad of related purposes. This then serves to build in a certain adaptive instability into language, since any particular coalition of meanings may eventually collapse and require reinterpretation. Grammars are thus viewed as a set of partial solutions to the mapping problem, each representing one pathway through the constraints imposed by cognitive content and cognitive processing. No solution is perfect, and each one is constantly subject to change; but every grammar used by a community of human adults and acquired by their children has to meet certain implicit but implacable limits of tolerance.

This last point is eloquently illustrated by the inventions and adjustments that take place during creolization, the process by which a pidgin code formerly used only by traders suddenly has to serve as a full-fledged native language for a community of users. As Bickerton (1984), Sankoff (1980), and other Creole scholars have shown, pidgin codes subjected to the pressures of full language use evolve within one generation the grammatical forms that are needed to express complex ideas within a cohesive oral narrative. A similar process has been observed in the acquisition of American Sign Language by deaf native speakers. Deaf children often receive their sign language input in a grammatically incomplete form – either from hearing teachers who acquired the language in adulthood, or from deaf parents who also acquired ASL late in life. Newport and Meier (1985) have shown how deaf children systematize this impoverished input, regularizing certain principles and extending others to cover new cases. Goldin-Meadow (1982) has studied the most extreme case of this type where deaf children with hearing parents create a small pidgin gestural system in order to express their most basic communicative intentions. Two or three generations of this process are apparently sufficient to turn an unsystematic gestural system into a full-fledged human language.

For Creole scholars like Bickerton (1984), the rapid and predictable course of creolization can only be explained with recourse to an innate and domain-specific "language bioprogram," much like the universal grammar envisioned by Chomsky (1965) and Lightfoot (1982). We would argue, instead, that creolization (and related diachronic phenomena) reflect formal constraints that inhere in the mapping problem itself. Consider the forces that operate to create a soap bubble: the sphere that forms is the inevitable result of an attempt to simultaneously attain maximum volume with minimum surface area. Similarly, universal aspects of human grammar may emerge inevitably whenever universal categories of thought have to be mapped efficiently onto a limited channel.

Functionalism and Biology

All this is not to say that the Competition Model denies the importance of biology. Indeed, there has been a great deal of misunderstanding on this particular point. We think that much of this misunderstanding comes from a failure to distinguish between innateness and domain-specificity. The innateness issue has to do with the extent to which human language is determined by the unique biological heritage of our species. But this biological heritage may include many capacities that are not unique to language itself: our large and facile brain, our particular social organization, our protracted infancy, and a variety of unknown factors that may contribute in indirect but very important ways to the problem of mapping universal meanings onto a limited channel, and to the particular solutions that we have found to that problem. Hence, the human capacity for language could be both innate and species-specific, and yet involve no mechanisms that evolved specifically and uniquely for language itself. Language could be viewed as a new machine constructed entirely out of old parts (Bates, 1979).

Piaget made this critique of Chomsky's linguistic nativism in 1958 (Piaget, 1970) and the force of his criticism has not been diminished by the years. At issue is the difference between innateness and inevitability. Outcomes that are inevitable on structural grounds do not have to be innate. Indeed, an outcome that is insured by problem-solving constraints may be much more robust across a range of situations than an outcome based entirely on direct genetic guidance. In an edited volume documenting an historic encounter between Piaget and Chomsky (Piaget, Chomsky, & Piatelli-Palmarini, 1980), we find Piaget criticized as an "antibiological behaviorist." Our own position has been misunderstood in the same way. In this light, we would like to state as explicitly as possible that we view grammar as a biological system. However, the universal properties of grammar are only indirectly innate, being based on interactions among innate categories and processes that are not specific to language. In other words, we believe in the innateness of language, but we are skeptical about the degree of domain-specificity that is required to account for the structure and acquisition of natural languages.

Qualitative and Quantitative Variation

Like other biological systems, natural languages display a great deal of in-traspecies variation. Although the constraints imposed by the mapping problem are heavy, and the class of possible solutions is finite, the number and range of language types that are possible seems to be quite extensive. Languages differ qualitatively, in the presence or absence of certain linguistic devices (e.g., word order constraints, case marking), but they also differ quantitatively, in the extent to which the "same" linguistic device is used at all and in the range of functional roles that the "same" linguistic device has come to serve.

We will give a number of examples of quantitative differences between languages throughout this volume. One particularly important example has to do with the relative strength of word order versus subject-verb agreement as cues to sentence meaning. In English, word order is a strict and highly valid cue to sentence interpretation and that order is usually Subject–Verb–Object or SVO. In Italian, on the other hand, word order can be varied extensively for pragmatic purposes. This is illustrated in the following imaginary restaurant dialogue taken from Bates, MacWhinney, and Smith (1983):

1. SVO: *Io mangerei un primo.* (I would eat a first course.)
2. OSV: *La pastasciutta Franco la prende sempre qui.* (Pasta Franco it orders always here.)
3. VSO: *Allora, mangio anche io la pastasciutta.* (Well then, am eating also I pasta.)
4. VOS: *Ha consigliato la lasagna qui Franco, no?* (Has recommended the lasagna here Franco, no?)
5. OVS: *No, la lasagna l'ha consigliata Elizabeth.* (No, the lasagna it has recommended Elizabeth.)
6. SOV: *Allora, io gli spaghetti prendo.* (In that case, I the spaghetti am having.)

This short and realistic conversation contains all possible orders of Subject, Verb, and Object. Some of these require particular intonation patterns to sound exactly right, and some are definitely better with particular grammatical markers like the object clitic. But all these orders can be found in a large enough sample of free speech, and all of them occur at some point in the input received by Italian children (Bates, 1976).

At one level, the sentences given above simply serve to illustrate well-known qualitative differences between languages: Italian has word order options that do not exist in English at all. However, this qualitative variation also has quantitative implications. We have demonstrated in several different experiments that Italian listeners "trust" word order – even good old-fashioned Subject–Verb–Object order – less than their English counterparts. Given a sentence like "The pencil hits the cow," English listeners from ages 2 to 80 have a strong tendency to pick the pencil as the agent/subject. Given the Italian equivalent *La matita colpisce la vacca*, Italians are much more likely to choose the cow as the agent/subject. Hence a qualitative difference in the availability of word order types has a quantitative effect even on that subset of grammatical structures that both languages share (e.g., SVO order).

This point is made clearer still by observing the reaction of subjects to a semigrammatical sentence like "The cow are hitting the horses." English listeners do not like this sentence very much, but in a forced choice situation they overwhelmingly choose the cow as the subject of the verb. In other words, they "distrust" morphological cues to meaning, preferring to rely on word order instead. Speakers of richly inflected languages with variable word order like Italian or Hungarian do not behave this way at all; they "trust" their morphological cues, and rapidly choose the plural noun as the subject of a plural verb regardless of constituent order.

This division between inflected and uninflected languages is useful but it is still too discrete to account for the variation that we have observed to date. Instead, there are degrees of "word order dependence" or "morphological dependence." For example, German seems to stand somewhere in between the Italian and English extremes described above: There is more reliance on grammatical morphology than in English, but more reliance on word order than in other richly inflected languages (MacWhinney, Bates, & Kliegl, 1984). Results from Chinese are particularly interesting in this regard (Kilborn & Ito, this volume). Mandarin Chinese has very little inflectional morphology, and no morphemes at all to indicate agent/object relations. Nevertheless, when lexical semantics and word order are placed in competition, native speakers of Chinese base their interpretations on lexical rather than syntactic cues. As we shall see in several chapters to follow, these differences of degree are principled, reliable and predictable. They follow from statistical as well as structural facts in the languages studied to date. For example, the weak word order effects in Chinese sentence comprehension make sense in light of (1) the frequency with which the subject is omitted in Chinese (reducing the utility of preverbal position as a cue to meaning) and (2) the availability of certain marked and noncanonical word orders in both formal and informal speech.

Most of the examples presented in this book come from studies of sentence comprehension. But we have also uncovered some interesting quantitative differences in the domain of sentence production. For example, Bates and Devescovi (this volume) have described some robust differences between Italian and English in the use of relative clauses. The structural options available in the two languages are the same, at least for the set of structures studied by these investigators. In both languages, it is perfectly grammatical to describe a picture of a monkey eating a banana by saying either "A monkey is eating a banana" or "There is a monkey that is eating a banana." English speakers typically use the first option. By contrast, Italian speakers describing exactly the same pictures, under the same conditions, are three to five times more likely to produce a relative clause. This crosslinguistic difference in relative clause use is already well-established in children by the age of three, and it tends to persist even in elderly patients who have suffered left-hemisphere damage. How can we capture a quantitative difference between two structures that are equally grammatical from a traditional grammatical perspective? To be sure, there are some differences between the two languages in the range of functions that control these particular forms. In particular, Italians appear to use the relative clause as a kind of topic marker. But in addition to (and perhaps because of) these differences in function, there are also clear processing differences between English and Italian in the "accessibility" of the relative clause. Function and frequency codetermine the selection of grammatical forms in sentence production (together with a number of other processing factors like recency and point of commitment – see Bates & Devescovi, this volume, for details).

Our emphasis on quantitative variation is probably the greatest point of divergence between the Competition Model and other functionalist theories. With some exceptions, functional grammars tend to state the relationship between form and meaning in terms that are both direct and discrete: "Use structure X if and only if semantic factors Y and pragmatic conditions Z are met." From this point of view, human language use should be perfectly predictable from meaning. Imperfect, probabilistic mappings between form and function would then reflect a failure on the part of the linguist (or psycholinguist) to provide an adequate account of the rich array of contextual factors governing the formal device in question. It is important, of course, to dig as deeply as possible into the contextual motivation underlying the use of forms. Work by Gee and Savisir (1985) indicates how much we can sharpen our understanding of the use of linguistic devices by a sensitive study of the context of their uses. However, such studies focus on qualitative aspects of language functioning, seldom recognizing the fundamentally probabilistic nature of language processing.

The emphasis in the Competition Model on probabilistic rules does not mean that we ignore the powerful laws that separate one language from another. After all, the values "0" and "1" do exist even in a probabilistic system, and an adult native speaker may come to know with some certainty that a particular structure is impossible in his or her language. The difference between our characterization of adult knowledge (i.e. "competence to perform") and the characterizations offered in most competence models lies in our ability to capture the many values that fall between 0 and 1. We describe linguistic representations in terms of a complex set of weighted form–function mappings, a dynamic knowledge base that is constantly subject to change.

This quantitative approach has a number of advantages in the description of a language at a particular point in time (i.e., synchronics); but perhaps more importantly, quantitative description makes it easier to explain linguistic change (i.e., diachronics). In the evolution of a single language from one synchronic type to another, in the acquisition of language by children, and in the loss of language by individuals or by whole communities, we need an appropriate means for characterizing what it means to be "in between" structures. A theory phrased entirely in terms of discrete, qualitative rules cannot serve this purpose – whether or not those rules make reference to cognitive content.

There are at least two traditions within functionalist linguistics that do deal directly with quantitative facts about language use. The first is laid out most explicitly by Givón (1979, 1984), although it can also be found in work by Keenan and Comrie (1977), Kuno (1986), Hopper and Thompson (1980), and many others. Givón's approach to quantification is different from the one adopted here, in that it rests on ordinal rather than interval scales. He describes "clines" or "dimensions" of topicality, foregroundedness, and other communicative functions along which different linguistic forms can be ordered. On the foregroundedness cline, explicit noun phrases are higher in foregroundedness than pronouns, pronouns are higher than zero anaphors, and so on. Many of the ordinal claims that result from this kind of scaling have been verified in detailed text analyses in a variety of structurally distinct language types. However, this approach makes no predictions about the distance between different steps on the foregroundedness scale (or any other functional cline). In the terms of measurement theory, clines make predictions only about ordinal relations on scales. We believe it is now possible to go further by specifying precise degrees of correlation between forms and functions. That is, we can now work with interval, rather than ordinal, scales.

An attempt at interval scaling can be found within the variable rule school of sociolinguistics led by Labov. As elaborated in Sankoff (1978), variable rule theory represents an effort to state directly in the grammar the probability that a given rule will apply within a particular social context. Researchers working with variable rule theory have described in detail the statistical variation that can be observed in a large number of linguistic forms, ranging from *tu* and *vous* in French Canadian to /s/-deletion in Puerto Rican Spanish. These alternations are not random; they cannot be explained by attaching a coin-flipper to a discrete rule. Rather, the observed alternations are quite lawful and are conditioned by a variety of factors in the phonological, syntactic, and discourse context of the alternation. Labov has explained these statistical regularities with a device called a "variable rule," that is, a rule with an explicitly stated weight or probability on its application.

Labov's use of variable rules to estimate parameter strengths is in the best tradition of mathematical psychology. Sankoff's log-linear instantiations of those models are close mathematical cousins of the maximum likelihood models used by psychologists such as Anderson (1982) and Massaro (1987) to study information integration, an approach which in turn serves as the basis of our most recent work in statistical modeling (McDonald, this volume). The cognitive assumptions underlying variable rule theory are quite familiar to psychologists, since so much of psychological theory is stated in terms of activation and strength. Like Labov, psychologists generally believe that it is possible to build a precise theory of imprecise phenomena. Statistical regularities and lawful gradations must be described and explained. They are part of the native speaker's knowledge of his/her language, and they are an important source of information (not just an unfortunate form of noise) for the language learner. Physicists have lived with the fundamental indeterminism of physical reality for most of this century. Perhaps it is high time that linguists and psycholinguists follow suit. Along these lines, the Competition Model can be viewed as the psycholinguistic analog to quantum theory in physics.

Levels of Evidence for Functionalism

Different kinds of functionalist claims require different kinds of evidence. This is a point that we have made in several places (Bates & MacWhinney, 1982; Bates, MacWhinney, & Smith, 1983; Bates & MacWhinney, 1987), but it is sufficiently important that we think it deserves reiterating here. We distinguish four different levels of functionalist claims, ordered from weakest to strongest (in the sense that claims at the higher levels presuppose that claims at the lower levels are true). Level 1 focuses on the role of cognitive and communicative functions in the evolution of language proper, and in the history of individual languages. Claims at this diachronic level need not (as we shall see) have implications for current language use by adults, language acquisition by children, or the proper characterization of grammatical knowledge. Level 2 is a synchronic variant of Level 1, focusing on the causal relationship between form and function in real-time language use by adult speakers of the language. Level 3 presupposes, but also goes beyond Level 2, focusing on the causal role of cognitive and communicative functions in language acquisition by children. Finally, Level 4 is reserved for the claim that facts from Levels 1 through 3 play a direct role in the characterization of adult linguistic competence. The Competition Model includes claims at Levels 1 through 3; functional grammars reside at Level 4. Let us examine these four levels one at a time, in order to clarify exactly what kinds of claims are involved in the Competition Model. This will hopefully help the reader to evaluate the relationship between theory and evidence in the chapters that follow.

Level 1 – Language History

Claims at Level 1 constitute a kind of linguistic historical evolutionism, which holds that functional constraints have played a role in determining the forms that grammars take today. Where did the tiger get his stripes? Why do giraffes have long necks? Why do grammars have relative clause markers? A great deal of work in functionalist linguistics focuses on the possible functional origins of grammatical structures during language evolution. For example, Givón, Sankoff, and others discuss the development of relativization structures from deictic elements. Many writers discuss how agreement marking on the verb arises from the fusion of pronominal elements to the verbal stem. Givón (1984) and Bybee (1985) discuss the development of aspectual markings and tense markings from general verbs such as "have," "go," and "be" that become coopted into particular grammatical functions. Grammaticalization is the process by which relatively transparent lexical combinations become conventionalized into grammatical morphemes; in the course of this process, through use with a larger and larger array of lexical items, the original meaning of the proto-morpheme may become "bleached."

Historical functionalism is the weakest kind of functional claim, because it carries no necessary consequences for the psychological relationship between form and function in a living native speaker today. Evolution is littered with examples of vestigial forms, structures, and behaviors that were selected at one point to serve a function that is no longer relevant. For example, humans still have wisdom teeth, an appendix, and the Babinski reflex, although none of these structures serve the purposes for which they originally developed. Because we are no longer toothless by the age of 20, wisdom teeth no longer serve the function of providing us with replacements for lost teeth; the appendix no longer serves as a digestive organ, although it may now play a role in the immune system; and the Babinski reflex is no longer needed to prepare us for falling out of trees, since we no longer live in trees. It is both logically and biologically possible that pieces of grammar also have achieved a certain functional autonomy (i.e., vestigiality) in present-day language use. However, we suspect that vestigial forms are relatively rare in language, because there are too many competing pressures on real-time language processing to permit waste. As soon as forms start to seem vestigial, the frugal aspects of the human mind begin to subject them to reinterpretation (MacWhinney, in press). To justify this claim, we need to spend some time carefully analyzing the different kinds of causal relationships that can exist between cognitive functions and grammatical forms.

Icon, Index, and Symbol

Peirce (1932) has offered a taxonomy of sign–meaning relations that is useful in characterizing cause-and-effect relationships at Level 1. According to Peirce, a sign or signal can come to stand for its referent in one of three ways: iconic, indexical, and symbolic determinism. If any of these three relations holds, then there is a functional relationship between the sign and its referent. Some researchers (e.g., Petitto, 1987) seem to equate functionalism with iconicity, believing that evidence against iconicity constitutes evidence against functionalism. This is not true, since a sign is functional whenever any of these three relations hold.

Iconic Determinism.   Iconicity refers to a literal physical resemblance between a sign and its meaning. A picture of a house looks like a house; the line drawing of a man or a woman on a restroom door tell us which sex may use the facilities; a picture of a cow at a cattle crossing warns drivers to slow down because a large animal may be crossing the road. Although the idea of iconicity is an appealing one, in reality most iconic signs bear only a partial, often minimal, resemblance to their referents – a fact that becomes clear to the traveler in Europe struggling to decipher international highway signs and symbols next to hotel listings in the Michelin guide. Hieroglyphic writing systems have an iconic base, but the physical resemblance between sign and referent is usually evident only after the learner has been told the meaning ("Oh yeah, I guess that does look sort of like a house...."). There is good reason to believe that iconic relations are rare and evanescent in the evolution of language. In the lexicon of spoken languages, we find identifiable iconic relations in only a handful of onomatopoaeic expressions like "sneeze" and "bang." At the sentence level, it is even harder to find transparent examples of an iconic relationship between meaning and form. One possible candidate is the relationship between degrees of pragmatic emphasis and degrees of phonological contrastive stress (Bolinger, 1986). However, a close analysis shows that contrastive stress also interacts with canonical word order and a host of other grammatical conventions that bear no one-to-one, isomorphic relation to meaning.

The minor role of iconicity in language evolution is particularly clear in studies of sign languages (Klima & Bellugi, 1979; Newport & Meier, 1985). For example, Hoffmeister (1978) has shown that, despite the transparent iconicity of the signs for locative relations like "in," "on," and "under," deaf children make the same kinds of mistakes displayed by hearing children (e.g., they tend to place objects in boxes and on tables, regardless of the language input, evidently relying more on their knowledge of canonical events than the relationship expressed in the language). And Meier (1987) has shown that verb agreement in ASL is determined by morphological rather than iconic factors. The minimal contribution of iconicity to language acquisition and language use has occasionally been cited as evidence against a functional approach to grammar (e.g., Petitto, 1987). However, we think this conclusion is unwarranted, because there are still two viable routes for functional determination of form: symbolic and indexical determinism.

Symbolic Determinism.   There are many areas where a weaker form of functional determination holds: symbolic determinism. In Peirce's terminology, a symbol is a sign that comes to stand for its referent simply because a community of users has agreed to use the sign in this way. There is no "natural," discoverable link between a symbolic sign and its referent, and if the community of users that established such conventions should disappear without a trace, the probability that another community would assign the same sign to the same meaning is astronomically small. In other words, symbolic signs are completely arbitrary. Symbolic determinism appears to be the predominant form of sign–meaning relationship within the lexicons of spoken languages, and it operates within the grammar as well (Langacker, 1987).

But notice that what is arbitrary in a symbolic relation is only the specific choice of a sign to go with a referent. The basic decision to choose a sign to express a particular referent is not arbitrary at all. Rather, it is governed by the pressure of fundamental communicative functions. For example, the Italian language needed some kind of symbol to fill out the conditional paradigm, expressing the counterfactual status of a third person plural verb. Could a language get by without such verb markers? Yes. Chinese has no explicit verb morphemes to convey counterfactual reasoning – a fact that has misled some Western researchers into believing that the Chinese cannot think in counterfactual terms (Bloom, 1981). However, as Au (1983, 1984) has shown, Chinese does make use of lexical markers to indicate the same meanings that are conveyed by modal verbs in English, and by conditional suffixes in Italian. When those markers are removed (as in Bloom's experiments), Chinese subjects do indeed fail to demonstrate counterfactual reasoning. But when Au provided her Chinese subjects with the appropriate lexical cues, they performed just like English subjects on counterfactual conditionals; conversely, when Au removed the counterfactual markers in her English materials, English subjects performed just like the Chinese in Bloom's experiments. We accept Au's conclusion that the concept of underlying counterfactuality is a cognitive/communicative universal. Every natural language will evolve some means of expressing this idea, but the particular means selected to carry out this work may vary markedly from one language to another.

Symbolic determinism is, then, a form of functional causation. Grammatical symbols can carry out communicative work without bearing a literal physical resemblance to their associated meanings or functions. Sometimes the functional base of a grammatical symbol may be difficult to discern (more on this below), but the lack of an iconic relationship between form and function does not mean that no relationship exists at all. This is particularly true when we recall that grammatical devices can evolve in the service of cognitive processing as well as cognitive content. For example, gender markers in German bear only the most indirect and infelicitous relationship to sex. There is no obvious semantic basis for classifying "little girl" as neuter, "sun" as feminine, and "moon" as masculine. And yet, gender markers may be crucial in helping the listener to keep track of referents across a complex passage of discourse (see Kilborn, 1987, for a demonstration of the role of German morphological markers in lexical recognition). Tags of some kind are needed to do the necessary communicative work; it is not obvious why gender was borrowed for that purpose in the first place, but if gender were not available then some other distinction would have to be drafted into service.

Indexical Determinism. The third kind of sign–referent relation in Peirce's taxonomy is the most subtle and the most difficult to explain. And yet we think that this form of determinism may play a particularly important role in the evolution of grammar. An index is a sign that comes to stand for its referent not because of physical resemblance, nor because of an arbitrary decision by a community of users, but because the sign participates in some natural and discoverable way with the event or object that it represents. Thunder is an index for a coming storm; smoke is an index for fire; the sound of footsteps in the brush is an index of coming danger for small forest animals. Like icons, but unlike symbols, indices bear a natural relationship to their referents. However, the "natural" relationship between an index and its referent must be discovered. The relation between an icon and its referent is so transparent that no real process of discovery is required. The relation between a symbol and its referent is so arbitrary that there is no preset relation ready to be discovered. Only in the case of the index can we say that there is a preset relation that must be discovered through learning and exploration. We must learn that lightning precedes thunder. Once we have learned and elaborated the connections between these phenomena, the relation then seems natural. However, if we are not aware of the natural link that binds sign and referent together, the relation may seem quite opaque. For a new learner, it may be impossible to distinguish between indices and true symbols (i.e., the arbitrary sign–referent bonds discussed above). Hence, an index may be learned by rote (see Bates, 1979, for a further discussion of this point).

Many so-called iconic signs are actually indices, or at least, mixtures of iconic and indexical relations. Consider, for example, the use of footprints as a clue to the presence of a large animal. The footprint bears an iconic relationship to the animal's foot; however, the foot itself stands in a part–whole relationship to the animal we are looking for. This part–whole or participatory relationship is in fact an index. Hence the chain of meaning that lies behind the use of a footprint as a signal is a mixture of iconic and indexical relations.

Some more interesting and illuminating examples of mixed sign relations come from American Sign Language. For example, the ASL sign for "nurse" is a cross signed on the upper arm. This sign does not look like a nurse at all. But it does look like the red cross on a nurse's sleeve, an entity which in turn forms a part of (i.e., participates in) the complex of features that make up our concept of nurses as a class. There is also a sense in which this mixed iconic/indexical relation is quite arbitrary (i.e., symbolic). Why choose the red cross on the sleeve, and not some other part of the nurse-concept, as the part that will be chosen to stand for the whole? In fact, some signed languages form their signs by choosing an altogether different bit of a complex meaning to serve as the basis for an iconic/indexical sign (e.g., a nurse's cap). There is, then, a certain degree of arbitrariness in the particular choice of parts to stand for a whole – a kind of sign relationship called "metonymy."

The possible role of indexical determinism in signed languages is clear. But what possible role could this kind of causation play in a spoken language? Silverstein (1976a) has argued that much of language is indexical in nature, and that indices are the basis and indeed the definition of that aspect of language called "pragmatics." The paradigm case of indexicality in language can be found in pronouns and other forms of deictic reference. The pronoun "it" can take on meaning only via its relation to the context in which it is uttered: in the nonverbal context (so-called exophoric reference), in past verb discourse (anaphoric reference) or, less often, in the discourse that is about to be uttered (cataphoric reference). Pronouns provide the most obvious illustration of linguistic indexicality, but many more subtle forms could be mentioned. In general, a relationship between a sign and a meaning is indexical whenever the understanding of that sign is at least partially dependent on aspects of the context in which the sign is used.

We think that the concept of indexical determinism can be usefully extended to several other aspects of language use and language change. These include (1) the metaphoric extension of signs, (2) the reinterpretation of the meaning of signs, and (3) pressures on the shape of signs that arise from processing. In each of these cases, language processing itself produces a "natural" link between form and meaning – one based on participation or indexicality rather than iconicity or physical resemblance.

Metaphoric Extension. Metaphoric extension is an extremely common process in language, in which a form is extended to convey a meaning that is only indirectly, partially, or peripherally related to its semantic core (Lakoff & Johnson, 1980; Lakoff, 1987; MacWhinney, in press). We are usually aware of poetic metaphors like "John is a young lion," somewhat less aware of metaphors that have attained an idiomatic status like "John spilled the beans", and perhaps even less aware of metaphors in which a concrete sensorimotor process is extended to cover abstract cases like "John was unable to convey his thoughts to her." The formation of new compound words such as "couch potato," new derived words such as "teach-in," and new inflected words such as "hacked" (in the computational sense) all require the active utilization of metaphorical extension. These issues are discussed further by MacWhinney (in press). For present purposes, we would simply like to note that metaphor is a kind of indexical relation. One meaning or piece of meaning that we would like to express overlaps with or participates in another. The "borrowing" of forms is caused by (or enabled by) this overlap in meaning.

Reinterpretation.   Whenever forms begin to lose their functional motivation, reinterpretation works to breathe new life into them. Reinterpretation takes advantage of the fact that natural language is based on richly confounded coalitions of overlapping functions and forms (the same situation that is responsible for metaphoric extension, above). The notion of sentential subject serves as a particularly good example of a form–function coalition to illustrate this point. At the surface level, we find several morphosyntactic devices that tend to be assigned to the same element of meaning. In English, each sentence has an element which (1) is expressed as a noun phrase (a pronoun or an explicit noun), (2) agrees with the verb in person and number, (3) tends to appear in preverbal position, and (4) carries nominative case if it surfaces as a pronoun. These morphological and positional facts cooccur so reliably that we tend to think of them as obligatory rules, operating as a block (although this cooccurrence can break down, legally or illegally – more on this point later). In addition, we find a set of "optional" formal devices that are also correlated (albeit less strongly) with the subject coalition. For example, the subject is more likely to be a definite noun phrase, and more likely than other arguments of the verb to be modified by a relative clause.

Agent-mapping devices like nominative case and topic-mapping devices like definiteness are correlated at the surface level because agent meanings and topic meanings are correlated at the semantic level. But where does the semantic correlation come from? Agency and topichood are both important and common meanings in human discourse. Hence, they each deserve high priority access to the "real estate" provided by the grammar. This might lead (and occasionally does lead) to a situation of competition in which semantic and pragmatic roles struggle for control over important grammatical options. Fortunately, however, the roles of agent and topic are usually assigned to the same referent. That is, the agent of an action is more likely than any other semantic role to serve as the topic of a passage of discourse, and the topic of a given discourse is particularly likely to be the protagonist in some human drama (the agent of an action, or a closely related role such as the experiencer of an emotion or state). This kind of semantic/pragmatic overlap no doubt derives from social universals: we like to talk about ourselves and our activities. In fact, in oral discourse the topic is also particularly likely to be the speaker or the listener. This social universal results in a statistical bias toward first or second person subjects – a fact that has also been conventionalized into some grammars (e.g., so-called "split ergative" languages – see Silverstein, 1976b). For present purposes, the point is that the statistical overlap between agent and topic at the level of meaning results in a tendency for many natural languages to assign agent and topic marking devices together as a block. Across generations, this cooccurrence of form may lead to a "reinterpretation" of the relation between forms and meanings, particularly when some of the dominant form–meaning relations have become "bleached" through overextension. This is a kind of linguistic guilt-by-association. For example, Bates et al. (1982) have shown that Italian adults tend to interpret definite nouns as the agent of a transitive action. Definiteness is in the subject coalition primarily because of its association with topichood (in particular, the portion of topichood that is contributed by givenness); however, the long association between topic and agent has led to a situation in which definiteness can also be used as a cue to agency. This kind of plurifunctionality is, we will argue, the rule rather than the exception in natural language. One-to-one mappings between form and function are rare. Under the real-time pressures of adult language use, redundancy is welcome. As a result, double function mitigates against the existence of vestigial grammatical devices. For example, suppose the functional link between definiteness and topichood in Italian were to erode over time (for reasons that need not concern us here); the definite/indefinite contrast might be taken over in the service of transitivity, that is, as a cue to "who did what to whom." MacWhinney (in press) offers some examples in terms of verbal and case marking in Hungarian.

Darwin made extensive use of the principle of double function to salvage the principle of natural selection (Gould, 1983). Near-perfect adaptations like wings or eyes are easy to explain within a creationist framework, but they present problems for the Darwinian point of view. What possible function could have been served by two-thirds of an eye or seventy-five percent of a wing? And yet, if those forms evolved from other forms, something must have kept them going on their way toward their ultimate functions of seeing and flying, respectively. Darwin's answer was that the intermediate forms are maintained by different functions altogether, permitting gradual selection of the new activity over generations. For example, it appears to be the case that wings evolved from membranes that initially served the function of helping to maintain body heat. Indeed, the flapping motion that is part and parcel of flying in the current organism may also have originated from this original heat-maintenance function. Nature is apparently content to pass on half-baked jobs from one generation to another, lending the necessary time for better mechanisms to evolve, as long as the intermediate forms are contributing to survival and reproductive success. Vestigial forms will also be tolerated if they don't get in the way, but they are more likely to be maintained if they can be "recycled" (cf. reinterpreted) in the service of some other function. If we think of language in these biological terms, then it becomes clearer how some of the more exquisite structures of grammar could have evolved in the first place.

Processing Determinism. Psycholinguists have often noted that the shape of the communicative act in which a given device participates feeds back on that device to determine or influence its shape. The device will not "look like" its meaning (iconic determinism), but it nevertheless has to adjust to real-time processing pressures if it is going to convey that meaning. The speech event in which the device participates places constraints on where the device should occur in the speech stream (position), and how much time it should take (length).

The marking of relative clauses can be used to illustrate several different forms of processing determinism. The basic function of the relative clause is to identify the head of the relative (Keenan & Comrie, 1977). As MacWhinney and Pléh (in press) note, this function is best served when the language has clear ways of marking the identity of the head of the relative clause and the role of the head in the relative clause. If one were to ignore processing considerations, there are many ways of marking these relations that one could imagine. Consider three marking techniques that are almost never used: (1) the presence of a relative clause could be marked at the beginning of the clause, (2) the identity of the head could be marked by agreement particles on the main verb, and (3) the role of the head in the relative could be marked by prefixes on the head. In Downing's (1978) survey of relative clause marking types in 52 languages, we find that none of these three techniques are used. Rather, languages tend to use markings that are far easier to process. The identification of the head of the relative clause is usually done by placing the relative directly before or after the head. However, this particular solution sometimes means that the relative clause may interrupt a main clause. Kuno (1973) and Hakuta (1982) argue that this kind of interruption can be costly for two reasons. First, because relative clauses are longer than most modifiers, the main clause has to be held open for a rather long time. Second, because relative clauses resemble main clauses in many respects, there is a potential for confusion (e.g., which verb goes with which noun). One way to relieve the burden on processing is to transpose the relative clause to the end of the sentence. Many languages do this by attaching special markers to the head to indicate that an extraposition has occurred. This type of marking, along with the various other markers of relative clause structure, can be understood as an indexical marking whose shape is governed by processing determinism. In general, there are a small number of high-probability solutions to the relative clause-marking problem. The exact solutions chosen by a particular language depend on the presence of other structures in that language.

Another example of processing determinism is found in the tendency for languages to place their modifiers in one preferred position (i.e., before or after the noun), or in the tendency to line noun and verb inflections up together on one side of the root word (usually as suffixes). As discussed by Vennemann (1974), it may simply be easier in both production and comprehension to locate all forms of a given type in the same general area. This pressure is not an absolute, and exceptions occur in every language (e.g., articles, numerals, and a handful of frequent adjectives occur before the noun in Italian, whereas other modifiers occur after the noun). However, as Hawkins (1983) has pointed out, there are implicational regularities in the order in which modifiers "drift" from left to right across the course of language change (e.g., numerals, articles, and relative clauses tend to be the last to move from an old position to a new one). Hence, pressures toward typological conformity may interact with other factors like the size of the unit to be moved during a transitional phase (which would mitigate against movement of large units from a well-established slot) and the frequency of the unit (e.g., articles and numerals may have been so heavily over-learned in a particular position that they resist a system-wide change).

We suspect that pressures of this sort are responsible for most of the cross-language regularities that have been described within purely structuralist theories like the theory of Government and Binding (Chomsky, 1982). Consider, for example, the correlations between pro-drop (i.e., the tendency for a language to omit subject pronouns in freestanding declarative sentences), the presence of rich inflectional morphology on the verb, and the availability of lexical expletives. The Competition Model attributes the ability to omit pronouns to the presence of clear subject marking on the verb. Where this verbal marking is not available, subject pronoun omission is disfavored. If the identity of the subject is clearly marked by morphological means, then at least one functional pressure toward lexicalization of the subject has been removed.

These correlations between pro-drop and agreement marking are high, but they are not perfect. For example, Chinese permits subject omission despite its impoverished system of inflectional morphemes. German does not permit pro-drop, even though German has far more inflectional morphology than Chinese. Within formal theory, such exceptions would have to be explained by postulating yet another parameter as a part of the innate language organ. The Competition Model seeks explanations for these exceptions in other parts of the linguistic system. For example, it may be that the extensive elaboration of topic marking in Chinese is what permits the dropping of pronouns without agreement marking on the verb. In German, on the other hand, pronouns may be retained because they provide clear marking of gender features which control identification of subsequent anaphoric reference. In general, exceptions are less painful for a functionalist theory in which features like pro-drop reflect many competing functional conditions that could be satisfied in several different ways. Nonetheless, it behooves us to point out exactly what those functional conditions are, and how they have been satisfied from one language to another. At the present time, there is no full functionalist account for the regularities described by Government and Binding Theory, although Kuno (1986) presents analyses of parts of the total picture. Our point is, simply, that an adequate functionalist account of these phenomena will necessarily include a description of pressures that operate across the system as a whole. Such systemic pressures come not from the cognitive content of grammatical forms, but from the many different and often competing demands of perception, production, learning, and memory.

Level 2 – Language Use

At Level 2 we find claims about *in vivo* causal relationships between form and function, constraints that operate in real-time language use. This is a synchronic version of the diachronic claims at Level 1. We set these out as two separate levels because in fact we cannot assume that old cause-and-effect relationships are still operating in today's grammar. As we noted earlier, it is at least logically possible that certain forms once served a communicative function but now have no clear communicative role. Such vestigial forms would motivate a distinction between Level 1 functionalism and Level 2 functionalism. But there is also a second and more compelling reason to keep Levels 1 and 2 separate: Many of the functional constraints that we have described so far are large-scale effects that are visible only across many generations, collective effects of communication among many different individuals. We cannot assume that each of these cause-and-effect relationships is detectable, or, for that matter, operative at all in a single speaker. Historical language change may be the linguistic equivalent of population genetics, with facts and principles that depend upon but also transcend knowledge of the individual organism.

Two kinds of methods have been used to establish the existence of "live" cause-and-effect relationships in individual language users. Linguists tend to make use of text analysis, demonstrating that particular target forms are always or typically used only in a certain set of functional/communicative contexts (for example, Zubin, 1977, 1979). Psycholinguists are, instead, more likely to manipulate putative cause-and-effect relationships directly. In studies of sentence production, functional conditions are manipulated as independent variables (e.g., agency, givenness, topicality); the linguistic devices that speakers produce under those conditions serve as the dependent variable(s) (e.g., a particular word-order configuration, case markers, contrastive stress, or pronominalization). This logic is reversed in studies of sentence comprehension: Surface forms are presented to subjects in different competing or converging combinations (i.e., as independent variables); the meanings or interpretations that the subjects derive serve as dependent variables. This kind of design characterizes most of the comprehension and production studies described in this volume. Because the second half of this chapter and many of the other chapters in this book are devoted to an elaboration of Level 2 functionalism, we will not spend our time here repeating discussions that the reader will encounter later.

The various caveats about cause and effect that we raised at Level 1 apply just as seriously at Level 2. First, there are many types of functional determinism at work in adult language use. Second, form and function stand in a many-to-many relationship. Therefore, we are likely to obtain a distorted view of reality, if we restrict ourselves to simple one-to-one manipulations in our experimental designs. Third, we are usually dealing with quantitative rather than qualitative effects when we manipulate form–function relations. We must be prepared to accept "maybe" as an answer; in fact, we ought to have theories that are powerful and precise enough to predict the proper degree of "maybe" in a given experimental design. This may require us to move toward increasingly complex designs, employing the powerful multivariate tools that have been developed in other social sciences (e.g., economics) to model a multilayered reality. Computer simulation may also become an important tool in the construction of psycholinguistic theory, permitting researchers to manipulate more variables than the "eyeball" can handle.

With these caveats in mind, Level 2 research can tell us a great deal about the "ecological niche" of a given linguistic form. When and why do we use the passive? What are the functions conveyed by aspect marking? However, this kind of result does not require us to conclude that form–function mappings play any role at all in acquisition, nor are we forced to conclude that form–function correlations belong in a structural description of the language. Such claims belong at the next two levels.

Level 3 – Language Acquisition

Level 3 functionalism claims that language acquisition is guided by form–function correlations. The child can only exploit form–function correlations in acquisition if such correlations actually exist. Hence, claims at Level 3 presuppose the plausibility of claims at Level 2. However, a different kind of evidence is needed to prove that children actually take advantage of these correlational facts. After all, many of the complex discourse functions that motivate adult grammar may be entirely opaque to the child. And it is demonstrably possible for children to learn aspects of language that they do not understand at all. For example, children acquire linguistic categories like gender at a relatively young age, despite the fact that these categories have no obvious semantic/pragmatic base. In the case of linguistic patterns like gender marking, language acquisition becomes a problem of pattern detection that may or may not require the application of innate linguistic knowledge. We suspect that more general principles of pattern detection and distributional learning are sufficient for the task – but that is an empirical question, perhaps the most important question in language acquisition research.

In the Competition Model, language acquisition is characterized as cue-driven distributional analysis. Primary among the various cues the child detects are those involving form–function correlations. Children take advantage of form–

function correlations in the course of language learning, insofar as they are able to understand and formulate the relevant dimensions of meaning. In addition, however, they are also capable of detecting certain distributional facts in the sound stream even in the absence of an interpretation for those facts. They can treat sound as an object, just like any perceptual object, and pick up recurring patterns whether they understand them or not (MacWhinney, 1978, 1982, in press; Bates, Bretherton, & Snyder, 1988). However, this process is greatly enhanced when meaning is available (1) to motivate the child's attention to the relevant facts and (2) to add critical patterned information of its own.

An adequate account of language development will necessarily involve a mixture of function-driven and form-driven learning. In underscoring the role that meaning and cognition play in language acquisition, many of us in the functionalist camp have neglected the other half of the story, that is, the fact that language learning is also a perceptual-motor problem. The emphasis on function-driven learning and the relative neglect of form-driven learning in some of our writings (Bates & MacWhinney, 1979, 1982) has resulted in some misunderstandings that we would like to begin to rectify here. These misunderstandings relate to (1) the relation between cues and functions, (2) the role of cues in distributional learning, and (3) the role of reinforcement in learning.

Cues and Functions. It has in fact been argued that the acquisition of "purely formal" linguistic patterns constitutes clear disconfirmation of the Competition Model and any other functionalist theory of language learning (Chien & Lust, 1985; Hyams, 1986; Levy, 1983b, Meisel, 1986). We cite these articles only because they make the analysis of the relevant issues so clear. Many other papers based on similar analyses could also be cited. Levy (1983b) presents an argument of this general type based on her analysis of the acquisition of gender in Hebrew and other languages. However, it turns out that what Levy calls "formal" patterns are really simple surface phonological cues and not deep abstract concepts in a formalist universal grammar. As Zubin and Köpcke (1981, 1986), Köpcke and Zubin (1983, 1984), and Taraban, McDonald, and MacWhinney (in press) have shown, the surface phonological shapes of words provide children with a great deal of information about category assignment. MacWhinney (1978) emphasized the importance of such information in language learning. However, it is misleading to call surface phonological cues "formal patterns" since they do not force the child to abstract formal categories based on the principles of universal grammar. Garden-variety principles of learning and pattern detection may be sufficient.

Meisel (1986) presents a more general challenge to the functional view of language acquisition. Observing aspects of grammatical development in a French-German bilingual child, he demonstrated that there are large differences between the child's two languages in the age at which forms with the "same" meaning are acquired (see also Slobin, 1973). He assumes, reasonably enough, that the bilingual child brings one and only one set of cognitive prerequisites to bear on learning her two languages. Hence, any difference in onset time between the two target grammars must be due to something other than cognitive content. Up to this point, we agree completely with Meisel's reasoning. However, he then goes on to conclude that this "something" must be the innate and grammar-specific language acquisition device that Chomsky has foreseen in his writings on Universal Grammar. We see no reason to opt for this particular explanation of the developmental pattern. There may, for example, be differences between the child's two target languages in the perceptual, motor and/or memory demands associated with "equivalent" linguistic forms. The problem with Meisel's line of reasoning is that he is comparing a radically simplistic functionalist account with a not-yet-fully-specified autonomous syntactic account. Our work on the Competition Model suggests that the truth lies somewhere in between. Later on we will give examples of "cue cost" effects on learning in languages that are otherwise quite similar, lending support to our interpretation.

Hyams (1986) states the autonomous position in even stronger terms. In reviewing studies of grammatical development in Italian, Hyams notes that Italian children acquire many aspects of gender, number and person agreement at a very young age (see also Bates, 1976; Caselli & Pizzuto, 1988). Furthermore, the Italian child provides agreement on all the appropriate nouns, pronouns, adjectives and verbs – not only those that correspond to a semantic core such as "concrete object" or "physical action." Given the generality of agreement phenomena in early Italian (i.e., the fact that they transcend concrete semantic categories), Hyams concludes that the child must control abstract notions like "noun phrase" and "verb phrase." From this conclusion, she goes on to a stronger point: the child could not possibly learn such abstract categories, so they must be given in the innate and language-specific knowledge that children bring to bear on the acquisition problem. But of course this need not follow. Suppose (as we do) that children are simultaneously learning vertical correlations between form and function (i.e., semantic control), and horizontal correlations among surface forms (e.g., the markings that characterize agreement). A number of experimental and computational studies have shown that this kind of simultaneous learning is possible and perhaps desirable (e.g., Valian & Coulson, 1988; St. John & McClelland, in press). Suppose also that this combined horizontal/vertical learning is carried out by a learning device that accepts partial information. In fact, we know that multiple fallible cues can lead to surprisingly robust learning (Taraban et al., in press). In short, Hyams is mistaken in her belief that imperfect correlations between form and meaning cannot in principle account for the acquisition of grammatical categories.

Chien and Lust (1985) devised an interesting experimental test of the functionalist claims of the Competition Model. Their test was based on the imitation of sentences in Chinese that show equi-NP deletion. They gave children Chinese sentences like "Xiaohua, father like father watch TV," which means something like "As for Xiaohua, (her) father likes (her) father to watch TV." They then asked children to imitate these sentences and found that, beginning around age 3, they tended to delete the second mention of the subject noun "father" rather than the topic noun "Xiaohua." They take these results as evidence that young Chinese children have an abstract category of "subject" that is not identified "with closely related and highly accessible semantic/pragmatic concepts" (p. 1373). While accepting the results of this study as reasonable, we believe that they provide little evidence against the functional analysis of the subject category. Both Bates and MacWhinney (1982) and MacWhinney (1977) note that there is no reason that a topic and an agent cannot coexist in the same sentence. It is true that the first argument of the verb "like" is not as agential as the first argument of a verb like "hit." However, it still contains many elements of the cluster of meanings which we refer to as "agent" including "perspective" and "source of volition."

There is an important leap that Chien and Lust, Levy, Meisel, and Hyams all make in their arguments: children acquire regularities in their input that have no transparent semantic base; therefore, learning must be based on purely linguistic categories that are free of cognitive content. Since it is not clear where else those linguistic categories might come from, they must be innate. Hence, the existence of distributional learning serves as evidence in favor of innateness! We think this logic is flawed and the conclusions are incorrect. But we can also understand why researchers might have been led to such reasoning, reacting to earlier more unidimensional formulations about the "critical" role of meaning in the acquisition of grammar (Bloom, 1974; Bowerman, 1973; Schlesinger, 1974).

Form-Driven Learning. In order to correct these misunderstandings, we would like to first clarify our own position on the role of form-driven learning in language acquisition. In our earlier papers we made a distinction between two types of distributional learning. The first type is what MacWhinney (1975, 1982) called "item-based frames." A good example of an item-based frame is the English indefinite article. As Katz, Baker, and Macnamara (1974) discovered, very young children can use the absence of the article before a word to infer that that word is probably a proper noun, rather than a common noun. If the children are told "show me Zav," they tend to hand the experimenter a figure of a human. If they are told "show me a zav," they tend to hand the experimenter a nonhuman object. MacWhinney (1982, 1985, in press) argued that children were using this syntactic frame to "abduce" the semantics of the nonce word "zav." Working with the acquisition of gender and case marking in German,

MacWhinney (1978) noted that children used a similar mechanism to learn the genders of new nouns. Although this type of learning is clearly form-based, it relies on the existence of a clear syntactic/semantic relation between the operator word and the word whose semantics are being learned.

In our early papers on the functional bases of syntax (Bates & MacWhinney, 1979, 1982; MacWhinney, 1982) we noted the importance of this simple type of form-driven learning, while questioning the importance of a more extensive sort of distributional learning scheme proposed by Maratsos and his colleagues (Maratsos & Chalkey, 1980; Maratsos, 1982). Maratsos argued that children could extract abstract linguistic classes entirely on the basis of distributional evidence – without reference to correlations between form and meaning, and without reference to innate clues about the structure of linguistic categories. To illustrate, take the syntactic category "verb." Verbs tend to occur within reliable paradigms: The same lexical item that ends in "-ing" in one context will also end in "-ed" in another context. These elements will also have certain positional privileges relative to members of other paradigms (e.g., nouns, prepositions). Maratsos argued that children are capable of detecting these regularities in their data, without mapping those regularities onto any a priori category. At first this pattern of correlations may be extended only to particular lexical items, perhaps only to those words that carried the information in the first place. However, with enough experience of this kind the child can learn to make systematic predictions: Given a nonsense word that ends in "-ing" in a particular context, the child can predict that the same nonsense word will end in "-ed" in another context. The child does not even have to know the meaning of the word to reach this conclusion. The prediction is based, instead, purely on distributional facts. At some point late in this process we can say that the child possesses the abstract category "verb." Note that this is quite similar to the "item and arrangement" approach to grammatical categories, and the "substitution and contrast" approach to grammatical induction proposed by American structuralists before the onslaught of generative grammar (e.g., Harris, 1951; see Gazdar et al., 1985, for a modern version of phrase structure grammar).

To make a long story short, as both Maratsos and we developed our ideas further, the gap between our respective formulations continually narrowed. Maratsos increasingly stressed the role of meaning as providing cues used by the distributional learning mechanism. We became increasingly comfortable with a general distributional learning mechanism within which the various cues to which we had drawn attention could play a role. Recent developments in connectionist theory (Rumelhart & McClelland, 1986) have provided us with an algorithmic way of understanding how various cue types can interact within a general framework of distributional/cue-driven learning. Within this new framework, our earlier differences with Maratsos become nothing more than debates about the relative strengths of cues at different points in development.

We see now that the important issue is not whether learning is driven by form or by function. The answer to that question is that it is driven in both ways. The basic scheme for learning is a meaning-driven distributional analysis. The important issue now is whether learning can take place without *a priori* semantic or syntactic categories. Here Maratsos agrees with us in questioning the quick recourse to nativist explanations.

Language acquisition is a perceptual-motor problem. The child is trying to extract patterns, islands of regularity that can be isolated within a noisy sound stream. This is the perceptual side of the problem, and it is subject to all the vicissitudes of perceptual learning and pattern recognition in any domain (much more on this below, and in other chapters throughout this volume). Once patterns have been isolated, the child will also try to reproduce them. This is the motor side of the problem, and it can only be understood within a much broader theory of motor learning. All of our claims about form–function mapping presuppose this perceptual-motor framework. Forms exist, and they must be perceived before any mapping can occur at all (Golinkoff et al., 1987). We do not see why this admission should lead one to question the functionalist enterprise. Indeed, within a highly interactive theory we should expect to find intimate causal relationships among phonetic, articulatory, grammatical and semantic facts.

What these various controversies have served to obscure is the fact that a matrix of correlated features will be acquired more easily if it includes meanings and uses that are transparent to the child. This is the essence of form–function mapping, the meaning-driven aspect of distributional learning. Functional correlations facilitate the acquisition of form for two reasons. First, regular mappings between form and function constitute a large part of the information that is available to the child. Second, communicative functions can drive the learner in a rather special way, by directing attention to regularities in the linguistic environment. The child is scanning the input for ways to convey interests and needs, trying to extract information that will help in predicting the behavior and attitudes of other people.

Reinforcement. Meaning contributes to the acquisition of grammar by providing both information and motivation. This emphasis on the motivation of grammar makes some of our colleagues nervous; they fear that it smacks of American behaviorism from James to Skinner. In fact, we reject the Skinnerian view that reward and punishment determine learning. We are more comfortable with the treatment of reinforcement offered by Tolman (1922). Tolman was viewed as an outlaw and a mystic by many of his contemporaries, because he argued that rats and other beings (e.g., people) operate on the basis of their expectations and their theory of the world. In Tolman's cognitive learning theory, reinforcement facilitates learning by motivating the organism to attend to regularities in the environment. The learning itself is driven by these attended regularities, and not by arousal, drive reduction, or any other direct and mechanistic definition of reinforcement (cf. Hull, 1943).

But even within this framework, we must insist that reinforcement means something very special in our species. As Piaget has argued, children are inherently motivated to learn, and will do so in the absence of any reinforcement other than the sheer joy of finding out how things work. In a socially motivated species like ours, this includes a drive to find out how other people work. Human children want to behave like others in their community and engage in imitation, with or without an extrinsic reward. They also want to know how other people think, and begin to build a "theory of mind" as early as the second year of life (Bretherton, McNew, & Beeghly-Smith, 1981). From this point of view, language is precious stuff indeed, providing the key to successful participation in a society. This is surely enough motivation even for such a daunting task as the acquisition of German gender, or acquisition of the mysteries of WH-movement.

Level 4 – Competence

It is possible to accept functionalist claims at Levels 1 through 3 without accepting the further claim that these form–function relations must be stated within the grammar, that is, within an abstract description of the rules and regularities that comprise the ideal speaker-listener's knowledge of his or her language. From a nativist perspective (e.g., Pinker, 1984, 1987), it is quite possible to argue that children use semantic bootstrapping to discover certain boundaries in their language; once those boundaries are discovered (e.g., once they know what nouns and verbs look like in this language), they can then instantiate a whole set of innate categories and principles. From this point on, the old semantic prototype becomes irrelevant (sloughed off like the tadpole's tail or the chrysalis from which the butterfly emerges).

We tend instead to favor an alternative view of semantic bootstrapping. Semantic/pragmatic prototypes remain at the core of all or most linguistic categories, showing up in a wide array of adult linguistic behaviors (Bates & MacWhinney, 1979 and 1982; see below for details). Does this mean that we espouse Level 4 functionalism, i.e., the claim that linguistic competence must be described in functional terms? We cannot answer that question at this point. No functionalist grammar has yet been formulated with enough internal detail to constitute a model of competence in any human language. Indeed, there is no grammatical theory of any sort that has yet met this challenge, and debates about what a competence model should look like are all currently based on nothing but fragmentary analyses. In lieu of a convincing competence model, we have contented ourselves with a characterization of competence to perform, describing the kinds of representations that could underlie the Level 2 and Level 3 findings in our crosslinguistic work to date.

As we shall see in more detail below, the native speaker's latent knowledge can be described in terms of a network of weighted connections: correlations between forms and functions, correlations among forms themselves, and correlations or points of overlap between particular communicative functions or meanings. Borrowing a term from Marr (1982), who described aspects of visual perception in terms of a "2.5D sketch" (a two-dimensional description annotated with three-dimensional information), we could characterize the representational component of the Competition Model as Functionalist Level 3.5. It is a compromise that stands somewhere midway between a description of linguistic behavior and a characterization of competence.

This is our position on the matter right now. But let us put the same question a different way. Could the representational component of a performance grammar ever replace the Level 4 competence models offered by linguists? In considering this question, we are drawn to a useful set of contrasts offered by Pinker and Prince (1988) in their critique of the connectionist approach to language acquisition described in Rumelhart and McClelland (1987). Connectionist models provide a characterization of the "microstructure" of cognition, a subsymbolic level of analysis in which knowledge is represented in terms of many simple "on-off" units that are massively interconnected. This level of organization is intentionally "brainlike," in that it has certain properties in common with the organization of neural nets. To some extent, these systems can mimic the operation of traditional cognitive models, which are instead inspired by the organization of digital computers with discrete symbols and rules or procedures for manipulating those symbols. And yet it is not at all obvious where these "rules" and "symbols" are located in a connectionist model. At best they are emergent properties of lower-level units; at worst, they may play no role at all. Pinker and Prince describe three different relationships that could hold between a connectionist model and traditional rule-based accounts of cognition.

1. Implementational connectionism: This term refers to an approach in which there is an isomorphic relationship between the facts expressed in a connectionist format and at least some subset of the facts expressed in a traditional rule-based symbolic mode. Connectionist representations add nothing new (except to show how symbols and rules might be implemented in a neural net), and new facts could still be discovered at the symbolic level using traditional representations and traditional investigative techniques. This is plainly the most palatable version of connectionism for Pinker and Prince, since it poses no challenge to the modes of inquiry that they value.
2. Eliminative connectionism: This term refers to the belief that connectionist accounts completely eliminate the need for higher-order descriptions. Notions like "symbol" and "rule" are viewed as epiphenomena of facts at the subsymbolic level. They may provide a convenient shorthand for the description of finer-grained phenomena, but they have no explanatory value. This is the version of connectionism that Pinker and Prince find most objectionable (see also Fodor & Pylyshyn, 1988).

3. Symbolic-revisionist connectionism: This phrase refers to an approach that rec-
    ognizes the value of descriptions at both the symbolic and the subsymbolic level.
    However, it is argued that the two levels are not equivalent. In particular, discoveries
    at the subsymbolic level can constrain the class of psychologically and biologically
    plausible symbolic theories.

The limitations of a purely qualitative approach are particularly clear in some
recent attempts to apply Chomsky's theory of principles and parameters to
language acquisition data (Chomsky, 1982 and 1986; Hyams, 1986; Roeper and
Williams, 1987). Parameter theory represents the first serious attempt within
generative grammar to provide a typology of natural languages. This typology
is based on a small set of structural dimensions or "parameters" along which
natural languages may vary; each parameter represents two or more possible
forms that a supposedly innate principle can take. For example, the null subject
parameter captures the fact that natural languages either do or do not permit
subject ellipsis in a free-standing declarative sentence. Other parameters that
have been proposed include order relations among the constituents of a phrase
(e.g., "head first" or "head final"), and the presence or absence of a canonical
order for the major constituents of a sentence (e.g., "configurational" versus
"nonconfigurational"). Although the list of possible parameters is still open
(i.e., some await discovery; others may prove not to deserve parametric status),
it is generally believed that the list is finite and rather small; furthermore, most
investigators hope that the parameters will prove to be orthogonal (i.e., setting
along one parameter is independent of setting along another). Parameter theory
is, then, an excellent example of a theory based entirely on discrete, qualitative
principles. There is still some controversy within generative grammar circles
concerning the "right" application of parameter theory to language learning (e.g.,
whether or not all children begin with a universal default setting, and/or whether
parameters "mature"), but most interested theorists agree that a parameter setting
process of some kind would greatly simplify the child's learning problem. In
order to figure out what kind of language s/he has to learn, the child simply has
to listen for the right kind of positive evidence (e.g., the referentially empty
pronoun in a sentence like "It is raining," a phenomenon that supposedly
occurs only in a language with obligatory subjects). When these "triggers"
are encountered, the child can immediately draw a whole series of conclusions
about the nature of her/his target language.

Unfortunately, there is a very bad fit between this theory and the messy
empirical facts of language acquisition. In its original form, parameter theory
requires all children to begin with the same default setting (i.e., the so-called
subset principle). Within this framework, it is difficult to understand how
Turkish, Italian and English children could look so different at the stage of
first word combinations (or, for that matter, in the one-word stage – Slobin,
1985). Worse still, any serious version of parameter theory predicts abrupt

transitions, developments in which a whole host of correlated phenomena appear simultaneously, with no turning back. For example, Hyams (1986) claims that English children begin with the default assumption that they are learning a pro-drop language; this explains why subject omission is possible in Stage I English. Children supposedly "switch" to the obligatory subject setting only after they have encountered the appropriate triggering evidence (e.g. referentially empty pronouns; modal auxiliaries that can be moved out of the verb phrase). At a global level, the evidence supports Hyams's argument: some time before their fourth birthday, normal English children produce empty pronouns, acquire the auxiliary system, and stop omitting obligatory subjects. However, parameter setting can be distinguished empirically from garden-variety learning *only* if these events occur in a "special" time-locked fashion: triggers precede parameter setting, and once the parameter is set, the relevant phenomena are set in place simultaneously and very fast. These requirements are not met in the existing data for English. For example, Maratsos (1988) has shown that English children cease to omit the subject many months before they have acquired the auxiliary system. Conversely, Loeb and Leonard (1988) have shown that some English children fail to produce obligatory subjects even though they demonstrate productive control over "empty" subject pronouns (e.g., the "it" in "it is cold"). In short, the facts of English language learning support a model in which these diverse aspects of grammar are acquired gradually, in a potentially variable order. They "hang together" no more or less than any of the other morphosyntactic changes that take place between the ages of 20 and 40 months. (See Hyams, 1987, for a revised proposal, in which the triggering evidence for obligatory subjects in English comes from the nonuniformity of verb conjugation – a proposal which, in our view, suffers from even more serious empirical problems).

Finally, if we assume that English and Italian children have the "same" setting at Stage I, then we should expect them to omit the subject at a similar rate. However, our own data for English suggest that very young children produce the subject more than fifty percent of the time in their first word combinations; by contrast, very young Italian children may produce no lexical subjects at all for the first weeks or months of multiword speech (Bates, 1976). In other words, English and Italian children differ on the pro-drop parameter *before* the relevant parameter is set. These results are not compatible with Hyams's theory, but they *are* compatible with a quantitative theory like ours, i.e., a theory in which children are sensitive to the statistical properties of their native language from the earliest stages of language learning. The Competition Model does have nonlinear mechanisms that allow for abrupt transitions when they occur, but it can also account for the much more general phenomenon of gradual, statistically driven change.

In the ongoing argument about the relationship between symbolic and subsymbolic structure, some of our colleagues have suggested that the relationship is analogous to the contrast between Newtonian and quantum mechanics. Deterministic Newtonian mechanics suffice for most macro-level problems (e.g., building a bridge or launching a missile); indeterministic quantum mechanics come into play only for micro-level problems (e.g., research on subatomic particles). This analogy is quite appealing to those who prefer an implementational form of connectionism, because it makes the subsymbolic approach irrelevant for most problems in cognitive science. But we think another analogy from physics may be more useful: the contrast between wave and particle theories of light. It is now generally agreed that this is a false opposition. Light displays both wave and particle properties, and both must be considered simultaneously for a complete account of the relevant physical and mathematical facts. In the same vein, a complete account of language may require simultaneous consideration of its symbolic and subsymbolic properties. This may be the most useful way of characterizing symbolic-revisionist connectionism.

Our approach to the relationship between rules and probabilistic representations corresponds best to the symbolic-revisionist approach. We recognize the value of linguistic descriptions that are cast in a traditional rule-based format. But we also believe that the underlying facts of human performance constrain the set of competence models that are likely to lead to real discoveries. This is the major reason why we cast our lot not with the "ruling party" of MIT generative grammar, but with the functionalist "loyal opposition."

The Competition Model

Before describing the basic tenets of the Competition Model, we should explain why we call this a model and not a theory. We are trying to account for a range of crosslinguistic data within a unified framework, but the framework itself cannot be disconfirmed in any single critical experiment. A model must instead be evaluated in terms of (1) its overall coherence, (2) its heuristic value in inspiring further research, and (3) its performance compared with competing accounts. Components of a model are tested one at a time, and if predictions fail, modifications are made and new concepts are introduced. Ideally, these new concepts should have an independent motivation (i.e., they should not be added merely to save the model), and they should lead to new discoveries in their own right. But the framework as a whole will be rejected only if (1) it loses coherence, weighted down by circularities and ad hoc assumptions, (2) it loses its heuristic value, and/or (3) a better account of the same phenomena comes along.

From these three points of view, the Competition Model has fared rather well so far. We began with a set of broad assumptions about the functional bases of language, the importance of crosslinguistic comparison, and the need to account for quantitative as well as qualitative facts about language structure and language use (cf. Bates, 1976; MacWhinney, 1978; Bates & MacWhinney, 1979, 1982). To account for our first demonstrations of crosslinguistic variation in performance, we appealed to a single quantitative principle: cue validity, that is, the information value of a given linguistic device as a cue to an underlying meaning or intention (MacWhinney et al., 1984). With this single principle, we were able to quantify with some precision the degree of informativeness that the "same" structure carries in two different languages. We knew that this minimalist approach was much too simple; no single principle, however powerful, can account for all the complexities of language processing. The real test of our model has come from the failures of cue validity, failures that have helped us to discover a range of interesting constraints. Many of these new constraints fall within a general category that we have called cue cost, that is, processing limitations that mute or augment the speaker-listener's ability to take advantage of different information types. Others have to do with different aspects of cue validity itself, including the contrast between overall cue validity and conflict validity – a discovery that helps us to understand how relatively rare phenomena in the language can play a role in acquisition and processing, providing an explanation for certain late developments that were difficult to explain in any other way. For present purposes, the important point is that these new constraints all have independent motivation. They have enriched the model, but they do not exist solely to keep the model going.

After many years of research, much of it summarized in this volume, the Competition Model is now competitive. It will undoubtedly be replaced by or merged with its competitors at some point down the road, when enough crosslinguistic data have accumulated to challenge the statements offered here. Indeed, many of the authors in the present volume have pointed out fundamental problems that do not yet have adequate solutions. But, if we are successful in inspiring more crosslinguistic research on language processing, then the model has served its purpose. We will describe the model and its supporting data in three sections: the structure of the system, processing dynamics, and acquisition.

The Structure of the System

Our understanding of the structure of the language processing system can be expressed in terms of five key concepts: two-level structure, direct mapping between these levels, cue validity, cue strength, and coalition between forms and functions.

Two-Level Structure

Only two levels of informational structure are specified a priori in this model: a functional level (where all the meanings and intentions to be expressed in an utterance are represented) and a formal level (where all the surface forms or expressive devices available in the language are represented). We assume that mappings between these two levels are as direct as possible. Intervening layers will emerge only when they are essential for processing to take place in real time. These layers are the products of the meaning-driven distributional analysis described previously, and neither their content nor their structure is specified in advance of language learning.

The two-layer system of form–function mappings that we have described elsewhere constitutes a kind of perceptron (Rosenblatt, 1959; Minsky & Papert, 1969; Rumelhart & McClelland, 1986). It is known that perceptrons can learn any linearly separable combination of inputs and outputs, and that they cannot learn a host of other important second- or third-order relationships such as (for example) the relationship of "exclusive or." In our work with Italian, Hungarian, and Dutch, we have encountered a variety of compound cues to sentence interpretation that seem to defy a linearly separable representation. This means that the two-layer approach that we have specified elsewhere has to be modified to permit the emergence of intervening layers.

To illustrate, consider the interaction of word order and contrastive stress in Italian (Bates et al., 1982; MacWhinney et al., 1984). For adult Italians, word order cues are essentially uninterpretable without additional information of some kind. As we have noted, Italians will attend preferentially to lexical and/or morphological cues if these are available; if the sentence is semantically and morphologically ambiguous, then pragmatic and/or prosodic cues come into play. However, word order and stress cues are never evaluated separately; instead, they are interpreted jointly in complex configurations, as follows (keeping in mind that these results are always probabilistic):

	Default Stress	First Noun Stressed	Second Noun Stressed
NVN	SVO	OVS	OVS
NNV	random	random	SOV
VNN	random	VOS	random

Notice that stress and word order do not combine in a linear fashion. The "same" prosodic cue can take on different meanings depending on its syntactic environment; conversely, the "same" word order information can take on new meaning, or even reverse its meaning, when stress cues are added. This nonlinear relationship is also supported by the reaction time data: stress speeds up performance on NNV and VNN, but slows down performance on canonical NVN strings. We suggest that the relationship between contrastive stress and word order in Italian constitutes a kind of exclusive-or problem. These cues simply do not "add up" in the orthogonal fashion required for learning in a two-layer perceptron. There is no single formula, no one weighting of the cue "stressed noun" that will yield the above pattern. The interpretation of stress depends entirely upon the word order environment in which it occurs. This is not the only possible configuration; we find equally complex interactions between word order and stress in German, but with different results. Kail (this volume) reports similar nonlinear interactions between word order and pronominal object clitics in French and Italian: the mere presence of a morphologically ambiguous clitic in an NVN suspends the usual SVO interpretation. This kind of cue interaction appears to be widespread in adult sentence comprehension.

There are a variety of ways in which we can complicate our simple two-layer model in order to represent such compound cues. Of these, the most attractive is the "hidden unit" model of Rumelhart, Hinton, and Williams (1986). The "back propagation" algorithm of Rumelhart et al. provides a robust learning rule of the type that Minsky and Papert thought was only possible for the two-layer perceptron. In our work on the acquisition of German case and gender marking, we (Taraban et al., in press) have found that systems utilizing hidden units can provide us with powerful ways of understanding developmental patterns. The acknowledgment that intervening layers can emerge through learning is a new feature of the model (cf. Bates & MacWhinney, 1979, 1982, 1987; MacWhinney, 1978, 1982). In this regard, it is interesting that the above order/stress configurations are acquired late by Italian children (Bates et al., 1984). They begin with a linear interpretation of each variable (e.g., treating stress as a cue to the agent role regardless of word order environment), and reach the above nonlinear combinations sometime after the age of five. Kail and Devescovi (personal communication) report a similar late onset for the nonlinear interactions between word order and object clitics.

Direct Mapping

In the Competition Model the mapping between form and function is stated as directly as possible – in two layers or (as described above) with intervening layers that are the minimum required for learning in a particular language. Since the principle of direct mapping has been a source of some confusion, it may be worth our while to underscore what this principle does and does not mean within the Competition Model.

First, direct mapping does not mean that relationships between form and function are necessarily one to one; indeed, we assume that one-to-one mappings are rare in natural languages, which are instead composed primarily of many-to-many relationships (polysemy, homophony, syncretism – see coalitions, below).

Second, direct mapping also does not refer to the direction in which information flows during sentence interpretation, that is, the question of serial versus parallel processing. A great deal of research in psycholinguistics from 1960 to 1980 focused on precisely this issue: which stages occur first in processing, and which stages can be skipped. In a typical modular model of sentence processing of the sort that underlay most psycholinguistic research in the 1960s

(Fodor, Bever, & Garrett, 1974, Massaro, 1975), processing was assumed to go through these stages: peripheral auditory processing, phonemic encoding, lexical look-up, phrasal construction, full sentence parsing, and then semantic interpretation. These processes were not supposed to interact and were supposed to occur in a serial pipelined fashion. In the 1970s, a large number of studies appeared demonstrating context effects on processing at both the phonological and syntactic levels, effects that made this serial pipelined flow of information difficult to defend (Warren & Warren, 1970; Marslen-Wilson, 1975).

Some researchers believed that the subsequent abandonment of serial processing signaled the end of a modular view to language processing, in favor of an approach in which meanings are mapped onto sound strings directly, without passing through separate processing units. However, alternative accounts are now available that salvage autonomy/modularity within a more parallel system (Swinney, 1979; Tanenhaus, Leiman, & Seidenberg, 1979; Tanenhaus, Carlson, & Seidenberg, 1985). McClelland's Cascade Model (1979) is of this type. In a cascade model, given a complex Input A, the phonetic/phonological module goes to work in extracting recognizable packages of sound, and passes those patterns directly to the other modules in a rapid and constant cascade. After this point, several alternatives are possible (and they are not mutually exclusive). The grammatical module may go to work directly on that part of the phonetic input that it recognizes (e.g., closed-class morphemes), while the lexical module works on all the meaningful units that are passed up from the phonological processor; alternatively, the grammatical processor may have to wait just a short time for the lexical/semantic processor to recognize possible information about word class (e.g., nouns versus verbs) and/or to separate out closed- and open-class information, passing these relevant bits onto the grammar in another rapid and continuous cascade. Both the lexical and the grammatical processor may in turn pass their products on to a general information processor that assigns final interpretations; or they may employ some kind of a shared blackboard on which partial products are written until there is a coherent parse. The main point is that, in a cascade-type model, modular processes can go on in parallel; cascades may impose short time delays as information passes from one module to another, but these delays may be so brief that they defy measurement. For example, it may be that modularity obtains for a period of only one millisecond.

The principle of direct mapping is not proposed as an alternative to serial processing, but rather as an alternative to certain forms of modularity. Modularity postulates the computational independence of data sources and computational differences between the various modules that have evolved to deal with each data source. By contrast, the principle of direct mapping emphasizes (1) the mixed nature of input to the language processor, and (2) the homogeneity of processing across different data types. By mixed data types we mean that the language processor can make use of compound cues that cross traditional boundaries (e.g., segmental phonology, suprasegmental phonology, morphology, the lexicon, and positional frames). The above example of word order/stress configurations in Italian illustrates this claim. By homogeneous processing we mean that different sources of information (morphological, phonological, lexical, and syntactic) are processed in a similar fashion, via a common set of recognition and retrieval mechanisms. This may be regarded as a strong form of lexicalism. That is, the native speaker learns to map phrasal/prosodic configurations onto propositions, using exactly the same learning principles and representational mechanisms that he uses to map single words onto their meanings (see Bates, Bretherton & Snyder, 1988, and Bates & Wulfeck, this volume).

Cue Validity

The major predictive construct in the Competition Model is cue validity. Following Brunswik (1956) and Gibson (1966), we argue that human beings possess psychological mechanisms that lead them to act in accordance with the validity or information value of cues in their ecology. Validity is an objective property of the cue itself, a property of the perceptual environment relative to some organismic state. Because of this, cue validity is not a circular notion; it can be measured directly in samples of spoken or written language, and used to derive predictions concerning language processing by adults and/or language acquisition by children.

MacWhinney (1978), MacWhinney, Pléh, & Bates (1985), and McDonald (1986, this volume) have analyzed cue validity into three components:

1. *Availability* represents the extent to which a cue is there when you need it. In the scheme of McDonald (1986), availability is best expressed numerically as the ratio of the cases in which the cue is available over the total number of cases in a task domain. For example, the availability of the cue of preverbal position is very high in English, but relatively low in Italian. This reflects the fact that subjects are frequently omitted in Italian, leaving many verbs in sentence-initial position.

2. *Reliability* represents the degree to which a cue leads to the correct interpretation when you count on it. Reliability can be expressed numerically as a ratio of the cases in which a cue leads to the correct conclusion over the number of cases in which it is available. For example, preverbal position is a highly reliable cue in English, where it is almost always assigned to the agent of a transitive action; it is a very unreliable cue in Italian (when it is available at all), since OV and SOV constructions are both possible and likely. "Overall cue validity" is defined as the product of availability times reliability. Given the reliability and availability calculations described above, this necessarily means that the cue validity of preverbal position is very high in English and very low in Italian – a fact that is reflected in the performance of English and Italian listeners in our sentence comprehension experiments.

3. *Conflict validity* is yet another way in which the validity of a cue can be measured. When estimating conflict validity, we look only at those cases where two or more cues conflict. These relatively infrequent competition situations are the denominator for calculations of conflict validity; for any given source of information, the conflict validity estimate is the number of competition situations in which that cue "wins" (i.e., leads to a correct interpretation), divided by the number of competition

situations in which that cue participates. Overall validity and conflict validity are two mathematically distinct and partially dissociable measures of information value. Because they are theoretically and empirically distinct, these two validity estimates can account for different aspects of language processing and language acquisition.

The distinction between overall validity and conflict validity constitutes one of the most important discoveries in our fifteen years of crosslinguistic research. Overall validity can explain many phenomena, but some puzzling exceptions remain that can only be explained by considering the way that cues behave in conflict situations. As we shall see below, conflict validity has been particularly helpful in explaining certain late and/or U-shaped developments in children, and in explaining how relatively infrequent structures can influence adult performance. The two forms of cue validity also have a principled and very natural realization within a connectionist architecture, as by-products of learning with hidden units (Taraban et al., in press).

Cue Strength

To model the organism's knowledge about the validity of information, we postulate a subjective property of the organism called cue strength. This is a quintessentially connectionist notion, referring to the probability or weight that the organism attaches to a given piece of information relative to some goal or meaning with which it is associated. In other words, cue strength is the weight on the connection between two units.

In our psycholinguistic instantiation of this idea, each link between a given surface form and an underlying function is given a weight or strength. With this kind of mechanism, no sharp line is drawn between probabilistic tendencies and deterministic rules. An obligatory relationship between form and function is nothing other than a connection whose strength approaches unity. This permits us to capture statistical differences between adult speakers of different languages, and it permits us to describe facts about language change (in language history and/or in language learning) in gradual and probabilistic terms; we are not forced to postulate a series of all-or-none decisions in which parameters are definitively set and rules are added or dropped.

We view development as the process whereby, under ideal conditions, the value of cue strength converges on the value of cue validity. As a result, the order of importance of cues to meaning for adult speakers ought to closely reflect cue validity estimates. This simple prediction has been confirmed repeatedly in our own crosslinguistic studies, and in work by our colleagues around the world. However, in many cases, estimates of the relative validity of each cue type have been based on the knowledge of informal language use in each language, and not on precise tabulations of cue validity in texts. Therefore, these studies can only test ordinal predictions (e.g., the prediction that word order will be stronger than subject-verb agreement in English, with the opposite pattern occurring in Italian and German – MacWhinney, Bates, & Kliegl, 1984). In more recent studies (especially McDonald, 1984, this volume; Sokolov, this volume), estimates of cue validity have been made directly in sample texts. This permits the experimenter to work with a more precise interval scale, predicting not only the rank order of cues in each language but also the relative distance between ranks. Both approaches have met with considerable success, although interval scaling provides a much stronger and more interesting test of the model.

Table 1.1 summarizes the results of our experiments on sentence comprehension in adult native speakers of different languages. In almost all of these experiments, adult native speakers were presented with a series of simple transitive sentences composed of two concrete nouns and a transitive action verb. On each item, they are asked to decide which of the two nouns is the actor/subject (i.e., "Whodunit?"). Although the linguistic devices that are tested vary from one experiment to another, the materials always include some orthogonal set of competing and/or converging cues to sentence meaning: different levels of word order, animacy/reversibility, grammatical morphology (including case marking, subject–verb agreement, agreement between objects and clitic pronouns, and reflexive markers), prosodic contrasts, and in a few experiments, different forms of topicalization. The impact of cue validity on performance is assessed by evaluating the overall variance accounted for by each independent variable, as well as the extent to which each variable contributes to determining the "winner" in situations of competition and/or cooperation (including "conspiracies" of two or more weak cues against one strong one). McDonald and MacWhinney (this volume) have carried the estimation of cue strength considerably further, using maximum likelihood procedures to construct statistical models of cue interaction, models which provide a single goodness-of-fit statistic for the performance of individuals or groups in our sentence processing experiments.

Before describing the data obtained with this method, a few words are necessary to defend the method itself. In order to test the predictions of the Competition Model, we have to examine situations of both competition and convergence. This requires orthogonalization of factors that are usually confounded in natural language use (cf. Massaro, 1987). In some experiments, in some languages, the resulting stimuli contain a mix of grammatical and semigrammatical stimuli. For example, English experiments may include sentences like "The horse are hitting the cows"; sentences in Hungarian or Turkish may include a large number of ungrammatical sentences with no case contrast (e.g., with both nouns taking nominative case marking). It has been argued that these semigrammatical sentences may evoke abnormal processing strategies that are unrelated to the processes used in normal sentence comprehension.

Given the important role that this particular method has played in our crosslinguistic research, we have taken this criticism seriously. Our answer

Table 1.1. *Order of importance of cues to actor assignment across languages*

English

Adults: SVO > VOS, OSV > Animacy, Agreement > Stress, Topic

5 - 7:   SVO > Animacy > Agreement > NNV, VNN, Stress

Under 5: SVO > Animacy > Stress, SOV, VSO > Agreement

Italian

Adults: SV Agreement > Clitic Agreement > Animacy > SVO > Stress, Topic
          (NNV, VNN interpretable only in combination with stress, clitics)

Under 7: Animacy > SVO > SV Agreement > Clitic Agreement > SOV, VSO
          (no interactions of NNV,VNN with stress, clitics)

French

Adults: SV Agreement > Clitic Agreement > Animacy > SVO > Stress

Under 6: SVO > Animacy > VSO, SOV (agreement not tested)

Spanish

Adults: Accusative preposition > SV Agreement > Clitic Agreement > Word order
          (animacy not tested)

German

Adults: Case > Agreement > Animacy > SOV, VSO, SVO

Dutch

Adults: Case > SVO > Animacy

Under 10: SVO > Case > Animacy

---

comes in several parts. First, the use of semigrammatical stimuli has many precedents in other areas of cognitive science; it is, for example, similar to the use of visual illusions by Gestalt psychologists to discover interesting facts about perceptual principles that are confounded in the real world. Such procedures are defensible if they lead to results that make sense within a coherent theory of normal processing. Second, we have obtained comparable results in studies with and without semigrammatical stimuli. For example, case-ambiguous sentences occur naturally in both German and Serbo-Croatian; hence, all stimuli in an orthogonalized design are grammatical and ecologically valid. The same design in Hungarian or Turkish necessarily involves the use of ungrammatical stimuli. Nevertheless, the effects of competition, convergence, and conspiracy are quite similar across all these languages. This point was made most clearly in a study of Hungarian sentence processing by MacWhinney, Pléh, and Bates (1985). Case marking is mandatory and unambiguous in Hungarian, except for a small set

Table 1.1. *(cont.)*

Serbo-Croatian

Adults: Case > Agreement > Animacy > SVO, VSO, SOV

Under 5: Animacy > Case > SVO, VSO, SOV > Agreement

Hungarian

Adults: Case > SV > Agreement > SVO, SOV > Animacy > V – O agreement

Under 3: Animacy > Case > SVO > Stress (agreement not tested)

Turkish

Adults: Case > Animacy > Word Order

Under 2: Case > Word Order (animacy not tested)

Hebrew

Adults: Case > Agreement > Order

Under 10: Case > Order > Agreement

Warlpiri

Adults: Case > Animacy > Order

Under 5: Animacy > Case > Order

Chinese

Adults: Animacy > SVO

Japanese

Adults: Case > Animacy > SOV

---

of noun-phrases marked in the possessive. MacWhinney et al. first examined the relative contributions of case marking, word order, and semantics using stimuli that included ungrammatical case-ambiguous sentences like "The horse-nominative is kicking the cow-nominative." These results were compared with those of a second experiment with a similar design, using possessive sentences in which case-ambiguous combinations are grammatical (e.g., "Your red-possessive is hitting my blue-possessive"). The main effects and interactions among variables were quite similar in these two experiments, suggesting that the presence of semigrammatical stimuli does not evoke strategies that are qualitatively different from those observed with normal sentences only. Finally, we have also conducted a number of studies varying methodological factors: randomized designs compared with blocked designs, with or without instructions that focus subjects' attention on their processing strategies, with or without instructions forcing subjects to respond as quickly as possible. The crosslinguistic results that we have obtained to date appear to be quite robust, replicating across all these methodological conditions. Furthermore, most of our crosslinguistic effects are extraordinarily large, accounting for 20–50% of the experimental variance. Strategies that are this robust must reflect something solid and real. We are convinced that our subjects respond in this laboratory situation by assimilating both grammatical and ungrammatical sentences to the representations and processes used in everyday life.

As shown in Table 1.1, many different hierarchies of cue strength have now been observed across languages. The functional differences that we have discovered so far suggest the need for a new functional taxonomy of languages, a taxonomy that may not always correspond to the formal distinctions of typological linguistics. Traditional taxonomies are based upon contrasts such as the presence or absence of case marking, the pro-drop parameter (e.g., whether or not a language can omit the subject of free-standing declarative sentences), and the default word order used in a language (including the postulation of certain "non-configurational" languages that may have no basic word order at all). Our data present problems for all these classic dichotomies.

First, word order has proven to be a more important cue in German (a case-marked language with rich inflectional morphology) than it is in Mandarin Chinese (a language with very little grammatical morphology overall, and no inflections of any kind to mark transitive relations). This pattern is not compatible with a sharp dichotomy between case-marked and noncase-marked languages.

Second, findings about French, Italian and English present problems for a theory that emphasizes the pro-drop parameter (Rizzi, 1982). These are all languages without case inflections, and in which SVO is the basic or default word order. However, Italian permits considerably more word order variation, and sentences without overt subjects are both permissible and frequent. French and English both require overt subjects, including dummy subjects like the "it" in "it is raining." Furthermore, at least for sentences without clitic pronouns (see below), deviations from canonical SVO are rare in French. Nevertheless, Kail and her colleagues have shown that French is functionally more similar to Italian than to English (Kail, this volume, McDonald and MacWhinney, this volume). In particular, semantic and morphological cues are much more important than word order for sentence interpretation by French adults. We will offer some explanations for this pattern shortly; for now, the point is that these findings on linguistic performance do not fit a formal classification based on the pro-drop parameter.

Yet another surprise comes from experimental results in Warlpiri (Bavin & Shopen, this volume). Warlpiri is a so-called nonconfigurational language in which word order should in principle have no effect at all on sentence processing. It is true that Warlpiri adults pay more attention to morphological and/or semantic cues than to word order; however, they also have a significant tendency to choose the first noun in NVN constructions, particularly when no other contrasts are available. In this respect, Warlpiri is not functionally very different from Italian or French. In fact, English is the one truly exotic language – the only language we have studied to date in which word order is the most important determiner of sentence meaning across all tested morphological and semantic/pragmatic conditions. Insofar as ninety percent or more of the existing research in psycholinguistics is based on the performance of English subjects, this is a worrisome finding indeed.

Coalitions and Prototypes

What we have described so far is the relationship between a single cue (e.g., preverbal position) and a single function or meaning (e.g., the actor role). This kind of relationship is depicted in Figure 1.1a. In natural languages, such mappings of a single form onto a single function are quite rare. Rather, languages make extensive use of polysemy, thereby producing grammatical systems in which the same form can map onto several functions, while the same function can map onto several forms. For example, preverbal position is associated not only with the actor role, but also with the potentially dissociable notion of discourse topic. These two functions, in turn, are also associated with other surface forms – for example, agreement with the verb in person and number. Taken together, these many-to-many mappings comprise a series of subsystems which we refer to as coalitions. A very simple coalition of this sort is illustrated in Figure 1.1b.

The paradigm case of a many-to-many mapping, exploited in most of our experimental work to date, is the mapping underlying the category of "sentence subject." This mapping is based heavily on the activation of concepts such as "agency" and "topicality." By labeling a node in a figure such as Figure 1.1b as expressing "agency" we may seem to be indicating that we view "agency" as an impenetrable unitary concept. In fact, we realize that concepts such as "agency" have a fine-grained and distributed internal structure of their own. In particular, agency is an emergent grouping of such underlying features as humanness, animacy, intentionality, and motion. None of these features may be either necessary or sufficient to activate the agent role (Hopper & Thompson, 1980). The particulars of language processing and development require that we dig continually deeper into the microstructure of these grammatical categories.

It is not enough to focus simply on the connections between functions and forms. In order to fully understand the structure of coalitions like the "subject" coalition, we need to also look at the correlations and connections between functions and between forms. We will call the connections between forms and

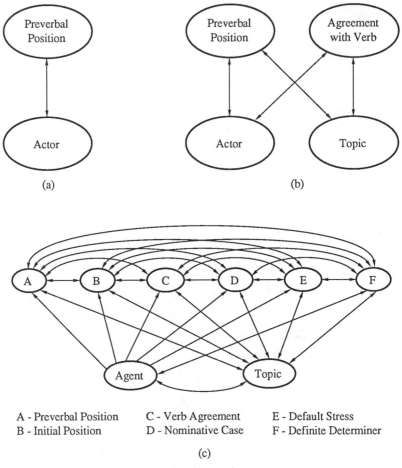

A - Preverbal Position   C - Verb Agreement   E - Default Stress
B - Initial Position   D - Nominative Case   F - Definite Determiner

(c)

Figure 1.1. Three ways of viewing form–function mapping.

functions "vertical connections" and the connections between forms or between functions "horizontal connections." Figure 1.1c indicates the fact that all forms on a level are potentially connected with double horizontal lines. At the level of horizontal form–form correlations, we can specify the probability that any given pair of forms will cooccur: the probability that a noun mapped onto preverbal position will also agree with the verb in person and number, receive nominative case, occur with definite determiners, and so forth. These correlations among forms are particularly likely to vary from one language to another. For example, in English, preverbal position and subject–verb agreement tend to be assigned as a block; in Italian the correlation between these two forms is considerably lower. Subjects are more likely to be definite in both English and Italian, but definiteness is much more highly correlated with the other subject devices in Italian. These distributional facts comprise an important part of the input to small children, and as we have noted earlier, it is possible in principle for children to detect such form–form correlations without necessarily detecting their associated meanings.

At the level of horizontal function–function correlations, we specify the probability that any given pair of functions will cooccur: the probability that an entity serving as the topic for a particular comment is also the agent of a transitive action, similar to the speaker with a similar perspective on the situation, and so forth. Languages do not choose these functional correlations randomly. Instead, these correlations reflect "natural" tendencies in human experience that tend to recur across natural languages. For example, the correlation between agent and topic reflects a high-probability tendency for speakers in all cultures to talk about their own activities and the actions of those who are near and dear to them. Hence, horizontal correlations at the functional level are considerably less likely to vary from one language to another.

Between these respective "horizontal" levels of form and function, there are also a set of "vertical" weightings that represent the probability in a given language that an individual function will be mapped with a particular form. With these connections we can, for example, capture the following differences between Italian and English:

1. the probability that the topic of a discourse will be assigned preverbal position (more common in Italian),
2. the probability that the agent will be assigned preverbal position (more common in English), and
3. the probability that the agent/topic will be marked with definite determiners (more common in Italian).

Again, note that many of these language differences are statistical rather than obligatory in nature. Although such performance facts typically fall outside the purview of a grammar based on rules, they are exactly the kind of fact that we are trying to capture in our model.

Finally, as we noted earlier, it may be necessary to postulate more than two layers in order to capture nonorthogonal relationships like the exclusive-or (i.e., in order to solve the perceptron problem). We have argued that such intervening layers may develop through experience, in neutral "hidden units" such as those described by Rumelhart, Hinton and Williams (1986) or Taraban et al. (in press; see also MacWhinney et al., this volume). The organization of stress and word order in Italian is a case in point, as is the relationship between pronominal object clitics and word order in Italian and French. Figure 1.2 illustrates a hypothetical fragment of the subject system in Italian, demonstrating how word order and stress cues may be organized together into blocks (i.e., "grammogens"), units which in turn serve as the input to assignment of the actor role.

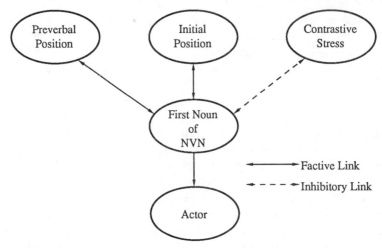

Figure 1.2. Hypothetical fragment of the subject system in Italian

These correlational relationships constitute an application of prototype theory to the domain of grammatical categories (Bates & MacWhinney, 1982). In other words, when we say that a mature speaker "knows" the set of connections described in Figure 1.1c, we mean that he "knows" the internal composition of a prototypic subject in his native language. All of the critical predictions of prototype theory follow from this claim.

1. Family resemblance. In less-than-ideal communicative situations (where the proposition to be expressed does not contain a prototypic subject), the set of surface forms that comprise "subject" in this language will be assigned by family resemblance through "best fit" or "maximum overlap" with the prototypic subject. Membership in the subject category is a matter of degree.
2. Heterogeneous membership. A grammatical category will contain members that overlap with the prototype but not with one another (e.g., sentences in which the subject is a nontopicalized agent versus sentences in which the subject is a nonagentive topic).
3. Maximum distance from other categories. Grammatical knowledge involves reciprocal relations among neighborhoods of categories, where category assignment is the joint product of maximum overlap with the category that is ultimately assigned, and minimum overlap with competing categories that could have been assigned. Hence, assignment of the subject role involves not only a calculation of goodness-of-fit to a prototypic subject, but also a calculation of goodness-of-fit to other grammatical categories (e.g., prototypic object).

Through generations of experience with the competition process, languages have evolved to exploit natural coalitions whenever it is possible to do so. Nevertheless, it does occasionally happen that functions which prototypically "go together" have to be split apart and assigned to different items in order to express an idea adequately. To illustrate, consider what happens when the coalition between agency and topicality breaks down in English and Italian.

This can occur, for example, when we need to topicalize "the ball" even though "John" did the hitting. In such cases the grammar has to determine which of the two elements should "win" access to devices like preverbal positioning and verb agreement. We have classified solutions to this problem into two basic types: "compromise" and "divide the spoils."

A typical compromise solution, provided by both English and Italian, is selection of the passive (Bates & Devescovi, this volume): the patient/topic "ball" wins access to the major subject devices, but the agent is placed in a special "by clause" that signals its continued semantic role. In terms of prototype theory, this is the kind of "hedging" and category–mixing that often occurs when categorization decisions have to be made for peripheral members. In a sense, it is a sentence-level analog to word-level expressions like "An ostrich really is a bird," designed to mark explicitly the peripheral status of a category assignment.

Topicalization is an illustration of a typical "divide the spoils" solution. In topicalization in Italian, preverbal position is assigned to the topicalized patient, but verb agreement is still assigned to the agent. In other words, the set of surface devices comprising "subject" is split up and assigned to separate elements. This kind of splitting does occur in English (e.g., in informal constructions like "Now that I'd really love to see!"), but such forms are much less frequent and considerably more constrained in English than they are in Italian. The highly correlated subject devices in English tend to be assigned as a block, whereas the lower correlations among the same devices in Italian permit the coalition to be split up more easily in nonprototypical situations.

The point is that a series of compromises are made in both sentence comprehension and sentence production. The ideal situation does not always hold. In fact, the fully prototypical instance of a category such as "subject" may actually be fairly rare (like the "ideal member" that is extracted but never taught in studies of artificial category learning such as Posner & Keele, 1968). This is possible because our knowledge of a "prototypic subject" is the emergent property of a great many weightings between individual forms and functions. It is the result of a lifetime of distributional analysis, and not a template derived from any single instance of grammatical learning. To understand how such a system works in real time, we turn to the processing dynamics of the Competition Model.

Processing Dynamics

Competition

The model assumes dynamic control of the mapping of form onto function in comprehension, and the mapping of function onto form in production. This mapping is understood to be governed by a system of parallel activation with strength-based conflict resolution much like that found in word-level processing models such as Thibadeau, Just, and Carpenter (1982) or McClelland and Rumelhart (1981). The Competition Model extends these word-based models to the sentential level to account for assignment to grammatical roles and other parsing decisions in comprehension.

To illustrate what we mean by this, consider the word-recognition system modeled by McClelland and Rumelhart, to account for experimental findings by Glushko (1979). People know how to pronounce a "new" or nonexistent string like MAVE, even though they have never seen it before. Usually they will pronounce it to rhyme with CAVE, but occasionally they will pronounce it to rhyme with HAVE. Glushko suggested that speakers make their decisions not by applying an abstract set of phonological rules, but by a process of analogy. Specifically, when the letter string MAVE appears, all of the existing words that overlap partially with this nonsense string are activated simultaneously. Each of the real word candidates has a basic activation level reflecting (at least in part) its baseline frequency in in the language. The decision about how to pronounce this nonsense input, and the time taken to reach that decision, emerge out of the competition among all of these partially overlapping "demons": HAVE, as well as CAVE, SAVE, RAVE, MANE, MATE, CANE, and so forth. In the case of MAVE, the high-frequency candidate HAVE does occasionally win out, but it is usually overwhelmed by the greater number of word candidates with a long vowel. In general, decisions are a combined product of the number of different types in the competition pool, and the activation weights associated with each type.

A phrase-structure analog to this process can account for a number of robust phenomena in our crosslinguistic sentence comprehension data. As we have noted, there are massive differences between languages in the way that listeners respond to word order variations. Most of these differences follow directly from calculations of cue validity as described above. For example, Italians make greater use of both semantic contrasts and subject–verb agreement than their English counterparts; English listeners make greater use of word order than any other cue. In addition, however, we have also uncovered some interesting new information about the specific strategies used in different languages to deal with word order configurations. For example, English listeners not only have an overwhelming SVO strategy to deal with NVN sentences; they also have very strong and reliable VOS and OSV strategies to deal with the two respective noncanonical word order types. For every language that we have looked at, we have discovered some set of word order biases that do not follow in any straightforward or obvious way from known facts about basic word order types in the language. That is, the word order biases cannot be attributed to any single phrase structure "template."

However, we discovered that these word order and/or order/stress biases can be accounted for by the parallel activation of all the partially overlapping word order types in the language. That is, if a phrase structure analog to the MAVE example is going on, we should get exactly the results that we have obtained in all of the languages examined so far. Suppose, for example, that we line up all the possible phrase structures for talking about "John hit the ball" in English. Ignoring morphology, looking only at the "islands" of constituent ordering that we see (e.g., treating a cleft sentence like "The one who HIT the BALL was JOHN" as a VOS), it is clear that SVO is the statistically predominant ordering in English, followed by OSV and VOS. Carrying out a similar exercise in Italian, we find a much weaker bias toward SVO, with essentially random probabilities for SOV versus OSV and for VOS versus VSO – unless we take stress into account. For French, alternative word orders are possible only in the presence of a complex set of clitic markers. And yet, in experiments by Kail (this volume), French listeners behave almost exactly like Italians, distrusting word order and making decisions primarily on the basis of semantic and morphological cues – even though Kail did not provide clitics to "release" word order variation. The behavior of French adults with respect to phrase structure possibilities makes sense only if they are engaged in a process that involves a competition among partially as well as completely overlapping phrase structure candidates. In other words, the cliticized word order variations of French are somehow "echoing" in the listener's mind and influencing a decision about how to treat a novel sentence stimulus without clitic markers.

To what extent is a parallel system of this sort affected by the relative frequency of phrase structure types? A complete answer to this question must await more detailed calculations of the statistical structure of informal language use than we have available at this time. However, it is worth pointing out that absolute frequency may be of limited importance in the kind of nonlinear system of activation and competition that we have postulated here. As we will lay out in more detail in the section on acquisition below, conflict validity may be more important for adult speakers than overall cue validity. For example, our native informants assure us that word order variations are considerably less frequent in French than they are in Italian – even within the kinds of cliticized structures described by Kail (this volume). If performance were driven entirely by frequency, we should expect more differences between Italian and French adults than we have observed so far. The same should be true even if performance were based on the more complex notion of overall cue validity, because overall validity is at least a partial function of the availability (hence, frequency) of a cue. However, if adults are strongly affected by conflict validity (i.e., the trustworthiness of a cue in competition situations), then the absolute frequency of certain word order variations may be far less important than the clarity with which a prediction based on word order is disconfirmed in a reliable subset of sentence types.

Ongoing Updating

The processes of comprehension and production have to unfold in real time. There are constraints on the order in which cues are made available, and the order in which interpretations based on those cues are activated and selected.

In order to control the interaction of the various cues that impinge on sentence comprehension, we believe that the parsing system engages in an ongoing updating of assignments of nouns to case roles. For example, when parsing a sentence such as "The dogs are chasing the cat," the assignment of "dogs" as the agent is first promoted by its appearance as the initial noun. Then the fact that "are chasing" agrees with "dogs" in number further supports this assignment. Finally, when the singular noun cat appears postverbally, its binding to the object case role further supports the candidacy of "dogs" as the agent. Thus, at each point in sentence processing the mapping from the lexical item "dogs" to the agent role is updated. In this particular case, each updating increased the strength of this assignment. In other cases – particularly in languages that permit a great deal of word order variation – assignments may wax and wane in strength across the course of sentence processing. As a result, the competition pool expands and contracts across the course of sentence understanding, until a solution is reached. Because each language designs cues to permit ongoing updating, and because competing parses are maintained in parallel, the need for backtracking is minimized (Marcus, 1980).

The processes of competition and ongoing updating must take a somewhat different form in sentence production (Bates & Devescovi, this volume). In comprehension, the listener is not "in the driver's seat." Unsure of the speaker's intended meaning, the listener must be prepared to reject an early interpretation in favor of one that proves to be more appropriate later on. Hence, the degradation of "losers" may be gradual, permitting a less probable interpretation to come back to life if it is needed (this is why listeners are not compelled to follow the same garden path over and over again; they can learn from experience when forced to backtrack). In production, the speaker knows (more or less) what meaning is intended, making possible early commitments to a particular set of form–function mappings. Furthermore, if the utterance is going to come out right (i.e., as a relatively well-formed structure in the language), commitments will have to be made rather quickly – the sooner the better. There are only so many ways to express the same thought in a given language, and the pool of alternatives shrinks rapidly from the first word that the speaker selects (Bock, 1982). Although we adopt the view that comprehension and production make use of the same system of representations, we acknowledge that the real-time exigencies of processing may be quite different – a point that is important for language acquisition as well as adult language use and may prove to be particularly important in accounting for language breakdown in brain-damaged adults (Bates & Wulfeck, this volume).

A serious test of these claims about ongoing updating will require a move toward more on-line methods than we have adopted to date, particularly in the domain of receptive processing. In almost all of our sentence comprehension work, decisions are made at the end of the sentence. We have examined end-of-sentence reaction time data in several experiments; in general, the results support the predictions of the model (competition items take longer to resolve, convergence decreases reaction time). But there are some interesting exceptions that suggest a closer look at moment-to-moment decision making.

MacWhinney and Pléh (this volume) examined aspects of sentence inter-pretation in Hungarian, using stimuli in which a competition between cues occurs either early or late in the sentence. They report that reaction times are longer, even though decisions are the same, when the competition occurs relatively late. This result is compatible with the "rich get richer" principle in parallel distributed processing models like the one proposed by McClelland and Rumelhart (1981): The earlier a cue occurs, the sooner it can begin to inhibit its competitors; hence, more activation is required to "beat down" an interpretation that gets off the ground relatively early.

Confirming cues do not necessarily speed the processing of a sentence. Kail (this volume) has shown that the presence of a clitic pronoun can actually slow processing in both French and Spanish even though it eventually aids in the interpretation of the sentence. Devescovi (in progress) reports similar findings for clitics in Italian. An analogous slowing with the presence of a subject–verb agreement cue has been noted by Kail for Spanish, and in our own unpublished data on reaction times in English. However, no slowdown in processing has been noted for use of the agreement cue in French or Italian; in these languages, a subject–verb agreement contrast always results in faster reaction times.

How do we put these contradictory results together? The Competition Model clearly needs to be enriched with on-line information about the way listeners distribute their attention and make predictions across the course of sentence processing. It appears that listeners can often make up their mind more quickly on the basis of incomplete information. Having to pay attention to additional information can slow down processing unless (a) use of that cue is entirely automatic, and/or (b) the cue is expected and eagerly awaited.

These processing effects appear to interact with something that Kail (this volume) and Sridhar (this volume) both call "canonicity." Canonical, default word orders profit least from additional morphological information, a result that is magnified by (a) the importance of the word order cue in a given language, (b) the relative cue validity of the. morphological cue itself, and (c) the probability that these word order and morphological cues should occur together. We have to conclude that cues are not simply added up in a bottom-up fashion. Reaction times can be slowed by cues that the listener typically does not use (e.g., subject–verb agreement in English), and by unexpected configurations of cues (e.g., clitic pronouns and/or contrastive stress in sentences with default word order – turning a configuration that is usually pragmatically neutral into a marked variant). This slowing occurs even if the sentence interpretation is still a product of combined cue strengths. Effects of this kind require a better understanding of the dynamics of "horizontal" interaction between cues, including top-down inhibitory effects that vary in strength over time.

We are currently turning to a variety of on-line methodologies to investigate these and other aspects of real-time processing in the Competition Model. Kilborn (1987) devised an on-line version of our basic interpretation task, permitting subjects to make decisions as quickly as they can, before the end of the sentence if they prefer. His results for German and English are quite compatible with results obtained off-line: German subjects make their decisions on the basis of morphological information, with assignments occurring as soon as all the relevant information is available; English subjects base their decisions almost entirely on word order, and make those decisions as soon as the word order configuration itself is clear (e.g., immediately after the verb in NVN strings). Kutas and Bates (1988) have investigated event-related brain potentials to semantic and grammatical violations, in English monolinguals and in Spanish-English bilinguals. Their results provide further on-line support for the claim that Spanish and English listeners attend to different aspects of the same sentence input. English listeners show little or no reaction to violations of grammatical morphology (Kutas & Hillyard, 1983). By contrast, Spanish-English bilinguals show large cortical responses to morphological violations, in both of their languages (although the effects appear to be stronger in Spanish).

Other on-line techniques applied by members of our research team include word monitoring (Kilborn, 1987), error detection (Wulfeck, 1987), and a probe-identity task that can be used to test the degree to which a given noun is acceptable as the referent for pronouns and other anaphors (MacDonald & MacWhinney, in preparation). By focusing on the temporal microstructure of language processing, we hope to provide a stronger test of the Competition Model, discovering new constraints on cue validity that are not apparent from off-line methods. This brings us to the issue of processing costs.

Processing Limitations

So far, we have sketched out a processing system that has no fundamental resource limitations. In this simple system, cue strength is a direct function of cue validity. Even if a cue is hard to process and maybe even hard to hear, we would expect it to be a strong cue according to this simple model. We know, of course, that this simple account is wrong. But what we did not know in our earlier research was exactly how these limitations affect processing and development. In the last few years we have learned more about two major types of processing limitations: perceivability and assignability. We refer to these two types of limitations as "cue cost" factors to distinguish them from the "cue validity" factors we discussed above. Each of the two cue cost factors was foreshadowed by Slobin (1973) who described a set of "operating principles" that favor simplicity and locality of grammatical marking. The Competition Model adds to Slobin's insights primarily by providing detailed experimental evidence for such limitations, and explicit computational statements about the interactions among processing constraints (MacWhinney, 1987).

Perceivability

The most obvious limitation on processing is the low-level limitation dictated by the perceivability of the stimulus. Consider, for example, the example of subject–verb agreement in spoken French, as it is displayed by the contrast between these two sentences:

Elle mange.	She eats.
Elles mangent.	They+FEM eat+PL.

For most French verbs, in most conjugations, the clear-cut written difference between the singular and plural form of the verb is entirely inaudible (i.e., *mange* and *mangent* are pronounced the same way). Even though the agreement contrast is distributed quite faithfully through written texts of French, it is an imperceptible cue in the oral language. Cue validity means very little if a cue cannot be heard at all.

MacWhinney et al. (1985) have shown that less drastic differences in the perceivability of cues can also have a significant impact on the way those cues are used in sentence interpretation. In Hungarian, accusative case marking is a highly available and reliable cue. However, sometimes the accusative is hard to detect. When the accusative follows a dental or alveolar consonant, as in *mokus-t*, it is fairly difficult to identify with certainty. However, when the stem ends with the letter *a* as in *pipa,* the final *a* lengthens and changes its height. The distinction between the nominative *pipa* and the accusative *pipát* is quite clear and easily detected. In sentence interpretation experiments with adults and children, this difference in the perceivability of cues interacted with cue validity in determining the probability that a Hungarian listener will rely on case information. If case competed with other cues (e.g., word order and semantics), the strong vowel form of the suffix quite clearly "won" the competition; but if the weaker consonant form was involved, listeners would often (though not always) take the "conspiracy" of order and semantics into consideration in making their decision. In such cases, they would often mishear the case marking in a way that matched the default interpretation of the syntactic structure. MacWhinney et al. suggest that this is a morphological version of the "phoneme restoration effect" of Warren and Warren (1976), for example, the tendency to hear a stimulus like "(cough)-eel" as "wheel" or "meal," depending on the sentence context. Another way of putting it is that a lifetime of not being sure whether a case contrast is there or not has led listeners to "distrust" that cue, even in those instances when it is perceived.

In a sense, perceivability and availability are similar notions: a cue is not available from the organism's point of view if it cannot be perceived. Remember, however, that we are separating cue validity (an objective property of the linguistic environment) from cue strength (a subjective property of the organism). This move is necessary in order to keep validity from turning into a circular notion. We calculate cue validity from samples of real language use (oral or written). There is nothing in the text itself that tells us which cues are easiest to perceive, and to what extent. Indeed, estimates of perceivability may vary markedly from one listener to another (children versus adults, young adults versus older adults with hearing problems – see Bates & Wulfeck, this volume). Some of our ongoing work on "listening through noise" is designed to provide more independent motivation for perceivability and other aspects of cue cost (e.g., Kilborn, 1987).

Assignability

The second "cue cost" factor is what we call "assignability." The principle of ongoing updating outlined above is based on the assumption that the processing system tries to assign cues to meanings as rapidly as possible, integrating each fragment of sound and meaning into one or more larger structures that are compatible with all the information obtained up to that point (Bransford, Barclay, & Franks, 1972; Kintsch, 1974; Van Dijk & Kintsch, 1983). The amount of memory required for integration is relatively low when attachments between units can be made locally (Frazier, Clifton, & Randall, 1983; Ford, Bresnan, & Kaplan, 1982; Frazier, 1985; Small, 1980). Memory load increases when integration must be delayed until more information is received. Cues to sentence meaning can be ranked along a dimension called "assignability," referring to the amount of material that must be held in memory before a meaning assignment can be made.

Case morphology and agreement morphology provide an interesting contrast along this particular dimension of cue cost. In languages like Turkish or Hungarian, with unambiguous case systems, a case suffix can lead to the assignment of a semantic role as soon as it has been recognized and integrated with its (usually adjacent) noun stem. Ammon and Slobin (1979) and Johnston and Slobin (1979) refer to these as "local cues." Many forms of agreement morphology are, instead, "topological cues." For example, Italians cannot make use of number agreement in the third person until they have heard the verb and all its associated nouns. If the verb is third person singular, but both the nouns are also third person singular, then the agreement cue is completely ambiguous and provides no information. The same is true for agreement between the object and a clitic pronoun.

If the processing system is under stress, and/or if the processor has limited auditory storage, topological cues or cues that are low in assignability may become so costly to handle that they are abandoned despite their information value. Bates and Wulfeck (this volume) have provided some evidence to suggest that case cues are better preserved than subject–verb agreement in aphasic adults, presumably because of the extra processing load imposed by agreement cues that span several different elements of the sentence. Some implications of assignability for language acquisition by children are discussed in the next section.

Acquisition

Cue-Driven Learning

Within our model, language learning is viewed as a process of acquiring coalitions of form–function mappings, and adjusting the weight of each mapping until it provides an optimal fit to the processing environment. This is quite similar to the process that Gibson (1969) describes as "detection of invariance" and/or "acquired distinctiveness of cues." We have offered some strong predictions about language acquisition across natural languages, claiming that cue validity will determine the order in which grammatical devices are acquired. In other words, children are sensitive from the beginning to the information value of particular perceptual patterns, and will go to work first on those forms that promise a greater "payoff." With some interesting exceptions which we will discuss in more detail below, the data summarized in Table 1.1 provide strong evidence for the role of cue validity in language acquisition.

The same results also disconfirm many putative universals of acquisition. For example, several authors have previously claimed that children will acquire semantic cues to meaning before they understand the word order principles of their language (Strohner & Nelson, 1974). Our data suggest that this proposed universal is much too simple. In our own English-speaking subjects, SVO word order is the first cue to have a significant effect on sentence interpretation (in children as young as 28 months), and canonical order remains the strongest cue to meaning from 2 through 82 years of age (remaining strong even in so-called agrammatic aphasic patients – see Bates & Wulfeck, this volume). By contrast, semantic cues are far stronger than word order at every stage of development in Italian, from 2 through adulthood. Figure 1.3, which is based on data in Bates et al. (1984), plots the percent of experimental variance accounted for by the

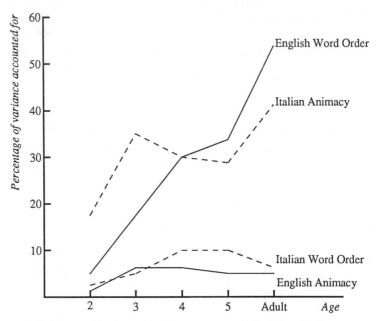

Figure 1.3. Variance resulting from main effects across ages in English and Italian.

respective main effects of word order and animacy, in each language, at each age.

Another putative universal involves the claim that children will acquire word order cues before they master grammatical morphology (Pinker, 1982). This is certainly true for children acquiring English. However, as Slobin and Bever (1982) have shown, Turkish children have attained adultlike use of case morphology as a cue to sentence meaning by the age of 2; they show no sensitivity at all to canonical SOV word order until 4–5 years of age, and even then the effect remains (as it is for adults) extremely small. Case suffixes are established somewhat later for Serbo-Croatian and Hungarian children, compared with their Turkish counterparts, However, there is no point in development in which canonical word order is more important than case in any of these languages.

A similar analysis can be applied to the use of morphology versus semantics. Figure 1.4 compares the developmental course of these two cue types in Serbo-Croatian and Hungarian (where the amount of experimental variance accounted for by each type of cue is plotted over age). In Serbo-Croatian, where case contrasts are frequently ambiguous, children begin with a bias toward semantic information. Semantically based interpretations drop off and case becomes dominant by 5 years of age. In Hungarian, where case contrasts are very rarely

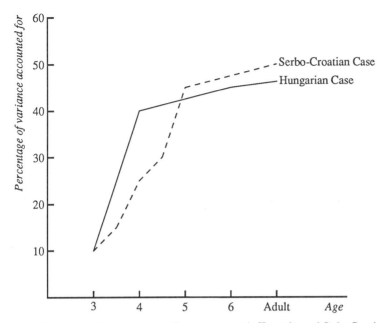

Figure 1.4. Variance resulting from main effects across ages in Hungarian and Serbo-Croatian.

ambiguous, semantic and morphological cues are roughly equivalent in strength at age 3, and case is firmly established as the dominant source of information by age 4. Hence there is a one-year difference between these two languages in the relative strength of case cues. This difference is quite compatible with the differential validity of case in the two languages.

In short, there appears to be no single, universal schedule of development in sentence comprehension. Children may begin by attending to word order, semantics, and/or grammatical morphology, depending on the relative validity of those cues in their native language. We have, however, uncovered a number of surprisingly late developments in sentence interpretation, delays that do not follow in a straightforward fashion from overall cue validity. Many of these late phenomena can be explained by distinguishing between overall cue validity and conflict validity.

Conflict Validity and Acquisition

McDonald (1986, this volume) has shown that the course of acquisition cannot be understood without recognizing the importance of the concept of "conflict validity." The contribution of conflict validity to acquisition represents one of the most important discoveries in our years of joint research. In the earliest stages of learning, children appear to respond primarily on the basis of overall availability (corresponding roughly to frequency, albeit frequency from the point of view of those meanings that are of interest to the child). After this initial phase, across the first years of language learning, development appears to be controlled primarily by reliability. However, once the bulk of language-specific learning is complete, children begin to fine-tune the system (Karmiloff-Smith & Planck, 1980; Karmiloff-Smith, 1986; McDonald, 1986). They begin to take note of relatively rare situations in which two or more cues compete, and reset form–function mappings to favor those cues that win in such conflict situations. Hence, conflict validity dominates the last phases of language learning, and may in some cases result in U-shaped functions and radical restructurings of the system as a whole (Bowerman, 1982, 1983, 1987).

It may be helpful to think of language learning in terms of the "80/20 rule." This rule holds that, in solving real-life problems, one often gets 80 percent of the gain in 20 percent of the time. This is also true in language. Using availability and reliability as guides, the child can correctly interpret the overwhelming majority of the sentences of his language. However, there often remains a residual set of sentences where full learning depends on attention to particular conflicts between cases which are only rarely encountered. There is evidence that certain late developments in language relate to the problems involved in acquiring a final set of dominance relations. McDonald (1986) has observed a dominance effect in the acquisition of Dutch. In sentences with a pronominal direct object, Dutch allows OVS word order to produce the Dutch equivalent of "Him saw I." For adult subjects, the usually weaker case cue dominates over the strong word order cue in sentences like these. The same relationships present serious problems for Dutch children as old as 8 years. Another example comes from Warlpiri (Bavin & Shopen, this volume), a language in which children must acquire a variety of dominance relations in order to disambiguate case markers. Again, there is evidence here that children find dominance relations hard to learn. Such late developments appear to occur somewhere between 6 years of age and adulthood. This "second phase" of language acquisition is the period in which interpretations based on overall cue validity give way to interpretations based on conflict validity.

This insight can help us to understand a result for French that we initially found very puzzling (Kail, this volume). As we noted earlier, French adults behave very much like Italians in our sentence interpretation experiments: a heavy reliance on grammatical morphology, followed by semantics, with relatively little use of canonical or noncanonical word order strategies. Nevertheless, French children seem to behave much more like young speakers of English: SVO is the first and most important cue to meaning from 2 through 6–7 years of age. Somewhere between 6 years to adulthood, French children must go through a radical reorganization of their comprehension system, switching from word order dominance to a primary reliance on morphology and semantics. This

U-shaped function can be explained if we remember that canonical word order is often violated in French – but only in complex cliticized structures within informal adult speech. These segments of the input constitute the conflict cases – in contrast with Italian, where word order violations abound even in very simple sentences spoken to children below the age of two (Bates, 1976). In French, violations of canonical word order violations contribute primarily to conflict validity; in Italian, word order variation influences overall cue validity.

The generality of this progression from overall validity to conflict validity has also been demonstrated in an unpublished experiment by McDonald and MacWhinney on artificial concept learning in adults. In acquiring a set of nonverbal concepts, adult subjects went through the same stages of acquisition that we have just described for children: an initial phase in which responses are controlled primarily by cue availability, followed by a lengthy phase of learning controlled primarily by overall cue validity, with the last phase of learning (i.e., the phase of "fine-tuning") driven primarily by cue dominance in conflict cases (see McDonald, this volume). Hence, the phenomena that we have observed in child language acquisition may reflect a much more general fact about distributional learning.

One way to account for these findings is by simply postulating a shift from overall validity to conflict validity as a general law of learning. However, a deeper and more unified explanation for the same phenomena comes from theories of learning in artificial neural networks (Rumelhart, Hinton, & Williams; 1986). In the Rumelhart et al. formulation, learning takes place through "back propagation" (also called the "generalized delta rule"). Specifically, learning takes place when there is a discrepancy between the desired output (the output presented by the teacher/environment) and the actual output (the output predicted by the system at its current level of learning, in the presence of a given input). At each output node, the degree of discrepancy is noted and propagated back through all input-output connections leading to that node. Each of the intervening weights is adjusted in strength (increased or decreased) in proportion to the degree to which that particular weighted connection was responsible for the final error (i.e., in proportion to "blame"). During the bulk of learning, many adjustments are made on any given trial (i.e., blame is widely shared). In the final stages of learning, far fewer errors are committed. Because the weights are changed only when errors are committed (i.e., when predictions are disconfirmed), relatively rare conflict situations begin to control the late phases of learning. As Taraban et al. have shown, the shift from overall cue validity to conflict validity that we have observed in our experiments can be simulated in a connectionist network that employs back propagation. With a constant and unchanging input, and a constant and unchanging learning device, we can obtain U-shaped functions and late developments of the sort that are observed in human language learning (McDonald, this volume; MacWhinney, this volume).

We think that the enriched notion of cue validity can account for many of the late developments observed to date – but not for all of them. Language acquisition is also affected by endogenous changes in information processing capacity. These include changes in cue cost (due to increases in perceptual acuity and/or memory), and a series of conceptual developments that we will refer to with the term functional readiness.

Cue cost in language acquisition

Cue cost is an obvious first place to look for constraints on cue validity in acquisition. Children are less developed organisms than adults, in perception, memory, motor skills. The costs of processing a given linguistic structure might well be expected to weigh more heavily for small children – perhaps enough to blunt the impact of information value on sequences of language learning.

The notion of assignability provides an explanation for one particularly puzzling delay in language learning. In MacWhinney et al. (1984) we have found that subject–verb agreement is an extremely strong cue to sentence interpretation for Italian adults; indeed, this cue appears to be just as important for Italians as case cues are for speakers of German, Hungarian, Turkish and other case-inflected languages. Similar patterns are obtained in Italian for agreement between the object and a clitic pronoun. Given these results, we should also expect very early acquisition of agreement by Italian children. And indeed, there is evidence available to suggest that Italian children mark agreement productively and correctly in their own expressive language by 2–3 years of age (although object/clitic agreement may come in somewhat later than subject–verb agreement). Nevertheless, in work still in progress, Devescovi and her colleagues have found that Italian children are unwilling to use agreement contrasts in sentence interpretation. Although there are reliable effects for both agreement contrasts by age 3, the effects are very small; semantic factors play a much greater role (accounting for 2–3 times more variance) until 6–7 years of age. Kail reports a similar late onset for both kinds of agreement in French, suggesting that the late use of agreement may be general phenomena. Finally, Devescovi et al. also describe a striking developmental contrast between case and agreement morphology within a single language. For Serbo-Croatian adults, case morphology is the most important source of sentence meaning; however, if case is ambiguous (which it often is in this language), Serbo-Croatian adults are strongly influenced by gender agreement markers on the verb. For Serbo-Croatian children, case (a local cue) becomes the dominant cue to meaning by age 4; gender agreement (a more distributed cue) is not used reliably for several more years.

The general picture appears to be one in which local morphology is acquired early, in accord with its cue validity, whereas more topological agreement cues are not used in sentence interpretation until 5–8 years of age – even if those cues are high in information value. Slobin (1985) has proposed a bias toward local marking as a general operating principle, in both comprehension and production (cf. Ammon & Slobin, 1979). However, given the disparity between production of subject–verb agreement (an early phenomenon) and use of the same forms in comprehension (a late phenomenon), Devescovi and Kail (this volume) both argue for an explanation based on the cue cost of agreement contrasts in receptive processing, in particular the memory costs involved in using cues that are low in assignability. In sentence production, the speaker presumably knows in advance "who did what to whom" and assignment of agreement markers can be made early, without waiting or holding extra material in memory. In sentence comprehension, the listener may not have prior knowledge about "who did what to whom." Under these circumstances, children may prefer to make tentative interpretations as soon as possible, using some combination of word order and semantic information, without holding elements in memory and comparing them to determine whether a usable agreement cue is available. This explanation leads to an interesting hypothesis in Italian: The memory demands of subject–verb agreement apply only for the third person; first and second person cues can be unambiguously assigned, the moment they are encountered, to the speaker and the hearer respectively. This fact leads to the prediction that Italian children will make use of first and second person agreement reliably before three years of age, on a schedule that parallels the appearance of these markers in their own speech production. Pilot results with a small number of Italian two- to three-year-olds lend support to this prediction (Devescovi, research in progress).

Perceivability is another source of cue cost that could in principle explain exceptions to cue validity in the development of sentence comprehension. MacWhinney et al. (1985) investigated the use of case suffixes by Hungarian children, comparing the two forms of the accusative described earlier: a -*t* suffix following a strong vowel (high in perceivability), and a -*t* suffix following a consonant cluster (low in perceivability). The more perceivable version of the case suffix was established approximately one-year earlier in sentence comprehension. The same finding may explain why there is approximately a one year overall difference between Hungarian and Turkish children in the onset of case morphology. Case is regularly and unambiguously marked in both these languages; however, the low perceivability of Hungarian case morphology after consonant clusters may delay the completion of case paradigms by Hungarian children compared with their Turkish age mates.

We are currently pursuing some extensions of the perceivability notion, in studies of the acquisition of clitic particles in Italian and French. These preverbal object markers are equally informative in both languages. However, French and Italian differ in the perceptual salience of object clitics in certain verb phrase environments. For example, the final *s* on the French plural object clitic *les* is silent in most environments; however, if the clitic is followed by a word beginning in a vowel (e.g., the participial construction *ont fait*, as in *les ont fait*), then the final s is pronounced – thus rendering the object clitic particularly salient. Compare this with the Italian *li hanno fatto*, in which the vowel-final object clitic is much less salient (blending into the vowel-initial sound of the participle that follows). If perceptual salience augments or degrades the effects of cue validity, then we should find differences between French and Italian in the relative strength of the clitic cue in a participial environment.

There are also some interesting differences between French and Italian in the perceptual similarity among object clitics, full subject pronouns, and articles. For example, the sentence initial sound *le* could signal at least three things in Italian: a third person feminine object clitic (as in *le vede* or "them-feminine sees"), a third person feminine article before a noun (as in *le donne* or "the women") and/or the first segment of a third person singular subject pronoun (as in *lei viene* or "she is coming"). Some preliminary evidence on pronoun interpretation by Italian children suggests that these potential ambiguities cause them considerable difficulty in the early stages. Confusions between object clitics and articles are also possible in French, but confusions between the object clitic and full subject pronouns are much less likely (i.e., compare *le* with the subject pronouns *lui* and *elle*). We are interested in determining the extent to which subtle phonological factors like these influence the acquisition of clitic forms as a cue to underlying semantic relations. Obviously this complicates any predictions based on cue validity, since a whole catalog of phonological factors would have to be taken into consideration. But if that is the way things are, so be it. Interactions between phonology and syntax may be inconvenient from a theoretical point of view, but they are certainly testable, and may play an important role in the acquisition of grammar.

Functional Readiness in Acquisition

Cue validity is calculated from the objective distribution of forms and their inferred meanings in a sample of text. Even if we assume that children can perceive all of the surface variations in their input language (i.e., horizontal correlations), we cannot assume that they are sensitive from the very beginning to all the meanings signaled by those forms (i.e., vertical correlations). A form–function mapping that is objectively available may be subjectively unavailable if the child has no understanding at all of the function, meaning, or intention signaled by a given linguistic form. The principle of functional readiness refers to the need for certain functions to develop before mappings from form to function can be made.

Consider, for example, the distribution of conditional and subjunctive markers in Italian. Although such forms are relatively rare in adult speech to children (compared with other verb inflections), they are no less frequent than many lexical items that children acquire well before the age of three. And they are associated quite clearly with their respective meanings. Nevertheless, Bates (1976) has shown that the conditional and subjunctive inflections are not mastered by Italian children until somewhere between 4 and 6 years of age. This fact can be explained in part by the cognitive difficulty of the counterfactual notions that underlie both of these verb paradigms. A similar argument can be made for the order of acquisition of locative terms within and across languages (Johnston & Slobin, 1979; Johnston, 1984), and for the relatively late appearance of devices for achieving discourse cohesion (Karmiloff-Smith & Planck, 1980). Children need some kind of guide to tell them when and where a given word, morpheme, or phrase structure should be used. If the children have no idea at all why adults are using a particular sound contrast, they may (a) fail to perceive it in the first place, (b) perceive it, but fail to integrate it well enough into memory for retrieval to take place, or (c) perceive and store the form as an arbitrary associate of a few lexical items (resulting in considerable undergeneralization).

This point may seem to contradict our earlier insistence that distributional learning is possible even in the absence of semantic interpretation. We argued that children could in principle treat distributions of sound like any other perceptual object, detecting and acquiring correlations between morphemes that have no clearcut meaning. Indeed, we must acknowledge such a process to account for the acquisition of German gender paradigms and/or the early appearance of certain forms of agreement marking in Italian. But notice that these latter phenomena are all tied to the lexicon, providing "hooks" on which to hang morphophonological variation. The child is interested in using a given word because she is interested in talking about the referent for that word. Reference provides a functional anchor for the word itself; the variations in sound associated with that word (gender, agreement, etc.) are detected, acquired, and reproduced in the service of reference.

Artificial language learning experiments by Morgan, Meier, and Newport (1987) and Valian and Coulson (1988) are particularly interesting in this regard. These authors presented adults with strings of symbols that obey a set of arbitrary combinatorial rules. These rules had to be learned under one of three conditions: (1) the formal relations in the grammar mapped onto semantic relations in an artificial object world, (2) the formal relations themselves had no semantic base, but each symbol had a constant referent in the same object world, or (3) the grammar had neither semantic nor referential correlates in the object world. Their results suggest that semantic relations may not be necessary for grammatical induction, but constant reference is very important for successful learning.

We suggest that the functional readiness principle is particularly important for sentence-level phenomena that have no clear referential base – that is, for syntactic principles which range across a wide variety of referents, as opposed to lexical/morphological regularities that can be tracked across the input because they have a recognizable referential "anchor." The child's attention is drawn to regularities of gender and other agreement phenomena because she is interested in the words that incidentally encode those regularities. The same child may not notice or use a phrase structure option in the language, if that phrase structure type is used by adults primarily for discourse purposes that are completely opaque to the child.

We suggest that functional readiness (a property of the child) interacts with conflict validity (a property of the environment). Specifically, changes in cognitive capacity may cause the child to notice conflict cases that she never noticed before. Prior to that point, the subjective input (i.e., the input attended to by the child) may actually be much smaller than the objective input (i.e., the input from the adult's point of view). With this idea in mind, we can provide a unified account for a range of late developments that have appeared in our crosslinguistic research to date:

1. a period around 4–5 years of age in which children overgeneralize some aspect of canonical word order (albeit in different ways, and to different degrees, from one language to another),
2. the shift away from word order dominance toward semantic and morphological strategies in French children after 6 years of age,
3. the appearance of VOS and OSV "second-noun strategies" in English children after age 6, and
4. the late appearance of word order and stress configurations in Italian children after age 6.

The lack of order/stress interactions in Italian is particularly puzzling, since the children are certainly sensitive to the absolute presence of contrastive stress. In fact, children in both Italian and French show a small but reliable tendency in the first years to choose the stressed element as the subject – exactly the opposite of the adult pattern. We have suggested elsewhere that this is essentially a nonlinguistic strategy: If you don't know what else to do, choose the noun that the experimenter said loudest. But it does show that children can hear the stress manipulation; why does it take them so long to use that information?

In the absence of these secondary adult word order patterns, Italian children develop a secondary strategy of their own: Generalize the first noun strategy derived from SVO to other word order types. This strategy starts between 4 and 5 years of age, and does not drop out until after the age of 9, when we finally see reliable use of stress to interpret NNV and VNN sentences. During this period of "word order overgeneralization," Italian children actually make more use of word order and less use of animacy than their adult counterparts (although word order never actually "wins out" over lexical semantics).

Kail (this volume) observed an even more dramatic version of word order overgeneralization in French children (discussed above). A much weaker version of first-noun overgeneralization has been noticed in Chinese (Miao, 1981), Hungarian (MacWhinney et al., 1985), Serbo-Croatian (Smith, personal communication), and Turkish (Slobin & Bever, 1982). In these studies, the overgeneralization of first-noun choice also starts around 4 years of age, although it drops out considerably earlier than it does in Italian or French. No such overgeneralization occurs in our data on English children. Other investigators have reported a tendency for English children to generalize SVO strategies to the passive – a strategy which, interestingly, also peaks between 4 and 5. But the first-noun bias is apparently not extended to NNV and VNN constructions in our research. Bates et al. (1984) suggest that the first-noun tendency is somehow blocked in English, because the English children are sensitive at some level to the factors that create VOS and OSV biases in adults. We will return shortly to an explanation of how this might occur.

Although these patterns vary markedly in size, range, and time of offset, some form of word order overgeneralization seems to occur reliably around age 5 across structurally and functionally distinct language types. The rise and fall of word order overgeneralization can be explained if we assume that the pool of phrase structure types impinging on sentence comprehension undergoes a series of changes during development. In the first phase (peaking between 4–5), evidence for basic or canonical word order accumulates and reaches a saturation point. Around age 5, there is a new influx of phrase structure types, including many complex phrase structures that violate canonical word order. These new entries in the competition pool serve to cut back the strength of canonical word order – to different degrees, and in different ways, depending on the input language. In part, this is the story that we told above, concerning a shift from overall validity to conflict validity. However, we think the reliable timing of this shift across languages can be explained if we also invoke the principle of functional readiness. In particular, we argue that children around age 5–6 begin to hear and to construct longer passages of oral and written discourse. This new contact with narrative speech brings the child into further contact with the sentential forms that adults use to create cohesive texts. Many of the phrase structure configurations that have a late effect on comprehension in our data fall into this category: relatives, clefts and related phrase structure types in English that are responsible for adult second-noun strategies, cliticized phrase structures in French that are implicated in the shift from order dominance to a morphological strategy, and word order/stress configurations in Italian.

Karmiloff-Smith (1979) provides independent evidence for a shift around 6 years of age, from a sentence-based grammar organized to express the semantics of simple events, to an intersentential grammar organized around the demands of discourse. For example, she describes a series of interesting errors that English and French children make around this age in the use of pronouns and determiners. These errors on structures that are produced flawlessly by much younger children can be explained on functional grounds: younger children use the same forms "exophorically" (to describe referents that are physically and psychologically present), whereas the older children are breaking into the more demanding "anaphoric" uses of the same linguistic forms (to describe multiple referents in a connected story, and/or to remind the listener of referents and events that occurred at another time and place). The same argument may apply to certain complex surface configurations that operate as a block (e.g., clefts), in the service not of sentence-level "event semantics" (e.g., who did what to whom) but rather, intersentential "discourse-level" semantics (e.g., how does this proposition contrast with a presupposition derived from previous discourse?).

If this argument is correct, then we have to predict parallels between comprehension and production in (a) the peak use of canonical phrase structures around age 5, and (b) a subsequent increase in discourse-based phrase structures after age 6. We do not yet know whether this is the case. It is certainly true that preschool children reliably produce only a subset of the possible phrase structure types in their language. However, we need more evidence about such things as the range and frequency of order/stress configurations for child speakers in "free word order" languages like Italian and Hungarian.

We also need to explain why English children fail to overgeneralize SVO to the same extent as children in the other languages studied to date. If they do not have the phrase structures responsible for the OSV and VOS biases of English adults, then why should any "blocking" occur at all? We may have to postulate a "two-tiered" membership in the competition pool of either word or phrase structure candidates. Active members in the pool are members that have been functionally assimilated (as defined above). These candidates exert the greatest force in a parsing decision. However, the child may well retain some memory of sentence types that he or she heard but failed to understand. If enough of these exceptions accumulate, they may serve to block certain generalizations that would be possible in their absence. This "second tier" notion is similar to the "waiting room" idea discussed by Ammon and Slobin (1979), and to the "file of unknown forms" in MacWhinney (1978).

The functional readiness principle can handle a variety of exceptions to cue validity. It is really a very simple notion, tantamount to "What you don't know can't hurt you (or help you)." And it may interact in interesting ways with the objective principles of overall validity and conflict validity. However, this principle can become completely circular if it is not used with caution. We need independent evidence for any and all claims that a given grammatical structure is "conceptually difficult" – evidence other than the mere fact that the structure in question appears late in development. Crosslinguistic research is one particularly helpful strategy in this regard, enabling us to separate conceptual difficulty (a dimension that should, in principle, apply equally across natural languages) from variations in structure. This is of course a major motivation behind the crosslinguistic methods pioneered by Slobin and his colleagues (Slobin, 1985). We hope that we have made some contributions here as well.

Conclusion

We suggested at the outset that a model must be evaluated along three dimensions: (1) its internal coherence (i.e., can it respond to the data without invoking ad hoc assumptions and/or circularities?), (2) its heuristic value, and (3) how well it compares with competing models in accounting for the same range of data. Let us now consider, briefly, how well the Competition Model stacks up against these three criteria.

With regard to internal coherence, the Competition Model is now considerably more explicit and detailed than it was more than ten years ago (when we first presented our joint work at the 1978 State of the Art conference organized by Gleitman and Wanner – see papers in Gleitman & Wanner, 1982). The principle of cue validity explains an extraordinary range of data, particularly when it is enriched by the distinction between overall validity and conflict validity. A number of interesting constraints on this powerful principle have also been discovered, particularly in the domain of cue cost. All of these constraints have an independent motivation, and they can all be investigated thoroughly and systematically (e.g., degrees of perceivability, assignability, or functional readiness). We have offered a series of explicit and testable claims about the structure of the system, processing dynamics and acquisition: Some of these claims are now precise enough to permit mathematical modeling (McDonald & MacWhinney, this volume), some progress has been made in the development of a realistic parser (MacWhinney, 1988), and there are now simulations of morphological learning that are consistent with the Competition Model (MacWhinney, this volume).

The heuristic value of the model in its present form also seems to be well-established. In addition to the research on normal processing and acquisition described here, the Competition Model has been applied successfully to language breakdown in adult aphasics (Bates & Wulfeck, this volume) and to sentence processing in bilinguals (Kilborn & Ito, this volume). Some further developments in the study of sentence production are described by Bates and Devescovi (this volume). Kail (this volume) underscores the importance of on-line investigations; her point is well taken, and first steps in this direction seem to be quite promising (Kilborn, 1987; Wulfeck, 1987; McDonald & MacWhinney, in press; Kutas & Bates, 1988). At the moment, at least, there seems to be no shortage of new ideas within this research framework – one of the major criteria for evaluating the success and utility of a model.

Finally, the Competition Model fares reasonably well against its competitors – primarily because there are no competitors. To our knowledge, there is no other comprehensive account of linguistic performance across natural languages. This is largely because no one else is trying to do what we are trying to do. There are three research currents that seem to speak to some of the same issues, but in reality the goals of these three other enterprises are quite different. A number of linguistic theories make interesting claims about crosslinguistic variations in competence. Such theories confine themselves to the study of the "core grammar," often focusing on structures involved in anaphora and case relations. Good examples of the application of linguistic principles to the study of competence in different languages can be found in the work on anaphora collected in Lust (1987) or the work on parameters found in Roeper and Williams (1987). This work attempts to look at variations in linguistic structure with an eye toward identifying a set of parameters which characterize the variation between languages. Having identified these parameters, workers in this tradition then hope that it might be possible to construct an identification procedure that would induce the proper grammars on the basis of sentences of the language and the innate constraints of universal grammar. This work seems to be a useful way of developing formal linguistic theory. However, it tells us little about linguistic performance and places relatively slight emphasis on the experimental verification of hypotheses. This is not a criticism of this line of work. Rather it is simply an observation that it is directed toward entirely different goals.

A much smaller group of investigators has used competence models to make strong claims about linguistic performance. The work of Berwick (1987) and Hyams (1986) is in this tradition. In principle it might be possible to use competence models to predict the quantitative data that are central to language acquisition. However, in practice, researchers trained in the tradition of competence theory have little understanding of the basic principles of experimentation and quantitative analysis that would be necessary to make strong links between competence and performance. Without such skills, these applications are necessarily doomed to failure when they come in contact with the realities of variability in language acquisition and processing data.

A third, extremely vital tradition is represented by the research collected in Slobin (1985). This tradition uses data on spontaneously occurring errors and early uses to abstract a set of "universal operating principles." These operating principles provide the child with biases toward preferring some grammatical forms more than others and hints about the best place to start in the process of acquiring a natural language. Although they seem to have considerable crosslinguistic generality, these operating principles were never intended to serve as a coherent theory of linguistic performance, in children or in adults. Rather, they constitute an ecologically valid set of strategies from which an integrated processing model can be constructed. In this way, work on operating principles can feed directly into work on the Competition Model.

The ultimate duty of a research model is to die for its science, providing hypotheses that are flatly and roundly disconfirmed. We fully expect that to happen to us as well, probably very soon. In the meantime, we hope that the success of our enterprise (and its failures) will encourage investigators to apply the crosslinguistic method in psycholinguistic research. To describe, predict, and explain human linguistic performance, we have to look outside the boundaries of English – an exotic code which is, according to Arnold Pick (1913), "An essentially formless language of high standing."

Part I. Sentence Comprehension

2 Cue Validity, Cue Cost, and Processing Types in Sentence Comprehension in French and Spanish

Michèle Kail

It has often been observed that children have a marked preference for one-to-one mappings between form and function (Slobin, 1973, 1977, 1982, 1985). Unfortunately for the child, natural languages seem to prefer much more complex, overlapping form–function relationships – a fact that has to be confronted in the course of language learning. To discover what it means to understand a sentence when multiple form–function mappings are available, a number of psycholinguists have tried to establish which cues subjects rely on and what strategies they apply during sentence comprehension. This of course calls for careful comparison of cues and of associated strategies within a crosslinguistic design. The idea that various message functions can be expressed by a *limited* number of competing linguistic devices – word order, lexical contrasts, morphological markings, intonation patterns – has been formulated in the functionalist, crosslinguistic model of sentence processing of Bates and MacWhinney (this volume). I shall assume familiarity with the major theoretical results and empirical findings associated with the model, whose value I have stressed elsewhere (Kail, 1983a, 1983b).

The initial version of the Competition Model (Bates & MacWhinney, 1982; Bates, MacWhinney, Caselli, Devescovi, Natale, & Venza 1984) focused on the relation between overall cue validity and cue strength. The current version of the model allows for a more complex relation among overall cue validity, cue cost, and conflict validity. These elaborations of the model were stimulated by several sources of data. In the present chapter, I will present data from French that were central in delineating the shape of these elaborations. In this discussion, I will refer to the initial version of the model as the "overall validity model." I will refer to the current version of the model as the "elaborated Competition Model."

In Experiment 1, I will show that, although the overall validity model can explain some of the facts noted for French, it nevertheless fails in its original form to account for the strength of animacy versus word order cues in adult French speakers, and for the sequence of acquisition of cues by French children. Specifically, we will see that there is a complete reversal in sentence processing

77

strategies, from an order-based strategy in French children to a lexically based strategy in French adults. The principle of conflict validity (McDonald, this volume) is required to account for this change.

In Experiment 2 (based on Kail & Charvillat, 1986), I introduce the notion of *cue cost* to account for several processing facts that cannot be explained by cue validity. One important cue cost factor revolves around the distinction between *local cues*, which can be interpreted as soon as they are processed, and *topological cues*, which are distributed across several continuous or discontinuous sentence elements. I will show that the order of importance of cues to sentence meaning in French and Spanish falls along a local-to-typological dimension. In addition, some of the reaction time findings in Experiment 2 violate the usual assumption in the Competition Model that speed increases with information. In some cases, converging morphological information actually slows down decision time – even though it increases the reliability of the decision itself. Some of these cases require us to invoke a notion of *canonical form*, that is, a default interpretation that listeners try to impose early in the sentence. The challenges posed by Experiment 2 can only be resolved through on-line research.

Selected Characteristics of French

Although numerous French-language psycholinguistic studies have examined sentence competition strategies and their emergence in the course of development (Sinclair & Bronckart, 1972; Noizet, 1977; Amy & Vion, 1976; Kail & Segui, 1978; Bronckart, Gennari, & de Weck, 1981; Kail, 1983c; Noizet & Vion, 1983), no single coherent picture, integrating these various findings, has as yet been drawn. To be sure, specific conclusions have been reached in connection with the interaction between such specific cues as word order, the animate/inanimate noun distinction, and morphological markers (Plas, 1981; Bronckart, Kail, & Noizet, 1983; Clark, 1986). However, even when limited models have been proposed and the necessity of crosslinguistic studies recognized (Ferreiro, Othenin-Girard, Chipman, & Sinclair, 1976; Kail & Weissenborn, 1984), none have ever fully adopted a comparativist approach. This is where the Competition Model, with comparative analysis at its core, can play a major role. Psycholinguistic research cannot be based on a mere juxtaposition of data from necessarily heterogeneous studies (Kail, 1987). Rather, our research must be organized around specific hypotheses which determine the choice of the language to be analyzed in terms of the constellation of processing cues that distinguish a given language from others.

Compared with languages such as English and Italian, for which the data are largely compatible with those predicted by the model, French offers a significant testing ground for the cue validity hypothesis owing to a number of special features of the language. Listed below are those linguistic characteristics of French that motivate the experiments reported later.

1. Word Order Cues

The canonical order of French is SVO. The first NP in a sentence is most frequently the agent, but canonical SVO is also preserved in sentences involving intransitive verbs (e.g., *mourir* or "to die") or elliptical transitives (e.g., *manger* – "to eat"; Segui & Kail, 1974). Unlike Italian and Spanish, which are also SVO languages, French does not permit subject ellipsis. Like English, French maintains SVO order through recourse to "dummy subjects" (e.g., *Il pleut* or "It is raining") or the kind of impersonal constructions often found in proverbs (e.g., *Rien ne sert de courir, il faut partir à point,* loosely translated as "Haste (it) makes waste"). Taken together, these facts mean that SVO constructions are both frequent and informative in French.

Despite its preeminence, the canonical SVO order occurs along with other orders imposed by syntactic, pragmatic or contextual constraints. VS order can be found in relativized object constructions, for example,

L'homme que connaît Jean pratique la médecine,

which means "The man that John knows practices medicine" and which contrasts with the SV stylistic variant

L'homme que Jean connaît pratique la médecine,

which means that same thing and more closely resembles the object relative construction in English. The latter variant, involving two contiguous verbs, is infrequent in French and has been shown to pose special processing problems for French children (Kail, 1975a, 1975b). An important difference between French and English is that French marks subject relatives with the pronoun "qui" and object relatives with the pronoun "que" whereas English uses one marker "who" for both purposes. However, Sheldon (1978) has shown that French-speaking children are slow to acquire full use of this case. This SV order is obligatory when the subject of the relative clause is pronominalized, as in

Le médecin qu'elle connaît emploie la médecine douce.
"The doctor that she knows uses natural medicine."

In such sentences the interpretation of the relative clause is facilitated by the fact that the pronoun is marked for nominative or accusative case.

A second major exception to SVO order is the use of SOV order. SOV order in French is primarily due to the existence of a double series of clitic pronouns: both preverbal direct object (*le, la, les*), and preverbal indirect object (*lui, leur*) pronouns. From the sentence

Le soldat montre la flèche à l'indien.
"The soldier is showing the arrow to the Indian."

all of the following may be derived:

Le soldat la montre à l'indien.
"The soldier it is showing to the Indian."
Le soldat lui montre la flèche.
"The soldier to him is showing the arrow."
Le soldat la lui montre.
"The soldier it to him is showing."

Although object clitics are marked both for gender and number, these forms are identical to the definite articles (*le, la, les*). This potential ambiguity between clitics and articles could present problems for left-to-right parsing in French. Indirect object clitics are unmarked for gender, and third person indirect object clitics follow the direct object clitic in both the indicative and imperative moods (*Montrez-le lui* – "Show it to him."). However, first and second person indirect object clitics precede the direct object in the indicative (*Le soldat me le montre* – "The soldier to me it is showing") but not the imperative (*Montre-le moi* – "Show it to me."). Obviously this complicates the statistical distribution of direct/indirect object ordering relative to the verb – a factor which may have implications for the utility of word order information in real-time sentence interpretation. For a further discussion of French clitic pronouns and the complex matter of their ordering, see Edmonds (1975), Gaatone (1976), Hurtado (1981), and Fernandez (1985).

The other exceptions to SVO order are fairly rare. VSO order is found in the interrogative form *Prend-il le train ce soir* ("Is taking he the train this evening?"). However, this form is infrequent in spoken French (Behnstedt, 1973). Canonical SVO is preserved instead thanks to three alternative devices:

1. final intonation rise (most frequent in the spoken language), for example, *Jean prend le train demain?* – "John is taking the train tomorrow?".
2. repetition of the subject by means of an inverted pronoun, for example, *Jean prend-il le train demain?* – "Jean is taking he the train tomorrow?".
3. formulaic *est-ce que?* – "Is it that?," for example, *Est-ce que Jean prend le train demain?* (Note that this interrogative expression may be combined with the full range of interrogative pronouns: *qui, ou, comment, pourquoi, quand, combien*, e.g., *Qui est-ce que tu as choisi?* – "Who is it that you chose?," *Combien est-ce qu'il vous doit?* – "How much is it that he to you owes?" As in English, questions containing interrogative morphemes normally have falling intonation.)

Finally, VOS is a very low frequency construction, observed in two cases:

1. right-topicalization as in sentences of the sort *Prend beaucoup de fleurs, ma soeur* – "Takes a lot of flowers, my sister."
2. imperatives (e.g., *Ecris les lettres rapidement, Paul* – "Write the letters quickly, Paul.").

Combinations of the above-mentioned factors (left- and right-topicalizations, clitic object pronouns) are responsible for extending the range of possible orders found in French through topicalization of the subject and object in accord with contextual or pragmatic constraints and the distribution of "new" and "old" information. Trévise (personal communication) has shown that the canonical form of the utterance *Jean aime les pommes* ("John likes apples") is in fact rather infrequent. Instead, she provides a list of over twenty variants of the utterance. The following selection may illustrate the complex interlocking ordering possibilities (where Sp and Op mean subject pronoun and object pronoun, respectively):

Jean il aime les pommes.	S SpVO
Il aime les pommes Jean.	SpVO S
Jean il aime les pommes Jean.	S SpVO S
Jean il les aime les pommes.	S SpOpV O
Jean les pommes il les aime.	S O SpOpV
Jean les pommes il aime.	S O SpV
Jean les pommes il aime ça.	S O SpVOp
Jean il aime ca les pommes.	S SpVOp O
Les pommes il les aime Jean.	O SpOpV S
Les pommes il aime ça Jean.	O SpVOp S
Les pommes Jean il les aime.	O S SpOpV

The extreme variability of ordering that is characteristic of French under these conditions is quite comparable to the ordering variability observed in Italian and Spanish (although clitic pronouns are not always necessary to "release" word order variation in those languages). Nonetheless, this variability clearly operates within definite limits. French does not allow subject ellipsis, and tends to conserve canonical SVO in many constructions. Whenever noncanonical order appears in simple sentences it cooccurs with specific phenomena such as cliticization. Thus, it may be claimed that French lies midway between English and either Italian or Spanish (i.e., the three other languages that are most relevant to the studies presented below) in terms of the rules or principles governing word order.

2. Prosodic Cues

It is important to differentiate a device like "contrastive stress," as found in English, from what we shall call French-style prosodic "highlighting." In English it is possible to place contrastive stress on a lexical item like "sailors" in the sentence:

"SAILORS make a mean fish stew."

Given the appropriate context, this may signal a contrast between the fish stew made by sailors and the rather ordinary fare which might be made by Kansas City taxi drivers (for example).

There is no exact phonological equivalent of this device in French, whose rhythmic accents regularly fall on the final syllables of phonological words, and are therefore entirely predictable (Wenk & Violand, 1982). The usual way for French speakers to translate a sentence with a stressed subject such as:

"JOHN is going to Philadelphia."

is through the use of clefting, as in

C'est Jean qui va à Philadelphie
"It is John who is going to Philadelphia."

From a *phonetic* standpoint, however, there is a phenomenon known in French as *mise-en-relief* which bears some resemblance to contrastive stress in English, since the first (or in some cases, the second) syllable of a word in French may be highlighted through an increment of intensity, accompanied by a sudden pitch-jump and greater duration of the syllable-onset. This device is essentially stylistic and is much recommended to French newsreaders and others in journalism schools these days in order to relieve the putative monotony attributed to strings of phonological words whose prosodic shape is felt to lack the fundamental frequency and variation that is supposed to capture and retain the attention of media consumers. Thus, in the following sentence pair:

a.   *La délégation néo-zélandaise est arrivée hier à Mururoa.*
b.   *La DElégation NEo-zélandaise est arrivée hier á Mururoa.*
     ("The New Zealand delegation arrived in Mururoa yesterday.")

in which the second (b) reading includes two highlighted (capitalized) syllables, there is no semantic (or pragmatic) distinction comparable to that embodied in the following pair of possible English sentences:

c.   "JOHN is quite a baseball player." (...unlike Bartholomew)
d.   "John is quite a baseball player." (...although he may be hopeless on the golf course)

Nevertheless, on the strength of the phonetic similarity between the two devices, the one meaning-bearing (in English) and the other stylistic (in French), and for the sake of experimental parallelism, we manipulated a highlighting variable in the studies reported below, naturally expecting it to behave in a manner unlike English-style contrastive stress, or the semantically informative role played by stress in Italian.

3. Animacy Cues

As in English, the animate/inanimate distinction is not morphologically marked on nouns in French. Rather, animacy is a lexical-semantic property of the noun itself. Many investigators have underlined the tendency for very young children to favor animate agents and inanimate patients (Brown, Cazden, & Bellugi, 1968; Brown, 1970; Slobin, 1968; Bowerman, 1973; de Villiers & de Villiers, 1974; Chapman & Miller, 1975). A considerable body of research testifies to an ordering strategy based on the animacy/inanimacy distinction which places animate entities preverbally and inanimate ones postverbally (Bloom, 1970; Bowerman, 1973; de Villiers & de Villiers, 1974; Chapman & Miller, 1975). By virtue of this strategy, children can produce reliable ordering of animates and inanimates in their expressive language without considering the role each item plays as agent or patient in a particular meaning structure. Similarly, in comprehension the child can supposedly short-circuit either a semantic or a syntactic analysis of the sentence, by assigning roles entirely on the basis of animacy.

In their study of comprehension, Sinclair and Bronckart (1972) found evidence of no such a strategy in French. They asked children ages 2–10 to act out sentences containing two nouns without articles and an infinitive verb in all possible orderings (NVN, NNV, VNN). For NVN sentences in which the first noun was inanimate, for example, "box open boy," the most frequent interpretation was patient-action-agent. This result differs strikingly from that obtained with English children (Bates et al., 1984), for whom an SVO strategy was dominant. But in the Sinclair and Bronckart experiment, the distinction between lexical-semantic and event probability strategies had not been taken into account. Chapman and Kohn (1978) have shown the importance of distinguishing between the two. Controlling for the development of event probability in their stimulus material, they discovered no evidence for a general semantic strategy for example, "agent-action." Children seemed to be influenced by event probability for familiar items (e.g., the knowledge that mothers feed babies and not vice-versa), but they relied on word order (or performed randomly) for items displaying no strong real world relationship.

In a number of experiments that focus on comprehension, a slow, gradual decline in the use of semantically based strategies has been recorded from age 1;11 to 12;0 (for an overview on English, see MacWhinney, 1982; for French, Bronckart, 1983). This is especially clear between ages 6 and 12, when ordering strategies become dominant. The decline is also sharper for active than for passive sentences. Dewart (1975), for example, asked children to choose referents in NVN sentences made up of nonsense words. At 3 years, children showed a very strong preference for animate referents for N1, but the preference had already begun to decay by age 5.

In a study of sentence production, Angiolillo and Goldin-Meadow (1982) have recently demonstrated that children take account of the actual roles played by linguistic entities (agent or patient) whatever the status (animate/inanimate) of the entities. However, work involving utterance completion and judgment tasks with adults in French and English has indicated a subject preference for sentences beginning with animate nouns (Clark, 1965, 1966; Jarvella & Sinnott, 1972; Segui & Chauvaut, 1974).

To summarize, at least three kinds of semantic strategies have been shown to play a role in sentence comprehension and production: animacy (an inherent property of lexical items), agency (the actual role played by a given referent in a transitive action), and event probability (an inherent property of the situation being described). The relative importance of these semantic strategies varies with age. Most important for our purposes, their developmental onset and offset differs from one language to another. It is not always the case that semantic strategies are "immature." For example, Bates et al. (1984) have shown that animacy plays a larger role in sentence comprehension for Italian adults than for Italian children between the ages of 4 and 6. And animacy is a more important cue than word order for adult speakers of several different languages studied within the framework of the Competition Model (see Bates & MacWhinney, in press, for a review). This point will be underscored when we present the results from Experiment 1 on French.

4. Topicalization

It is well known that the order of words in an utterance is not a matter of chance. Syntactic conventions are correlated with a variety of complex meanings and discourse functions. The different positions which may be occupied by each of the elements of discourse may be characterized in terms of "functions" or values (Halliday, 1967). In order to keep communication moving ahead, speakers are obliged to distinguish between prior information, matters already known to the listener (the "topic") and new information (the "comment" brought to bear on the former). As often noted in the literature (e.g., Clark & Clark, 1977), in simple declarative sentences, the grammatical subject constitutes old information and the predicate, the new information. In French, as in English, the subject most frequently precedes the verb. Hence, in discourse terms, the second part of the sentence usually carries the new information.

Research across a range of languages surveyed by MacWhinney and Bates (1978) indicates that young children place new information at the beginnings of utterances, followed by old or less focal elements of meaning. This order contrasts with a tendency in most natural languages for adults to begin the sentence with old or topicalized information, placing the new or informative aspect of the utterance in second position. In studies of sentence comprehension by adult subjects, Bates et al. (1982) have demonstrated a bias toward selecting the topicalized element as the subject of the sentence. However, this bias was quite marginal in English listeners; it played a much greater role in Italian, a language that varies word order extensively for pragmatic purposes. Insofar as French seems to stand midway between English and Italian in the availability and reliability of word order cues, we decided to examine the influence of topicalization on French listeners.

A different perspective on the distinction between old and new information is provided in research on the development of the definite/indefinite article contrast, in speech production by French and English children (Bresson, 1974; Maratsos, 1976; Karmiloff-Smith, 1979), and in comprehension by adults (Hupet & Le Bouedec, 1975; MacWhinney & Bates, 1978). Details of the article system vary from language to language, as does the moment of appearance (between

2 and 3 years for most Indo-European languages) of the first articles. In both languages, there appears to be a consistent relationship between definite articles and the presupposition of information considered old. This relationship seems to be respected from the earliest stages of article use. However, as Karmiloff-Smith (1979) has stressed, the first uses of the definite article are deictic, not anaphoric, and, hence, the connection between anaphoric givenness and the definite article is much closer in adults than in young children. In the work reported below, the definite/indefinite article distinction was examined for the adult subjects alone, as a way of operationalizing the influence of topicalization on sentence interpretation.

Experiment 1: Cue Validity in French Sentence Processing – a Crosslinguistic Comparison

The purpose of this study is to test a number of predictions made by the Competition Model using French-speaking adult and child subjects.[1] The specific goal was to determine how cues involved in sentence comprehension are ordered in terms of their strength in a language which shares certain features with English (basic SVO order, absence of subject ellipsis) and certain features with Italian (i.e., frequency of noncanonical orders), while exhibiting rather idiosyncratic behavior with respect to accent or stress. The adult version of the experiment constitutes a replication in French of the design described by Bates et al. (1982) for English and Italian. The child version of the experiment is a French version of the English and Italian experiment described by Bates et al. (1984).

Method

Stimuli

Four cue types were selected to conform with those used in experiments reported by Bates et al. (1982, 1984) for English and Italian. These included (1) word order, (2) animacy, (3) highlighting, and (4) topicality. Each of these four cues was treated as a factor in a fully crossed analysis of variance design. Each factor had three levels. Word Order had either NVN, NNV, or VNN. Animacy had either both nouns animate (AA), the first noun animate and the second noun inanimate (AI), or the first noun inanimate and the second noun animate (IA). Highlighting had either neither noun highlighted, the first noun highlighted, or the second noun highlighted. Topicalization had either neither noun topicalized, the first noun topicalized, or the third noun topicalized. Topicalization refers

---

[1] Experiment 1 was conducted by two of my students, A. Charvillat and C. Combier. Experiment 2 was conducted by A. Charvillat. My thanks go to M. Léveillé for her assistance in preparing both experiments.

to the fact that one of the nouns participated in preceding discourse material, thereby qualifying it for the definite article, with the other noun introduced by the indefinite article.

The animate nouns were: bear (*ours*), butterfly (*papillon*), camel (*chameau*), cat (*chat*), cow (*vache*), dog (*chien*), duck (*cane*), fish (*poisson*), giraffe (*girafe*), hippopotamus (*hippopotame*), horse (*cheval*), lion (*lion*), monkey (*singe*), pig (*cochon*), rabbit (*lapin*), sheep (*mouton*), turtle (*tortue*), and zebra (*zèbre*). The inanimate nouns were: ball (*balle*), cigarette (*cigarette*), cube (*cube*), eraser (*gomme*), glass (*verre*), hammer (*marteau*), pen (*stylo*), pencil (*crayon*), and pencil-sharpener (*taille-crayon*). And the transitive verbs were: bite (*mordre*), caress (*caresser*), feel (*sentir*), greet (*saluer*), hit (*frapper*), kiss (*embrasser*), lick (*lécher*), push (*pousser*), and upset (*renverser*).

For example, a NNV stimulus with two animates was: *Le chien le chat embrasse* "The dog the cat is kissing." A VNN stimulus with an inanimate first noun and animate second noun was: *Léche la gomme un lapin* "Licks the eraser a rabbit."

The design was orthogonalized, permitting us to assess the effects of cue convergence, cue competition, and coalitions among cues of varying strength. More often than not, the stimuli that make it possible to study cue competition are semigrammatical sentences. It has been claimed (Cromer, 1976) that for such sentences, answers may be random, especially on the part of children. Nevertheless, if it can be shown that adults from different language backgrounds respond in a consistent and language specific way, then the impact of such criticism should be weakened.   This is not to say that the processing of semigrammatical sentences is held to be identical to that of fully grammatical utterances, as will be made clear; but it is likely that processing will operate on the basis of the same relevant set of cues.

Subjects

Forty native French-speaking (middle-class) children from Paris suburban schools took part in the experiment. There were four age-groups for the children, each consisting of five girls and five boys. The mean ages of each group were 2;6, 3;6, 4;6, and 5;6. Thirty native French-speaking adults, for the most part psychology students at the University of Paris, participated in the adult version of the experiment.

Procedure

All of the child subjects were tested individually. For the children the factor of topicalization was not included. Children had to act out, with the help of experimental toys of identical size, each of 54 sentences (3 word order × 3 animacy × 3 highlighting × 2 replicates) given orally with standard intonation by the experimenter. The experimenter made sure that each of the actions denoted by the verbs and the names of the objects were understood by the children before beginning. To prevent the children from relying on event probabilities arising out of particular lexical combinations (Chapman & Kohn, 1978), the items were counterbalanced and also designed in such a way as to permit direct comparison with English and Italian results.

The 30 adult subjects were also tested individually. Each heard 81 sentences in the full four-factor design (3 word order × 3 animacy × 3 topicalization × 3 highlighting). Half of the subjects were asked to identify "the subject of the sentence, hence the actor." The other half were asked to identify "the actor, hence the subject of the sentence." This double formulation left subjects the option of spontaneously adopting a syntactic and/or semantic strategy. The sentences were grouped into nine blocks of nine items, each block involving the nine possible word order × highlighing combinations in one of the three animacy conditions and one of the topicalization conditions. The order of the triplets within the blocks and the order of presentation of the blocks were randomized for each subject.

Results

The discussion of the results will be in five sections: (1) the results for word order, (2) the results for animacy, 3) the results for highlighting, 4) the results for topicalization, and 5) the significant two-way interactions.

1. Word Order

In general, the French children's performance looked much like their English counterparts. As expected, there was a significant main effect for word order among the children, $F(2,72) = 75.41$, $p < .0005$. Canonical NVN sentences were consistently processed using a strict first-noun-as-agent or SV strategy. In the results presented by Bates et al. (1984), choice of first noun on NVN strings was much stronger in English children than in Italian children, at every age. However, Italian children generalized their (weaker) first noun strategy on SVO to both of the noncanonical word orders, resulting in SOV and VSO biases. French children, like the English children in the Bates et al. study, showed no such overgeneralization. Their strict order strategy, evident in the youngest age group (2;6), is consistently applied to all canonical occurrences from 3;6 and reaches a plateau at 4;6 (93%) and 5;6 (97.5%). Performance on noncanonical sequences (VNN and NNV) is random at 2;6. At 3;6, our subjects appear to adopt a strategy which designates the lexeme closest to the verb as agent, as found in earlier work (Kail & Segui, 1978).

For adult subjects, there was a significant main effect for word order both in terms of the percent of the first noun as agent, $F(2,58) = 13.03$, $p < .0005$, and in

Table 2.1. *Percentage choice of first noun as agent by French children*

	Word order			Animacy			Highlight			Topic		
	NVN	VNN	NNV	AA	AI	IA	0	1	2	0	1	2
2;6	62.0	42.0	40.5	50.0	48.5	46.0	47.5	58.0	39.0			
3;6	81.0	59.5	42.5	62.0	67.5	54.0	57.5	70.5	55.0			
4;6	93.0	57.0	50.5	70.0	90.5	40.5	65.0	70.0	66.0			
5;6	97.5	63.5	41.5	70.5	82.0	49.5	65.5	66.5	69.5			
Adult choice	67.0	50.0	57.0	61.0	89.0	25.0	61.0	59.0	54.0	58.0	64.0	52.0
Adult latency	-120	-30	+140	+240	-160	-80	+10	-30	-10	+100	-60	-40

terms of reaction times, $F(2,58) = 13.55$, $p < .0005$. As expected, the first noun was chosen most often in canonical NVN triplets (67%). It should nevertheless be noted that this SVO interpretation was considerably less frequent for French adults than for French children at 5;6 – the first of several sharp differences between children and adults revealed in this experiment.

Though no specific strategy guides the choice in VNN items (50%), there is a significant tendency for French adults to choose the first noun as agent in NNV sequences (57%). This strategy is probably related to SOV constructions in French when the object is a clitic pronoun. With regard to reaction times, NVN is processed more rapidly (–120 ms) than VNN (–30 ms) or NNV (+140 ms). Note, however, that VNN sequences are processed more quickly than NNV, even though listeners have a somewhat more consistent way of interpreting the latter. In this respect, the choice/reaction time findings are not as consistent as the results reported by Bates et al. (1982) for English and Italian adults.

2. Animacy

For French children, there was a significant main effect of animacy, $F(2,72) = 13.47$, $p < .0005$. For semantically reversible AA items, children tended to choose the first lexeme as agent. For contrasting items, they tended to choose the animate noun as agent. However, analysis by age-groups reveals that this lexical distinction is not used consistently to determine the agent until as late as 4;6. This finding contrasts with previous results obtained in similar experiments on French (e.g., Noizet, 1977; Vion, 1980; Bronckart et al., 1981), but can be explained by the abstract nature of the cue when not buttressed by strong event probabilities. It may be observed that the effect of the animacy cue is highest at 4;6. This *increase* in animacy for French children occurs at the same age at which animacy begins to *decrease* for Italian children. In Italian, this is also the same age at which children begin to overgeneralize SVO to the other two word orders – a strategy that we do not see in the development of French. We are reminded, again, that the use of animacy cues in sentence interpretation depends upon the language being acquired. It is not necessarily an immature strategy that disappears with the onset of grammar.

This point is underscored by the findings for French adults. To our surprise, adult French subjects behave much more like adult Italians in their use of lexical information. The animacy factor is quite reliable, $F(2,58) = 97.19$ $p < .0005$. Direction and consistency of noun choice coincides with our predictions: AI > AA > IA. Furthermore, animacy had a major impact on reaction times, with subjects performing more slowly when no animacy contrast is available (AI = -160 ms, IA = -80 ms, AA = +240 ms). As we shall see in more detail below, it is fair to say that there is a dramatic switch in preferred strategies from 5;6 to adulthood: French children rely more on word order, whereas French adults rely more on semantic contrasts.

3. Prosodic Highlighting

In children, highlighting clearly affects processing, $F(2,72) = 11.57$, $p < .0005$. Highlighting one of the two nouns increased its chances of being chosen as agent, especially if the highlighted noun was also the first noun. Developmentally, this pattern is the opposite of that found for word order and animacy. The youngest age groups (2;6 – $F(2,18) = 8.33$ and 3;6 – $F(2,18) = 2.51$, $p < .0005$) chose the highlighted nouns as agents; no such strategy was evidenced at ages 4;6 and 5;6. This is precisely the pattern reported by Bates et al. (1984) for Italian children and MacWhinney and Price (1980) for English-speaking children, i.e., a tendency to choose the stressed noun as agent which decreases over age. Because this "Pick the loud noun" strategy runs in the opposite direction from stress effects in Italian and English adults (who are biased against choosing the highlighted noun as subject), Bates et al. and MacWhinney and Price suggest that this is an immature and essentially nonlinguistic strategy that is rapidly replaced by language-specific structural information.

There was no significant main effect for the highlighting cue in the choice behavior of adult subjects, and no effect at all on reaction times. However, the presence (vs. absence) of highlighting in a stimulus item did interact with several other factors, particularly word order (see Table 2.2). The primary (albeit minor) effect of highlighting seems to be the reduction of a canonical word order strategy. In the absence of highlighting, the first noun was chosen as agent – particularly on NVN items. But if one of the two nouns were highlighted, there was an increase in the tendency to treat the second noun as the agent. This is similar to the patterns reported by Bates et al. (1982) and MacWhinney, Bates,

Table 2.2. *Percentage choice of first noun as agent in word order by animacy interaction in French children and adults*

		2;6	3;6	4;6	5;6	Adults
	AA	65.0	82.0	98.5	100.0	68.0
NVN	AI	61.5	85.0	98.5	98.5	93.0
	IA	59.0	77.5	82.0	93.5	39.0
	AA	45.0	71.0	58.5	73.5	54.0
VNN	AI	36.5	59.0	87.5	77.0	84.0
	IA	43.5	47.5	25.0	40.0	11.0
	AA	40.0	33.5	52.5	38.5	61.0
NNV	AI	46.0	57.5	85.0	70.0	89.0
	IA	35.0	36.5	14.0	15.0	19.0

and Kliegl (1984) for Italian adults – except that the order and stress interactions seem to be more robust in that language. Indeed, given the claim that French makes no structural or semantic use of contrastive stress at all, it is interesting that we found any consistency in the use of highlighting to interpret simple sentences.

4. Topic

This cue was only investigated in adult subjects. Here the main effect reached significance in both the choice, $F(2,58) = 11.44$, $p < .0005$, and latency, $F(2,58) = 4.62$, $p < .025$, analyses. In general, topicalization increased the listeners' tendency to choose that noun as the agent – particularly if the noun was N1.

5. Interactions

To summarize, French children seem to behave very much like English children, as though they were acquiring a rigid word order language. However, French adults seem to behave much more like Italian adults, showing strong effects of animacy, weaker effects of word order, and consistent albeit secondary use of pragmatic information (i.e., highlighting and topicalization) to interpret simple active declarative sentences. This developmental switch-over becomes still clearer when we examine some of the more detailed interactions concentrating on situations of cue competition and cue convergence. Only the major findings obtained for child and adult subjects will be reported, and this will be done separately for children and adults.

A significant overall order × animacy interaction was evident in children, $F(4,144) = 9.87$, $p < .0005$. For *canonical* sequences, children relied on the syntactic cue in their interpretations. Indeed, their preference for the first

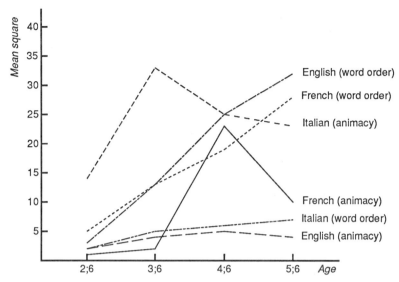

Figure 2.1. Mean squares of word order and animacy effects in French, English, and Italian children.

noun on NVN sentences was equivalent for AI and AA forms. And in cases of competition (IVA), syntactic information appeared to be preferred. For *noncanonical* sequences, children relied on semantic information to interpret the sentence. Thus, in competition items, the strategy that requires selection of that noun closest to the verb as agent was overridden.

From two years of age, word order is the most important cue to meaning for French children – in particular use of a canonical SVO pattern to interpret NVN strings. The dominant strategy used for noncanonical items (NNV, VNN) is a "proximity strategy" (the noun closest to the verb = agent), which appears around age 3;6. The animacy cue is first used around 3;6 and becomes much stronger at 4;6. But it never reaches adult levels in these ages (see below). Intonational highlighting has no effect beyond the youngest age groups, who attribute agent status to the highlighted noun. In cases of competition between syntactic cues and lexical-semantic cues, canonical word order systematically wins out. With reference to noncanonical orders, results indicate that the first noun is taken as agent from 5;6, as reported by Sinclair and Bronckart (1972) and Kail and Segui (1978). Semantic strategies are always secondary, although the use of lexical information does increase consistently from 2 to 5 years of age. This syntactic/semantic tradeoff is clearly illustrated in Figure 2.1, which presents the amount of experimental variance accounted for by the respective main effects at each age.

French children make greater use of semantic information than do English children, and more use of syntactic information than do Italian children. Overall, their performance is closer to that of the English subjects, as shown by the analysis of cue coalition and competition. More specifically, the French children seem to perform like English children on canonical sentences and like the Italian children on noncanonical items. This behavior tends to confirm the idea that the status of both grammatical and "semigrammatical" sentences depends on the relative weights of the different cues in a language. This can also be seen from Figure 2.2, which illustrates interactions of animacy, word order, and age in each of the three language groups (French, English, and Italian).

Interestingly, this would support the concept of French as an "intermediate" language and fit in with the assumption that young children use the most reliable and available cues in their language, i.e., word order and animacy. However, the behavior of French children is strikingly *unlike* the behavior of French adults. In the adults, all the interactions for noun choices reached significance except the interaction between topic and highlighting. In general, these complex interactions reflect confirmation of the convergence, coalition, and competition patterns predicted by the Competition Model. Let us see why this is the case.

The word order × animacy interactions for choice, $F(4,116) = 4.60$, $p < .005$, and latency, $F(4,116) = 5.09$, $p < .001$, can be said to fulfill the coalition and competition "contract." First, when the two cue types point to the same subject-agent candidate, choice consistency is higher and reaction times shorter than when order alone is available. Second, competition between these cues retards processing and lowers consistency, with listeners showing a clear preference for animacy. However, the force of semantic information exceeded expectations, since it was hypothesized that syntactic information would prove a tougher opponent. French adults are not behaving like speakers of a rigid word order language.

The word order × topicalization interaction was not significant for latencies, but did conform to the model's predictions for choice, $F(4,116) = 5.28$, $p < .001$. The coalition of word order with topicality made choices more consistent than did word order alone, but word order fostered greater consistency on its own than when competing with topic.

In order to explain the significant animacy × topicalization interaction, $F(4,116) = 16.85$, $p < .005$, conditional weights have to be considered. Semantic information generally outweighs pragmatic information. However, when word order and semantics are in competition, pragmatic effects play an important role. If the first noun of an NVN string is inanimate and the second noun is animate, French listeners tend to choose the second noun as agent. However, if the inanimate first noun is topicalized, then pragmatic factors seem to tip the balance toward choice of the first noun as the agent. This is a classic example of a coalition effect in the Competition Model.

The word order × highlighting interaction does reach significance for noun choice, $F(4,116) = 6.87$, $p < .0005$, despite the lack of a significant main effect

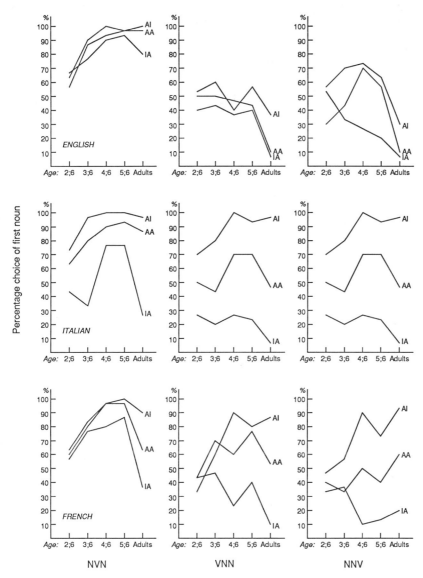

Figure 2.2. Choice results within languages and age groups.

for highlighting. Highlighting thus plays the role of a secondary cue and may act in concert with a well-established syntactic strategy. In particular, highlighting seems to reduce the tendency for listeners to interpret syntactic strings in their canonical form. It is as though a marked prosodic pattern tells the listener to be wary of default interpretations.

The animacy × highlighting interaction also reached significance for choice, $F(4,116) = 2.72$, $p < .025$. Coalition and competition predictions concerning the two cues are borne out with the exception of those triplets involving highlighting of an animate N1 in initial position (i.e., the AI items). In other words, this weak cue can only have an effect when stronger cues are absent, or in competition.

Higher order interactions also support the *extended coalition principle*, which states that three cues pointing to the same interpretation are better than one or two. Regarding the results of competition among three cues, an estimate of relative strength was based on their mean squares in the ANOVA. With these rankings, we advanced and largely confirmed a series of predictions, in line with the competition and conspiracy principles described by Bates et al. (1982). For example, a coalition between a strong and a very strong cue leads to better performance than the strongest cue alone, even if weak competition is present (where "better than" means more consistent choices and shorter processing times).

Crosslinguistic comparisons confirmed the prediction that French would lie in between English and Italian in the application of word order principles. But we did not expect to find French listeners performing so closely to the Italian model. French is closer to Italian in the overall strength of canonical word order. Furthermore, whereas English subjects show a consistent second noun strategy in processing NNV and VNN items, the French, like the Italians, are far slower and less systematic in interpreting noncanonical structures. Whereas the English continue to favor syntax when in competition with semantic information, the dominance of semantics is almost as striking in French as it is in Italian. These findings are quite surprising for a language which, after all, shows relatively strict SVO order. At first glance, this appears to constitute a case in which sentence interpretation cannot be directly related to overall cue validity (i.e., that of word order). Obviously, the overall validity seems to require a more precise formulation. We will return to this point shortly.

6. Adult Processing of Canonical and Noncanonical Sentences

The unexpected weight of the animacy factor in adults might be due to an overextension to NVN canonical sequences of semantic strategies which are heavily relied upon in noncanonical sequences. To investigate this possibility, we reexamined the adult data for NVN sequences. This analysis considered the percentage of N1 as agent choice as well as the percent of subjects who clung to a single strategy (i.e., for whom between 6 and 9 responses out of the 9 items per configuration were of the same type). It may be noted that a number of researchers (e.g., Vion, 1980; Bronckart, 1983), have spoken of the need to restrict the term "strategy" to subjects' systematic behavior.

For AVI sequences, where animacy and word order point to the same agent-candidate, N1 choice reached the level of 93%; all subjects except one (97%) favored an N1-as-agent strategy.

For IVA sequences, where the two cues are in competition, N1 choice reached 39%; noncanonical sequences of the same configuration (IAV + VIA) yielded a 15% first noun choice. Given these numbers, it is obvious that at least some subjects are splitting their strategies: using word order for some items (NVN) and semantics for others (NNV, VNN). In that sense, subjects do not divide neatly into "word order types" and "semantic types." Within the IVA sequences, we can also discern a continuum of individual differences: 30% of the subjects use a first-noun-as-agent strategy, 42% a second-noun-as-agent strategy, and 28% favor no single strategy. These results suggest that most French adults are sensitive to the competition between order and animacy, vacillating back and forth between solutions to the problem. The results are not a consequence of averaging together the performance of "pure" word order strategists and "pure" lexical strategists. Individual differences are a matter of degree.

In AVA sequences, without animacy contrasts, subjects were expected to rely on the word order cue; in fact the first-noun-as-agent strategy is less prevalent than anticipated for an SVO language. The data show a 68% first noun choice. Although a majority of subjects (56%) use a first-noun-as-agent strategy, a few of them (16%) still use the second-noun-as-agent strategy, while a comparatively greater number (28%) rely on no single strategy at all.

The reaction time data put these individual differences in a different kind of perspective. In AVA sequences those subjects (56%) who use the expected first-noun-as-agent strategy show reaction times which are shorter than their own overall mean (based on all 81 stimuli). Those subjects using the unexpected second-noun-as-agent strategy show reaction times that exceed their own mean value. When subjects follow a first-noun-as-agent strategy, they are able to reach a decision regarding the identity of the agent right at the beginning of the sentence. Having reached this decision so early, their response latencies are quite short. If, on the other hand, subjects are applying a second-noun-as-agent strategy, they must wait until the end of the sentence until they find out who was the agent. Because of this wait, their latencies are longer.

Discussion

The main findings for this study may be summarized as follows:

1. Word order and animacy are the major factors governing interpretation in French (as well as English and Italian). Topicalization and highlighting are secondary cues which operate primarily in conjunction with animacy, word order or both.
2. Like the Italian adult subjects, French adults rely on semantic factors but also make greater use of topicalization. They are less systematic and slower than English adults in processing noncanonical sentences. And many of the subjects are also less systematic and slower than English adults in processing AVA strings where SVO receives no competition from animacy.

3. French children do not act at all like French adults. It would therefore be necessary to revise the claim that the emergence of cues in a language is determined by the overall validity of cues in the adult language. Like their English counterparts, French children make greater use of canonical word order and much less use of semantics in the interpretation of simple sentences.

How do we interpret these findings? It was expected that French would behave more like a word-order language, but the data for adult subjects indicate that French and Italian are very close in processing terms despite certain differences with respect to cue validity.

As we pointed out earlier, a variety of orders are used in informal French in the presence of clitic pronouns – despite the reliability of SVO when clitics are absent. These alternative orders may attenuate the effect of word order in favor of the animacy contrast in cases of competition between the two cues. Because there are so many alternative phrase structures available in French when clitic pronouns are present, these competing structures are activated through partial overlap even though the simple sentences that we presented to the subjects had no clitic particles in them. The competing phrase structures create interference that ultimately reduces the strength or effectiveness of an SVO interpretation – particularly in a situation where other cues (e.g., semantics, highlighting, topicalization) are competing with canonical SVO. McDonald (1984) has shown that adults are particularly sensitive to such conflict sentences, even though they are rare in absolute number. Unlike children, who respond primarily to overall validity, adults pay particular attention to conflict validity, picking out cues that are strong in conflicts, although they are lower in overall validity.

It may be that French children have relatively less experience with and sensitivity to the kinds of complex cliticized constructions described earlier. Since these are the constructions that conflict with canonical word order in French, we can thus explain why the French child relies on canonical word order in situations where a French adult relies on semantics.

Another kind of challenge for the overall validity model involves the notion of cue cost. We observed individual differences among French adults with regard to their preferred processing strategy, differences which were reflected in the time these subjects took to process the "same" sentence stimuli. In particular, subjects who rely heavily on semantic factors also take longer to process canonical AVA strings. This can be explained if we assume that subjects who rely on canonical order can make their decision in an NVN string as soon as they encounter the verb; subjects who are basing their decisions on a semantic contrast instead cannot reach a decision until all three constituents are available. Obviously, there are costs incurred in the French listener's decision to ignore canonical word order in favor of other factors. This kind of finding requires an integration of the notion of "cue cost" into the Competition Model (Kail & Charvillat,

1986). Cue cost, which must be distinguished from cue validity, refers to the differential processing demands imposed by different kinds of cues. If cue cost is high enough, a listener may ignore a given source of information in favor of a less available and/or reliable source that is nevertheless easier to use. Bates and MacWhinney (1987) have discussed several sources of cue cost, including "detectability" (i.e., the ease with which a given cue can be perceived in real-time sentence processing). In Experiment 2, we will focus on another kind of cue cost, based on the distinction between local processing and topological processing in sentence comprehension.

Experiment 2: Cue Cost and Processing Types in French and Spanish

Experiment 2 is part of a series of studies designed to evaluate the relationship between the notions of cue validity and cue cost in sentence processing. In this study, we will focus on the differential costs involved in the processing of local and topological cues, defined as follows:

Local processing refers to the identification and interpretation of a linguistic cue within a single lexical word without consideration of the other words in the clause. Examples of cues that lend themselves to local processing include lexical animacy information as well as features such as gender, number, and case and that are either marked by inflections or inherent in lexical items.

Topological processing refers to the identification and interpretation of linguistic cues coded across words. Examples of cues that require topological processing include word order relations, suprasegmental stress patterns, as well as lexical and/or morphological agreement markers that span two or more potentially discontinuous items across a sentence.

This local/topological contrast should not be viewed as a dichotomy; rather, cue processing can be said to lie on a continuum from maximally local to maximally topological. For example, the agreement between an article and the associated noun phrase typically involves a very short segment of speech (except for the unusual case where a long list of modifiers intervenes). Agreement between a clitic object pronoun and an object noun phrase may apply over segments up to several sentences long.

The contrast was first introduced into the psycholinguistic literature by Ammon and Slobin (1979) and Slobin (1982). In a study of the acquisition of causal terms, they showed that children acquire grammatical cues that are marked on the stem (i.e., a causative inflection) earlier than cues which are distributed across the clause (e.g., periphrastic causatives like "Make to fall"). Presumably, topological cues are more costly to process because they make greater demands on short-term memory, and because they require some additional operations of comparing and cross-referencing the elements held in a memory store. Broadly applied, this distinction crosses the traditional boundaries between syntactic, semantic, and pragmatic cues and leads to a new formulation of the question of processor autonomy.

In the present experiment involving adult subjects, the cues selected are primarily syntactic and morphological cues that vary along the local/topological dimension. French and Spanish were chosen because of the contrasts they offer with respect to these cues.

The first goal of this research was to determine the weight of each of the following cues for the two languages: (1) word order, (2) object clitic pronouns, and (3) verb agreement. In Spanish an additional important cue was examined, namely the preposition *a* which obligatorily precedes animate objects of a transitive verb. A further goal of the study was to establish whether the ordering of cues on a continuum from most local to most topological processing types could be related to their respective weights. Within this framework, the correlation between cue cost and a cue's position on the continuum was investigated. For present purposes, cue cost is indexed by two associated phenomena: ease of access to functional relations (reflected in consistency of choice behavior), and processing economy (in terms of time gained or lost in reaching an interpretation). Before presenting experimental particulars, it will be helpful to describe some relevant contrasts between Spanish and French.

1. Word Order

Linguistic typologies classify both French and Spanish as canonical SVO languages. However, whereas SVO is relatively strict in French (particularly in the absence of clitic markers), Spanish allows a considerable range of orders depending on various contextual or pragmatic constraints. In simple active declarative structures, the nominative pronoun is usually dropped in Spanish. This, of course, is not possible in French. Both languages permit noncanonical word orders as occasioned by specific communicative needs. However, word order variation in French requires the introduction of a clitic pronoun, a nominative pronoun, or both (particularly in SOV structures – see previous sections). Interrogative forms in Spanish do not change basic SVO order. In this sense, Spanish resembles informal French.

With regard to relative clauses, it should be noted that in Spanish the object of the main clause may be topicalized, as in:

Al medico que mi vecina conoce Juan no quiso pagar.
"The doctor my neighbor knows John did not want to pay."

This is only possible in French if the main clause includes a clitic pronoun:

Le médecin que connaît ma voisine, Jean n'a pas voulu le payer.
"The doctor whom knows my neighbor, John did not want to pay him."

In Spanish, as in Italian, word order variation appears to be considerably less constrained than in French. In Experiment I our French listeners showed surprisingly weak word order effects. Nevertheless, we would still expect French listeners to rely more on word order than their Spanish counterparts, particularly in an experiment in which it is possible to rely on morphological cues.

2. Object Clitic Pronouns

Both French and Spanish make extensive use of clitic object pronouns, unlike either English or German. But there are differences in the ambiguity, and hence relative cue validity, of clitic pronouns in the two languages. In French, the pronouns *le, la*, and *les* are doubly ambiguous. First, the pronoun *les* is ambiguous in gender, serving as the plural for both masculine and feminine forms. Second, all these pronouns are homophonous with articles in French (including feminine singular *la*, masculine singular *le*, and masculine/feminine plural *les*). This presents obvious problems for left-to-right parsing, since a listener might be tempted to misassign a clitic pronoun as the article of some noun phrase to come. (For discussion of the complex problem of double cliticization, see Weissenborn, Kail, & Friederici, in press.)

In Spanish, the object clitic pronouns *le, la, lo, les, las,* and *los* are not ambiguous with regard to gender. Only three of these forms (*la, las,* and *los*) are homophonous with articles. However, *le* and *les* display case ambiguity, as they can be datives and accusatives. A further complication of regional variants (e.g., *leismo, laismo,* etc.) did not arise in the experiments reported below, since these variants are generally rejected by the Spanish Academy which provides a thorough set of usage rules.

In French, third person dative clitic pronouns (*lui, leur*) are lexically ambiguous with regard to gender. *Lui* also shows case ambiguity since the nominative has the same form, whereas *leur*, which is also a possessive adjective and pronoun, displays intersystem ambiguity. In Spanish, *le*, and *les* exhibit lexical ambiguity with respect to gender and to the contrast between accusative and dative case. However, this potential source of case ambiguity is often overcome by a unique feature of Spanish: The pronoun *se*, the use of which is obligatory in double cliticization, is substituted for the dative *le* or *les* when an accusative clitic pronoun is still to come. *Se* is lexically ambiguous with regard to both number and gender, and it is also homophonous with the reflexive pronoun. But it does serve as a "warning" to the listener that both an accusative and a dative clitic are occupying preverbal position. This prevents the listeners from mistakenly classifying the first clitic encountered as an accusative when a dative is in fact intended. Taken together, these facts suggest that the system of clitic pronouns is somewhat more reliable (i.e., less often ambiguous or misleading) in Spanish, compared with French.

3. Verb Agreement

Spoken French also differs from Spanish in the ambiguity of its inflectional system. Verb agreement is quite regular and transparent in Spanish, with explicit marking of number and person. The French system is often misleading, particularly in the ambiguity of first conjugation verbs in the present tense (indicative and subjunctive), as shown in the following example:

	French	Spanish
Singular		
1st person	chante*	canto
2nd person	chantes*	cantas
3rd person	chante*	canta
Plural		
1st person	chantons	cantamos
2nd person	chantez	cantais
3rd person	chantent*	cantan

*same pronunciation

In this conjugation, there is no agreement cue for number in the third person at all in French. In Spanish each cell of the first conjugation paradigm has an unambiguous form.

4. The Preposition A

In addition to the above agreement markers, and to word order principles, Spanish makes extensive use of the preposition *a*, a particle that occurs directly before the patient to signal its accusative role. This preposition is not always available as an indicator of the patient role. According to traditional accounts, the presence of *a* depends on the nature of the object: animate patients require the *a*, whereas a specified patient and/or a singular patient more often require the preposition than would a generic patient and/or a plural patient. This is an area where regional variation is considerable. For instance, in Latin America, one finds *a* used before inanimate objects. According to Pottier (1968), the *a* may be used when a speaker wishes to attribute subjectivity to an object (e.g., *Salvo a una ciudad*, or "I save a city"). But despite its imperfect availability the *a* particle serves as a caselike, maximally local cue for the object where French has no cue at all.

There are also several restrictions on the reliability of *a*. One major use of the preposition is as a marker of the infinitive, as in *voy a cantar* "I-am-going to sing." However, this use can be easily separated out by noting that when *a* is followed by an infinitive ending in *-ar*, *-er*, or *-ir*, it is not a case marker. A second use of *a* is as a marker of the dative, as in *Juan le dió el libro a Maria*, "Juan gave the book to Maria." However, this use of *a* can also be separated out by noting that *a* only marks the dative when there is also a bare postverbal noun to serve as object. Finally, the preposition can also be interpreted as a locative as in *Juan trajó el libro a Barcelona*, "Juan took the book to Barcelona," or *Juan corrió a Barcelona*, "Juan ran to Barcelona." This locative reading of *a* will often be in competition with the case marker reading. Although the preposition is initially unreliable as a case marker, its reliability increases as the learner sorts out the cues which help distinguish between the alternative readings.

These cues in French and Spanish could be ordered on a processing type continuum from local (the preposition *a*) to topological (word order). Two other cues, verb agreement and clitic pronouns, embody local features that assign coreference (assignment of the subject for verb agreement, and of the coreferent of the pronoun for clitics). However, these agreement cues also involve topological processing, insofar as two potentially discontinuous elements are required to make an agreement "match." In addition, because cliticization interacts extensively with constituent order, it falls still further along the proposed topological continuum. If we are correct in our assessment of the processing costs involved in topological processing, then the relative processing difficulty imposed by cues to sentence meaning should be: preposition *a* < subject–verb agreement < object clitics < word order. These processing demands should interact with the relative validity of cues (in French and Spanish, respectively) to create the final hierarchy of strength reflected in adult sentence processing. In particular, given its low cost and relative high validity (at least as available and reliable as the above agreement cues), the Spanish particle *a* should be an exceptionally strong cue to meaning.

Method

Stimuli

There were a total of 54 reversible test sentences for each subject. Each sentence consisted of a verb in the third person singular or plural and two common nouns, singular or plural, with the definite article. The sentences were constructed by the selection of twelve nouns referring to agents. There were the six masculine nouns – gardener, cook, baker, street-sweeper, handyman, fisherman – and their six feminine equivalents. The verbs "move along," "fall," and "turn" were used in periphrastic forms in order to ensure distinctive pronunciations between singular and plural third person occurrences in French, *fait tomber* versus *font tomber*. Thus there was a contrast between *fait tomber* "he made fall" and *font tomber* "they made fall." In Spanish versions, the singular/plural verb marking meant that the verbs could be presented in the usual present tense forms.

Word order was either NVN, NNV, or VNN. Three combinations of clitic pronouns were investigated: C0, no clitic pronoun; C1, the clitic favors the choice of the first noun as agent (i.e., N2 is the clitic pronoun's coreferent); and C2, the clitic favors the choice of the second noun as agent (i.e., N1 is the clitic pronoun's coreferent). Examples of C1 are: *Le pêcheur la fait tomber la balayeuse* and *El cocinero a la barrendera la mordió.* Examples of C2 are: *Le pêcheur le fait tomber la balayeuse* and *El cocinero a la barrendera lo mordió.* Three combinations of agreement are:

1. AO, agreement is ambiguous (both N1 and N2 are either singular or plural) as in *Le cuisinier fait avancer le pêcheur* or *El cocinero empujó al pescador*;
2. A1, verb agrees with N1 as in *Le pêcheur les cuisiniers le fait tomber* or *El pescador a los cocineros les empujó*; and
3. A2, verb agrees with N2 as in *Le pêcheur les cuisiniers le font tomber* or *Al pescador los cocineros le empujaron.*

The first three factors were varied in both languages. The fourth factor was only varied in Spanish. This factor had two levels:

1. P1, where the preposition designates N1 as agent, as in *La panadera empujó a los carteros*; and
2. P2, where the preposition designates the first noun as the object and N2 as the agent, as in *A los cocineros la jardinera besó.*

As mentioned above in connection with Experiment 1, it is necessary to use artificial stimuli to test cue competition. Although it might seem unnatural to present subjects with sentences in which cues generate contradictory interpretations, for example, *Le pêcheur les cuisiniers le fait tomber*, it is precisely the outcome of the competition between cues that makes it possible to evaluate the relative strengths of the various competing cues.

A three-factor, three-level design in French gave 27 combinations, each of which was presented twice. In Spanish, the same procedure provided 54 combinations through the addition of the preposition *a* at two levels. The lexical material (nouns and verbs) was randomized for each subject.

Subjects

Twenty-five middle-class adult subjects took part in the experiment, including 15 French native speakers and ten Spanish native speakers. All were university students. The French subjects resided in Paris, and the Spanish all lived in Madrid and spoke the educated dialect of that city.

Procedure

The procedure was similar to that used in Experiment 1. Half the subjects were instructed to give the noun which was the subject of the sentence, hence the agent of the action, and half were instructed to give the noun which was the agent of the action, hence the subject of the sentence. Subjects were also warned that they might hear some rather odd sentences. The sentences were read with standard intonation, insofar as possible. As for Experiment 1, the two dependent variables were percent choice of the first noun as agent and latencies in milliseconds.

Results

The ANOVA for choice of subjects-agents in French yielded significant main effects for word order, $F(2,28) = 19.58$, $p < .0005$, clitic, $F(2,28) = 77,28$, $p < .0005$, and agreement, $F(2,28) = 68.61$, $p < .0005$. Word order and clitic also produced main effects on latencies, $F(2,28) = 7.58$, $p < .005$ and $F(2,28) = 4.03$, $p < .025$, but verb agreement did not.

For Spanish, there was no main effect of word order on choice, but significant main effects were noted for clitic, $F(2,18) = 17.03$, $p < .0005$, agreement, $F(2,18) = 7.64$, $p < .005$, and, above all, preposition, $F(1,9) = 563.47$, $p < .0005$. Significant main effects on reaction times were obtained for Word Order, $F(2,18) = 4.19$, $p < .05$, Clitic, $F(2,18) = 4.00$, $p < .05$, and Agreement, $F(2,18) = 7.95$, $p < .005$, but not for the Preposition. Now let us look in somewhat more detail; first, at the results for choice, and then, at those for reaction times.

1. Choice (Main Effects)

Preposition.   The preposition *a* is the most decisive cue in Spanish. If the first noun is preceded by *a* it is chosen as the agent only 5% of the time; if the second noun is preceded by *a*, it is chosen as the agent only 6% of the time. Hence this particle operates much like deterministic accusative markers in a case-inflected language, effectively preventing the noun it precedes from attaining agent status.

Word Order.   Summed across morphological conditions, French listeners showed the following word order biases: SVO on NVN (62%), SOV on NNV (57%), and VOS on VNN (45%).

In Spanish, where the main effect of word order is not significant, there were also no individual effects of canonical versus noncanonical order. For Spanish adult subjects, word order does not seem to play a role in sentence interpretation – at least not when it is combined with so many other, more powerful cues.

Clitic.   French and Spanish adults take account of the information provided by clitic pronouns in the expected direction, that is, when the object clitic agrees with one of the nouns, they choose the other noun as agent. But the effect is stronger in French. The effect of clitics might be larger in Spanish if no *a* particle were available; but in the present context, this agreement cue is clearly swamped by the local accusative marker.

Agreement.   In both languages, adults are found to process verbal inflections in the expected direction when assigning functional roles. French speakers choose

Table 2.3. *Mean effects of factors within languages*

		% Choice of first noun		Latency (msec)	
		French	Spanish	French	Spanish
Word order	NVN	62	49	1900	1220
	NNV	57	52	2650	1520
	VNN	45	49	2270	1290
Clitic	C0	60	52	2010	1160
	C1	78	54	2490	1450
	C2	27	45	2330	1420
Agreement	A0	63	51	2380	1000
	A1	83	56	2350	1530
	A2	19	45	2090	1500
Preposition	P1	–	95	–	1310
	P2	–	6	–	1380

the first noun as agent 83% of the time when it is the only noun that agrees with the verb. In Spanish, this noun is chosen 56% of the time. When the second noun is the only noun that agrees with the verb, the figures are 81% second noun choice for French and 55% second noun choice for Spanish. Once again, we see that the Spanish *a* particle has overwhelmed the effects of any other morphological marker.

Taking the mean squares of the variance as a measure of the different cues' weight, the same ordering was discovered for both languages. In French the order was: agreement > clitic > word order. In Spanish the order was: preposition > agreement > clitic > word order. These orderings are, it may be noted, comparable to those established on the basis of processing types: from most local to most topological. *In both languages, the more local a cue, the greater its strength.* Not only does cue cost interact with cue validity, a local marker may (in the case of the Spanish accusative marker) completely eclipse morphological cues of roughly equivalent availability and reliability. Having completed our analysis of the results for choice we now turn to an analysis of the results for latencies.

2. Latencies (Main Effects)

Word Order. In post hoc analyses of word order types for French, canonical NVNs (with an average latency of 1900 msec) elicit faster responses than the other two orders (NNV = 2650 msec; VNN = 2270 msec). In Spanish, NVN and VNN sequences are processed equally fast (averaging 1220 and 1290 msec, respectively), but latencies for NNV were longer (1520 msec). Notice that the latency data do not map onto consistency in choice behavior in any clearcut way – particularly for Spanish. Cue validity and processing cost are not isomorphic, as we noted in Experiment 1.

Clitic. In both languages, listeners were slowed down by the presence of clitic pronouns. In both languages, there was no significant difference in reaction times between sentences with clitics agreeing with the first noun and clitics agreeing with the second noun. This finding could reflect a major discrepancy for the overall validity model, which predicts faster decisions as information increases. We will return to this point later, after determining whether the increased processing cost is contributed exclusively by the competition items (as predicted by the model), or by the absolute presence of an additional cue in a competing or a converging direction.

Agreement. Verb agreement appears to be processed differently in the two languages. The agreement marker produced no simple, main effect on latencies in French. In Spanish, ambiguous agreement (AO) yielded the shortest latencies (1000 msec). The processing of both A1 (verb agreement with the first noun) and A2 (agreement with the second noun) was significantly longer (1530 and 1500 msec, respectively). Again, we have a discrepancy with the original Competition Model. Cues which clarify sentence interpretation (reflected in choice behavior) should speed up reaction times relative to sentences without those cues. The question is, again, are these processing costs imposed exclusively by competition items, or by an addition of information in any direction?

Preposition. The preposition *a* was always present and yielded equivalent latencies whatever the position of the noun it preceded. This finding is undoubtedly related to the finding that word order is not an important cue in Spanish. We can also explain the fact that mean overall latency for Spanish subjects (1340 msec) was shorter than that for the French (2270 msec): availability of the preposition *a* permits efficient local processing for Spanish listeners, at minimal cost.

To explore the cost issue for other cues – especially clitic pronouns and verb agreement – we need to examine the rate of increase or decrease in processing time of the utterances in which they add converging information, as compared with those where they are not available. This leads us to more detailed consideration of the higher order interactions.

3. Interactions (French)

All the two-way interactions for choice reached significance in French, as did those for latencies.

Table 2.4. *Word order by clitic and word order by agreement in French adults*

		% Choice of first noun			Latency (msec)		
		NVN	NNV	VNN	NVN	NNV	VNN
	C0	73	63	42	1540	2300	1930
Clitic	C1	80	83	71	1840	2990	2630
	C2	33	26	21	2320	2660	2000
	A0	76	61	51	1930	2460	2500
Agreement	A1	91	84	72	1860	2650	2530
	A2	20	27	11	1910	2840	1530

Word Order × Clitic. The competition and coalition principles, with respect to canonical order (NVN) and clitic pronouns, successfully account for most of the results obtained for choice and latencies. Competition between the word order cue and the clitic cue is resolved in favor of the information supplied by the pronoun, for both canonical and noncanonical word orders. Furthermore, for all order types, behavior is more consistent when word order and clitic information converge, and less consistent when they compete. Nevertheless, processing time is shorter in the *absence* of a pronoun (Table 2.4), even if the clitic information and the order information lead to the same conclusions. This kind of discrepancy between sentence interpretation and reaction time data has not been reported to date for experiments of this kind (but see unpublished data for English, cited by Bates & MacWhinney, this volume).

Word Order × Agreement. The coalition between NVN order and agreement results in more consistent choice behavior, as predicted. And agreement wins out in competition with word order, to an even stronger degree than we obtained in the above competition between word order and clitic pronouns. For example, when NVN disagrees with the clitic marker, subjects chose the first noun only 33% of the time (Table 2.4); but when NVN disagrees with the agreement marker, subjects chose the first noun only 20% of the time.

But the effects of interacting order and agreement cues on latency are not so clearcut. Converging agreement information leads to a slight reaction time advantage for NVN items, a larger advantage for VNN items, but a fairly significant reaction time loss for NNV. As with the similar effect found in Experiment 1, these results present problems for a nondynamic account. More information does not necessarily lead to faster reaction times. The explanation of this difference between NNV and the other two orders may well be based on the fact that the number contrast between the two nouns cannot be evaluated until the verb is processed. In NNV sequences the verb occurs at the very end of the clause and attachment of the subject to the verb is therefore delayed to the last moment. This delay is reflected in slower reactions times. Examples of such on-line accounts are given by MacWhinney (1987).

Clitic × Agreement.   In general, the results of this interaction support the competition principle: Choices are more consistent and reaction times are faster when clitics and agreement markers converge, compared to items where the same markers lead to opposite results. When the two sources of information do compete, agreement information seems to be stronger. Collapsing across word order types, choice of first noun on A1C2 items is 62%; choice of first noun on A2C1 items is 47%. (Keep in mind that A1 and C1 both mean that the cues favor the first noun as agent; similarly, A2 and C2 both mean that the cues favor the second noun as agent. Since A is an agent-marking cue and C is an object-marking cue, this terminology is potentially confusing.)

The surprises come not from competition items, but from convergence items. A coalition of two morphological cues should lead to accelerated processing, when cue combinations are compared with items in which either cue operates alone. This prediction was only partially supported in our data. Converging agreement information does seem to increase processing speed, relative to the same clitic conditions without an agreement contrast. But converging clitic information seems to *decrease* speed, relative to the same agreement conditions without clitics. To clarify this situation, let us turn to the three-way interactions involving word order types.

Word Order × Clitic × Agreement.   This very complex set of interactions among cues is summarized in Table 2.5. In canonical NVN sequences, French adults choose the first noun 100% of the time in this experiment when no contrasting morphological information is available (compare this with the relative distrust of a SVO strategy in Experiment 1, where they were led to expect competitions from animacy). Obviously, a convergence of morphological information with NVN could not possibly increase this perfect performance. Based on the Competition Model, however, we would predict that an SVO interpretation will be faster when word order and morphology converge. This is particularly likely given the fact that either of the morphological cues defeat word order in a competition. Nevertheless, as can be seen from Table 2.5, processing time is markedly slower when additional morphological contrasts are provided on an NVN structure – even if they all converge on the same interpretation. Obviously, there is an added processing cost involved in the computation of agreement information. This differs from studies of Italian and German, where the topological cue of subject–verb agreement always seems to speed decision making, compared with word order and/or animacy cues alone (MacWhinney et al., 1984).

Table 2.5. *Word order by clitic and verb agreement in French adults*

		% choice of first noun			Latency (msec)		
		NVN	NNV	VNN	NVN	NNV	VNN
C0	A0	100	77	47	1260	2790	2210
C0	A1	100	100	80	1360	2020	2390
C0	A2	20	13	0	2010	2100	1190
C1	A0	100	93	93	2000	2050	3110
C1	A1	100	90	87	1300	2330	2640
C1	A2	40	67	33	2210	4600	2130
C2	A0	27	13	13	2530	2560	2160
C2	A1	73	63	50	2930	3590	2560
C2	A2	0	0	0	1490	1830	1280

In noncanonical sequences, the results are more staightforward. For both NNV and VNN items, subjects are faster and more consistent when information from either or both morphological cues converges on baseline word order interpretations. And of course, morphological cues win out when they compete with the much weaker biases that French subjects display for NNV and VNN in the absence of morphological contrasts (i.e., SOV and VOS, respectively). So the failure of added information to lead to faster latencies occurs primarily with canonical word order strings. We will consider some explanations for these phenomena shortly, after examining the data for Spanish.

4. Interactions (Spanish)

With the sole exception of the clitic × agreement × preposition interaction, none of the interactions reached significance for choice. However, most of the interactions were significant for latency.

Word Order × Clitic. For Spanish, as for French, clitic pronouns tend to slow down reaction times (Table 2.6). However, the direction of effects is different for the various word order types. On NNV orders, the reaction times to C0 items are 1370 msec and C1 items 1400 msec; but for C2 strings (where N2 = agent), reaction times are considerably longer (1790 msec). Apparently, Spanish listeners do not expect an OSV construction to be indicated by a clitic. For the other two orders, reaction times are faster on C2 items than on C1 items. Taken together, these findings suggest that, in the presence of an object clitic, Spanish listeners expect to find the following interpretations: OVS, SOV, and VOS. We can only assume that these are cliticized orders most often encountered in informal conversation – an empirical question, but one that we cannot answer here.

Table 2.6. *Word order by clitic in Spanish adults – latency in msecs.*

	NVN	NNV	VNN
C0	1000	1370	1110
C1	1440	1400	1510
C2	1220	1790	1250

Table 2.7. *Word order, clitic, and verb agreement by preposition in Spanish adults – latency in msecs.*

		P1	P2
Word order	NVN	1220	1220
	NNV	1410	1630
	VNN	1310	1280
Clitic	C0	1060	1250
	C1	1290	1700
	C2	1260	1180
Agreement	A0	1030	970
	A1	1000	2060
	A2	1900	1100

Word Order × Preposition.   Processing time is the same for NVN and VNN sequences, whatever the local information carried by the preposition (P1 or P2). But latency increases for NNVs if the preposition precedes the first noun (P2), which of course makes the second noun the agent. It is not the case simply that Spanish listeners are surprised by OSV constructions, with an accusative marker in sentence-initial position, since they apparently have no difficulty with OVS constructions. Rather, it may be that their difficulty with OSV is due to a tendency in Spanish to prefer the object either immediately before or immediately after the verb.

Clitic × Preposition.   In P1 items, clitic pronouns slow down reaction times regardless of whether they compete or converge (Table 2.7). On P2 items, we find that clitic pronouns follow the principles of the Competition Model, increasing speed in a convergence and slowing things down in a competition (Table 2.7). In some ways, these results are similar to the three-way word order × morphology interactions in French: Morphological cues tend to slow down the interpretation of canonical sentence frames and speed up the interpretation of a noncanonical order. P1 items are canonical, reflecting statistically predominant word orders in which the agent/subject is located in first position and the accusative-marked patient/object is located in second position. Spanish clitics,

Table 2.8. *Word order by clitic by verb agreement in Spanish adults – latency in msecs.*

	NVN			NNV			VNN		
	C0	C1	C2	C0	C1	C2	C0	C1	C2
A0	840	1250	760	870	930	1680	790	1010	900
A1	1030	1490	1410	2040	1510	1750	1260	1930	1340
A2	1130	1580	1490	1200	1780	1940	1300	1610	1520

like most French agreement markers, slow down processing in these more canonical sentence frames regardless of the contribution that the added morphology makes to sentence interpretation. By comparison, P2 items are noncanonical, reflecting word orders in which the accusative-marked patient/object is the first noun phrase to appear. Spanish clitics, like French agreement markers, can speed up sentence interpretation in a noncanonical frame. This kind of finding will clearly require some refinement of the Competition Model.

Agreement × Preposition. Competition between subject–verb agreement and the accusative marker produces longer processing times (see Table 2.7). But coalition effects are not so clearcut, and depend once again on canonicity. For the more canonical P1 items (where N1 is the agent), additional and converging information from a subject–verb contrast slows processing down. For the less canonical P2 items (where N2 is the agent), the addition of a converging agreement cue speeds up processing. This is similar to our findings for the interaction between the preposition *a* and clitic pronouns.

Word Order × Clitic × Agreement. This analysis (see Table 2.8) collapses across the all-important accusative-marking preposition in Spanish, which (as we have seen) does have important implications for the interpretation of reaction time data. For noncanonical word orders, the fastest processing occurs in the *absence* of additional information from either subject–verb agreement or clitic pronouns. This is also true for canonical NVN strings, with one exception: AOC2 sentences. These are NVN strings with no subject–verb agreement contrast, where the clitic pronoun signals that N2 is the agent – hence forcing an OVS interpretation. At first glance these patterns seem to run against all the predictions of the Competition Model. Converging morphological information ought to speed processing, especially in a richly inflected language like Spanish. However, before we interpret these findings further, we have to examine interactions involving the all-important preposition factor. As we shall see, these reaction-time results can be explained by once again invoking the notion of canonical expectations.

Table 2.9. *Word order by verb agreement and preposition for Spanish adults –
latency in msecs.*

	NVN			NNV			VNN		
	A0	A1	A2	A0	A1	A2	A0	A1	A2
P1	910	950	1790	1320	990	1910	870	1050	2010
P2	980	1070	1000	1000	2530	1370	930	1960	940

Word Order × Agreement × Preposition. In general, these findings (see
Table 2.9) obey the competition principle: the longest reaction times within
any word order type are obtained when agreement and the prepositional cue
compete. Hence, even though the prepositional cue clearly does determine
Spanish sentence interpretation, this powerful cue "suffers" markedly when it
conflicts with another important source of morphological information – a fact
that is reflected in processing time even if it does not appear in choice behavior.
However (again), the interactions provide less evidence for the predicted effects
of coalitions. For NVN items, the addition of a converging agreement contrast
results in a slight slowing down of reaction times – and in this case, the
processing cost occurs for both canonical P1 and less canonical P2 items. The
same is true for the less common VNN constructions – and once again the
added cost of a morphological contrast occurs for both P1 and P2 constructions.
The addition of agreement morphology provides a savings in time for only
one condition: P1/A1/NNV, which is, of course, interpreted as an SOV, where
the first noun agrees with the verb while the second noun is preceded by the
accusative *a* marker. This is a particular "good" example of a noncanonical word
order construction in Spanish, but it is not the only one. No single principle is
likely to account for these patterns. We have to take canonical expectations into
account, and the notion of "canonical form" depends in turn on the language
and the set of cues in question.

Clitic × Agreement × Preposition (For Choice). This was the only significant
interaction in the analysis of choice in Spanish. Because most of the cells in
the design are close to the ceiling (due to the overwhelming strength of the
accusative preposition *a*), it seems best not to interpret this particular three-way
interaction.

Discussion

The major results of Experiment 2 may be summarized in relation to the
principles of local processing, left-to-right processing, canonicity, and perceptual
salience.

Local Processing and Sentence Interpretation.   In both languages, the syntactic cues used to determine functional relations are ordered in terms of the processing types with which they are associated, from the most local to the most topological. In French, the hierarchy of cue strength is verb agreement > clitics > word order. This result parallels the findings in Experiment 1, where animacy (a cue that permits more local interpretations) wins over word order in competition situations. Hierarchical ordering can be predicted on the basis of processing cost, interacting with the availability and reliability of cues. In fact, processing cost may be more important than cue validity, given the extent to which French adults avoid the use of the relatively valid word order cue.

In Spanish, the results obtained are even clearer: Along a proposed local to topological continuum, the preposition *a* requires a minimum amount of storage and cross-referencing for interpretation to occur. Analyses of choice behavior show that the preposition *a* is a maximally effective cue which effectively blocks the impact of any other grammatical form. The major difference in overall processing times for the two languages (1340 msec for Spanish, 2270 msec for French) is no doubt attributable to the effect of this very powerful caselike cue, which operates as an *absolute signal*.

Left-to-Right Parsing and Canonicity.   Most of the predictions based on the competition principle were confirmed: Behavior is less consistent, and reaction times are slower, when two or more cues compete, compared with situations of convergence and/or with individual cues operating in isolation. On the other hand, I uncovered a number of problems for the simple overall validity model. In the analyses of choice behavior, responses were generally more consistent as information converged – as the overall validity model would predict. But analyses of reaction time data yielded a different picture. Those configurations in which verb agreement and/or clitic pronouns are absent (A0C0) often yield the shortest reaction times. This surprising pattern was found in both languages, albeit in rather different combinations.

For example, both clitics and subject–verb agreement markers tend to slow down French listeners in NVN strings. By contrast, converging morphological cues can speed up response time on noncanonical orders. Hence, the contribution of additional cues interacts with canonicity. In Spanish, the situation was somewhat different: converging morphological cues interacted primarily with the position of the preposition *a*. In the statistically predominant P1 items, where N1 is the agent and N2 is the accusative-marked patient, additional morphological information (particularly object clitics) tended to slow down the listeners. In the more unusual P2 configurations (where N2 is the agent, and the accusative-marked N1 is encountered first), additional morphological cues could result in a slightly faster response.

But canonicity does not account for every exception to the coalition principle.

There are interactions related to the relative positioning of cues that require a new kind of explanation. To account for data like these, we would invoke the on-line principle proposed by MacWhinney, Pléh, and Bates (1984, p. 783). As the parser progresses, it accumulates evidence that strengthens or weakens the candidacy of each noun for the agency role. Our data add much more detail to this initial claim. In canonical situations, the listener may have a strong initial expectation that has to be overcome by lexical or morphological cues that point in another direction. But whether the configuration seems canonical or not, the relative processing cost of cues (particularly their local/topological status) will also play a role in determining when and to what extent a listener is willing to entertain an alternative interpretation. For example, it could be said that in Spanish there is no other true syntactic decision beyond that supplied by the case markings. We have proposed that the other available cues are used merely as checks on earlier choices made. However, because the accusative *a* is homophonous with other uses of the same prepositional form, the listener may be somewhat wary when that particle occurs in a less likely position (i.e., in our P2 items). Such suggestions are currently being evaluated in on-line research which should make it possible to determine at what point in the course of sentence processing subjects actually take account of the various cues.

As observed by Frankel and Arbel (1982), off-line research cannot choose between alternative hypotheses concerning the point at which cues are selected: This could take place before "an accessing of alternative assignments of sentence relations, or a selection between alternative assignments of sentence relations could occur after the various indications of different cues have been computed and after the respective assignments of sentence relations have been accessed" (p. 451).

It is interesting to compare the results obtained for adult Spanish subjects with those reported for Hebrew (Frankel, Amir, Frenkel, & Arbel, 1980; Frankel & Arbel, 1981; Frankel & Arbel, 1982) because of the relationship between the available cues for sentence interpretation. In Hebrew, word order is relatively free, with SVO dominant in the modern variety of the language, as in Spanish. Hebrew has a prepositional case mark *et* which comes before the direct object of a transitive verb much like the Spanish preposition *a*, which precedes an animate direct object in Spanish. In addition, Hebrew has postpositional inflections which mark gender and number agreement between the (noun) subject and verb. Hebrew gender inflection is fusional with number on nouns and verbs, and with verb tense as well.

Frankel et al. (1980) report a dominant strategy for Hebrew children (aged 3 to 11 years) which takes the first noun in a sentence as agent. (This strategy was especially evident in NVN and VNN sequences.) However, whenever object marking and gender agreement jointly designate the second noun as agent, choice of N1 falls by 50 percent. As a result, the combined effect of local cues is seen to outweigh that of word order for all age groups. Furthermore, the effect of object marking is systematically greater than that of gender marking. Frankel and Arbel (1982), referring to an earlier study with adult subjects, report that the influence of the accusative marker was so great that it would have taken an especially large number of different sentences to arrive at an adequate test of the interactions involving other types of cues. They thus chose to eliminate the accusative contrast from subsequent research.

Such predominance of one cue in the case of Hebrew adults is entirely compatible with our Spanish data. The question remains of course whether it is justified – ecologically and methodologically – to discard sentences, in this instance high frequency sentence types, because of their borderline status with reference to the predictions of a probabilistic model of sentence processing which is based on the make-up of the various available cues. In fact, such sentences make it possible to discover the economical processing strategies which characterize the adult user of a particular language. Furthermore, the work of Frankel et al. (1980) indicates that the dominance of such a strategy, as was found in Spanish children (Kail & Charvillat, 1985), develops gradually over time.

Detection of Local Cues and Perceptual Salience. The effectiveness of accusative case marking through *a* in Spanish seems to be related to two features: pre-positioning with respect to a noun candidate for the accusative function, and morphemic autonomy. The latter introduces a distinction between the above mentioned languages and languages with flectional accusative markers taking the form of an affix (usually a suffix), such as Turkish (regular, systematic marking) or Serbo-Croatian (unsystematic marking involving phonetic ambiguity). In an early formulation of his operating principles, Slobin (1982) proposed that "if an analytic and a synthetic option are available for expression of the same notion, prefer the analytic option." In other words, use syntax rather than morphology: words are clearer than affixes (Berman, 1982). Comparing Turkish and Serbo-Croatian to Italian and English (languages without inflection), Slobin and Bever (1982) showed that Turkish children succeed very early in understanding simple sentences lacking the animacy contrast, even though they do not make use of word order in assigning roles. This fact and others (Hakuta, 1982; Weist, 1983) have cast doubt on hypotheses founded on the myth of a universal natural order.

In their work on Hungarian, MacWhinney et al. (1985) take up the question of cue detectability. Direct objects of the verb in Hungarian are always marked by an accusative suffix placed on the noun. This suffix is composed of the phoneme *t*, sometimes preceded by a linking vowel (e.g., *ház* 'house'; *házat* house-ACC). Although Hungarian is closely related to Turkish (basic SOV, highly regular accusative suffixation), Hungarian children (aged 2;6–3;5) make use of the accusative cue in fewer than 70% of the cases, whereas Turkish children (aged 2;6) already use the cue 80% of the time. MacWhinney et al. have suggested that this difference might be attributable to a blurring of the phonetic distinction between the accusative *t* and the possessive marker *d*, along with the fact that in certain cases, for example, *mokus-t* squirrel-ACC, a very careful pronunciation is required for the case marking to be audible. This work thus stresses the role of phonological processing in sentence comprehension, a problem which has been somewhat more neglected in this area than elsewhere (cf. lexical access studies).

More specifically, the MacWhinney et al. results make clear the effects due to interaction between "syntactic expectations" and what they term "phonemic restoration," effects which are totally compatible with the Competition Model. In terms of the processing cost approach which is being examined in this paper, it is clearly important to take account not only of a marker's detectability, but also of its *anticipation function*. By anticipation function, I refer to the set of hypotheses which, at a given time *t*, may be entertained in connection with an utterance string. In this respect, one of the functions of clitic pronouns would be to anticipate the transitivity of the verb and to permit earlier syntactic closure. Naturally, in a language such as French the anticipation function is somewhat weakened by the fact that phonemically identical strings (*le, la, les*) correspond to both the clitic pronoun and definite article morphemes. Clearly, several dimensions are involved in the promotion of a syntactic cue to best possible signal status. Among those highly valued are perceptual clarity, form/function transparency, regularity, and the availability for preassignments. This is to draw attention to the fact that within the useful distinction between local and topological processing, finer distinctions must still be considered. Furthermore, the notions of cue validity, cue cost, and cue detectability are dynamic (in the developmental sense) and are no doubt at least partially dependent on the task set. This is readily apparent in some results that we have obtained for French children aged 4;6–6;6, which reflect a cue hierarchy (word order > clitic > verb agreement) that is the mirror image of that obtained for adult subjects, whereas Spanish children of the same age groups show the same cue hierarchy (preposition *a* > verb agreement > clitic and word order) as Spanish adult subjects.

MacWhinney et al. (1985) state that the two determinants of cue validity develop by moving on from the most available cue to the most reliable cue. This progression, attested to in the elimination of errors and overgeneralizations, arises out of the child's growing awareness of the success of a strategy founded on one or another cue, and of his or her increasing awareness of the cost of implementing the cue. But cost also changes over time with capacity (e.g., increases in memory and efficiency).

Conclusion

It is important to consider the effect of accumulating more and more varied data in terms of the validation and/or enrichment of the Competition Model. It seems that the model can be characterized formally in terms of two separate levels: that of its primitives or axioms (e.g., direct mapping between the formal and functional levels of cue competition) and that of the derived notions (e.g., cue strength, cue validity), which constitute a body of empirically disconfirmable hypotheses.

Research within, or inspired by, the Competition Model framework has led to a number of reinforcements and innovations, including two aspects of cue cost: cue detectability (Macwhinney et al., 1985) and local versus topological processing (Kail & Charvillat, 1988). With regard to sentence comprehension, developmental hypotheses formulated in terms of overall cue validity would clearly seem to be oversimplified. It may be expected that on-line research in this area will lead to further refinements that will better account for those areas presently neglected (e.g., automaticity of access, or the functional readiness principle).

The model should therefore be regarded more as providing a framework for *empirical* investigation than as a set of powerful axioms from which one might derive a *logically* sound body of theory. It is, of course, highly unlikely that such a model could be proposed at the present time. Nevertheless, the notion of competition, which lies at the core of the model under consideration, has a theoretical value which extends beyond the areas of speech production and comprehension (Norman, 1981).

In evaluating the explanatory power of Slobin's operating principles, Bowerman (1985) gives a number of examples in conflict with the predictions of certain operating principles. The notion of competition makes it possible to resolve the discrepancy between the principles and the facts; Bowerman shows how competition between different ways of expressing the same (or nearly the same) meaning favors an approach less dependent upon inherent mapping preferences than Slobin's. She also draws attention to the fact that the available crosslinguistic data on language acquisition provide no support for claims of inherent predispositions with regard to how meanings should map onto linguistic forms. This is not to favor one explanation over another, but rather to call for a coherent theoretical framework which could accommodate both the role of certain predispositions (e.g., the intrinsic notion of relevance in young children) and the flexibility characteristic of acquisition. The immensity of the task before us does not escape MacWhinney et al. (1985): "The question is whether it will be possible to provide a full account of sentence processing that is based upon the competition between a set of cues. We have begun to construct this elaboration, but it is clear that there is still a great deal of work to be done" (p. 207). Such has also been the motivation for this research into child and adult speakers of French and Spanish. The results described here have contributed to changes in the original Competition Model. Moving the Competition Model into the area of on-line research will undoubtedly bring about further change.

3   The Development of Role Assignment
in Hebrew

Jeffrey L. Sokolov

Hebrew is a language that has been revived from near extinction. It nearly became extinct after the destruction of the second temple when Jews migrated from Israel and attempted to assimilate to new cultures. The revival of Hebrew occurred as part of a nationalist movement that began when Jews started to populate Israel toward the end of the nineteenth century. Because Modern Hebrew is based on earlier written versions of Hebrew, most notably Biblical, it was an enormous task to transform it into the language spoken by a nation's children. One indication of the size of this task is the story of the first native speaker of Modern Hebrew. The story tells of a certain Hebrew scholar named Ben-Yehuda who decreed that his son would hear only Hebrew during the whole length of his childhood. He went so far as to not allow his son to play with other non-Hebrew speaking children. The boy did eventually grow up to speak Hebrew as a first language (although legend has it that he didn't speak until after his tenth year). In fact, he became a respected scholar of the Hebrew language. Since the time of Ben-Yehuda, there have been three generations of native Hebrew speakers. Each generation has been instrumental in creating Hebrew as we know it today: a Semitic language that has many interesting linguistic features including a rich system of verbal morphology, a variable word order, and case inflections. These features and how children acquire them have now been extensively investigated by Israeli psycholinguists (Berman, 1985; Dromi, 1979; Frankel & Arbel, 1981; Levy, 1983a; Walden, 1983). This chapter will focus specifically on how the child learns to use these features to assign various grammatical roles.

When children try to understand sentences, they have to figure out who did what to whom. This problem can be thought of as the role assignment problem. One part of this problem is deciding who is the actor. This subproblem can be refered to as the actor assignment problem. A large body of developmental psycholinguistic research has addressed this problem. It has been examined in French (Sinclair & Bronckardt, 1972; Kail, this volume), in Turkish (Slobin & Bever, 1982), in Italian (Bates, McNew, MacWhinney, Devescovi, & Smith, 1982; Slobin & Bever, 1982), in Dutch and German (McDonald, 1984), in Serbo-Croatian (Slobin & Bever, 1982), in Hungarian (MacWhinney, Pléh, & Bates, 1985; Pléh, this volume), in Japanese (Hakuta, 1982; Kilborn & Ito, this volume), and in English (Sheldon, 1974). For Hebrew, Frankel and Arbel (1981) and Frankel et al. (1980) have studied how children learn that surface structure cues such as word order, subject–verb agreement, and an object marker provide solutions to the actor assignment problem. Frankel and Arbel interpreted their results as suggesting that "the likelihood of assigning the agent relation to the first [versus] the second noun of Hebrew utterances systematically varied with the relative weights of cues that supported and opposed each assignment" (1981, p. 112). However, they did not propose any explanation for how children might be deriving these cue strengths. One goal of the present chapter is to propose and test such an explanation.

A second aspect of the role assignment problem is the task of deciding who is the patient. This problem can be called the patient assignment problem. This problem only arises when the main verb is transitive. When it is intransitive, the role assignment problem is simply the actor assignment problem. This is because the intransitive subject is really an actor in the prototypic sense. The patient assignment problem is not simply the obverse of the actor assignment problem, since it is often the case that the patient is not simply the noun that is not the actor. Sometimes there are several non-agentive nouns. Sometimes there is only one noun. Sometimes the patient is pronominal; sometimes it is reflexive; sometimes it is reciprocal. Cues to patient selection help children decide among all these alternative assignments of the patient role. Hebrew provides a particularly rich set of cues for patient assignment. These include word order, case marking, and verbal morphology. This aspect of the role assignment problem has remained largely unstudied (but see Sokolov, 1988, discussed below).

In addition to solving the "who did what to whom" puzzle, children are often faced with a third aspect of the role assignment problem. This problem involves assigning oblique roles (such as locative, instrumental, or comitative) to nouns in sentences. In Hebrew, this problem is generally indicated not only by the verb, but also by prepositions or prefixes. As we will see from some previous research (Berman, 1985; Dromi, 1979; Rom & Dgani, 1985), Hebrew also provides several cues to oblique role assignment. In this chapter, we will investigate the development of Hebrew-speaking children's solutions to all three role assignment problems. The theoretical framework for the investigation will be the Competition Model as described by Bates and MacWhinney (this volume).

The Competition Model

A major tenet of the competition model is that different languages employ different grammatical cues in wide and varied ways to assign grammatical functions. For example, although both nouns are equally probable actors in the English sentence, "The boy kissed the girl", English speakers will consistently assign the role of actor to the first noun. In fact, the word order cue is so strong in English that English-speaking subjects will even assign the role of actor to the "eraser" in "The eraser kicked the horse" (Bates, McNew, MacWhinney, Devescovi, & Smith, 1982). Interestingly, however, Italian-speakers behave in a very different manner. Given the corresponding Italian sentence, they tend to assign the role of actor to the *horse*. In other words, word order is a strong cue for actor assignment for speakers of English, whereas animacy is a strong cue for speakers of Italian. One of the goals of the Competition Model is to provide an account for why speakers of these and other languages attribute high *cue strengths* to certain grammatical forms and low ones to others.

The Competition Model proposes that a form which is high in *cue validity* (Brunswik, 1956) will eventually also come to have high *cue strength*. Cue validity is defined as an objective property of the stimulus to be measured by text counts. Cue strength is a psychological property to be measured in psycholinguistic experimentation. Learning involves bringing cue strength into tune with cue validity. The higher the validity of a cue, the earlier it will be acquired. To have high validity, a cue must be both *available* and *reliable*. For a cue to be fully available, it must be present each time the task it supports is performed. For example, since English uses SVO word order to assign grammatical case roles, the SVO cue is extremely high in availability. If a cue is fully reliable, its use should never lead to an erroneous interpretation of the sentence.

Availability and simple frequency are not equivalent constructs. First of all, availability is computed without consideration of the frequency in which a given task (e.g., actor or patient assignment) is performed. Availability is independent of task frequency because it is defined here as the percentage of times that particular cues are present *within* a given task, and not *across* tasks. Secondly, within a task, availability takes into account more than the simple presence or absence of a given cue. This is true because the availability of a cue is lowered when the cue is present but not informative. Such a situation is often true of the subject–verb agreement cue for actor assignment. One such a case occurs in Hebrew when a sentence consists of a transitive verb and two singular masculine nouns. The subject–verb agreement cue is present (i.e., both nouns are marked in terms of number and gender); however, it does not provide a contrast between the two nouns. On the basis of agreement alone, we cannot tell which noun is the subject/actor. We must rely on other cues for this information.

If the range of role assignment tasks can be represented as in Figure 3.1, then it is easy to provide a quantitative definition for the notion of cue validity (McDonald, 1984). For each particular role assignment task, *availability* equals the proportion of utterances in which a given cue is available to help perform the task divided by the total number of utterances. *Reliability* equals the proportion of utterances in which the cue is reliable divided by the total number of times it is

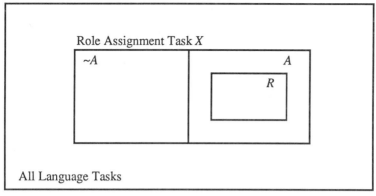

Figure 3.1. Defining cue validity in terms of availability and reliability, where *A* = availability and *R* = reliability.

available. *Validity* is the product of availability and reliability: the proportion of utterances in which the cue is reliable divided by the total number of utterances.

These equations provide a guide for computing estimates of the validity of grammatical cues directly from sample texts. The strength of a grammatical cue in sentence comprehension can be determined by devising an experimental task which requires subjects to interpret sentences where cues are set in competition with one another. The manner in which subjects resolve this conflict determines which cue is the strongest one for them. According to the Competition Model, there should be a significant correlation between cue validity and cue strength. Since cue validity makes predictions concerning cue strength, such a correlation would indicate that cue validity is a significant predictor of cue strength. Since cue strengths are different for different languages, if cue validity is going to be successful as a mechanism of language development it must be computed and tested across different languages.

McDonald (1984, 1986) performed one such test. She calculated cue validity estimates from actual English and Dutch texts and then performed an experiment with English and Dutch monolinguals to test the predictions made by the estimates. Her analysis generated predictions across two languages with three different syntactic constructions (standard NVN, relative clauses, and datives) tested in each. All of the predictions concerning the relative initial strengths of word order, animacy, and case inflections made by the model were supported by the data. Five of the correlation coefficients were above 0.9, while one, for simple English NVN constructions, was 0.63 (the correlation approached a significant probability value at 0.07).

Another tenet of the Competition Model is that young language learners are creating and storing direct connections between forms and functions. The model eliminates any intermediate levels of representation, such as phrase-structure rules. This claim finds support from the work of Rumelhart and McClelland (1987) who have demonstrated in a number of simulation models that systematic behavior need not be governed or "explained" by explicit rules. When considering the traditional role of rules in linguistics and child language, this might appear to be a radical claim. However, when considered in the context of current linguistic and psychological theories, it does not seem so radical. We see a move away from rules to lexical representations in linguistics (Bresnan, 1982) and to connectionist structures in psychology (Rumelhart & McClelland, 1987; McClelland & Kawamoto, 1986; MacWhinney, 1987). We do not know yet how far we can go without explicit rules, but it has become clear that they are not necessary for many aspects of the acquisition of grammar.

The Competition Model has also been employed to account for developmental differences. The model predicts that the earliest mappings between grammatical cues (forms) and grammatical roles (functions) should be derived from cue validity. In other words, in solving the role assignment problem, young children should be sensitive to both the availability and reliability of the grammatical cues of their language. However, as children get older and are exposed to grammatical forms repeatedly, they should begin to trust the most reliable cues irrespective of their availability (MacWhinney, 1978). This is because reliable cues lead to correct interpretations more of the time than unreliable ones. In more quantitative terms, this would predict that cue validity would be strongly correlated with cue strength for the youngest children, whereas cue reliability would be more strongly correlated with cue strength for the older children.

McDonald (1984) hypothesized that developmental change is driven by situations in which cues conflict with one another. The conflict cases are crucial because in such cases only the most reliable cues support correct interpretations. Thus children can maximize the number of correct interpretations they make by weakening unreliable cues in conflict situations. She tested this hypothesis by analyzing the conflict sentences in her English and Dutch corpora. She found that for English, word order is both the most reliable cue in the text counts and the strongest cue for both younger and older subjects. In contrast, the results for Dutch indicated that as subjects became older, they shifted their allegiance from the most available and reliable cue (noun animacy) to a cue (case inflections) that was highly reliable in conflict cases. Although McDonald (1984) has proposed that adult performance can best be predicted by the reliability of cues in conflict situations (conflict reliability), another possibility is that adults attend to the reliability of cues over both conflict and non-conflict situations. Unfortunately, conflict reliability and overall reliability are usually confounded in natural languages so it is nearly impossible to test which is the better predictor of adult performance. Since overall reliability is simpler to compute, we will use this measure to predict adult performance.

Given these findings, a basic prediction of the extended Competition Model is that cue validity should predict cue strength for young children but that cue reliability should be a better predictor of the older children's performance. The main goal of the present chapter will be to determine whether or not this model can successfully account for the three major role assignment problems in Hebrew. If the model proves unsuccessful, we will attempt extensions to account for the data. Of particular interest as a possible extension to the model are information-processing constraints, also referred to as *cue cost*. Bates and MacWhinney (1987) discuss evidence indicating that the more difficult it is to process a cue, the less subjects will rely upon it. Perhaps processing constraints are useful in accounting for aspects of the role assignment problem in Hebrew. If so, it will be interesting to see for which aspects they are important. In addition, given the mathematical framework provided by McDonald, if it is possible to justify a cardinal ordering of cues based on processing constraints, we should be able to derive equations similar to the ones given for cue validity. Although the scales for validity (which are numerical) and cost (which would be cardinal) would not be identical, we should still be able to measure the contribution of processing constraints to the role assignment problem more precisely than we could otherwise. Following a discussion of the relevant properties of Hebrew, the remainder of the chapter will focus on these tests with the methodology described above.

Some Properties of Hebrew

Up to this point, the Competition Model has been successful in accounting for several important findings in the crosslinguistic literature on language acquisition. However, no one has yet provided an articulation of the Competition Model for Hebrew. Hebrew has a unique configuration of both word order and structural cues for actor assignment, a particularly rich set of cues for patient assignment, and both analytic and fused oblique role assigners. For the actor assignment problem, the relevant cues include word order, subject–verb gender agreement, and absence of the object marker. For the patient assignment problem, the relevant cues include word order, subject–verb agreement, case marking, verbal derivations, and reflexive noun phrases. In addition, Hebrew verbs can signal several candidates for the identity of the patient: transitive, reflexive, reciprocal, inchoative, intransitive, and passive. These cues provide Hebrew speakers with expectations leading to one of these types of patients. In the sentences we will examine, the patient is expressed either as a direct object or by reflexive marking on the verb. Similarly, the actor is always the subject. Of course, in the general case, actors are not always subjects and patients are not always objects. However, for the verb types we are examining, the cues to the subject are also cues to the actor and the cues to the object are also cues to the patient. For oblique roles, Hebrew provides its listeners with a large and varied group of prepositions or prefixes. Although objects are often marked with a special object marker, not all transitive sentences need include an object marker. Some may in fact be marked by a preposition as in *hu hirbits la xamor* "He hit at-the donkey."

Word Order

The basic word order of Hebrew is SVO. This means that the preverbal noun is usually the subject and the postverbal noun is generally the object of the verb. In simple transitive sentences, the subject tends to be the actor and the object tends to be the patient (although this is not necessarily the case all of the time). One exception to this is the passive construction where these grammatical roles are reversed. However, SVO is not the only allowable order in Hebrew. For example, Hebrew allows VSO ordering (e.g., *yesh li kova xadash* "be to-me a-hat new" = "I have a new hat"). Berman (1978) notes that in literary Hebrew, where a complement or an adverbial phrase is preposed, the verb of the complement or adverbial must precede its subject noun phrase, for example, *biglal shtut ibed ha-saxkan et yitrono* "Because-of a-mistake lost the-player OM his-advantage." This example of VSO ordering differs from the previous one in that the verb is transitive. It also provides an example in which the verb and object are separated such that the object is not simply the postverbal noun. Pragmatically governed orders, such as left dislocation or topicalization and right dislocation, are also allowed in Hebrew. Although such dislocations generally include pronoun-copying (e.g., "Ronnie, I don't want to play with him"), copying the pronoun is not obligatory (Borer, 1984). It is important to note that for both left (OSV) and right (VOS) dislocations, the object precedes the subject of the sentence. These examples of nonstandard word orders affect the reliability of word order as a cue to role assignment. The more flexible word order proves to be in Hebrew, the lower will be its reliability.

Subject–Verb Agreement

Hebrew uses gender, number, and person agreement between the subject and the verb of a sentence to mark the identity of both the subject and the object. If there are two nouns and only one agrees with the verb, then that is the subject and the object must be the other noun. If both nouns agree with the verb, then some other cue must differentiate between them. For example, in the sentence *ha-kelev likek et kol ha-yeladot* "The-dog-MASC licked-MASC OM all the-girls-FEM," *kelev* agrees both in gender and number with the verb, while *yeladot* does not. However, if the sentence was *ha-kelev likek et ha-yeled* "The-dog-MASC licked OM the-boy," then the agreement cue would fail and both word order and the accusative marking would be the only available cues. Although agreement is not available all of the time, when it is available, it is extremely reliable.

Although gender agreement is pervasive in Hebrew and is determined by the gender of the noun, gender inflection is highly irregular. In fact, the system is governed by morphophonological rules and fits a characterization similar to the one that Köpcke and Zubin (1983) have provided for German. All nouns are either masculine or feminine with a semantically motivated contrast for animate nouns only. The linguistic gender of inanimate nouns is semantically empty. Singular nouns ending in an *a* or *t* are typically feminine. Other nouns are masculine. However, there are many exceptions in both directions (e.g., *ceva* "color" is a masculine noun). The choice of the plural suffix is determined by the gender of the noun, *-ot* for feminine and *-im* for masculine. This is also highly irregular (e.g., *xalonot gdolot* "windows-MASC big-MASC-PL"). In addition, plural inflection may involve a transformation of internal vowels (e.g., *sefer-sfarim*).

Object Marking

Another form that Hebrew uses to signal grammatical functions is the object marker. The particle *et* assigns the role of direct object to the noun it precedes independently of the number or gender of that noun. Thus it is a cue that the object is participating in a transitive relation. Conversely, it is also a cue that the nonmarked noun is the actor of the sentence. In passive constructions, the object marker is absent. Such passive constructions are marked by passive verbal morphology. The patient is generally in preverbal position, whereas the agent (if there is one) is in postverbal position and is marked by a preposition (Berman, 1985). Frankel and Arbel (1981) note that the object marker has many of the features which typify the highly regular inflectional system of Turkish (Slobin, 1985). According to them, "it is syllabic, stressed, obligatory, nonsynthetic, only indicative of a grammatical role, and consistently applied"' (p. 104). This description appears to be inaccurate on three accounts. First, the object marker is almost never stressed. Second, it is only obligatory when the noun it precedes is definite. When the object is indefinite, the accusative is always omitted. This significantly lowers its availability. Third, although the object marker generally appears in its nonsynthetic form, it is often the case that in fluid conversation, the object marker and the definite article become fused (*et ha-* → *ta*). In addition, when the object is a pronoun, a series of suppletive forms are used which fuse the pronoun with the object marker. The following examples should help to clarify the various conditions of usage for the object marker:

Dan ra'a et ha-yeled.   Object marker: object is a definite common noun.
"Dan saw OM the-boy."

Dan ra'a et bno.   Object marker: object is fused with a possessive determiner.
"Dan saw OM his-son."

Dan ra'a et Yehuda.   Object marker: object is a proper noun.
"Dan saw OM Yehuda."

Dan ra'a oto.   Object marker: object is pronominalized.
"Dan saw OM-him."

Dan ra'a yeled.   No object marker: object is indefinite.
"Dan saw a-boy."

Like subject–verb agreement, the object marker is not always available; however, when it is identifiable it is always reliable. For cases in which the verb is transitive, there is some ambiguity as to whether the morpheme *et* encodes an accusative case marking or a feminine suffix (e.g., *menagev-et* "towelling"). For example, if the sentence *menagev et Rut* is an example of VO ordering with subject ellipsis, then the *et* is an object marker. However, if the word order of the sentence is VS with object ellipsis (which is possible though somewhat rare), then the *et* is a feminine suffix on the verb. Since it is possible to mistake the singular feminine suffix for the object marker, the object marker is not a completely reliable cue.

Marking of Oblique Arguments

Oblique roles, such as dative, instrumental, and locative, are signaled by various prepositions and prefixes (called here prepositionals for simplicity). Examples of some of these and the roles they signal are presented below:

Recipient: *Dan natan* le-*rina et ha-sefer.*
                "Dan gave *to*-Rina OM the-book."

Benefactive: *hu kana* le-*xulam kartisim.*
                "He bought *for*-everyone tickets."

Instrument: *Dan patax et ha-mgera* ba-*mafteax sheli.*
                "Dan opened OM the-drawer *with*-the-key of-mine."

Comitative: *Dan halax ha-ira* im *axoto.*
                "Dan went to-town *with* his-sister."

Goal: *Dan hevi ugot* la-*msiba.*
                "Dan brought cakes *to*-the-party."

Source: *Dan lamad italkit* me-*ha-shxenim.*
                "Dan learned Italian *from*-the-neighbors."

Note also that the preposition *le* "to" can be fused with the definite article *ha* as in the prepositional phrase *la-msiba* "to-the-party." As in English, each prepositional can encode several different roles depending on the action being performed. Because of this, they tend not to be very reliable. Hebrew prepositionals can occur in three forms (as coined by Dromi, 1979):

1. Enclitic prefixes: bound morphemes attached directly to the noun.
   be "in" + *oto* "car" → *beoto* "in a-car"

2. Separate word prepositions: morphemes that are represented in the orthography as separate words. *al* "on" + *gag* "roof" → *al ha-gag* "on the-roof"

3. Fused forms: these are prepositions that have been pronominalized.
   le "to" + *hu* "him" → *lo* "to-him"

Verbal Derivations

Along with other Semitic languages (e.g., Arabic), Hebrew has a rich system of verbal morphology for assigning grammatical relations, such as the identity of the patient. Hebrew verbs are derived from a root consisting of three or four consonants. Each root generally has associated with it an abstract meaning. For example, the triconsonantal root *l-b-sh* is associated with "dressing." This root is used to build the transitive *hilbish*, as in *aba hilbish et ha-yeled* "Father dressed OM the-boy," the reflexive *hitlabesh*, as in *aba hitlabesh* "Father dressed (himself)," and several other forms all of which share the *l-b-sh* consonantal pattern and the meaning of "dressing." Hebrew scholars have provided names for the verb patterns based on their different morphological patterns. Each verb pattern is named after its conjugation of the root of the verb "to act" (*p-a-l*). For example, the *hitCaCeC* pattern (where *C* is a consonant) is named *hitpa'el*. This is the verb pattern in which the root *l-b-sh* is conjugated as the reflexive *hitlabesh* "dress-REFL."

For the purpose of the present research, only three verb patterns from the seven possible were selected for use. The chosen patterns are the *pi'el*, *hif'il*, and *hitpa'el* patterns. *Pi'el* and *hif'il* were chosen because of their transitive functions, despite the fact that they are not exactly equivalent (cf. Bolozky & Saad, 1983), whereas *hitpa'el* was chosen because of its reflexive function. Transitive and reflexive functions were singled out because of the ease in which they translate into picture stimuli. In addition, the verbal system is not entirely consistent: the same function may be expressed by more than one pattern and the same pattern may encode more than one function. For example, the *hif'il* pattern encodes both a transitive and an inchoative function and the hitpa'el pattern encodes intransitive, reflexive, reciprocal, inchoative, and iterative functions. To sum up, Hebrew verb patterns are not highly valid cues. This is mainly because they do not map onto grammatical relations in a consistent manner.

Reflexive noun phrases

One way of marking reflexivity is to use the *hitpa'el* verb pattern. Reflexive verb morphology can also be paraphrased by a transitive verb pattern together with a reflexive noun phrase. For example, a speaker of Hebrew might say *ima hilbisha et acma* "Mother dressed-TRANS OM herself" instead of *ima hitlabsha* "Mother dressed-REFL." However, it is ungrammatical to say *ima hitlabsha et acma* "Mother dressed-REFL OM herself" which would provide redundant coding of reflexivity. Note that two transitive cues – a transitive verb pattern and the object marker – combine with a reflexive cue – the reflexive pronoun – to signal a reflexive interpretation. In addition, the reflexive pronoun agrees in number and gender with its referent. Hebrew uses the reflexive *hitpa'el* verb pattern discussed in the last section to refer to everyday physical

Table 3.1. *Summary examples of the relevant properties of Hebrew*

1. **Word Order**

   SVO: *ima ohevet et aba.*
         "Mother loves OM father."

   VOS: *ohevet et Dani, Rut?*
         "Loves OM Dani, Rut?"

   OSV: *et Dani Rut ohevet.*
         "OM Dani Rut loves."

   VSO: *biglal shtut ibed ha-saxkan et yitrono.*
         "Because-of a-mistake lost the-player OM his-advantage."

2. **Subject–Verb Agreement**

   Available   *ha-kelev likek et kol ha-yeladot.*
                  "The-dog(m) licked all the-girls."

   Not Available *ha-kelev likek et ha-yeled.*
                  "The-dog(m) licked OM the-boy."

3. **Object Marking**

Dan ra'a et ha-yeled. "Dan saw OM the-boy."	Object marker:	Object is a definite common noun.
Dan ra'a et bno. "Dan saw OM his-son."	Object marker:	Object is fused with a possessive determiner.
Dan ra'a et Yehuda. "Dan saw OM Yehuda."	Object marker:	Object is a proper noun.
Dan ra'a oto. "Dan saw OM-him."	Object marker:	Object is pronominalized.
Dan ra'a yeled. "Dan saw a-boy."	No object marker:	Object is indefinite.

activities usually performed upon one's own body, such as washing, drying, and combing. In contrast, the reflexive noun phrase is the syntactically productive means for forming a reflexive in Hebrew. It obeys similar constraints to the "-self" construction in English. Since a verb pattern is used to encode reflexive relations for common activities, we might expect the reflexive noun phrase to be infrequently used. If so, this would lower its validity considerably. The previous discussion of Hebrew is summarized in Table 3.1.

By now the reader has a basic understanding of the principles of the Competition Model and the cues employed by Hebrew to assign actors, patients, and oblique roles. In the next three sections, we will present the available data on the development of strategies for dealing with the various role assignment problems and the implications of these data for the Competition Model. Each section will focus on a single role assignment problem and the ability of cue

Table 3.1. *(cont.)*

---

4. **Oblique Argument Marking**

    Recipient: *Dan natan* le-*rina et ha-sefer.*
                "Dan gave to-Rina OM the-book."

    Benefactive: *hu kana* le-*xulam kartisim.*
                "He bought for-everyone tickets."

    Instrument: *Dan patax et ha-mgera* ba-*mafteax sheli.*
                "Dan opened OM the-drawer with-key of-mine."

    Comitative: *Dan halax ha-ira* im *axoto.*
                "Dan went to-town with his-sister."

    Goal: *Dan hevi ugot* la-*msiba.*
                "Dan brought cakes to-the-party."

    Source: *Dan lamad italkit* me-*ha-shxenim.*
                "Dan learned Italian from-the-neighbors."

5. **Verbal Derivations**

    l-b-sh   *hilbish:*   *aba hilbish et ha-yeled.*
                        "Father dressed OM the-boy."

              hitlabesh: *aba hitlabesh.*
                      "Father dressed (himself)."

6. **Reflexive Noun Phrase**

    aba hilbish et acmo.
    "Father dressed OM himself."

---

validity to predict the results for that subproblem. In order to test the cue validity hypothesis, both cue strength and cue validity must be derived so that the amount of correlation between them can be determined. So to accomplish the main goal of testing the notion of cue validity, three subgoals must be performed: (1) The strengths of the experimental cues must be determined; (2) the validity of these cues must be estimated; and (3) a regression analysis between cue strength across ages and cue validity must be performed. We will begin our examination of Hebrew with the actor assignment problem.

Actor Assignment

Frankel et al. (1980) and Frankel and Arbel (1981) performed two experiments exploring the acquisition of three cues to actor assignment: word order, subject–verb gender agreement, and the object marker. In the first experiment, Frankel et al. (1980) devised test sentences which set the two morphological cues in competition with the word order cue. They did not, however, include test sentences which set the morphological cues in competition with one another. The subjects in this study were seventy monolingual middle-class Israeli females from the following age groups: 3, 4, 5, 6, 7, 11, and adults. The sentence stimuli consisted of seven sentence patterns distributed across three different word orders (NVN, NNV, VNN). There were three tokens of each of the seven different sentence types. The sentence stimuli were recited orally to the children. The youngest children were asked to enact the sentences with toys, whereas the 11-year-olds and adults were simply asked to indicate the actor of the utterance.

The results indicated that, with the exception of the NNV utterances, the actor was identified with the first noun more often than the second one in sentences in which only the word order cue was available. For the NNV sentences, the 4-year-olds and adults were more likely to chose the second noun as actor than the first. In these cases, subjects responded by using a proximity strategy (cf. Bates et al., 1982). In other words, subjects chose as actor the noun closest to the verb for these sentences.

The same word order effects were obtained for sentences which included the morphological cues. However, the presence of the object marker and agreement cues functioned to either override or strengthen the assignment supported by the word order cue. When the object marker and the agreement cues supported the first noun as actor, the tendency to go with the first noun as actor was strengthened. However, when the object marker and the agreement cues supported the second noun as the actor, subjects relied upon the morphological cues over the word order cue. Actor assignments to the first noun also increased or decreased as a function of the morphological cues when they were presented alone. However, the effect of the object marker was greater than that of the agreement cue.

Cue Strength

Although this experiment demonstrates that all three cues have significant effects on children's sentence processing, the results cannot be matched to any quantitative predictions based on cue validity. The Frankel et al. (1980) experiment did not set all three cues in competition with one another. In a second experiment, they did set all three cues in competition with one another. This experiment permitted a more complete assessment of relative cue strength.

In this experiment, as in the first, Frankel and Arbel constructed test sentences which set the two morphological cues, gender agreement and the object marker, in competition with word order. The subjects in the study were eighty monolingual Hebrew-speaking females. There were twenty subjects from each of four age groups: 4, 6, 8, and 10. The procedure was the same as in the first experiment. The sentence stimuli consisted of nine different sentence types. Subjects were presented with five different tokens of each sentence type. The word order cue (NVN) in each of the sentence types supported the first noun in

Table 3.2. *Sentence stimuli for the Frankel and Arbel (1981) experiment*

Sentence type	Word order	Object marker	Gender agreement	Example
A	N1			*ha-kelev doxef ha-doobee* "The-dog pushes the-bear."
B	N1	N1		*ha-kelev mezeez et ha-kof* "The-dog moves OM the-monkey."
C	N1	N2		*et ha-kelev mezeez ha-doobee* "OM the-dog moves the-bear."
D	N1		N1	*ha-yalda mezeeza ha-yeled* "The-girl moves(f) the-body."
E	N1		N2	*ha-yeled doxefet ha-yalda* "the-boy pushes(f) the-girl."
F	N1	N1	N1	*ha-isha mezeeza et ha-ish* "The-woman moves(f) OM the-man."
G	N1	N2	N2	*et ha-yeled mezeeza ha-yalda* "OM the-boy moves(f) the-girl."
H	N1	N2	N1	*et ha-na'ara doxefet ha-na'ar* "OM the-lass pushes(f) the-lad."
I	N1	N1	N2	*ha-ish mezeeza et ha-isha* "The-man moves(f) OM the-woman."

the sentence as the actor. The various sentence types represented all possible combinations of the three cues and are listed in Table 3.2.

The results indicated that all three cues affected subjects' performance. Word order had an effect when it appeared alone, in conjunction with other cues, and in conflict with the other cues. However, of all three of the cues, subjects were most likely to trust the object marker. They tended to follow the interpretation supported by the object marker more often than the one supported by gender agreement. Even when the object marker was in conflict with both the word order and gender agreement cues, it was able to override the opposition. Although Frankel and Arbel noted that word order became a less effective cue as children became older, it was not until adulthood that gender agreement was able to overtake it in strength.

These observations are corroborated by a further analysis of the Frankel and Arbel data. Recall that in order to test the cue validity hypothesis, we need to obtain a measure of the strength of each of the three cues. These cue strengths were obtained by using the program STEPIT (Chandler, 1969; McDonald & MacWhinney, this volume). STEPIT works by modeling each of the nine sentence types in the experiment with a particular equation. Each equation is based on the multiplicative model of information integration proposed by Massaro (1987). For example, the following equation was used to model the sentence type in which gender agreement was set in conflict with word order [e.g., *ha-yeled mezeeza ha-yelda* "The-boy moves-FEM the-girl"]:

$$\frac{ORDER \times (1 - AGR)}{[ORDER \times (1 - AGR)] + [AGR \times (1 - ORDER)]}$$

According to this analysis, each cue strength maps onto an unknown parameter in the model. For example, the ORDER parameter in the above equation would represent the cue strength for the SVO word order cue. By iteratively adjusting each parameter, the program minimizes the squared deviations between the observed (from the experimental data) and predicted (from the equations) points. The output of the program is a set of parameter values for each of the three cues which represent each cue's strength value.

The results of the STEPIT analysis are graphed in Figure 3.2. For each of the four age groups the relative rankings are the same: object marker > word order > gender agreement. Since the error terms (the RMSD) for each of the age groups are low, we can conclude that the multiplicative model provides a good fit of the data. With one exception, these results corroborate Frankel and Arbel's observations. The exception is that, whereas Frankel and Arbel interpreted their data in such a way that the word order cue seems to be decreasing in strength, the STEPIT analysis shows that the word order cue remains at around the same strength level with minor fluctuations. In contrast, the two morphological cues appear to be increasing in strength as the children become older.

Cue Validity

Two corpora of sentences from Hebrew were analyzed to determine the availability and reliability of the three cues. The first corpus consisted of 223 clauses taken from *hame'ahev The Lover'* by A. B. Yehoshua (starting with the new chapter on page 97 and skipping over a poetic section on page 99 and ending in the middle of page 102). The text is a dramatic novel about the breakup of a family. The sentences excerpted from the novel are taken from two different sections. One section highlights an older man who is bemoaning his dull life, whereas the other section features his teenage daughter who is visiting a friend's house. Since the goal of performing a distributional analysis is to gain an estimate of the cue validity that is reflected in the input to children, it is important to verify that the same calculations across different genres of text provide similar results. To provide such a verification, a second corpus was also analyzed. This corpus consisted of 142 clauses taken from adult input to five Israeli children in the Child Language Database Exchange System (CHILDES) in the Psychology Department at Carnegie Mellon University (Dromi & Berman, 1986; Berman & Dromi, 1983; MacWhinney & Snow, 1985). Thus, the two corpora have been

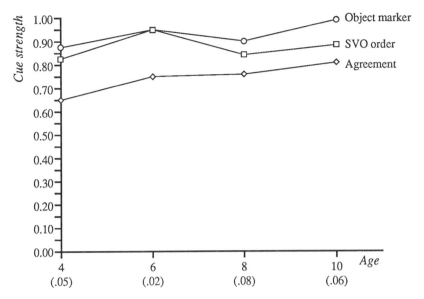

Figure 3.2. Strengths and RMSDs for actor assignment cues across ages. Root mean squared deviations between predictions based on all cue strengths and observed data in parentheses.

takcn from very different sources: one from a fictional novel and the other from adult conversational input. If similar cue validity results are obtained from both corpora, then we can be reasonably sure that these estimates reflect the general linguistic input provided to children. However, to be absolutely sure, a much larger corpus of widely varying examples would have to be analyzed. Until such an analysis is performed, the results from this analysis of cue validity can only be considered estimates.

Each clause in the corpus was coded as to which noun was the actor. Next, each of the three cues was analyzed as to whether or not it was available and reliable in signaling which noun was the actor. To clarify the coding system for the reader, the analysis performed on the larger corpora will be duplicated on a small subset of sentences taken from the corpora (OM = object marker, AGR = subject–verb gender agreement):

		Actor	*OM*	*AGR*	*Order*
1.	*Tali lokaxat et ha-mivxan.*	N1	N1	F/M	NVN
	"Tali grabs-FEM the-test."				
2.	*ma he ta'ama?*	N2	absent	-/F	whNV
	"What she tasted-FEM?"				
3.	*lo over zman rav.*	N1	absent	M	VN
	"Not pass-MASC time much."				
	= "Much time did not pass."				

To compute the cue validity of the SVO word order for these three sentences, its availability and reliability must be computed first. The cue is present in sentences (1) and (3), so its availability is 66%. However, the VN configuration in sentence (3) maps onto a VS ordering which is not consistent with the SVO cue. So for the two sentences in which the cue is available, it is reliable only 50% of the time. Therefore, the validity of the SVO word order cue for the three sentences is 33%.

Before presenting the results, it is important to describe two of the coding conventions that were employed. First, the gender agreement cue was considered available only when it provided a contrast between two competing nominals. In sentence (1), such a contrast exists because N1 (feminine) agrees with the verb and N2 (masculine) does not. In contrast, in sentence (3), only N1 agrees with the verb. Sentence (2) provides a special case in which N2 and a question word are competing for the role of actor. Since such question words agree with masculine singular verbs, the agreement cue does provide a contrast and is considered available for these sentences. Second, the validity of the object marker was only encoded for sentences in which an object was expected for the verb (i.e., transitive sentences). Since agreement was only considered available when it provided a contrast between two nouns, this convention was decided upon to make the analysis for agreement and the object marker comparable. Counting the agreement and object marker cues as available only when they provide contrastive information represents a departure from McDonald's (1984) method for computing availability. Within the functionalist perspective of the Competition Model, it seems reasonable to consider a cue to be available only if it contributes a unique piece of information to the role assignment problem. This distinction also serves to highlight the earlier point that availability is not equivalent to simple frequency. This analysis was performed on both corpora to derive estimates of cue validity for each of the three cues.

The results of the cue validity analyses for both corpora are listed in Table 3.3. The two corpora yielded the same ranking: word order > gender agreement > object marker. However, the conversational input taken from CHILDES proved to be more complex and varied than the input taken from the novel. Other than the standard SVO order, there were examples of OSV, *gam lo et ze ata mexapes* "Also not at that [do] you look for" and VOS, *tagid li xamud* "Tell me honey." The OSV example also provides a case in which the object marker conflicted with the order cue. In all, there were two cases of such a conflict in the CHILDES corpus. In each of these cases, the correct interpretation was supported by the object marker rather than the word order cue. Another difference between the two corpora was the large proportion of transitive sentences which included object ellipsis in the conversational input. In contrast, the language employed in the novel contained less variation and fewer interactions among cues. In fact, the SVO word order achieved an availability

Table 3.3. *Validity estimates for actor assignment cues*

	NOVEL			CHILDES			Average		
	Avail	Rel	Valid	Avail	Rel	Valid	Avail	Rel	Valid
Object marker	0.40	0.81	0.33	0.19	0.81	0.16	0.30	0.81	0.24
SVO order	0.95	0.99	0.94	0.72	0.99	0.71	0.84	0.99	0.83
Agreement	0.47	1.00	0.47	0.29	1.00	0.29	0.36	1.00	0.36

score of .95 for this corpus. This finding underscores the importance of basing cue validity estimates on "real speech." After all, this is the kind of input that is most relevant to language acquisition by children and everyday language use by adults.

Cue Cost

The relationship between cue validity and cue strength is based on the hypothesis that children are performing a distributional analysis of the incoming data in such a way that a cue's availability and reliability determine its validity and ultimately its strength. Such a mechanism does not take into account the processibility of a given cue. A cue can be easy to process on two fronts (MacWhinney et al., 1985): detectability and assignability. For a cue to be detectable, it must be perceptually salient. An assignable cue is one that can be immediately bound to a grammatical function during processing. This simply suggests that local cues, such as inflections, are easier to process than global cues, such as word order (Ammon & Slobin, 1979). Perhaps the more *costly* it is to process a given cue, the less likely children are to rely upon it to interpret their language.

In describing the object marker, Frankel and Arbel (1981) list several reasons why it might be such a strong cue (see earlier quote). One of these reasons is that the object marker is syllabic. If we assume that syllabic cues are more detectable than cues which are embedded within lexical items or affixed to them, we can hypothesize that the object marker is a highly detectable cue. Second, Frankel and Arbel (1981) note that the object marker resembles a class of cues that Ammon and Slobin (1979) have singled out as particularly easy to process. They identify these cues, which they call *local cues*, as "surface markings which [assign] the roles of particular [nouns]" (p. 16). They are called local cues because they minimize the amount of time that the cue must be held in working memory before the information it signals can be utilized. In the terminology of the Competition Model, local cues are highly assignable. Perhaps the object marker is such a strong cue because it is both reasonably valid and easily processed.

In contrast, gender agreement is a difficult cue to process. Bates and MacWhinney (this volume) and Kail (this volume) argue that it is low in both detectability and assignability. Their claim for detectability is based on the observation that number agreement in Italian and French is virtually imperceptible in spoken language. Although we believe that gender agreement in Hebrew is perceptible, it is not highlighted by stress or intonation. If a cue is difficult to detect in speech, then it cannot be a very strong cue for listeners. For assignability, Bates and MacWhinney (this volume) note that in order to use agreement correctly, "the child must store (1) the noun that will ultimately agree with the verb, (2) the verb itself, and (3) one or more competing noun phrases which could also agree with the verb (thereby rendering agreement information ambiguous and useless)." This problem is made even more difficult in a pro-drop language where the subject of the sentence is often not explicitly marked by a subject noun phrase.

Although word order is not as easy to process as the object marker, it does not have all of the problems associated with gender agreement. Word order is more difficult to assign but at the same time more easily detected. It is difficult to assign because it is a global, rather than a local, cue (Ammon & Slobin, 1979). However, it is essentially impossible to somehow ignore the order in which words occur in the input. Word order information is easily detected, as an inevitable by-product of sequential recognition and classification of lexical items. Content words should be much easier to detect than inflections because they can either be stressed or carry intonational marking or both. They are also more likely to be bounded by pauses than are inflections.

According to this analysis of cue cost, the following ranking is suggested for the three cues: object marker > word order > agreement. If we translated this ordinal ranking into a cardinal one, we could assign the highest number (3) to the object marker and the lowest one (1) to agreement. Although this procedure is admittedly ad hoc, by attributing a cardinal ordering to cue cost we are able to submit it to a regression analysis with cue strength just as we will be doing with cue validity.

The Results for Actor Assignment

In order to examine the relationship between cue validity, cue cost, and cue strength across the different age groups, a regression analysis was performed. The results, given in Table 3.4, indicate that the predictions made by the cue validity hypothesis are not fully met. Overall cue validity accounts for an average of only 2% of the variance (the correlation coefficient squared) for the four-year-olds and 8% for the six-year-olds. In contrast, the cue cost hypothesis fared much better: There are strong positive correlations between cue cost and cue strength across all age groups. Since cue cost is a strong predictor of cue strength across all the age groups, it appears that it is not subject to developmental differences. Initially, the product of availability and cue cost is

Table 3.4. *Correlation matrix between the predictors and cue strength for the actor assignment cues across ages*

		Age			
		4	6	8	10
Availability	NOVEL	.23	.39	.01	-.22
	CHILDES	.17	.34	-.05	-.28
	Average	.20	.37	-.01	-.25
Reliability	NOVEL	-.68	-.56	-.84	-.93
	CHILDES	-.67	-.55	-.83	-.93
	Average	-.67	-.55	-.83	-.93
Cost		.94	.87	.99	.99
Availability × *Reliability*	NOVEL	.13	.30	-.09	-.32
	CHILDES	.12	.29	-.09	-.32
	Average	.13	.29	-.09	-.32
Availability × *Cost*	NOVEL	.78	.87	.62	.42
	CHILDES	.55	.69	.36	.13
	Average	.68	.80	.51	.29
Reliability × *Cost*	NOVEL	.99	.96	.99	.95
	CHILDES	.99	.96	.99	.95
	Average	.99	.96	.99	.95
Availability × *Reliability*	NOVEL	.66	.78	.48	.27
× *Cost*	CHILDES	.49	.63	.29	.06
	Average	.59	.71	.40	.17

a good predictor, but as subjects get older, the amount of variance accounted for by the combined product of availability and cost appears to be decreasing. Finally, although there are strong negative correlations between cue reliability and cue strength across all age groups, the product of reliability and cue cost is the best predictor of cue strength accounting for an average of 95% of the variance across ages.

What accounts for the decrease in the combined product of cue availability and cue cost? Of the three cues, gender agreement is the one which undergoes the most change developmentally. For the four-year-olds, the gender agreement cue is fairly weak. However, as the children get older it increases in strength to the point that it almost overtakes the word order cue. In fact, Frankel and Arbel (1981) report that adults trust the agreement cue when it conflicts with word order. Since gender agreement is the most reliable cue from among the three tested, its increase in strength could explain the increased importance of reliability relative to availability in the equation with cue cost.

According to the Competition Model, developmental change is driven by situations in which cues conflict with one another. This is because cues that win in competitions with other cues generally have a higher reliability than those that lose. To test this hypothesis, we collected all of the conflict sentences in both corpora and looked to see which cues won the competition in such cases. In the set of conflict sentences that we collected, there were two cases in which gender agreement conflicted with word order. There were no cases of conflicts between the object marker and gender agreement. In each of these cases, the correct interpretation of the sentence was supported by the agreement, and not the word order, cue. We can infer from this analysis that gender agreement is a more reliable cue in conflict situations than word order. Since such conflict sentences are somewhat rare in the Hebrew input, it would take time for them to have an effect on children's sentence comprehension. This would account for the gradual increase in strength of gender agreement, which culminates in the eventual overtaking of word order for adults.

Thus, it appears that the acquisition of the gender agreement cue is delayed by its low processibility and morphological complexity. As Berman (1985) notes:

Perhaps the most complex morphosyntactic task for the Israeli child, and one which is as crucial as a developmental criterion for Hebrew as is the acquisition of auxiliary patterning in English, is the learning of grammatical agreement – from subject to main-verb in number and gender and, in past and future tense, also in person... (p. 273)

However, as children begin to master this system (Levy, 1983a, 1983b), they must then attend to conflict cases in order to increase the strength of the gender cues in their system.

However, if cue reliability is such a strong predictor of cue strength then why are the correlations between the two measures so consistently negative? One reason why the correlations are so strongly negative might be that while the object marker is rated as the least reliable cue, it is in fact the strongest cue for subjects. If subjects were not confused by those instances in which the form *et* encoded a feminine verbal suffix, they could have attributed a higher reliability rating to the object marker than expected by our measure of cue reliability. Perhaps after encountering a feminine subject, subjects were able to anticipate a feminine verbal suffix. Since the main word order of Hebrew is SVO, this seems possible. If this is the case, then the prediction made by the Competition Model, that as children get older they should attend to more reliable cues irrespective of their availability, is confirmed.

To summarize the results for actor assignment, overall cue validity appears to be a weak predictor of young children's performance. Instead, there was evidence for the importance of cue reliability and cue cost as predictors of cue strength. The more costly it is to process a cue, the less likely subjects are to rely upon it. This finding suggests that when there are large differences in cost across cues, cue cost should be a more powerful predictor of subjects' performance than cue validity. In other words, if a cue is difficult to process, subjects are not likely to rely upon it no matter how available and reliable it is. Reliability also plays an important role in predicting developmental differences. In particular, reliability provides an account for the increase in the strength of gender agreement with development. This claim is supported by the observation that as children get older, they tend to rely less and less upon cue availability whereas the product of cue reliability and cue cost remains a highly successful predictor.

Patient Assignment

We began our examination of the actor assignment problem with a presentation of the experimental data on cue strength and then turned to an analysis of cue validity. We will do the same for the patient assignment problem. Where the organization of this section will depart from that of the earlier one is with regard to cue cost. This is due to differences between the two role assignment problems and the cues employed to solve them. The actor assignment cues differed markedly in cue cost with gender agreement being a rather costly cue to process. However, the patient assignment cues vary much more on the semantic dimension, since they are cues not just to who is the patient, but also to the exact role of the patient (e.g., reflexive, transitive, reciprocal, etc.). In light of this, the section will not include an analysis of cue cost for the patient assignment cues.

Cue Strength

Sokolov (1988) conducted an experiment to measure the strengths of six cues to patient assignment. These cues were: the object marker, postverbal noun, reflexive noun phrase, and three verb patterns. As in the Frankel experiments, test sentences were constructed which set these cues in conflict with one another. The subjects were forty monolingual native speakers of Hebrew in the following age groups: 4, 5, 7, 9, and adults.

In order to distinguish a real understanding of the different verb patterns from simple rote memory for each individual verb form, *novel* verbs – verbs that children could not have memorized – were used. Such verbs were formed by taking the consonantal root from nouns and forming denominal verbs from them in the sense of Clark and Clark (1979; see also Bolozky, 1978). For example, the verb root *p-j-m* was extracted from the noun *pajamot* "pajamas" and used to derive the transitive verb *lepajem* "to pajama (someone)" and the reflexive verb *lehitpajem* "to pajama (oneself)." *Lepajem* was used instead of the more normative *lefajem* to maintain phonological similarity with the nominal. Since Berman (1985) summarizes evidence that Hebrew speaking children are adept at dealing with such allomorphic alternations, similar allomorphic adjustments were performed with some of the other denominal verbs. The denominal verbs then presented the children with a task that measured their reliance on the verb patterns as separate from specific knowledge of lexical items. In all, eight denominal verbs were employed in the experiment.

Three verb patterns from the seven possible were selected for use in the experiment. The chosen patterns are the *pi'el*, *hif'il*, and *hitpa'el* patterns. *Pi'el* and *hif'il* were chosen because of their transitive functions, despite the fact that they are not exactly equivalent (cf. Bolozky & Saad, 1983), whereas *hitpa'el* was chosen because of its reflexive function. Two transitive verb patterns were selected to allow maximal preservation of the morphophonology of the noun in the formation of the denominal verbs. For example, *masaixa* "mask" was conjugated in the *hif'il* pattern using *himsix* rather than in the *pi'el* pattern using *misex*. Children should be better able to comprehend denominal verbs that are phonologically similar to their nominal counterparts.

The experiment involved two stimulus manipulations: verb pattern and sentence type. The verb pattern varied across two levels (transitive and reflexive). The sentence type varied across six levels, as shown in Table 3.5.

Subject–verb agreement was not manipulated as an independent factor: both nouns in the sentences were of the same number, gender, and person. Since there were three cues, eight different sentence types were possible. However, since it is meaningless to present an object marker in the absence of an object, the two conditions in which the object marker would have been presented alone have been deleted. By crossing the factors of sentence type and verb pattern, twelve experimental cells were generated that result in twelve different experimental sentences. Of these twelve sentences, eight are ungrammatical. A rationale for the use of ungrammatical sentences in this task can be found in MacWhinney et al. (1985) and in the various other articles in the current volume.

The subjects were requested to perform a sentence–picture matching task. Each test sentence was recited orally to the subjects and they were required to point to the picture whose meaning they felt corresponded to the meaning of the sentence. There were four pictures in each stimulus set: a picture depicting a transitive relation, a reflexive relation, a distractor picture (both people from the previous two pictures), and an identifier picture. The identifier picture depicted the nominal item whose consonantal root was used to derive the alternative verb patterns. The characters in the pictures were given the common Hebrew names which the children were taught before the beginning of the experiment. For example, the four picture types for the verb root *l-p-j* from *pajamot* "pajamas" depicted: (1) identifier – a pair of pajamas; (2) transitive – a boy putting pajamas on another boy; (3) reflexive – a boy putting pajamas on himself; (4) distractor – two boys standing while doing nothing.

The results indicated a complex set of interactions involving all three of the experimental factors. Overall, subjects were more likely to trust the transitive

Table 3.5. *Sentence type (with Object marker = OM, Postverbal noun = PostN, Reflexive noun phrase = ReflNP)*

Type	OM	PostN	ReflNP	Verb	
A	+	+	+	Trans:	*Yehuda mepajem et acmo et Dani.*
					"Yehuda pajamed OM himself OM Dani."
				Refl:	*Yehuda mitpajem et acmo et Dani.*
					"Yehuda pajamed-REFL OM himself OM Dani."
B	+	+	−	Trans:	*Yehuda mepajem et Dani.*
					"Yehuda pajamed OM Dani."
					Refl:*Yehuda mitpajem et Dani.*
					"Yehuda pajamed-REFL OM Dani."
C	−	+	+	Trans:	*Yehuda mepajem et acmo Dani.*
					"Yehuda pajamed OM himself Dani."
				Refl:	'*Yehuda mitpajem et acmo Dani.*
					"Yehuda pajamed-REFL OM himself Dani."
D	−	+	−	Trans:	*Yehuda mepajem Dani.*
					"Yehuda pajamed Dani."
				Relf:	*Yehuda mitpajem Dani.*
					"Yehuda pajamed-REFL Dani."
E	−	−	+	Trans:	*Yehuda mepajem et acmo.*
					"Yehuda pajamed OM himself."
				Refl:	*Yehuda mitpajem et acmo.*
					"Yehuda pajamed-REFL OM himself."
F	−	−	−	Trans:	*?Yehuda mepajem.*
					"Yehuda pajamed."
				Refl:	*Yehuda mitpajem.*
					"Yehuda pajamed-REFL."

verb patterns than the reflexive one, but the exact degree to which they did this was dependent upon the particular configuration of cues in each sentence type and the subject's age. More specifically, when a transitive verb pattern was presented with a reflexive noun phrase (an ungrammatical construction), subjects tended to trust the reflexive cue; also, when the reflexive verb pattern was presented with both the object marker and postverbal noun or even with the postverbal noun alone (again ungrammatical constructions), subjects tended to trust the accusative cues. In other words, children tended to trust the markings on nouns (and pronouns) more than the verb patterns when these sources of information were set into competition with one another. However, there was a significant increase in reliance on the verb pattern as subjects' age increased. In fact, as subjects became older, they demonstrated a greater tendency to trust *both* the reflexive verb pattern and the reflexive noun phrase.

Once again, the STEPIT program (Chandler, 1969) generated the strength

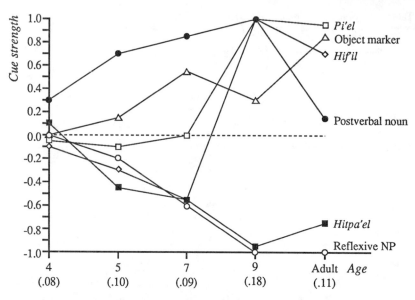

Figure 3.3. Strengths and RMSDs for patient assignment cues across ages. Root mean squared deviations between predictions based on all cue strengths and observed data in parentheses.

values for the six cues, using a multiplicative model (Massaro, 1987). The results are presented in Figure 3.3. They are presented so that strong transitive cues have high positive values, whereas strong reflexive cues have strong negative values. This way of displaying cue strengths makes clear the contrast between transitive and reflexive cues. The possible strength values range from -1.00 to 1.00. With one exception, the results indicate that the four-year-olds appear to be performing by chance. The one exception is the postverbal noun which is functioning somewhat weakly as a transitive cue. A partial explanation for why the four-year-olds could be performing so poorly is that the denominal verb task is too difficult for them. If they are not able to make productive use of the denominal verbs, then the effects of the different verb patterns would be meaningless. This appears to be the case since Berman and Sagai (1981) and Walden (1983) report that Israeli children do not begin to understand the root plus pattern morphology of Hebrew in the abstract until around five years of age. However, this would not explain their lack of use of both the object marker and reflexive noun phrase. In contrast, the behavior of the five-year-olds reveals a differential treatment of several of the cues. They do not, however, appear to have established a clear separation between the transitive and reflexive cues. Finally, by the age of seven and upward, children in the study began responding systematically to the various cues, including a near complete separation between the transitive and reflexive cues. The cue strengths from the STEPIT program corroborate the results from the analysis of variance in that they both show the reflexive cues starting out weaker than the transitive ones, but eventually overtaking them.

Cue Validity

Each clause in both corpora was coded for the identity of the patient. Hebrew verbs can signal several types of candidates for the role of the patient:

1. Intransitive: There is no patient.
2. Transitive: The patient is the noun most closely involved in the action of the verb (Hopper & Thompson, 1980).
3. Reflexive: The patient is coreferential with the actor.
4. Reciprocal: The patient is cotemporaneously engaged in an action with the actor.
5. Inchoative: There is no patient and the subject is undergoing a state change.
6. Passive: The patient is the agent.

Next, each of the six cues was analyzed as to whether or not it was available and reliable in signaling the role of the patient. To clarify the coding system for the reader, the analysis performed on the larger corpus will be duplicated on a small subset of sentences taken from the corpus (VP = verb pattern, OM = object marker, PostN = postverbal noun, Refl NP = reflexive noun phrase):

	Relation	VP	OM	Post N	Refl NP
1. *hu mitkase bi-smixa* "He covered-REF in-a-blanket."	reflexive	*hitpa'el*	absent	present	absent
2. *aval Erlix mitatsben* "But Erlich became-nervous."	inchoative	*hitpa'el*	absent	absent	absent
3. *ha'alimut lo martia ota* "The-violence did-not frighten her."	transitive	*hif'il*	present	absent	absent

To compute the cue validity of the object marker for these three sentences, its availability and reliability must be computed first. The cue only occurs contrastively in one of three sentences, so its availability is 33%. In the one sentence where the cue is available, it is reliable. Thus, for these three sentences, the object marker is 100% reliable. Finally, since cue validity is the product of availability and reliability, the cue validity of the object marker in this example is 33%. The exact same analysis was performed on both corpora to derive estimates of cue validity for each of the six cues.

Before presenting the results, it is important to explain several coding conventions. First, why is the validity of the object marker computed across all sentences instead of just those with transitive verbs? In English, the cue validity analysis for patient cues would only be computed for transitive verbs. This is because for an intransitive verb-stem like "walk" there would be no sense in looking for cues to the patient, since the verb stem itself does not set up an expectation for a patient. English has some transitive verbs that are homophonous with intransitive verbs, but which have quite different meanings.

Table 3.6. *Validity estimates for patient assignment cues*

	NOVEL			CHILDES			Average		
	Avail	Rel	Valid	Avail	Rel	Valid	Avail	Rel	Valid
Pi'el	0.17	0.72	0.12	0.20	0.93	0.18	0.18	0.82	0.15
Hitpa'el	0.16	-0.17	-0.03	0.05	-0.57	-0.03	0.10	-0.37	-0.03
Hif'il	0.15	0.82	0.12	0.12	0.76	0.09	0.13	0.79	0.10
Postverbal noun	0.35	0.48	0.18	0.28	0.57	0.16	0.32	0.53	0.17
Object marker	0.20	0.81	0.16	0.14	0.80	0.11	0.17	0.80	0.13
Reflexive NP	.0001	-1.00	-.0001	.0001	-1.00	-.0001	.0001	-1.00	-.0001

MacWhinney (1987) discusses how these compete with one another. In Hebrew, the transitive-intransitive boundary is still more permeable. Given the correct derivational markings, nearly any Hebrew verb could be transitive. Moreover, the greater tendency to omit transitive objects in Hebrew means that often the derivational markings are the only cue to whether the sentence is transitive or intransitive. This explains why it is important to compute the cue validity of the object marker across all predicates in Hebrew. Second, as noted earlier, there is some ambiguity as to whether the morpheme *et* encodes an accusative case marking or a feminine suffix (e.g., *menagev-et* "towelling"). To capture this ambiguity, the analysis of the availability of the morpheme *et* included both cases in which it encoded an accusative case marking and cases in which it encoded a feminine suffix on transitive verbs. Third, both the standard form of the object marker (i.e., *et*) and the pronominalized form (e.g., *oto* "him") were accepted as coding an accusative marking. In such cases, the pronominalized form was not considered to indicate a postverbal noun. Fourth, postverbal nouns were accepted as available when they were preceded by prepositions (both separate words and prefixes). However, no complex noun phrases were accepted as postverbal nouns. Fifth, idioms or verbless copular constructions were dropped from the analysis.

The results of the cue validity analyses for both corpora are given in Table 3.6. Once again transitive cues are given positive values whereas reflexive ones are given negative ones. None of the six cues proved to have high validity ratings in either corpus, largely because of low availability scores. This is probably due to their more specialized function, that of signaling the role of the patient.

For the fictional novel, the postverbal noun was the most valid cue of the six. It correctly interpreted 18% of the sentences. The next strongest cue was the object marker, followed by the verb patterns, followed by the reflexive noun phrase. For the adult input, the *pi'el* verb pattern was the strongest cue. The postverbal noun and object marker were the next strongest cues. These three cues were then followed by the other two verb patterns and the reflexive noun phrase.

Although the two corpora yield similar cue validity ratings, there are two main differences: First, the *pi'el* pattern is used more reliably in the adult input than in the novel. Second, greater use of object ellipsis in the adult input over the novel has led to a decrease in the validity of the object marker and postverbal noun. An interesting interpretation of this (which would be consistent with a functionalist account of language) would be that the increase in validity of the *pi'el* pattern serves as compensation for the decreased validity of the other two cues. With these two exceptions noted, the cue validity results from the two corpora make similar predictions regarding the initial strength values of the cues.

The reflexive noun phrase did not appear in either corpus. Since it is possible that the chosen texts underestimate the frequency of the reflexive noun phrase, a separate check of its frequency was calculated. This check was based on the full sample of available on-line Hebrew-language transcripts in CHILDES. The corpus consisted of a collection of speech samples from Israeli children in the database (Berman & Dromi, 1983; Dromi & Berman, 1986). The on-line corpus totals approximately 45,915 utterances of both adult and children's speech. Despite the large number of utterances, the reflexive noun phrase appeared in children's speech only four times (N=3, Average Age: 4;2) and in adult's speech only twice (N=2) for a total of only 6 utterances. Thus the two corpora do not appear to underestimate the frequency of the reflexive noun phrase.

The Results for Patient Assignment

To test the degree to which the ranking of cues predicted by cue validity actually matches the one obtained by cue strength, a regression analysis was performed. The results are given in Table 3.7.

Beginning with the five-year-olds, there are strong positive correlations between cue validity and cue strength. These strong correlations provide evidence supporting the cue validity hypothesis. In addition, despite the fact that the correlations for the four-year-olds are rather low (for reasons listed earlier), the one cue that appears to have been any use to them (the postverbal noun), is exactly the cue that is predicted to be strong by cue validity.

Recall that the Competition Model predicts that as children get older, they should begin to attend to the most reliable cues irrespective of their availability. Indeed, as children became older, the amount of variance accounted for by reliability increased more than that for availability and eventually overtook overall cue validity as a predictor of cue strength. Since all VS constructions provide examples of conflict sentences, this shift may be at least partially due to cue conflicts. For these sentences, the postverbal noun is not the patient and either the object marker or subject–verb agreement provide the necessary cues for proper role assignment.

Table 3.7. *Correlation matrix between the predictors and cue strength for the patient assignment cues across ages*

		Age				
		4	5	7	9	A
Availability	NOVEL	.66	.76	.83	.64	.44
	CHILDES	.46	.80	.83	.86	.65
	Average	.58	.80	.85	.76	.55
Reliability	NOVEL	-.14	.31	.52	.87	.94
	CHILDES	-.14	.41	.59	.94	.97
	Average	-.14	.37	.56	.91	.96
Availability × *Reliability*	NOVEL	.13	.74	.81	.90	.82
	CHILDES	.08	.64	.71	.92	.83
	Average	.11	.72	.78	.93	.84

Despite the fact that cue reliability accounts for an average of 92% of the variance in the adult data, availability is a better predictor for ages 4, 5, and 7. Let us look in detail at the development of each of the five cues with an eye to understanding why reliability does not have a strong impact at first.

The Object Marker.   Previous research (Frankel & Arbel, 1981; Frankel et al., 1982; Rom & Dgani, 1985) has shown the object marker to be an excellent grammatical cue. In addition, the results of each of these three studies demonstrated that as children get older, the object marker goes from being a good cue to an excellent one. The present research replicates these findings. In addition, the analysis of reliability provides a possible account for why the object marker is not an excellent cue for the youngest children. It is possible that the delayed use of the object marker by young children stems from problems they might have in distinguishing it from the singular feminine suffix on verbs. However, the pattern of results can be accounted for by two other hypotheses: (1) Young children are confused by the inclusion of the object marker in the reflexive noun phrase (e.g., *et acmo* "himself"); and (2) Young children have difficulty detecting the object marker when it is fused with pronominals (Rom & Dgani, 1985). At this stage of the research, the data do not allow for a separation of these competing hypotheses.

The Reflexive Noun Phrase.   According to the Competition Model, in order for children to create a mapping between a particular function and a particular form, they must have encountered them together enough times to actually construct such a mapping. In the case of the reflexive noun phrase, children have few opportunities to construct such a mapping. In other words, children simply might not have been exposed to the cue enough times to learn that it is a rather reliable one. However, the more children are exposed to the reflexive noun phrase, the more they learn that it is the productive means for expressing reflexivity in Hebrew. This would account for the increase in strength of the cue across time. By the time children are nine years old, they are able to understand that the reflexive verb pattern typically encodes a small number of common physical activities, such as hair-combing and tooth-brushing, and the reflexive noun phrase can be used to productively generate other reflexive relations.

The Hitpa'el Verb Pattern.   The *hitpa'el* pattern can be mapped onto five different functions. Since the cue is low in reliability, it is also low in validity. If the cue is low in validity, what leads to its increase in cue strength between the ages of four and nine? One possibility is that children are learning that the *hitpa'el* pattern is really a better cue at signaling some function other than the ones we listed earlier. If so, children must be hearing certain, albeit rare, constructions which help them to better define the cue. An example of such a construction might be right dislocations (e.g., *ima mitlabeshet, Avi* "Mother is dressing-REFL, Avi"). In right dislocations, the verb pattern is pointing to a reflexive interpretation, whereas the nominal is pointing to a transitive interpretation. In such a situation, children must decide whether the sentence is transitive or not. Presumably, they learn that these constructions are definitely not transitive. That is, they learn that *hitpa'el* is not truly multi-functional. Rather, it is a cue that the sentence is *not* transitive. Children presumably also learn that there must be some other cue which determines the exact role of the patient in relation to the predicate – either intransitive, reflexive, reciprocal, iterative, or inchoative. For example, children might learn that *hitpa'el* denominals dealing with clothing articles tend to be reflexive (as in the present experiment). Since the newly defined cue is unifunctional, it is more reliable. Since the cue is more reliable, it is also more valid. This accounts nicely for the rise in strength of the *hitpa'el* pattern shown in Figure 3.3. This is also an example of development being driven by sentences in which cues conflict.

The Pi'el and Hif'il Verb Patterns.   The results for *pi'el* and *hif'il* show that children do not trust these cues until they are nine years old. Interestingly, as the *pi'el* and *hif'il* patterns gain in strength, the object marker and postverbal noun lose it. We would like to argue that these two findings are related. In order to do so, we must first review certain aspects of the cue validity results.

Recall the difference in the cue validity results for the fictional and conversational corpora. The cue validity estimates for the object marker and postverbal noun were high for the novel, but somewhat lower for the conversational input. The validity results for the *pi'el* verb pattern were exactly the opposite: low for the novel and higher for the conversational input. Recall that in the cue validity analysis, we noted that the validities of the object marker and postverbal noun were lower because there was a large amount of object ellipsis in the conversational input. The *pi'el* verbal cue appears to compensate for the absence of the accusative cues in conversation. In other words, since the accusative cues were no longer very available, the *pi'el* verb pattern became a more important cue.

Since ellipsed objects can only be recovered from the discourse context, object ellipsis is a discourse phenomenon. Therefore, the compensation provided by the *pi'el* verb pattern for the deleted accusative cues is also a discourse phenomenon. If, as recent research indicates (Karmiloff-Smith, 1982), children become sensitive to discourse-based constraints by the age of nine, then perhaps the increase in reliance on the *pi'el* verb pattern reflects this shift from sentence-based to discourse-based constraints. The older children may be realizing that the *pi'el* verb pattern is a better cue than the accusative cues because the accusative cues are subject to object ellipsis.

This interpretation works for the *pi'el* pattern, but what about the *hif'il* pattern which actually shows a decrease in validity from fiction to conversation? One explanation is that children may be generalizing their reliance on the *pi'el* pattern to the *hif'il* pattern. This generalization is possible only when children come to the realization that both verb patterns are members of the same morphological system – something they do before the onset of discourse-based processing (Berman, 1982; Walden, 1983). Finally, although the object marker is reliable enough to recover from discourse-based cue validities (its cue strength is strong for the adults), the postverbal noun is not (hence a low cue strength for the adults).

The Postverbal Noun.   The postverbal noun is high in availability but low in reliability. The Competition Model therefore predicts that the postverbal noun should become increasingly weaker as a cue to transitivity for older children. In fact, the experimental results indicate that as the reflexive noun phrase and *hitpa'el* pattern increase in strength, the postverbal noun decreases in strength. Indeed, the data show the influence of the postverbal noun decreasing exactly for those sentence types in which it is in competition with the reflexive cues. The simplest explanation for this result is that the reflexive cues have become strong enough to beat out the postverbal noun. Although such an explanation might adequately account for the results, it leaves an important question unanswered: If subjects are relying solely on the reflexive cues, to what role are they assigning the postverbal noun?

In order to utilize all of the information presented in the experimental sentences, subjects must be able to perform a more complex application of the available cues.   Rather than considering only sentential constraints in role assignment, they must also consider a more sophisticated application of grammatical cues. Two possible examples of such complex cue application have been identified:

1. *Vocatives*: Children may consider the sentence *Yehuda hitlabesh Dani* "Yehuda dressed-REFL Dani" to be an example of right dislocation and assign the postverbal noun to the role of the vocative.
2. *Marking Insertions:* Unmarked nouns in Hebrew are less frequent than marked ones. The older subjects may insert a marking (e.g., comitative or locative) to make the sentences more plausible. An example might be *Yehuda hitlabesh im/al-yad Dani* "Yehuda combed-REFL with/next-to Dani."

These strategies involve the resolution of an apparent cue conflict by making a finer distinction concerning the role of the postverbal noun.

In sum, we have hypothesized that the differences in performance between the younger subjects and the older ones can be attributed to an increased reliance on cue reliability, discourse-based constraints, and complex cue application. However, an alternative hypothesis is that the older subjects are affected by the ungrammatical stimuli in a way that the younger ones are not. In fact, some of the performance shifts described earlier happen to appear around the age that other researchers (Beilin, 1975) have noticed an increase in meta-linguistic ability. Could increased meta-linguistic awareness have led to the observed results? There are three arguments which refute this claim. First, much of the previous research on actor assignment by Bates and MacWhinney and their colleagues (summarized in Bates & MacWhinney, this volume) have used ungrammatical stimuli and obtained systematic results, even with very young children. Second, MacWhinney et al. (1985) explicitly manipulated the grammaticality of their experimental stimuli and found that subjects responded similarly to both the grammatical and ungrammatical stimuli when other factors were held constant. Third (and most important), the exact nature of the shift in the present experiment is such that the cues which are most detrimentally affected appear to be exactly those cues which are governed by functional or discourse-based constraints. If we subscribed to the hypothesis that increased metalinguistic awareness could explain the differences between the younger and older subjects, we would expect cues which are sensitive to discourse features to simply increase in strength.

To conclude this section, the results for patient assignment indicate that cue validity does correlate with cue strength for all but the youngest age groups. The younger children did not use the reflexive cues contrastively with the transitive ones. However, as they became older the reflexive cues became very strong. Although cue validity accounts for a large percent of the variance in the regression analysis with cue strength, other factors also come into play. Two major factors were hypothesized: an increasing reliance on cue reliability across ages and discourse-based constraints for the *pi'el* verb pattern and the postverbal noun. Given the large amount of object ellipsis in the conversational input, it is not surprising that discourse-based processing strategies were discovered for patient and not actor assignment. The shift from sentence-based to discourse-based processing has been discussed by Bates and MacWhinney (this volume) in terms of *functional readiness* (see also Slobin, 1973). The principle of functional readiness states that "children will not acquire a complex form until they can assimilate it ... to an underlying function." The data for the *pi'el* verb pattern and the postverbal noun appear to support this notion.

Oblique Role Assignment

The prepositionals that encode oblique roles in Hebrew fall under a category that has been much studied in child language. One of the earliest and perhaps most influential study has been that of Brown's (1973) analysis of the acquisition of fourteen grammatical morphemes. Among the fourteen morphemes studied by Brown were two English prepositions, "in" and "on," both of which encoded locative relations. The results from longitudinal studies of three children indicated that these two prepositions were among the earliest morphemes to be acquired. Brown considered three separate determinants of the order of acquisition of the fourteen morphemes: frequency in parental input, semantic complexity, and grammatical complexity. He found that frequency did not appear to be a significant contributor. In contrast, the data did support both formal and semantic complexity as significant determiners of the order of acquisition. Unfortunately, Brown found it very difficult to separate the predictions of grammatical complexity from those of semantic complexity. In Hungarian, MacWhinney (1976) has noted that differences in the emergence of Hungarian inflections could be directly attributed to nonmorphological factors, since Hungarian inflections "differ little in terms of formal complexity" (p. 409). The order of acquisition of grammatical morphemes he reports for Hungarian, where morphological complexity is not a factor, is much like that reported for Indo-European languages. This suggests that semantic complexity is a major determiner of the order of acquisition of oblique role markers.

As noted earlier, Hebrew prepositionals have a rather complex morphology. Not only do they come in three forms (enclitic prefixes, separate words, and fused forms), many of these forms are irregular. Therefore one might expect that formal complexity might play a heightened role in the acquisition of Hebrew as opposed to Hungarian. To address this question, Dromi also analyzed the different morphological forms of the locatives produced by the children in her study. She found that the children preferred enclitic prefixes over separate words. For example, *le* "to" was preferred over *el*, and *mi* "from" was preferred over *min*. In discussing this finding, she stated:

The frequency of use of the two different forms in adult speech and especially in mothers' input to young children is another important factor to consider. Although there is no empirical data to support my claim, it is my impression as a native Hebrew speaker that the prefixed prepositions are more frequently produced by adult speakers. (p. 559)

In fact, Dromi's intuitions are supported by our analysis of the cue validity of Hebrew prepositionals. Although this analysis will be described in greater detail later in this section, the results indicated that input frequency does affect which form the child prefers. Out of 124 adult utterances containing prepositionals in the conversational input from CHILDES, 28 included *le* and 6 included *mi*, whereas there was not a single utterance including either *el* or *min*. Interestingly, for each example in which morphological complexity could be cited as the determinant of the rate of acquisition in the Dromi study, there is a conflict with input frequency. The complex forms are simply rather rare in the input. This finding suggests that frequency is affecting the form that children choose to express the underlying notions encoded by Hebrew prepositionals.

Reliability and frequency do seem to affect children's solution to the role assignment problem regarding locatives. However, we do not yet have a quantitative measure of the effect. We also do not know how children treat these prepositionals when they encode functions that are not locative, such as possessive or range. To remedy this situation, the remainder of this section presents a detailed analysis of the results of a study by Rom and Dgani (1985) on case marking pronouns in Hebrew.

In examining the development of prepositionals in language production, we cannot apply the same cue-based analysis that was used for language comprehension. Nonetheless, we can look at (1) the strength of each prepositional in elicited production; (2) the relative frequencies of the different prepositionals; and (3) the extent to which polysemy cuts into the reliability of each prepositional. Thus the analysis for production looks at production strength, frequency, and reliability whereas the analysis for comprehension looked at cue strength, availability, and reliability.

Production Strength

The production strengths for the oblique argument cues were obtained from a study performed by Rom and Dgani (1985) of the acquisition of three case-marking prepositionals in Hebrew. The child's task was to answer questions, such as *shel mi ha-perax ha-ze?* "Whose flower is this?," with the appropriate case-marked prepositional in either prepositional or pronominal form. The three prepositionals of interest were: *shel* as possessive, *et* as accusative, and *al* as locative. The subjects were 105 children between the ages of 2;0 and 5;5 divided into seven age groups. The experimenters were interested in exploring the interaction between semantic and pragmatic factors and morphological factors. In analyzing their data, Rom and Dgani looked at children's performance with

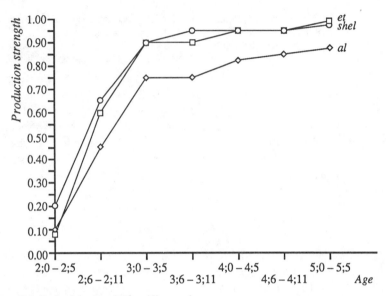

Figure 3.4. Production strengths for oblique assignment cues across ages.

the prepositionals collapsed across the different morphological forms which were elicited. They found that the children were better at producing both *shel* and *et* than they were at producing *al*. The results of this analysis are presented in Figure 3.4 (as percentages rather than total number correct).

To analyze the effects of morphological complexity, Rom and Dgani compared children's performance on the second person singular feminine fused forms for each of the prepositionals. They found a significant difference between *shel-ax* and both *ot-ax* and *al-ayix*. They interpreted these results as supporting the view that there was a morphological rather than semantic basis for acquisition: *Shel-ax* is learned faster than *ot-ax* (which can be encoded in two ways, *et* and *ot-*) and *al-ayix* (which is inflected in an irregular way). This interpretation is further supported by the finding that there is no significant difference between the prepositionals, holding morphological complexity constant (using the first person plural form).

For the purpose of testing the production validity hypothesis, the performance of the children on each preposition collapsed across the various morphological forms was employed as the measure of production strength. This is the best measure we can obtain since an elicited production experiment of this type cannot include any instances of competition among the different prepositionals or their functions. Since there are no competitions among cues, a STEPIT analysis is not necessary. The production strengths are given in Figure 3.4.

Production Validity

All the utterances from both corpora were submitted to a production validity analysis. The sample included 223 utterances from the text of a fictional novel and another 142 utterances from adult conversational input to children. The analysis measured the frequency and reliability of all the prepositionals in both corpora to the functions that they encoded. Production validity differs from cue validity in that it measures relative frequency rather than the more specific notion of availability. In the novel, there were twenty-one prepositionals that encoded eighteen different oblique roles; in the conversational input, there were ten prepositionals that encoded fifteen different oblique roles. As these numbers indicate, many of the prepositionals were multi-functional. The following example should help to clarify the analysis:

	Oblique	Prep
1. *ze sipur* al *Zehava ve shloshet ha-dubim.*	Range	*al*
"This is a story on Goldilocks and the three bears."		
2. *efshar lesaxek* al *ha-gag.*	Locative	*al*
"It's possible to play on the roof."		
3. *ima bishla daysa.*	—	—
"Mother cooked porridge."		

The cue validity analysis for oblique roles differs from that of actors and patients in that instead of availability, the analysis codes the frequency of each prepositional from among the total number of sentences in the corpus encoding *oblique* roles. This is because it is unreasonable to assume that every utterance sets up an expectation for an oblique role. In the example above, to compute the production validity of the preposition *al* for three sentences, we first note that example (3) does not encode an oblique role. Therefore, the total number of examples in which *al* could have occurred is two. Since it occurs in both examples, *al* has a frequency of 100%. However, it encodes a locative function in only one of the two examples. Therefore, it has a reliability of 50%. Finally, the product of the results for frequency and reliability yields a validity rating of 50% for the locative preposition *al* in this example.

A measure of production validity was calculated for the three prepositionals in the Rom and Dgani study. The three prepositionals were: *shel* for possessive, *et* for accusative, and *al* for locative. The results, which are listed in Table 3.8, were the same for both corpora: *et* > *shel* > *al*. Neither of the three cues had very high validity ratings. This is mainly because there were many different prepositionals encoding many different functions in the corpora.

The Results for Oblique Role Assignment

The results of the regression analysis between production validity and production strength are presented in Table 3.9. The two-year-olds perform quite

Table 3.8. *Production validity estimates for oblique assignment cues*

	NOVEL			CHILDES			Average		
	Avail	Rel	Valid	Avail	Rel	Valid	Avail	Rel	Valid
shel	.12	.86	.10	.09	.91	.08	.105	.885	.092
et	.20	.82	.16	.18	.82	.14	.190	.820	.156
al	.07	.31	.02	.14	.29	.04	.105	.300	.031

poorly. This is consistent with previous results (Dromi, 1979; Berman, 1985) which indicate that it is not until around the age of three that children gain much mastery over Hebrew prepositionals. However, for all the other age groups there are strong positive correlations between production validity and production strength. Although production validity is an excellent predictor of production strength (accounting for 58% of the variance averaging across all age groups), production reliability is an even better predictor. It accounts for 86% of the variance. This result supports the claim (Slobin, 1973; Dromi, 1979) that children search for one-to-one mappings between forms and their functions.

It is also possible that Rom and Dgani are correct in claiming that morphological factors determine the rate of acquisition of Hebrew prepositionals. One way to test this claim is to construct a quantitative analysis similar to the one performed for cue cost in actor assignment. According to the analysis of Rom and Dgani *shel* is less complex than both *et* and *al*. This suggests the following cardinal ranking: *shel* = 2, *et*, *al* = 1. To test the predictions made by the morphological complexity hypothesis, a regression analysis was performed. The results, listed in Table 3.9, indicate that morphological complexity, though not as successful as production reliability, is a reasonably good predictor of production strength. The most interesting finding is that morphological complexity is an extremely good predictor of the performance of the youngest subjects. However, from age two on upward, its ability to predict production strength diminishes greatly. Children's initial ability to process these prepositionals appears to be greatly influenced by their morphological complexity. As children begin to gain some mastery over them, production reliability becomes a more important determiner of performance. One plausible account for this result is that children cannot successfully perform distributional analyses until after they can map complete morphological paradigms onto their respective functions. This entails categorizing all of the allomorphic tokens of an inflectional form to be of the same type. For example, children must recognize that both the standard *et* and pronominalized *oto* are tokens of the same object marker type. Only after children begin to map both of these forms onto roughly the same function, can they begin to respond based on the frequency and reliability of the morphological

Table 3.9. *Correlation matrix between the predictors and production strength for the oblique assignment cues across ages*

		Age						
		2;0-	2;6-	3;0-	3;6-	4;0-	4;6-	5;0-
Frequency	NOVEL	-.30	.58	.79	.62	.79	.79	.89
	CHILDES	-.96	-.35	-.06	-.30	-.06	-.06	.11
	Average	-.64	.22	.50	.28	.50	.50	.64
Reliability	NOVEL	.40	.97	1.0	.98	1.0	1.0	.97
	CHILDES	.46	.99	.99	.99	.99	.99	.95
	Average	.44	.98	.99	.99	.99	.99	.96
Morphological complexity		.98	.73	.50	.69	.50	.50	.34
Frequency × complexity	NOVEL	.54	1.0	.97	1.0	.97	.97	.92
	CHILDES	.34	.96	1.0	.97	1.0	1.0	.98
	Average	.50	.99	.98	1.0	.98	.98	.94
Reliability × complexity	NOVEL	.86	.93	.78	.90	.78	.78	.65
	CHILDES	.87	.92	.76	.90	.76	.76	.64
	Average	.86	.92	.77	.90	.77	.77	.65
Frequency × reliability	NOVEL	-.09	.74	.90	.78	.90	.90	.97
	CHILDES	-.30	.58	.79	.62	.79	.79	.89
	Average	-.18	.67	.86	.71	.86	.86	.94
Frequency × reliability	NOVEL	.53	1.0	.98	1.0	.98	.98	.92
× complexity	CHILDES	.48	.99	.99	1.0	.99	.99	.94
	Average	.51	.99	.98	1.0	.98	.98	.93

paradigm as a whole. At this stage in the research this proposal is merely intriguing. Further research is necessary to substantiate it.

Conclusion

The data presented in this chapter paint a picture of a young language learner who creates and strengthens mappings between various forms and functions. The strengths of these mappings determine how a given cue is to be utilized in language comprehension and production. They also help to determine the rate at which grammatical forms are acquired. Children are apt to acquire cues that represent strong form–function mappings before those that represent weak ones. To a large extent, children's form–function mappings are determined by the availability and reliability of a given form toward a given function. In addition, children are able to recategorize forms as to their function if a relatively simpler form-function mapping exists. We saw an example of this with the *hitpa'el* verb pattern which is an unreliable cue when seen as a reflexive indicator, but a highly reliable one when seen as an indicator of nontransitivity. Similarly, young children are also attempting to determine the range of particular morphological paradigms (Slobin, 1985) so that they can recognize which of several paradigmatic forms map onto a single function. The high correlation between morphological complexity and performance for the two-year-olds' solutions to the oblique role assignment problem provides evidence for this process.

Although children may not have a long-term memory limitation for storing form–function mappings, they do appear to be limited in their ability to process certain types of cues in real time. In particular, those cues which are either hard to detect in the speech stream or require storing a large amount of information in short-term memory pose problems for sentence processing. Although Hebrew-speaking children tend not to rely upon highly valid but costly cues (e.g., word order in actor assignment), they do rely upon less valid but easily processed cues (e.g., the object marker). For patient assignment, there is also some evidence that the acquisition of the reflexive noun phrase is delayed because it is a cue that is low in assignability. However, the case for the reflexive noun phrase is not as clearcut because it appears so infrequently in the input. Perhaps it appears in the input so infrequently precisely because it is difficult to process.

There is also evidence that as children get older and become exposed to some grammatical forms repeatedly, they begin to trust the most reliable cues irrespective of their availability. This is because reliable cues lead to correct interpretations more of the time than unreliable ones. It is hypothesized that this change is driven by situations in which competing cues are in conflict. Early in development, the strongest cues are usually the most valid ones. But since validity is defined in terms of both availability and reliability, these cues need not be the most reliable. Since, in conflict cases, only the most reliable cues support correct interpretations, the only way the child can maximize the number of correct interpretations is to weaken the most unreliable cues in such situations. Conflict reliability appears to contribute to the increase of gender agreement over word order for actor assignment and the increase of the reflexive noun phrase over all the other cues for patient assignment in adults.

In addition, the results for patient assignment indicate a shift from sentence-based to discourse-based processing. As noted by Karmiloff-Smith (1982), this shift takes place primarily after children are seven years old. We see evidence for this in the decrease in strength of the accusative cues for patient assignment and the increase of the *pi'el* verb pattern. Since the discourse-based notion of object ellipsis leads to a decrease in the availability of the accusative cues, the *pi'el* verb pattern is called upon to compensate. This suggests that children are not able to consider discourse-based form–function mappings until they are cognitively equipped to do so (Slobin, 1973; Bates & MacWhinney, 1987).

As a final observation, we would like to claim that any model of language acquisition must necessarily consider the status of children's sentence-processing abilities. This is because the processes of language acquisition and sentence processing are intertwined in a nearly inseparable manner. In other words, any characterization of the child language-learner is also an implicit characterization of the child sentence-processor. Assuming this to be true, we would like to leave the reader with a set of parsing principles which are consistent with the data presented in this chapter:[1]

1. As noted in the first section, lexical representations drive all processing. All the grammatical information that is necessary for successful parsing to take place is stored in the lexicon. Although this hypothesis was not previously discussed in the paper, the evidence from undergeneralizations of Hebrew verb patterns (Berman, 1982) and error-free production of governed prepositionals (Berman, 1985) suggests that Hebrew verbal morphology is learned on a verb-by-verb basis.
2. Nonlexical cues are based on grand analogies derived from the lexicon. For example, if the majority of verbal entries in the lexicon state that preverbal nouns tend to be actors, then this tendency will be reflected in sentence-processing. Within this framework, phrase structure rules can be considered an epiphenomenal result of analogical processing.
3. During parsing, role assignments are governed by a mathematically based probabilistic integration of cue strengths (McClelland & Kawamoto, 1986).
4. Cue strengths are based on cue validity, conflict reliability, cue cost, and formal complexity.
5. The information provided by cues is utilized immediately or as soon as possible (Marslen-Wilson & Tyler, 1980; Thibadeau, Just, & Carpenter, 1982). This process involves a cumulative and ongoing updating of strength values for various assignments.

It is our hope that further research will be conducted in order to substantiate or refute each of these principles.

In conclusion, the main finding of the present study is that the distributionally based notion of cue validity is predictive of the actual strength of cues as they are used by listeners and speakers of Hebrew to assign actor, patient, and oblique roles. Since cue validity is not defined in terms of cue strength, the predictions of the experimental results involve no circularity. By performing a distributional analysis of the validity of the cues employed by a particular language, it is possible to predict the strengths of the earliest form–function mappings in children. However, the success of the cue validity hypothesis is not complete. In order to fully understand the process of language development, we must also take into account cue cost, morphological complexity, and discourse-based constraints.

---

[1] Many of these principles are shared by already existing parsers: Sokolov (1985), MacWhinney (1987), McClelland and Kawamoto (1986). Both the Sokolov and McClelland/Kawamoto parsers have already been implemented and successfully parse a portion of English.

4   The Development of Sentence Interpretation in Hungarian[1]

Csaba Pléh

Some basic grammatical features of Hungarian

Case marking and agglutination

The Hungarian language provides a variety of interesting grammatical features which can be exploited in studies of sentence processing. Hungarian is an agglutinative language with a very rich case system. Case marking itself means that nouns carry markers of their grammatical role on themselves. Agglutination is something more than that. It also means that most of the interesting grammatical distinctions are carried by bound morphemes – mainly suffixes going back to free morphs (function words) – and grammatical distinctions build up in a "bricklike" manner: a separate identifiable morpheme corresponds to each grammatical distinction. Grammatical morphemes are strictly ordered following the stem. Thus, in a certain sense the system is more transparent than the flexional one familiar from Indo-European languages where several grammatical distinctions are marked by one single morpheme (think about the singular and the plural accusative in Latin) and where the same grammatical distinction is marked by different morphemes in different stem classes. Some basic features of the system will be presented with regard to the nominal paradigm since most of the experiments to be reported will deal with it. For a good structural characterization of Hungarian see Lotz (1939) which is still the best source. For a psycholinguistically oriented characterization see MacWhinney (1985).

Agglutination in the nominal paradigm basically means the following: Nouns are marked for case and number with two distinctive markers with fixed order: stem + number + case marker. Thus the nominative *fiú* (boy) takes the *-t* accusative marker in the singular to give the form *fiú-t*, becomes *fiú-k* in the plural nominative (the plural marker being *-k*), and is *fiú-k-at* in the plural accusative.

---

[1]   The studies reported here were carried out with support from the Hungarian Ministry of Education. Writing of the paper was facilitated by support from the MacArthur Foundation during a visit to Carnegie Mellon University. The author would like to thank Brian MacWhinney for his help in the common experiments and in discussions concerning this paper as well.

There are over 20 cases in the nominal paradigm. Besides the zero marked nominative and accusative, the instrumental-commitative, the dative and the different adverbial relations (in, to, from, at, etc.) also carry different case markers. There are no stem types similar to the ones in Indo-European languages; all stems take the same marking to code the same grammatical relation.

Deviations from Transparency

This indeed seems to be a very transparent system to acquire and to use. There are, however, two major deviations from this transparency. First, although there are no stem types with different endings in different classes, some stems undergo characteristic modifications as a result of morphophonemic rules. The marker for the accusative, for example, is always *-t*. This is however, as MacWhinney (1978) has phrased it, only a "common denominator" of the different modifications stems undergo when in the accusative. It can be attached directly to the stem as in some stems ending in a short vowel, for example, *maci* "bear" *maci-t*, or in some stems ending in consonants, for example, *mókus* "squirrel" *mókus-t*. Vowel lengthening can occur in stems ending in a short *-a* or *-e* as in *macska* "cat" *macská-t*. The case marker can also be preceded by a linking vowel in some of the stems ending in a consonant as in *zsiráf* "giraffe" – *zsiráf-o-t*, and vowel shortening can also occur with long *-é-* or *-á-* in closed final syllables as in *tehén* "cow" – *tehen-et*. These modifications are only semiarbitrary: They usually correspond to the phonological nature of the stem and follow sophisticated morphophonemic rules. There is no need here to go into the details of the system. MacWhinney (1978) gives a rather extensive summary.

Table 4.1 gives a few examples for the different stem types. It should be clear from the examples that when a child learns Hungarian he or she has to acquire these lawful modifications besides the common form of the morphological marker for certain grammatical relations. As a matter of fact, some of the most detailed examples for learning the morphophonemic rules in a language with rich morphology come from studies on the Hungarian nominal system (MacWhinney, 1978; Réger, 1979). The system has relevance for the process of understanding as well: The different allomorphs have to be mapped onto the same basic relationship during perception.

Notice a few things in connection with Table 4.1. First, all the case markers containing a vowel or involving a linking vowel obey either fronting vowel harmony, like the inessive *-ban* and *-ben*, or fronting plus rounding harmony like the stative superessive *-on, -en, -ön*. We won't deal with this issue here; it is worth noting, however, that the actual number of allomorphs to be taken into account is much larger due to vowel harmony, and vowel harmony certainly

Table 4.1. *Morphological patterns of some Hungarian nominal stem types*

Case	I Clustering	II Vowel length	III Vowel shorten	IV Linking vowel	V Dropping vowel
Nominative	*mókus* squirrel	*macska* cat	*tehén* cow	*zsiráf* giraffe	*majom* monkey
Accusative	*mókus-t*	*macská-t*	*tehen-et*	*zsiráf-ot*	*majm-ot*
Dative	*mókus-nak*	*macská-nak*	*tehén-nek*	*zsiráf-nak*	*majom-nak*
Instrumental	*mókus-sal*	*macská-val*	*tehén-nel*	*zsiráf-fal*	*majom-mal*
Illative	*mókus-ba*	*macská-ba*	*tehén-be*	*zsiráf-ba*	*majom-ba*
Inessive	*mókus-ban*	*macská-ban*	*tehén-ben*	*zsiráf-ban*	*majom-ban*
Elative	*mókus-ból*	*macská-ból*	*tehén-ből*	*zsiráf-ból*	*majom-ból*
Sublative	*mókus-ra*	*macská-ra*	*tehén-re*	*zsiráf-ra*	*majom-ra*
Superessive	*mókus-on*	*macská-n*	*tehén-en*	*zsiráf-on*	*majm-on*
Delative	*mókus-ról*	*macská-ról*	*tehén-ről*	*zsiráf-ról*	*majom-ról*
Plural	*mókus-ok*	*macská-k*	*tehen-ek*	*zsiráf-ok*	*majm-ok*

facilitates segmentation in perception by giving a cue to the integrity of the word.

Notice also that in the different types indicated in the table the stem modifications entail different oppositions between the cases. In Type I all the singular and all the plural forms are contrasted in that all the plural forms do take the linking vowel. In Type II the singular nominative is contrasted with all the other forms due to lengthening. In Type III the singular accusative and all the plural forms take the vowel shortened form; thus the contrast is between the singular accusative plus plural and the rest of the singular paradigm. Type IV is the same as Type III in this respect whereas in Type V all the plural forms (because of the linking vowel) and all singular forms allowing a linking vowel (i.e., the ones that are not syllabic) take the vowel dropping stem allomorph.

During real-time processing, the different stems thus allow different conclusions at different points concerning the possible roles the noun can play in the given sentence. Notice also that some stems are inherently more difficult with regard to perceptual identification of certain endings, and some stem alterations – most notably linking vowels – may have been preserved in the language exactly to enhance perceivability.

The other deviations from the transparency of the system concern the unequivocal correspondence between case markers and basic syntactic or semantic relations in the sentence. Consider the nominative–accusative distinction which should ideally always correspond to the subject–object distinction on the syntactic level and to the agent–object distinction in terms of semantic cases. There are two deviations from this one-to-one correspondence. Certain relations may be unmarked, and certain relations may be marked with varying endings.

Let us see examples for the first deviation. There are semantic objects which allow the omission of the accusative on them. Most notably, Hungarian nouns also enter a paradigm of possessive marking where the morpheme that precedes the case marker indicates the number and person of the possesor. Thus *ház* "house" becomes *ház-a-m* "my house" and *ház-a-d* "your house". In these two forms that is in the singular first and second person possesed forms the distinction between the nominative and the accusative is almost obligatorily neutralized. Thus a sentence such as "The cat is chasing my dog" would be in Hungarian *A macska kergeti a kutyá-m* without the otherwise obligatory accusative *-t*.

Specific deviations from obligatory and unique marking appear in expressions for possession. Ordering in these constructions is always possessor-possessed in Hungarian, and the fact of possession is only marked on the possessed by the third person form of the possessive marking mentioned above. For example, an expression like the "boy's father" would be translated as *a fiú ap-ja* which would be in a literal translation "the boy father+possessed". From our point of view this means that the nominative cannot be mapped directly onto an agent or subject role without further considerations. On the basis of similar facts, Szabolcsi (1987) argues that although Hungarian is a non-configurational language by and large, it still has configurational islands where word order only differentiates between the very different meanings of (1) and (2).

1. *A réz az arany helyettesítője.*
   The copper the gold replacement+POSS. (Copper replaces gold.)
2. *Az arany a réz helyettesítője.*
   The gold the copper replacement+POSS. (Gold replaces copper.)

There are several further discrepancies from a one-to-one correspondence between morphological case marking and syntactic and semantic roles. In multiple possessive constructions, the dative is used to mark the possessor. Or, as pointed out by Zsilka (1966) and extensively surveyed by Moravcsik (1978), the semantic object can be marked in the same transitive event either by the accusative or an oblique case depending on the completeness of the action, similar to the difference in English between "He painted the house" and "He put paint on the house."

In one word thus there are discrepancies from one-to-one mapping between the morphological case system and syntactic and semantic relations both in the sense that the same marker can carry different distinctions and also in the sense that the same distinction can be marked by different devices. We will see some of the processing implications of this fact later on.

Word Order

Word order of the main constituents in Hungarian sentences is basically free. One can think of this in terms of a tradeoff between morphological marking of syntactic-thematic roles and ordering: Since the thematic roles are marked on the nouns themselves word order is "freed" to serve other purposes. How do we have to interpret this freedom of word order? First of all, it only relates to the freedom of ordering of the major constituents. Words within a noun phrase, for example, are rather strictly ordered as: Art Adj N. The fixed position of adjectives is easily understood if we consider that they do not agree with the head noun of the noun phrase. Furthermore, the lack of the copula in the present tense would change the function of the attributive adjective into a predicative one between (3) and (4).

3. *A fekete fiú...*
    The black boy...
4. *A fiú fekete.*
    The boy black

Second, and more important for our present purposes, freedom of word order only means that all the possible permutations of S,V, and O can produce grammatical sentences. In the terminology of the language typologist, however, there are still neutral or basic orders among these. With definite objects the basic order in transitive sentences is SVO, while the neutral word order with indefinite objects is SOV (Dezső, 1982).

The newer literature on Hungarian word order has tried to find some regularities behind this freedom. Works in the functionalist sentence perspective tradition starting from Dezső and Szépe (1974), Kiefer (1967) , and Elekfi (1969) have all suggested that ordering is somehow related to the topic-comment organization of Hungarian sentences.

É. Kiss (1981a, b) represents a curious blend of traditional speculation concerning the topic-comment motivation of Hungarian sentence structure and recent work in Government and Binding theory. In her formulation the terms Topic and Focus become syntactic positions, that is, landing sites for the elements effected by transformations, in an invariant syntactic configuration.

In this framework the base structure of a sentence would consist of an unordered set of major categories and the verb. Movement rules would allow the movement of one of the categories into immediately preverbal position which is the focus position of the sentence, the default option being the verb itself as focus. Another optional movement rule could move other categories before the focus thereby constituting the topic of the sentence.

The focus also carries the main stress of the sentence. Therefore, any structures which emphasize other elements than the immediately preverbal one are ungrammatical.

The neutral, default option – with no contrastive stress – would be the verb itself as a focused element. Thus the simple sentence "The boy chases the girl" would have among others the following possible readings in Hungarian.

5. *A fiú kergeti a lányt.*   SVO   "The boy chases the girl."
6. *A fiú kergeti a lányt.*   SVO   "It's the boy who chases the girl."

7. *A fiú a lányt kergeti.*   SOV   "It's the girl the boy chases."
8. *A lányt kergeti a fiú.*   OVS   "It's the girl the boy chases."

The facts are clear; not all linguists are happy with the interpretations, however. The system leaves the status of so-called basic or contextually neutral order obscure: it would predict verb initial sentences to be the most neutral (no movement transformations are applied here), but for native speakers these structures are clearly marked. Some linguists argue that the basic SVO order should still be preserved in grammatical theory (Horvath, 1986); some others take issue with the exact formulation of the movement rules (Kenesei, 1984). The details of the debate would lead us too far into the intricacies of Hungarian word order and contemporary schools of formal linguistics. We will see, however, that the problem of word order has to be raised in connection with the studies of sentence understanding as well even if the issue is not a life-or-death matter there. The traditional typological approach (Dezső, 1982) here suggests that there are two basic word orders for sentences in Hungarian: SVO for definite objects and SOV for indefinite objects. We will present some psychological evidence supporting this position.

Agreement and Pro-drop

Correlatively with its agglutinative structure Hungarian has an elaborate verbal conjugation system with two types of agreement built into the system. Finite verb forms do agree with the subject in number and person, and also show an agreementlike phenomenon with regard to the object. Namely, a different conjugation pattern is used with intransitive verbs and verbs with an indefinite object on the one hand and transitive verbs with a definite object on the other hand. What is important in this introductory context is the following: corresponding to these agreement phenomena, Hungarian freely drops pronouns both in the nominative and the accusative case.

Experiments on Understanding Simple Sentences

The above characterization of some basic features of Hungarian grammar immediately raises some questions concerning sentence understanding. For example, what is the relationship between case marking and word order in understanding, how do the intricacies of the morphophonemics affect understanding, and so on. The experimental work summarized here tried to attack most of the issues trivially raised by the grammar of Hungarian. Its motivation partly came, however, from present theories of crosslinguistic differences as well.

In several experiments we were trying to use very simple and direct methods to address these issues. Namely simple "off-line" sentence interpretation was used where children are asked to enact the sentences they are told with simple toys while adults are asked to say as fast as possible "who" did the action of the sentence. Even though these methods are very simple and rather unsophisticated compared to the methodology of some of contemporary psycholinguistics they do show some robust and hopefully nontrivial results.

The Overwhelming Importance of Case Marking

The object as we have seen above is rather clearly indicated in Hungarian by the marker -*t*. It is quite natural to expect an exclusive use of the case marker in the interpretation of simple transitive sentences. Two sorts of evidence support and at the same time qualify this idea. In a series of experiments designed in the framework of the Competition Model, where different possible determiners of sentence interpretation – case marking, animacy of the nouns, word order and stress – were orthogonally varied, children and adults had to interpret simple sentences like (9)–(11). Case marking was by far the most important single determinant of sentence interpretation from the youngest age group – 3 years – in MacWhinney, Pléh, and Bates (1985) and Pléh and MacWhinney (1985).

9. *A macskát átugorja a kutya.*
   The cat+ACC over-jumps the dog+NOM.
10. *A macska átugorja a kutyát.*
    The cat+NOM over-jumps the dog+ACC.
11. *A macska átugorja a kutya.*
    The cat+NOM over-jumps the dog+NOM.

As Figure 4.1 shows, as a function of the selection of the first noun depending on which noun carried the case marker, there was a strong reliance on case marking throughout. There was, however, considerable development with age in the importance of this factor. Whereas in 3-year-olds case marking has accounted for 12.5% of the total variance in the experiment, at age 4 its explanatory value increased to 50.8%, at 6 to 64%, and from then on it has remained constant to adulthood (64.8%). Notice that the numbers are not higher only because – due to the sentences with no case marking, one-third of the entire list – our subjects had to use other possible clues to interpretation with many of the sentences.

Another sort of experimental evidence for the overwhelming importance of case marking comes from a different type of experiment also devised in the framework of the Competition Model. MacWhinney and Pléh (in preparation) asked adults to interpret sentences where case marking was set into competition with agreement between the verb and the potential subjects in number as well as another agreement: the agreement in definiteness between the verb and the potential objects. To get an idea of the tasks the subjects faced compare (12) and (13) where in (12) there is no competition between number agreement and case marking whereas in (13) there is: case marking favors the first noun as subject-agent whereas agreement favors the second.

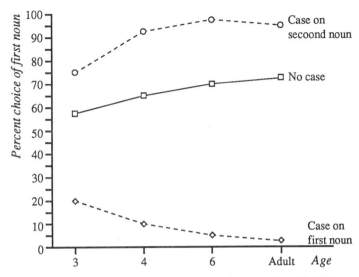

Figure 4.1. Selection of first noun as agent as a function of case marking (MacWhinney, Pléh, & Bates, 1985).

12. *A kutya kergeti a macská-t.*
    The dog+NOM chases the cat+ACC.
13. *A kutyá-k kergeti a macská-t.*
    The dogs+NOM chases the cat+ACC.

In one study half of the sentences were without case marking, in another only one third. In the first experiment, number and definiteness on the nouns as well as animacy were varied, whereas in the second, besides case marking the number of the nouns, the type of the conjugation on the verb (definite or indefinite) and the number of the verb were varied. Table 4.2 shows the variance explained by each variable in the two experiments.

The picture was rather straightforward: If agreement was at variance with case marking, case marking always won. This amounts to say that even in ungrammatical sentences – since all of the interesting, competitive cases were ungrammatical – the most important grammatical feature in the language practically washes out any other possible sources of decision.

So far, so good: In a language where case marking is systematic it is used as the almost exclusive feature to base interpretation on. There was no need for much psycholinguistics to learn that. There is reason for some reservation in the data themselves, however. If we consider the age trend shown in Figure 4.1 we can see that children in the youngest age group did not follow case marking in about 20% of the time, whereas even younger (2;6) Turkish children follow case marking in over 80% of the time according to the data of Slobin and Bever

Table 4.2. *Proportion of variance explained in two experiments where different factors were competing for the subject role (MacWhinney & Pléh, in preparation)*

Factors	Case	Noun number	Noun definit.	Noun animacy	Verb number	Verb definit.
Experiment 1	29.7	6.5	0.6	1.9	not used	not used
Experiment 2	41.3	0.4	0.0	not used	0.5	0.0

Table 4.3. *Percentage of children with no mistakes with case marked sentences of different word orders, six tokens by sentence types (Pléh, 1981)*

Age	3;9	4;5	4;9	5;5
n	33	41	61	43
SVO + SOV	58	66	75	86
OVS + OSV	30	36	45	58

(1982). In another experiment (Pléh, 1981) using only grammatical, that is, case marked, sentences the percentage of children showing no mistakes at all with a given sentence type (6 token sentences were used for each type) indicated even more clearly that case marking was not all of the story. As Table 4.3 shows, sentences with the object preceding the subject lead to difficulties even in older children if we applied more absolute criteria.

Thus, Hungarian children do rely on something else than case marking. In the following we will examine what other strategies they use as well as the reasons for using them.

The First-Noun-as-the-Agent Strategy

As one of the first attempts to apply the notion of perceptual strategies in psycholinguistics, Thomas Bever (1970) proposed a strategy according to which NVN sequences are interpreted as agent-action-object sequences. This strategy is formed and overgeneralized in English-speaking children around the age of four (Bever, 1970, 1971) causing a misinterpretation of passive and certain cleft constructions. One of our first attempts to address the issues of the language specific factors in sentence processing dealt with this problem: Does the strategy appear even in children acquiring a free word order case marking language?

As the data from 178 children in Table 4.3 show there certainly is a strong bias toward using the first-noun-as-the-agent strategy. In fact the age trend of the use in this strategy also seemed to correspond to the one found by

Table 4.4. *Average correct percent choice of bilingual and monolingual Hungarian and Russian children between 4 and 6 with subject first and object first sentences (Pléh, Jarovinskij, & Balajan, 1987)*

	Monolingual		Bilingual	
	S first	O first	S first	O first
Hungarian	92	74	98	92
Russian	96	86	93	79

Bever: performance with subject initial grammatical sentences (i.e., transitive sentences with one nominative and one accusative noun) was superior to object first sentences in the four age groups on the average by 6.5, 13.4, 10.1, and 7.9%. Thus the overgeneralization of a word order based interpretation was strongest in Hungarian children roughly in the same ages as in English-speaking ones. It should be kept in mind, however, that in Hungarian children the tendency was much weaker than in the English-speaking ones.

As the middle line in Figure 4.1 (the ungrammatical sentences with no case marking) shows, the same tendency was observed in the experiments using more varied sentence material by MacWhinney et al. (1985). The age trend was basically the same – the big shift, the reliance on order, appeared around four years of age, with the mean selections of the first noun as agent option being 58, 67, 71, and 73% in the four age groups. Notice at the same time that the first-noun-as-the-agent strategy in the same experiment was rather weak in connection with grammatical sentences that had case marking. This can best be seen if we compare correct performance in those word orders where the subject preceded the object (SOV, SVO, VSO) against correct performance in those where the object preceded the subject (OSV, OVS, VSO). The corresponding figures in the four age groups were: 74–69%, 93–91%, 98–95%, 98–96%. Thus, the superiority of the subject first sentences was between 3% and 5% only. We will return to the reasons for this discrepancy between the results of the different experiments later on.

In another study comparing Hungarian-Russian bilinguals and their monolingual controls, four word orders (SVO, OVS, SOV, OSV) were used with four token sentences for each in both languages (Pléh, Jarovinskij, & Balajan, 1987). The subjects were 4- and 6-year-old nursery school children. As Table 4.4 shows, there was a relatively strong first-noun-as-the-agent strategy observed in both languages but it was remarkably weaker in the bilinguals in their dominant language. (All the bilinguals were living in Budapest, and their dominant language according to vocabulary data was clearly Hungarian. See Jarovinskij, 1979.)

What are the reasons behind using an order based strategy in a language which clearly marks the grammatical roles on the nouns (agent, object, etc.)? We were looking for the answer to this question in two segments of the language: First, there are constructions where accusative case marking is almost obligatorily missing; second, there are stems where accusative marking is present but hard to detect.

Order Based Strategy When Case Is Missing

As was mentioned in the grammatical introduction, sentences containing a first or second person possessor are neutralized with regard to the accusative. In two experiments reported by MacWhinney et al. (1985) this possibility was exploited by using sentences which had *two* possessively marked nouns in them with neither in the accusative, like (14) and (15) below.

14. *A szarvas-od átugorja az oroszlán-om.*
    The deer-yours over-jumps the lion-mine.
15. *A szarvasom átugorja az oroszlán-od.*
    The deer-mine over-jumps the lion-yours.

These sentences – though perfectly grammatical – are structurally ambiguous: The two nouns are equally good candidates in them for both the agent and the object roles. A rather strong first noun strategy was observed with similar sentences. In the experiment using a stem type free of confounding phonetic effects (see about this below) average first noun selection over the "mine-yours", "yours-mine", and "yours-yours" versions was 85, 92, and 84% in 4- and 6-year-olds and adults.

In another yet unpublished study (Pléh, in preparation) nursery school children were asked to interpret similar sentences as (14) and (15) but supplemented with "trapping" versions like (16) and (17) where a possessively unmarked nominative also appears. In these sentences the possessive has to be the object by default. Part of the rationale to do this study was to see when children learn to overcome the traps introduced by the overgeneralization of the first-noun-as-agent strategy.

16. *Az oroszlán megsimogatja a tigris-em.*
    The lion+NOM pets the tiger-mine.
17. *A tigris-ed megsimogatja az oroszlán.*
    The tiger-yours pets the lion+NOM.

Sentences with noun pairs with identical possessive markers (M-M "mine-mine" or D-D "yours-yours"), differing markers (D-M and M-D), topicalized nominatives (nominative, "zero" – M or D) and topicalized possessives with sentence final nominatives (M or D – nominative) were used with 4 tokens for each type. All sentences were in an SVO order, all nouns were names of animals (animate), and all stems allowed an easy identification of ending. Over-generalization of the first noun strategy would best be indicated in performance with sentences like (17) where this strategy leads to misinterpretation since the

Table 4.5. *Interactions between age and stem type in percent first noun choice in nouns with various possessive endings (Pléh, in preparation)*

Age	n	Identical M-M D-D	Different M-D D-M	Nom first No-M No-D	Nom second M-No D-No
3 years	4	75	74	69	65
4 years	15	78	68	69	65
5 years	25	79	77	82	61
6 years	51	94	94	95	57
Mean		86	78	78	62

fronted possessively marked noun which is a good candidate for the agent role is the only candidate for the object role in this sentence.

Table 4.5 shows the basic results obtained on 95 children. There was a significant main effect of the noun-combination type $F(3,273) = 1.68, p < 0.0001$. Its basic meaning is indicated by the overall means on the table: The first noun selection strategy proved to be the strongest if the two nouns were marked identically, on the one hand, and its effect was reduced when it led to wrong interpretations [nominative second sentences like (17) above]. However, there was a strong interaction with age: $F(3,273) = 5.29, p < 0.0001$. This interaction had the following main sources. Differences in first noun selection between sentences where this leads to correct interpretation (zero first) and where it does not (zero second) only appear after 5 years of age. The difference between zero first and zero second in the four age groups was: 4, 4, 21, and 38%. Thus, again, strong signs for a first noun strategy were found together with some indication that it is overruled when misleading, after 5 years of age as was the case for English-speaking children.

In summary, experiments with sentences where case marking can be deleted show that the order based strategy is indeed very strong in those islands in the language where it is almost necessarily called for as the basic remaining means to convey grammatical information. These sentences show us how strong the order based strategy can become (compare the percentages obtained here with the ones in sentences with case marking) if there is no case marking and also indicate one source for the application of this strategy in Hungarian. Let us turn to the other source: complications in identifying the nominally present case marking.

The Case of Hard to Detect Cases

As was mentioned in the grammatical introduction, one systematic deviation from the transparency of the system is related to the morphophonemic variations stems undergo with certain endings. We have noticed in several experiments that these intricacies of Hungarian morphophonemics might be the basic factors behind the emergence of order based, and possibly other, supplementary strategies of interpretation. There are three different versions of these effects but they all go back to the same source: failure to identify uniquely the ending due to phonetic-acoustic factors. People, especially children, may map the marked accusative into the unmarked nominative, they may map the unmarked nominative into the marked accusative, and they may map some other marked ending into the accusative.

Failure to "Hear" the Accusative

In the Hungarian-Russian bilingual sentence interpretation experiment already mentioned above (Pléh et al., 1987) we have noticed that in object-fronted sentences (OVS and OSV orders) performance varied according to the type of the stem carrying the accusative marker. "Difficult" and "easy" stems were distinguished both in Hungarian and in Russian. In Hungarian "difficult" has meant stems like Type I discussed in connection with Table 4.1, that is, stems where the accusative -t is directly attached to a consonant at the end of the stem thereby producing a consonant cluster. "Easy" stems in the Hungarian data meant types where the accusative was attached directly to a stem ending in a short vowel like maci "bear" – maci-t or stems where there was a linking vowel correlated with a vowel drop inside the stem like majom "monkey" – majm-ot. Incidentally, it is worth mentioning that the first "easy" variety also belongs to Type I in Table 4.1, and the second to Type V, the latter being the hardest to master in production (MacWhinney, 1978). From the point of view of perceptual identification, however, it is not the "formal" stem type that matters but acoustic confusability which is related to stem types but not in a one-to-one way.

In the Russian material easy and difficult were defined in a different way. Stems which belong to the feminine declensional class and take the unique -u marker for the accusative were treated as easy ones like sobaka "dog" – sobak-u "dog/accus" while the ones belonging to the masculine declensional class and therefore taking the overloaded -a marker for their accusative like tígr "tiger" – tígra "tiger/accus" were classified as difficult ones. The specific difficulty associated with these stems, where only names of animals were used, was the following: children could treat the fronted accusative masculine as a nominative feminine because -a is a gender changing derivational suffix as well.

Table 4.6 shows that in both languages there was a tendency to misinterpret the sentence initial difficult objects more frequently. In other words this corresponded to the first-noun-as-agent strategy since no similar differences in mistakes appeared when the object was following the subject. The other noteworthy thing was that bilinguals – especially in their dominant language – were much more sensitive to endings: they had a much weaker tendency to

Table 4.6. *Percentage of mistakes in object initial sentences with easy and difficult stems in the bilingual study (Pléh, Jarovinskij, & Balajan, 1987)*

	Monolinguals		Bilinguals	
	Easy	Difficult	Easy	Difficult
Hungarian	18	35	8	8
Russian	12	38	10	27

mistakenly map the difficult sentence initial object onto the agent role. This may mean that since they were acquiring two case marking languages simultaneously the "Pay attention to the ends of the words!" strategy as put forward by Slobin (1973) was selectively reinforced in their case resulting in earlier development of fine morphophonemic sensitivity.

It is worth noting another issue in connection with this experiment. It was already mentioned that there were some discrepancies among results concerning the strength of the first-noun-as-the-agent strategy in our other experiments. These discrepancies might very well be related to the nature of the stems used, which was not a systematically varied factor in the first studies. In Pléh (1981), where a relatively strong first-noun strategy and misinterpretation of initial objects were found, one-third of the nouns used belonged to the difficult stem category, whereas in the sudy of MacWhinney et al. (1985) less than 10% of the nouns belonged to this type. This fact can easily explain the less pronounced initial object misinterpretations found in this latter study.

Another yet unpublished experiment (Pléh, in preparation) was done to look for the systematic effects of difficulties in identifying the accusative on the first-noun-as-the-agent strategy. This is not redundant compared to the above results since the conclusions there were drawn on the basis of *post hoc* considerations. Children between 3 and 6 had to enact sentences all of which were of an NVN order, and had names of animals in them. Thus, both animacy and word order were kept constant. All sentences had one noun in the accusative and one in the nominative. Two factors were varied: position of the subject (SVO and OVS) and the types of the two stems. Difficult-Difficult, Difficult-Easy, Easy-Easy, and Easy-Difficult configurations were used. The two factors were crossed and there were 3 token sentences for each difficulty and subject position combination. The difficult stems were of the consonant cluster ending types, while the easy ones of the simple linking vowel types (Type IV in Table 4.1). Notice that with these types of difficult stems there are two possible difficulties: not hearing the accusative, that is interpreting *mókus-t* ("squirrel+acc") as *mókus* ("squirrel/nom") or hearing the final sibilant as a consonant cluster, thus interpreting *mókus* as *mókus-t*.

Table 4.7. *Percentage of correct interpretation as a function of stem type and subject position (Pléh, in preparation)*

	Stem types				
	D-D	D-E	E-E	E-D	Mean
Subject first	95	95	94	92	96
Subject second	75	83	94	86	84
Mean	85	89	94	89	90

Table 4.7 summarizes some of the results. There was a significant main effect of stem type $F(3,273) = 4.50$, $p < .005$. Easy-Easy stems gave the best results, followed by Easy-Difficult and Difficult-Easy, and naturally the configuration where both stems belonged to the Difficult type resulted in most mistakes. There was an age effect which is not shown on the table. Five- and six-year-olds performed much better (90% and 93% correct interpretation) than younger children (the means being 69% and 80% for 3- and 4-year-olds). This effect was highly significant, $F(3,91) = 14.12$, $p < .0001$. The age trend had a significant interaction with stem type, $F(9,273) = 2.51$, $p < .01$. The meaning of the interaction was basically that development was slowest in the Difficult-Difficult configurations. The means indicated in Table 4.7 are more interesting for us at the moment than the details of the age trends. Besides the stem type effect there was a significant main effect of subject position, $F(1,91) = 4.30$, $p < .0001$. Taken in itself this main effect meant a 12% overgeneralized first-noun-is-the-agent strategy. The strong interactions between stem type and subject position, $F(3,273) = 7.49$, $p < .0001$, deserve special attention. There were no differences depending on the positions of the subject if both nouns were of the easy stem type. In all other configurations mistakes only appeared when the object was fronted. Thus, there was a tendency to map a fronted object onto the agent role (D-D and D-E) or to map a backgrounded subject onto the object role (E-D) if the stem "allowed" for such mishearings. This latter effect was much weaker. This is an even clearer demonstration of what MacWhinney et al. (1985) had termed the effects of syntactic expectations on phonemic factors of understanding: If the stem ending is hard to detect there is a tendency to force it into the canonic role connected to the given position, but no mapping problems arise when the difficult form is in its expected position.

Adding an Accusative Where It's Missing

In the experiments of MacWhinney et al.(1985) with possessive endings already referred to, actually two stem types were included and, as a control, sentences with no case marking were also used. The first stem type was of the vowel lengthening variety (Type II in Table 4.1) where the singular nominative contrasts with all the other endings in that it ends in a short vowel whereas the others all take the vowel lengthened stem variety (see *macska* "cat" – *macská-t*). Because of this feature it is very hard to mishear the nominative as accusative. On the other hand the second stem type they used was the consonant cluster variety discussed above where it is easy to imagine such a mishearing provided there is no case marker in the sentence (see *mókus* – *mókus-t*).

The expected difference was indeed found between the two stem types: with sentences where no ending was on the nouns in the clearly differentiable type the selection of first noun in 4- and 6-year-olds and adults was 53, 70, and 72%, whereas in the difficult stem type it was 80, 82, and 85%. The difference indicates again that the first-noun strategy is more readily activated if there is a chance to mishear the second stem as accusative. Similar results were reported by Lengyel (1982). He compared the interpretation of ungrammatical sentences by Russian and Hungarian children between 4 and 10 and found that with stems like *macska* there was less tendency on the part of Hungarian children to impose an SVO interpretation on NVN strings than with Russian children. He interpreted the difference as suggesting that whereas in the Russian sentoids only one morphological factor was missing, namely the case ending, in the Hungarian versions two things were missing: the case ending and the stem alteration.

Mishearing Something Else for Accusative

In the experiments of MacWhinney et al. (1985) the stem types were also varied in connection with the possessive sentences used. The potential for assimilation to the accusative is just the reverse here compared to the case of ungrammatical sentences with no case marker. Namely, the second person possessive form of the vowel lengthening type is very similar to the accusative: *macskád* "cat-yours" and *macská-t* "cat+acc." This is due to the already mentioned fact that vowel lengthening stems take the lengthened allomorph in all their forms but the singular nominative added to the not so accidental phonetic similarity between the accusative *-t* and the possessive *-d*. (They probably can be traced back historically to the same morpheme.) On the other hand, stems ending in consonant clusters in the accusative take the linking vowel in possessive forms (as well as for example in the plural). Thus while their accusative is hard to hear it is well differentiated from all possible other forms of the noun (compare *oroszlán-od* "lion-yours" with *oroszlán-t* "lion+acc.").

Table 4.8 shows for the two most relevant stem types, where a -D-M and -M-D configuration was used, that the tendency to impose a first-noun-as-the-agent strategy depended on stem type. In the stem type where the -D ending was easily assimilable to the accusative a clear difference emerged between the

Table 4.8. *Percentage selecting the first noun as a function of stem type and configuration of the possessive markers (MacWhinney, Pléh, & Bates, 1985)*

	Easy to assimilate stems		
	4 years	6 years	Adults
M-D	81	95	91
D-M	71	86	66

	Difficult to assimilate stems		
	4 years	6 years	Adults
M-D	87	94	87
D-M	86	91	84

two configurations: first noun selection was promoted by -D on the second noun and reduced if the first noun sounded more like the accusative. Notice that the contrast is larger in adults: they had listened to tape recorded sentences whrereas children were told the sentences. In the nonassimilable stem type no similar contrast emerged: first-noun selection was overwhelming in both configurations.

The Problem of Basic Word Order from a Psycholinguistic Perspective

As was mentioned in the grammatical introduction, contemporary Hungarian syntacticians have fierce debates on whether one can talk at all about basic word orders in a language like Hungarian where basic grammatical role distinctions are not coded by word order and at the same time all word order variants do indicate a certain type of discourse segmentation, that is, in a sense all variants are "marked." We have seen that a radical interpretation of this approach implies that, if anything, only verb initial structures could be treated as basic word orders in Hungarian, which is clearly against our intuitions.

We have already seen some evidence related to the issue of basic word order: The fact that naive people apply an order based strategy when facing difficulties of interpretation suggests that in the "psychological model" of sentences order plays a role even in a formally nonconfigurational language. There is a further issue besides the use of order based strategies: Are there any word orders which lead to easier processing indicating thereby that some sort of a basic word order or canonical order is activated? In Hungarian grammar usually two types of basic word orders are postulated (provided, if any): SVO for transitive sentences with a definite object and SOV for transitive sentences with an indefinite object. The SOV order is supposed to be the older one, with the other, verb-middle pattern arising gradually as the definite verbal conjugation has evolved (Dezső, 1982).

Table 4.9. *Latencies of interpretation (milliseconds) as a function of word order and accusative assimilability of the nouns (MacWhinney, Pléh, & Bates, 1985)*

	NVN	NNV	VNN	Mean
Non ass. − assim.	2206	2294	2538	2346
Assim. − non ass.	2525	2546	2492	2521
Means	2365	2420	2515	2434

Some evidence for the primacy of both will be presented from our experimental data.

SVO with Definite Objects

In the studies on simple sentence interpretation performed in the framework of the Competition Model, consistently faster interpretation times were found for verb middle structures (NVN) than for the other two orders (VNN and NNV). This effect was observed both for sentences with case markers and sentoids with no case marker (Pléh & MacWhinney, 1985) and was interpreted as a sign of the primacy or prototypicality of the SVO order with definite objects.

Similarly, if there was no accusatively marked noun in the sentence but the stem types used allowed a projection of the SVO pattern onto the sentence, very fast reaction times appeared in the experiment with possessive nouns (MacWhinney et al., 1985). As Table 4.9 shows, not only were NVN orders allowing for an SVO interpretation interpreted faster on the average, they were especially fast when the second noun could be "misheard" as an accusative.

Similar tendencies were also observed in connection with the first-noun selection strategy: This type of interpretation strategy was strongest in sentences to which the SVO pattern could be applied.

The particular position of the SVO pattern with definite object sentences shows up also during processing of more complicated sentences. MacWhinney and Pléh (1988) have shown in a reading time experiment using rather complicated relative clause structures in Hungarian that reading time of the entire sentence was shorter if the main clause contained a verb middle structure (SVO or OVS), and it was particularly speeded up with SVO main clause orders. This finding, summarized in Table 4.10, is particularly interesting since in the experiment the continuity of the main clause pattern was broken up at different places by the inserted relative clause. It seems to be that the SVO pattern is activated and "hold active" even if it is temporarily interrupted by a dependent clause.

Notice one further fact in connection with Table 4.10. Not only were verb-middle structures in general easier to process but sentences where the

Table 4.10. *Reading times of relative clause structures as functions of word order in the main clause (MacWhinney & Pléh, 1988)*

	SOV	SVO	VSO	OSV	OVS	VOS
Reading time (sec)	6.03	5.74	6.17	6.38	5.94	6.32

subject preceded the object were in general faster to read. SOV, SVO, and VSO orders took on the average 5.98 seconds to read while OSV, OVS, and VOS took 6.21 seconds. This result suggests that speakers of Hungarian even after they managed to base their sentence interpretation almost exclusively on morphological markers still apply a strong expectation that the subject should be sentence initial (topic) or at least precede the object.

There is some further evidence which suggests that the prototypical perspective Hungarian speakers expect a sentence to have is a rather rich cluster of features. There is evidence for the following expected features of a sentence initial, perspective giving, topicalized noun:

1. Perspectives Should be Grammatical Subjects.   This is supported by all the above discussion which implies that sentences where the topic coincides with the subject are easier to understand. Further support for this idea comes from researches on intersentential anaphora interpretation. Since in Hungarian there is no gender the entire process of anaphora interpretation is based on the relationships between subsequent clauses and sentences. Out of the many factors considered here a basic one is the grammatical role. Subjects are very frequently deleted in subsequent sentences and the default interpretation is that they are coreferent with the subject in the antecedent sentence (Pléh & Radics, 1978). In several experimental studies (Pléh, 1983; Pléh & MacWhinney, 1987) using Hungarian equivalents of sentences like (18)–(21), characteristic processing differences were found in the sentences containing the anaphoric reference as a function of the antecedent. The first two columns in Table 4.11 clearly show that both in an acoustic task where phoneme monitoring was used as an indicator of processing difficulty and in a sentence reading paradigm the agent–grammatical subject–topic correspondence gave a better perspective to the sentence thereby making it easier to integrate and interpret the subsequent anaphora.

18. The boy noticed the man. Went over to him.
        nomin   accus
19. The boy met with the man. Started to talk to him.
        nomin   instrum
20. The boy remembered the man. Gave him some advice.
        nomin   oblique
21. To-the-boy pleased the man. Went over to him.
        dative   nomin

Table 4.11. *Phoneme monitoring times at critical points following the anaphoric coreference and reading times of sentences following different antecedents (Pléh, 1983; Pléh & MacWhinney, 1987)*

Semantics	Agent-Object		Agent-Commit.		Exper.-Object		Exper.-Object	
Marking	nom	acc	nom	inst	nom	obl	dat	nom
First NP	nom	acc	nom	inst	nom	obl	nom	dat
Phoneme monit. (mseconds)	639	664	634	654	671	691	636	608
Reading time (seconds)	2.61	2.84	2.41	2.95	2.50	2.60	2.84	2.60

2. Perspectives or Topics Should be Animates.   In the competition type of experiments several data indicate that animacy is an important factor of sentence interpretation in Hungarian children at the first stages of their development, before case marking starts to dominate the entire picture. It is used, however, if not as a determinant of interpretation, as a very strong expectation, even by adults. In the experiment with possessive markers, for example, faster reaction times were obtained if the first noun was animate compared to when it was not. This effect was especially clear when the NVN order and the animacy were consonant: Interpretation time was 2200 milliseconds for NVN orders with an animate topic, as opposed to 2700 milliseconds for NNV orders with an inanimate topic.

In as yet unpublished experiments the main factor varied according to manipulations of the Competition Model was the agreement between the verb and the subjects (MacWhinney & Pléh, in preparation).   Only NVN (verb-middle) orders were used in this experiment.   The main result in connection with animacy interesting for us at this moment was that when the first noun was animate and the second inanimate, SVO orders produced a 2560 milliseconds mean reaction time, whereas OVS orders took 2800 milliseconds.   At the same time having an inanimate object fronted in the OVS order did not cause such conflicts as reflected in the 2480 milliseconds mean reaction times.   Thus additional evidence on adults was gained here that sentence initial animate subjects make for good topics or perspectives of a sentence.

Some data also indicated that not only do we expect an animate topic-perspective but we also expect that something closer to the ego of the speaker is used as the perspective of the sentence.   This concept used following MacWhinney (1977) and Ertel (1977) could be tested in our experiments since possessive nouns with both "mine" and "yours" endings were used.   If the speaker's ego-centered "mine" was ahead average reaction times were 2425 milliseconds, whereas if the "yours" was fronted reaction times increased to 2682 milliseconds when all other factors, especially phonetic similarity between the "yours" ending and the accusative -t, were controlled.

3. Topics or Perspectives Should be Definite.   This is a common observation emphasized many times since Clark and Haviland (1977) published their given-new contract principle.   As Clark and Clark (1977) summarize this side of the contract: Subjects make better topics than other NPs, and, in general, definite topics are better than indefinite ones. In the studies mentioned above several times, varying agreement between the verb and the nouns, an originally unexpected finding of ours supported this conception. In the study we were looking for, among other things, effects of the definiteness of the object on interpretation conflicts since in Hungarian there is a definiteness agreement between the object and the verb. Rather than this, it was found that Hungarian adult listeners, in general, expect to have a definite subject as the topic of the sentence; that is, a strong effect of definiteness for agent selection was found. In the study where both verbs and nouns were varied according to number and definiteness as well as case, sentence initial definite nouns were selected as agents 59% of the time (on a random basis the value should be 50% since case was systematicaly varied), whereas if the sentence initial noun was indefinite this value dropped to 48%. The coalition between the subject role and definiteness in sentence initial (topic) positions was also indicated by the fact that if the subject is indefinite in an SVO construction, interpretation slows down to 2,036 milliseconds compared to the case when it is definite (1,896), whereas in OVS constructions sentence initial definite objects result in slower interpretation (1,923 milliseconds) than sentence initial indefinite objects (1,836).

4. Semantically More Involved Participants Make Better Topics.   This is a trivial claim in the case of sentences with an active verb which denotes physical activity.   However, what happens if sentences are used where there is no real actor and surface marking deviates from the prototypical in the sense that a nonagent participant is coded in the nominative.   An interesting example of this is provided in Hungarian by certain experiencer constructions such as (21) where the experiencer – the one who "does the liking" – is in the dative case, whereas the object of the psychological relationship is in the nominative.

Using anaphora interpretation as a test of the "naturalness" of different orderings the following was found. After sentences like (21) the dative experiencer in the antecedent behaves like the nominative agents and experiencers following frames like (18)–(20). In 80% of the cases the antecedent dative was felt to be the subject of the second sentence if there was a pro-drop there (Pléh, 1983). Furthermore, as the processing load data in Table 4.11 show, structures were easier to process if the dative-experiencer was in the topic position. If there was an experiencer in the nominative then the nominative fronted constructions led to easier coreference identification. Thus, the most prototypical, best case is for subject, agent, nominative, and topic to coincide; if there is no agent in the sentence then the expectation is to have the semantically most active participant to become the topic, independent of the surface marking.

SOV with Indefinite Objects

The basic word order of sentences with indefinite objects is an issue not easily amenable for direct experimentation, especially in its developmental aspects. The reason for this is very simple: Prototypical sentences with an indefinite object in Hungarian are the ones where the level of transitivity in the sense of the language typologists (see Moravcsik, 1978) is low; action and its object are only partially differentiated, and compared to real transitives, the object in a sense only modifies the verb and concretizes its meaning. Typical sentences with object with no modifier would be things like "beer-drinks," "bread-eats," and "wood-cuts" with the necessary accusative on the object. The methodological problem for the psycholinguist with structures entailing such activities is simply that it is difficult to build up a real differentiating enactment type of task since the other participant (the object) is not a possible agent with these verbs, unlike the pet ones used in word order research like "chases."

The linguistic issue related to these structures is also rather complex: Some lexicalist syntactic approaches claim that in similar structures the objects belong to a larger class which cuts across traditional part of speech categorizations and which could best be labeled as *verbal modifiers* following Ackerman (1984) and Komlósy (1985). Verbal prefixes (locative or perfective bound morphemes), certain types of infinitive phrases ("wanted to drink"), and certain idiomatic expressions ("came to himself") also belong to this class. What is interesting about this class is that its members have a specifically assigned linear position in the sentence: They take the immediately preverbal slot otherwise occupied by the focus.

With regard to the neutral word order of sentences with an indefinite object two types of indirect data were gathered on similar constructions by Pléh, Ackerman, and Komlósy (1987). In adult subjects, paired relatedness judgments of each of the word pairs in sentences like (22) had shown that the strongest "togetherness" is felt by the subjects concerning the verb and the bare noun as object of the sentence. Furthermore, these judgments showed a stronger connection between indefinite objects and their verbs than between the verb and its definite object.

22. *A férfi sört ivott a kertben.*
   The man beer+ACC drank the garden+INESS.

This fact does not tell us anything, however, about basic word order here. In another experiment with 4- and 6-year-old children where elicited imitation (sentence repetition) was used, two types of evidence were obtained for the canonic or basic nature of SOV order with similar constructions. First, the repetition task was much easier for the children if the sentence was in a canonic (SOV-like) order: They were able to retell much more of the irrelevant material in the sentence besides the basic grammatical relations compared to the case when the modifier (O) was moved far away from the verb. Second, when the sentence was ungrammatical and contained two possible modifiers at the "O-slot," children tended to restructure the sentence: either they made a definite object out of the indefinite O which allows for other modifiers, for example perfective verbal prefixes in the sentence, or they omitted the other modifier (for example, the verbal prefix) and kept the SOV pattern.

Thus, there is some evidence that not only do children treat the SOV pattern as the basic one with indefinite objects but they also tend to realize the different behavior of seemingly similar constituents (the object) in the definite and the indefinite patterns.

Brain Asymmetries and Sentence Understanding

In connection with the studies on word order based strategies in Hungarian a specific "side issue" has been raised regarding the relationship between the development of brain asymmetries and sentence understanding strategies. In one of the few attempts to address this issue on large-scale empirical material, Thomas Bever (1971) had shown on American nursery-aged children that the development of dichotic asymmetries (as an index of the development of increasing left hemisphere specialization for language processing) is related to the appearance of order based strategies. One interpretation of this finding could be that the left hemisphere is the special serial order hemisphere and, therefore, order based strategies should be connected to it in any language.

Some empirical results seriously question this generalization. In the studies of nursery school children looking for the presence of the first-noun-as-the-agent strategy we have found that in Hungarian the opposite was true. Table 4.12 shows data from 178 children between the ages of 3 and 6, according to ear preference (Pléh, 1982). "Right ear" preferent children are supposed to be left hemisphere lateralized for language. In contrast to Bever's result we found that only children showing no signs of clear language lateralization showed an overgeneralized order based strategy which is indicated by a larger difference between correct percentage for subject first and object first sentences.

Notice especially that in children showing a reversed ear preference the order strategy was especially very weak. This negative finding left open several

Table 4.12. *Correct interpretation of sentences as a function of ear preference in a dichotic task in nursery school children (Pléh, 1981)*

	Right ear prefer	Left ear prefer	No ear prefer
Subject first sentences (%)	93	87	93
Object first sentences (%)	83	81	80

possibilities. One could argue that in a language where case marking is the basic cue to understanding, order based strategies belong to the less mature ones and with the development of lateral brain asymmetries they should be reduced and replaced by strategies specifically based on morphology.

In further studies we have made some attempt to clarify the issue of what sort of interpretation strategies do lateral asymmetries become connected to. In the unpublished research already referred to several times (Pléh, in preparation) data both on the order strategy in the possessive experiment and ending detection difficulty were compared to dichotic asymmetries. Concerning purely order based strategies the findings were even more negative than in the previous study: the error percent in constructions where a possessive noun (neutralized for accusative-nominative differences) was fronted followed by a clear nominative subject at the end of the sentence were 38, 38, and 41% in the right ear, left ear, and no ear preferent groups, respectively. On the other hand, as Table 4.13 shows, ear preference had some relationship to morphological sensitivity. In the analysis of variance computed from the data presented in the table, a significant ear preference by subject position interaction was found, $F(2,100) = 3.02$, $p < .05$. We should recall here that the general tendency was easier interpretation in sentences with an SVO order than sentences with an OVS order. This interaction means again that the order effect or overgeneralization of an order based strategy was clearly weaker in children with a strong left brain–right ear preference. There was a significant ear preference by subject position by stem type interaction as well, $F(6,300) = 3.43$, $p < .005$.

The meaning of this interaction was rather straightforward. Order based strategies appeared especially in children with left ear preference in sentences where a difficult accusative was fronted. They made 28% mistakes with OVS sentences beginning with a difficult accusative whereas the right ear preferent group made 17%, and the groups showing no ear preference made only 14% mistakes.

The specific behavior of the left ear preferent group is a bit surprising, since many studies group the children on the simple presence or absence of ear preference rather than the actual side of the preference. If we disregard this discrepancy and treat the left ear preferent children as ones where there is insufficient lateralization of speech processing to the left hemisphere, this study

Table 4.13. *Percent correct interpretation as a function of stem types, ear preference and the position of the subject (Pléh, in preparation)*

Ear preference	Left		Neutral		Right	
Word order	SVO	OVS	SVO	OVS	SVO	OVS
Difficult-Difficult	98	65	93	79	95	77
Difficult-Easy	96	78	97	92	94	88
Easy-Easy	91	89	92	89	95	92
Easy-Difficult	87	86	98	85	92	92
Total	93	80	95	84	94	87

gives some support to the hypothesis that in a case marking language like Hungarian left hemisphere based strategies might be related to fine morphological sensitivity rather than simply use of order as a cue. As Bever (1971, p. 234) has put it in his original formulation, *"the dominant hemisphere is the locus of the behavioral strategies of speech comprehension*: these strategies are acquired by the young child as functional lateralization develops as component of adult perceptual mechanisms." It seems to be that the left hemisphere might be the site of rather different strategies of this sort depending on typological characteristics of the language.

Three Approaches to Crosslinguistic Differences in Understanding

In the experimental psycholinguistic literature of the last decade a growing interest toward crosslinguistic comparisons can be observed. This is all the more understandable since most of the ambitious processing models have been put forward on the basis of material gained from a single language, English, which is remarkably unique in relying mainly on word order to convey grammatical information. The motivation for comparative work is two-fold: On the practical level it is only natural that, if one wants to build up workable models of understanding for a given language, data from the language are needed. On the other hand, in a more ambitious plan, data obtained from languages of different structure may be used to address theoretical issues connected to the universality of the models proposed solely on the basis of English language data.

One can approach crosslinguistic differences in understanding with three attitudes. The first is an unqualified universalistic attitude which claims that certain factors have unconditional predominance and priority in understanding and especially in its development. Thus, for example, strategies of understanding based on word order would be primary even in languages with a free word order to be substituted only later on by strategies based on features more specific to the given language, most notably case marking. This universalistic attitude exists both in a form closely tied to the universalistic approach in linguistics (e.g., Pinker, 1984) and in the form of universal expectations based on cognitive universals (Sridhar, this volume). For a characterization of the universalistic trend see Bates, MacWhinney, Caselli, Devescovi, Natale, and Venza (1984).

The second approach could be labeled as qualified universalism. Its advocates claim universal mechanisms with language dependent particularities. They suggest that the process of understanding is basically the same in all languages; however, the characteristics of the given language decide which features of all the possible ones are predominantly and primarily used in the given language to direct "syntactic understanding."

The two best known rival versions of this approach are taking diametrically opposed attitudes concerning the presupposed common, universalistic mechanisms as well as concerning the way crosslinguistic differences are organized and how they evolve in the child. The "canonic forms" hypothesis put forward by Slobin and Bever (1982; Slobin, 1981) is basically a holistic conception. Sentences are understood with reference to prototypical well formed sentence patterns which develop in children by coupling prototypical situations to the clearest encoding features for the given situation in the language. The approach is holistic in the sense that the prototypical sentence patterns act like "good Gestalts," that is, at the beginning all sentences are understood with reference to them. The child tries to fit every sentence to a small set of prototypical sentence forms. The approach is holistic in the further sense that understanding is based on entire sentence forms rather than isolated features of the input string.

The other approach taking the "universal mechanisms" attitude is the Competition Model put forward by Bates and MacWhinney (1982; Bates, McNew, MacWhinney, Devescovi, & Smith, 1982; MacWhinney, Bates, & Kliegl, 1984). Its basic premise relevant at this point is that understanding develops through perceptual abstraction of the relevance of given cues in the language.

The cues are isolated features of the input strings rather than characteristics of global sentence patterns. In the process of understanding, the cues act according to their relevance to code certain grammatical distinctions. They are acting in processing ungrammatical strings as well as well formed sentences, and the output of understanding is a result of computations made on the basis of separate cues. This approach is analytic compared to the "canonic forms" theory in two respects: It deals with isolated features of sentences, and it considers understanding or interpretation performance as an arithmetic product of different vectors. To put it in a metaphoric way, whereas in the "canonic forms" approach understanding is an issue of goodness of fit where a distance metric is used, it is a question of arithmetic equations according to the Competition Model.

There is a third possible approach: the typological one. One can very well imagine that, similar to linguistic typology, not only would the "content" of processing be different between languages but the mechanisms used as well. With regard to the above presented holistic-analytic issue one could hypothetize that, though in some languages processing is mainly made with reference to entire sentence patterns, and decisions are based on larger chunks of inputs, in other languages relatively short input chunks make possible grammatical decisions and in this sense the entire processing model is more analytic.

Although the data presented here on Hungarian do not provide direct evidence, they strongly suggest that in Hungarian this latter might be the case. That is, in the process of sentence understanding a more "on the spot" analytic type of mapping might go on compared to English where there is more need for overall sentence patterns to arrive at grammatical distinctions. Some other types of research, on line studies of sentence understanding, propositional integration, and accessibility within compound sentences suggested similar things: Hungarian speakers seemed to access the grammatical relations immediately upon attending the case markers, did not wait until the end of the clause with grammatical assignments, made predictions faster on the spot, etc. (Gergely, 1985). If this more analytic image of processing in Hungarian proves to be true we may have a strong case for typologically specific processing models in speakers of different languages which may even correspond to typologically different strategies developed by the left hemisphere. However appealing this typological perspective may sound it will have to be able at the same time to account for effects of word order in Hungarian which are "canonic form"-like phenomena in a basically analytic processing model. It may very well be that in the field of processing typology we will have to use the approach so familiar from other branches of social science. First, radically different ideal types will be postulated to be replaced by "mixed" type models more fitting to the varieties of real-life phenomena.

5   Cues to Sentence Interpretation in Warlpiri

Edith L. Bavin and Tim Shopen

Recent studies have shown that, in the early stages of language development, children utilize different cues for sentence processing depending on the nature of the language being acquired (Bates, McNew, MacWhinney, Devescovi, & Smith, 1982; Bates, MacWhinney, Caselli, Devescovi, Natale, & Venza, 1984; MacWhinney, Bates, & Kliegl, 1984; Slobin 1981, 1982; Slobin & Bever, 1982). For example, Slobin (1981) found that Turkish children would not respond consistently to utterances that lacked the necessary case marking. However, when case markings were used, Turkish two-year-olds did respond consistently to all six possible word orders of subject, object, and verb. This evidence indicates that case marking is a salient cue in sentence processing in Turkish from an early age, but that word order is not. MacWhinney, Pléh, and Bates (1985) report parallel findings for Hungarian. In English, on the other hand, there is no case marking, and word order is the dominant cue for children from 28 months of age.

Warlpiri[1] is a language of a type quite different from the Eurasian languages that have been the focus of earlier research. It is a Pama Nyungan language that is learned as a first language by children in the Yuendumu community located in the center of Australia about 300 km northwest of Alice Springs. A particularly unique aspect of Warlpiri is the extent to which it displays a "nonconfigurational" syntax. Hale (1983) distinguishes between two types of languages: configurational languages, such as English, and nonconfigurational languages, such as Warlpiri. Configurational languages have standard treelike structures for the verb phrase or the noun phrase. Nonconfigurational languages have a flatter structure which allows all the elements of the sentence to attach directly to the S node. The contrast between configurationality and nonconfigurationality is taken by many as a fundamental "parameter" of human language. Hyams (1986), Pinker (1984, 1987), and Roeper (1987) argue that in order to learn language, a child simply needs to find out the correct values for his language on a small number of such parameters. In acquiring Warlpiri, this would mean that the child could use the fact that many word order variations

[1] The research was funded by the Australian Research Grant Scheme and the Australian Institute of Aboriginal Studies. Many thanks to the Yuendumu community for allowing the research, and to Roger Wales for some advice on statistical analysis.

185

occur in the language as evidence that Warlpiri is nonconfigurational. Similarly, the child who is learning English would have to use the rigidity of the word order structures he observes to infer that English is configurational. The basic thrust of the parameter-setting proposal is that the decision to treat one's native language as either configurational or nonconfigurational (or any corresponding reformulation of this contrast) is a fairly sharp and precipitous decision, probably occurring over a matter of a few days, weeks, or perhaps a few months.

In addition to being nonconfigurational in terms of word order, Warlpiri also uses a rich and often complex system of morphology, including both ergative and other case markings. In this work, we are interested in understanding how young children learn to deal with the word order variation introduced by the nonconfigurational nature of Warlpiri and how they come to use this complex system of morphological markings to interpret sentences. Before examining the data, we will discuss some of the properties of Warlpiri that are relevant here.

Properties of Warlpiri

In Warlpiri, there is no necessary correlation between word order and the grammatical or pragmatic functions of noun phrases. Because of this, Warlpiri can be called a free word order language. A transitive sentence can have any of the six possible word orders of subject, object, and verb (SVO, SOV, VSO, VOS, OVS, and OSV) and a Warlpiri speaker will count them as repetitions of the same utterance. This means that, for each of the example sentences we give below there are always alternate word orders which we do not give. There are morphological and intonational means available for focusing elements in the clause; in addition, word order may have a subtle focusing effect though not in any predictable way. Two of the morphemes that may be used to focus a noun phrase are *ju* and *jala*. The form *ju* is used to focus a nominal which the speaker assumes represents old information for the hearer, whereas *jala* has an added element of meaning: the hearer should have known the identity. *Jurlpu-ju* "bird-FOCUS" used in a text would imply that the bird has already been introduced as a participant and is given some prominence in the particular clause. *Jurlpu-jala* would imply "It was the bird; you should have known." Other languages discussed in the current volume such as Italian, Turkish, and Hungarian also allow all six possible word orders and these word order variations, along with variations in stress, often express different types of focusing. In Warlpiri, focusing is expressed mainly by specific morphemes and intonation.

Warlpiri uses case markings to show the functions of nominals in the clause. The language uses ergative case for most transitive subjects and absolutive for intransitive subjects and most objects. The use of case markings makes it possible for the elements of a noun phrase to be discontinuous. A head and a modifier separated from each other carry the same case. For example, the ergative case is marked on both *jarntu* "dog" and *wita* "little" in the following sentence. (Note that the elements to be matched are discontinuous, but they could also be contiguous.)

1. *Jarntu-ngku   yalkurnu   wati   wita-ngku.*
    dog-ERG   bite_PAST   man   little-ERG
    "The little dog bit the man."

This freedom of order for modifiers and heads is a distinctive feature of Warlpiri. Other languages discussed in this volume such as Hungarian or Turkish have free word order for major constituents, but they retain strict order within the NP and show very little tolerance for separation or extraposition of elements from the NP. The fact that Warlpiri permits separation of a head from a modifier is made possible by the clear case marking on *both* constituents – a cue that is not found in Hungarian and Turkish.

Warlpiri uses case agreement not only to mark which modifiers go with which nouns; it also uses case agreement to mark part–whole relationships and nominal-adverbial modifications. The examples in (2) illustrate case agreement in these types of constructions:

2a. *Karnta-ngku   wirriya   parnparnu   rdaka.*
    woman-ERG   boy   touch_PAST   hand
    "The woman touched the boy on the hand."

Here the hand is understood as belonging to the boy because both nouns are unmarked and hence absolutive.

2b. *Ngarrka-ngku   marlu   panturnu   pirli-ngka-rlu.*
    man-ERG   kangaroo spear_PAST hill-LOC-ERG
    "The man speared the kangaroo on the hill."

Here the man is understood as being on the hill because both nouns carry the ergative case.

Although the case markers in Warlpiri carry a large functional load, they are not always "available" because the language allows ellipsis of the core arguments (i.e., ergative, absolutive, and dative). A system of cross-referencing is used to mark the person and number of subjects and objects, and in discourse these cross-reference markers are often the only overt representation of these arguments. All the examples we have given so far have used third person singular arguments for which the cross-reference markers are zero-morphs. However, there are distinct cross-reference markers for all other subjects and objects: first and second person singular dual and plural, third person dual and plural, and third person singular dative. Whereas nouns and independent pronouns follow an ergative-absolutive pattern, the pronouns which mark cross-reference follow the nominative-accusative pattern, as in (3).

3a. *Nyanyi   ka-rna-ngku.*
    see   AUX-1sgSUB-2sgOBJ
    "I am looking at you."

3b.   *Nyanyi   ka-npa-ju.*
     see   AUX-2sgSUB-1sgOBJ
     "You are looking at me."
3c.   *Yani   ka-rna.*
     go   AUX-1sgSUB
     "I am going."
3d.   *Yani   ka-npa.*
     go   AUX-2sgSUB
     "You are going."

The subject cross-reference markers are always used, although in imperatives only number is marked. However, the use of the object cross-reference markers is variable: indefinite, nonhuman objects are not usually cross-referenced. The cross-reference markers are clitics attached to an auxiliary base which generally occurs in second position in the clause, as in (3). If there is no auxiliary base the clitics are attached to the first constituent of the clause, as in (5b) and (5c). Third person absolutive objects are not always cross-referenced; plural forms may be used for cross-referencing nonplural arguments under certain conditions. Moreover, dative objects take precedence over absolutive objects according to Hale (1973, 1982), although we have found some variability. For the younger speakers there are some neutralizations taking place in the cross-referencing system, and also some innovations in the forms being used (Bavin & Shopen, 1987; Bavin, 1989).

Complex noun phrases illustrate another property of Warlpiri. When more than one word is contained in a continuous noun phrase, only the last one is required to carry case marking; the others may appear without case marking. For example,

4.   *Jarntu   wiri   yalampu-rlu   kuyu   ngarnu.*
    dog   big   that-ERG   meat   eat_PAST
    "That big dog ate the meat."

We have noted that the cross-referencing system follows a nominative-accusative pattern, whereas the nouns and independent pronouns follow an ergative-absolutive pattern. In fact, there are three case frames for transitive verbs: ergative-absolutive, absolutive-dative, and ergative-dative. The most common and frequent is the ergative-absolutive frame. The three case frames are illustrated below:

5a.   *Karnta-ngku   pakurnu   ngarrka.*
    woman-ERG   hit_PAST   man_ABS
    "The woman hit the man."
5b.   *Karnta-rla*   *rdipija*   *ngarrka-ku.*
    woman-ABS_3_SG_DAT   meet_PAST   man-DAT
    "The woman met the man."
5c.   *Karnta-ngku-rla*   *warrurnu*   *ngarrka-ku.*
    woman-ERG-3_SG_DAT   seek_PAST   man-DAT
    "The woman looked for the man."

There are also transfer verbs with an ergative-absolutive-dative case frame, and ergative-dative verbs derived from ergative-absolutive ones with a modification in meaning (attempted action rather than completed). Verb compounding is productive: preverbs are combined with verb stems; in some instances preverbs govern a dative argument which is added to the arguments of the verb stem. For example, *paarrpardimi* "fly" is a one-place predicate, whereas *jurnta-paarrpardimi* "fly away from" is a two-place predicate with the additional argument taking the dative case.

So the child must learn which case frames are used with each verb. There does seem to be some semantic correlation between the verb and case frame selected, but it is not always easy to predict which case frame a verb will take. Hale (1982) argues that the principle which governs the selection of the ergative-absolutive case frame is the notion of cause. When the subject of a two-place predicate causes a theme to be affected, it is marked with the ergative case. Examples include *kijirni* "throw," *pakarni* "strike," and *yarlkirni* "bite." The agent (ergative) does not have to deliberately cause the theme to be affected. Thus *kijirni* "throw," which is ergative-absolutive, can be used when something is accidentally released or dropped. Agents can be inanimate; rocks, wood, and grass are some of the objects that can cause something to be affected by an action, as in the following:

6. *Katurnu*   *kurdu   watiya-ngku.*
    press_down_PAST   child   wood-ERG
    "The wood pressed down on the child."

Verbs of perception and verbs such as *mardarni* "hold" also have the ergative-absolutive case frame.

For absolutive-dative verbs, the subject is generally an experiencer, whereas the (dative) object is not directly affected by the action. Verbs that fall into this case frame include *wangkami* "speak to" and *rdipimi* "encounter." The only simple verb stem that is subcategorized for the ergative-dative frame is *warrirni* "look for, seek." Other verbs can, however, appear with this case frame (compound verbs and ergative-absolutive verbs with a modification in meaning). The role of the dative case marker seems to be the marking of nonaffectedness of the argument.

To summarize, the choice between ergative-absolutive, absolutive-dative, and ergative-dative marking for transitive verbs is governed by complex semantic principles. These principles are probably not immediately obvious to the language-learning child who may have to learn these case frames for each verb individually at first.

A second major factor affecting ease of acquisition with the competition model is the detectability of a marking. Many Warlpiri grammatical markers are easily identified in the sound stream because there is relatively little fusion (except in the cross-reference marking pronouns; see Bavin & Shopen, 1987).

For example, number and case are signaled by separate morphemes, as can be seen in the words listed below:

7. *wirriya*   *wirriya-jarra*   *wirriya-patu*
    boy   boy-DUAL   boy-few
    wirriya-rlu   *wirriya-jarra-rlu*   *wirriya-patu-rlu*
    boy-ERG   boy-DUAL-ERG   boy-few-ERG

Nouns can carry a number of endings but the word is usually easy to segment into a sequence of morphemes that each convey one meaning. Consider, for example, the following two ergative nouns that could each serve as the subject of a transitive sentence. The (a) version means "the one with two children" and the (b) version "the two that each have a child."

8a. *kurdu-jarra-kurlu-rlu*
     child-DUAL-with-ERG
8b. *kurdu-kurlu-jarra-rlu*
     child-with-DUAL-ERG

Some of the case markings have phonologically conditioned allomorphs. For example, the ergative takes one of four shapes, *rlu, rli, ngku,* and *ngki.* The variant *rli* is used following high front stem vowels, and *ngki,* the variant of *ngku,* is used under the same conditions. This vowel harmony rule applies throughout the language so the dative also has allomorphs (*ku* and *ki*). These phonological conditionings of allomorphs do not affect the ease with which words are segmented and do not seem to cause problems for acquisition. The alternation between *rlu/rli* and *ngku/ngki* is conditioned by the length of the stem and does cause some confusion in production, although there is no evidence that the alternation leads to difficulties in detection. There are some exceptions to the rule that words of two syllables take the allomorphs *ngku/ngki* and these must be learned as exceptions. An example is *nyiya-rlu* "what-ERG" which is often produced by the children as *nyiya-ngku.*

Other markers are a bit more difficult to detect. The ergative and dative are monosyllabic; they are often unstressed and then lose their syllabicity. The syllabic pronunciations of the ergative allomorphs *ngku/ngki* and *rlu/rli* are fully voiced, whereas those of the dative *ku* and *ki* are often voiceless. When the ergative and dative lose their syllabicity, the consonant that remains to mark ergative or dative is difficult to detect because a following word always begins with a consonant. For example, notice the shortened form of the ergative in example (9):

9. *Wati-ng(ki)*   *nyangu.*
    man-ERG   see‗PAST
    "The man saw something."
    = watiŋɲaŋu

Also notice the shortened form of the dative in the following; the only trace of the case marking in (10) is in the lengthening of the velar stop:

10. *Karnta-ku   ka   pardarni wati.*
    woman-DAT AUX   wait_for   man
    "The man is waiting for the woman."
    = kaṇtak:a paḍaṇi wati

An assignable cue is one that can be immediately and locally bound to a function. Case marking is a local cue. But, when more than one word is contained in a continuous noun phrase in Warlpiri, only the last one is required to carry the case marking. In example (4), there is only one case marker for the three word noun phrase, but in (11), two nominals carry the ergative case.

11. *Wirriya-rlu jurlpu luwarnu   wiri-ngki.*
    boy-ERG   bird   shoot_PAST big-ERG
    "The boy shot the bird, the big one (=boy)."

Here *wirriya* "boy" must be matched with *wiri* "big," but the allomorphs for the ergative are *rlu* for one nominal and *ngki* for the other, because the words differ in length.

So far we have discussed problems with the detectability and assignability of case markers in Warlpiri. There are also major problems involving the "reliability" of these markings. These reliability problems arise because of homophony between grammatical markings. There are homophones for the four allomorphs for the ergative case: *ngku*, with the variant *ngki*, is also the clitic for the second person singular object, whereas *rlu*, with the variant *rli*, is the clitic for the first person dual inclusive subject. This homophony can lead to confusion [see examples (12) and (13)]. The form *rla* is one of the allomorphs of the locative as well as the third person singular dative cross-reference marker. As well as being the dative with the meanings "to, for, from," *ku/ki* is used in possessive constructions related to kinship. In perfective clauses the cross-reference markers are generally attached to the end of the first constituent of the clause, and if this constituent is a noun or noun phrase, the cross-reference markers can be mistaken for ergative case markers. The following examples illustrate some of the homophonous forms:

12. *Nyalali-rli   nyangu.*
    girl   see_PAST
    a. "The girl saw it."
    b. "You and I saw the girl."
    c. "They saw the girl."
13. *Karnta-ngku nyangu.*
    woman   see_PAST
    a. "The woman saw it."
    b. "He/she saw you as a woman."

In (12a) *rli* has the ergative meaning; in (12b) it has the meaning "first person dual inclusive subject"; in (12c) it has the meaning "third person plural subject." The forms *rlu* and *rli* are being used by speakers under 20 years of age in place of the traditional plural subject forms *lu* and *li*. In (13a), *ngku* has the ergative interpretation and in (13b) it has the meaning "second person singular object."

As noted above, the dative signals a wide range of meanings. The principles of agreement with secondary predicates mean that the core case markers have a wide distribution. For example, ergative case marking may appear on a locative as in (2b). The child must acquire the knowledge that a case marker may be used for agreement as well as to mark a grammatical function. The absolutive case is not reliable as a marker of object because it can be used for transitive subjects also, with verbs that take the absolutive-dative case frame. These properties all affect the *reliability* of case as a cue in sentence processing.

In addition to being high in homophony and, hence, low in reliability, case markers are not always *available*. Because there are three case frames for transitive verbs, the ergative does not always signal the subject and the absolutive does not always signal the object. Because nominals and their case markers may be ellipsed, the case markers are not always present. And because the ergative case marker may be left off *ngaju* "I" and *nyuntu* "you_SG" in certain conditions (Laughren, 1977), the ergative marker is not always present.

In summary, because case markers are not fully reliable or available and there is some cost in their detectability and assignability, their acquisition should be delayed and the young child should often be forced to rely on other cues to determine propositional structure. These other cues should include semantic cues and probability based on knowledge of the world. We do not think that stress is a potential cue because in adult speech it does not serve reliably to identify subjects or objects. Rather, as in English, stress in Warlpiri serves to emphasize any part of the clause.

The Acquisition of Warlpiri

In our initial investigations into sentence comprehension by Warlpiri children, we presented test sentences using the three case frames for transitive verbs. The children were asked to act out the sentences, which represented the six possible word orders of subject, object and verb. All the sentences were reversible in that each one contained two animate nouns. Subjects were 89 Warlpiri children aged from 3 years to 11. The results of the test reported on in Bavin and Shopen (1985) revealed that the Warlpiri children did not perform much above chance level until they were 5. This is in contrast to the results of the Berkeley cross-linguistic studies (Slobin, 1982) in which it was found that the youngest Turkish children tested (2 years) averaged more than 67 percent correct for agent-patient transitive sentences. These results also contrast with reports of early learning of case marking in Polish (Weist, 1983), Hungarian (MacWhinney, 1985), and Samoan (Ochs, 1982). We proposed that a number of factors influence the comparatively "late" acquisition of case markers: ellipsis of core arguments in the input data, the use of three case frames for transitive verbs, and the presence of homophones for the ergative and dative case markers. Although the ergative-absolutive is the most frequent marking type (and the first acquired according to the study), the use of dative case on a core argument with certain verbs and in certain situations tends to reduce the availability and reliability of ergative-absolutive marking and thereby tends to delay the overall acquisition of the system.

Although children under 5 years generally did not perform well on the comprehension test, they can *produce* ergative and dative case markers in appropriate contexts (Bavin, to appear). But it is not common to find a transitive sentence with two overt arguments produced by such young children.

Our early findings led us to investigate what cues the Warlpiri children would use in sentence processing before they had mastered the case system. In the next section we will discuss the study we designed to investigate this.

Design of Study

Subjects

Fifty Warlpiri children from Yuendumu participated in the test. Ten children were used for each of the five age groups, 3, 4, 5, 6, and 7 years. In fact the youngest child was a few days under 3. Subjects were used only if they were able to name all the practice items and could follow the directions for the practice sentences. With the one exception noted above, we were unable to get reliable responses from children under 3. Presumably the fact that Warlpiri children have very little practice in following directions (since they are not expected to) has some bearing on this. The children learn most things by observation, receiving very little verbal instruction. In addition to the fifty children, we tested six adults aged between 20 and 30 years on part or all of six of the eight tests described below (Tests 1, 3, 5, 6, 7, and 8) to find out what strategies adults would use in interpreting utterances with and without the necessary case markings. In those sentences that included case marking, adults *always* chose the noun with ergative case marking as actor, even when this created a conflict with probability. In the absence of case marking, semantics and event-probability were stronger cues than word order. These adults were all bilingual, but dominant in Warlpiri. The children were not bilingual. English is definitely a foreign language in the community, and the children have not had enough contact with English to be bilingual.

Materials

A total of 78 transitive sentences were included in the test. The subjects were asked to act out the sentences using toy animals, people, and objects. For each test item, two objects were set out and then the sentence was read. The children were asked to listen to the sentence before attempting the action. All conversation with the children was in Warlpiri. The testing took place in a variety of places, usually sitting on the ground in the shade outside, or in a building in the community.

The Eight Individual Tests

The study comprised a series of eight tests designed to compare the roles of animacy, case marking, verb semantics and word order as cues in early sentence processing. We split the eight tests into two groups. The items within each group were presented in random order. The sentences were all composed of one verb and two nouns. The animate nouns were: *puluku* "cow," *karnta* "woman," *nantuwu* "horse," *maliki* "dog," *wati* "man," *purlka* "old man," *marlu* "kangaroo," *warnapari* "dingo," *lingka* "snake," and *wardapi* "goanna." The inanimate nouns were: *pirli* "stone," *parraja* "cooliman," *watiya* "stick," *parla* "leaf," *marna* "grass," *yakajirri* "berry," and *karli* "boomerang." The verbs varied from test to test, but they were always in the past form.

Test 1: Subject Animacy × Word Order: Reversible Verbs

For the first group of sentences, we used a 2×6 design. All the verbs used took the ergative-absolutive case frame, and so in all examples subjects were marked. All the verbs used in this section allowed either animate or inanimate subjects. The verbs were *katurnu* "pressed down on," *parnparnu* "touched," and *yurnturnu* "capsized, tripped." All sentences contained one animate and one inanimate noun, and for half the sentences the animate was marked as subject; for the other half, the inanimate was marked as subject. The word orders were SOV, OSV, SVO, OVS, VSO, and VOS. In presenting the results, the SOV, SVO, and VSO orders are combined as SO orders. The OSV, OVS, and VOS orders are combined as OS orders. We decided to collapse the orders into these two groups because we found no differences between the three orders within each group; furthermore, we found no greater accuracy or preference for SVO orders.

Three sentences were used in each of the 12 cells for a total of 36 sentences. The inanimate nouns were names of common objects and the animate nouns were terms for humans or animals. Example sentences are given in (14), (15) and (16):

14. *Puluku-rlu   katurnu   pirli.* (SVO)
    cow-ERG   press_down_on_PAST rock
    "The cow stepped on the rock."
15. *Maliki yurnturnu watiya-rlu.* (OVS)
    dog   trip_PAST   stick-ERG
    "The stick tripped the dog."

Table 5.1. *The percentage of correct responses for animate and inanimate subjects by word order type*

		SO	OS	Both
Age 3	Animate	50.0	53.3	51.7
	Inanimate	50.0	50.0	50.0
	Both	50.0	51.7	50.8
Age 4	Animate	73.3	70.0	71.7
	Inanimate	50.0	46.7	48.3
	Both	61.7	58.3	60.0
Age 5	Animate	76.7	70.0	73.3
	Inanimate	63.3	46.7	55.0
	Both	70.0	58.3	64.2
Age 6	Animate	83.3	93.3	88.3
	Inanimate	53.3	30.0	41.7
	Both	68.3	61.7	65.0
Age 7	Animate	100.0	86.7	93.3
	Inanimate	76.7	70.0	73.3
	Both	88.3	78.3	83.3

16. *Parnparnu   marlu   parla-ngku.* (VOS)
    touch_PAST   kangaroo   leaf-ERG
    "The leaf touched the kangaroo."

The results indicate that the children have not entirely mastered the ergative case marking until the age of 7 years. Until that age, the overall percentage of correct responses was not more than 65% (see Table 5.1). Adults' responses for these sentences were 100% correct. Table 5.1 summarizes the cell and marginal means for Test 1.

The analysis of variance showed significant main effects for animacy, $F(1,45) = 7.241$, $p < .01$, age, $F(4,45) = 5.904$, $p < .001$, and word order, $F(1,45) = 5.264$, $p < .05$. None of the interactions were significant. At all ages, children were more likely to choose an animate noun as the subject. Except for age 3, the children correctly identified the subject more frequently if it preceded the object. As they got older, children were increasingly accurate in their choice of the subject.

We also computed the number of animates chosen as subject regardless of whether the noun was marked as subject or not. At age 3 some children chose the animate noun as subject in all the sentences, whereas others always chose the inanimate noun as subject. However, the overall percentage of correct choices at age 3 was 50.8%. Choice of the animate noun as subject increased to 61.7% at age 4, 59.2% at age 5, and then peaked at 73.3% at age 6, after which it declined to 60.0% at age 7 and 50.0% for the adults.

The analysis of variance showed that animacy was a stronger cue than word order. We can see this not only in the F values, but also by noting that the

Table 5.2. *The percentage of correct responses in Test 2*

	Animate subjects	Inanimate subjects	Overall
Age 3	86.7	23.3	55.0
Age 4	81.7	38.3	60.0
Age 5	81.7	40.0	60.8
Age 6	91.7	61.7	76.7
Age 7	95.0	71.7	83.3

difference between animate and inanimate responses is higher than between the word orders. For both ages 5 and 6, the difference between scores for inanimate subjects preceding objects versus those following objects is high. When an inanimate noun is marked as subject and it follows the object, the children in those two groups (5 and 6 years) will frequently make the error of choosing the animate noun as subject.

Test 2: Subject Animacy × Word Order, Nonreversible verbs

The design of Test 2 followed the design for Test 1, but the verbs were chosen from those that take only animate subjects. These verbs were: *ngarnu* "ate," *jampurnu* "licked," *parnti-ngangu* "smelled," *nyangu* "saw," and *yalkurnu* "bit." This means that half the sentences violated selectional restrictions on the animacy of the subject. Two example sentences follow:

17.   *Jampurnu   nantuwu-rlu   parla.*   (VSO)
      lick_PAST   horse-ERG   leaf
      "The horse licked the leaf."
18.   **Puluku   nyangu   pirli-ngki.*   (OVS)
      cow   see_PAST   rock-ERG
      "The rock looked at the cow."

When using the verb *nyangu* "saw," we used a divider between the two toys and the child was required to move the agent around the divider to demonstrate the action "see." To demonstrate the action "lick," the child was required to pick up the agent and have it make contact with the other object. By comparing the results for the sentences in Test 1 with those in Test 2 we could evaluate the role of verb semantics as a cue in processing.

Table 5.2 gives the percentages of correct responses. They indicate that animacy was a particularly important cue in determining the subject of sentences with nonreversible verbs.

The main effect of animacy was highly significant, $F(1,45) = 59.75, p < .0001$, as was the main effect of age, $F(4,45) = 7.16, p < .001$. Note that the verbs in Test 2 sentences were selected because they require animate subjects. For all five groups there was a higher percentage of correct responses for those sentences that contained animate subjects in Test 2 (Table 5.2) than for those in Test 1 (Table 5.1). With the exception of age 6, the reverse is true for sentences with inanimate subjects. The main effect of word order was not significant and there was no significant interaction of animacy with word order.

Comparison of Tests 1 and 2

The only difference between Tests 1 and 2 was that in Test 1 the verbs were reversible, whereas in Test 2 they were nonreversible. We submitted the results from Test 1 and Test 2 to a single analysis of variance. We found no significant main effect for the factor of reversibility. However, there was an interaction between animacy and reversibility, $F(1,45) = 5.007$, $p < .05$. There was no interaction between word order and reversibility, although there was a significant three-way interaction between reversibility, animacy, and word order ($p < .05$). There was also a significant interaction between age, animacy, and word order, $F(4,45) = 3.06$, $p < .05$.

Each of these is significant at only the $p < .05$ level and the relation among the interactions is fairly complex. The interaction between animacy and reversibility appears at all ages except at age 7. The three youngest groups chose more animate nouns as subjects in Test 2 than in Test 1 (81.7% vs. 50.8% at age 3, 71.7% vs. 61.7% at age 4, and 70.8% vs. 59.2% at age 5). However, there is much less difference between the percentage of animates chosen in the two tests for the 6-year-olds (73.3% vs 65.0%) and the 7-year-olds show no difference at all (60.0% vs. 61.7%). However, independent of reversibility, there is a main effect of animacy in both tests, since, if the children had only been using case markings as the cue in interpreting the sentences, there should have been a 50% score for choice of animate noun as subject.

The interaction of word order with reversibility and animacy is due to a tendency for animacy to overcome word order with nonreversible sentences. In addition, the interaction of age with animacy and word order was due to a tendency for older subjects to pay somewhat more attention to word order when it contradicted animacy. Together, these interactions indicate that all subjects rely particularly strongly on animacy for nonreversible verbs, even when the word order has the object before the subject. Figures 5.1 and 5.2 show that, at the younger ages particularly, animacy is a more salient cue for Test 2 than for Test 1. That is, the children are more likely to select an animate noun as subject when the verb requires an animate subject. Older children can violate this requirement when the case marking indicates an event such as "The rock looked at the cow." By 7 years of age, the child is clearly able to override nonreversibility and use the ergative case marker as the cue for identifying subjects. However, for reversible verbs there is not a sharp conflict between animacy and case marking.

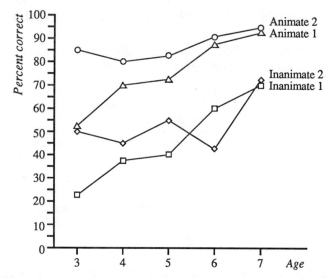

Figure 5.1. The percentage of correct responses for animate and inanimate subjects in Tests 1 and 2.

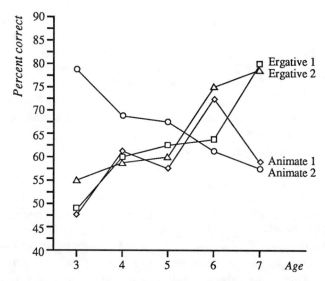

Figure 5.2. The choice of case marked noun vs. the choice of animate noun in Tests 1 and 2.

Test 3: Word Order × Animacy × Reversibility (No Case)

This test was composed of twelve sentences with no case markings, half containing the reversible verbs of Test 1 and half containing the nonreversible verbs of Test 2. Each sentence had an animate and an inanimate noun. Half the sentences had the animate noun before the inanimate and the other half had the reverse. So the orders were AI and IA, where A stands for animate noun and I stands for inanimate noun. The design was 2×2×6. As in Tests 1 and 2, all six word orders were used, although they are merged into SO and OS types in the analysis of variance.

Two example sentences for this set follow. Note that these sentences are ungrammatical because there is no case marker.

19. *Parnparnu   wati   watiya.*   (VNN)
    touch_PAST   man   stick
20. *Marlu   yakajirri   ngarnu.*   (NNV)
    kangaroo   berry   eat_PAST

As in Test 2, reversibility was a significant variable in that more animates were chosen as subjects for nonreversible sentences than for reversible ones, $F(1,45) = 5.725$, $p < .05$. Both reversibility and animacy are stronger cues than word order. In reversible sentences, word order played a slightly more important role than it did in nonreversible sentences (see Table 5.3). This was reflected in a significant interaction of reversibility with word order, $F(1,45) = 8.199$, $p < .01$.

For the adults, we only included sentences with reversible verbs. There was too much variation in the responses to say there was one overriding strategy, but adults tended to choose the animate noun as subject. Overall for the groups, the difference between how many first nouns were chosen as subject in the reversible sentences versus the nonreversible was significant. More animates were chosen for the nonreversible sentences than for the reversible, regardless of whether they were first or second nouns. For all groups, more inanimate nouns were chosen in the reversible than the nonreversible sentences.

Test 4: Word Order with No Other Cues (No Case Marking)

Test 4 was composed of six sentences with nonreversible verbs and no case marking. These sentences were used to test for a word order bias when no other cue was available. Three sentences had both nouns animate and three sentences had both nouns inanimate. Three word order variations (NNV, NVN, and VNN) were used for each of these two types of sentences.

No significant results were found. Overall, only the 5-year-olds showed a strong bias toward first noun as subject when no other cues were available. The 4-year-olds tended to take the first of two animates, and the 5-year-olds the first of two inanimates (see Table 5.4).

Test 5: Word Order × Probability (with Case Marking)

In this test we examined the effect of event probability on subject choice. To do this, we used verbs which are inherently reversible, but for which some

Table 5.3. *The choice of first noun as "subject" in Test 3*

	Reversible		Nonreversible	
	AI	IA	AI	IA
Age 3	53.3	46.7	73.3	20.0
Age 4	73.3	46.7	83.3	23.3
Age 5	56.7	70.0	76.7	33.3
Age 6	90.0	36.7	60.0	26.7
Age 7	63.3	30.0	63.3	20.0

Table 5.4. *The percentage of first nouns chosen as subject (no case)*

	AA	II
Age 3	56.7	60.0
Age 4	66.6	56.7
Age 5	76.7	76.7
Age 6	56.7	63.3
Age 7	56.7	70.0

constellations of actors are more likely than others. The test included six sentences with probable events and six with improbable events. The improbable events used the verbs of the probable events, but reversed the actors. In addition, we varied the order of the noun with ergative marking. In half of the sentences, the noun with ergative marking occurred first; in half it occurred second.

We determined which events to include by asking adults in the community. For example, a snake biting a woman is a common occurrence, but a woman biting a snake is just as unlikely as a man biting a dog. Only those sentences for which ten adults agreed were likely events, or were unlikely events (often accompanied with much laughter) were used. All nouns in these sentences were animate to control for an animacy bias. Examples follow:

21. *Purlka   yalkurnu   maliki-rli.*
     old man   bite_PAST   dog-ERG
     "The dog bit the old man." (OS order, likely event)
22. *Karnta-ngku   maliki   jampurnu.*
     woman-ERG   dog   lick_PAST
     "The woman licked the dog." (SO order, unlikely event)

The results in Table 5.5 show a significant developmental trend; as the children get older they have a higher percentage of sentences correct. The main effect of age was significant, $F_{(4,45)} = 3.086$, $p < .05$. At each age level, the difference between the number of probable subjects and improbable subjects identified

Table 5.5. *The percentage of correct responses in Test 5*

	Improbable	Probable	Overall
Age 3	40.0	75.0	57.5
Age 4	40.0	81.7	60.8
Age 5	48.3	78.3	63.3
Age 6	65.0	86.7	75.8
Age 7	70.0	88.3	79.1
Adults	100.0	100.0	100.0

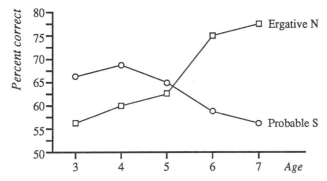

Figure 5.3. The choice of case marked noun versus the choice of probable subject.

correctly was significant. Word order was not significant. For the adults, the case marked noun was selected as the subject.

Figure 5.3 shows that by age 6 case marking comes to have more weight as a cue for identifying the subject of a sentence than does knowledge of probable events. Comparing Figure 5.3 with the results for Test 2 in Figure 5.2, we see a similar developmental pattern in terms of increasing reliance on case as a cue in sentence processing.

Test 6: Word Order and Probability (No Case Marking)

Six sentences without case markings were included to compare the roles of word order and probability as cues in sentence parsing. In three sentences the unlikely agent was the first noun; in three others the probable agent was the first noun. Table 5.6 shows the results for these sentences.

Across groups, the first noun was chosen as subject less than 30% of the time if it was an improbable subject. Word order is not a strong cue when it is in competition with probability. The main effect of probability was highly significant, $F(1,45) = 147.254$, $p < .0001$. For the adults, the most usual strategy was to interpret the sentence with its probable reading.

We can compare the results from Test 6 (Table 5.6) with those of Test 3

Table 5.6. *Probability of the first noun as subject and its effect on the choice of the first noun as "subject" in Test 6*

	Improbable	Probable
Age 3	30.0	70.0
Age 4	26.7	80.0
Age 5	23.3	96.7
Age 6	26.7	90.0
Age 7	43.3	83.3
Adults	100.0	100.0

Table 5.7. *The percentage of correct choices by word order and animacy type*

		SO	OS
Age 3	AA	63.3	46.7
	II	53.3	46.7
Age 4	AA	73.3	76.7
	II	66.7	66.7
Age 5	AA	86.7	70.0
	II	83.3	56.7
Age 6	AA	96.7	70.0
	II	63.3	76.7
Age 7	AA	96.7	90.0
	II	73.3	73.3
Adults	AA	100.0	100.0
	II	100.0	100.0

(Table 5.3), since both tests had sentences with no case marking. The figures in the two tables (5.3 and 5.6) indicate that animacy persists as a cue in sentence processing for a longer period than probability when it is in competition with word order and no case is marked. For the 7-year-olds, when the improbable subject was the first noun, 43.3% chose it as subject. In comparison, only 30% chose the inanimate as subject when it was the first noun in reversible sentences and 20% when it was the first noun in nonreversible sentences.

Test 7: Word Order × Animacy Type (with Case Marking)

Six sentences included only animate nouns, and another six included only inanimate nouns. All had a case marked subject and in each set of six there were three sentences in which the subject preceded the object; in the others it followed the object. The verbs were selected from those that allow inanimate subjects. These items were included to see if word order was used as a cue when no animacy cue was available. Table 5.7 summarizes the results.

Adults were always correct on these sentences, relying on case marking as their cue to sentence interpretation. The children were less consistent. They were more likely to score correctly when two animates were included than when two inanimates were included. Except for the 3-year-olds and the 6-year-olds, the scores for the second noun subjects were higher when both nouns were animate than when both nouns were inanimate. For all groups, the scores for first noun chosen as subject were higher with two animates than with two inanimates. It is clear that, from age 4 on, children are making increasingly reliable use of the case marker as a cue to sentence interpretation. However, even at age 7, the use of this cue is not fully stabilized. Word order was a significant variable, $F(1,45) = 4.645$, $p < .05$, as was animacy type, $F(1,45) = 9.220$, $p < .01$. The interaction between word order and animacy type was not significant overall. Note that the effect of animacy type was stronger than that of word order.

Test 8: Case Frame by Word Order

We included a set of twelve sentences to compare the children's performance with ergative-absolutive case marking and ergative-dative case marking. The nouns were all animate. The ergative-absolutive verbs were *pungu* "attacked" and *yunturnu* "capsized, tripped." The ergative-dative verbs were *warrurnu* "sought" and *nyangu* "looked for." The results are summarized in Figure 5.4. This figure shows the percentage of correct responses by case frame.

Adults performed correctly on all these sentences. The 4-year-olds had a 70% correct score for both case frames. In this condition, there was no competition from animacy or probability. Although the 5-year-olds had a higher score than the 4-year-olds in the ergative/absolutive case frame sentences (85%), their score was lower for the ergative/dative sentences (56.7%). This result indicates that the 5-year-olds expect a transitive sentence to have the canonical form of an ergative/absolutive case frame (see Bavin & Shopen, 1985a).

Table 5.8 summarizes the results by word order. For the ergative/absolutive sentences there was a word order bias favoring the SO order. This is particularly noticeable for the 6- and 7-year-olds. For the 4-year-olds there was a 13% difference for OS sentences between the ergative-dative and the ergative-absolutive case frames, indicating that, for this age group, the easiest sentences to process are those with the first noun marked as object and the second marked as subject. For the 5-year-olds, there was a 40% difference for OS orders between the ergative/absolutive and the ergative/dative case frames. The first case marked noun was taken as subject, regardless of the case form. For the 6-year-olds there was a clear preference for the first noun as subject for both case frames, and this pattern extends to age 7. Across groups, the percentage correct for SO word order is higher in ergative/absolutive sentences than in ergative/dative sentences. This shows that two case marked nouns in one sentence may cause some confusion in terms of identifying the subject.

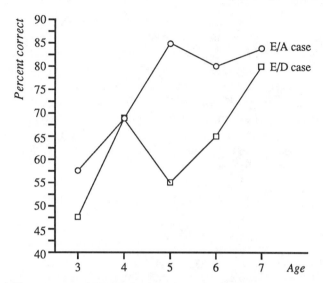

Figure 5.4. The percentage of correct responses by case frame.

The effect of age was significant, $F(4,45) = 5.368$, $p < .01$. Word order was significant, $F(1,45) = 23.151$, $p < .0001$. Case frame was also significant, $F(1,45) = 8.777$, $p < .01$.

Conclusion

We have seen that, for Warlpiri children under the age of 5, semantic and pragmatic cues in sentence processing are much stronger than case marking. Starting at the age of 5, case marking becomes a stronger cue than the semantic and pragmatic cues, and by the age of 7 it is the predominant cue in all conditions tested. We created two tests (1 and 2) with transitive sentences each having an animate and an inanimate noun. The two conditions differed only in verb semantics. The differences in results between these two conditions demonstrate that from an early age verb semantics plays an important role in restricting the choice of subject until the case system has been mastered.

Word order is the weakest cue. When it is in competition with animacy and probability, it is not a highly valued cue. When we removed animacy and probability as cues in the test situation, word order became a stronger predictor of responses. There was a trend for the first noun to be chosen as subject but not for all age groups and not for all conditions.

These results provide a nice illustration of the basic principles of the Competition Model. Like the other free word order case-marking languages that have been studied – Turkish and Hungarian – Warlpiri shows only a marginal use of word order as a cue. It is not a reliable cue in the input and children do

Table 5.8. *The percentage of correct responses by case frame and word order*

		E/A	E/D
Age 3	SO	63.3	53.3
	OS	53.3	43.3
Age 4	SO	73.3	60.0
	OS	66.7	80.0
Age 5	SO	96.7	70.0
	OS	83.3	43.3
Age 6	SO	96.7	90.0
	OS	63.3	53.3
Age 7	SO	96.7	90.0
	OS	73.3	76.7
Adults	SO	100.0	100.0
	OS	100.0	100.0

not attempt to rely on it. However, Warlpiri differs from Turkish and Hungarian in that the learning of its case-marking system is heavily burdened by problems with detectability, availability, and reliability. In this regard, it is more like the case-marking systems of Serbo-Croatian or German which come in much later than those of Turkish and Hungarian (Smith, 1985; MacWhinney et al., 1985; Mills, 1986). In learning Warlpiri case marking, children must first overcome problems in detecting the affixes. Then they must attempt to sort out the homophony by attaching each homophone to the correct set of cues. During this process of sifting out cues and homophones, they must still continue with the work of understanding sentences. To do this, they make use of animacy, verb reversibility, and event probability.

These data provide no evidence of any sudden emergence of either the case system or any other indicator of the "nonconfigurational" status of the language (Hale, 1983). There is no evidence that at some point the child decides to set a particular "parameter" on the language, as suggested in accounts such as those of Hyams (1986), Pinker (1984, 1987), and Roeper (1987). Instead, the evidence indicates a slow continual growth in understanding of a rich and complex system of case marking that the child eventually controls despite initial problems with detectability, availability, and reliability.

Part II. Sentence Production

6 Cognitive Structures in Language Production: A Crosslinguistic Study

S. N. Sridhar

Introduction

Over the last two decades, solid advances have been made in the study of sentence production. Researchers have begun to address the difficult problem of identifying the variables affecting the syntactic structure and content of sentences. A number of theoretical proposals delineating the assumed effect of perceptual, attentional, and discourse-related factors have appeared, along with limited empirical evidence investigating those variables. This literature has been reviewed in Clark and Clark (1977), Flores d'Arcais (1975), MacWhinney (1977), Osgood and Bock (1977), Sridhar (1980), and Bock (1982). Although many of these variables (e.g., perceptual salience, ego involvement) are presumed to be universally applicable, the empirical support adduced, however, has been based for the most part on data from English and Dutch.

This paper is intended as a modest contribution to several interrelated issues in current psycholinguistic research: (a) What factors beyond those invoked in autonomous models of grammar determine the syntax and semantics of sentences? (b) Are these factors language-specific or are there universals of language performance? (c) Is it possible to demonstrate empirically the operation of putative psycholinguistic universals? The basic hypothesis of this study is that a number of crucial properties of human language – including word order, clause order, choice of perspective, structure of locative expressions, degree and type of elaboration of referential expressions, negation, transitivity, and a host of others – are determined by universal cognitive principles involving the perceptual, motivational, and communicative dynamics of human information processing. This hypothesis, in a less elaborate form, was first tested in an informal experiment by Charles Osgood (see Osgood, 1971), in which a small number of English speakers were asked to "simply describe," in single sentences, a set of simple states and actions designed to induce certain basic cognitive distinctions such as that between figures and grounds, given and new information, and so forth. The results obtained led to a crosscultural extension of the "simply describing" paradigm, involving some fourteen language-culture communities in different parts of the world, and a large number of functional factors hypothesized to affect sentence form and content. In this paper, I shall discuss a subset of the results from this experiment – those that deal with the effect of perceptual and attentional factors – with reference to ten languages from different parts of the world. I must emphasize that the experiment involves a large number of other functional hypotheses and other languages than those reported on here. The data have not yet been fully analyzed and interpreted, so the present paper should be regarded as preliminary and tentative. The paper is also highly abbreviated, focusing on the presentation of the theoretical and empirical outlines of the current experiment at the expense of a review of the interesting and important related literature including the work of Levelt, McNeill, Tomlin, Bock, and Johnson-Laird. A more detailed account, covering several additional hypotheses and related results, may be found in Sridhar (1988).

Theoretical Background

Two sets of performance principles underlie the specific predictions tested here about universal characteristics of sentences that "simply describe" certain types of perceptual scenes: (1) a set of Perceptual Principles – deriving from the information orderings determined by prelinguistic perceptual experience; and (2) a set of Salience Principles – deriving from the momentary interests and motivations set up in speakers by the informational input.

Perceptual Principles

The intimate connection between language and perception is, of course, obvious: "the perceptual system is the primary means through which language acquires a semantics" (Pylyshyn, 1978, p. 174). The well-known work of Berlin and Kay (1969) on color terms, H. Clark (1973) on spatial and temporal expressions, Bierwisch (1967) on semantic universals, E. Clark (1973) and others on overextensions in child language, among many others, demonstrates that a number of aspects of language are perceptually anchored.

The first set of performance principles is based on the hypothesized continuity between the cognitive structures developed in prelinguistic, perceptual information processing and those later utilized in language processing. According to Osgood's "Naturalness Principle," "the more sentences correspond in their surface forms to the cognitive structures developed in prelinguistic perceptuo-motor experience, the earlier they will be understood and produced by children and the more easily they will be processed in both comprehending and expressing by adults" (1980, p. 111). These prelinguistic perceptual structures, according to Osgood, are partly innate and partly learned. They include innate properties such as Gestaltlike predispositions, and the tendency to organize behavior hierarchically and to differentiate units within each level componentially, and learned traits such as the distinctiveness of componential meaning features and the significance of feature combinations.

The work of Gibson (1969), Bower (1974), and others on human perceptual development shows that infants as young as 22 weeks display quite sophisticated perceptual discriminations (as indexed, e.g., by visual trackings and fixations). (1) Infants attend to "point-at-able" entities (particularly animates) involved in both action and stative relations; (2) they distinguish between the sources (agents) and the recipients (objects) of action relations and between the figures and grounds of stative relations (Golinkoff, Hirsh-Pasek, Cauley, & Gordon, 1987); (3) they follow entities involved in temporal sequence of events; (4) they find change of state more salient than constant states.

These findings provide a developmental backdrop for a series of perception-based performance principles which are outlined below in the form of a set of specific hypotheses.

Hypothesis 1. In describing perceptual scenes, figures of states and sources of actions tend to be (a) chosen as perspectives; and (b) expressed earlier in the sentence than grounds of state and recipients of action, respectively.

The hypothesized correlation between perceptual prominence and sentence-initial placement follows up on MacWhinney's observation that "the starting point is always the first element to attract the listener's attention" (1977, p. 155). Note that the initial position is also, in the overwhelming majority of the world's languages, correlated with the subject relation in unmarked sentences.

Given several alternative aspects of a perceptual scene that may be verbalized, the second hypothesis predicts which aspect will be selected for expression:

Hypothesis 2. Natural perceptual salience yields a continuum of expressive preference: actions > changes of states > constant states.

This hypothesis is based on the relative informativeness of the three types of relations and is related to the natural tendency to attend to change and movement, especially when movement is controlled by an identifiable entity.

The third hypothesis concerns the choice of expressions for describing objects in spatial relations. As Clark, Carpenter, and Just (1973) have observed, the structure of the human perceptual system is constrained in such a way that "the only visible, fully perceptible part of the perceptual field is that quadrant of space in front of the perceiver and above ground level..." (p. 238). This fact yields the "rule": "People prefer to code the locations of objects positively, where upwardness and forwardness are positive dimensions" (ibid). Based on this observation, the following hypothesis is proposed:

Hypothesis 3. Given that the primary perceptual receptors of the human organism are located on top of and in front of the body, people will tend to describe (a) vertical arrays from top down, that is, by locating objects at the top with reference to those below; and (b) horizontal arrays from front to back, that is, by locating objects near to the perceiver with reference to those away from the perceiver.

The final perception-based hypothesis relates to the order of expression of temporally related events. Given that in prelinguistic experience, events prior in time must be prior in perceptual processing, it is assumed that this order is carried over into linguistic processing.

Hypothesis 4.   The natural order for describing temporally related events will be one that retains the order in which the events are ordinarily perceived in non-linguistic experience.

Salience Principles

The principles discussed in the previous section refer to the description of "unmarked" perceptual inputs. However, these principles may sometimes reinforce and sometimes conflict with other functional principles. The most important of the latter group are Salience Principles that reflect the transient motivational states set up in speakers by the perceptual input.

Linguists and psychologists have invoked salience to account for a variety of phenomena, ranging from contrastive stress to word order and grammatical relations. Wundt (1901, in Blumenthal 1970, p. 29), Bloomfield (1914, pp. 113–14), and Jespersen (1924, pp. 167–8) are among those who have proposed a correlation between high attentional value and (either directly or indirectly through subjectivalization) sentence-initial placement of a constituent. Bloomfield is, however, the only one to claim that the salient constituent may also be displaced to the end of the sentence. However, this is not inconsistent with the position of the Prague School linguists who claimed that the communicative dynamism of the sentence leads to the "new" information being placed after the "old" information. We will return to this point later. Fillmore (1977, pp. 74–8) has proposed a "saliency hierarchy" or hierarchy of importance, which determines which element in the situation (or the "cognitive scene") gets included in the perspective from which the situation is described in the sentence, i.e., foregrounded. The elements of this hierarchy include humanness, change of state, totality, and definiteness. In Chafe's (1977) theory, "conceptual salience" (resulting from information value and ego involvement), rather than the placement of a particular sentence constituent, determines which aspect of a situation gets verbalized. MacWhinney (1977) shows that the "starting points" of sentences tend to serve one of the four functions: (1) agent, (2) given information, (3) attentional focus, and (4) perspective. Elaborating the notion of "perspective," he points out that speakers tend to prefer starting points that are "above" to those that are "below" and large starting points to small ones.

The notion of salience and its linguistic correlates proposed here draws upon the ideas referred to above. Three determinants of salience are proposed: (1)

vividness, the intrinsic meaningfulness of entities, defined both denotatively (e.g., human, animate) and affectively (e.g., intense codings for evaluation, potency, and activity on the semantic differential scale); (2) speaker motivation (e.g., ego involvement, perceptual focus); and (3) topicality, the relatively high availability of the meanings of recently processed entities.

Given the current state of knowledge regarding the relationship between information structure and grammatical relations, no claim is made about the grammatical relation assigned to the salient constituent. However, it is predicted that the salience of a constituent would result in its being placed either initially or finally in the sentence, at the attentional foci for the hearer.

Hypothesis 5. Constituents rendered salient by their (a) intrinsic semantic vividness, (b) motivation of speaker, or (c) topicality (recency of prior cognizing) will tend to be placed initially or finally.

There is quite a bit of preliminary evidence supporting or consistent with the five hypotheses listed above. I will not review that literature here (see Sridhar, 1988) for an extensive critical discussion) except to note that almost all of the studies in question deal with a single language, most often English.

Method

Design

The hypotheses outlined above were among those tested in a crosslinguistic sentence production experiment. The relevant cognitive distinctions were embodied in a color film that contained seventy perceptual scenes and ran for an hour. The subjects were instructed to describe each scene in a single sentence. There were two reasons for using the film medium: (1) subjects had to be provided controlled "raw material" for their sentences without using language for this purpose, since language was the dependent variable; (2) the inputs had to be held constant across a diverse range of socio-cultural experimental situations.

The film featured a male "actor" and various everyday objects (e.g., balls, blocks, dolls, spoon, plate, cup, etc.) taking part in various action and stative relations. The composition of the scenes and the order of their appearance were designed to create a variety of cognitive contrasts and presuppositions which served as the independent variables.

Various cinematographic techniques were used to code the perceptual dimensions being studied. The contrast between a new perception and a familiar perception was encoded by the contrast in the film between first versus repeated presentation of an entity. Negation was encoded by the absence of objects that had been seen in an immediately preceding scene. The distinguishing use of modifiers was encoded by the presence of similar but not identical objects in arrays. Salience was encoded by greater relative size, camera focus, and presence of humanlike entities, and so forth. It is important to keep in mind

Table 6.1. *A selection of the languages involved in the "simply describing" experiment*

Language (variety)	Collection site	Basic word order	Language family	Number of subjects
Cantonese	Hong Kong	SVO	Sino-Tibetan	37
Modern Hebrew (Israeli)	Haifa	SVO	Afro-Asiatic (Semitic)	26
Finnish	Jyvaskyula	SVO	Uralic (Finnic)	29
Slovenian	Ljubjana	SVO	Indo-European (Slavic)	18
English (American)	Champaign	SVO	Indo-European (Germanic)	30
Spanish (Mexican)	Mexico City	SVO	Indo-European (Romance)	34
Hungarian	Budapest	SOV/SVO	Uralic (Ugric)	34
Japanese	Tokyo	SOV	Altaic (Japanese)	37
Kannada	Mysore	SOV	Dravidian (South)	30
Turkish	Ankara	SOV	Altaic (Turkic)	25
Total				300

that the film was designed to control not only the perceptual stimuli themselves but the speakers' construal of the stimuli. Though total control can never be established, the systematic manipulation of the content of the scenes and the contexts (sequence) in which they are presented permits us to focus on the speakers' construal of the stimuli on the basis of the contrasts within minimal pairs of scenes.

Since the functional principles tested in this study are based on assumptions about panhuman perception, they are expected to hold for all languages. Hence, a crosslinguistic design was adopted. The film has been shown in fourteen language communities around the world so far, and data from ten languages have been analyzed and will be reported on here.

The ten languages (see Table 6.1) in the present sample include languages of different basic word orders (SVO and SOV), structural types (inflectional, isolating, agglutinating) and cultural backgrounds.

The subjects in the ten language groups were 300 undergraduate students (approximately half of them were male and half female) and all native speakers of their respective languages. The subjects were instructed to "simply describe" each scene on the film in a single, simple sentence, in such a way that a six-year-old child, who himself did not see the film, could understand what they saw.

Data Processing Procedures

The data, consisting of more than 21,000 sentences (70 sentences for each subject, an average of 30 subjects for each of the ten languages), were first transliterated in the Roman script, then translated morpheme-by-morpheme into English, and finally freely translated into idiomatic English by linguistically trained native speakers fluent in English. The morpheme-by-morpheme translation, which preserves the grammatical peculiarities of the original descriptions, formed the basis of the analysis, with the free translation serving as an interpretive guide.

Results

I shall use the following conventions in discussing the results. For each hypothesis, I shall (1) repeat the statement of the hypothesis, (2) describe the relevant scenes on the film that serve as test cases, (3) report the pattern of the results, and (4) discuss the results. For want of a better language, I shall describe the perceptual inputs in rudimentary English sentences but put them in small print to emphasize their nonlinguistic status. (Ideally, a videotape should accompany this paper!) It should be kept in mind that although the total number of responses for each scene is potentially 300, there were a small number of responses that were judged invalid because the subject either (1) did not describe that particular scene, because he/she did not look up at the screen in time, (2) wrote an incomplete or unintelligible response, or (3) wrongly identified the crucial entities/actions involved. Such invalid responses – fortunately, a very small percentage of the total – are disregarded in calculating the percentages and significance of the results.

Hypothesis 1. Figures of state and sources of action tend to be (a) chosen as perspectives; and (b) expressed earlier in the sentence than grounds of state and recipients of action, respectively.

Among the many scenes that are relevant to this hypothesis, scenes (1) and (2) may be regarded as representative of the stative and action relations in question.

1. ball on table
2. man rolls ball on table

Hypothesis 1 predicts that these scenes will be described from the perspective of the figures (ball and man, respectively) and that constituents expressing these entities will precede those expressing the ground (table). In the case of scene (1), all 296 of the valid responses used sentences with the ball as the grammatical subject. In the case of scene (2), except for 16 subjects who used constructions such as passives – perhaps in order to maintain continuity with the previous scene – there were 280 responses with the man as the grammatical subject. Not surprisingly, there were no sentences of the type "The table is holding/supporting the ball" or "The ball is rolling on the table."

The prediction about linear order was also strongly supported; the orders of mention of the ball (figure) and the table (ground) for scene (1) were as follows:

figure–ground order	=	206	(70%)
ground–figure order	=	76	(26%)
other	=	14	(5%)
total relevant cases	=	296	
invalid responses	=	4	
total	=	300	

Interestingly, 60 out of the 76 responses with the ground–figure order (e.g., "On the table a small ball is") came from the four SOV languages, Japanese (24), Kannada (21), Turkish (8), and Hungarian (7). This may be due to the strong tendency in SOV languages to place the locative constituent first, a preference seen most clearly in the case of Japanese and Kannada in this data. An additional factor may be the perception of the ball as an indefinite entity (though it had figured in earlier scenes) due to the treatment of each scene as a separate, self-contained event. Whereas most sentences with the figure–ground order made a definite reference to the ball, a majority of those with ground–figure order treated the ball as indefinite. This particular use of the indefinite needs further exploration. However, the fact remains that crosslinguistically, a strong majority of sentences show a figure–ground order.

As for scene (2), 280 out of 296 (93%) valid responses had the expected figure–ground order, placing the agent (man) before the object (ball). Sixteen sentences were passives or related structures, with the object placed prior to the agent. There were no language-specific effects.

Hypothesis 2. Natural psychological salience yields a continuum of expressive preference: actions > changes of state > constant states.

Of the many scenes relevant to this hypothesis, the results for scene (3) will be analyzed as a representative sample.

3.   three identical blocks on table; man takes two end blocks / man leaves middle block.

Fully 100% of the subjects (297 valid responses) described the action of taking, with 61 subjects (20%) describing, in addition, the constant (end) state as well. None described only the resultant constant state.

Hypothesis 3.   Given that the primary perceptual receptors of the human organism are located on top of and in front of the body, people will tend to describe (a) vertical arrays from top down by locating objects at the top with reference to those below, and (b) horizontal arrays from front to back

> *by locating objects near to the perceiver with reference to those away from the perceiver.*

Scene (4) showed a vertical array, with a ball placed on top of a tube (a hollow paper towel cylinder) which itself was placed on a plate.

4. ball on (top of) tube (which is) on plate

Hypothesis 3 predicts that the ball will be described as being on (top of) the tube and the tube on the plate. This is because the objects on top (ball, tube) are expected to be located with reference to the objects below them (tube, plate) rather than the other way around. The upper part of the array (ball on tube) was described as follows:

ball on tube	=	257	(89%)
ball at the end of tube	=	26	(9%)
tube holds/supports ball	=	6	(2%)
tube under ball	=	1	
total valid responses	=	290	
invalid responses	=	10	
total	=	300	

Note that the overwhelming majority described the array as expected. Subjects did not locate the tube with reference to the ball by giving descriptions such as "The tube is under the ball," although this would have been a perfectly logical and grammatically permissible response. The description of the ball being at the end of the tube may have been an artifact of a too-literal translation (20 of the 26 subjects who gave this response were Finnish speakers, using the term *paasa* "in the end of"). If these responses are included in the "on" category, nearly all subjects used the order predicted by the hypothesis.

The position of the tube vis-à-vis the plate was not described as uniformly. The responses were as follows:

tube on plate	=	179	(62%)
tube in plate	=	98	(34%)
plate has a tube	=	6	(2%)
others	=	7	(2%)
total valid responses	=	290	
invalid responses	=	10	
total	=	300	

Although nearly two-thirds of the subjects did specify the vertical dimension with "on" or its equivalents, about a third of the subjects encoded the array in terms of a content-container relationship. This was understandable, given the fact that the plate was 6 cm wide, whereas the tube was only 3 cm wide.

The second part of the hypothesis – relating to the description of horizontal arrays – was tested in several scenes, but I shall discuss only two of them here. Scenes (4) and (5) form a sort of minimal pair for the elicitation of spatial deictic terms. Both show the actor moving one block half way around another block. Note that the scenes could be described either from the subjects' own (egocentric) point of view (which is also the camera view), or from the point of view of the actor. Given that the position closer to the reference point (subjects or the actor) would be designated the "front" and that further away would be designated the "back," the hypothesis predicts that the scenes would be described from the subjects' own (egocentric) perspective, resulting in descriptions like "The man moves the blue block in front of the yellow block" for scene (4) and "The man moves the yellow block in back of (behind) the blue block" for scene (5).

4.   man moves blue block in front of/in back of yellow block
5.   man moves yellow block in back of (behind)/in front of blue block

The results for scene (4) are as follows:

man moves blue in front of yellow	=	168	(63%)
man moves blue in back of yellow	=	27	(10%)
man moves blue around (etc.) yellow	=	71	(27%)
total valid responses	=	266	(89%)
invalid responses	=	34	(11%)
total	=	300	

The unusually large number of "invalid" responses was due to subjects either missing the scene completely, failing to complete their sentences, or erroneously identifying the moved and stationary blocks. The response category "around (etc.)" is nonspecific or neutral with regard to the ego/alter-orientation. Discounting these two categories of responses, we are left with nearly two-thirds of the subjects describing the scene from a specific point of view. Of these subjects (n = 195), 168 (or 86%) described the scene from an egocentric point of view, using the equivalent of "in front of." Only 27 subjects (or 14%) described the scene from the actor's point of view. (There were no significant language-specific effects in the responses.) This pattern of results, of course, is exactly as predicted by Hypothesis 3.

This preference for egocentric perspective is found in the description of scene (5) as well. Of the 225 subjects who explicitly used the front/back dimension, 78% described the scene egocentrically using expressions such as "The man moves the yellow block behind the blue block," while only 22% adopted the actor's point of view. The slight drop in the egocentric descriptions of scene (5) as compared to (4) is probably due to the fact that the choice of an egocentric perspective in (5) necessitates the use of the "marked" member of the deictic pair, "behind."

Hypothesis 4 posits a correlation between the perceived temporal order of perceptual events and the order of expression of linguistic units encoding those events:

Hypothesis 4.   *The natural order for describing temporally related events will be one that retains the order in which the events are ordinarily perceived in non-linguistic experience.*

One of the scenes relevant to this hypothesis is (6):

6. green ball rolls and hits red ball; (and then) red ball rolls and hits yellow ball

Although events shown in scene (6) may be represented in different orders by the use of sequential adverbs such as "then," "before," "after" and their equivalents, the hypothesis predicts that given the unmarked or neutral condition embodied in the perceptual input, the descriptions will tend to reflect the real-time sequence of events.

The results strongly support the hypothesis. The typical response was a coordinate sentence in which the first clause expressed the perceptually prior event and the second clause the second event. Fully 100% of the 224 valid responses used this order. Of the remaining 76 responses, 45 involved wrong identification of the color of the balls (e.g., "The green ball hit the yellow ball and the yellow ball hit the red ball"), 27 sentences were passives or related object-fronted sentences (wrongly) conflating the objects of the two separate actions (e.g., "the red and yellow balls are hit by a green ball"), and four were incomplete. Significantly, of the subjects who identified the two actions separately, every single one had the order of clauses correspond to the order of occurrence of the events.

The set of hypotheses discussed above may be regarded as "obvious" in some sense. Because they deal with the most fundamental principles of perception and their reflection in language, they have an all-too-familiar ring to them, but they are not obvious in the sense of being "logically inevitable." I now turn to a set of not so obvious phenomena, those involving the effects of perceptual salience on sentence structure.

Hypothesis 5. *Constituents rendered salient by their (1) intrinsic semantic vividness, (2) speaker motivation, and/or (3) topicality will tend to be displaced from their canonical positions for either prior or subsequent expression.*

Scenes (7), (8), (9), and (10) test the effect of the salience of the object/recipient (as opposed to the source) of action on word order. Scene (7) served as the "control" condition in which a simple action relation, not involving any induced salience effect, was given as input.

7. Black ball rolls and hits yellow ball.

Here, the canonical word order is expected, with the constituent representing the source of action preceding the object. Scenes (8), (9), and (10) embody three putative determinants of salience, namely relative greater size (8), perceptual focus induced by zooming (9), and attributed humanness of the object (10), respectively.

8. big black ball on table
   small black ball rolls and hits it
9. yellow ball (camera closeup) on table
   black ball rolls and hits it

10. doll on table
     black ball rolls and hits it

The hypothesis predicts that the salience of the object would lead to initial placement or at least leftward movement of the constituent expressing the object of action.

The results reveal interesting, if slightly complicated, patterns. In addition to sentences with unmarked word order, three types of topicalized structures were produced: (1) object-fronted active sentences, (2) object-fronted passive sentences, and (3) two-sentence descriptions in which the first, typically an existential sentence, established the object and the second described the action in terms of what happened to the object. These structures are illustrated in the following sentences (the numbers preceding the sentence refer to the scenes being described).

Two sentence descriptions (Japanese):
7.   *Teiburunoueni   kiiroi   tamaga   ari   sono*
     table   on   yellow ball (S.)   is   that
     tamani   kuroi   tamaga   butsukatte
     ball-acc.   black   ball (S.)   hit
     "There is a yellow ball on the table. It is hit by a black ball."

Object fronting (Hungarian):
9.   *A   sárga   golyót   ellöki   a fekete*
     the   yellow   ball-acc.   away-hits   the black
     "The yellow ball is hit by the black one."

Passive (Spanish):
10. *Una   muñequita   pequeña   esta   golpeada   por   una   bola   negra*
     a   doll-little   small   is   hit   by   a   ball   black
     "A little doll is hit by a black ball."

These topicalized structures may be regarded as responses supporting the hypothesis. The two-sentence descriptions are included in this category because they are essentially structural paraphrases of sentences containing relative clauses modifying the object: Note that the object constituent precedes the agent in the order of description. In any case, single sentence descriptions are reported separately to facilitate analysis. The results are given in Table 6.2.

Several observations need to be made about the complex pattern of results in Table 6.2. First, it is clear that some experimental conditions were more successful in inducing salience effects than others: Thus in scene (8), the relative bigness of the object failed to produce noticeable word order effects, whereas perceptual focus induced by zooming in scene (9) was more effective in this respect. The most successful determinant was the pseudo-humanness of the doll in scene (10). Second, the languages differ sharply on the basis of structural type in their use of topicalization: The four SOV languages show very little difference in topicalization across the four scenes, whereas the SVO languages (with the marked exception of Hebrew) show considerable sensitivity to salience in terms

Table 6.2. *Topicalization via passive, object-fronted active, or with object-existential first sentence (single sentence descriptions in parentheses)*

Language	Scenes						
	7 Control		8 Size salience		9 Zoom salience		10 Human salience
Cantonese	6	(3)	5	(3)	9	(5)	17	(13)
English	6	(4)	7	(5)	16	(14)	17	(14)
Finnish	2	(–)	1	(1)	2	(1)	10	(10)
Slovenian	2	(–)	5	(2)	8	(6)	11	(10)
Spanish	13	(3)	13	(2)	16	(10)	23	(15)
Hebrew	13	(–)	12	(–)	16	(1)	19	(1)
Hungarian	13	(11)	17	(15)	21	(19)	27	(9)
Japanese	25	(20)	29	(25)	33	(21)	36	(25)
Kannada	24	(12)	24	(12)	20	(10)	23	(9)
Turkish	13	(13)	16	(16)	15	(14)	17	(15)
Totals	117	(66)	129	(81)	156	(101)	200	(131)
Invalid/neutral	28		19		22		3	
Percentages	43%		48%		56%		67%	

of word order shifts. Clearly, topicalization is not correlated with salience in SOV languages, although Hungarian and Japanese use this device slightly more than the others. These results suggest that the surface manifestations of functional distinctions are often mediated by typological, and indeed language-specific, constraints (see Bates & MacWhinney, 1982, p. 175). However, at least with regard to the first five SVO languages listed in Table 6.2, it is clear that salience does affect constituent order significantly.

The second type of salience tested involved the increased information value of an unexpected occurrence found in scene (11):

11. block on table; (suddenly) a spot (a circle of light) appears on block

The sudden and unexpected appearance of the spot induced word order shifts, as predicted. Most descriptions had the spot as the subject, which was moved to the right of the verb in most SVO languages, and placed preverbally but not initially in SOV languages. The Cantonese and Turkish sentences below are illustrative of the patterns. (The tones are not marked.)

Verb–Subject Order (Cantonese)
Yat   hak   lahpfong   tai   dik   mahtgin   keihjung   yat
one   black   cube   shape   adj.m.   suddenly   object   among them
min   dhat   cheutyihn yat   baahk   yuhn   dim
one   side   appear   one   white   round   shape
"A black cube-shaped object. On its side suddenly appears a white round shape."

Table 6.3. *Syntactic shifts due to "surprise" salience*

Language	Verb-subject syntax	Preverb subject syntax	End-state description
Cantonese	32	1	–
English	6	18	6
Finnish	25	–	4
Hebrew	19	3	2
Slovenian	13	–	5
Spanish	25	1	7
Total	120	23	24
Hungarian	10	20	3
Japanese	–	26	3
Kannada	–	10	20
Turkish	–	14	11
Total	10	70	37
Invalid:	17		

Preverbal Subject Order (Turkish)

Siyah	*kipin*	*ortasinda*	*beyaz*	*bir*	*notka*	*belirdi*
black	cube-gen.	center-its-at	white	a	spot	appeared

"A white spot appeared in the middle of a black block."

The results for this scene are given in Table 6.3. The category "end-state description" refers to those responses which did not encode the action but encoded the resulting state (e.g., "There is a spot on a/the block," etc.). Disregarding the end-state description responses, the number and percentage of subjects using VS and SV syntax are as follows:

	VS syntax	SV syntax
SVO languages	120 (84%)	23 (16%)
SOV languages	10 (12%)	70 (88%)

Note that most SVO languages exhibit a dramatic shift to VS syntax, whereas SOV languages do not. Also, within SVO languages, English is an exception, with the majority of English speakers expressing the subject in the canonical, sentence-initial position. The lack of movement in SOV languages needs further study. Since, as it has often been observed, the preverbal position is the focal position in SOV languages, the sentences may involve a vacuous application of a movement rule. It is interesting to speculate whether some other type of movement, say, placement of sentence subject to the right of the object, would take place if the subjects were to describe a transitive surprise action rather than an intransitive one as in scene (30).

Conclusion

The major findings of the study concerning the effect of perceptual and salience variables may be summarized as follows.

1. Nominals denoting figures of states and agents of actions consistently precede those denoting grounds and patients. They also tend to be expressed as sentence subjects.
2. Speakers tend to express changes of state overwhelmingly more often than accompanying constant states.
3. Vertical arrays are described such that the object on top is located with reference to that below, leading to the use of the unmarked "above" rather than the marked "below."
4. In horizontal arrays, objects closest to the perceiver (ego) are located with reference to those farther from ego, resulting in a preference for "X in front of Y" over "Y in back of X."
5. The order of clauses expressing perceptual events corresponds to the sequence of events in perception.
6. Entities rendered salient by virtue of their intrinsic meaningfulness (e.g., humanness), or perceptual focus, tend to be expressed sentence-initially, at or near the beginning of the sentence in SVO languages, leading to the use of object-fronted topicalized sentences.
7. "Surprise subject" contexts lead to disruption of normal word order: leading to VS syntax in SVO languages (except English) and SV order in SOV languages.

As noted earlier, in this paper I have discussed only a subset of the hypotheses and results of the experiment. Other hypotheses, having to do with pragmatic principles such as Grice's maxim of Quantity and Searle's notion of "fully consummated reference," and a variety of presuppositional and discourse factors are discussed in Sridhar (1980, 1988). Those works also contain detailed descriptions of the experimental design and analytical procedures, relevant theoretical and empirical studies, as well as speculations on the explanations for some of the language-specific effects.

The findings reported here are significant from the point of view of theory, method, and data for a number of reasons. They demonstrate that (1) it is possible to test the effects of specific cognitive variables on sentence production by systematically manipulating the content and context of perceptual inputs; (2) a number of properties of the form and content of sentences describing everyday states and actions are determined in a major way, though not exclusively, by fundamental principles of human perception and cognition; (3) all languages possess structural devices to express certain fundamental cognitive distinctions; and (4) the effect of the perceptual variables is mediated via structural constraints.

This study, therefore, lends strong support to the functionalist program in linguistics and psycholinguistics. It shows that psycholinguistics need not limit itself to the task of testing the psychological validity of the constructs proposed in linguistic theory; it can successfully propose and validate explanatory theories that relate language to other higher mental functions. However, the functionalism supported by the findings of this study is not of the naive variety that treats linguistic structure as a mere epiphenomenon of cognitive structures, rather it is a complex functionalism that recognizes the independent effect of typological constraints on language structure. Although the relative contribution of autonomous syntactic variables and functional (cognitive) variables is far from clear, the results of this study demonstrate, at the least, that the strong version of the autonomous syntax model should be rejected.

Furthermore, the impressive consistency of most of the results across the range of diverse languages in the sample underscores the viability of crosslinguistic designs in psycholinguistic experimentation. Such designs also help us to test whether the structural equivalences established in contrastive linguistics are also functionally comparable. For example, the differential use of word order shifts to encode salience in SVO and SOV languages discussed earlier shows that formal equivalence (e.g., availability of topicalization, passivization, etc.) does not necessarily entail functional equivalence.

The perceptual principles discussed above do not, of course, operate in isolation. The effects of other variables (discourse structure, pragmatics, socio-cultural constraints, etc.) as well as the interaction of all these have to be studied. Nevertheless, the impressive effects of perception on sentence structure found in a wide range of languages included in this study will help establish the role of cognitive structures as one of the powerful, and universal, determinants of the structure of human language.

7 Crosslinguistic Studies of Sentence Production

Elizabeth Bates and Antonella Devescovi

A model of sentence production must provide an account of the process by which native speakers select a set of expressions to convey meaning. It should predict the forms that a speaker will use in a given context, and explain why the speaker chose this particular expression out of a range of well-formed alternatives. And if it is based upon general principles of real-time language use, then the model should also predict qualitative and quantitative differences in sentence production among speakers of structurally and functionally distinct language types. In other words, it should have crosslinguistic generality.

To meet these goals, we must rely on a combination of linguistic and psycholinguistic data. Unfortunately, as we move from qualitative studies of linguistic form to quantitative studies of language use, the available crosslinguistic literature moves perilously close to zero. Comparative and/or typological studies of linguistic structure are abundant (e.g., Greenberg, 1966, 1974; Keenan, 1978; Hawkins, 1980). Comparative studies of form–function relations are less common, most of them produced by a small group of functional grammarians (Comrie, 1981; DeLancey, 1980; Duranti & Ochs, 1979; Foley & Van Valin, 1984; Givón, 1979; Keenan & Comrie, 1977; Li & Thompson, 1976). Comparative studies of the statistics of language use are rarer still, restricted primarily to sociolinguistic research carried out by Labov and his colleagues, under the rubric "variable rule theory" (Cedergren & Sankoff, 1974; Labov, 1986). Crosslinguistic differences in the accessibility of comparable structures have been studied by only a handful of psycholinguists working within the functional tradition (MacWhinney & Bates, 1978; Sridhar, 1988, this volume; Perdue & Klein, this volume).

There are good reasons for this trend. Crosslinguistic research on sentence production inherits all the well-known problems involved in achieving experimental control over speech production, particularly when we are aiming at the higher levels of sentence planning. The most popular models of speech production are based primarily on naturally occurring or experimentally induced speech errors; as a result, these models tend to revolve primarily around issues in lexical access, and the local morphosyntactic context of a single lexical item (Dell, 1986; Garrett, 1988; Stemberger, 1985b). Goldman-Eisler (1968) pioneered the use of hesitation data as a source of information about higher-level sentence planning, but there are limitations on the applicability of such suprasegmental (hence phonological) information for a theory of syntactic choice. Other studies have focused on those factors that influence the "starting point" of a sentence (see MacWhinney, 1977, 1985 for a review of this literature). This phenomenon is of course related to the speaker's choice of morphosyntactic frames (Bock, 1982), but it can tell us relatively little about the on-line organization of the sentence from that point on.

The fact is that it is difficult to control and/or monitor syntactic planning beyond the first constituent. In studies of receptive processing, we have rigorous control over both the independent and the dependent variables. Furthermore, there is usually only one dependent variable at issue (e.g., time to push a button). Hence, studies of receptive processing tend to be restricted to more manageable many-to-one designs. In sentence production, there are a great many ways that a speaker can respond, even within a well-structured experimental design. To derive dependent variables from the many responses produced by adult or child subjects, the experimenter has to develop an n-dimensional coding scheme – a process which may also require calculation of interrater agreement for difficult classifications. Things are even more complicated at the analysis stage. With multiple dependent variables, we have to choose between the questionable procedure of conducting many separate analyses of variance, or applying new multivariate techniques that many readers in the field still find difficult to follow.

An alternative is to focus only on the subset of responses that meet criteria of theoretical interest, for example, looking at the proportion of all utterances in which the passive voice was used. This single dependent variable can then be used within a more classic statistical design. However, if we elect this alternative, then a great deal of information is lost. For example, Bock (1986) has demonstrated that syntactic structures like the passive can be "primed," through previous exposure to a sentence that contains the target structure but no overlapping lexical items. However, she was able to use less than 50 percent of the responses produced by her subjects across the relevant priming conditions. Although this is an important study (to which we will return below), this much selectivity limits the generalizability of results. Tannenbaum and Williams (1968) tried to get around this kind of problem by instructing their subjects explicitly to produce either an active or a passive sentence for each picture stimulus; a letter A or P in the corner of the slide signalled which form should be produced. On each item, subjects were also asked questions pertaining to either the agent or the patient of a transitive action (e.g., "What happened to the cow?"). With this design, Tannenbaum and Williams were able to show that passives are produced more quickly with a patient probe than an agent probe, permitting them to conclude that pragmatic conditions influence the access and/or production of grammatical forms. However, the forced-production situation itself is so unnatural that it is difficult to draw firm conclusions about the relationship between grammar and pragmatic context.

We have no new solutions to these well-known methodological problems, but we believe that a crosslinguistic approach can provide new insights.

To assist us in this difficult enterprise, we have drawn on several English-based models of sentence production (e.g., Bock, 1982, 1986; Dell, 1986; Garrett, 1988; Stemberger, 1985b). And we have adopted some of the methods pioneered by investigators working primarily in English (e.g., Tannenbaum & Williams, 1968; Goldman-Eisler, 1968). But our emphasis on crosslinguistic data has resulted in a somewhat different view of the same events. To capture differences between languages, we have made use of the Competition Model, a framework for the crosslinguistic study of language processing developed by Bates, MacWhinney, and their colleagues (see Bates & MacWhinney, this volume). To date, this model has been applied primarily to the study of receptive language, in particular sentence comprehension. As we shall see, crosslinguistic studies of production require some additional principles and constraints.

This chapter is organized in three parts: a discussion of sentence production within the Competition Model, a brief review of our previous crosslinguistic results in this domain, and three new studies focused primarily on differences between English and Italian in the production of complex sentence structures.

Sentence Production in the Competition Model

The Competition Model is a good framework for investigating crosslinguistic differences in sentence production, primarily because it is the only comprehensive processing model that has ever been applied across distinct language types.[1] Our account of sentence production is based upon four types of information: form (the structural options that are available in each language), function (the meanings or communicative goals that control each structural option), distribution (statistics that capture the cooccurrence probabilities among forms and functions in each language), and accessibility (differences between languages in the ease with which a target structure can be accessed and produced). The first two can be described in qualitative terms; the last two require quantification along ordinal or interval scales. In addition, the notion of accessibility requires a specification of the internal conditions that make it "easy" or "hard" to retrieve

---

[1] There are a number of comprehensive theories of competence that have been offered to explain structural differences across languages – notably the theory of principles and parameters offered within Government and Binding Theory (Chomsky, 1982; Rizzi, 1982). Although there have been a few efforts to apply these principles to child language acquisition (cf. Hyams, 1986), statements about performance have been restricted to occasional footnotes on the possible intervention of frequency or memory constraints, usually offered to explain aspects of language behavior in children that do not fit the theory (see Rizzi, 1982, p. 525).

and produce a given configuration of sounds, when frequency and informativeness are held constant. Let us begin by considering how the representational component of the Competition Model can be applied to the study of production, and then go on to some ideas about processing that motivate the studies presented here.

The Structure of the System

We start with the simplifying assumption that comprehension and production are served by the same set of representations: a weighted set of horizontal and vertical connections that include (1) horizontal correlations among surface forms (including lexical items, morphological markers, positional cues, and prosodic contours), (2) horizontal correlations among overlapping categories of meaning and communicative intent, and (3) vertical correlations that connect forms to functions. Within this framework, a grammatical notion like "subject" is viewed not as a single symbol or relation, but as a coalition of many-to-many mappings between surface forms (preverbal position, agreement with the verb in person and number, nominative case, etc.) and underlying meanings (e.g., a topicalized human agent of a concrete transitive action).

For descriptive convenience, we refer to "macrostructures" such as subject–verb agreement or preverbal position as though these were primitive and unitary. In fact, these symbols are shorthand for complex patterns of interrelated sounds. Similarly, we also assume that macroconcepts like agent and topic have a distributed internal microstructure, comprising notions such as humanness, intentionality, movement, and so forth. This distributed view of grammatical structure also permits us to represent complex second- and third-order relations among grammatical categories, nonlinear combinations of cues of precisely the sort that a two-layer perceptron cannot learn (see Bates & MacWhinney, this volume). For example, we have shown that adult Italians can only interpret word order configurations in the presence of certain patterns of intonation. The "same" word order pattern can change or even reverse its meaning, depending on prosody; and the "same" prosodic cue means very different things in different word order environments. Hence, word order and stress cues are clearly not additive; they have to be evaluated together, in complex configurations that we have called "grammogens." In this chapter, we will present related evidence from sentence production, suggesting that phrase structures like the relative clause are accessed by a process similar to the on-line access of individual lexical items (cf. Bock, 1986). We will also argue that there are crosslinguistic differences in the accessibility and deployment of complex phrase structures and/or phrase structure fragments. This kind of result can be accommodated within the same kind of multi-layered connectionist system that Bates and MacWhinney have proposed for sentence comprehension.

The assumption that comprehension and production share the same representations follows logically from a major principle of the Competition Model: cue validity, or the information value of a given expression for a target meaning. We have argued that cue validity is an objective property of the linguistic environment, vis-à-vis some meaning or set of meanings of interest to the child or adult listener. Cue strength is a property of the organism, reflecting the strength of the same form–function mapping from the organism's point of view. Under ideal conditions, in a mature native speaker, with the costs of processing held constant, cue strength will be isomorphic with cue validity. For our purposes here, this means that comprehension is driven by the statistical facts of language production, and vice versa. The two modalities interact to determine the shape of the representations that underlie language use (i.e., competence-to-perform – see Bates & MacWhinney, this volume, for a discussion of the difference between this kind of knowledge and linguistic competence in the strict sense).

If this assumption is correct, how can we explain the enormous developmental lag that is so often observed between comprehension and production, in both lexical and grammatical development (Bates, Bretherton, & Snyder, 1988; Golinkoff, Hirsh-Pasek, Cauley, & Gordon, 1987)? One alternative is to ascribe the differences to processing constraints, an approach similar to the one that many psychologists have taken to explain differences between recognition and retrieval without invoking two separate memory stores (Kintsch, 1974). This brings us to a discussion of processing dynamics.

Processing Dynamics

In the Competition Model, comprehension and production share the same set of representations (determined by cue validity), but a different set of cue cost factors is at work in each modality. We suggest that comprehension is governed by uncertainty, a condition in which vertical mappings from form to meaning are paramount whereas horizontal constraints on coherence and well-formedness are relaxed. Production is governed by commitment, a condition in which the goodness-of-fit between form and meaning (i.e., vertical constraints) may be relaxed while horizontal constraints (i.e., the drive to produce coherent and well-formed speech) are correspondingly increased. These differences in the apportionment of control arise from differences in the ways that the two modalities operate over time.

In both modalities, the set of possible form–function mappings is continually updated as new information comes in. In comprehension, new fragments of meaning are created and new attachments are made (i.e., qualitative change), and competing interpretations wax and wane in strength across the course of sentence understanding (i.e., quantitative change), until one interpretation emerges as the clear winner. A related process of ongoing updating takes place in sentence production. As the speaker begins to formulate his or her meaning, several possible "starting points" compete; once a starting point is selected, the range of possible completions begins to constrict rapidly, until there are no more choices to be made. Comprehension and production differ primarily in the rate at which these competitions have to be resolved. Losers can degrade slowly in comprehension, fading away like old soldiers. But losers must be jettisoned rapidly in production, to prevent any possibility of return. These quantitative differences represent a realistic response to the different responsibilities of speaking and listening.

In sentence comprehension, the incoming utterance is produced by somebody else; therefore the listener has to be prepared for the unexpected. The utterance may be ill-formed (particularly when we are listening to an incompetent speaker, e.g., a child or a foreign adult), and the message itself may be quite surprising. Under these conditions of uncertainty, the listener has to keep his options open as long as possible. The interpretation cannot be dictated too quickly by top-down semantic-pragmatic expectations (i.e., coherence relations at the level of meaning), or by the precise bottom-up characteristics of the utterance itself (i.e., well-formedness relations at the level of form). Coherence relations can play an advisory role, activating a set of competing interpretations for an incoming utterance; principles of well-formedness can serve as a guide to perception, activating likely completions for the utterance as it unfolds (e.g., the prediction that a singular feminine determiner will be followed shortly by a singular feminine noun). However, the final interpretation (i.e., "the winner") is dictated primarily by the vertical fit between meaning and form. These constraints can be embodied at relatively little cost in a parallel parser, where losers can remain active and available (albeit at low levels) just in case things go wrong. This property can also explain how we recover from garden path sentences, that is, how we are able to find a secondary reading without falling into the same error all over again.

In sentence production, we are the ones in control, responsible for the simultaneous creation of both form and meaning. We cannot tolerate very much error, and we cannot afford to change our minds too often. Under the joint constraints of speed, coherence, and well-formedness, we are forced to make commitments relatively early in the formulation of an utterance. We cannot afford to keep competing alternatives around too long, because they can create patterns of interference that lead to speech errors (Dell, 1986; Stemberger, 1985b). Under these conditions, the "best utterance" does not always win. We do not always have time to locate exactly the right expressions, and we do not always say exactly what we mean (Tannen, 1986). Moreover, we are not always careful in formulating meaning itself; we sometimes make it up as we go along, falling back on prepackaged or prototypical ideas ("Lousy

day, huh?" "So tell me, how's Betty?" "She didn't! Did she really?").
This aspect of sentence production is underplayed in many theories of speech
production, where flowcharts of the planning process start at the bottom with
a box that contains a complete idea waiting for expression. In our extension
of the Competition Model, we want to account for sentence production under
more realistic conditions. We are particularly interested in spoken production,
rather than written production. In written production, time constraints are greatly
relaxed; we can formulate our meanings carefully, and select exactly the right set
of expressions to get our message across. Hence written production bears more
resemblance to comprehension, in the extent to which competition is driven
by vertical mapping (i.e., goodness-of-fit), with competing alternatives held in
mind at length until a clear winner emerges.

Of course these differences between comprehension and production are only
a matter of degree. In the long run, we all try to say just what we mean, and as
cooperative listeners we give our partners the same benefit of the doubt (Grice,
1975; Sperber & Wilson, 1986). Speakers can buy time and preserve meaning in
the formulation of speech by dividing the problem of commitment into two parts:
local commitments and long-range commitments. Local commitments include
category assignments (at the level of form) and role assignments (at the level
of meaning) within the immediate word or phrase environment. At a minimum,
these commitments must be sufficient to insure that the right morphological
markers are provided for each lexical item. The sooner these local decisions are
made, the better. Longer-range commitments are (by definition) those that can
be postponed beyond the immediate word or phrase. We propose that speakers
work to maximize local commitment (to avoid speech errors) while avoiding
long-range commitments as long as possible (to maintain flexibility). In any
given language, speakers will fall into preferred speech patterns that represent
a compromise between these two goals. This is one area in which we can
expect to find interesting crosslinguistic differences in speech production, when
meaning is held constant.

To illustrate this point, consider the production of noun phrases in English,
Italian, and German. It is quite common for adult speakers of English to lengthen
or repeat articles and other determiners, as though they were stalling for time
while searching for the right noun (e.g., "Yes, well, that's the, uhm... the...
hypothesis that we had in mind..."). In English, we can get away with such a
ploy, because the article itself carries few commitments. Production of an article
signals our intention to produce a noun (as opposed to a pronoun). But this still
leaves us with a lot of options (namely, every lexical noun in the language!). In
Italian, this trick will not work as well. Because the Italian article agrees with its
noun in gender and number, choice of an article commits the speaker to a subset
of possible lexical selections. In German, the article also carries information
about case. Hence, assignment of an article in German represents assignment

of the sentence role that will be carried by the noun that follows (i.e., a long-distance commitment). The "same" decision has very different implications for sentence planning in English, Italian, and German.

On the other hand, English speakers have much less flexibility in sentence planning once they have chosen a noun phrase to begin their sentence. English rigidly preserves word order; hence, choice of a sentential starting point almost always constitutes choice of the subject role, which in turn conditions the kind of verb that can be used. By contrast, Italian permits all possible orderings of subject, verb, and object. The first noun mentioned need not be the subject of the sentence. As Duranti and Ochs (1979) have shown, this gives Italian speakers an option in sentence planning that is much less common in English. In a rapid-fire conversation with several participants, Italians tend to produce a particularly large number of left-dislocated OVS or OSV structures, compared with rates of noncanonical word order production in conversations with only two participants. Duranti and Ochs explain this fact in terms of conversational management. In competing for the conversational floor, a speaker can produce a relevant noun phrase quickly (thereby staking out his claim), without making any commitments to the sentence structure that must follow. Having grabbed the floor, the speaker can then go on and complete the sentence in several different ways, including assignment of the floor-grabbing noun to the object role.

There are other crosslinguistic differences that need to be taken into consideration for an adequate model of sentence production in real time. These include (of course) the presence or absence of rules and constraints, differences in the meaning and frequency of equivalent morphosyntactic structures, articulatory costs associated with equivalent forms, and so on. In this paper we will explore one piece of the larger crosslinguistic picture. We take as our point of departure a well-known but poorly documented difference between these two languages: Italians tend to produce longer and more complex sentences than their English counterparts, in written prose and in speech production. This difference is folk knowledge among professional translators, and it appears to be built directly into typewriter keyboards: To type a period in Italian, one has to hit a shift key!

Presumably this inconvenience can be tolerated because Italian sentences tend to last a very long time. We will provide evidence in favor of this crosslinguistic claim in three different studies of sentence production in adults, and we will also show that the difference is established for at least one complex structure by 3 years of age. These effects are explained by (1) universal semantic-pragmatic constraints, (2) crosslinguistic differences in the meanings that govern the "same" linguistic form, (3) crosslinguistic differences in the statistical distribution of equivalent phrase structures, and (4) differences in the point at which the components of a complex phrase structure have to be accessed and deployed (i.e., long-distance commitment).

To set the stage for these new data on the production of complex syntax, let

Table 7.1. *Picture stimuli in the given-new task*

Series	Structure	Sample sentences
1	(A)V	A (bear, mouse, bunny) is crying.
2	A(V)	A boy is (running, swimming, skiing).
3	(A)VO	A (monkey, squirrel, bunny) is eating a banana.
4	A(V)O	A boy is (kissing, hugging, kicking) a dog.
5	AV(O)	A girl is eating (an apple, a doughnut, ice cream).
6	AV(Prep)L	A dog is (in, on, under) a car.
7	AVPrep(L)	A cat is on a (table, bed, chair).
8	AV(O)D	A woman is giving a (present, truck, mouse) to a girl.
9	AVO(D)	A cat is giving a flower to a (boy, bunny, dog).

Note: A = agent. V = verb. O = object/patient. Prep = preposition. L = location. D = dative object.

us briefly review some crosslinguistic differences in the production of "local" morphosyntactic elements.

Review of Previous Findings: The Given-New Task

The given-new task was originally designed by MacWhinney and Bates (1978), in a study of pragmatic constraints on sentence production by adult and 3–5-year-old child speakers of English, Italian, and Hungarian (10 in each age × language group). It has also been used extensively in more recent crosslinguistic studies of sentence production in normal and aphasic speakers of English, Italian, German, Hungarian, Turkish, and Chinese (see Bates & Wulfeck, this volume, for a review). In this procedure, subjects are asked to describe a series of static three-picture cartoons illustrating simple intransitive, transitive, dative, and locative events (summarized in Table 7.1). In each cartoon sequence, one element is varied across the three pictures while the other elements remain constant. For example, a little girl is pictured eating an ice cream cone in Frame 1, an apple in Frame 2, and a cookie in Frame 3. Hence, these stimuli provide semantic constraints (the pictured events) and pragmatic constraints (the given-new manipulation) on several aspects of sentence form including lexicalization and ellipsis, pronominalization, and definiteness. Results to date can be summarized briefly as follows:

Lexicalization and Ellipsis. There is a universal tendency to omit old information more often than new, a tendency that we have now documented in normal and brain-damaged adults, and in children as young as 2–3 years of age (see also Sridhar, this volume). However, there are also some interesting crosslinguistic and developmental effects on lexicalization and ellipsis. For example, levels of ellipsis are higher in Hungarian (18%) and Italian (12%), compared with English (8%). Part of this effect comes from the fact that Italian and Hungarian are both "pro-drop" languages (Rizzi, 1982), that is, languages that permit omission of the subject in free-standing declarative sentences. But there are other, less obvious differences in ellipsis as well, including a greater tendency for Italian speakers to omit the direct object (a finding that may receive a partial explanation in the studies of complex syntax reported below).

The developmental findings also provided some surprises. Ordinarily, one might expect crosslinguistic differences to grow in magnitude over time, as children move away from "universal child language" (Slobin, 1985) toward more language-specific patterns of production. However, the opposite was true for patterns of ellipsis in the MacWhinney and Bates study, where language differences were greatest among the 3-year-olds! There are two related explanations for this effect.

1. First, older children tend to lexicalize more of the pictured material; hence, language-specific patterns of ellipsis are exaggerated in the youngest children because they are omitting more material overall.
2. Second, although the given-new constraint is already operating by 3 years of age, children become more sensitive to this constraint as they grow older; hence, when pragmatic conditions are held constant, children move from default production of high-frequency patterns, to patterns that are more appropriate for the discourse situation.

So the pattern of decreased language differences over time is perhaps not as surprising as it seems at first glance. Nevertheless, there is a useful message here: Because very young children are sensitive to the statistical properties of their native language, they may actually present an exaggerated version of their native-language profile under some discourse conditions. We will refer to this developmental pattern as crosslinguistic convergence.

Pronominalization. Rates of pronominalization were slightly higher overall for old information – another pragmatic universal, but one that also interacts with a number of different crosslinguistic and developmental factors (see Sridhar, this volume). Use of subject pronouns was highest in English (15%), compared with Hungarian (6%) and Italian (3%); this of course reflects the fact that overt subjects are obligatory in English. However, Italians and Hungarians also increase their use of subject pronouns when the agent role is in focus, suggesting that pronouns play a more contrastive role in languages that permit subject omission (see also Giuliani, Bates, O'Connell, & Pelliccia, 1987). Overall rates of pronoun use tend to decline with age (as children lexicalize more and more of the pictured material). But this finding also interacts with language: in contrast with the above findings for ellipsis (where language differences decrease over time), language differences in pronoun use increase with age. We will refer to this developmental pattern as crosslinguistic divergence.

Definite Reference.   The data on article use reflect one more pragmatic universal: Definite articles are used more often with given information, indefinite articles are used more often with new information (see Sridhar, this volume). But this linguistic fact also interacts with language and age. Definite articles are more common in Italian and Hungarian, whereas indefinites are more common in English. This finding reflects known differences among the three languages in the pragmatic factors governing definiteness, with more default use of definite reference in the two richly inflected languages. Age effects across the three languages are compatible with previous reports for English only: Indefinite forms tend to increase with age, perhaps because younger children are more likely to take an exophoric "here and now" stance in describing the pictures laid out before them (thus using a definite "the" even for a referent that has not been named before). Language-by-age interactions on definiteness suggest a pattern of crosslinguistic divergence, with language differences increasing in magnitude between 3 and 5 years.

Article Omission.   We have also looked at an aspect of article use that is independent of the given-new manipulation. Bates, Friederici, and Wulfeck (1987b; see Bates & Wulfeck, this volume) report that article omission occurs more often in their English subjects (including fluent aphasics, nonfluent aphasics and normal controls), compared with normal and aphasic speakers of German and Italian. These omissions are particularly likely in sentence-initial position (e.g., "Girl eating an ice cream..."), and they seem (if anything) to be governed more by phonological constraints than any known pragmatic or semantic variable. Because MacWhinney and Bates did not analyze article omission patterns in their original study, we went back to their transcripts for English and Italian children and adults. In our reanalysis of these data, we found a pattern similar to the one reported by Bates et al.: significantly more omission of the article in English ($F(1,72) = 12.99, p < .001$). There was no main effect of age, and no interaction. In fact, this crosslinguistic difference appears to be well established by the age of 3, with English children omitting the article twice as often as their Italian counterparts. Once again, we find that very young children are sensitive to statistical as well as structural features in their input language.

Word Order Variation.   MacWhinney and Bates report significantly more use of noncanonical word order in Italian and Hungarian. However, there are no simple effects of the given-new manipulation on this syntactic variable (see also Bates,

Friederici, Wulfeck, & Juarez, 1988; Bates & Wulfeck, this volume; Sridhar, this volume). Pragmatic word order variation seems, instead, to be motivated by much more subtle discourse factors – a point to which we will return in the studies below. Not surprisingly, language-by-age interactions are also subtle and complex, varying with stimulus type. On some items, language differences are larger among the older children (i.e., crosslinguistic divergence). But there are other items in which language differences decline with age (i.e., crosslinguistic convergence).

To summarize so far, pragmatic universals create broadly similar patterns of reference across the languages studied to date (i.e., lexicalization and ellipsis, pronominalization, definiteness). But we also find crosslinguistic differences in the function and frequency of analogous linguistic forms (e.g., rates of definite reference, article omission, subject omission, pronominalization, and word order variation). All these factors seem to be operating early in language acquisition, beginning by at least 2–3 years of age. So language acquisition and language use are jointly affected by the functional range and statistical distribution of lexical and grammatical forms.

This approach to language acquisition and language use would be more convincing if we could show that function and frequency affect not only the elicitation of single elements (e.g., content words, articles, inflections) but also the access and deployment of complex sentence frames. The rest of this paper will be devoted to crosslinguistic differences in the production of complex syntax, starting with our reanalysis of the given-new data.

Three Studies of Complex Syntax

Study 1: Relative Clauses in the Given-New Task

MacWhinney and Bates obtained a rather surprising crosslinguistic result that is not discussed in their original paper, in part because the finding did not follow from the functional theories of grammar that they set out to test. Specifically, Italian speakers seemed to produce an inordinately large number of relative clause constructions. A language-by-age analysis of variance that we have conducted with the MacWhinney and Bates data reveals that Italians produce relative clauses in their picture description six or seven times more often than their English-speaking counterparts ($F(1,72) = 160.01$, $p < .0001$). There is also a main effect of age ($F(3,72) = 5.15$, $p < .003$) and a significant age-by-language interaction ($F(3,72) = 5.47$, $p < .002$), illustrated in Figure 7.1. In the overall effect of age, relative clause use increases up to age five and then drops off slightly. However, an examination of the language-by-age interaction shows that this age effect is due entirely to developmental changes among the Italians. The developmental function for English is essentially flat, with speakers producing fewer than one relative clause apiece at any age level. Furthermore,

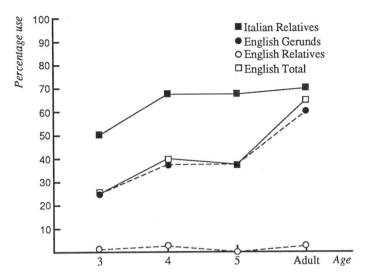

Figure 7.1. Usage of gerunds versus relatives across ages in Italian and English

although the Italian relative clause bias does show some increase between 3 and 5 years, it is already very strong among the youngest children in our study (occurring in 52% of their picture descriptions).

Where does this robust crosslinguistic difference in syntactic complexity come from? It cannot be attributed to any known structural difference between the two languages, that is, to the presence or absence of a clearcut grammatical rule. Consider the following sentences:

1a. A monkey is eating a banana.
1b. *Una scimmia mangia una banana.*
2a. There is a monkey that is eating a banana.
2b. *C'e' una scimmia che mangia una banana.*
3a. There is a monkey eating a banana.
3b. *C'e' una scimmia mangiando una banana.*
4a. Here we have a monkey. He's eating a banana.
4b. *Qui abbiamo una scimmia. Mangia una banana.*

All four descriptions are perfectly grammatical in English, and their translations are all equally grammatical in Italian. But there are marked crosslinguistic differences in the acceptability and/or accessibility of these four alternatives in the given-new task. Among English speakers, Type 1a is by far the most common (i.e., a simple declarative sentence). Types 3a and 4a also occur with some regularity, but the relative clause construction (2a) is rarely produced. Among Italian speakers, relative clauses (2b) are the most common response, although descriptions with one or two simple clauses (Types 1b and 4b) do occur. Constructions in which a gerund modifies the noun subject (Type 3b) are quite rare.

There seems to be a complementary distribution here between relative clauses in Italian, and gerundive constructions in English. To the extent that this is true, we would not want to conclude that Italians produce more complex syntax per se, because the underlying forms of the two construction types are equally complex (at least in some syntactic theories). With this thought in mind, we gave subjects credit for use of complex syntax if they produced either a relative clause or a noun modified by a gerund. The analysis of variance was then repeated using number of complex forms produced as the dependent variable. The crosslinguistic difference was still significant ($F(1,72) = 10.16$, $p < .002$), as was the main effect of age ($F(3,72) = 8.43$, $p < .0001$). This time the age-by-language interaction failed to reach significance. We conclude that this use of complex syntax is significantly higher in Italian, at every age from 3 to adulthood (see Figure 7.1).

When we first encountered this unexpected pattern, we considered an explanation based on crosslinguistic work in functional grammar by Li and Thompson (1976). These investigators have proposed a division of natural languages into two categories: topic-dominant and subject-dominant. In topic-dominant languages such as Tagalog, the subject role is strongly identified with topicality. This alignment has several consequences, but the most interesting one for our purposes involves definite reference: Indefinite subjects are ungrammatical, and Tagalog equivalents of sentences 1a and 1b are thus precluded. If a Tagalog speaker wants to assign the subject role to a new discourse element, he must first topicalize that element in a prior sentence or clause – as in sentences 2a through 4b. In subject-dominant languages such as English, the subject role is usually assigned to the highest semantic argument of the verb (i.e., to the agent, or to the most agentlike element), whether or not that element is the discourse topic. As a result, indefinite subjects are perfectly acceptable (although they are statistically less common than definite subjects, due to a universal albeit imperfect correlation between subjecthood and topicality in all natural languages). Italian may lie somewhere in between the topic-dominant and subject-dominant poles: sentences with indefinite subjects are possible (as in 1b), but they are not preferred. Relative clauses provide one solution to the problem: an indefinite subject is introduced in an existential matrix clause (i.e., "There is a monkey..."), turning it into the definite subject of an embedded predicate ("...who is eating a banana").

To test this hypothesis, we divided all the picture descriptions in the given-new task into those with definite subjects, and those with indefinite subjects. In Italian, 72% of the indefinite subjects were modified by a relative clause, but the same was also true for 64% of the definite subjects. In English, 69% of the indefinite subjects took a clausal modifier (usually a gerund); only 31% of the definite subjects were modified in this way. We must conclude that the relative clause bias in Italian does not exist solely to avoid indefinite subjects. In fact, we have found a striking crosslinguistic difference in the opposite direction. Consider the following sentences:

5a. Here is the monkey that is eating a banana.
5b. *Qui c'e' la scimmia che mangia una banana.*

These sentences are grammatical in both languages, but under very different functional conditions. In English, 5a can have one and only one meaning: The monkey in question is being distinguished from some other monkey who presumably is not eating a banana. In Italian, 5b can also be used noncontrastively, to describe a situation with only one monkey. To clarify this point, consider the following sentence pairs:

6a. Here is John who is kissing Mary. (restrictive clause)
6b. *Qui c'e' Giovanni che bacia Maria.* (restrictive clause)
7a. Here is John, who is kissing Mary. (nonrestrictive clause)
7b. *Qui c'e' Giovanni, che bacia Maria.* (nonrestrictive clause)

With proper nouns, the restrictive relative clause appears to be completely unacceptable in English; the Italian equivalent is perfectly acceptable. We conclude that relative clauses serve a different range of functions in the two languages. In Italian, subject-modifying relatives can be used to distinguish between competing referents (as in English). But they also serve a more general topic-marking function. They are used to introduce new (indefinite) referents, but they can also be used to place established (definite) referents into discourse focus. In this last respect, the relative clause marker *che* can be viewed as an Italian analogue to the topicalizing *wa* particle in Japanese (Delancey, personal communication).

We conclude that the "same" structure serves a different range of discourse functions in English and Italian. However, this is still rather weak evidence for our earlier claim that Italians produce more complex syntax overall. There are many other complex constructions that we have not yet examined. And there are also other versions of the relative clause itself, in addition to the topicalizing relatives that we have described so far. For example, nonrestrictive relatives are sometimes used to link together two components of a complex event, as in the following example:

7a. The dog bit the cat, who then bit the mouse.

We will refer to this second usage as the continuation relative. In the next study we will again compare relative clause production in English and Italian, using a more complex and heterogeneous stimulus set to elicit a broader range of discourse forms.

Study 2: The Pixolation Film

In this study, we have used a set of moving picture stimuli designed by MacWhinney and Bates, using a combination of live action and pixolation (animation created by filming a succession of slightly different tableaux with inanimate objects and toys). This color film is patterned in many respects after the stimuli used by Sridhar (this volume), within the large-scale crosslinguistic study of sentence production that he conducted with Osgood. Like the Osgood–Sridhar film, our stimuli were designed to reflect a range of basic event types (e.g., intransitive, transitive, directional locative), viewed from several different discourse perspectives. The segments emphasize different contributions to the underlying semantic role of "agent" (e.g., degrees of animacy, prior possession of the agent role, first mover within an individual scene), and different contributions to the pragmatic role of "topic" (e.g., givenness, salience, point of view established by camera angle). Because so many different discourse factors are represented in the film, no attempt was made to provide a full orthogonal design; instead, viewers are given an array of partially overlapping event constraints similar to the landscape of competing and converging factors that are typically encountered in real narratives.

Although this nonorthogonal design provides some advantages, the necessary analyses are quite complex – one reason why our use of this film has lagged in favor of the tighter experimental studies described throughout this volume. Computerized transcripts of film description data are now available for three languages: English (adults and 3–8-year-olds), Hungarian (adults and 3–8-year-olds), and Italian (adults only). For our modest purposes here, we have analyzed the data for 25 Italian and 25 English adults, extracting information about the use of simple and complex sentence structures to describe transitive events. Table 7.2 describes the 31 transitive events in the film that were selected for the present study. These segments include single events involving two participants (e.g.,"a toy horse chases a moving apple"), as well as compound events involving at least two actions by two or more protagonists (e.g., "a toy fish bumps into a flowerpot, and then bumps into a toy TV"). Hence, the stimuli are rich enough to elicit both topicalizing and continuation relatives, on first mention (when all participants are new) and on later mentions (when we might expect definite reference across the board).

We coded all the actions described by our subjects along the following dimensions: whether the subject of each action predicate was definite or indefinite, and whether the action predicate was contained within a simple sentence, a relative clause, or a participial/gerundive form (e.g., "a horse chasing a cow" or "a cow chased by a horse"). Relative clauses were further divided into topicalizing relatives and continuation relatives (as defined in the previous study). We also noted whether speakers introduced the subject of a subsequent action predicate with a separate existential sentence (e.g., "In this picture I see a cow. The cow chases an apple around the stage...").

Results confirm and extend the findings reported in Study 1. English speakers used significantly more simple sentences in their film descriptions: an average

Table 7.2. *Description of transitive items in pixolation film*

1. An apple chases a stool.
2. The apple chases a dog.
3. A cow chases a zebra.
4. The zebra chases a seal.
5. A camel chases a giraffe.
6. A bottle chases the camel.
7. A chair chases a table.
8. A hippo chases the chair.
9. The apple chases the cow.
10. A tree pulls a walrus.
11. The tree circles an alligator.
12. The tree pushes a penguin.
13. The tree chases a panther.
14. The tree falls on a bear.
15. The tree pushes a sheep.
16. The tree hits a gorilla.
17. The tree pulls a camel.
18. A buffalo pushes the tree (tree is active).
19. The buffalo pushes the tree (tree is neutral).
20. A bottle hits the goat; the goat hits a lock.
21. A block hits a pipe; the pipe hits a dog.
22. A giraffe hits a stool; the stool hits a tree.
23. A gorilla chases a camel.
24. The gorilla chases a stag.
25. The gorilla chases an elephant.
26. A hippo hits a ladder; the ladder hits a lock.
27. A lion hits a spool; the spool hits a ball.
28. An orange hits a basket; the basket hits a table.
29. A cow hits a basket; the basket hits a TV.
30. A chair hits a fish; the fish hits a TV.
31. A flowerpot hits a ball; the ball hits a pig.

of 23.2 per speaker, compared with 12.5 in Italian ($F(1,48) = 13.26, p < .001$). Sentences with a topicalizing relative were far more common in Italian: an average of 13.8 per speaker, compared with .28 in English ($F(1,48) = 31.45, p < .0001$). Gerundive/participial constructions were again more common in English (averaging 2.1 per subject, compared with only .04 for Italian). However, when gerunds, participles and relative clauses were added together to create a single measure of complex syntax, the language difference was maintained ($F(1,48) = 20.98, p < .0001$). These results were (again) largely independent of definite or indefinite reference; relative clauses were produced more often on first mention, but Italians also used them to topicalize a definite element mentioned in a previous frame.

We found no difference between English and Italian in the tendency to set elements up with an existential sentence (e.g., "Here we see a cow and an apple..."). If we had found such a difference, we might conclude that the complex syntax observed in Italian derives from a cultural rather than a linguistic bias, perhaps reflecting a tendency toward more careful and complete descriptions of the filmed events (an alternative interpretation that we will consider once again in Study 3). Finally, we also compared English and Italian subjects in their production of continuation relatives, that is, a very different descriptive use of the relative clause. Although these structures were indeed more common in Italian, rates of production were quite low in both languages (2.00 in English, 2.76 in Italian) and did not reach statistical significance.

So far we have evidence for greater syntactic complexity in Italian for only one structure, in one function slot: a topicalizing relative clause, used to place both definite and indefinite elements into discourse focus. There is a trend toward more production of continuation relatives as well, but this trend is certainly not sufficient to establish general claims about the accessibility of complex syntax in Italian. We looked for several other sentence types in the data set (including passives), but these forms were too infrequent to permit statistical analysis. In the next study, we use a new animated film that elicits higher rates of complex sentence production, within an orthogonal design that can display the interacting effects of language, event type and discourse constraints.

Study 3: The Animated Film

Table 7.3 summarizes the structure of a black and white animated film designed by Bates and Wulfeck, illustrating simple and complex events with one, two, and three animate participants. The 12 simple events include three intransitives, three transitives, three datives, and three directional locatives. The 12 complex events all involve three participants and one repeated transitive action. These are divided into four basic event types, each designed to encourage use of a different target sentence structure (Table 7.4).

We do not assume that these events will be 100% successful in eliciting the target sentence frames, nor do we assume that they will be equally successful. In fact, one of the purposes of this design is to assess language differences and age differences in the accessibility of the target structures under different pragmatic/semantic conditions.

The animated film represents an interesting extension of the given-new manipulation described in Study 1. Here we are manipulating role constancy instead of (or in addition to) referent constancy. The four complex sentence types described in Table 7.4 follow from a proposed universal semantic/pragmatic tendency to maintain perspective across two consecutive action descriptions – particularly when those action descriptions are housed in a single sentence.

Table 7.3. *Simple and complex events in the animated film*

Simple events
Intransitives
  1. A frog hops.
  2. A dog runs.
  3. A bird flies.

Transitives
  4. A bear licks a tiger.
  5. A kangaroo hits a zebra.
  6. A horse bites a goat.

Directional locatives
  7. A baby crawls under a table.
  8. A lion walks into a cage.
  9. A snake slides onto a rock.

Datives
10. A man gives a flower to a woman.
11. A girl shows a balloon to a boy.
12. A bunny throws a stick at a pig.

Complex events
ABAC
13. A snake bites a horse; the horse bites a sheep.
14. A penguin touches an owl; the penguin touches a rooster.
15. A mouse jumps over a worm; the mouse jumps over a butterfly.

ABCB
16. A turkey pecks a turtle; a chicken pecks the turtle.
17. A gorilla hugs an elephant; a tiger hugs the elephant.
18. A dog walks on a seal; a cat walks on the seal.

ABBC
19. A lion bumps a bear; the bear bumps a camel.
20. A boy kisses a girl; the girl kisses a baby.
21. A monkey pets a skunk; the skunk pets a pig.

ABCA
22. A bunny hops on a cat; a frog hops on the bunny.
23. A cow butts a donkey; a ram butts the cow.
24. A squirrel pushes a bird; a fox pushes the squirrel.

For example, the constant agent structure of complex event type 1 encourages speakers to assign the subject role to A in both action descriptions. The pragmatic constraints of givenness and newness permit omission of the constant agent and the constant action on second mention. The best solution to both these constraints is a single sentence with a conjoined object (e.g., "An A hits a B and a C"). Similar competition/convergence analyses can be offered for event types 2, 3, and 4 – resulting in the gapped, conjoined, and relative clause structures predicted in Table 7.4. In this highly constrained experimental situation, we

Table 7.4. *Complex events and predictive sentence forms*

Event type	Target structure
Constant agent (A → B; A → C)	Conjoined object ("An A hits a B and a C")
Constant patient (A → B; C → B)	Conjoined subject ("An A and a C hit a B")
Flow of action (A → B; B → C)	Continuation relative ("An A hits a B, which then hits a C")
Role switch (A → B; C → A)	Voice shift ("An A hits a B and then gets hit by a C")

can obtain a rigorous test of the proposed Italian advantage in production of complex syntax.

Further information about pragmatic effects on syntax is obtained by adding external discourse probes. In simple events, speakers in all the languages we have studied to date have a strong tendency to assign the subject role to the agent; lacking an agent, they will assign subjecthood to the next element on an active-passive hierarchy (e.g., Fillmore, 1968). However, these default assignments can be overridden by an external discourse probe that places the patient of a transitive action into discourse focus (e.g., "Tell me about the B"). Under these conditions, the named element is often promoted to the subject role regardless of other constraints from agency, animacy, and/or perspective maintenance. In English, this situation typically results in production of a passive sentence (Tannenbaum & Williams, 1968). Previous studies in our laboratory using this animated film suggest that passives are produced at a high rate, in both the simple and complex events, when the experimenter asks about a nonagentive element – although this tendency is much weaker in small children, and does not reach adult levels until 12 years of age (Marchman, Bates, Good, & Burkhardt, 1988). In the present study, we expect to obtain comparable results for English and Italian adults (i.e., successful elicitation of the passive with an appropriate discourse probe). However, there may be differences in overall rate of passive production, and in the kinds of passives that are produced.

Sixty subjects participated in Study 3: 30 native speakers of Italian and 30 native speakers of English, all college students at a large urban university. An additional sample of ten English speakers was added later, for reasons described below. Within each language, subjects were evenly divided into two conditions: free description and probed description. In the free description condition, the film is stopped after each complete event, and subjects are cued to begin their description in any way they see fit. In the probed condition, the film is stopped at the same point, but subjects are asked to describe the scene they have just witnessed in response to a question from the investigator (i.e., "Tell me about the X"). Discourse probes were balanced evenly across all the pictured elements, in several different random assignments (the single element in intransitives; both agent and patient in transitives; both agent and location in locatives; agent, patient and dative in datives; A, B, and C elements in the complex events). We will first describe evidence for production of gapping, relative clauses, and conjoined phrases (i.e., the target structures in Table 7.4), in both the free and probed conditions. Then we will describe elicitation of the passive, concentrating on the discourse probe condition.

Gapping, relatives and conjoined phrases

All film descriptions were coded for the presence or absence of gapping, conjoined phrases, and/or a continuation relative clause. On each of the 12 complex event descriptions, subjects received a score of 1 if any of these target forms were produced. This yes-or-no scoring yields a possible range of 0–12, with 0–3 on each of the four event types. These scores were entered into a $2 \times 2 \times 4$ mixed analysis of variance. Language (English versus Italian) and condition (free versus probed) were between-subject variables, and event type (ABAC, ABCB, ABBC, ABCA) was a within-subject variable.

There was a large and reliable main effect of language, ($F(1,28) = 25.9$, $p <$ .0001), with more complex syntax produced overall by the Italian subjects. Italians produced one or more of the complex target forms on 53.3% of their scene descriptions (averaging 6.4 out of 12 possible overall). By contrast, English subjects produced complex forms on only 29.2% of their scene descriptions (averaging 3.5 out of 12). However, language did not interact with any other variable. Hence, the "Italian advantage" appears to be distributed across the board in this situation. The effects of condition and event type are essentially the same in both languages.

There was also a strong main effect of event type, ($F(3,84) = 39.4$, $p < .0001$), suggesting that there are indeed differences among the four events in the success with which they elicit the target sentence frames. Production of complex syntax was highest for the constant agent scenes (ABAC); these elicited an average of 2.08 complex forms out of 3 possible, consisting almost entirely of picture descriptions using a conjoined object (i.e., "An A hits a B and a C"), or gapping constructions with the verb repeated (i.e., "An A hits a B and then hits a C"). Constant patient scenes (ABCB) elicited an average of 1.21 complex forms from each subject, consisting primarily of sentences with a conjoined subject (i.e., "An A and a C hit a B").

These were followed by the flow-of-action scenes (ABBC), averaging .95 per subject (consisting primarily of continuation relatives). Role switch items resulted in the smallest number of complex constructions overall (.73).

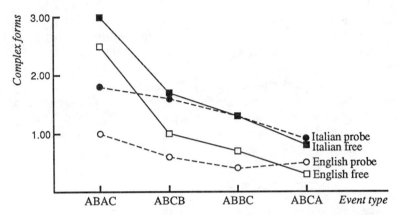

Figure 7.2. Number of complex sentence forms for the four event types in Italian and English, with and without probes.

This rank-ordering is consistent with the functionalist principles outlined earlier. They represent different degrees of convergence among (a) the default tendency to assign subjecthood to the agent of an action, (b) a tendency to maintain perspective between clauses, keeping the same element in the subject role whenever it is possible to do so (maximized in ABAC items), (c) a tendency to omit redundant/repeated elements where possible (maximized in ABAC and ABCB items), and (d) a tendency to assign the subject role to elements that have already been mentioned before (promoted in ABAC and in ABBC items). On role switch items (ABCA), perspective can be maintained only if the speaker is willing to produce a switch between active and passive voice (e.g., "An A hits a B and then gets hit by a C"). Although such utterances do occur (particularly in Italian), they are usually avoided in favor of a description with two different subjects, in two full clauses (e.g., "A hits B, and then C hits A").

We also found a small but reliable main effect of condition, ($F(1,28) = 8.39$, $p < .01$), and a significant condition × event type interaction, $F(3,84) = 16.7$, $p < .001$. This interaction is illustrated in Figure 7.2, plotted separately for English and Italian to demonstrate just how similar the findings are in each language despite overall differences in level. The condition × event type interaction provides further support for a functionalist interpretation of the rank ordering among the four event types.

Although there is slightly more production of complex syntax in the free condition, Figure 7.2 shows that this effect comes primarily from the ABAC items. In free description, ABAC items provide an ideal fit to default assignments in sentence production: Subjecthood goes to the agent in both events, perspective is maintained between events, and repetition of the same element in the same sentence role encourages subject omission on the second mention. In the probe condition, each element (A, B, or C) is probed equally across speakers and events. The speaker never knows what perspective the experimenter is going to impose with his annoying questions, and as a result, default assumptions are suspended across the board. When this default advantage is removed, differences among the four event types are greatly reduced.

To summarize so far, results from both the free and probed conditions confirm the hypothesis that complex syntactic structures (gapping, conjoined phrases and continuation relatives) are produced more easily in Italian. However, in both languages we also find evidence for universal semantic/pragmatic constraints on syntactic form (i.e., effects of role and referent constancy). Let us turn now to the effects of language and discourse probes on production of the passive.

Elicitation of the passive

Three different passive production scores were assigned for each of the 24 simple and complex items, in both the free and probed condition. The first score reflects production of "true" passive forms with an auxiliary verb and a participle; although we also noted whether or not the "by" phrase was produced, production of passive verb morphology alone was sufficient for a score of "1" on any given item. Second, we counted all items in which some kind of lexical passive was produced. In English, this was usually a "get" passive; in Italian, a much broader range of forms qualified as lexical passives (see below). The third score reflects total passives produced, with true passives and lexical passives combined.

All forms of the passive were rare in the free description condition, particularly for the 12 simple events. A few were produced in the complex events, to maintain constant perspective on elements that switch between agent and patient roles. However, this phenomenon was significantly more common in Italian. In the free condition, English speakers produced an average of only .15 utterances with a voice switch (1.25% of all complex event descriptions); in the same condition, Italians produced an average of .93 utterances with a voice switch (7.75%). These ratios went up markedly in the probed condition, where English speakers produced an average of 1.4 utterances with a voice switch (11.7%), and the Italian average went up to 2.47 (20.6%). A language × condition analysis of variance on these figures yielded significant main effects of language, $(F(1,28) = 12.74, p < .001)$ and condition $(F(1,28) = 28.58, p < .0001)$, but no significant interaction.

Not surprisingly, production of the passive was higher across the board in the probed condition, when the experimenter focused on a nonagentive element. Furthermore, rates of passive production followed a hierarchy from "most patientlike" to "least patientlike." This point can be made most clearly by describing results for the simple and complex events separately.

On the 12 simple events, passive production broke down as follows (summarizing across languages and across passive types): 75% passive production when the patient of a transitive action was probed, 36% when the dative was probed, only 8% when a locative element was probed, and no passives at all (0%) when the experimenter asked about the agent (in transitives and datives) or the actor (in locatives and intransitives). On the less prototypical dative and locative items, true passives constituted only 32% of all the passive forms produced, compared with 58% on the prototypical patient probes. So "degree of patienthood" and "degree of passivehood" appear to be correlated. Nevertheless, speakers were still quite sensitive to the nonagentive probe on the dative and locative items. They managed to find some way to place the probed element in the subject role on 48% of the datives (e.g., "The little girl is looking at the balloon that the boy is pointing to") and 30% of the locatives (e.g., "The cage entraps the lion" or "The table covers the baby").

The four complex event types create another rank order of "passivizability," reflecting the combined effects of primacy, recency and agency. Consonant with the data on simple events, passives were never produced if the probed element only played an active role (element A in ABAC, ABCB and ABBC; element C in ABCB and ABCA). The highest rates of passive production were obtained when C was probed in ABBC items (83.3%) and ABAC items (83.3%). C plays a purely passive role in both these cases, and it is involved only in the last event (i.e., a recency effect). By contrast, much lower rates of passive production (46.7%) occur when A is probed in ABCA items. The "first impression" of A as an active element seems to be just as important as the "last impression" of A in the patient role – a primacy/recency tradeoff. Finally, participant B is always the patient in the first scene; when B is probed, this fact seems to determine rates of passive production regardless of B's fate in the second act: 63.3% in ABAC, 73% in ABBC, 63.3% in ABCB, and 67% in ABCA. The rank order is similar if we restrict our attention only to true passives: highest when patient C is probed (52%), lowest when patient A is probed (23%), with in-between values when patient B is probed (37%).

These data provide further evidence for universal semantic/pragmatic constraints on syntactic form. However, we did not obtain a significant crosslinguistic difference in the total number of passives produced, for either the simple or the complex events. Overall, Italian speakers produced an average of 6.53 passive descriptions, compared with 7.53 in English ($t = 1.01$, $p < .40$). And when we focused only on production of "true" passives, we actually obtained a trend in the opposite direction: 4.93 full passives in English, compared with 2.73 in Italian ($t = 1.85$, $p < .08$). The source of this trend was clarified when we returned to the transcripts. Although there was no significant difference between the two languages in the total number of lexical passives produced, there was a considerable difference in variety. In English, lexical passives consist almost entirely of the so-called get passive (e.g., "The sheep got bitten by the snake"). In Italian, we instead find a range of different lexical forms. Some examples include the following:

...si prende una bastonata da...	"...gets himself a beating from..."
...ha ricevuto delle leccate dal...	"...received some lickings from..."
...viene morso dal...	"...comes bitten by..."

There seems, then, to be a larger choice of lexical passives in Italian. Notice that the English translations for these different lexical forms involve at least two prepositions ("by" and "from"). As Clark and Carpenter (1989) have argued, "by" and "from" share the semantic notion of "source," and perhaps for that reason they are often confused in the first production of passive forms by English-speaking children. In Italian, all the lexical passives (as well as the true grammatical passive) share the same preposition *da*. Hence, they are arguably closer together on both semantic and phonological grounds. In any case, this final difference between English and Italian in the number of different passive forms produced does reach significance by a one-tailed t-test (t = 2.02, $p < .03$).

To summarize, we find an Italian advantage in the production of complex syntactic structures involving two predicates. This includes a greater propensity to shift voice from active to passive in a single sentence, including gapped constructions with a single overt subject (e.g., "A hits B and then gets hit by C"). On the other hand, Italians have no advantage in the overall number of passives produced; they actually produce slightly fewer true grammatical passives, due perhaps to the greater array of lexical passives that are available and accessible in this language. These findings provide quantitative support for our earlier claim that complex syntax is more accessible in Italian; they also help to set qualitative boundaries around the supposed Italian advantage.

Before seeking a psycholinguistic interpretation of these findings, we once again entertained the possibility that Italians produce more complex syntax for cultural rather than linguistic reasons. Our subjects are all middle-class college students at an urban university. Nevertheless, it is at least possible that our Italian students are better educated and/or more articulate than their American counterparts. Some support for this view comes from developmental findings with English-speaking children, using the same film description task. Marchman et al. (1988) found a steady increase between 3 and 12 years of age in the number of picture descriptions produced with gapping, conjoined phrases, relative clauses and/or passives of any kind. They also found a developmental shift in the same age range, from a predominant use of lexical passives (e.g., "got hit") to a predominant use of grammatical passives (e.g., "was hit"). These developmental findings provide only a partial fit to the crosslinguistic differences observed here. The Italian advantage in production of gapping, conjoined phrases, and continuation relatives does resemble a developmental effect; but there is no comparable crosslinguistic difference in either the number or kind of passives produced. Nevertheless, we pursued the hypothesis that Italians are "simply smarter," by testing an additional sample of ten English speakers drawn from an (arguably) more elite academic group: graduate students and postdoctoral fellows at the University of California, San Diego, all of whom are engaged in constant use of formal English prose, both written and spoken. Half the subjects were randomly assigned to the free condition, and the other half were tested in the probe condition. None of these subjects were aware of the purpose of the study, or the crosslinguistic findings that prompted our request.

Results were quite straightforward: the elite English sample did not differ significantly from English undergraduate students on any of the target measures; by contrast, significant differences between these English subjects and the Italian groups were obtained in the total number of gapped constructions, conjoined phrases and continuation relative clauses they produced, in the same directions reported above. Patterns of passive production were identical to the results obtained with younger college students (i.e., there was no crosslinguistic difference in the overall number of passives produced, but elite English speakers produced a somewhat smaller array of lexical passives than we found in Italian college students).

Although one could presumably carry this effort further (testing Shakespearean actors, novelists, and professors of English literature), we are now convinced that the crosslinguistic differences observed in Studies 1–3 are based on linguistic/psycholinguistic differences between the two languages, and not on differences in culture or educational level. At least within the kind of picture and/or film description task that we have used here, native speakers of Italian appear to have an advantage in the production of some (but not all) complex syntactic forms. When the material to be described is held constant, they produce a large number of relative clauses (existential and continuation relatives), a higher proportion of gapped and conjoined phrases, and more shifts of voice to maintain a constant perspective. However, in response to discourse probes focused on a nonagentive element, Italian and English speakers are equally likely to produce a passive form. So the Italian advantage appears to be restricted to "interclausal syntax," that is, devices that maintain perspective and pack two predicates into a single sentence frame. We are now beginning to examine crosslinguistic differences in the production of complex syntax in a range of different discourse conditions (e.g., informal conversation), with children and adults, to test the generality of these findings.

Conclusion

We have provided substantial evidence for universal semantic/pragmatic effects on the production of complex syntax. These include the functional contrast between given and new information, manipulations of discourse focus, role constancy and perspective maintenance, and, of course, the objective structure of the event to be described. At the same time, we have also shown that certain complex syntactic structures are accessed more easily by native speakers of Italian, compared with native speakers of English tested in the same situation. Where does the Italian advantage come from?

Cultural factors could of course play some role. We have (we believe) eliminated the argument that Italian college students are better educated or more articulate than their U.S. counterparts, because the Italian/English difference was maintained when we tested an elite sample of adult subjects who live their lives within the walls of academe. Is it possible that the crosslinguistic difference is actually caused by the U.S. educational system? Classical English may be the language of Shakespeare, but American English is the language of Hemingway. American students are taught to write in short clear sentences, an experience that might feed back on their oral narratives as well. The crosslinguistic difference that we have observed here might be reduced if we compared Italians with products of the British public school system. However, the effects of literacy are probably not sufficient to account for all our findings. Italian children produce far more relative clause constructions by the age of 3, well before they encounter the written conventions of their language.

Some of the crosslinguistic effects that we have observed may derive from differences in the range of meanings served by the "same" form. The topic-marking function of relative clauses in Italian is a case in point, resulting in use of this form in contexts that are impossible in English (i.e., as the noncontrastive modifier of a definite noun phrase, including proper nouns). But we have also found crosslinguistic differences that have no obvious functional explanation, based instead on stylistic and/or phonological factors. This point is illustrated by the tendency for English speakers to omit articles in sentence-initial position – a pattern is already apparent in the earliest stages of language learning, and may actually be magnified in the speech of brain-damaged adults. For example, Bates et al. (1987b) report that nonfluent Italian aphasics provide the article more than 75% of the time; in the same picture description task, English patients provide the article less than 30% of the time. In deciding which elements to encode in their slow and effortful speech, aphasic patients may exploit all legal opportunities for omission, creating exaggerated versions of pragmatic, stylistic, and/or phonological patterns of omission in their language. This is analogous to the "crosslinguistic divergence" profile that we reported above for patterns of lexicalization and ellipsis in small children. In our view, these are best viewed as statistical/distributional effects, where the sheer frequency of a lexical or morphosyntactic type makes it more accessible for language learning and adult language use.

In the Competition Model, function and frequency are not mutually exclusive explanations. If a surface form serves a wider range of functions in one language (or one individual), then it will be called into service more often. The more often it is used, the lower its threshold of activation. In the model that we sketched out earlier, frequent use may increase the candidacy of a structural type to the point where it is sometimes chosen even under nonoptimal conditions, in place of a form that is higher in cue validity but also higher in cue cost. The relative clause difference that we have documented here may reflect the joint effects of function and frequency, operating synergistically to create a "descriptive habit" in native speakers of Italian. The combined availability and reliability of the Italian relative clause also makes it an attractive linguistic object for small children, whether or not they have fully grasped the topic-marking function that justifies frequent use of this object in the adult language.

This line of argument can be extended in a speculative but interesting direction to account for the other crosslinguistic differences observed in Study 3, that is, differences in "interclausal syntax." We have done a reasonably good job of delineating functional differences between English and Italian in the use of a topic-marking relative clause. We have no comparable evidence for a crosslinguistic difference in the functions served by gapping, continuation relatives, conjoined subjects, and/or conjoined objects. There may be differences between the two languages in the degree to which sentence planning is controlled by perspective maintenance, reflected in a slightly greater production of picture descriptions with a voice switch in Italian. This would be compatible with our earlier argument (based on Li & Thompson, 1976) that Italian falls somewhere in between English and Tagalog on a continuum from "subject dominance" to "topic dominance." However, we think that some additional factors may be operating to increase syntactic complexity in Italian, related to the issues of accessibility and commitment that we raised in the introduction.

Specifically, we would like to propose that the subcomponents of a complex two-predicate sentence are more accessible in Italian, because they have separate functions elsewhere in the grammar. Two facts about Italian go into this argument: Subjects can be omitted in a free-standing declarative sentence (i.e., "pro-drop"), and the order of major constituents can be varied within a simple clause (i.e., OV and VO, SV and VS). Armed with these facts, consider the on-line problems involved in the planning and execution of the complex two-predicate sentences described in Table 7.4. In Italian, phrases like "and hit the cow" can play several different roles: as an independent clause with an omitted subject (VO), as an independent clause with a right-dislocated subject (VS), and as a subcomponent within a larger gapped construction (SVO and VO). In English, the same passage never appears as an independent clause; it can only be used as a subcomponent within a larger sentence.

From the point of view of the listener, this means that there is more potential for ambiguity in Italian (a risk that is presumably reduced by the wealth of morphological markings in that language). However, from the point of view of the speaker this structural ambiguity may provide two advantages. First, because the various bits and pieces that are needed to compile a complex form have a separate life in Italian, they may have lower activation thresholds. They should be easier to "get at" if the speaker decides they are needed. Second, given the flexibility of word order and ellipsis provided by their language, Italian speakers do not have to commit themselves to a complex form quite so early in sentence production. They can begin a sentence from any of several points of view, and flesh out the details later. By contrast, an English speaker has very few structural options left once the first noun phrase is chosen. Because commitments have to be made so early in English, speakers may stick to simple sentences as a "safe harbor." If this analysis is correct, then it may also account for the fact that true passives are (if anything) more frequent in English, whereas a wider array of lexical alternatives are chosen in Italian. In both languages, speakers try to obey the experimenter's discourse probe by starting their descriptions from the suggested point of view, but obedience has its costs (i.e., the usual agent → subject mapping is precluded). Under these costly conditions, English speakers need to commit themselves quickly to a passive structure. Under the same conditions, Italians can afford to be more "relaxed," moving in a variety of different directions at a (slightly) more leisurely pace.

We are aware that this proposal is frustratingly imprecise, but we think it has promise. The twin notions of accessibility and commitment could be explored in more detail, using on-line measures that provide precise information about the point in time at which commitments are made, and the amount of time it takes to stage utterances that vary in accessibility from one language to another. These two ideas also have implications for the development of complex syntax in children. We may be able to move beyond a view of grammatical rules as discrete objects that are "acquired" in a single moment, focusing instead on developmental changes in the conditions under which syntactic knowledge is accessed and deployed.

Part III. Special Populations

8　Sentence Processing Strategies in Adult Bilinguals

Kerry Kilborn and Takehiko Ito

Bates and MacWhinney and their colleagues (1981, 1982, 1984) have shown that native speakers depend on a particular set of probabilistic cues to assign formal surface devices in their language to a specified set of underlying functions. The research program encompassed by their approach to language processing has extended from describing crosslinguistic processing differences in even typologically similar languages (e.g., English and Italian, both SVO languages), to charting the pattern of acquisition of grammatical "rules" in the first language, and more recently to crosslanguage investigations of "characteristic" neurological-based language deficits.

A natural extension of this broad experimental effort is in a field that involves issues of both language learning and sentence processing in adults: late second language acquisition. Given the large volume of data already collected from monolingual speakers, we are now in a position to begin exploration into bilingual sentence processing strategies. In this chapter we report on sentence processing experiments carried out with adults who speak two or more languages. The notion that cues vary in strength has proven valuable in describing the psychologically relevant features of different kinds of languages; it may also provide a window into the psycholinguistic properties of second language acquisition.

Students of language study come from many schools; not all share our assumptions or biases regarding the kinds of questions that are germane to second language acquisition, nor what constitutes an answer to those questions. For this reason, we will briefly review a small part of the history of second language acquisition research that lies behind the work presented here. We will focus on two issues: the influence of first language acquisition research on work in second language learning, and the role of rules in characterizing language acquisition of either kind.

The Roots of Second Language Acquisition Research

The study of second language (L2) acquisition has closely followed developments in first language (L1) research. In this regard, the central empirical issue has been whether the paths taken by the learner during the course of L1

257

vis-à-vis L2 acquisition are fundamentally different, or, in important ways, the same. Many, if not most, attempts to answer this and related questions employ proven research paradigms borrowed directly from L1 research. For example, a replication (Dulay & Burt, 1974) of Roger Brown's (1973) now-classic "morpheme order studies" showed that nonnative speakers from very different language backgrounds acquire a subset of English grammatical morphemes in a characteristic order, much in the same way children learning English as L1 do. Although it is not within the scope of this chapter to explore the long-standing relationship between L1 and L2 research, this one influential study serves to remind us that L1 and L2 research are both concerned with types of language acquisition (Anderson, 1984). The emphasis placed by L1 researchers on universals spilled over into L2 research, with a corresponding deemphasis on language differences.

The more recent emphasis in first language acquisition research on crosslinguistic comparisons of L1 learning has had undeniable impact on work in L2 acquisition. For the first two decades of child language research as a field in its own right, the vast majority of studies were carried out in English. It was recognized by many researchers that problems arose when general claims were based on language specific findings. Slobin and his colleagues (1967, 1973, 1977, 1982, 1985) spell out clearly the need to collect systematic data from a wide range of languages before we can hope to gain a sound understanding of the principles underlying language acquisition. Berman (1984), in a review of Slobin's contribution to the crosslinguistic study of L1 acquisition, points out that the same rationale applies to L2 research: the most fruitful approach involves applying the same types of research paradigms to two or more languages. What is more, this approach to bilingual language use offers an important contribution to crosslinguistic research in general: the processing system(s) employed in the service of two languages can be evaluated within single subjects, who provide their own control for many of the extraneous factors (e.g., cognitive level, socioeconomic status) that contribute to variance in most studies. The studies we report below are precisely of this kind.

The Role of Rules

Formal linguistics has long provided child language researchers with at least some of the theoretical tools necessary to ply their trade. In spite of having to deal with frequent shifts in linguistic theory, L1 researchers have borrowed heavily from formal linguistics to describe the state of the language systems they observe. Not surprisingly, the descriptions are typically in terms of rules, which are defined for the present purposes as a statement of the conditions that require, in discrete and categorical terms, the presence or absence of a given linguistic form. As we shall see, a formal description of language acquisition may be possible in terms of rules, but rules may be a less useful construct in building a performance model that accounts for the developmental aspects as well as the "steady-state" features of first and second language acqusition.

Like the majority of models of L1 acquisition, most models of L2 acquisition also emphasize the role of rules. Though different models may disagree or remain vague on how the learning mechanism that manipulates rules works, they do agree in principle on the end result: a language is acquired when the rules of the target language are internalized.

One such model in which rules play a central role, the Interlanguage Hypothesis (Selinker, 1972; Selinker, Swain, & Dumas, 1975; Corder, 1983), has been and continues to be influential in both theoretical and applied linguistic areas. According to the Interlanguage Hypothesis, a second language learner has at any given point in the acquisition process an interim stage grammar. This interim, or interlanguage, grammar changes in response to incoming data, so that with continued exposure to sufficient and appropriate input, the interlanguage grammar, by a series of successive approximations, moves closer and closer to the standard grammar of the target language. The interlanguage grammar is described in terms of its component rules (which may be derived from the target language, from the native language, or "invented" by the learner). At any one point in time, however, the L2 speaker's interlanguage grammar is relatively static. One of the advantages to this characterization of L2 acquisition is that it helps to account for the fact that many L2 learners seem to stop making much progress after some point (which varies from learner to learner), and never move beyond the final interlanguage grammar they acquire. In Selinker's terms, the interlanguage "fossilizes." We will return to the issues raised in the interlanguage literature in the discussion section, where we will point out several ways in which a probabilistic model of language processing can account in a somewhat different way for much of the same data.

The notion of a rule may, however, be too rigid to adequately capture a process as complex and dynamic as language acquisition. Rule-based models have two major shortcomings. First, they tend to be "all-or-nothing": Either a rule is present or it is not. We are often faced with the problem of how to talk about having "some but not all" of a language, but it is decidedly unsatisfactory from a formal theoretical perspective to frame the issue as learning or losing "part" of a rule. A second language learner may use or comprehend a passive in the appropriate discourse context only about half of the time, or usually but not always apply a vowel harmony rule correctly. But what position could half of a passive, or seventy-five percent of a vowel harmony rule hold in a learner's L2 grammar? Second, rule-based models derive from theoretical accounts of single linguistic systems, considered one at a time. This is desirable from a linguistic point of view, but it may not account in a natural way for the real-time processing considerations that constrain actual language use, for a learner's incomplete (L1 or L2) grammar, or for the possibility of interference and transfer between linguistic systems.

If we choose to characterize the expanding language system of a second language learner in terms of rules, we risk overemphasizing the aspects of language performance which easily fit the rules we have adopted, and missing other, potentially crucial aspects of the acquisition process which do not conform to our rule system. This is clearly the case with both aphasia and L1 acquisition (especially in light of recent crosslinguistic findings in these areas; this volume), but it is perhaps most obvious in L2 acquisition. For this reason, we will discuss the L2 learner in terms of a "partial" language system, as compared with the complete L1 system in the same individual, or in native speakers of the target language. Unless language acquisition follows the lines of linguistic rules absolutely, we may be forced to reconsider the usefulness of linguistically derived rules in describing such cases; when behavior deviates from the rules, our explanations become necessarily ad hoc.

An alternative approach to linguistic description goes under the heading of functional linguistics (Givón, 1979; Dik, 1978). The main tenet of functional linguistics is that forms in any natural language perform in the service of function. The strongest version of functionalism holds that a one-to-one relationship exists between form and function in a language. In fact, as we shall see, many-to-many mappings are the rule in natural languages. The functional approach bears quite different implications for the acquisition and processing of language than a rule-based account. On the latter version, acquisition is characterized by the internalization of the abstract rules which govern relationships between grammatical entities in the target language. Once in place, the rules themselves are an integral part of the processing system. A functional account does not necessarily entail the rejection of rules as components at a formal level of description. However, rules need not constitute the actual substrate of acquisition or processing. According to a functional account, the learner must pay attention to the way in which particular forms map onto particular functions. When form–function mappings are clear and direct, they can, like rules, operate in a discrete, categorical fashion. However, as we shall see, discrete, categorical behavior does not always characterize the the language processing system, nor its operation at any stage of (first or second) language acquisition.

It is important to note that a functional view of language acquisition does not necessarily entail the summary rejection of rules. Labov (1975, 1986) discusses the notion of variable rules, which allow for considerable variability in the application as well as the acquisition of grammatical features. This may be one way to bridge the gap which currently exists between models of language performance, such as the Competition Model, and accounts of language learning based on competence-oriented linguistic theories.

A functional perspective may thus help explain what appears to be a "partial" language system in a second language learner. Certain form–function mappings may be learned before others due to a variety of factors (attention, availability, etc.), so that the L2 learner may appear to have only part of a rule. A model of language performance which provides a principled account of what it means to have a "partial" language system is the "Competition Model" of Bates and MacWhinney. This model is a probabilistic theory of grammatical processing which developed out of a large body of crosslinguistic work in adult and child language, as well as in aphasia (Bates & MacWhinney, 1981, 1982, 1984, etc.). Since the studies discussed here are interpreted on the basis of the Competition Model, we will briefly describe the features of the model relevant to a study of bilingual sentence processing.

The Competition Model

The Competition Model derives from a consideration of the functional aspects of mapping linguistic forms to underlying meaning. Since this is a performance model, which attempts to describe real world language behavior, the resolution of form–function relations during processing must take place in real time. The model adheres to functionalist tenets in that form–function mappings are made as directly as possible. However, the strong functionalist position which posits one form to one function is rejected in favor of a multiplicity of form–function mappings: natural languages rarely make use of one-to-one mappings; rather, a single form can map onto many functions, and a single function can map onto several forms. The probabilistic feature of the Competition Model leads to the treatment of statistical tendencies and obligatory rules as quantitatively rather than qualitatively different. This is important because relations between surface forms and functions can be described in terms of strength or degree of interaction. Particular instances within the system of many-to-many form–function mappings in a given language are assigned weights in this model. This is done according to the statistical distributions of certain constructions, for example, how often or how reliably a given form is used to perform a given function. The sources of information a listener uses to decide which function is meant to be expressed by a given form are referred to as "cues." The usefulness of a particular cue is determined by its availability and reliability. For example, animacy may be heavily depended upon when an animate–inanimate distinction is present, as in "The boy broke the window," but not in "The ball broke the window."

A related feature of the Competition Model for the study of bilingual sentence processing is that it predicts the gradual emergence of conventions or rules, via a continuous increase in the strength or "determining force" (MacWhinney, Bates, & Kliegl, 1984; McDonald, this volume) of statistical form–function assignments. The implication for L2 acquisition is a strong one: The application of cues in form–function mapping in L2 ought to approach distributionally predicted levels as fluency in L2 increases. However, as noted earlier, L1 strategies may strongly interfere or interact with appropriate L2 strategies.

The Competition Model allows for a test of at least four hypotheses of bilingual sentence processing.

1. First language (L1) strategies may be applied to both languages.
2. A second set of strategies is acquired and applied exclusively in the context of L2, so that the learner behaves essentially as a monolingual in each language.
3. L2 strategies are not only applied to L2 but may even supplant L1 strategies.
4. New strategies may be adopted in the course of L2 learning, and become assimilated into one amalgamated set that is applied to processing in both languages.

These are not mutually exclusive in a developmental model; each of these possibilities might be true at some point in the process of acquiring a second language. Furthermore, these different hypotheses point out that a single level progression from beginner to fluent bilingual is only one of several possible courses for second language acquisition to follow. If L2 learning turns out to be more or less unidimensional, it would be rather convenient for the model we have adopted here. If, on the other hand, there are many routes to fluency, any model will have to be considerably more complex than the the Competition Model in its current form, whether rules are incorporated in some form or not.

In what follows, we will examine the evidence from a number of studies derived from the Competition Model, including L1 and L2 speakers of English, German, Italian, Spanish, Dutch, and Japanese. As we proceed, we will track which of the above hypotheses receive support from the data and which do not. As we shall see, results do support the use of probabilistic models instead of rule-based models, to capture the "in-between" status of the processing characteristics in second language users. At the same time, however, the second language results also look quite different than comparable studies of first language acquisition within the Competition Model, and may suggest some further constraints on the learning component of that model.

Before we begin, it will be useful to first establish a convention for referring to the various language groups included in these studies. We shall adopt the following terminology: For example, in referring to a group of native English speakers whose second language is Dutch, we will use the label ED (English-Dutch), placing the native language first and the second language second. Likewise, native Dutch speakers whose second language is English will be referred to as DE. Similarly, when a DE group is tested in their first language (Dutch), we will use the label DE1 (Dutch-English in L1); when DE subjects are tested in their second language (English), we will use the label DE2 (Dutch-English in L2).

Experiments in the Competition Model Paradigm

In this section we will examine six studies which use variations of a sentence interpretation task designed to set up various "coalitions" and "competitions" among a restricted set of grammatical entities (e.g., word order, animacy, agreement, case inflections, etc). Though the studies reported here vary in details, in each one we are interested in the probabilistic nature of processing strategies in bilingual individuals. In particular, we are concerned with the question of whether L1 strategies "invade" into processing in L2. Taken together, their findings may give us some insight into what it means to have a "partial" language system.

The first studies from the point of view of the Competition Model asked whether first language (L1) strategies "invade" into processing in the second language (L2). In other words, does an adult bilingual depend to some extent on L1 strategies in order to map surface forms onto functions in L2? If this kind of process proves to be available to skilled bilinguals, then we can address a further set of questions regarding the acquisition process at earlier stages (e.g., what does it mean to be "between" languages? What influence does the processing structure of L1 have on L2? Does this influence vary as a function of fluency, age, and context of L2 acquisition?).

Case studies of Italian-English and German-English bilinguals

Having performed numerous investigations of sentence processing in adults and children in a variety of different languages, Bates and MacWhinney (1981) extended their Competition Model paradigm to look at whether L1 strategies impinge on processing in L2 (or vice versa) within a single individual. They carried out a pilot study with native German and native Italian speakers using a sentence interpretation task adapted from earlier studies of sentence processing in monolinguals. Subjects heard sentences containing two nouns and a verb, orthogonalized along the dimensions of order (NVN, NNV, VNN), agreement (first noun, second noun, or neither noun agrees with the verb in number), and animacy (both nouns animate, first animate and second inanimate, first inanimate and second animate). The result is a 2(language) × 3(word order) × 3(agreement) × 3(animacy) design in which cues are set into competition and coalition with one another. The task was to simply identify the actor ("who did it?") in each sentence heard.

From the pattern of responses to the test questions set up in this manner, a picture of the relative strength of different combinations of cues to sentence interpretation emerges. Although too few subjects participated for extensive statistical analyses, the results of these case studies, shown in Figures 8.1, 8.2, and 8.3, were very much in keeping with the idea that L1 strategies play a central role in early L2 processing. The performance of the Italian bilinguals in English exactly paralleled results from monolingual Italians: Agreement was stronger than animacy, which was in turn stronger than word order. One German subject also used monolingual German processing strategies to interpret English sentences. The other German subject, also an extremely fluent bilingual, used processing strategies similar to native speakers of English (comparable testing of the same individuals in German was not carried out). These pilot results suggest that L1 strategies operate during processing in L2, and that use of language-appropriate strategies may interact with level of fluency.

The fact that processing strategies appropriate to L1 carry over to L2 provides strong support for the form–function model of representation in the Competition Model. However, at least one problem also emerges at this point: Despite many years of exposure and a high level of fluency in English, one native German still interpreted English sentences on the basis of form–function mappings appropriate to German. Such persistence of L1 strategies is not accounted for by the current version of the Competition Model; it seems instead to reflect an extraordinary insensitivity to cue validity in L2. We will return to this and other problems for the Competition Model raised by second language acquisition research in the discussion. We turn first to another study which provides further evidence for the invasion of L1 strategies into L2 processing.

Sentence Processing in English-Chinese Bilinguals

Miao (1981) studied the role of two cues, word order and animacy, in the processing of Chinese by native Chinese speakers and by English-speaking second language learners of Chinese. The basic word order in Chinese is SVO, and there are no inflectional markers for transitivity. Other word orders, such as SOV and OSV, also occur in colloquial speech, but these are accompanied by obligatory morphological marking with respect to subject/object roles. Furthermore, the topic, which may not be the subject or the agent, is often associated with the first position in Chinese sentences, whereas subject roles are frequently not expressed overtly at all (Li & Thompson, 1976).

Subjects in Miao's study were eight native Chinese speakers and eight native English speakers who had studied Mandarin for more than three years (six had been in China for two or more years). Subjects enacted simple sentences consisting of two nouns and a verb in Chinese, drawn from a list of animate and inanimate nouns (without morphological markers) and transitive action verbs, and varied orthogonally in order (NVN, NNV, VNN). Miao hypothesized that word order ought be a dominant cue in sentence interpretation in Chinese. Contrary to expectation, however, she found that native Chinese speakers relied more heavily on semantic cues than on syntactic ones. Although there was a slight tendency to choose the first noun in NVN sentences (68.1% of the time, compared with 42.4% in VNN and 56.3% in NNV sentences), these

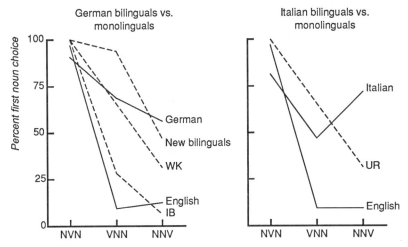

Figure 8.1. Word order main effects (for items that are ambiguous with regard to agreement and animacy) for native speakers in their first languages (solid lines) and for bilinguals tested in English as a second language (broken lines).

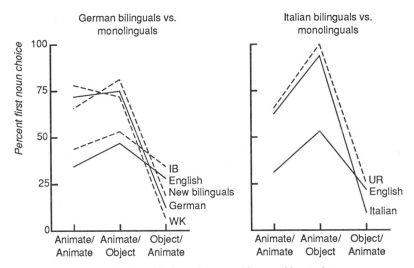

Figure 8.2. Animacy main effects (for items that are ambiguous with regard to agreement, summed across word order conditions) for native speakers in their first languages (solid lines) and for bilinguals tested in English as a second language (broken lines).

differences did not reach significance, suggesting that word order is not a particularly important source of information in Chinese sentence processing. Compare these findings with those from the use of the animacy cue: Chinese subjects chose the first noun 86.1% of the time if it was animate and the second

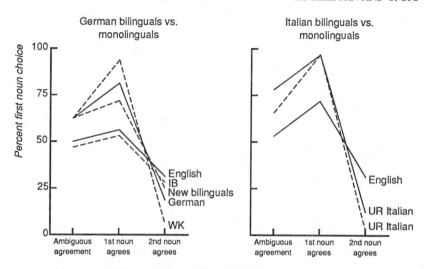

Figure 8.3. Main effects of subject–verb agreement (summed across word order and animacy conditions) for native speakers in their first languages (solid lines) and for bilinguals tested in English as a second language (broken lines).

noun inanimate. When the first noun was inanimate and the second animate, the *second* noun was chosen as agent 81.9% of the time. When both nouns were animate, performance was near chance level (62.5%). Clearly, Chinese subjects make more use of semantic cues than word order cues in interpreting simple sentences, contrary to initial expectations based entirely on typological considerations. However, given what we know about the low reliability of word order in informal Chinese, perhaps this is not surprising (see below).

In contrast to native speakers of Chinese, Miao found that EC2 speakers did rely heavily on word order as a cue to sentence meaning. Regardless of animacy relations, EC2 subjects consistently chose the first noun of NVN strings as the agent (91% first noun choice). In VNN orders, the first noun was chosen 33% of the time, and in NNV orders 72.2% of the time. EC2 speakers also tended to choose the animate noun over the inanimate noun as agent (84% first noun choice in AI, 40.3% in IA, 72.2% in AA), but this bias was less overt than in the strategies adopted by native speakers.

Why did native Chinese speakers depend most heavily on semantic features in Chinese, a language which provides consistent word order information? There are at least two factors that may militate against a strong word order strategy in native Chinese speakers. Although the apparent weakness of word order as a cue to sentence meaning seemed surprising at the time, we have since learned that on-line competition from other word order types within the language diminishes the strength of the canonical order, even in morphologically impoverished settings (see below). Second, as Miao points out, the dominant role played by the subject-as-agent in other SVO languages such as English may be partly undermined by the importance of the topic feature in Chinese. As noted earlier, the subject is often omitted altogether in Chinese sentences, and is explicitly marked when it occurs in noncanonical orders. The topic, which tends to occur in sentence-initial position and may or may not be the subject or the agent of the sentence, may be afforded a relatively high status in real-time processing strategies in Chinese. These findings have been replicated by Tzeng and Hung (1984).

Word order was the primary cue for EC2 speakers in Miao's study, however. These subjects are native speakers of English, a language in which, as we have seen, word order as a cue to sentence meaning typically "wins" over-whelmingly in competition with other cues. Miao's study provides evidence that processing strategies appropriate to L1 may carry over to processing in L2. However, while we can be fairly certain that at least some transfer such as this is likely to occur, the characteristic second noun strategy in English NNV sequences was not found in Chinese NNV sequences, which suggests that simple transfer cannot completely account for the L2 findings in Miao's experiment.

Sentence Processing and Cue Validity

McDonald (1986, 1987a, this volume) developed a model of cue mapping which posits that the the first cues to be assigned form–function mappings in a language-to-be-learned will be the most valid ones over all sentences, and that a cue's final mapping strength will depend on how it performs when it is in conflict with other cues in a sentence. McDonald obtained validity and strength estimates from samples of texts in each language tested. Using this model to predict trends in second language learning, she examined the notion that as fluency increases in a second language, the cue weights (i.e., a measure of the consistency with which a particular cue wins in competition with other cues) used by the learner gradually shift from the first language norm to that of the second language.

The cues tested by McDonald included word order, animacy, and case inflection, presented in the context of NVN sentences, relative clauses, and dative constructions. Subjects were first and second language learners of German, English, and Dutch, grouped according to their overall proficiency in L2, who performed a sentence interpretation task in both L1 and L2. The results showed that as the level of fluency increased, cue weights approached those predicted by frequency counts in the target language. In other words, L2 strategies were built up gradually in a more or less linear fashion following the principles of cue validity. Although different languages provide different strategies, the same principles apply to the establishment of form–function mappings in L1 and in L2.

To recap the findings so far, we have seen that transfer of L1 strategies to L2 processing does occur; however, L2 strategies are adopted as well, and may be accounted for in terms of the strength and reliability of cues in the target language. These results support predictions made by the Competition Model. In the sections to follow, we will review further evidence from a variety of languages. As we shall see, although generally supportive, the data raise several challenges to the Competition Model account of acquisition and performance in L2.

Sentence Interpretation in Dutch-English Bilinguals

On the surface, Dutch and English, both Germanic languages, have many features in common. Both locate articles and other modifiers before the noun, both make case distinctions only only on personal pronouns, and the canonical word order for simple, active declarative sentences is Subject-Verb-Object (SVO). Given the large degree of similarity between English and Dutch, we might expect to find little crosslanguage variability in processing strategies. However, there are some important differences between Dutch and English which, depending on what kind of model we choose to explain processing behavior, lead to different predictions about how the two languages are processed.

One such difference is the relatively rich morphological system in Dutch, versus the impoverished one in English. Dutch provides a fairly regular set of distinct markings, mainly on verbs, for tense and number agreement. English has vestiges of such a system, but morphological cues in English are neither consistently available, nor consistently reliable when they do appear. Another difference is related to word order. The basic or canonical word order for Dutch as well as for English has typically been considered to be SVO. Whereas English fits this classification rather cleanly, Koster (1975) has shown that Dutch may fit the formal category of SOV better, chiefly because the presence of an auxiliary (e.g., *zullen* "shall" to mark the future, or *zijn* "be" to mark the passive and some types of past tense) requires that the main verb in infinitive or participle form be postposed:

No auxiliary: *Piet   ziet   de   kat.*
                 SUB   VERB   ART   OBJ
                 Pete   sees   the   cat
                 "Pete sees the cat."

Auxiliary: *Piet   zal   de   cat   zien.*
                 SUB   AUX   ART   OBJ   VERB
                 Pete   will   the   cat   see
                 "Pete will see the cat."

Other sentence forms are also possible in Dutch. For example, a very frequent form for questions in Dutch is VSO:

Ziet	*Piet*	*de*	*kat?*
VERB	SUB	ART	OBJ
Sees	Pete	the	cat?

"Does Pete see the cat?"

In English, VSO is not a possible configuration, if the V is taken to be a main verb, rather than an auxiliary. Verb-final clauses also occur in Dutch, but only in subordinate clauses, such as sentential complements and relative clauses (the latter of which requires an obligatory relative pronoun [e.g., *De man, die de vrouw sag was...* – The man (whom) the woman saw was...]).

If language processing is based on the application of rules, then we would not expect to find a difference between Dutch and English on simple, auxiliary-free SVO forms, which map onto the same functions in each language. However, the Competition Model holds that processing strategies in a particular language are a product of the processing system's sensitivity to the full distribution of form–function mappings in that language. A particular form's distribution will overlap with that of other forms in the language to the extent that the two are structurally similar, on the one hand, and functionally similar, on the other. So an incoming sentence form activates all of the potential interpretations which are, to a greater or lesser degree, compatible with the input. The greater the degree of compatibility, the more a particular form is activated, and eventually only one interpretation "wins." If the presence of partially overlapping structures (e.g., SOV and SVO word orders in Dutch) in a language can impinge on sentence interpretation, then we ought to find that Dutch, which allows much more word order variation than English, differs from English in this dimension.

Kilborn and Cooreman (1987) presented sets of Dutch and English sentences to native Dutch speakers who were advanced (post-graduate) students of English. Twenty subjects each received 54 sentences in each language consisting of two nouns and a verb, and indicated which noun they thought was the actor or subject. The independent variables were language (Dutch and English), word order (NVN, VNN, NNV), agreement (Ag0, Ag1, Ag2), and animacy (AA, AI, IA).

Although there were main effects of each of the three main variables, the most important findings here involve the interactions in which the language variable participated. Language interacted independently with word order and with agreement, and it also participated in one three-way interaction (language × animacy × word order). We will limit our discussion here to the language × word order interaction, as it nicely illustrates the direction of the findings in general.

The solid lines in Figure 8.4 show the Language × Word Order interaction for the Dutch-English bilinguals. Three word order permutations were possible: NVN, VNN, and NNV. In both Dutch and English, SVO is the basic or canonical word order for active, declarative sentences (no auxiliary forms were presented),

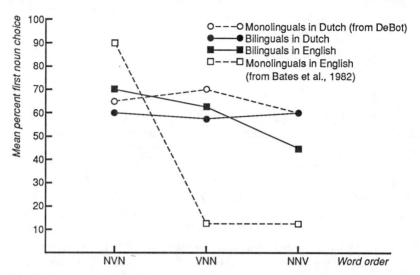

Figure 8.4. Language by word order interaction (noun choice): comparison between bilinguals and monolinguals in Dutch and English.

which corresponds to NVN. Nevertheless, a difference in percent choice of first noun as actor emerged across languages in the canonical NVN word order: Subjects chose the first noun as actor 61% of the time in Dutch, in contrast to 68% choice in English. In the noncanonical order conditions, subjects chose the first noun 59% and 58% of the time in Dutch for VNN and NNV, respectively. In English a different picture emerges: First noun choice rate was 62% in VNN, but dropped to 44% in NNV orders. A post hoc analysis showed that the source of the interaction was in the different interpretations given NVN and NNV orders for English as compared with Dutch.

The broken lines in Figure 8.4 illustrate data from similar sentence interpretation tasks carried out in a monolingual setting with native speakers of Dutch (De Bot, personal communication) and English (Bates et al., 1982; MacWhinney et al., 1984). These results provide a useful reference point against which we can compare the performance of bilingual subjects in each of the languages in question. Overall, our subjects' performance in Dutch closely parallels the results reported by De Bot for native Dutch speakers in a Dutch-only version of the sentence interpretation task, which clearly indicates the robustness of the paradigm. The monolingual English data shown have been replicated a number of times; the effects of word order, animacy, and agreement in English are surprisingly consistent across studies (Bates et al., 1982; MacWhinney et al., 1984).

The Dutch bilingual subjects' performance in English suggests further evidence for invasion of L1 into L2: the results are markedly "Dutch-looking" in both languages. However, when the results in English do diverge from those in Dutch, it is in the direction of the monolingual English findings. Figure 8.4 shows that DE2 subjects, like native English speakers, preferred the first noun in NVN strings, although to a lesser extent. (broken lines show data from Bates et al, 1982, for comparison). DE2 subjects, again like monolingual English speakers, also showed a second noun strategy in NNV sentences, although again less pronounced. The main difference emerged on VNN sentences: DE2 subjects chose the first noun 62% of the time, in contrast to only a 15% first noun choice by English monolinguals.

Two factors contributed to these findings. First, word order does not appear to command as much attention in Dutch as do animacy and agreement cues. In order of relative strength, processing cues in Dutch line up as follows: agreement > animacy > word order. Thus, even in English, DE2 subjects continued to exhibit Dutch-like processing biases, and so were not much affected by variations in word order. This is consistent with the fact that Dutch, which has a relatively rich verb agreement system, allows more word order variation than English. Second, the first noun bias on VNN sentences can be accounted for in terms of transfer from Dutch. In particular, VNN strings were interpreted as VSO, which happens to be the predominant question form in Dutch. For these subjects, the relative strength of the frequent Dutch question form may "win" in competition with other potential interpretations, including English VOS.

One difference between this study and previous ones was the use of a within-subject design, providing a control for much of the extraneous variance introduced when comparisons are made simultaneously across subjects and across languages. This underscores even more strongly the finding that L1 strategies invade into processing in L2, providing more support for the Competition Model account of second language acquisition. However, one other aspect of the results from this study deserves mention. Within the constraints just described, Kilborn and Cooreman identified two subgroups of Dutch speakers who appeared to attend more consistently to either animacy cues or agreement cues, and a third subgroup which used an amalgam of those two cues. Subjects in each subgroup applied their biases to both Dutch and English. As we shall see, the potential for individual differences poses special challenges to the Competition Model. We will return to this issue in more detail when we discuss similar subgroup differentiation observed in different language groups by Harrington (1987) and Wulfeck et al. (1986).

Sentence interpretation in Spanish-English bilinguals

In a recent study, Wulfeck et al. (1986) examined the performance of Spanish-English bilinguals on a sentence interpretation task. Twelve subjects each received 54 sentences in each language. Sentences consisted of two nouns and a verb, and subjects were instructed to indicate which noun they thought was the actor or subject. The four factors manipulated as independent variables included language (Spanish and English), word order (NVN, NNV, and VNN), animacy contrasts (AA, both nouns are animate; AI, first noun animate and second noun inanimate; and IA, first noun inanimate and second noun animate), and agreement contrasts (ambiguous agreement, Ag0, in which the verb agrees with both nouns, versus first noun agreement, Ag1, or second noun agreement, Ag2).

Recall the four possible outcomes that we suggested at the outset: (1) Bilinguals may use interpretation strategies appropriate to their native language in both L1 and L2 (i.e., depend on L1 cues to sentence meaning in L2); (2) they may switch over and apply L2 strategies to both languages; (3) bilinguals may look just like monolinguals in each of their languages; and (4) bilinguals may apply a combination of L1 and L2 cues, resulting in a strategy amalgam that is neither exclusively L1 nor L2 in character.

The results from this study supported not one but two outcomes: One group of subjects did not employ distinct processing strategies for either language, but rather seemed to apply an amalgam of processing strategies drawn from Spanish and English. A second, distinct group applied Spanish-like strategies to the same degree in both languages. Figures 8.5 and 8.6 show the findings for both groups with respect to word order and agreement, respectively. The solid lines represent the bilingual subjects from this study. The broken line shows findings from an earlier study of this type with monolingual speakers of English (Bates et al., 1982), and serves here as a useful point of reference. Group 1 adopted word order, the dominant cue from their second language (English), followed to a lesser extent by agreement and animacy, which are generally the strongest cues in Spanish. These subjects seem to operate with the same merged hierarchy of strategies for both languages. Group 2 showed only slight sensitivity to word order cues, instead depending heavily on agreement, followed by animacy cues. This Spanish-dominant processing strategy was also applied equally to both languages. The difference between merged-hierarchy and Spanish-dominant strategies could not be explained in terms of any obvious group factor (e.g., age of second language learning, fluency, educational level).

Taken singly, either a Spanish-dominant processing strategy or an amalgam of English and Spanish strategies would present no problem to the Competition Model account of language acquisition. They might each represent different stages along a continuum of sensitivity to L2 cues. However, given that the observed differences between individuals in this study cannot be related to fluency or other factors, we are faced with having to account for these differences in bilingual processing styles. Crosslinguistic work has shown that there is tremendous variability in the way natural languages divide up the tasks of assigning surface form to underlying function. The processing mechanism

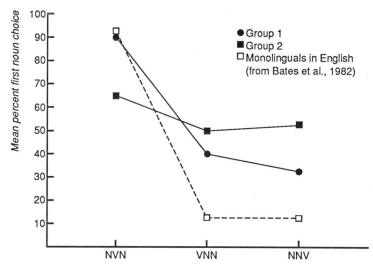

Figure 8.5. Group × word order interaction in English.

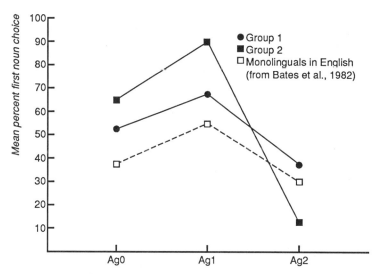

Figure 8.6. Group × agreement in English.

that must deal with such potential variability must also possess considerable flexibility. The findings reported by Wulfeck et al. (1986) provide solid evidence for such flexibility within individual speakers, indicating that alternate routes are available to L2 learners, rather than a series of way stations along a single learning process. We will get back to the issue of individual differences and alternate learning routes shortly.

Sentence Processing in Italian-English and English-Italian Bilinguals

Gass (1987) looked at sentence interpretation strategies of L2 speakers of English (L1 Italian) and L2 speakers of Italian (L1 English). Subjects heard sentences containing two nouns and a verb, in which three cues, word order, animacy, and topic, were varied orthogonally. Topicality was indicated by the phrase, "As for X," which preceded each sentence. Subjects were instructed to indicate which noun they thought was the actor or agent in the sentence.

Gass found that in Italian, native English (EI2) speakers tended to adopt animacy as the primary cue to agency, the same cue that native Italians used most. In English, however, Italian-English (IE2) bilinguals continued to depend heavily on animacy relations, in contrast to native English speakers, who focused instead on word order. Gass claims that these results reflect a potential universal in second language acquisition. Specifically, semantics may be a stronger or more central strategy than one based on syntax. For this reason, it is in some sense easier for native English speakers to drop word order and pick up animacy in Italian than it is for native Italian speakers to let go of a semantic strategy when they interpret English sentences.

While a "semantic primacy" effect is an interesting proposal, we shall see in the next section that the picture is not so simple. Gass's findings are contradicted by the results of English-Japanese bilinguals, who appear to apply a "meta-word-order" strategy which overrides the semantic bias in Japanese.

Sentence Interpretation in Japanese-English and English-Japanese bilinguals

We will review two studies in this section. Harrington (1987) investigated sentence processing strategies in Japanese L2 speakers of English, with monolingual control groups in both English and Japanese. The cues to sentence meaning in Harrington's study included word order, animacy, and contrastive stress. In the second experiment, Ito (in preparation) looked at advanced and beginning L2 speakers of Japanese and English, and included monolingual control groups in each language as well. Word order and animacy were systematically varied, and an additional factor, morphological marking of topic (the particle *wa*) and subject case (the particle *ga*), was included as well. Before turning to these studies in detail, we will briefly discuss some relevant typological differences between Japanese and English.

1. Word Order.   As we discussed earlier, English is a rigid SVO language. Recall that although some minor variation occurs in colloquial speech (e.g., such as OSV and VOS orders in left and right dislocations), other possible orders (OVS, SOV, VSO) are not acceptable. Also, as we have seen, English lacks a rich system of inflectional morphology. Consequently, word order is the primary source of information about case roles in English sentences.

Japanese is an SOV language. However, in contrast to English, considerable word order variation is permitted, providing the verb remains in last position and the appropriate grammatical morphemes are included when required. The role of word order is not to mark case relations, as in English. Rather, word order serves pragmatic purposes in Japanese, highlighting particular elements of a sentence.

2. Animacy. English permits a wide range of noun types to function as subjects. Other languages, however, are much more restrictive, typically allowing only animate entities to be subjects. This is the case in Japanese, in which only humans and some higher animals are permitted to be subjects.

3. Stress. In English, contrastive stress is used for pragmatic purposes, mainly to focus attention on certain elements in a sentence. As Harrington (1987) succinctly points out, the subject in English does not usually receive contrastive stress, since the subject position is "typically associated with given information." Japanese, on the other hand, may or may not provide contrastive voice stress to this same end. Instead, contrastive particles such as *wa* play the role in Japanese filled by stress in English (see Kuno, 1973).

4. Case/topic marking. Japanese also has a set of noun-suffixing particles which function as case and topic markers. The subject marker *ga* and object marker *o* are nonobligatory, and are usually used to indicate old information. These case particles are often replaced by the topic marker *wa*, which conveys new information. Much of the word order variation in Japanese is due to the presence of these particles (see Clancy, 1985). In addition, since animates are more likely to be topics due to discourse-pragmatic reasons (Givón, 1979), the topic marker *wa* is more likely to be attached to animate elements in a sentence than to inanimate ones. Since topics tend to be animate *and* are typically marked by *wa*, the distributions of "animate" and "topic" overlap, making it difficult to distinguish in practice between dependence on Japanese morphosyntactic features and more general semantic strategies during processing.

Sentence Processing in Japanese-English Bilinguals

Harrington (1987) performed a sentence interpretation study in which word order, animacy, and contrastive stress were set into competing and converging combinations. Subjects tested in English were 12 native English controls and 12 native Japanese ESL learners, all of whom had been enrolled in an English program for a maximum of five months. An additional 12 native Japanese subjects were tested in Japanese. Each subject received 81 test sentences, which were adapted from Bates et al. (1982).

The results included a language × word order interaction. The native English controls (E1) exhibited the characteristic pattern of noun choice across the three word order types: In NVN, the first noun was chosen 81% of the time, compared with 35% for NNV and 33% for VNN. In native Japanese (J1), word order had virtually no effect on noun choice: The first noun was chosen in Japanese NVN 59% of the time, in NNV 56%, and in VNN 54%. In the L2 test group (JE2), native Japanese speakers performing the task in English chose the first noun 68% of the time in NVN sentences, 59% in NNV, and 56% in VNN. Note that neither Japanese group exhibits any bias toward the canonical word order in Japanese, SOV (=NNV). However, although it was not reported whether the difference between groups on NVN was significant, the JE2 group did appear to lean toward the first noun in English NVN (68%), falling midway between English and Japanese L1 speakers. This suggests the possibility that the JE2 learners in this study were at least aware of the utility of word order as a cue in their second language, and is compatible with the pattern of within-subject divergence reported earlier for Dutch-English bilinguals.

The animacy condition yielded differences across languages as well. In Japanese, native speaker controls (J1) chose the animate noun over the inanimate noun overwhelmingly, 98% first noun choice in AI, and .03% in IA. In AA combinations, first noun choice was 69%, suggesting a weak first noun effect. In English, animacy produced much less pronounced differences. Monolingual English controls (E1) chose the first noun in AI pairs 75% of the time, compared with 23% in IA pairs, while selection was random (50%) in AA pairs. By contrast, the JE2 group appears to have used an amalgam of native English and native Japanese animacy strategies. First noun choice for AI and AA pairs paralleled the results for Japanese, 93% and 67%, respectively. In IA pairs, however, JE2 speakers chose the inanimate noun 23% of the time, which was just as often as the native English controls. This suggests that even in these novice L2 speakers, there is some sensitivity to the acceptability of inanimate nouns as subjects, contrary to convention in their native language.

There was no effect of stress in either language. According to Harrington, trends in the data suggest that there was some avoidance of the first noun when it was stressed, which is consistent with the pragmatic function of stress to signal new information (case and topic particles were not included in this study).

To summarize, there were two areas in which Japanese L2 learners of English differed from monolingual controls. First, JE2 speakers showed a bias toward the first noun in canonical NVN sentences in English, but no second noun strategy in noncanonical orders. This is consistent with all of the studies that we have reported, so far, in which bilinguals show any sign at all of sensitivity to processing strategies characteristic of native English speakers. Second, JE2 learners depended more heavily on animacy cues in English than E1 native speakers, in keeping with the use of a semantic strategy by monolingual controls in Japanese. However, JE2 subjects showed as much willingness to select an inanimate noun as subject as monolingual English E1 speakers, in strong contrast with J1 controls. Thus, evidence both for transfer of L1 strategies and acquisition of L2 cues was found.

One apparent inconsistency also emerged from the findings with monolingual English controls. Although native Japanese speakers did evidence a strong tendency to use animacy as a cue to sentence meaning in both Japanese and English as L2, English speakers in this study also used the animacy cue to a greater extent than was found in previous studies. Harrington, noting this difference, performed post hoc analyses which revealed that the lean toward animacy in English was due to the use of that cue by one subgroup of English speakers, whose performance closely paralleled that of the Japanese groups. We have already seen evidence from both Spanish-English and Dutch-English bilinguals for individual differences in bilingual processing which carry across languages; these recurring within-language differences point to a need to account in a principled way for individual differences in L2 acquisition. We will return to this issue later.

We turn first to two experiments by Ito (in preparation) which also involved English and Japanese. In Part 1, two groups of native Japanese speakers, one fluent and one nonfluent in English, and a native English control group (i.e., advanced JE2, novice JE2, and E1, respectively) performed an English sentence interpretation task in which word order and animacy cues were systematically varied. In Part 2, two native English groups, one fluent and one nonfluent in Japanese, and a native Japanese control group (i.e., advanced EJ2, novice EJ2, and J1, respectively) performed a similar task with the same cues in Japanese, but with the additional cue of topic/case particle (*wa/ga*).

Sentence Processing by Japanese-English Bilinguals in English. Three groups participated in this part of Ito's study, a monolingual English control group (E1), an advanced Japanese-English bilingual group (native Japanese speakers studying at an American university, advanced JE2), and a novice Japanese-English bilingual group (native Japanese speakers in a Japanese university, novice JE2).

The group × word order interaction in English is shown is Figure 8.7 (for purposes of comparison, the results from monolingual Japanese speakers on the same task are included as well). Native English speakers exhibited the characteristic first noun strategy on NVN sentences (87% first noun choice), and the equally characteristic second noun strategy in noncanonical strings (18% first noun choice in VNN, 23% in NNV). By contrast, both groups of Japanese-English bilinguals made much less use of word order distinctions. The advanced JE2 group did exhibit a preference for the first noun as agent in NVN orders (86%), but choice fell within chance levels for VNN (42%) and NNV (47%).

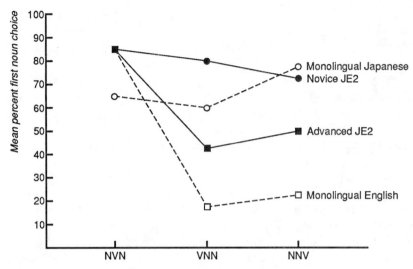

Figure 8.7. Group × word order interaction in English.

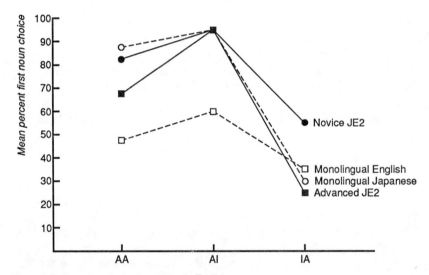

Figure 8.8. Group × animacy interaction in English.

The novice JE2 group tended to choose the first noun regardless of word order (85% in NVN, 79% in VNN, and 72% in NNV). The absence of a consistent word order strategy in these bilingual subjects suggests that sentence processing in English is guided by some other factor.

The group × animacy interaction, illustrated in Figure 8.8, shows clearly what that other factor is. Both advanced and novice JE2 groups depended heavily on animacy as a cue to sentence meaning in English. When an animate noun preceded an inanimate one, the animate noun was chosen 96% of the time by both advanced and novice JE2 subjects. When an inanimate noun came before an animate noun, the inanimate one was chosen only 23% of the time by advanced JE2 subjects, and 55% (at chance) by novice JE2 subjects. This reflects the tendency of the latter group to select the first noun in all sentence types in English, and probably also reflects more differentiation between canonical and noncanonical orders in the advanced JE2 group. When both nouns were animate, some preference for the first noun emerged in both bilingual groups, 69% for the advanced and 84% for the novice JE2 group. In contrast, the animacy cue played a relatively minor role in the sentence processing strategies of monolingual E1 speakers. Native English controls chose the first noun in AI pairs 60% of the time, compared to 33% of the time in IA pairs. Choice in AA pairs was random.

The strong preference for animacy as a cue to sentence meaning in English in Ito's study provides further evidence for the transfer of a semantic strategy characteristic of Japanese into processing in English as a second language. These results essentially replicate the findings reported above from Harrington (1987), and they are consonant with Gass's claim about a "universal" semantic bias. Also, a weak but consistent first noun strategy in English NVN sentences was evident in Ito's findings, as well as the lack of a second noun strategy in noncanonical NNV and VNN strings. However, as Figure 8.7 shows, both bilingual groups tended, albeit weakly, to move away from the native Japanese norm in the direction of the native English use of word order, which suggests that even though the bilingual subjects made more use of animacy than word order, both advanced and novice bilingual groups may be sensitive to the role of word order as a cue in English. We will return to this point later.

This tendency was somewhat more pronounced in the advanced bilingual group than in the novice group, suggesting that overall level of fluency may be an important factor in the use of language-specific strategies. When the advanced JE bilinguals diverge from the novice group in the use of word order, it is even further in the direction of the native English controls. This suggests that, even though their overall pattern of responses is more similar to Japanese than to English norms, the more advanced speakers of English as L2 are using English-like strategies a greater proportion of the time than novice speakers.

Sentence Processing by English-Japanese Bilinguals in Japanese. In this experiment, three groups, native English speakers who are teachers of Japanese (advanced EJ2), native English speakers who are students of Japanese (novice EJ2), and a monolingual Japanese control group (J1), performed a sentence interpretation task. The factors varied included word order (NVN, VNN, NNV) and animacy (AI, IA, AA). In order to investigate the role of morphological markers for nonnative speakers of Japanese, Ito introduced the case-marking particles *wa* and *ga* as an additional factor in this experiment. We will discuss this factor separately. We turn first to the use of word order and animacy in L2 speakers of Japanese.

Japanese sentences without particles.   Figure 8.9 shows the group × word order interaction. This figure shows that both advanced and novice EJ2 speakers are affected more by the word order cue than J1 speakers. The monolingual J1 subjects chose the first noun 67% of the time in NVN, 63% in VNN, and, in keeping with a view of Japanese as an SOV language, 77% of the time in canonical NNV orders. (Note that this is somewhat contradictory with Harrington's results, in which J1 subjects showed no preference across all of the orders.) In contrast, advanced and novice EJ2 subjects chose the first noun in NVN as subject 58% and 67% of the time, respectively. In the other two word order conditions, the nonnative groups were nearly identical, preferring the first noun only 44% (advanced) and 43% (novice) of the time in VNN orders, and 88% (advanced) and 90% (novice) of the time in NNV orders. This pattern of responses by the EJ2 subjects is not what we would expect if subjects were relying on English strategies, particularly in the case of NNV orders. We will return to this finding shortly.

Figure 8.10 shows the group by animacy interaction. In Japanese, EJ2 speakers depended on animacy as a cue to sentence meaning, as did the J1 controls. This contrasts with the JE2 groups in the above studies by Ito and by Harrington, in which subjects were found to continue to rely in English on the same cue (i.e., animacy) that "wins" in their native language. Animacy is a cue which is normally assigned peripheral status in native English processing strategies. This appears, then, to be evidence that these EJ2 speakers were able to acquire the use of a cue that is appropriate to processing in Japanese.

However, several interesting differences emerged between the nonnative speakers and the native controls, differences which point to L1 intrusion into L2 processing. The effect of animacy seems to have been compromised in EJ2 subjects by a tendency to choose the first noun in IA combinations. In particular, in the IA condition, animacy competes with an interpretation based on the canonical SOV word order in Japanese. Japanese control subjects were much more likely to continue to depend on animacy in these cases, ignoring competition from the word order cue. EJ2 speakers, however, were more likely than their monolingual J1 counterparts to choose an inanimate noun if it came first, making them less consistent in their application of the prevalent Japanese strategy. The solution settled on by these EJ2 subjects indicates an elevated sensitivity to word order, which might be expected given the extreme weight placed on word order as a cue to sentence meaning in their native English. Recall that both advanced and novice EJ2 groups interpreted NNV sentences as SOV. However, an SOV word order strategy (appropriate for Japanese) runs

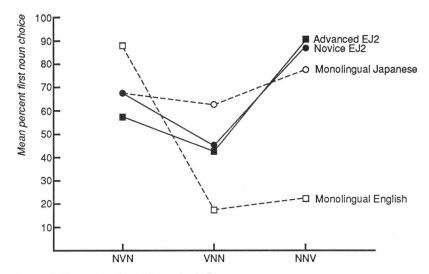

Figure 8.9. Group × word order interaction in Japanese.

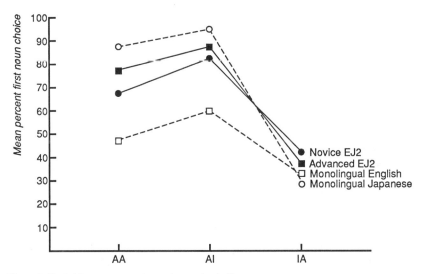

Figure 8.10. Subject group × animacy interaction in Japanese.

directly counter to the OSV bias native speakers apply to English. This provides a third kind of problem for the Competition Model.

We would like to suggest that the direct transfer of L1 strategies to L2 sentence processing, which is predicted by the Competition Model, is not the only kind of transfer. In particular, what may account for this finding is not the intrusion of a *language-specific* strategy, but rather an awareness of the potential for word order as a cue to thematic roles in sentences. This suggests a new kind of transfer: The L2 speakers in this study may have adopted a "meta-word-order" strategy in their approach to processing in Japanese. The instantiation of this strategy may indeed reflect the use of a word order strategy, but one based on knowledge of the canonical order in L2, and not on the particular orders found in L1. This suggests some potentially important complications for the Competition Model, to which we shall return shortly.

Japanese sentences with particles.   In order to investigate the role of morphological markers for nonnative speakers of Japanese, Ito introduced the case marker *ga* and the topic marker *wa* as an additional factor in the original design. As a reminder, recall that *ga* normally marks the syntactic subject, whereas *wa* signals the topic. Three separate combinations of *wa* and *ga* particles were constructed: sentences including *wa/ga* versus *ga/wa* particles (appended to the noun phrases in that order) were set up in order to test the relative "strength" of each particle in competition with the other and in different orders; in other sentences, each particle was included by itself, appended to either the first or second noun (*wa/0* versus *0/wa*, and *ga/0* versus *0/ga* combinations), in order to establish the individual contribution of each particle in different sentence positions. Percentage of first noun choice by advanced and novice EJ2 speakers and by monolingual J1 subjects in each condition is shown in Figures 8.11, 8.12, and 8.13.

Sentences with ga *alone.*   The percentage of choice for nouns with *ga* as agent in 0/*ga* and *ga*/0 sentences are shown in Figure 8.11. Although all of the groups significantly preferred the noun with *ga* to the unmarked noun, differences across groups emerged only when the subject marker was attached to the first noun in the sequence. In this condition, Japanese monolinguals always chose the marked noun as agent (100% for *ga*/0), whereas the marked noun was chosen by advanced EJ2 subjects about 82% of the time, and by novice EJ2 subjects 75% of the time.

Sentences with wa *alone.*   As shown in Figure 8.12, all subjects tended to choose the noun marked with *wa* more than the unmarked noun, but differences between groups were not statistically significant. If we compare the results from *ga* sentences, Japanese monolinguals appear to prefer *ga* over *wa* as the agent marker, whereas no difference is apparent in the use of these two markers in isolation by EJ2 subjects.

Sentences with ga *and* wa.   When these topic and subject particles are set into competition with one another, considerably more variation across subject groups emerges. Figure 8.13 illustrates this group by particle interaction. When *ga* and *wa* appeared together in a sentence, these two particles worked competitively as cues to agency. Japanese monolinguals tended to choose *ga* considerably more than *wa* as the agent-marking device, and the same tendency, albeit weaker, was evident in the advanced EJ2 subjects. Japanese monolinguals preferred *ga*

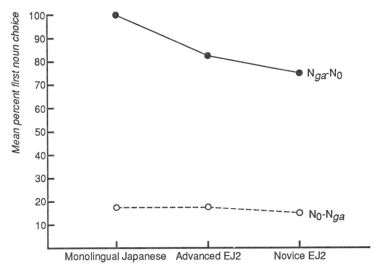

Figure 8.11. Group × sentence type ($N_{ga} - N_0$ vs. $N_0 - N_{ga}$) interaction.

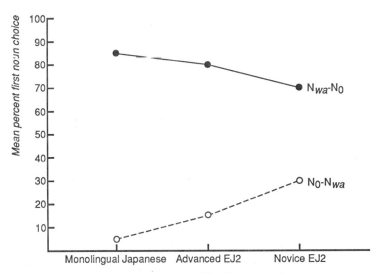

Figure 8.12. Group × sentence type ($N_{wa} - N_0$ vs. $N_0 - N_{wa}$) interaction.

over *wa* even when the two markers were in competition, regardless of order, choosing *ga* 87% of the time in *wa/ga* orders, and 78% of the time in *ga/wa* orders. Advanced EJ2 subjects also chose the *ga*-marked noun at higher than chance levels, 67% of the time in *ga/wa* orders and 69% of the time in *wa/ga* orders. However, novice EJ2 speakers preferred *wa*-marked nouns as agents in

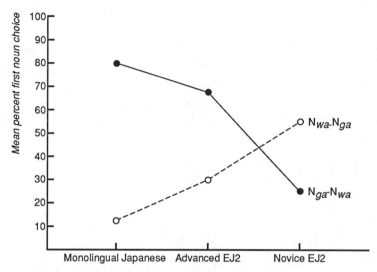

Figure 8.13. Group × sentence type ($N_{ga} - N_{wa}$ vs. $N_{wa} - N_{ga}$) interaction.

ga/wa orders (75% chose *wa*), but exhibited no preference in the opposite order (44% chose *ga*). To summarize, native Japanese and advanced EJ2 speakers preferred the noun with the subject marker *ga* as agent over the noun with the topic marker *wa*, whereas the novice EJ2 speakers preferred the topic-marked noun.

A subsidiary analysis showed a group × word order × particle interaction as well. Summarizing this interaction, the Japanese monolinguals overwhelmingly ignored word order, attending instead to the morphological case particle contrasts. The advanced EJ2 group, though less consistent in their dependence on this cue, showed a similar pattern. In contrast, the novice EJ2 group was largely unaffected by the presence or absence of particles of any kind in NVN and VNN orders. Rather, the word order cue appeared to "win" over competing morphological cues in these subjects. This finding is consistent with the observation made earlier that English-speaking subjects, perhaps due to their habitual tendency to utilize word order cues in their native language, may place unusually heavy emphasis on word order as a cue in Japanese as L2. What is interesting in this regard is that EJ2 novices gravitate toward SOV, a word order that is not valid in their native language. They seem to have elected a short cut to sentence interpretation, based on the "metaprinciple" that word order is important.

Discussion

The Competition Model, a functional performance model of language processing, has served as the foundation for a variety of empirical investigations into the nature of adult processing (Bates et al., 1982; MacWhinney et al., 1984), language acquisition (Bates et al., 1984), and language breakdown in aphasia (Bates et al., 1985; Wulfeck et al., 1986). One of the foremost strengths of the Competition Model is its applicability across many language types, an aspect which distinguishes it from the majority of other models of language processing, which are based largely on work in English. This same crosslinguistic utility affords one other obvious application of this approach: the exploration of second language acquisition. The studies reported in this chapter represent the "first generation" of second language acquisition research based on the Competition Model. These experiments were carried out by various researchers, in different settings, in different languages, with slightly varying methodologies, and they were generated independently, taking off from the promise offered by one very tentative pilot study (i.e., Bates & MacWhinney, 1981). In a sense, however, their differences provide a strong test of the universality of the concepts proposed by the Competition Model to explain the real-time processing characteristics of individuals who speak more than one language.

One goal shared by all of the studies discussed here is to identify the conditions under which a second language speaker's two language systems may interact. This interaction may take various forms; in the context of these studies, we have observed different kinds of transfer reflected in the strategic variations adopted by bilinguals in the sentence interpretation tasks. It is in this context that we can identify whether and to what extent (1) strategies appropriate to first language processing are applied to the second language; (2) a "switchover" to L2 strategies occurs; (3) appropriate L1 strategies are adopted for each language; or (4) an amalgam of L1 and L2 processing strategies leading to an "in-between" stage in interpreting L1 sentence cues exists.

Understanding a "Partial" Language System

The Competition Model has offered one way to define what it means to be between languages, without necessary reference to rules. An important aspect of this approach is that it allows us to characterize the partial language system of the learner as the result of a general learning mechanism and its sensitivity to the cue distribution that defines the target grammar. This is accomplished via an account of how various cues to assigning formal surface devices to underlying functions can operate. The notion that cues can vary in strength suggests a straightforward way to acount for many of the findings reported here; in conjunction with this, the competition or convergence of cues helps explain how different strategies may be adopted at different times in the course of acquisition. Cues may be "tuned" according to various factors, some under learner control (e.g., vocabulary size in L2, attention to particular elements in discourse, etc.), and some in the language/structural domain (e.g., absolute frequency of lexical items, particular grammatical constructions, specific global constraints on WO, subject-topic cohesion, etc.). This has obvious implications for any situation in which languages come into contact. For example, a foreign language teaching program that emphasizes aspects of the language-to-be-learned, which are likely to encounter interference from the "linguistic underground" of the native language, may facilitate learning.

Bilingual Sentence Processing: Implications for the Competition Model

The studies of bilingual sentence processing based on the Competition Model have shown that three problems exist for a straightforward application of the notion of cue validity to second language acquisition. The first problem is the persistence of L1 strategies in L2 processing even after decades of exposure and practice in L2. Second, individual variation, both within and across languages, has consequences for the generality of the performance aspect of the model. Third, the model's account of transfer or intrusion from L1 into L2, based on a more or less direct invasion of L1 cues, is challenged by evidence for a "meta-strategic" level of transfer, which may involve conscious manipulation of rules. We will discuss each of these problems in turn.

1. Persistence. One of the central assumptions of the Competition Model is that processing is essentially cue-driven. A language processing system that takes full advantage of the cues provided by the language would certainly be sensitive to the often vast differences across languages, and thus we would expect to find that bilinguals are able to realign their own processing strategies to suit the available cues. As we have seen, however, the sometimes stubborn application of L1 strategies to L2, despite lengthy exposure to L2, shows incredible insensitivity to the very cues that are supposed to lie at the heart of the process.

There are two ways to reconcile the phenomenon of persistence with the underlying principles of the Competition Model. One way involves a property of the learning mechanism recruited in the service of language. Although it seems incredible on the surface that core L2 strategies are resisted despite years of exposure, it may be the case that this persistence results from the statistics of massive overlearning of L1. Once established, cue weights may be difficult to change; in other words, what appears to be extensive exposure to L2 may not begin to compare with the amount of exposure experienced by L1 learners (whose cues, incidentally, generally have no crosslanguage competition). This notion could be tested by simulations in which cue weights are adjusted according to relative amounts of exposure.

A second way out of the persistence problem is provided by the observation that natural languages contain a large degree of redundancy. This redundancy may permit L2 speakers to "reconfirm" their old (L1) tunings often enough to stave off the rare disconfirmations. For example, not all NVN strings in German require an SVO interpretation, but each instance which does so would tend to "shore up" a native English speaker's already well-established bias in that direction.

The cue settings made in the course of L1 acquisition have been seen to persist far into L2 acquisition, perhaps indefinitely. Although it is possible that vastly different mechanisms are at work in L1 versus L2 acquisition, the Competition Model suggests another possibility. L1 and L2 acquisition may differ not as much in terms of their underlying properties as they do in the emphasis placed on the imperativeness of making complete and unambiguous form–function assignments. The strength, and later persistence, of L1 cues may derive from principles of optimality, which demand that the L1 learner establish the best, most complete form–function assignments possible, regardless of cognitive "cost." L2 acquisition, on the other hand, is more likely to reflect principles of economy, since the L2 learner is primarily motivated to learn to communicate efficiently and quickly, even if it means failing to achieve nativelike performance on some parameters.

2. Individual Differences. The issue of individual differences has arisen consistently in work with second language learners. As suggested earlier, it is possible that each of the four bilingual sentence processing possibilities suggested by the Competition Model (i.e., L1 strategies applied to L2, L2 strategies acquired correctly, L2 strategies come to supplant L1 strategies, and the acquisition of an amalgam of L1 and L2 strategies) are observable at some point. Indeed, they may be observable within a single individual, depending on a variety of factors. Both input conditions, such as formal language instruction versus naturalistic acquisition, and output conditions, such as code-switching or social register, may be factors in individual differences. In any case, it is not unreasonable to assume that individuals will differ in the particular path they take to fluency in a second language.

In several of the studies discussed here, researchers report finding individual differences among subjects of different language groups. Wulfeck et al. (1986) identified two subgroups among native Spanish speakers. One subgroup depended heavily on a word order strategy, whereas agreement and animacy cues dominated the processing strategy of a second subgroup. Interestingly, each subgroup applied their particular strategy to processing in both Spanish and English. Kilborn and Cooreman (1987) found essentially the same dichotomous strategy differences in native Dutch speakers. Again, it appears that subjects applied the strategy they settled on uniformly across their two languages.

Individual differences have also been observed in monolingual processing, albeit to a lesser extent. Bates et al. (1982) observed patterns of individual differences within groups of monolingual native speakers of Italian and of English. The so-called least English group of E1 speakers showed unusually strong interest in animacy cues. The so-called least Italian group of Italians showed an unusual interest in SVO word order. Nevertheless, subsidiary analyses showed that the direction of other language-specific differences remained the same even within these extreme language groups. For example, "least Italians" were still more influenced by topicalization and contrastive stress cues than "least English." The outlaws retained recognizable signs of their native language.

Harrington (1987) observed that animacy was more pronounced in his monolingual English subjects than in previous studies. He attributed this finding to the presence of two subgroups within the English group, one which relied on word order, as expected, and one which relied on animacy, much in the same way as his Japanese subjects did. McDonald (this volume) identified individual differences in the way certain cues were applied by native speakers of German, Dutch and English. Although some subjects were quite consistent in their form–function mappings, others were much less so. For instance, case inflection may dominate all other cues for some subjects, whereas for others different cues may at times be the strongest.

Kail (this volume) found that some adult native speakers of French differed in their use of word order and animacy cues. On NVN strings, which are interpretable as SVO, the canonical word order in French, most F1 subjects relied on word order. But with noncanonical NNV and VNN orders, a syntactic strategy gave way to a semantic strategy in many F1 subjects. Kail suggests that subjects may in fact be sensitive to the competition between word order and animacy, and split their strategies accordingly. And, as we might expect, subjects differed to some degree in their tendency to treat canonical and noncanonical orders differently, underscoring the point that even "individual differences are a matter of degree."

Just as alternative sentence processing strategies may be open to individuals, there may be alternative segmentation routines available at the phonemic and syllabic levels. Cutler, Mehler, Norris, and Segui (1986) show that adult French speakers use syllabic speech segmentation regardless of whether the words heard were French, in which words are easy to syllabify, or English, in which words do not have clearly bounded syllables. English listeners, however, do syllabify in the same way, whether in English, or in French. Cutler et al. propose that speakers have a range of segmentation procedures available to them; the one they typically use will tend to be the most efficient one for the language they speak. This may also involve mixing segmentation routines when necessary.

Returning to sentence processing, Bates et al. (1982) suggest several possible sources for such differences: an agreement versus animacy bias may have independent psychological status; or subjects may simply choose one of several possibilities and stick with that one. As noted earlier, Gass (1987) has suggested that semantics may be a "universally" stronger force than syntax, and thus more prone to be the cue which carries over to L2 processing. But this suggestion runs directly counter to the stronger "meta-word-order" strategy observed in many EJ2 speakers. Faced with a limited number of cues to choose from, none of which is particularly overwhelming, individual preferences may determine what strategy will win.

McDonald (1986) points out two other potential causes for individual differences: First, because in most cases subjects are required or encouraged to respond within a very short time (typically 2 seconds or so), some subjects may not have enough time to completely resolve the conflict in a sentence. Second, the nature of the immediately preceding context may influence the mapping strength of cues in the current sentence, in turn influencing the interpretation of the sentence. The repeated finding of similar subgroup differentiation in the context of even typologically different languages suggests that this effect is not accidental or due to language-specific factors. Moreover, it sounds a cautionary note by indicating that individual differences may be an important factor in any language processing study, and especially in within-subject comparisons of bilingual language use.

3. Language Transfer: Strategies and Meta-Strategies. The studies discussed in this chapter provide extensive evidence for the invasion of L1 strategies into L2 processing. The Competition Model handles this direct transfer without problem: the L2 speaker continues to rely on cue weights assigned to various form–function mappings in L1. Although the Competition Model accounts in a straightforward way for basic transfer phenomena, other findings reported here provide a challenge. In particular, native English speakers interpreted NNV sentences in Japanese as SOV, which is the canonical word order in simple, declarative sentences in Japanese. Based on the Competition Model, two alternate strategies are predicted. First, L2 strategies may be adopted. If subjects had followed this course, they would have shown no preference for either noun in NNV strings, relying instead like native Japanese on semantic features of the nouns. This was clearly not the case. Second, transfer or intrusions from L1 into L2 processing ought to involve cues which are "imported" as directly as possible from L1. Though this does not mean that L1 cues cannot interact with L2 cues, it does mean that the cues which are incorporated into the L2 processing strategy should be drawn from the same level of processing. For example, the model would predict that if an English word order-based strategy invades into Japanese processing, native English speakers ought to treat Japanese NNV strings as if they were English NNV strings, that is, as OSV. However, contrary to the Competition Model notion of transfer, these subjects preferred the SOV reading, at a much higher level than evidenced by native Japanese.

We are led to a different kind of explanation, one which may require some modification of the crosslanguage transfer component of the model. Recall that the canonical word order in Japanese is SOV, which was precisely the interpretation of NNV strings made by novice Japanese L2 speakers. Clearly, simple transfer of a particular word order bias cannot account for this result. What transfer may consist of in this case is the *top-down* application of a strategy from L1, producing an almost rulelike effect: Word order is still at the core of the native English speakers' L2 processing strategy, just as it is in L1. However, rather than an English-specific SVO bias, what invades is a higher level strategic bias to pay attention to word order as a cue to sentence meaning. Note that this involves a very different level of processing than the one assumed by the Competition Model.

The course of a meta-strategy would go something like this: English speakers may notice that the least complex sentences are most often of the SOV form in Japanese. This S-first property may then be extrapolated to aid in the interpretation of subsequent input, on the assumption that word order properties ought to be relatively invariant. More complex constructions, however, may include many instances in which this assumption would be incorrect. Japanese speakers, and fluent L2 speakers, are able to depend on other types of information, such as case and topic marking morphology, which present problems for the on-line interpretation of Japanese by less fluent speakers. Of course, the phenomenon may be much more general: When all else fails, or input is hard to separate out, the learner may adopt the strategy of attending to global, robust features of the grammar. The issue remains the same, however, since the L2 features which appear robust to a beginning learner are likely to be the ones which are near the core of L1.

The meta-word-order strategy was observed only in novice L2 learners, but not in more advanced learners. This is not surprising, since if such a meta-word-order strategy exists, then we would not expect it to persist for long. For one thing, increasing familiarity with appropriate L2 cues and their clear advantages in a real-time processing system ought to lead to a gradual fading of initially useful but slower rule- or monitor-driven approaches. This view is consistent with the Monitor Theory of second language learning proposed by Krashen (1978, 1982). According to Krashen, the early stages of second language learning are characterized by the more or less conscious monitoring of L2 input and output, based on the learner's knowledge of the rules of the target language. Eventually, these rules are internalized, and though they form the basis for efficient, rapid L2 processing, the monitor itself no longer plays an active role in comprehension or production.

Without further evidence we cannot know whether such meta-level strategies actually constitute some level of processing, and lead to transfer, or whether they are merely epiphenomena, perhaps specific to the narrowly defined tasks used in these studies. Two kinds of data would have a bearing on this issue.

First, assuming that such rulelike transfer does occur, we ought to find similar meta-strategies involving other cues, such as agreement or animacy, in native speakers of languages in which those cues play a more central role than they do in English. Indeed, what we have taken to be a more or less direct transfer, as in the application of agreement cues by native speakers of German to English as L2, may also involve higher level strategies. One way to distinguish between simple transfer and a purported meta-strategy is to set up a processing task so that the L2 speaker has the opportunity to use a rule that native speakers of that language generally do not use, as we observed in the novice L2 learners of Japanese.

The second kind of evidence that would be relevant here involves performing machine-based simulations of L2 acquisition. Simulation studies of L1 acquisition have shown that complex, apparently rule-driven behavior can "fall out" of a system that includes no explicit rules, a general learning function based on analogy, and fairly minimal input. Rumelhart and McClelland (1986) used such a system to show that English past tense rules, including many instances of irregular verbs, could be simulated in great detail, including the characteristic U-shaped function corresponding to an initial rote period during which children simply copy the correct verb forms, followed by an error-prone period, during which the past tense "rule" is overgeneralized, followed by the gradual settling in of both regular and irregular forms. Rumelhart and McClelland suggest that this is one instance in which apparently rule-governed acquisition may not involve rules at all, but is instead a solution which emerges from a limited set of nodes with changeable interconnections.

Likewise, a meta-strategy in L2 processing may be the result of preset cue mappings in L1 which interact with incoming information about new cue mappings in L2; the apparently rule-governed behavior in this case, as in the case of past tense acquisition in English, may be another instance of an emergent solution in the context of acquiring a complex communication system. In this view, the rule which appears to underlie the processing behavior is not necessarily a component of the processing system itself, but is rather an emergent property of a system which is subject to a wide range of constraints. These may include restrictions on short-term memory, on the ability to process competing information sources (e.g., cues) in parallel, and especially in the case of novice L2 learners, a lack of automatic access to a variety of processing factors (e.g., lexical meanings may initially require some sort of look-up function which may interfere with other levels of processing simply because it takes time).

It is clear now that, at the very least, L2 learning offers a qualitatively different perspective on the general questions of representation and learning of language. We believe that this perspective can be broadened by further work, guided by a functional view, in the area of L2 acquisition.

9   The Learner's Problem of Arranging Words

Wolfgang Klein and Clive Perdue

"I see another language as distorted English and then I try to work it out." (attributed to a linguist)

In the course of the acquisition of a second language in everyday communication, the learner passes through a series of more or less elaborate repertoires of linguistic devices that allow him to express himself and to understand others with varying degrees of success when he tries to communicate with his social environment.[1]   Repertoires of this sort we call *learner varieties*. We may assume that both the internal organization of a learner variety and the transition from one variety to the next are systematic in nature and that because of this systematicity, both "the internal organization of learner varieties" and "the logic of development" are problems worth studying.

This paper deals with the first of these problems, the internal organization of learner varieties, and more particularly with the question of how learners arrange words in their utterances if their repertoire is still very limited and most of the normal syntactic devices of the target language are not yet available to them. Its aim is therefore to attempt to find out what other organizational principles they can call on to make themselves understood. We think that the investigation of learner varieties should eventually deepen our understanding of the acquisition process, through a study of the second problem: the logic of development. Moreover, is should also cast some light on language and its functioning in general, and it is this latter aspect that motivates the present study.

Why should the investigation of the use of almost pathologically restricted systems such as elementary learner varieties tell us something that could not much more easily be uncovered by looking at normal, fully developed language, whose investigation is more advanced in many respects? In full-fledged languages, the interplay of forms and functions is extremely intricate and tight – they have a much higher degree of integration when compared to

---

[1]   The study reported here is part of a larger crosslinguistic project on adult second language acquisition. First analyses of the data were presented at a colloquium "Acquisition d'une langue étrangère" in Aix-en-Provence, May 1984, and at the University of California, Los Angeles, February 1985. We are grateful to our colleagues within the project, and to the participants of the Los Angeles seminar for their help and advice. We would especially like to thank Maya Hickmann, Eric Kellerman, Brian MacWhinney, and Christiane von Stutterheim for their detailed comments.

292

learner varieties, in which there are only a limited number of lexical items, and where the means available to indicate their interrelation within more complex units are dramatically restricted. The advantage of learner varieties is that it is relatively easier to disentangle the web of forms and functions and to study their interplay.[2]

This becomes particularly clear when looking at the way learners arrange words in their utterances. It has often been argued that for any type of language use descriptions in purely syntactic terms – case marking, government, or word class membership – do not suffice to cover all of the regularities that govern the internal organization of utterances in discourse. It has also been argued that nonsyntactic organizational principles – such as "information distribution" or "theme-rheme structure" – emerge particularly clearly in learner varieties simply because syntactic devices expressing these functions are less available: A learner variety which has no inflection cannot use case marking or agreement, for example.

But how can we develop a sound analysis of this aspect of utterance organization, given that concepts such as "theme," "focus," or "background" are much less clear and solid than, for example, morphological case marking? The obvious thing to do is to give them a more precise definition, or even better, to adopt or to develop a conceptual framework of which they constitute an integral part, and where they are related to syntactic concepts, such as "subject," "verb," "nominative," and so forth. It would then be possible to apply concepts of both types to the analysis of data from specific languages or varieties and to try to uncover the language-specific principles which determine the make-up of utterances in that language or variety. By comparing the language-specific givens, we may eventually be able to state more general constraints on the internal organization of utterances in discourse.

There is no a priori reason why such a procedure should not work. But in practice, it has led to an impressive mess. Over the last ten years, there has been much discussion about topic-oriented versus subject-oriented languages (kindled, especially, by Li & Thompson, 1976), and the outcome of this discussion is not fully convincing. It seems that despite considerable efforts to define these terms and related ones, different authors analyze the same phenomena in different ways; and their application across languages is anything but consistent and therefore lacking in comparability. Maybe this need not be so, but it *is* so. Consider, for example, the notion "subject": In languages such as English,

---

[2] We do not claim that learner variety utterances are in any sense closer to some "underlying semantic representation." If it is difficult – as we shall see – to substantiate claims about the overt structure, one can hardly see how we could make claims about the structure of the underlying representation; as a consequence, statements about "closeness" between these two levels ("higher semantic transparency") seem hard to verify. (Personally, we agree with Lancelot & Arnault, 1664, that written French best mirrors one's thoughts.)

German, or Italian, for which a long research tradition exists, there is usually little disagreement over what the subject of a given sentence is (for simple clauses at least); but by and large, the subject is case marked and movable in German, not case marked, movable and occasionally "null" in Italian, and neither case marked nor movable in English. In what sense, then, are we dealing with the same phenomenon? (For a careful examination of the relevance of "subject" for German, see Reis, 1982.) Needless to say, the situation is much less clear for "topic," where even for the most studied languages it is often debatable what the topic of a given utterance is. Consequently, we feel that universal statements based on "topichood" or "subjecthood" should be treated with suspicion.

The situation is even worse if we try to analyze learner variety utterances using such categories directly. What criteria allow us to label a lexical item "subject" rather than "topic" in an utterance which lacks all morphological marking, whose word order could be otherwise in a particular variety, and which even lacks a finite verb? Constructions of this sort are quite typical for learner varieties, as we shall see in what follows. Note that the problem is not just to establish a clear definition of these concepts which makes them consistently applicable to all languages; it is equally important to have a workable operationalization which allows for consistent analysis of given utterances in individual languages (and varieties), especially if these languages have received little or no description so far, as is clearly the case with learner varieties. Thus, von Stechow (1981) gives a clear and convincing definition of "topic" and "focus" in terms of formal semantics (see also Klein & von Stechow, 1982); but there is no direct way from these definitions to the concrete determination of what the "topic" in a given utterance is. We do not wish to say that the present unsatisfactory situation can never be remedied; we are simply saying that the many attempts along the lines mentioned above have led to numerous practical problems.

In what follows, we will try a different, more modest approach to the problem of arranging words in utterances. It is basically inductive and has at least the advantage of being controllable and easily applicable. In the next section, we will briefly explain what we have in mind.

The Learner's Problem of Arranging Words

At any point in time, an adult learner (as any other speaker) can draw on different kinds of cognitive resources whenever he wants to communicate. First, the adult learner already knows a language. This allows him to draw upon both the specific expressive devices which constitute that language and the semantic and cognitive categories that underlie them, such as modality, deixis, agency, or whatever. Second, the adult learner already knows about language and communication in general. He knows that he has to monitor for communicative success, that speaker and hearer have differing background knowledge, that there are social conventions for determining who is allowed to talk to whom, and so forth. Possibly, he does not know how these functions are concretely realized in the language he has to learn and in the culture which he enters (or invades), but he knows that such rules and influences do exist. Third, the adult learner has a lot of nonlinguistic information about the world and, thanks to his eyes and ears, about the situation in which he is communicating. Fourth, he knows bits and pieces of the target language from what exposure to it he has had. Obviously, these resources may be very different from learner to learner, and also change for any given learner over time.

Suppose now that you are an adult Italian worker who has been living and working in England for about six months. You have already learned, perhaps, a number of proper names, such as *John*, *Peter*, and *Mary*, as well as some base forms of verbs, such as *love*, *come*, and *kill*. You have learned that the proper nouns denote human entities and that the verbs denote the actions these entities can accomplish. You have no inflection, hence no case morphology or agreement (that is, your learner variety is quite restricted). Suppose now that on some occasion and for some reason, you want to express the thought that Peter is in love with Mary. You are able to denote some components of this thought, Mary by *Mary*, Peter by *Peter*, and that relation by *love*. But this does not suffice: somehow, the words must be arranged. This follows from the fact that language is linear (there are no hierarchical complications here). But this arrangement must also be done in such a way that the listener is able to derive the intended thought from what is uttered.

There are two extreme possibilities with respect to the six theoretically possible arrangements. One possibility is that there might be no restrictions at all in your learner variety. In this case, it is unlikely that you will get your message across since your utterance is in many ways ambiguous. In this case, the language analyst has nothing to say with respect to the organization of your utterance, he must just wait for a more advanced learner variety. The second possibility is that there may be restrictions of some sort. The obvious question then is: In what terms can they be stated? This is the case that will interest us.

We and others have considered a variety of possible influences on the selection of the first noun in our hypothetical learner variety utterance. (Sridhar, this volume, discusses a number of such influences on sentence formulation in adult native speakers.) Among the most important are:

I. a. The shortest unit (in terms of phonemes) is first. Behaghel (1923) proposed this as a general influence on all of syntax. However, we take this tendency to be a consequence of other facts.

   b. The verb comes first. This case makes sense only if the learner indeed distinguishes verbs from other word classes in his variety and if the analyst can perceive the distinction. This is by no means trivial; we might ask what a "verb" is if there is no tense, inflection, or agreement. Thus, one might argue that the distinction between *love* (verb) and *love* (noun) totally collapses in this variety (Klein 1984).

c. That NP which is morphologically unmarked (nominative) comes first. This is actually impossible in this particular variety, as it was defined above, since it has no morphological marking at this time. So, if "subject" is defined as a syntactic category on morphological grounds, then there is no point in speaking of subject in this variety at all.

II. a. If the thought to be expressed corresponds to an action or activity, then that entity which performs the action ("agent") is named first. If there is no action or activity, the choice is free.

b. Animate entities are named first; if there are more than one of them, the choice is free, unless one of them is human; then this one comes first.

III. a. An entity which was referred to before comes first; if there are more than one of them, the choice is free.

b. That entity which first comes to the speaker's mind comes first.

c. That entity which is dearest to the speaker's heart comes first.

d. That entity which the speaker thinks to be best known to the listener comes first.

IV. Some combination of these influences determines the word order. For example, if the thought in the learner's mind involves an action with an animate and an inanimate participant, then the animate participant comes first unless the inanimate participant was mentioned before, then this one comes first, and so on.

The last possibility is envisaged by Bates and MacWhinney (this volume) when they note that fully developed languages integrate several of these influences into particular "coalitions." They hold that concepts such as "subject" and "topic" can be defined on the basis of such combinations. Learner varieties can also express such coalitions, as we shall see.

The actual impact on learner varieties of the kinds of influences I–III listed above is open to speculation. The alternative approach, mentioned above, to an *a priori* definition of, for example, "topic" would try to determine which influences are indeed operative in utterances in discourse, and then aggregate them to complex interactions of these influences, exemplified by IV. It is here that the analytic task is easier for the study of learner varieties than of full-fledged languages. As a competent communicator, the adult learner will use the limited possibilities he has to maximal effect, and the principles underlying this use will emerge more clearly precisely because the linguistic means they apply to are limited.[3] Thus, a careful analysis of learner variety texts should provide both a deeper insight into the inner organization of learner varieties and an exemplification of the general principles that obtain in the organization of adult native languages. The definition of concepts such as "subject," "theme,"

---

[3] One can imagine a mirror argument for child language acquisition (see, e.g., Karmiloff-Smith, 1981): The child uses a relatively greater command of vocabulary and utterance-internal structures to solve the relatively more complex problem of arranging the utterances into coherent discourse, for example, by manipulating individual utterances in order to allow a "discourse theme" to appear consistently in utterance-initial position.

and "focus" should then derive from the regularities that could be observed in studying these varieties.

What causes a learner to obey one of these influences in his learner variety production rather than another? Various answers are possible; we will mention and briefly comment upon four of them. The first answer to this question is that it could be the case that the influence already holds in the learner's first language and that this influence is simply transferred over to the target language. This is probably the most common explanation, and there is no doubt that transfer of this sort can influence the structure of learner varieties. However, for transfer to occur, the learner must both perceive (however wrongly) a possible L1-L2 equivalence and have *some L2 means* to operationalize this perception in production. In this sense, transfer resembles many other domains in that, the more you know, the more kinds of mistakes you are able to make.

A second possible reason for adopting one of the influences noted above is that the learner assumes that it holds in the target variety. This sounds almost trivial. Why, after all, should a learner use a rule if he does not think it holds in the language to be learned? But in real-time communication, the learner is often forced to apply rules he is totally uncertain about or which he even thinks to be false with respect to the target language. This situation is familiar to any speaker of a second language; but it has also been reported for child language (see Klein, 1983, Chapter 8).

A third possible reason for obeying a particular influence is that the influence may be based on a universal constraint. Claims to this effect have often been advanced in the literature (for example, Gass, 1984; Rutherford, 1984); they are sometimes seen as an alternative to transfer hypotheses (although the choice is not mutually exclusive). There are various ways in which we might conceive universal constraints to operate.

1. Constraints could function as "generative" universals in accord with a Chomskyan "universal grammar." The proposals here involve concepts such as "subjacency," "specified subject condition," and so forth. (See Chomsky, 1982; Hornstein & Lightfoot, 1981; Felix, 1984). If there are indeed constraints of this sort, then they do not say very much about utterance organization in learner varieties that are as elementary as those discussed here. It is hard to see how a constraint such as "subjacency" or even a universal phrase structure constraint could restrict[4] the possible word orders in the "Peter is in love with Mary" example.

2. Constraints could function as "statistical" universals, in the sense of the Keenan-Comrie hierarchy of noun phrase accessibility (Keenan & Comrie, 1977; Hawkins, 1983; Gass, 1984; Comrie, 1981). Universals of this kind may serve as heuristic guidelines: They give the researcher an idea of where to look for interesting

---

[4] Note that this is not an argument against the existence of such constraints or even the constraining force of universal grammar in language acquisition, both first and second. Universal grammar in this sense resembles a husband who comes to the kitchen and offers his helping hand when the washing up is done except for three spoons and a saucepan.

phenomena. But they raise some of the same problems as UG (e.g., not all learner varieties actually have relative clauses) and all of the problems which we briefly discussed above. So long as we do not have criteria for what a "subject" is in learner variety utterances (and elsewhere), universals of this kind are of little help (Perdue, 1984).

3. Constraints could be "pragmatic" universals of the type enumerated in III, such as "from known to unknown" (Behaghel, 1923–32) or "me first" (Cooper & Ross, 1975; see also Silverstein, 1976b). We think that universal influences of this sort indeed play an important role in the organization of learner varieties. They are not particularly clear, however, and we think it might be more practicable to describe first what is indeed operative in learner varieties in these terms and then look for possible extensions and generalizations of the results, rather than stating a universal and then applying it to learner varieties. Thus the study of learner varieties may help in providing a better description of these universals, as we suggested above.

For both the generative and statistical universal constraints, the same objections hold that have been made in connection with transfer and its possibility. To be operative, both kinds of universals require that the learner have considerable knowledge of the language to be learned. This is much less the case for pragmatic universals which are less tied to the specifics of a given language and as such can be assumed to be broadly shared by competent communicators. These pragmatic constraints therefore tie in well with a fourth, and rather different, answer to the question why a learner might prefer a specific constraint over another, which is that the learner may assume that following this constraint makes his utterance better understandable (or understandable at all). This possible and plausible answer is unlike the first three in that it speaks of the speaker's state of knowledge of the listener. Having determined the listener's state of knowledge, the speaker may still need to rely on what he knows about pragmatic and statistical constraints.

We think that, in reality, all of these factors influence the way in which the learner organizes his utterances, and the way in which they interact with each other can only be determined by comparing learner varieties under varying conditions: with different target languages, different source languages, and at different developmental stages. The following study is a step in this direction.

Before turning to the data in detail, it might be useful to have a more global look at the procedure. In what follows, we shall analyze three relatively long texts from three learners, all of them foreign workers who developed their learner variety by everyday contact in the host country rather than in the classroom. The L1-L2 combinations are Italian-German, Italian-English, and Spanish-French; that is, there are three target and two source languages. The text is a retelling of a part of a silent movie to another person, who had seen the preceding part of the movie together with the learner. This defines a controllable background – we have at least a partial control of the speaker's and the listener's shared knowledge. We also know the general shape of the information that the speaker is trying to communicate. Obviously, our understanding of this information is not perfect, but it is reasonably clear. We have chosen to analyze a full text, rather than individual sentences, because a full text allows us to control for introduction, maintenance and shift of referents under varying circumstances. We also have a reasonable control over the temporal and spatial organization of the whole story. This kind of data gives us good, although by no means ideal, material for verifying a whole series of possible influences or constraints of the types listed above. There are three methodological problems, however, which deserve mention:

1. The data analyzed here are limited both in size and type. It may well be that the learner, under different circumstances, organizes his utterances in a different (or partly different) way. This can only be determined by examining other types of data. Indeed, in the context of the project in which this study was done, a wide range of data was collected; we plan to extend the present analysis by including other text types at a later stage.
2. It is often very problematic to interpret utterances in learner varieties. There is no "native speaker" that could be asked whether a certain construction is impossible, or (and this is far more problematic) what a certain utterance that was recorded some time ago really means. As a consequence, most samples of learner varieties contain certain utterances that are wildly ambiguous or simply uninterpretable.
3. Finally, we are faced with all the practical problems of analyzing recorded spoken language. Learner variety samples show many false starts, hesitations, or self corrections. This is not a problem in principle (and indeed may provide us with helpful additional insights), but in practice, it is a challenge for any reliable analysis. We will be confronted with numerous problems of this sort. In general, the examples presented in this paper are "edited" to exclude obvious false starts, breakdowns, hesitations, interjections, and metalinguistic questions such as "correctly speaking?" Readers who wish to study the full un-edited corpus are welcome to contact us directly.

So much for the aims and the general background of the present study. Now we will move from the fog of theoretical considerations into the swamp of empirical facts.

The Data

Our data come from the European Science Foundation project entitled "Second Language Acquisition by Adult Immigrants." The project was set up as a coordinated, comparative study taking place with identical schedules and identical data-collection procedures in five European countries, England, France, Germany, the Netherlands, and Sweden. In each country, we studied the acquisition of the local language by adult speakers of Arabic, Spanish, Finnish, Italian, Punjabi and Turkish. The pairings of source languages (SL) and target languages (TL) are such that comparisons can be obtained on the acquisition of one TL by speakers of two different SLs as well as the acquisition of two different TLs by speakers of the same SL: We can have, therefore, at least some means of distinguishing in the acquisition process between phenomena specific to one SL-TL configuration and more general phenomena. The overall aim of the project is to isolate the factors which determine the structural properties and tempo of the acquisition process in four major domains of investigation, one of which is the arrangement of words in learners' utterances. For a complete description of the aims and methodology of the ESF project, see Perdue (1984b).

The present paper reports on a small part of the full database collected in the larger project. Here we present a pilot analysis of one specific activity – a film-retelling task. This activity took place during the first half of data-collection with the three informants mentioned above.

The Charlie Chaplin Study

The project researchers working in Heidelberg made a montage of extracts from Charlie Chaplin's film *Modern Times* which lasts about twenty minutes and is divided into two main episodes, described below. The procedure for the activity is simply that a researcher and an informant watch the first episode together, then the researcher leaves the room while the informant watches the second episode. The researcher returns immediately after the end of the film in order to listen to the informant retelling the second episode.

Episode 1: America 1930 – Poverty, Hunger, and Unemployment.   Charlie gets into a demonstration against unemployment, is mistaken for the leader and put into prison. At dinner one of his fellow prisoners hides heroin in the salt cellar, and Charlie helps himself to it by mistake. The drug gives him a heroical force: He foils an attempt to escape and frees the director, who, in gratitude, releases him with a letter of recommendation for a job. Charlie is not too enthusiastic about this because he feels he is better off in prison than at liberty. Parallel with this we see a second story: A young girl (whose father is a widower, unemployed, and without the means to feed his three children) steals food for her family. Her father is shot in a demonstration, and the children are sent to an orphanage. The girl manages to escape at the last moment.

Episode 2: Determined to Return to Prison.   Charlie finds work in a shipyard. He clumsily causes the launching of a ship that was not finished. He is immediately fired and is all the more determined to go back to prison. The girl roams through the streets, hungry, and steals a loaf of bread. When she tries to escape she runs into Charlie and both fall to the ground. A woman, who watched the theft, calls the baker. A policeman comes to arrest the girl. Charlie tries to claim responsibility for the theft but it doesn't work. The girl is marched off to prison. Charlie tries again to get back into prison. He goes into a restaurant, eats as much as he can, calls a policeman from the street and tells him that he has no money to pay the bill. He is arrested. In the police car he again meets the girl who stole the bread. In an accident they are both thrown out of the car. The girl suggests that he escape with her, and he does. They rest for a while in the garden of a middle-class house, and watch the couple who live there say a tender good-bye to each other in front of their house. Charlie and the girl dream of such an existence. A few days later the girl has a surprise for Charlie: she has found a house. Of course, it is a ruined cabin in a miserable condition, so that a series of hilarious accidents happen when they first come to see it. But they don't let this disturb their happiness. In the last scene we see them walking down a long road that disappears into the horizon.

If we assume that the learner participates cooperatively, that is, that he wants to try to get his listener to understand the story he retells rather than confuse him, then this task is interesting for our present purposes for two major reasons. First, this is a complex verbal task: The speaker retells part of a relatively complex story, consisting of events whose relationship to each other must be specified. Within each event, the speaker has to tell who did what to whom, introducing new characters and maintaining reference to characters who are already on stage. The main characters are male (Charlie) and female (the girl) and they act and are acted upon. Their stories, which run in parallel during the first half of the film, intertwine during the second half, necessitating a choice on the part of the learner as to which of them is central in each event.

Second, this task is interesting because, as in the study by Sridhar (this volume), we have partial control over what is mutually known or unknown to the learner and the listener at the beginning, in that we have the film to compare with his production. This partial control gives us, therefore, a partial idea of what the speaker *maximally* wants to retell (given the cooperation assumption above). The comparison between an imposed message and the speaker's actual production is highly interesting as it is safe to assume that he does not have the TL means to fulfill his wish (or what we hypothesize to be his wish). On a conceptual level, it is then at least plausible that he will reorganize the story to a certain extent in order to achieve the double (and not necessarily compatible) purpose of accommodating his message to the means available while ensuring comprehension on the part of the listener. It is in this interplay of conceptualizing and formulating that the semantic/pragmatic "universals" we listed earlier may emerge particularly clearly in his speech, since both are available to him to a large extent irrespective of his knowledge of the TL, and assumed by him to be available to his listener. Thus, at the inter-utterance level, discourse organization principles (von Stutterheim, 1986) carry much communicative weight, and interact with utterance-organizational principles such as those mentioned earlier, because it is these principles that are the least dependent on specific elements of a TL.

Italian-German: Vito

After some remarks on Vito's biography and communicative behavior, we will briefly sketch his linguistic repertoire at the time of the interview and then give a detailed analysis of approximately his first twenty-five utterances describing the "shipyard" episode in order to illustrate both the typical features of this learner variety and the practical problems involved in this type of analysis.

Vito was born in 1948 near Palermo (Sicily). At the time of the recording (1983), he had been living in Germany for about eighteen months, but still had a very limited command of German, which reflects his very limited contacts with German speakers. His wife is Italian, they have no children, and he works in the kitchen of an Italian restaurant. He is however talkative, outgoing, and very interested in things linguistic, as his metalinguistic behavior shows. While retelling the film, he often interrupts himself and asks for a word or expression with the "formulaic" questions: *Was ist der Name?* "What is the name," *Was Name diese?* "What name this?" Occasionally, he checks the correction of his own speech: *Richtig spreche?* "Correctly speak?" We also find less apparent traces of metalinguistic activity: (1) his production seems carefully planned, with clear prosodic phrasing of each word; (2) when quoting speech – a metalinguistic device he and other informants often use – his production appears to be closer to the German standard than when he is reporting events or providing background material. This variation leads us to distinguish three types of utterances: those based on formulaic metalinguistic speech such as *Was ist die Name?*, those involving the narration proper including the story line and background material, and those based on quoted speech. The distinction between these three types of utterances is best illustrated by Vito's use of the copula: It never occurs in narrative utterances, it sometimes occurs in quoted speech, and it frequently occurs in formulaic utterances as part of the formula. In what follows, we will omit formulaic utterances from analysis as Vito does not himself "arrange" the words in them, and point to other differences between narrative utterances and quoted speech. Some rare instances of quoted speech are apparently induced by the intertitles of the film. The intertitles were only briefly shown on the screen and written in three languages (German, Turkish, and Italian); one would assume Vito to focus on the Italian version, but on occasion he clearly registered and reproduced the German one.

Vito's Linguistic Repertoire

Considerations of space force us to be very brief here. In particular, problems encountered in assigning words to classes are not dealt with; some of them emerge clearly in the next section. For a detailed analysis of Vito's lexicon see Dietrich (1984) and for an exhaustive analysis of Vito's means of referring to space see Becker (1984). Some overall aspects of Vito's system are:

1. Vito has no inflexional morphology (except in some instances of quoted speech), hence no case marking, no agreement, and no tense.
2. In this text, he uses about sixty different nouns, forty verbs, a dozen adjectives (in epithet and attribute function), and about ten adverbs of time, place and modality.
3. He uses three articles – *da* "the", *diese* "this, that", and *eine* "a" – and, very rarely, the quantifiers *viel* "much", *all* "all", and *zwei* "two". *Eine* is also used as a numeral.
4. He has a minimal pronominal system (Klein & Rieck, 1982): *ich* "I", *du* "you", *mir* "me" (after a preposition, and possibly *Sie*, polite "you", these appearing essentially in quoted speech. Otherwise he has just one pronominal form (*sie*) and one adjectival form (*seine*) for the third person. *Zusammen* "together" is occasionally used as an argument of the verb to denote Chaplin and the girl. *Diese* can be used alone, deictically and anaphorically, under conditions described in the next section.
5. He uses one preposition – *in* – very frequently, and half a dozen others occasionally. *In* is highly overgeneralized to denote all kinds of spatial relations. His negatives are *nix*, which is frequent, and *keine*, which is less so. The latter, a TL determiner, is used by Vito before nouns, but also as an alternative to *nix* as a sentence negator. Both may be used together in one utterance.
6. Finally, he uses the utterance connectors *und* "and", *aber* or **pero** "but", and *oder* "or", To mark a restart, he uses **alora** "then", which is the only Italian word he uses with any frequency. We ignore these connectors when assigning words to positions (initial, final) *within* the utterances examined below. (In what follows, source language sequences are bounded by *, pauses indicated by +, and a short text omission indicated by ...).

The Shipyard Episode

The retelling task starts with the scene where Chaplin leaves prison with a letter of recommendation. Chaplin and the letter are both mentioned in the interviewer utterance immediately preceding V1:

V1.   *sie*   *habe*   *brief*   +   *brief*   *für*   *gefängnis*
        she   have   letter   letter   for   prison

The intended meaning of the utterance is fairly clear – Chaplin has/had a/the letter from prison. Vito's lack of tense-marking makes it impossible to determine the tense of the verb in this passage. For simplicity's sake, we will therefore use present tense forms in the glosses. The utterance structure before the pause is NP1 V NP2 :

1. NP1 refers to Chaplin. *Sie* corresponds to a pronoun of the TL ("she" or "they") although the appropriate TL-form would be *er* "he". As Chaplin was mentioned in the immediately preceding utterance, Vito starts his task with an anaphoric pronoun (in preverbal position).
2. V denotes a stative relation.
3. NP2 also denotes a previously mentioned entity, but the internal structure of this NP is N. We cannot however draw any firm conclusions as to the referential status (definite or indefinite) of this N: It would be equally appropriate to refer back to – "the letter" – or reintroduce – "a letter" – in this context.

NP2 is related to the (appositional) sequence after the pause. It is hard to see, at this point, whether this sequence is a mere "postscript" or rather a disguised relative – "...letter, (which was) from..." Note, however, that *gefängnis* is a bare noun and is situationally defined (both interviewer and informant know about the prison from watching the first half of the film together). As a shorthand, we will sometimes use the term "thematic" to indicate a referent that has been explicitly referred to, pointed to, or which any adult speaker would infer, to the exclusion of other possible referents, in a given situation.

V2. *komme in eine baustell + baustell vielleicht*
      come   in a   building site building site perhaps

The intended meaning before the pause is again clear: Chaplin comes to a building site. The structure is V PP, where PP is directional. *Komme* denotes an action and seems to have standard German meaning here; we infer that this was performed by the individual referred to in initial position in the immediately preceding utterance. Note that this does not allow us to state that V2 contains a zero anaphor. What we have are two possible conditions for leaving a referent unexpressed: (1) either it was thematic immediately before, or (2) it was in initial position in the immediately preceding utterance.

The PP corresponds to the TL pattern, except that *eine* is invariant in Vito's variety, thus we cannot assume the correct TL accusative marking. Note that the building site is introduced into the discourse, appropriately, by a noun accompanied by the indefinite article. The sequence after the pause may be glossed as something like: "a sort of building site" (it is of course a shipyard). We take it to be a "postscript" – one of the possible analyses of V1. Note that the now contextually given part of the sequence – *baustell* – is in first position and is not accompanied by an article.

V3. *diese mache schiff*
      this   make   ship

The structure of V3 is clearly NP1 V NP2.

1. NP1 refers to an entity mentioned in the immediately preceding utterance. There, it occurred postverbally and had a different semantic role. Thus, we may say that *diese* goes with "reference maintenance" but also with "position shift" and/or "role shift."
2. *Mache* clearly denotes an action, hence *diese* is an agent, although one would not normally consider a shipyard to be an agent; hence, standard semantic processes that allow us to go from "the shipyard" to "the people at the shipyard" also apply to *diese* here.
3. *Schiff* introduces a new referent. It is unclear whether it is specific or generic or singular or plural. V3 can be glossed either "this one is building a ship" or "this is one of those that builds ships". This example therefore still does not allow us to assign clear referential status to bare nouns.

V4. *kleine schiff mache*
      small   ship   make

Although the specific versus generic interpretations are still possible, the latter seems less likely, the more so since the "reality check" of the film shows just one small ship being built. The structure is clear – NP V – but perplexing. NP is a "patient," the agent is unexpressed, we can infer "shipyard" from conditions (1) and (2) of V2 for leaving a referent unexpressed, and again we see no justification for postulating zero anaphora (where would we place it?). But it is hard to see why the order is NP V rather than V NP, unless the choice between the two is random. If it is not random, several possibilities come to mind:

1. There might be a structural principle at work (roughly: if an utterance contains one NP, it occurs preverbally irrespective of its semantic role), but this seems to be falsified by V2 and by numerous subsequent examples.
2. It may be that different semantic roles of NPs are associated with specific positions, but it is hard to see a great difference between the relation of *schiff* to *mache* in V3 and the relation expressed here.
3. More plausibly, the different orders of V3 and V4 may be based on the discourse organizational principle "go from given to new," except that here we have a (focussed?) case of going from "new" to "given" (cf. also the occurrences of *baustell* in V2). But standard assumptions about "given-new" distribution are perhaps too general in any case.

We will forego further discussion of V4 for the present, and return to it later when we can compare it to other similar utterances (V21).

V5.   *chef   arbeiter   rufe:*   "   "
        chief-   worker   calls

Here *rufe* introduces the quoted speech of V6, and the quotation marks – " " – indicate that *rufe* is a *verbum dicendi*. The intended meaning is obvious: "the foreman calls" and the structure is quite clear. The NP is definitely referring, introduces a new protagonist, but contains no article: What is meant is "the foreman of the shipyard" reference to the shipyard being left implicit. The semantic relation between this and V is agent-action.

V6.   *"Charlie Chaplin   +   ich   brauche   eine   holz"*
        "Charlie Chaplin   I   need   a   wood (log)"

It is clear from the intonation that the first NP is a vocative: We will have no more to say about it. The intended meaning of the sequence after the pause is clear and the whole construction is close to the TL pattern, as is often the case when Vito quotes speech. The structure is again NP1 V NP2, NP1 being a deictic pronoun "in the mouth" of the *chef arbeiter*. NP2 is nonreferential and contains, appropriately, the indefinite article.

V7.   *ich   brauche   eine   (keil)*
        I   need   a   (wedge)

V7 is a repetition of V6, and is separated from it by a metalinguistic passage in which Vito asks, and gets, the German word for "wedge" (*keil* is in brackets to indicate this):

V8.   *sie   nix   verstehn*
        she   no   understand

The most plausible interpretation of V8 is: "he does not understand," with "he" referring to Chaplin. Although "Chaplin" appears in the preceding utterance (if we ignore the repetition), it is a vocative, and contained in quoted speech, neither of which condition obtains in V8. It seems that conditions 1 and 2 of V2 for leaving a referent unexpressed are quite strict.

V9.   *nix komme eine keil,   eine holz, lang, zu   lange*
       no   come a   wedge, a   log, long, too long

If our conditions for leaving a referent unexpressed are correct, we have two alternative interpretations: *er kommt nicht mit einem Keil* "he doesn't come with a wedge", or *es kommt nicht ein keil* "it is not a wedge that comes". The second interpretation is perhaps more plausible, and since Vito uses *mit* "with" elsewhere, and with a "presentational" verb such as *komme*, it is not implausible that its argument appears postverbally. There are other instances of such presentational constructions in the text. The whole construction consists of two adversative components, roughly: "come not wedge – (but) log." It is interesting to note that the negation *nix* precedes the whole first clause although it only applies to the NP *eine Keil*. *Keil* and *Holz* are accompanied, appropriately, by the indefinite article: The referent of *eine holz* is introduced into the discourse here, whereas *ein keil* remains nonreferential.

V10.   *und sie spreche   " "*
       and she speak

The context makes clear that *sie* refers to the foreman. Assuming we were correct in interpreting *sie* in V8 as "Chaplin," we have to conclude that *sie* may refer to an entity introduced more than one utterance back in the discourse with the intervening material containing a possible referent for *sie*. *Sie* is again preverbal, and *spreche* introduces the quoted speech of V11 and V12,

V11.   *"diese nix"*
       "this   no (nothing)"

The meaning is clear, the structure too. The initial NP refers to the log mentioned in V9 – that is, more than one utterance back – although its referential status is complicated by the fact that "in the mouth" of the foreman it is deictic. With the *ich* of V6, *Charlie Chaplin* of V6 and *diese* here, we have items of quoted speech entering referential relations with elements of the surrounding text.

V12.   *ich wolle eine ...   (keil)*
       I   want a   (wedge)

Here *keil* is in brackets because Vito had to ask again for the word for "wedge." The meaning and structure of this utterance are clear; our remarks on the second part of V6 apply here too.

V13.   *sie   gucke eine   keil*
       you/she look   a   wedge

It is not clear whether the stretch of quoted speech stops at the end of V12 or V13. The intonation patterns of V12 and V13 are very similar: However, this interpretation necessitates analyzing *sie* as the polite address form, which Vito never uses elsewhere. Note, however, that this interpretation would give another example of Vito's production in quoted speech being relatively closer to the TL norm. Or, the meaning is "He (= Chaplin) looks for/sees a wedge." The indefinite article accompanying *keil* is appropriate for either gloss of the verb, and we have another example of preverbal *sie* jumping over an appropriate referent (*sie* in V10) and taking up a previously introduced referent.

V14. *hinten* + *eine grosse holz*
      behind (adv) a big log

This and the following utterances describe a complicated piece of business in the film, where Chaplin tries to remove a large wedge maintaining the timbering holding up the ship. When he succeeds in removing the wedge, the timbering collapses and the ship is launched. The structure of this utterance would correspond to the TL but for the absence of a presentative ("there's") between the adverb and the NP (i.e., "behind, *there is* a big log"). This NP is in final position and introduces – with appropriate *eine N* – a new referent. The structure thus shares one characteristic of the "presentative" interpretation of V9, providing indirect evidence for the plausibility of the latter interpretation. Similar examples follow.

V15. *komme diese nix weg*
      come this no off/away

It is unclear whether the intended meaning is "this does not come away" or "Charlie can't get this away" (German *bekommen* "get"). The latter interpretation would violate the conditions for leaving a referent implicit (see V2), which hitherto have seemed quite strict. The former interpretation would be totally consistent with previous uses of *diese* if its position were preverbal. One could appeal to V9 to explain the order *komme diese*, but this provokes further problems: *Komme* is not a presentative here, and *diese* is, of course, definite.

V16. *seine hand nix habe keine kraft weg diese*
      his hand no have no strength off this

"His hand was not strong enough to remove it." We may postulate two parts to this complex utterance: NP1 neg V (neg) NP2, and Adv NP3. NP1 is definite; *seine* seems to function like *sie* – it is (part of) a preverbal NP and can refer back several utterances to a NP already in preverbal position (*sie* of V13 in either interpretation of that utterance). V denotes a stative relation, as in V1. NP2 is either TL-like with *keine* as a determiner, or it can be analyzed as having a constituent negator *keine* corresponding to "not". In the second part of the utterance, *weg* functions as a sort of causative verb on the "patient" *diese*. This could explain the order V – *diese*, but example V18 below further complicates the picture. Note that *diese* in the utterances V15 and V16 refers to the same entity, that those utterances are adjacent, but that the semantic relation between *diese* and the Vs is different.

V17.   *sie   gucke   eine ...   (hammer)*
        she   look   a   (hammer)

Both meaning and structure are clear; the utterance adds nothing to what we already know.

V18.   *probiere   diese   weg*
        try   this   off/away

Again the agent is maintained and left implicit. *Diese* refers back, not to the hammer, but to the log. As in the case of *sie*, it can therefore "jump" appropriate referents, although here it has the same semantic relationship to the "verb" *weg* as in V16, and their relative order is reversed. As in the case of V4 and V9, an appeal to structural, semantic and discourse-organizational principles gives unconvincing answers: We have no real explanation at this point.

V19.   **pero*   sie   nix   gucke*
        but   she   no   look

Structure and meaning are again clear. The agent is maintained but not left implicit, perhaps because of the presence of a connective.

V20.   *diese   holz   sicher   schiff*
        this   log   safe   ship

Vito may have learned the (rare) German verb *sichern* "to make safe". But it is more plausible that he has learned to use the (common) adjective *sicher* "safe" as a verb (cf. *weg* in V16) relating two arguments. It would be pointless to postulate a "recategorization" of *sicher* from adjective to verb in a variety where derivational morphology is virtually nonexistent, and zero markings need as much justification in learner varieties as in other varieties. NP1 here is a kind of instrument and refers to an entity which is thematic, and which when last mentioned was in a patient relationship to the "verb". NP2 – *schiff* – most plausibly takes up the ship introduced in V3 – in the nongeneric interpretation of that utterance, and hence is definite.

V21.   *diese   schiff   arbeite   neue   schiff   bau*
        this   ship   work(er)   new   ship   build(ing)

Both the meaning and the structure of V21 are unclear. Vito seems to want to explain that, roughly, "This ship was being worked on ... was in the process of being built." *Diese schiff* is reintroduced explicitly. This, and other examples in the text, indicate that the "all-purpose" pronoun *sie* is in fact restricted in its use to refer to animates. We take *diese schiff* and *neue schiff* to be co-referential, the second NP providing a further specification. If we assume the same process to be at work in V4 above, where we had *kleine schiff*, then the specific, singular interpretation of *schiff* in V3 does seem more plausible.

The words *arbeite* and *bau* are (not surprisingly) morphologically undecidable between N and V, but as Vito's utterance patterns have overwhelmingly been (NP) V (NP) so far, we see little reason to postulate an utterance consisting of a string of NPs. As with *weg* and *sicher*, they are verb-like. Now, the NPs they associate with are in a relation of patient, not agent. There is no expressed agent. Vito appears to have a principle – and we will interpret V4 *kleine schiff mache* under this principle – that with verbs that are two-place (or can be two-place – *arbeiten*), and where the structure conveys the semantic relationship agent, patient, action, then the agent can be left implicit – for whatever reason: inferable in V4, unspecified in V21 – and the patient occupies preverbal position. One could call this a "passive": However, Keyser and Roeper (1984) and others point to a relatively wide-spread "ergative" use of action verbs in nonergative languages, such as in *der Laden schloss* "the shop closed", etc. It seems to us more plausible to posit such an "ergative" use in Vito's variety as it takes into account principles which explain other aspects of Vito's variety – word order, semantic role relationships – rather than appealing to "missing" copulas and verbal morphology in interpreting these utterances as "really" passives, or indeed to some otherwise unmotivated "fronting" operation. Speculative though this may be, it yields a consistent picture.

V22.	*Zwei*	*holz ...*	*sie*	*weg*	*eine +*	*diese*	*schiff*	*weg*
	two	log ...	she	away	one +	this	ship	away

V23.	*diese*	*schiff*	*weg +*	*sofort*	*meer ...*	*kaputt*
	this	ship	away	straightway	sea	destroyed

V22 and V23 close the shipyard episode (for reasons of space, we have omitted two utterances). They mean something like: "There are two logs ... he takes one away and he takes the ship away (the ship goes away). The ship goes away and straight into the sea (straightaway, there is the sea) and ... destroyed." The first part of V22 is a "presentational"; here Vito restricts himself to the focal part of the presentational, as the whereabouts of the logs are easily inferred from the preceding discourse (e.g., V20). The second part again contains the "verb" *weg*, associated with an agent (Chaplin, last referred to in V19 where again he was an agent) and a patient – the quantifier *eine* ("one of them"). The last part of V22 is ambiguous, given the principles we have established so far: Either the agent of the previous part of the utterance is left implicit, and the structure is "ergative," or *weg*, like *arbeit*, is either a one- or two-place "verb," and we have a one-place "verb" of locomotion here, similar to the nonpresentational *komme*. In either case, *diese schiff* functions as we now expect a NP containing *diese* to function: Its referent is inanimate. That verbs which may be one- or two-place function like other one-place verbs or like other two-place verbs does not surprise us. In V23, the first constituent is identical with the last constituent of V22, and the same remarks apply. The second constituent is ambiguous, given what we know so far: Either it is a "presentational" – *da war gleich das meer* "straightaway, there was the sea" – and we have a structure akin to V14, or *weg*, like nonpresentational *komme*, takes a directional adverbial – the bare noun *meer* – itself qualified by a temporal adverbial *sofort*. Finally, Vito says *kaputt*, which not only expresses the demise of the boat, but also the end of the episode.

Two Conclusions and a Lesson.   Two conclusions and a lesson may be drawn from our analysis of the shipyard episode. The lesson is the following: The methodological problems encountered in this type of analysis are severe. Inferring Vito's intended meaning is not always easy. This has consequences on all levels of analysis:

1. We distinguished two levels of discourse where Vito's production showed differences – the narration proper and quoted speech: assigning V13 to one level or the other leads to differing analyses, as we saw.
2. The segmentation of the speech stream into utterances is not always easy. In V1 we have hesitated between a "relative" and a "postscript" interpretation of the sequence after the pause – *brief für gefängnis*. Suppose now that Vito does indeed show traces of incipient subordination relations: we might then be justified in noting that of the three occurrences of *gucke* in the text, two have two overt NP arguments and one – in V19 – only one, and in assuming that the whole utterance V20 serves as its second argument "he does not see (that) this log supports the ship." But we have as yet no *overt* indications that Vito's production does contain subordination relationships.
3. Establishing tentative regularities and applying them to further utterances yields alternative interpretations – compare the "intransitive" versus the "ergative" interpretation of *diese schiff weg* in V22.
4. Finally, assigning words to classes (cf. *sicher*, *weg*), and, of course, establishing the meaning of individual words, is sometimes problematic.

These problems are compounded by what we may call the "closeness fallacy" – a methodological trap which creates a tendency to analyze learner variety utterances as minimally deviant from TL utterances. We are not convinced that we have avoided the trap (or indeed, if it is entirely avoidable), but we have come closer to avoiding it than in many other studies (including earlier versions of this paper), where the typical trap we fell into was the following: There is a learner utterance NP1 V NP2, we imagine a "corresponding" TL utterance NP1′ V′ NP2′ and note that NP1′ is its subject and NP2′ its object, *therefore* NP1 is the subject, and NP2 the object, of the learner utterance. What we have *tried* to do here is rather to capture regularities that are present in the text: (a) identify verbs and their overt arguments; (b) characterize the lexical properties of the verbs and the semantic relationship holding between them and their arguments; (c) characterize the referential status of the arguments: (d) try to find relationships between (b) and (c) on the one hand, and the internal structure and position of the arguments on the other hand. We have not relied on TL grammatical functions such as "subject" or "object", because they are in any case not foolproof, and call on phenomena such as verb agreement and case marking which are absent from this text, and because we are not tempted by arguments such as: "The subject is in preverbal position (in the TL), therefore the NP in preverbal position is the subject." This has also prevented us, so far, from postulating entities such as "zero anaphora." However, we dare to be less prudent in the following paragraphs.

The first, tentative, conclusion is then that the way Vito forms his utterances is related to the lexical properties of the verb.

1. The verb denotes an action. A first subclass – *mache, gucke, bau* – has either one or two overt NP arguments. In the latter case the preverbal NP denotes the "agent" and the postverbal NP the "patient" or "experiencer." If there is one overt argument, then if the patient is missing (one of the interpretations of V19), the rest of the structure remains constant; if the agent is missing, then either the agent is that of the immediately preceding utterance, and the rest of the structure remains constant, or the "ergative" structure occurs, and patient is preverbal. We will return to the ergative construction in a minute in order to see *why* it occurs. A second subclass has one or two overt arguments. These are inherently one-place verbs – for example, *komme* in V2 – and have the configuration agent–V, where the agent can be missing under the same conditions as for the first subclass, and where the whole configuration may be accompanied by a postverbal directional. There has only been one clear case so far – V2, there were competing analyses for V15 – but the remainder of the retelling contains many such examples.
2. The verb denotes a stative relationship (*habe, brauche, wolle, sicher*). Here, the structure is always NP1 V NP2, but the semantic relationships entertained between the verb and its arguments are very heterogeneous – possessor-possessed, instrument-patient, and so forth. Overall, one could imagine an "affectedness" hierarchy here, with the more "affected" NP being postverbal. We will return to this later.
3. Finally, there are a number of presentative or equative constructions in which there is not always an overt verb. A presentative consists of the NP that is presented, which may be preceded by an adverbial but need not be, as in V22. We have seen no equational constructions yet: They consist of two arguments, the first denoting what is defined or characterized – always an NP – the second being either an adjective or another NP.

The second conclusion is that of the central constituents of the utterances – NPs and Vs. Vs are invariant, but the internal structure of NPs varies. We may distinguish four cases:

1. NPs consisting of a noun, which is sometimes, but not always overtly determined.
2. NPs consisting of *sie* or *diese*. The former always denotes a human entity and always appears preverbally. The latter denotes inanimate entities and occurs preverbally and postverbally. There is a case we have not encountered yet, where, in postverbal position, *diese* denotes a human entity.
3. In quoted speech, there are some occurrences of *ich*, possibly *sie*, and, further on in the text, *du*.
4. Finally, there are cases where in order to understand the utterance, we have to infer a referent that is not overtly expressed.

We will now attempt to put the two conclusions together. Let us take the case where the two argument "action-verb" construction NP1 V NP2 introduces a participant into the discourse in NP1 position (say, *chef arbeiter*). He is the agent of the verb therefore, and is thematic. If, at more than one utterance's remove, he again becomes thematic *as agent*, he is referred to as *sie*, and *sie* is of course in preverbal position. The only cases with this construction where we do not get the configuration (NP1, *sie*) V NP2 are:

1. When the agent *remains thematic from the immediately preceding utterance*. We are now in a position to posit zero anaphora, since a structure Ø V NP2 aligns with all other instances of the two-argument action-verb structure, and we can predict under what discourse conditions the first place will be realized as NP, *sie*, or zero.

2. When the *patient* of the preceding utterance becomes thematic, and the agent is irrelevant (that the patient is thematic is marked both by preverbal position and by further determination or qualification). In this case we would *not* wish to posit a "zero anaphora" for the agent: there is not necessarily an appropriate referent available, and the possible configurations containing zero are nowhere matched by other, overt configurations in the text.

We may now turn back to the stative verbs, which also enter the configuration NP1 V NP2. Out of context, some of these utterances would seem to be reversible – here, we are appealing to our intuitive knowledge of the world – in the sense that *ich wolle eine keil* and *eine keil wolle ich*, and *sie habe eine brief* and *eine brief habe sie* would convey the same "message" to any (German-speaking) adult. On the other hand *diese schiff sicher holz* is less readily interpretable as "this log holds the ship up." Whatever the "semantic role hierarchy" may be, we conclude that for the less reversible cases, the NP higher up the hierarchy will be in NP1 position, and for the more reversible cases, discourse constraints – for example, "me first," what is thematic at that time – will determine the relative order of arguments.

The preceding two paragraphs may be seen as a first attempt to formulate, inductively, the "coalition" of constraints which govern the arrangement of words in Vito's utterances: For a structure NP1 V NP2, if the verb denotes an action, then NP1 will be filled by the agent, realized as a lexical NP, a pronoun, or zero, and so on. Obviously, these conclusions are tentative, and already have possible counter-examples. But the approach has been illustrated, and provides a good springboard for the more general analysis that follows.

Rudolfo and Ramon

Before turning to the utterance organization of all informants, we will sketch the social background and linguistic repertoire of Rudolfo and Ramon, the other two informants. Rudolfo is an Italian in his mid-twenties. After his "maturita," or high school diploma, in Italy, he worked for some time in an accordion factory, and then went to London, where he had been for 15 months at the time of the interview. After some months' work in an Italian restaurant, he found a job in a coffee-house where the language spoken is English. This job is his main contact with English, others being sport with English friends and one term of courses at a college of further education.

As was the case with Vito, it is necessary to treat separately (a) narration proper, (b) quoted speech, and (c) metalinguistic comments. In what follows, we will only consider (a) and (b), excluding, however, questions and commands (which only occur in quoted speech). Rudolfo uses about 20 verbs, including the copula. They occur in the base form or as base + *ing*; there is one "seen", one "fell", perhaps one "banged"; the copula almost never combines with base + *ing*. He increases his verb repertoire with "onomatopoeia," accompanied by gestures, which we will indicate as < crash>, < whoosh>, and so forth (see Ru13 below). Of the about 150 occurrences of lexical NPs in the text, about half are introduced by "the"; their usage seems to correspond to standard English. Bare nouns (except the name "Charlie") refer typically to indefinite or generic uncountables ("ham", "bread", "work"). There are about a dozen countable noncontextualized entities – that is, entities which cannot be assumed to be known to the listener – which are introduced by "one", "one lady", "one piece of wood", and less frequently by "a". About fifteen NPs show a somewhat more complex internal organization, for example "the other side", "the father girl"; some of them seem to include a relative clause; we will consider them later.

There are three deictic pronouns ("I", "me", and "you", only in quoted speech, (cf. Ru16 below) and two anaphoric pronouns, "he" and "they"; they refer to Chaplin or to the "father girl." There are no other anaphoric expressions, such as "this" and "that". Finally, Rudolfo uses a dozen prepositions/particles and five connectors: "and", "but", "after", "then", "when".

Lack of space prevents us from giving an utterance-by-utterance analysis of Rudolfo's retelling. To give some idea of his speech, however, there follow two short extracts: part of the shipyard episode, and part of the episode where the girl steals a loaf of bread and is finally arrested. In this transcription, parentheses indicate an unclear word, and the slash / a replanning on Rudolfo's part.

Ru1.   *e* the director prison give for Chaplin one piece of paper ... good for job

Ru2.   he go to the factory make the ship

Ru3.   (and) the manager: "its ok"

Ru4.   Chaplin ... take off the jacket

Ru5.   go to work

Ru6.   the boss tell: "give me one piece of wood ..."

Ru7.   Chaplin look for this one piece under the ship

Ru8.   (when) take off the piece

Ru9.   the ship go /

Ru10. the ship is not finish

Ru11. go to the sea

Ru12. and the girl ...(is) running ... away

Ru13.   <crash> with Charlie Chaplin

Ru14.   go to the street

Ru15.   the policeman take the girl

Ru16.   Chaplin tell: "is not the girl is me"

Ru17.   the girl go

Ru18.   (and) the policeman take ... Chaplin

Ramon, the third informant, comes from Chile, and is in his mid-twenties. After secondary education in Chile, he served an apprenticeship as a joiner. At the time of the interview, he had been in France about fifteen months, the same as Rudolfo in England, and somewhat less than Vito in Germany. His command of the TL is, however, intuitively much better than that of the other informants. This is probably due to two reasons: (1) as a political refugee, he was given a six-month French course on arrival; (2) the special SL-TL configuration "Spanish-French" allows the informant to perceive TL as closely related to SL on the level of lexis and, to a certain extent, of syntax (Noyau, 1984; Giacobbe & Cammarota, 1986). All initial learners in the Spanish-French part of the ESF project develop a vocabulary relatively fast in relation to other learners.

Metalinguistic asides are quite rare in Ramon's case. Quoted speech is frequent, however. It is almost invariably introduced by *dit*,[5] or *demande* (*à* NP) *qué*. Quoted speech and narration proper do not differ, except for the use of deictic pronouns and the occurrence of questions and commands. So we will include both in the following analysis, and metalinguistic asides will not be considered.

Ramon omitted the shipyard episode in his retelling: We give extracts of the bread-stealing episode, and the episode where Chaplin goes to the restaurant and gets arrested for not paying:

Ra1.   *depuis sé ... une femme qu' el est faim et volé un pain*
        since (=afterwards) it's a woman, who-she is hunger and steals a bread

Ra2.   *il sé trouve avec Chaplin*
        he (=she) is/finds herself with Chaplin
        (description of Chaplin thinking how nice prison would be)

Ra3.   *quand sé trouve la femme + pan!*
        when turns up the woman + pow!
        (= they collide and fall down)

Ra4.   *Chaplin il a le pain quand arrive la police*

---

5   It is often problematic to assign unambiguous correspondences between Ramon's pronunciation of verb forms and the written French form; for example, /truve/ may correspond to *trouvé*, *trouvait*, *trouver* or *trouvez*. For ease of reading, we succumb to the closeness fallacy ourselves, but note that the verb forms in what follows are highly overinterpreted.

Chaplin he has the bread when arrives the police

Ra5.   **bueno* la personne qué court devant la fille*
ok, the person who runs before (=behind) the girl
aussi sé trouve avec la police
also finds herself with the police(man)

Ra6.   *et lé demande qu'el a volé le pain*
and to-him asks who-she has stolen the bread

Ra7.   *Chaplin entre un magasin un magasin *trattora**
Chaplin enters a shop a shop *trattora*

Ra8.   *parce qu'il mange beaucoup de choses*
because he eats a lot of things

Ra9.   **y* bon après+il vu passer un police*
and well after he seen go by a police(man)

Ra10. *il appelle à le police*
he calls to the police(man)

Ra11. *bon et il né lé payé pas à la personne*
well and he not to-her pays not to the person
(= he doesn't pay the cashier)

Ra12. *bon *y* la police l'arrête*
well and the police(man) him arrests

Ra13. *après dans le voiture il sé trouve avec*
after in the van he finds/found himself with

la fille qué a volé le pain
the girl who has stolen the bread

As has been mentioned above, Ramon's vocabulary is comparatively rich, and he is hardly ever in need of a noun, a verb or an adjective. He also has a fairly rich verb morphology, although he is still far from having acquired the TL system. The base form (e.g. /truv/ "find," /envit/ "invite") is still dominant; but there are several infinitives, often with a preposition (e.g. *à vivre* "to live"), seven clear passé composé, (e.g., Ra13), one clear future, one possible imperfect, and a conditional.

There are two nominative pronouns, *il* and *el*, where both may correspond to standard French *il* or *elle* (Ra1, Ra2); we have transcribed the latter as *el*. This *el* and *les deux* are also used as anaphoric plurals. There is one oblique clitic pronoun, /le/ – transcribed *lé* – which corresponds to standard French accusative (*le*) and dative (*lui*) (cf. Ra6, Ra11). *Lui* "him", *moi* "me", and *elle* "her" are appropriately used as strong forms of these pronouns. There are no other anaphoric devices for NP, except one instance of *ça* "this" and a trace of *ce* in the set phrase /se/ (cf. Ra1) which probably comes from *c'est* "this is."

There are a number of prepositions, *à, de, dans, pour, avec, devant, en face de,* some of them strongly overgeneralized, and several connectors. Most important among them is /ke/ – transcribed *qué* – which functions as a relative pronoun – both "subject" and "object" – and as a complementizer after verbs of saying (cf. Ra 6). In the former function, the subject relative clause often, but not always, has a resumptive pronoun; compare Ra13 above with

Ra14.   *avec le police qué il a tombé ...*
         with the police(man) who he has fallen ...

Ramon makes extensive use of other connectors, as well, such as *et* "and", *mais* "but", *quand* "when", *après* "after", *avant* "before", *parce[ke]* "because", and others; their use sometimes deviates from TL use; thus, his *depuis* (standard French "since") means something like "after" (cf. Spanish *después*, as in Ra1).

Influences on Phrasal Construction

Earlier we listed various kinds of influences or constraints which the learner could follow in order to put his words together. One type was based on simple phrasal conditions, such as "Put the verb at the end" or "Put an NP into initial position." In this section, we will consider influences of this type. It will become clear that there are indeed restrictions statable in these terms but that they do not suffice to account for the learners' utterance structure. They must be completed by other constraints to which we will turn shortly.

Any description of possible phrasal constraints depends on which phrasal categories we assume to exist in the given learner variety. This is no trivial problem, and we will not go beyond the most elementary assumptions. As the detailed analysis of Vito has shown, and as is confirmed by an inspection of the complete data sets, there are at least the lexical categories N, V, Cop(ula), Art(icle), Adv(erb), Pro(noun), Pre(position) as well as the syntactic categories NP and P(rep + N)P. Other categories are disputable. Thus, Ramon clearly has complex verbs, consisting of Aux + V, and relative clauses; this is less clear for Rudolfo and unlikely for Vito. In what follows, we will start with the clear categories, and discuss additional possibilities, as they arise.

The Basic Patterns.   Ramon's constructions have either verbs or copulas and either one or two NPs. This gives us the following six basic patterns:

A1:	NP1 V
A2:	V NP2
B1:	NP1 V NP2
B2:	NP1 NP3 V
C1:	NP1 (Cop) {PP, Adv, NP2}
C2:	{PP, Adv} (Cop) NP2

All constructions may be preceded by a conjunction or some other sentence connector ("then," "now," etc.); all four V-constructions may be completed by an adverbial, that is, a spatial or temporal, sometimes modal, Adv (including, for Rudulfo and Ramon, "when-clauses") or PP. This adverbial is normally utterance-final; it may also appear in initial position, however.

Among all six patterns, A1, B1, and C1 are frequent; A2, B2, and C2 are rare and Rudolfo does not have them at all. Before considering them in more detail, we will first see how NP is expanded. This is obviously different for the three informants. It also depends on where NP appears in the pattern:

	Vito	*Rudolfo*	*Ramon*
NP1	Ø	Ø	Ø
	sie	"he", "they"	*il, el*
	diese (N)	–	–
	de N	"the" N	*le, la*, N
	ein N	"one/a" N	*un, une* N
	N	N	N
	name	name	name
NP2	all but	all but	all but
	Ø, *sie*	Ø, "he", "they"	Ø, *il*
			plus:
			Prep *lui, el*, N
NP3	–	–	*lé*

Note that, in Ramon's case, the Prep NP constructions whose NP is a clear argument of the verb (e.g., Ra10: *il appelle à le police*, cf. also the *lé* of Ra11) are assimilated to NP for the purpose of this analysis, limiting PP to cases such as *devant la fille, après l'accident* and so forth. In other words:

1. All informants have three types of lexical NPs[6] that can occur as NP1 and NP2.
2. All informants may have names in NP1 and NP2.
3. All informants have two anaphoric NPs, namely zero and "he" (and equivalents); they occur only as NP1.
4. Vito has in addition *diese* (N), which is anaphorical and may, but need not, have a lexical noun; it occurs as NP1 and NP2.
5. Ramon has anaphoric elements (*lui, el, lé*) as NP2 and NP3, too.
6. Ramon, finally, has a construction not mentioned so far: He may combine NP and *il/el* (e.g., Ra4: *Chaplin il a le pain*) in NP1 position.

Both the similarities and the differences raise interesting questions, to which we will return. Let us consider now the six basic patterns in more detail.

Verbs with One Argument. Rudolfo always uses pattern A1 to put an individual NP argument in initial position, whereas Vito and Ramon may also use A2, which puts the verb first. There is a clear condition for use of A2: They are "presentationals," in the sense already discussed, that is, they mark an "appearance on the scene," mostly with the equivalent of the verb "to come"

---

6 Lexical NPs may be expanded by some modifier in Rudolfo's and Ramon's case, for example an adjective or even a relative clause. There are also compound NPs, such as "father girl." Since we are not interested in NP-structure as such, and since these cases are rare anyhow, we will not consider them here.

(some of the examples quoted in this section have already been given; for ease of reference, they are repeated here):

V24. *sofort*   *komme* *chef* *bäckerei*
      immediately come   boss   bakery

Ra15. *après* *arrive* *otra* *personne*
       later   come   other   person

This is a first clear case which shows that purely syntactic criteria do not suffice to account for the regularities of utterance structure in learner varieties.[7]

It is worthwhile mentioning that the NP in pattern A1 may play different roles with regard to V. There are at least three types:

1. genuine intransitive constructions, with verbs such as "to go" and their equivalent;
2. "absolute" use of transitive verbs, such as "to pay," where only the agent is mentioned but not what is payed; and
3. "ergative" constructions, such as examples V4 or V21; in this case, no agent is mentioned but a kind of "object," affected by the action, is:

V25. *kleine* *schiff* *mache* (=V4)
      small   ship   make

Rudolfo has no clear cases of ergatives, Ramon has one where "Charlie" is clearly the topic:

Ra16. *Charlie +* *lé*   *doné* *la*   *liberté*
       Charlie   to-him give   the   freedom

since this is the first utterance of his retelling and is preceded by a metalinguistic passage where Ramon explicitly asks how one says *Carlitos* in French. Charlie is here the "beneficiary," and the "agent" is left unexpressed, presumably because it is felt by Ramon to be irrelevant.

We mention this heterogeneity of functions in order to stress again that the trivial but tempting rule, "Subject first," simply does not work; there is no or little morphological marking, positional criteria would beg the question (and fail for V NP), and semantic criteria give wrong results in the cases of the quasi-passive and of presentationals.

Verbs with Two Arguments. The clearly dominant pattern here is B1: NP1 V NP2. Only Ramon has NP1 NP3, where NP3 is the clitic pronoun *lé*.

Ra17. *la*   *police* *l'arrête*   (=Ra12)
       the   police   him arrests

---

7 Ramon also has V-NP in subordinate constructions: with *quand* in Ra3 and Ra9. However, it is difficult to tell whether the V-NP order is coincidentally only found in subordinate clauses containing presentational verbs, or whether it reflects the "stylistic inversion" (Kayne, 1972) of spoken French. Perhaps the class of "presentational" verbs will have to be modified in subsequent analysis: Véronique (1985), in a study of a Moroccan acquiring French, notes the V-NP order after verbs such as *marcher* "walk", *monter* "climb", and *partir* "leave" as well.

The distinction between "clitic" and "nonclitic" pronouns offers a straightforward explanation for the different orders NP NP V and NP V NP: It is just like in standard French. But note that this would be a strong (and perhaps fallacious) assumption, since it is arguable that "clitic" in Ramon's variety does not mean the same as "clitic" in the target variety – *lé* combines functions that are formally differentiated in French. He uses the corresponding nonclitic forms *lui* and *moi* only with prepositions, and it may well be that this is his criterion. Lack of space prevents us from further pursuing this point. This exception apart, note that B1 still does not solve the whole problem of arranging the words, since it leaves open which NP goes where. As we shall see, the solution must be based on semantic or "pragmatic" criteria.

Copula-like Constructions.   All informants have a copula. But since they often do not use it where both source and target language would require it (Vito uses it only in quoted speech), we prefer to speak of "copula-like" constructions. They have at least one NP argument, which Rudolfo always has in first position. Vito and – in at least one case – Ramon may have it in final position, too, and the difference is, again, whether it is a presentational or not. The less frequent structure C2 is then the stative counterpart to A2 (the "arrival on the scene"), and, as with A2, purely syntactic criteria are not sufficient to account for it. In the nonpresentational case, there may be a second ("predicative") NP, and again there is no syntactic criterion to decide which one comes first: With reference to the introductory quotation to this paper, the sequence "*A linguist is Peter" would be perfectly acceptable in German, for example.

Summary.   It seems then that the copula, where explicit, behaves like a verb with regard to positional restrictions, and we may sum up all positional restrictions in one rule, where V′ means V or Cop.

Rule A: *The basic pattern is NP1 V′ (NP2) except*
   (a) in presentationals, which have V′ NP2 (Vito, Ramon)
   (b) when one of two NP arguments is an oblique clitic; then the order is
       NP1 NP3 V (where NP3 is the clitic NP for Ramon)

This rule leaves open which NP – if there are two – goes where; it also does not explain the constraints which hold for the occurrence of anaphoric NPs. Finally, with the exception of place adverbials in copula-like constructions, it says nothing about the position of adverbials of place, time, and so forth. As has been said, they are mostly final, but sometimes initial, and we will not try to determine the conditions under which they appear.

Exceptions.   In a number of cases, it is simply impossible to confirm or disconfirm Rule A; the reasons have been extensively discussed and we will not take them up again. But there are three clear exceptions, too. First, there are some sentences with more than two overt NP forms: For example:

Ra19.   *il   ne   lé   payé pas à   la   personne*   (=Ra11)
        he   (not)   it   pay   not to the person

Lé most probably refers forward to *la personne*; thus there are two forms referring to the same argument of *payer*. These cases are too rare, however, to draw any general conclusions.

Second, Vito has at least two NP NP V constructions of the following type:

V26.   *Charlie   mit   de   polizei   gehe   in   gefängnis*
        Charlie   with the police   go   to   prison

Actually, the second NP is a PP, but it seems to function here like the second part of a conjunction "Charlie and the police go together ..." – a construction not dissimilar to pidgins and creoles. Again, there are not enough examples to draw any conclusions.

The third exception is more interesting: there are several relative clauses (Ramon) or constructions resembling relative clauses (Rudolfo). Recall that Ramon has a kind of relative pronoun *qué*, which seems to correspond to standard French *qui*:

Ra20.   ...   *la   fille   qué   a   volé   le   pain*   (=Ra13)
        ...   the girl   who has stolen the bread

If we analyze *qué* as a regular NP, then Rule A is saved: It also applies to relative clauses. There is one problem, however: Ramon's relative clauses often have an additional resumptive pronoun.

Ra21.   ...   *avec   le   police   qué   il   a   tombé*   (=Ra14)
        ...   with   the police   who he has fallen

This is a clear violation of Rule A, unless either we analyze *qué + il* on the same level as constructions such as *Charlie il a le pain* ("Charlie he has the bread") or we consider the *qué* in Ra21 to be the trace of a former stage where *qué* is a generalized marker of subordination, thus Ra21 is on a par with:

Ra2.   *il   pense   qué   c'est   mieux.*
        he thinks that its   better

Rudolfo has no relative pronoun, but some of his constructions resemble a relative clause:

Ru19.   One lady tell ... the man work in the backer

Ru20.   (Charlie) go to the factory make the ship (=Ru2)

One could save Rule A for this case by arguing that there is a zero-NP functioning as a relative pronoun after "the man" and "the factory", respectively (analogous to standard English constructions such as "there was a man came and asked for Fred"). This is a straightforward and therefore quite tempting description. But, as we have noted, one should be careful with postulating zero elements unless there is substantial evidence for a clear rule which controls the occurrence of the zero element – and in this case, we have only a couple of examples so far.

Semantic Constraints

If the learner wants to express the fact that Charlie has seen the policeman, Rule A provides him with some, but not with sufficient, information on how to put his words together: It tells him to put his word for "see" between his expression for "Charlie" and his expression for "the policeman"; but it does not tell him which NP comes first. Indeed, the English order expressing the idea "Charlie see policeman" can be expressed in French as "Charlie see policeman," "policeman Charlie see," "Charlie policeman see," "policeman see Charlie," "see policeman Charlie," or "see Charlie policeman." German allows both "Charlie see policeman" and "policeman see Charlie" for the same idea. Therefore, a learner cannot simply associate a fixed position with each verb. There must be additional criteria. In this section, we will consider possible semantic factors.

They may have to do either with inherent semantic properties of the referent – for example, whether the referent is animate, human, or whatever – or with properties relating to the verb or the whole activity, such as agentivity; we will call them "role properties." The example above suggests that inherent properties may be of little help: It is hard to image any semantic feature of either Charlie or the policeman which could serve as a base for their different position. In fact, an inspection of all examples shows that inherent semantic features play at most an indirect role: Animate human NPs strongly tend to occur in first position. But this is simply due to the fact that referents which function as an agent tend to be animate (cf. Silverstein, 1976b). An agentive verb such as "to make" may have nonanimate agents, however, as is illustrated by the following example (=V3):

V27. *diese*   *mache* *schiff*
      this (=shipyard)   make   ship

The crucial semantic factors (if any) are role properties rather than inherent properties. This is clearly corroborated by example V26. If there is a clear asymmetry between the two NPs, for example the one being an agent, the other not, then the former comes first. (We agree that this is not much of a surprise.) The problem is that not all utterances express actions with a clear agent. A principle such as "agent first" does not work for examples like the following ones (all taken from Vito):

V28. *Ich* *brauche* *eine* *keil*   (=V7)
      I   need   a   wedge

V29. *Ich* *wolle*   *eine* *keil*   (=V12)
      I   want   a   wedge

V30.   *Sie*   *habe*   *brief*   (=V1)
        She (=Charlie)   has   letter

V31.   *Diese*   *holz*   *sicher*   *schiff*   (=V20)
        This   wood   safe (holds)   ship

One might certainly argue that the relation between the two NPs in V31, though static, is more actionlike than, for example, the one in V29, and the "log," although not an agent, is at least more agentive in V31, when compared to the other NP referent "ship," as we have already argued above. So, one might replace categorical distinctions such as "agent" and other "case roles" by a scale which also extends over nonagentive relations. Looking through our examples, it looks as if the "degree of control" might provide us with such a scale: It reflects the degree to which one referent is in control of, or intends to be in control of, the other referents. The degree of control varies with the (nonnegated) relation: thus, "to make" provides us with a stronger control asymmetry than, for example, ownership, as in V3O, or intended ownership, as in V28 or V29. But in all of these cases, it gives us a semantic role asymmetry – an NP referent with "higher" intended control and another with "lower" intended control (for related insights, see the well-known studies of Hopper & Thompson, 1980; Silverstein, 1976b). This allows us to state the following rule:

Rule B: *The NP referent with highest control comes first.*

Admittedly, the relational property "being in control of" needs a more precise characterization, for example in terms of verb classes. But this being granted, Rule B solves a great deal of arrangement problems in sentences with two NPs. It does not work, however, for verbs which do not convey a control relationship such as the copula with two NPs, or uses of the verb "have" for property assignments (the sequence "*one handle has this cup" is very natural in German). The relation "x is y" seems to provide no semantic asymmetry. Hence, the difference between "The girl is the thief" and "The thief is the girl" – must be due to other factors, to which we will now turn.

Pragmatic Factors

There are two arrangement problems left, which cannot be accounted for by Rules A and B. These are the symmetric copula constructions and the specific occurrence restrictions of NP types: Anaphoric NPs, including zero, are subject to specific positional constraints. We will start with the latter problem.

As we have seen in the discussion of Vito, and as one would expect to find, the occurrence restrictions of these various NP types are closely related to whether a referent is first introduced, reintroduced, or maintained from some preceding utterance. An inspection of all examples leads to the following – quite straightforward – conclusions:

1. "the" + N (and equivalents) and names are used when the referent can be assumed

to be known to the listener, either because it was referred to before, or because it is associated with some entity referred to before, or because it can be assumed to be part of the listener's general knowledge;

2. "a" + N (and equivalents) is used for first introduction of a referent.
3. The use of bare N is not totally clear. It is often used to introduce or to maintain noncountables, but there are frequent exceptions. It may well be that the use of bare N reflects previous learning stages (for a more detailed investigation of this problem cf. Carroll & Dietrich 1985).
4. Zero and "he" are used to maintain a previously introduced referent (so do *diese* + N in Vito's case, and *lé/lui* in Ramon's).

This leaves us essentially with one important question: What causes the different types of maintenance – name, "the" + N, zero, "he" and equivalents? In Ramon's case, there is also the question of the conditions under which he uses NP + *il*.

In all cases, the referent has already been introduced. The difference between them apparently has to do with the nature of the referent (in these texts, human or not), and the position where it was previously referred to: in which utterance, and where in this utterance. We illustrate this with the first three utterances of Vito's text V1, V2, and V3 which we repeat here.

V32.   (Charlie is introduced in the previous discourse, which is not part of Vito's narration).

    sie habe brief ...

    Ø komme in eine baustell

    diese mache schiff

For zero to apply, two conditions must be met. Condition A is that the referent must be maintained from the immediately preceding utterance of the narrative text, and Condition B is that the referent must be in initial position. If Condition A is not met, *sie* must be used; if Condition B is not met, Vito uses *diese* (we will come to the other informants shortly). In practice, however, Condition A is often violated in that zero may jump over intervening utterances; but then, these utterances do not belong to the "plot line" of the story; they may give background information or be metalinguistic comments. In order to make Condition A more precise, we have to account for this difference in pragmatic function within the text. Also, Condition B seems to reflect some functional difference: Intuitively speaking, zero and (perhaps) "he" seem to require "topic maintenance," whereas the switch from *in eine baustell* to *diese* seems to reflect a transition from "focus" to "topic." Now, as we stated earlier, all of these terms are highly disputable. In what follows, we will work out a simple proposal to account for these problems in the present context.

Very often, a statement is used to answer a specific question, this question raising an alternative, and the answer specifying one of the "candidates" of that alternative. For example, the question "Who won?" raises an alternative of "candidate" persons – those who may have won on that occasion, and the answer specifies one of them. A question may raise all sorts of alternatives, for example, actions ("What did Charlie do?"), contents of prepositions ("Was Charlie *before* or *behind* the ship?"), etc. Let us call "focus" that part of a statement which specifies the appropriate candidate of an alternative raised by the question, and "topic" the remainder of the answer.

Now, not all texts are question-answer-sequences. But we may assume that any statement is an answer to an (implicit or explicit) question, which we will term *questio* to remind the reader that it is an analyst's construct. Thus, Vito's *Ø komme in eine baustell* is an answer to a (implicit) quaestio "What did Charlie do at that time?" whereas *diese mache schiff* answers an (implicit) *quaestio* "What did this baustell do?" Note that the two statements serve quite different functions within the whole narrative: The first indeed belongs to the "plot line" – the foreground of the story – whereas the second gives (relevant) background information: it does not answer the "key question" of the whole text, which is: "What happens with Charlie (and possible other protagonists)?" Thus, all utterances which answer the key *quaestio* belong to the foreground – they push forward the plot line – and all other utterances, no matter which (possibly very important) *quaestio* they answer belong to the background.

A narrative is an answer to a question-function Q_i where i ranges over time intervals:

Q1:   What happens with p at t_1
Q2:   What happens with p at t_2
Q_n: What happens with p at t_n

This question-function defines the foreground of the narrative:[8] all utterances which are answers to one of these questions are "foreground-utterances". It also defines topic and focus within each of these utterances: The topic of a foreground clause includes a time span t_i (which is mostly not explicitly specified but given by the sequential order, except for t_1) and a protagonist or the protagonist. The focus specifies the action or event at that time span (which means, incidentally, that foreground clauses normally cannot be imperfective or stative: One could characterize exceptions to this "norm" to a certain extent, but lack of space prevents us from doing so). The focus specifies then a possible "happening" at that time t_i with that protagonist p. Background clauses are normally linked to a foreground-clause; their internal focus-structure is quite different, depending

---

[8] Narratives may differ to some extent with respect to the "key question". We have chosen the relatively neutral formulation "happens with p," although it gives the protagonist (or protagonists) a somewhat passive role. Let us add that it might be more appropriate to characterize a narrative by two "key questions" (Q_0, P_i), where Q_0 refers to the "rooting" of the whole event in time and space (Labov's orientation): "When and where did a happen?" where a is the total event (one may indeed imagine a third "key question": "so what?"). This whole approach, which also applies to other types of texts, is worked out in more detail in Klein and von Stutterheim (1987); here we give only the rough idea.

on what information they specify. The overall structure of a narrative is then (A = foreground, B = background):

Q1   Q2   Q3 Q_n
(B) - A_1 - (B) - A_2 - (B) - A_3 - (B) - A_n - (B)

This structure plays an important role in the narratives of all informants. We noted that Rudolfo has a base form and a base + "-ing" form for V. It turns out that the latter massively occurs in B-clauses. Similarly, all "subordinate clauses" in Rudolfo's and Ramon's texts are of type B. There are also some immediate implications for word order to which we will turn in a moment.

Using the abbreviations T for topic and F for focus, we may now restate our observations in connection with V1–3 (repeated in V32 above): Zero maintains a referent from T in A_i to T in A_{i+1}, *sie* a referent from somewhere to T in A_i, and *diese* (N) from F in A_i to T in A_{i+1}. In other words: What matters for the use of the various types of NP is not only whether something is maintained or introduced, but also whether it goes from T to F (topic to focus), from F to T and so forth, and which clauses intervene.

An analysis of all of the texts shows the following regularities:

1. Transition from "nothing" to T (=first introduction): lexical NP (except *diese* + N in Vito's case). Note, however, that "the" is quite rare.
2. Transition from T to T ("topic maintenance"): zero, "he," "the" + N; zero only applies when the two clauses are adjacent, and where B-clauses do not normally interrupt adjacency of A-clauses. The difference between "he" and "the" + N is not totally clear; it seems, however, that "the" + N is used when there might be an ambiguity, e.g. when there is an intervening NP which could be misinterpreted as coreferential to "he."
3. Transition from F to T: "he" and, in Vito's case, *diese* + N.
4. Transition from "nothing" to F ("focus introduction"): lexical NP (or name), except *diese* (N); again, "the" + N is rare (it is only used when the referent can be assumed to be known, although it was not mentioned before).
5. Transition from T to F: There are few clear examples, probably lexical NP (or name) for Vito and Rudolfo as the following two utterances show:

   Ru24.   one man ... go to the work
           (his) wife kiss the man.

6. Transition from F to F: few clear examples, probably lexical NP (or name). (Note that this case *is* possible, as can be seen with *un police – le police* in Ra9 and Ra10.)

This leaves us with Ramon's *Charlie + il* construction. This pattern consistently serves to reintroduce a topic: It "highlights" that there is a new topic with respect to the preceding clause; but that the referent of this topic has already been introduced into the discourse.

So far, we have used the T/F distinction only to describe the regularities in the use of various types of NP. But apparently, it also has a direct bearing on the word arrangement problems. The crucial rule is quite simple:

Rule C: Focus comes last.

This rule is gross. In particular, it does not take into account the fact that both the topic-component and the focus-component usually have an internal organization. Still, it helps to answer some open questions. One of them is the "copula-problem." If a copula has two NP arguments, then there is no semantic criterion to decide about their order, as in the case of NP V NP. Here, Rule C puts that NP which is (or belongs to) F at the end. Rule C also gives a possible explanation of the word order in Ramon's and Vito's static (Cop NP) and dynamic (V NP) presentationals: It seems plausible to assume that in presentationals, the NP is the answer to the (usually implicit) *quaestio*, and hence, it comes last. Rudolfo, on the other hand, sticks to the strictly phrasal principle, "NP before V," which, defined in purely categorial terms, wins out in the competition with the pragmatic Rule C. And finally, Rule C provides us with an explanation of a problem which was mentioned only in passing: the position of (temporal and spatial) adverbials, which may appear in initial or in final position; as an inspection of the examples shows, this difference in position is clearly related to their function as part of the topic-component ("orientation") or as part of the focus component.

Summing up, we have found that three "pragmatic" factors play a role for the utterance organization in learner varieties:

1. Familiarity: Can a referent be assumed to be known to the listener, either by world knowledge, or by contextual information of various sorts?
2. Maintenance (vs. introduction): Is a referent first mentioned, or was it already referred to in a previous utterance?
3. Topic-focus structure: Does a constituent specify a candidate of the alternative raised by the *quaestio* of the utterance?

Conclusions

The objective of this paper was to analyze whether there are any principles according to which learners with a limited repertoire put their words together. It was shown – with some exceptions and some degree of uncertainty – that there are basically three rules which determine the arrangement of words in early learner varieties (plus one rule for the type of NP which may occur in a specific position): a phrasal, a semantic, and a pragmatic rule. In other words: All of the three possible kinds of constraints suggested in I, II, and III of the introduction indeed play a role. What we have not considered so far, is their possible interplay. What happens, for example, when Rule B, "low control unit last," and Rule C, "F last," are at variance, when, for example, a clear agent is in F? Apparently, our informants were quite skillful in avoiding such conflicts: There are few clear examples which would show how one factor is outweighed by another one.

But generally speaking, whereas Ramon and Vito allow for more pragmatic and semantic control of word order, as (spoken) French and German in general do when compared to English, Rudolfo favors a "coalition" of phrasal and semantic constraints: The NP is preverbal in presentationals, and the agent is preverbal in utterances with action verbs (the majority), which results in more frequent transitions from T to F, and F to T, than with the other two informants.

This brings us to a last point. We discussed some possible sources of word arrangement principles: source language, target language, and various kinds of universals. It seems clear by now that none of the three rules comes from a syntactic universal; Rules B and C possibly reflect cognitive universals. Where does Rule A then come from? There is no convincing answer at this point; but it corresponds neither to the phrasal constraints of Italian or Spanish, nor to those of the target languages except perhaps for English. It appears to be a genuine syntactic constraint on the three learner varieties considered here, resulting from the learners' interpretation of the input on the basis of their available linguistic knowledge.

10 Crosslinguistic Studies of Aphasia

Elizabeth Bates and Beverly Wulfeck

In this chapter, we will take a crosslinguistic approach to the study of language breakdown in aphasia. Like most researchers in this field, we accept the premise that the patterns of language breakdown observed in brain-damaged patients reflect some decomposition of a universal language processing system. Taken at face value, this claim appears to contradict many of the arguments offered in this volume, which are in favor of a highly interactive and interconnected model of language processing. It is relatively easy to see how traditional modular systems could break down one piece at a time, resulting in (for example) dissociations between grammar and semantics. It is much less obvious to see how an interactive, connectionist system could come apart at the seams.

Our answer to this challenge comes in two parts. First, we will review crosslinguistic evidence showing that the relationship between symptoms and mechanisms is much less direct than one might infer from the literature on aphasic speakers of English. These quantitative and qualitative variations in aphasic symptoms across natural languages can be captured quite naturally within the Competition Model, that is, the model of sentence processing developed by Bates and MacWhinney to account for findings across an array of languages that vary widely in the nature and richness of their morphological systems (Bates & MacWhinney, 1982, 1987, this volume; MacWhinney, Bates, & Kliegl, 1984; MacWhinney, Pléh, & Bates, 1985). Second, we will propose some further refinements of the Competition Model, to account for those patterns of dissociation that do appear to have crosslinguistic validity.

We will focus on the processing mechanisms proposed to underlie two different forms of language breakdown: Broca's (nonfluent) aphasia and Wernicke's (fluent) aphasia. Patients displaying these and related symptom patterns have been studied in several typologically distinct languages, permitting a test of two broad classes of theories of aphasia. *Syndrome-dominant models* (e.g., the closed-class theory of agrammatism) predict broad differences between patient groups, with relatively little differentiation as a function of language. *Language-dominant models* (e.g., the Competition Model) predict more differentiation as a function of language type, with few differences in the nature of grammatical breakdown among patient groups.

Our own crosslinguistic research on aphasia yields four conclusions, requiring a compromise between language- and syndrome-dominant models.

328

1. The "same" aphasic syndromes do look very different from one language to another. In fact, language differences account for more variance than patient group differences in all of our experiments to date.
2. Nevertheless, overlaid on these language differences we find strong evidence in both comprehension and production for a selectively greater impairment of grammatical inflections and function words.
3. This selective vulnerability of morphology is not restricted to agrammatics. It occurs in *every* syndrome that we have studied to date – although it may occur for different reasons in different patient groups.
4. The best way to characterize the breakdown of morphology is in terms of *accessing* rather than *loss*. That is, patients show an ability to retrieve and use morphological patterns correctly when there is enough redundancy in semantic/pragmatic functions or syntactic/morphological context.

We will review these findings briefly here, but we would also like to go beyond them, to determine *why* morphology appears to be so vulnerable to brain damage, and *whether* the apparent lack of differentiation between patient groups does not in fact belie qualitative differences in the causes of lexical/morphological breakdown. To provide an explanation for patterns of selective dissociation in aphasia – in particular, the selective vulnerability of grammatical morphology across languages – we will propose an extension of the Competition Model that incorporates features from several existing theories of lexical access (e.g., the Logogen Model, Morton, 1970; the Cohort Model, Marslen-Wilson & Tyler, 1980; the Trace Model, Elman & McClelland, 1984).

Specifically, we will propose a list of properties that increase or decrease the likelihood that a given lexical item will be retrieved for use in expressive language, and/or recognized and used in the course of receptive language processing. These *item access properties* apply to function words and content words alike, including both bound and freestanding items. However, individual items or classes of items can vary considerably in their strength or weakness along a given access dimension. For example, function words tend to be high in frequency but low in semantic content and/or imagery; content words, especially concrete nouns, often show an opposite profile. These properties may vary in importance at different moments in processing. Frequency may be most important in the first 50 milliseconds, whereas semantic content is more important further downstream. The timing and nature of frequency effects is also different in receptive and expressive language processing. Effects may also vary with task demands. For example, in studies of grammaticality judgment compared with studies of sentence comprehension, the strength of semantic effects can be reduced by instructing subjects to focus on linguistic form.

Our point is that dissociations can occur in a highly interactive system, if the whole system changes in ways that affect some items more than others. Selective sparing and impairment may result from perturbations in timing, from restrictions on a data source that is especially important for a given class of items, and/or through adaptations that the patient makes to his aphasic condition (that is, self-induced task demands). We do not have to postulate separate modules for each item type, or disconnections in the wires running from one component to another.

Syndrome Differences

Taxonomic approaches to language breakdown in aphasia have a long history. According to Lesser (1978), no fewer than 78 different subcategories have been proposed at one time or another to capture the range of variation observed in the linguistic symptoms of brain-damaged patients. Only two of these categories are really uncontroversial and known to occur across natural languages.

Broca's aphasia, also called nonfluent and/or motor aphasia, is characterized by slow and halting speech, reduction of phrase length and syntactic complexity, disruption of normal prosody or melodic line, and a tendency to omit grammatical function words. The patient may also experience difficulty in retrieving content words, although this is not the most striking symptom. In a prototypical Broca's aphasic, comprehension appears to be intact – at least at an informal, clinical level. The syndrome is usually (though not always) associated with damage to the anterior portion of the left hemisphere, in particular, a region of frontal cortex near the motor strip referred to as Broca's area.

Wernicke's aphasia, also called fluent and/or sensory aphasia, is characterized by fluent or even hyperfluent speech, with apparently normal melodic line (though subtle prosodic disruptions have been detected). These patients may produce lengthy sentences of considerable morphosyntactic complexity. However, their expressive language is far from normal, marked by severe word-finding difficulties, long passages of circumlocutionary speech (for example, "I know what it is but I can't think of its name"), substitution of one word for another (semantic paraphasias), neologisms (literal and/or phonemic paraphasias), and in the worst cases, long strings of jargon that are totally incomprehensible to the listener. Wernicke's aphasics also experience moderate to severe difficulties in language comprehension, a symptom that led to the earlier term "sensory aphasia." The syndrome is usually (though not always) associated with damage to the posterior areas of the left hemisphere, in particular a region of temporal-parietal cortex referred to as Wernicke's area.

These two key syndromes blend into others that share some of the same fluent or nonfluent features. For example, *pure anomia* refers to difficulty in retrieving content words in the absence of any other apparent language symptoms. Anomic symptoms can occur in conjunction with damage to almost any part of the left hemisphere. And many Broca's and/or Wernicke's aphasics, if they recover at all, resolve into something resembling an anomic syndrome (Holland, 1985). This fact is important for our purposes because it suggests that lexical problems play an integral role in all the major aphasic syndromes. In fact, we will argue later that morphosyntactic problems in aphasia may constitute a form of lexical impairment.

Grammatical impairments in aphasia have traditionally been divided into two categories: agrammatism and paragrammatism (Goodglass & Kaplan, 1983). These two forms of structural breakdown are, in turn, associated with the two major classes of aphasia described above. *Agrammatism* is defined as a marked reduction in phrase length and syntactic complexity, with omissions of inflections and grammatical function words that give the patient's speech a "telegraphic look." These symptoms are generally reported for Broca's aphasics. *Paragrammatism* is defined primarily in terms of substitution rather than omission errors, and is usually reported in fluent patients who suffer from moderate to severe word-finding problems; the same patients may also produce a large number of other substitution errors (that is, semantic and phonemic paraphasias), leading to the suggestion that paragrammatism and paraphasia have a common base. Although paragrammatisms are occasionally reported for patients from a variety of diagnostic categories, they are most often associated with Wernicke's aphasia – at least in studies of English, a point that we will take up shortly.

If the grammatical symptoms of Broca's aphasia were restricted entirely to expressive language, one might accept the classic argument that "telegraphic speech" reflects an effort to economize, primarily because of motor problems in speech production (e.g., Pick, 1913; for a discussion, see Gleason, Goodglass, Green, Ackerman, & Hyde, 1975). However, there are now a wealth of studies showing that Broca's aphasics also have difficulty in a variety of receptive language tasks, if those tasks require them to rely primarily on grammatical morphemes (Bates, Friederici, & Wulfeck, 1987b; Bradley, Garrett, & Zurif, 1980; Caramazza, Berndt, Basili, & Koller, 1981; Friederici & Schoenle, 1980; Friederici, Schoenle, & Goodglass, 1981; Goodglass, Blumstein, Gleason, Hyde, Green, & Statlender, 1979; Heilman & Scholes, 1976; von Stockert & Bader, 1976; Zurif & Caramazza, 1976). For example, Heilman and Scholes asked patients to interpret sentences like "He showed her the baby pictures" versus "He showed her baby the pictures," where selection of the matching picture revolves entirely around the patient's ability to process the nature and position of the grammatical function word "the." Despite the fact that their overall comprehension appears to be normal, Broca's aphasics perform well below age-matched normal controls on tasks like these.

Because such findings parallel the telegraphic nature of speech output in the same patients, they support a definition of agrammatism as a central processing deficit (Caramazza & Berndt, 1978, 1985; Zurif & Caramazza, 1976). From this point of view, Wernicke's aphasia could also be reinterpreted as a mirror image syndrome: difficulty with both the comprehension and production of content words, suggesting that there is selective impairment of semantics with selective sparing of grammatical structure.

At face value, such a double dissociation between grammar and semantics appears to provide strong evidence for a modular view of language, that is, a theory in which grammar and semantics are handled by separate and autonomous processors, each with its own neural architecture (Chomsky, 1980; Fodor, 1983; Gardner, 1983). But the initial characterization of agrammatism as a central processing deficit has proven to be far too simple, and subsequent research has led to a more complex view of the processing components that are dissociated in aphasia (Kean, 1985).

First, investigators are now questioning the idea that agrammatism involves an "across-the-board" impairment at every level of the grammar. Several studies have shown that word order is reasonably well preserved in both fluent and nonfluent aphasia (Ansell & Flowers, 1982; Bates, Friederici, & Wulfeck, 1987b; Bates et al., 1983; Bates, Friederici, Wulfeck, & Juarez, 1988; Goodglass, 1968; Kolk & van Grunsven, 1985). There are a few exceptions to this view in the literature that need to be accounted for (Saffran, Schwartz, & Marin, 1980; Schwartz, Saffran, & Marin, 1980; Tissot, Mounon, & Lhermitte, 1973; for detailed discussions, see Bates et al., 1988; Kolk & van Grunsven, 1985). Nevertheless, if there is such a thing as a central grammatical deficit, it seems to have its most severe and reliable effect on the patient's ability to retrieve inflections and function words, that is, what one patient called "those terrible little words" (Nespoulous, Dordain, Perron, Bub, Caplan, Mehler, & Lecours, 1984). Most patients seem to know *where* both open and closed class elements belong within a simple phrase, *if* they are able to retrieve those elements at all (a conclusion that is reinforced by our crosslinguistic findings – see below).

This kind of finding has led to a more restricted view of grammatical impairment, referred to as *the closed-class theory of agrammatism* (Bates et al., 1983; Bradley et al., 1980; Friederici & Schoenle, 1980; Kean, 1979; Zurif & Grodzinsky, 1983). According to this view, Broca's aphasia does involve a central grammatical deficit, demonstrated in both receptive and expressive processing. But its effects are restricted primarily to the retrieval and/or interpretation of closed-class elements, that is, freestanding grammatical function words and bound grammatical morphemes. This hypothesis deserves a rigorous test, because of its powerful implications for theories of normal and abnormal language processing. If we can show that agrammatism is limited to closed-class elements, then we will have markedly reduced the range of alternative explanations for language disorders in aphasia. If patients lose the ability to make use of closed-class vocabulary, while retaining their ability to use information about how vocabulary items are ordered in their language, then agrammatism – like anomia – could be viewed as a disorder of *lexical access*. We would still have to explain how different aspects of the lexicon can be dissociated from one another (e.g., content words versus function words, and, perhaps, nouns versus verbs). But we could at least begin by working with an array of existing theories of how individual lexical items are recognized and retrieved (Marslen-Wilson & Tyler, 1980; McClelland & Rumelhart, 1981; Morton, 1970; Small, Cottrell, & Tanenhaus, 1989; Swinney, 1979). Such a lexicalist conclusion would be much more compatible with the approach to sentence processing that we have taken throughout this volume.

There are now several different versions of the closed-class hypothesis (e.g., Bradley et al., 1980; Caramazza & Berndt, 1985; Grodzinsky, 1983; Kean, 1979; Zurif & Grodzinsky, 1982). For example, Zurif and Grodzinsky explain the impairment of closed-class elements in *grammatical* terms, based on a dissociation between "positional frames" (which presumably are not lost in aphasia), and a special vocabulary of morphological elements that are used to fill slots in those frames (see also Rizzi, 1982). By contrast, Kean offers a *phonological* explanation, based on the status of inflections and function words as "clitics," that is, one- or two-syllable elements that cannot receive stress under normal conditions. Goodglass and Menn (1985) suggest that closed-class morphemes are difficult for aphasic patients to access because they have little or no *semantic content*. All of these explanations are plausible – and they may in fact all contribute to the tendency for Broca's aphasics to omit closed-class elements in their speech, and to fail on receptive processing tasks that require the patient to rely on grammatical morphemes. However, several recent studies present problems for any version of the closed-class theory (see Goodglass & Menn, 1985, Badecker & Caramazza, 1985, for critical reviews).

The major problem revolves around the claim that agrammatism represents a central deficit. This position is summarized succinctly by Caramazza et al., (1981, p. 348):

Although it is possible that Broca patients may suffer from deficits in addition to this syntactic processing deficit, it should be the case that all patients classified as Broca's aphasics will produce evidence of a syntactic impairment in all language modalities.

However, there are at least some cases of expressive agrammatism in patients who do *not* experience difficulties in receptive processing of grammar (Kolk, van Grunsven, & Guper, 1982; Miceli, Mazzucchi, Menn, & Goodglass, 1983; Nespoulous, Dordain, Perron, Bub, Caplan, Mehler, & Lecours, 1984). These authors suggest that receptive and expressive agrammatism are actually different syndromes, occurring for different reasons. They generally occur together in Broca's aphasia, but either can occur in isolation.

The issue is complicated still further by studies showing that Broca's aphasics retain a surprising amount of sensitivity to violations of grammaticality (Crain, Shankweiler, & Tuller, 1984; Linebarger, Schwartz, & Saffran, 1983; Wulfeck, 1987; but see Zurif & Grodzinsky, 1983). What does the term "agrammatism" mean, in any version, if an agrammatic patient can make subtle judgments of grammatical well-formedness?

Further problems for the central deficit hypothesis come from studies suggesting that impairments of grammatical morphology are not unique to Broca's aphasia. For example, Caramazza et al. (1981) have shown that *both* conduction aphasia and Broca's aphasia can lead to receptive agrammatism. And as we shall see shortly, our own crosslinguistic studies show that morphology is selectively impaired in several different forms of aphasia.

Whether or not there is a single syndrome of agrammatism, there is still compelling evidence to suggest that closed-class elements are differentially sensitive to brain damage. We will show – we hope conclusively – that the closed-class theory does have crosslinguistic validity. Why is this important? Because the English language stresses word order principles at the expense of grammatical morphology, the finding that closed-class items are vulnerable in aphasia might reflect nothing more than a break in the "weak link in the chain." We will show instead that morphology breaks down in both comprehension and production, whereas sensitivity to positional information is maintained, even in languages with strong morphology and variable word order.

This suggests that the "special vulnerability of morphology" is a fact about aphasia, and not just a fact about English. And yet, as we shall see, the breakdown of morphology takes different forms depending on the patient's premorbid language. This leads us to a consideration of language-dominant models, designed to deal with crosslinguistic data.

Language Differences

The Competition Model provides a useful framework for crosslinguistic research on language processing in normal adults and children. But as we noted earlier, it is not immediately obvious how such a heavily interactionist model can account for double dissociations between major components of language. The answer lies in some recent modifications of the Competition Model, specifying different aspects of cue cost. Taken together, the principles associated with cue validity and the modifications associated with cue cost can be used to capture a range of language-based and syndrome-based facts about aphasia. Because the Competition Model is outlined in detail elsewhere in this volume (see especially Chapter 1), we will restrict ourselves here to a review of those principles that are particularly important for aphasia.

Lexicalism. The Competition Model is a lexicalist theory. That is, it attempts to account for both lexical and grammatical phenomena in terms of a single "dictionary" of content words and grammatical morphemes, annotated to include information about elements that typically occur to the left and right of each item. This lexicalist approach can be used to account for at least two aspects of language breakdown in aphasia. First, it is compatible with the well-established cooccurrence of lexical and grammatical deficits in fluent and nonfluent patients (e.g., Swinney, Zurif, & Nicol, in press; Milberg, Blumstein, & Dworetsky, 1988). Second, it is compatible with the finding that aphasic patients have difficulty accessing individual open and/or closed class items despite good preservation of positional frames: Even if the wrong item is retrieved within a given target class, there is still a great deal of active and often redundant information about the left- and right-hand context shared by items within that class. This suggests that patients are operating with a context-sensitive lexicon, one that exercises a parallel influence on lexical and grammatical processing.

Probabilistic Representations. The Competition Model is a probabilistic theory, in which the difference between obligatory rules and statistical tendencies is treated quantitatively rather than qualitatively. Two languages may both employ a set of rules or rule types that are equally obligatory from the point of view of a traditional competence model, and yet the strength of the mappings implied by those rules may differ significantly between languages. This aspect of the theory is particularly important for crosslinguistic aphasia research, because it helps us to understand why the "same" rule type (for example, subject–verb agreement) may be better preserved in both comprehension and production in one language than in another.

Cue Validity. Where do these differential probabilities come from? In the Competition Model, the probabilities or weights attached to forms and functions are derived from cue validity, referring to the information value of a given grammatical, phonological, or lexical cue to sentence meaning in a particular language. Highly informative cues are learned very early and play a major role in sentence interpretation throughout life. As we shall see, cue validity can also account for robust differences in sentence comprehension and production among aphasic speakers of structurally distinct language types.

However, Bates, MacWhinney, and their colleagues have now uncovered several clearcut exceptions to cue validity, particularly in language acquisition by children (Kail, this volume; Sokolov, this volume). These exceptions all seem to revolve around aspects of *cue cost*, that is, the processing costs incurred in using a particular form–function mapping. Some examples of cue cost with implications for aphasia follow.

Functional Readiness. This refers to the *cognitive costs* involved in acquiring and/or using a particular mapping, based on the assumption that conventional semantic/pragmatic functions vary in degree of conceptual difficulty. A cue may be highly informative; however, if it provides information about a concept that is exceptionally difficult in its own right (for example, counterfactual conditions, or complex text-cohesion functions), children may acquire that cue relatively late. This same principle has implications for the effects of brain damage on language processing. In adult patients, various forms of conceptual breakdown could result in loss or impairment of the same functions that develop late in normal children (for example, text cohesion in complex narratives). If this functional base is damaged, then the grammatical devices associated with those functions may be correspondingly impaired and/or difficult to access.

Perceivability. A morpheme that is high in validity may be difficult to use simply because it is relatively difficult to perceive. For example, MacWhinney, Pléh, and Bates (1985) have shown that phonologically salient case cues are acquired and used earlier than less salient cues that are equivalent in cue validity. This cue cost principle has clear implications for language processing in older adults. First, if an elderly patient's peripheral hearing is at all impaired (including subtle impairments that may be missed in global assessments of hearing ability), then the utility of these cues may fall well below the baseline levels established earlier in life. Second, if more central phonological mechanisms are damaged in some way, then the effects of phonological salience on grammatical processing may be magnified.

Assignability/Memory Load. Two cues to meaning may be equivalent in cue validity, but vary in the memory demands that they place on sentence processing. For example, "local" cues such as case suffixes on nouns can be used to bind or assign sentence roles as soon as they are processed; "global" or "long-distance" cues such as subject–verb agreement cannot be bound or assigned until the verb and all its noun arguments have been stored and cross-checked. This dimension of "assignability" seems to affect the order of acquisition of cues by children. For example, Hungarian children rely heavily on case cues to sentence meaning by the age of three; Italian children do not make heavy use of subject–verb agreement (an extremely strong cue for adults) until the age of 6. Bates and MacWhinney (this volume) argue that developmental limitations in short-term memory are responsible for such a massive difference in acquisition time for local versus global cues. This argument may be extended to memory limitations that result from brain damage in adults, placing agreement markers and other "long-distance" grammatical phenomena at greater risk.

These three potential sources of cue cost are not meant to be exhaustive; several others will be proposed later on, organized within a list of item access properties, that is, the internal conditions that affect a speaker/hearer in his efforts to locate the phonological forms (words, morphemes, suprasegmental units) associated with a given meaning configuration. We will suggest that language-specific differences in *cue validity* are preserved in aphasia, across a variety of syndromes. The syndrome-specific effects of brain damage are based primarily on aspects of *cue cost*, and presumably reflect some decomposition of the processing mechanisms that absorb these costs.

We will now turn to a brief review of our crosslinguistic aphasia results to date. Then we will sketch out a model of lexical/morphological access that is compatible with the Competition Model, a model that can be used to study the different patterns of lexical/morphological impairment that are observed in brain-damaged patients across natural languages.

Crosslinguistic Evidence

Subject Selection

In crosslinguistic research on language acquisition, children from different language groups are compared with one another on the basis of age, for example, 2-year-old Italians compared with 2-year-old Hungarians. In crosslinguistic research on aphasia, we must instead compare patients from the "same" clinical category, for example, Broca's and Wernicke's aphasics. This is no trivial matter. As we shall see, the "same" syndrome can take a qualitatively and quantitatively different form across natural languages. Morphological errors are surprisingly rare in many richly inflected languages, even among severely impaired nonfluent aphasics. And function words that are easily omitted in one language (for example, articles in English) are omitted much less often in a language in which the same function word carries a high information load (for example, articles in German). There is to date no clear metric for matching aphasic patients for severity of impairment across different language groups. We have discussed the problem of patient selection in several published papers, and will not belabor it here. Hopefully, our crosslinguistic project will ultimately contribute to a new set of standards for patient comparison across natural languages (see also Paradis, 1987).

To summarize our procedure briefly, patients are referred to us for testing by neurologists and speech pathologists at each research site, with a diagnosis of Broca's or Wernicke's aphasia (as defined above). We thus define patient groups *within* each language, according to their fit to a prototype used by neurologists and speech pathologists in that community. For example, a prototypic Broca's aphasic would show reduced fluency and phrase length, and a tendency toward omission of functors – *relative to normals in that language*. Hence, patients are matched across languages only in the sense that they represent different degrees of deviation from a prototype developed out of observed variation within each language group. In support of each classification, we are provided with neurological records (including CT scans in many cases), together with the results of standard aphasia batteries that are used at the respective research sites. To eliminate the possibility that a patient has changed status since the diagnosis provided at referral, patients are all screened in a biographical interview administered and recorded prior to testing. In addition, we exclude all patients with one or more of the following conditions:

1. history of multiple strokes,
2. significant hearing and/or visual disabilities,
3. severe gross motor disabilities,
4. severe motor-speech involvement such that less than 50% of subject's speech attempts are intelligible, or
5. evidence that subject is neurologically or physically unstable and/or less than 3 months post onset.

This permits us to compare the "best" and the "worst" patients across languages, as well as those who fit the mean.

At this point we have completed sentence comprehension and production studies in English, Italian, Serbo-Croatian and German (Bates et al., 1983; Bates et al., 1987a, 1987b, 1988; Smith & Mimica, 1985; Smith & Bates, 1987; Wulfeck, Bates, Friederici, MacWhinney, Opie, & Zurif, 1988). We have also tested normal Spanish-English bilingual controls, and applied those results to a case study of a Spanish-English bilingual patient suffering from a nonfluent, agrammatic aphasia in both languages (Wulfeck, Juarez, Bates, & Kilborn, 1986). More recently, members of our international team have administered the same comprehension and production tasks to 5–10 cases of Broca's and Wernicke's aphasia in Hungarian (Osmán-Sági & MacWhinney, in preparation), in Turkish (Talay & Slobin, in preparation), and in Chinese, including Mandarin and Taiwanese dialects (Tzeng & Chen, in preparation). Preliminary results are summarized in Bates and Wulfeck (1989). Because the details are available elsewhere, we can restrict ourselves here to a brief discussion of the most important findings to date.

Pragmatic Aspects of Production

Wulfeck et al. (1988) used a paradigm drawn from MacWhinney and Bates' (1978) crosslinguistic study of sentence production in normal adults and children. Broca's aphasics, Wernicke's aphasics, and normal controls in English, Italian, and German were presented with a series of three-picture "stories" in which one element is varied while the others remain constant (for example, a little girl eating an apple, then an ice cream cone, then a doughnut). This "given-new" technique permits us to observe pragmatic effects on several aspects of linguistic reference: lexicalization versus ellipsis (that is, whether the respective given or new objects and actions are mentioned at all), pronominalization (that is, whether nominal or pronominal forms of reference are used), and definite versus indefinite articles. This information was supplemented by transcribed biographical interviews for the German and Italian patients only, permitting analysis of subject omission and subject pronouns in a less formal situation, with a high proportion of first-person reference.

We found a complex interplay among four kinds of factors: syndrome-specific symptoms, universal pragmatic principles, language-specific rules, and patterns of reference that are specific to the discourse situation (that is, the contrast between picture description in the given-new task and self-description in the biographical interview).

Syndrome-Specific Patterns. We did find syndrome-specific symptom patterns in this and all the studies described below. Broca's aphasics produced fewer words overall, and they tended to omit closed-class elements, for example, articles and pronouns. Wernicke's aphasics tended to produce more "empty" pronominal forms than we find in normal controls. Both patient groups produced abnormally high levels of definite reference, suggesting that they are more likely to take a concrete "here and now" perspective in the picture description task. These symptoms are predictable, given the basis on which patients were selected for the study. More interesting for our purposes are the universal and language-specific constraints on reference that appeared in this study.

Universal Pragmatic Constraints on Reference. All patients in all language groups retained sensitivity to the given-new manipulation. Broca's aphasics, Wernicke's aphasics, and normal controls all tended to lexicalize new information more often than old. Conversely, ellipsis was more common for elements that were already established in the discourse situation, in every group. In addition, if patients produced articles at all, they tended to produce definite forms for old information and indefinite forms for new elements of discourse.

Language-Specific Constraints on Reference. Germans and Italians (including Broca's aphasics) used a higher proportion of definite articles, in keeping with known differences among the three languages in the rules that govern definite and indefinite reference. We also found strong evidence suggesting that aphasic patients retain language-specific constraints on the omission of subjects in freestanding declarative sentences (that is, the "pro-drop" parameter – see Bates & MacWhinney, this volume). In the biographical interviews (where first-person reference accounts for 60% of sentence subjects), Italian Broca's and Wernicke's aphasics both omitted the subject significantly more often than their German counterparts; conversely, German Broca's and Wernicke's aphasics produced a significantly higher proportion of subject pronouns. Hence, sensitivity to the pro-drop parameter appears to be preserved in aphasia.

Situation-Specific Constraints on Reference. The above language-specific effects on subject omission were observed only in the biographical interview, and not in the given-new task. The reason for this is clear: In the biographical interviews, where first-person reference predominates, speakers can take the subject of the sentence for granted most of the time; in the given-new task, which focuses exclusively on third-person reference, subject omission is relatively rare – even among nonfluent patients. Hence we can conclude that aphasic adults also retain sensitivity to situational constraints on forms of reference. They know that the "rules" of a picture description situation are different from the "rules" of informal conversation.

This study thus provides a valuable lesson for the study of grammatical symptoms in aphasia: The patterns of sparing and impairment that we observe in grammar are at least a partial function of those universal and language-specific pragmatic/semantic constraints that hold within and across discourse situations. The apparent preservation of sentence-level pragmatics in these patients provides important background information for studies of syntax and morphology.

Syntactic Aspects of Production

Bates et al. (1988) analyzed syntactic aspects of production in the same transcripts used in the above study of pragmatics (for Broca's, Wernicke's, and normal controls, in English, Italian, and German). This study focused primarily on word order, although other aspects of syntactic structure were considered, including the ordering relations that hold between open- and closed-class items.

Syntactic Complexity.   We found the same patient group differences in overall syntactic complexity reported by many other investigators: Broca's aphasics used less complex syntax than Wernicke's, who in turn produced fewer complex forms than normal controls. However, we were surprised to find that four of the Italian Broca's aphasics (and all of the Wernicke's) continued to produce the existential relative clause construction that is so frequent among normal Italians in a picture description task (that is, "There is a monkey that is eating a banana."). This language-specific difference in syntactic complexity is already well-established in children by the age of three (Bates & Devescovi, this volume). Our data suggest that the same structure may also be resistant to the effects of focal brain damage in Italian adults.

Canonical and Noncanonical Word Order.   We found no evidence whatsoever for an impairment of canonical SVO. In this simple picture description task, all three patient groups in all three languages relied overwhelmingly on SVO constructions, if they were able to produce a complete sentence at all. In fact, some patients seem to *overuse* canonical word order, clinging to it like a safe harbor.

There were some trends in the data suggesting that Broca's aphasics avoid some of the stylistic options available in their language. For example, there was a tendency for German normals – but not German aphasics – to use a Verb-Subject construction that is stylistically similar to VS variation in English (for example, "Here comes the rabbit..."), but far more frequent in German. However, the highly constrained picture description task elicited relatively little word order variation, even among German and Italian normals. For this reason, we compared results for the given-new task with use of word order by Italian subjects in the biographical interview. As expected, the informal interview situation elicited much more word order variation in normal Italian speakers. It also elicited significant use of noncanonical VS constructions in both Broca's and Wernicke's aphasics. The one clear patient group difference in word order variation that we obtained involves the much less frequent OV construction. Normals and fluent aphasics produced this structure; nonfluent patients did not, instead sticking with canonical VO. We conclude that preservation of word order in aphasia is not restricted only to canonical frames; noncanonical word order types may also be preserved, if they are particularly frequent and accessible in the patient's native language.

Preliminary results for Turkish, Hungarian, and Chinese support and extend these conclusions. The basic word order in Turkish is SOV, although many variations are possible. Talay and Slobin report that patients produce overwhelming proportions of SOV in the given-new task – indeed, more SOV than we might expect in a language that permits extensive pragmatic variation. Hungarian presents a particularly interesting test case: there are in fact two basic word orders in this language (SOV and SVO), depending on whether the object of the verb is definite or indefinite. Results to date suggest that *both* word orders are preserved in fluent and nonfluent aphasics; furthermore, patients are still sensitive to the subtle interaction between order and definiteness in this language. The basic word order in Chinese is SVO, although a number of topicalizing structures are also possible. SVO is indeed the predominant word order in the patients studied so far – but many of the Chinese aphasics, including some markedly impaired Broca's aphasics, still try to "stage" word order variations with appropriate topic markers (for example, an OSV order with the topic marker *ba* placed in correct position).

Constraints on the Order of Morphemes. The apparent sparing of word order principles in aphasia is not restricted to the order of major constituents. We find equivalent sparing of order information within grammatical morphology. On locative items in the given-new task, if our patients are able to produce locative markers at all, they invariably place those markers in the correct position in all the languages studied to date. This includes the locative prepositions of Indo-European, as well as the locative postpositions of Chinese.

The importance of order information *within* morphology is often overlooked by aphasia researchers. Even in so-called nonconfigurational languages, with ample variation in the placement of major constituents, there are always severe constraints on the position of bound and free morphemes. In principle, many different violations of morpheme order are logically possible across and within natural languages. And yet we never find patients producing errors like "dog the" or "ing-walk," in any of the languages that we have studied to date. Like the dog that didn't bark in a famous Sherlock Holmes novel, the absence of ordering errors in both syntax and morphology provides an important clue about the organization and breakdown of morphosyntax. We need to distinguish between *retrieval of morphological items* (a process that may be impaired in both fluent and nonfluent aphasia) and *knowledge of the positional privileges of those items once they are retrieved.* Although retrieval may be compromised, positional information seems to remain intact. This brings us to the next section.

Production of Morphology

The two studies reviewed so far suggest that both pragmatic and positional aspects of language are preserved in aphasic patients, compared with their well-documented problems in accessing content words and/or grammatical morphemes. In a third study (Bates, Friederici, & Wulfeck, 1988), we used the given-new transcripts for English, Italian, and German to conduct a detailed crosslinguistic comparison of morphological production in Broca's aphasics, Wernicke's aphasics, and normal controls.

Before we describe these findings, let us remind the reader of the traditional distinction between *agrammatism* (omission of inflections and functors) and *paragrammatism* (substitution of inflections and functors). In English, nonfluent Broca's aphasics are more likely to *omit* grammatical morphemes (producing what has been called "telegraphic speech"), whereas fluent aphasics are more prone to *substitute* grammatical morphemes, often as a result of a derailed search for the appropriate content word. However, several recent case studies have concluded that substitution is the prevalent pattern for "agrammatic" patients in richly inflected languages (Grodzinsky, 1982, for Hebrew; Kolk, van Grunsven, & Guper, 1982, for Dutch; Miceli, Mazzucchi, Menn, & Goodglass, 1983, for Italian). Our results support and extend this finding, challenging the traditional distinction between agrammatism and paragrammatism. We also show that patients retain a great deal of knowledge about the "morphological shape" of their language.

Overall Production of Function Words.   We first examined global differences in the production of open- versus closed-class lexical items, as a function of language and patient group. For this purpose, we calculated a "closed-class density score": a simple ratio of the total number of grammatical function words produced by each patient, divided by the total number of both open- and closed-class lexical items. Though this is admittedly a crude measure, it yielded robust differences among both language and patient groups. As we expected, given what we know about the morphological systems of these three languages, the closed-class ratios were ranked as follows: Italian > German > English. And as we also expected, given the clinical profiles that went into patient diagnosis within languages, the three groups' ratios were ranked as follows: Wernicke's > normals > Broca's.

However, on theoretical grounds, we were more interested in language-by-patient group interactions. According to syndrome-dominant models, we might expect aphasia to function as a "great equalizer," depressing between-language differences in the two respective patient groups. According to language-dominant models, life-long habits of grammatical morphology should be preserved, despite the demonstrable effects of focal brain damage, resulting in between-language differences within each patient group. In the three languages studied here, the language-dominant model provided the best overall fit to the data. Within each patient group, there were significant differences in morphological density, with Italian > German > English. This provides both a confirmation and a quantification of the case studies mentioned earlier: Broca's aphasia looks quite different in a richly inflected language, where substitution errors are more common than omission.

Article Omission. A second, more detailed analysis focused on the use of articles. This aspect of morphology contrasts markedly across these three languages. English has only three forms of the article ("the," "a," and "an"), encoding only the contrast between definiteness and indefiniteness. Italian articles are also inflected to agree with the noun in both gender and number (resulting in six definite and three indefinite forms). In German, critical information about the case of the noun is carried on the article, in addition to information about gender, number, and definiteness. Hence, these three languages form a striking continuum in the "information load" carried by the article, even when the material to be described is held constant. If aphasics tend to avoid those elements that present problems, then we might actually expect *more* article omission in German than in Italian, and in Italian compared with English. However, because these elements do carry so much useful information, they are omitted much less often by normal German and Italian speakers than by their normal Anglo-American counterparts (for example, in newspaper headlines and in informal conversation). The obligatory nature of article use might be reflected in aphasia as well.

In fact, we found a large and reliable interaction between language and patient group in the article data. Among the Germans, article use was observed by all three groups (in the 90% range), with no differences at all as a function of diagnostic category. Among the Italians, Broca's did produce significantly fewer articles than Wernicke's, and there was also a slightly lower use of articles by Wernicke's compared with normals. However, article omission averaged only 22% for the Italian agrammatic patients (and articles were furnished more than 30% of the time even by the most severely impaired Italian Broca's aphasic, whose utterances rarely exceeded one or two content words). Finally, among the English patients, Broca's omitted articles around 70% of the time, compared with 10–15% omission by normals. In fact, the "best" English agrammatic performed on this measure in the same range as the "worst" Italian.

Article Errors. Clearly, the Italian and German patients feel a strong, language-specific pressure to produce this aspect of grammatical morphology. Perhaps more important, they also produce the right form of the article more than 80% of the time: Percent substitution errors (over articles produced) averaged 17% for German Wernicke's, 16% for German Broca's, 2.7% for Italian Wernicke's, and 7.5% for Italian Broca's. It is interesting that the Germans produced roughly twice as many incorrect articles as Italians. This suggests that the size of the "article cohort" and/or the complexity of article choice may have an effect on item access: The more opportunities for error provided by the language, the more substitution errors we find in both fluent and nonfluent patients. It is also worth pointing out that gender and case errors both occurred in German. The existence of gender errors is interesting, since gender (unlike case) is an inherent property of the noun that is modified by an article. This suggests that the problem in article retrieval is not just a matter of role assignment at some abstract syntactic level; instead, it seems to involve selection of the correct item from an array of well-formed alternatives – in other words, it is a lexical problem.

Grodzinsky (1982) has put forth a related proposal to explain substitution errors in Broca's aphasia. However, he claims that Broca's aphasics select inflected forms *randomly* from a set of well-formed possibilities; this does not appear to be true in our data. Patients rarely made errors along more than one dimension. That is, they made errors of gender *or* number *or* case, but rarely an error of, for example, gender *and* case. Furthermore, they often stopped and corrected themselves after an error was produced. This suggests that the errors are definitely not random, but represent efforts to locate a specific target – similar to the *conducte d'approche* demonstrated by patients when they are trying to locate a content word. Once again, we conclude that grammatical disruptions reflect problems of access rather than a loss of grammatical knowledge.

The most important and perhaps the most disturbing finding was this: There were few differences between Broca's and Wernicke's aphasics in either the quantity or nature of article errors, in either language. To pursue this point, we carried out some fine-grained analyses of case errors in the German patients, particularly in the more complex dative structures. The results suggest (1) that substitution errors increase with sentence complexity, and (2) the error patterns of Broca's and Wernicke's aphasics may differ when patients are forced to produce the less frequent oblique cases. Specifically, the two patient groups seem to follow a different strategy in sentence planning. Broca's aphasics appear to be engaged in a strategy of avoidance. First, they try to avoid morphosyntactic structures that require an oblique case form. For example, given a dative picture of a mother giving a toy to a child, they may produce an utterance like "Mother give... girl have toy." This is not really a dative error, because the patient has set things up so that no dative is required. Second, when case errors are produced, Broca's tend to substitute a less marked case (usually the nominative) for an oblique case form. By contrast, German Wernicke's aphasics seem to plunge ahead into a complex sentence with no regard for the consequences; this sometimes leads to substitution of one oblique case for another, and may even include substitution of a marked form in place of a simple nominative. In short, the speed and nature of sentence planning is different in the two groups, a fact which results in subtle but interesting differences in the pattern of errors produced.

Case Errors in Other Languages. Much more detailed research on the morphological abilities and disabilities of aphasic patients is in order, in languages where there is enough grammatical morphology to provide a systematic test of competing hypotheses. We have begun such research with Hungarian and Turkish patients, using the same given-new paradigm. The results are preliminary, but they are already quite striking.

The Hungarian pattern parallels our findings for German, albeit at slightly lower levels of error. Patients produce the correct case suffix most of the time, with substitution rates of only 6–12% for both Broca's and Wernicke's aphasics. Given the enormous opportunity for error in Hungarian (where a given noun could appear in up to 100 different inflected forms), this performance is quite impressive. The only (subtle) patient group difference that is evident so far is a slight tendency for fluent patients to err more often by overproduction of oblique forms (as we found for German).

The Turkish Broca's and Wernicke's aphasics that we have studied to date rarely produce anything resembling a case error. These findings seem to parallel results by Slobin and Bever (1982) on the acquisition of case by Turkish children. Unlike children acquiring Indo-European case languages, Turkish children already have most of the adult case system under control in both comprehension and production by 2–2 1/2 years of age. Slobin and Bever attribute this early mastery of case to two factors: (1) Turkish case suffixes are extremely regular and semantically transparent (for example, there are no arbitrary distinctions of gender and/or morphophonological class); (2) the inflections carry stress, and are therefore quite easy for children to perceive. The same semantic and phonological factors may serve to "protect" case inflections in brain-damaged adults. These results cannot be explained by any simple model of grammar as a "mental organ" that is disconnected in aphasia. Processing factors seem to play a major role in determining degrees of sparing and loss within the grammar.

These findings appear to be quite general. With regard not only to article and case errors, but to many other aspects of morphology in our corpus, the most common substitution errors appear to be *legal within-class substitutions* (see also Miceli & Mazzucchi, 1985). Patients do not, for example, place verb inflections on a noun; furthermore, within a broad class (for example, verbs) they rarely make substitutions between different subclasses (for example, conjugating an *-are* verb like an *-ire* verb). In the same vein, although substitution and omission errors both occur, we have found no evidence to date for violations of morpheme order (for example, placing an article postnominally rather than prenominally). Patients are experiencing problems in item access; but they still retain a great deal of knowledge about the target.

Sentence Comprehension in Aphasia

We have now completed a study of sentence comprehension in English, Italian and German aphasics (Bates et al., 1987a), as well as two comparable studies of comprehension in Serbo-Croatian (Smith & Bates, 1987; Smith & Mimica, 1984). Preliminary evidence using the same procedure is also available for Turkish, Hungarian, and Chinese. Taken together, the comprehension results parallel our findings for production: selective impairment of morphology in the presence of spared semantic/pragmatic and syntactic abilities. However, we also have reason to believe that morphological impairments occur for different reasons in the two modalities.

In all these studies, we used the same enactment procedure that has been described throughout this volume: Aphasic patients are asked to interpret a series of simple sentences consisting of two concrete nouns and a transitive action verb. They enact the sentences with small plastic animals and/or objects; hence, a verbal response is not required.

Studies of Serbo-Croatian. In the first study applying this technique to aphasic patients, Smith and Mimica (1984) showed that Serbo-Croatian Broca's aphasics are significantly impaired in the use of case inflections as cues to agent–object relations, compared with age-matched controls. By contrast, they performed at normal or near-normal levels in the use of word order and semantic cues. Hence, case inflections also appear to be selectively vulnerable in aphasia.

Nevertheless, the ability to use case information was still available to these patients, under certain conditions. If word order and case cues converged, the patients performed much better than they did with word order cues alone. And when all three sources of information converged (that is, word order, case and semantics), the performance of Broca's aphasics was entirely normal. Cues to sentence meaning seem to act as retrieval cues for one another, working together to "boost" performance above threshold levels. Morphological information is not "lost" in aphasia; rather, it has become more difficult to access.

In a follow-up study, Smith and Bates (1987) took the accessing notion a step further, examining the interaction of cues within the "vulnerable" morphological component: Case, gender agreement, order and semantics were set into competing and converging combinations with one another. Subjects included agrammatic Broca's aphasics, age-matched normal controls, and fluent anomic patients. Normal controls performed much like college students in a related experiment: Case inflections were the most important source of information; gender agreement cues had the greatest impact on sentence interpretation when case was ambiguous; and both the semantic contrast and the "first noun" strategy were most evident when no morphological contrasts were available. Broca's aphasics, by contrast, were markedly impaired in their use of morphology – although case cues were stronger than gender, as we might expect in Serbo-Croatian. From the point of view of the "accessing hypothesis," the most important finding was a significant interaction among the various grammatical cues. If patients were presented with word order information alone, or a two-way combination of word order and case or word order and gender, performance was above chance but markedly worse than normal. However, when these three grammatical cues converged on the same interpretation, performance jumped to near-normal levels. This effect was clearly not additive; rather, the three cues apparently serve to boost response above some kind of accessing threshold.

A more surprising finding came from a comparison between Broca's and anomic aphasics. Although the anomic patients rarely produced morphological errors in production, they did demonstrate a significant impairment in the use of grammatical morphology to interpret sentences. Their performance was markedly better than that of Broca's aphasics, but it still raises questions for the idea that agrammatism is a unitary syndrome. Receptive and expressive agrammatism may occur for different reasons, in different patient groups.

Comprehension in English, Italian, and German. Bates et al., (1987b) pursued some of the same questions in a study of English, Italian and German aphasics – including Broca's aphasics, Wernicke's aphasics, and a series of neurological and nonneurological patient controls. Three factors were varied: word order, subject–verb agreement, and noun animacy (after MacWhinney et al., 1984). Results support the two Smith studies in Serbo-Croatian, and extend them in several ways.

First and most important, Broca's and Wernicke's aphasics in every language group retained normal and language-appropriate usage of canonical SVO. In fact, some patients (though not all) compensated for other problems by an *overuse* of SVO interpretations compared with normal controls. Most patients also showed language-specific strategies on the two noncanonical word orders, although these patterns were somewhat impaired.

Broken down by language, canonical SVO was the strongest cue to meaning for English patients, compared with either animacy or subject–verb agreement. The "secondary" VOS patterns of English were also still operating for most patients, albeit at lower than normal levels. Only the noncanonical OSV pattern showed signs of serious impairment or loss. German Broca's aphasics actually made *more* use of both SVO and VSO word orders than German controls, but their use of SOV was slightly reduced. Finally, Italian aphasics showed the same weak bias toward SVO displayed by Italian normals, with no bias at all on the NNV and VNN items.

In contrast with the word order findings, patients were all markedly impaired relative to college controls in their ability to use subject–verb morphology to interpret simple sentences. But even here, language-specific differences were maintained: Italian patients still made more use of morphology than their German-speaking counterparts, who in turn made more use of this information than English-speaking aphasics.

Morphology does appear to be selectively vulnerable in aphasia, although language differences in the degree of morphological impairment suggest that the deficit is better characterized in terms of access than loss. So far these results are entirely compatible with the closed-class theory of agrammatism, in its standard form. However, a comparison between patient groups provided a major surprise: The same closed-class "deficits" shown by Italian and German Broca's aphasics appear in Wernicke's aphasics. Insofar as there were any differences at all, Broca's were actually *more* adept at exploiting a convergence of grammatical cues than Wernicke's aphasics.

To pursue this issue in more detail, we have tested four other patient groups in Italian (that is, the language with greatest overall preservation of subject–verb morphology). These included anomics, neurological patients without focal brain damage, orthopedic patients with no neurological symptoms, and healthy older controls (the healthy controls were added in a study subsequent to Bates et al., 1987). The first three groups all demonstrated a selective impairment of morphology in comparison with young normals, though the orthopedic patients as a group fell somewhere between the neurological patients and the college students. Within these orthopedic patients we found a clear split: Some patients were comparable to college controls in their use of morphology; others showed the same "deficit" in use of agreement demonstrated by aphasics. A subsequent study using healthy older controls showed that the vulnerability of morphology in aphasia is not simply a function of age; healthy older Italians are indistinguishable from young normals in their overwhelming reliance on morphological cues to meaning. Hence, the form of receptive agrammatism tapped by this method seems to result from relatively general forms of stress – including hospitalization for hip fracture!

To summarize so far, aphasic patients preserve a control over morphology in sentence comprehension that is proportional to the strength of morphology in their native language. At the same time, however, the closed class is selectively vulnerable to brain damage, even in languages with a "strong" morphology. This "vulnerability" is found – at least in our experimental paradigm – in a variety of patient groups: Wernicke's aphasics, fluent anomic patients, and patients suffering from various forms of neurological and nonneurological stress. This suggests that receptive agrammatism need not occur in conjunction with disruptions in grammatical production. Morphology may be vulnerable to a variety of stress conditions, "shorting out" for different reasons in different patient groups.

Comprehension in Turkish and Hungarian. Preliminary findings from Turkish and Hungarian are particularly interesting from this point of view (Talay & Slobin, in preparation; Osmán-Sági & MacWhinney, in preparation). Recall that Turkish patients seem to produce virtually no case errors at all; Hungarian patients do produce errors, albeit at a rather low 6–12% rate. We might have expected parallel findings for comprehension: perfect preservation of case morphology in Turkish patients, with some evidence for impairment in their Hungarian counterparts. So far, that is not the result we have obtained. In both Turkish and Hungarian, Broca's and Wernicke's aphasics both demonstrate clear impairment in the use of case morphology as a cue to sentence meaning – although, in both languages, case is still operating at significant levels. These findings parallel our results for Indo-European languages to a surprising extent, providing evidence for a clear dissociation between comprehension and production in the degree to which morphology is compromised, within and across patient groups.

Many questions remain. For example, we have some evidence to suggest that long-distance cues, such as agreement marking on the verb, are more prone to disruption in sentence comprehension than locally marked cues, such as case markings. Use of long-distance morphology can be disrupted by almost any form of cognitive stress, including the sundry stresses associated with hospitalization in an older orthopedic patient. Impairments in case morphology are somewhat more restricted; for example, pure anomics show broad disruption of subject–verb agreement in Italian, whereas comparable patients show only slight signs of case impairment in Serbo-Croatian.

The role of perceptual factors is further underscored by a comparison within Hungarian of two forms of the accusative case suffix. In one set of inflections, the accusative syllable carries a strong vowel (for example, *macska* or "cat-nominative" becomes *macska't* or "cat-accusative"). In the other set, accusative marking consists only of a t-final consonant cluster (for example, *mókus* or "squirrel-nominative" becomes *mókus-t* or "squirrel-accusative." Like the Hungarian children in MacWhinney et al. (1985), Hungarian aphasics (both fluent and nonfluent) make more use of case information if the suffix contains a strong vowel.

Finally, we have some evidence on this sentence comprehension task in a Spanish-English bilingual aphasic. Bilingual patients represent an important test case for the conclusions yielded so far, because crosslanguage differences are housed within the same individual. Among the normal Spanish-English bilinguals that we have tested, some showed a strongly Spanish-dominant pattern, whereas others showed an English-based bias toward SVO, with strong Spanish-based agreement effects in the other two orders (Kilborn & Ito, this volume; Wulfeck, Bates, Juarez, & Kilborn, 1986). Extending these results to bilingual aphasics, we would predict that the English-based word order pattern will occur more often in brain-damaged bilingual patients, reflecting the greater resilience of word order strategies. For the one patient that we have tested so far, this prediction appears to be borne out. However, because we also find patterns of word order dominance is some normal Spanish-English bilinguals, this finding must be interpreted with caution (see also Vaid & Chengappa, 1988). We need to know more about the interplay between focal brain damage and premorbid language strategies in bilingual patients.

Summary of the Evidence

Our comprehension and production findings both suggest that morphology is selectively vulnerable to brain damage, compared with word order information (particularly canonical word order). However, we must also conclude that many factors influence sparing or impairment of morphology. This is particularly true in receptive processing, where we find evidence of morphological "deficit" even in some orthopedic patients. There may be many forms of receptive agrammatism, depending on the task and on the lexical and morphosyntactic factors that are varied within that task (cf. Caplan, 1985).

We also conclude that *some* language-specific morphological information remains, even if this is the most vulnerable component. This conclusion is compatible with a classic finding by Gleason et al. (1975) and Goodglass et al. (1979) with agrammatic patients who were retested across several weeks on the same elicited production items. The morpheme errors produced by these patients varied at every testing (for example, a patient might substitute "walking" for "walked" in one session, only to produce the opposite pattern of substitution in the next session). Clearly these patients have not lost the "engrams" for a particular morpheme; rather, their errors are statistical in nature, as though a fixed set of representations has been passed through a random noise filter of some kind. We conclude, then, that morphology is selectively impaired in aphasia – but the impairment lies at the level of item access, and not at the level of item loss.

A Model of Lexical/Morphological Access and its Predictions for Aphasia

To integrate the research described so far, and to guide future studies of language breakdown in aphasia, we propose some extensions of the Competition Model to lexical/morphological access, permitting us to pull apart the contribution of several different processing factors to the retrieval of content words, freestanding function words, and bound morphemes. This list of item access properties is built upon a large body of recent research on lexical access in psycholinguistics (Gordon, 1983; MacWhinney, in press; Marslen-Wilson & Tyler, 1980; Tyler & Marslen-Wilson, 1986; McClelland & Rumelhart, 1981; Morton, 1970; Rumelhart & McClelland, 1986; Salasoo & Pisoni, 1985; Selfridge,1959; Sternberg, 1966; Swinney, 1979; Swinney & Taylor, 1971; Taft & Forster, 1975). It is also compatible with a large-scale movement in formal linguistics in the direction of "lexicalism," that is, theories which account for many if not most grammatical phenomena within a richly annotated "dictionary" of individual lexical items (Bresnan, 1978; Pinker, 1981; MacWhinney, 1987). We are attempting a synthesis of these two literatures in our efforts to understand the nature of morphosyntactic breakdown in aphasia across natural languages.

But there are some serious *a priori* limits on this enterprise. Although a great deal is now known about lexical access, most of that information is focused on recognition or retrieval of *content words*. With a few notable exceptions (carried out in languages other than English – e.g., Burani, Salmaso, & Caramazza, 1984, for Italian; Eling, 1985, for German and Dutch; Katz, Lukatela, & McCann, 1983, for Serbo-Croatian; MacWhinney et al., 1985, for Hungarian), models of lexical access do not provide mechanisms to account for the way that bound grammatical inflections are interpreted or assigned. Findings relevant to grammatical morphology revolve primarily around the contrast between (1) content or open-class words, including most nouns, verbs and adjectives, and (2) closed-class words, including pronouns, articles and other determiners, prepositions, verb auxiliaries and copulas, conjunctions, and a heterogeneous set of high-frequency adverbials and other particles. In aphasia research, the term "closed-class" is sometimes used to refer *both* to freestanding function words and to bound morphemes. This usage is justified by the fact that omission and substitution errors in aphasia typically involve both kinds of morphology. As we shall see below, we think it is appropriate to treat bound and free items in a similar way. In fact, we think it is useful to handle *all* lexical items (closed- and open-class, bound and free) within a single lexicon; the dissociations observed between different kinds of items will derive from differences in the perceptual/motor and cognitive/semantic processing mechanisms that are involved in retrieving items from that lexicon.

What follows is a treatment of the open/closed-class distinction in psycholinguistics and neurolinguistics, as the starting point for a more general model of morphological access under normal and abnormal conditions. The discussion is divided into two parts: (1) issues relevant to the distinction between open- and closed-class items, and (2) a list of item access properties that could account for the differential behavior of these two classes of items within a single, unified lexicon.

The Open/Closed Contrast

As we might expect in such an active field, there are a number of controversial issues regarding the nature of lexical representation, and the mechanisms that access those representations. A thorough review of these issues is beyond the scope of this chapter. Instead, in sketching out our model we will take a stand on those issues that are critical to the predictions we can make regarding the distinction between open- and closed-class items, and the breakdown of morphology in aphasia: These are single versus dual representation, parallel versus serial processing, logogens as processing units, and morphological decomposition.

Single versus Dual Representation.   Open- and closed-class lexical items differ in a number of ways (Gordon & Caramazza, 1982), leading some investigators (Bradley et al., 1980; Friederici & Schoenle, 1980; Glanzer & Ehrenreich, 1979; Lapointe, 1985) to suggest that they actually belong to different lexicons or registers. Some major qualitative differences between the two vocabulary types include *set size* (the open class is called "open" because it is extremely large and constantly takes in new members; the closed class is called "closed" because it is relatively small, and because new members are rarely introduced), *frequency* (a kind of difference that has well-documented effects on perception and memory, although there are some qualifications in the highest frequency range, discussed below), and *function* (closed-class items carry relatively little semantic information, but they do generally serve some kind of clause- or phrase-building function). Other potential differences, to be discussed in more detail later, include *imagability* or *concreteness, phonological salience,* and *demands on short-term memory.*

Such differences in the characteristics of open- and closed-class items are used to build a plausibility argument for the theory that each class is mediated by a different mechanism and/or stored in a separate register. Other arguments in favor of the dual-representation approach come from data on the behaviors associated with each vocabulary type: differences in *development* (open-class words tend to be acquired earlier in development), *errors* (normal speakers tend to make different kinds of errors for the two word classes, including omission errors for the closed class and exchange errors for the open-class), and – most important for our purposes – differences in *patterns of breakdown in brain-damaged patients* (Broca's aphasics have greater difficulty with the closed class, whereas Wernicke's aphasics have more trouble with content words). There are a number of important qualifications on this last claim – as we have already seen in our own data on substitution errors for both anterior and posterior aphasic patients. But the possibility of a double-dissociation constitutes perhaps the most important argument in favor of the idea that the two vocabulary classes are mediated by separate mechanisms.

We will argue that the "dual lexicon" hypothesis is not the only way to account for qualitative differences in the characteristics of the items, and/or in the behaviors associated with each vocabulary type. It is possible that all vocabulary items are represented together in the same lexicon, and subjected to the same set of item access processes. However, because open and closed items are differentially responsive to the array of factors that influence access or retrieval, they behave quite differently in real-time language processing.

Let us offer a biological metaphor to explain this position, borrowed from D'Arcy Thompson (1917). Elephants and fleas both live in the same world, subject to the same physical forces. However, because of their weight and size elephants are much more affected by gravity than by surface tension; and because of their weight and size, fleas are more affected by surface tension than gravity. We need not postulate two worlds to explain the differential behavior of these very different animals; they live in the same world, but that world affects them differently. Similarly, open- and closed-class lexical items may be housed in the same lexicon, and subjected to the same set of access procedures. But because the items themselves are so different, the same access process will affect them differently.

As discussed by Gordon (1983), among others, the single-lexicon approach seems to provide a better fit to facts about the relationship between reaction time and frequency in different kinds of lists. But this approach is also sensible on historical grounds. Closed-class words typically evolve from freestanding function words in the history of individual languages (Cedergren & Sankoff, 1974; Givón, 1979). This means that, at some point in the history of a language, a number of items will have an "in-between" status that does not fall easily into either category. Even the synchronic classification of items into "closed" versus "open" is plagued with in-between cases. For example, prepositions have many of the characteristics of the closed class (a high-frequency, closed set of items that are used in phrase building, and rarely carry stress); but they also have characteristics of the open class (as heads of phrases, conveying some kind of concrete semantic relationship). And as Friederici has shown in several studies of German prepositions and locative particles (Friederici, in press; Friederici & Graetz, 1984; Friederici & Schoenle, 1980; Friederici, Schoenle, & Goodglass, 1981) these items also have an in-between status in the behavior of normal and aphasic speakers. In a similar vein, the contrast between free and bound items is often quite arbitrary, with many in-between cases. Indeed, the decision to classify an item as "bound" or "free" is often little more than a convention of written language. For example, there is a tendency for prenominal articles to be written as separate words, whereas postnominal articles (such as the article in Swedish) are usually written as part of the noun they modify.

Kean (1979) has shown how difficult it is to come up with a single definition that distinguishes between the open and closed class – and her own phonological definition has also come under fire (Black, 1980). We believe that the effort fails because the open/closed contrast is simply not a clean dichotomy. It may be better to view these two categories as "fuzzy sets," organized around prototypical members, with degrees of membership leading out to border cases that do not fit easily in either category. If we take this approach, then the graded nature of the open/closed contrast is captured much more easily by eschewing the two-dictionary theory in favor of a single, unified lexicon.

Parallel versus Serial Processing. One of the most important changes in recent psycholinguistic research is a movement away from traditional serial-search models (where items are examined and discarded one at a time until a match is reached), to parallel processing models (where all candidates are activated simultaneously, with decisions emerging through some kind of competition process that determines "goodness-of-fit" to the goal). Most modern theories of lexical access entail some form of parallel processing (e.g., Gordon, 1983; Marslen-Wilson & Tyler, 1980; McClelland & Rumelhart, 1981; Morton, 1970; Sternberg, 1966). These models vary in other ways – in particular, the importance of word-initial phonetic information in establishing the pool of competitors or "cohort" (Marslen-Wilson, 1987; Salasoo & Pisoni, 1985), and whether or not "top down" contextual information can have an effect before the cohort is established by phonetic "bottom-up" data (Swinney, 1979; Swinney & Taylor, 1971; Swinney, Zurif, & Nicol, 1989; Van Petten & Kutas, 1987). They also differ on questions like the role of facilitation versus inhibition in "spread of activation" through the system, and the difference between "partial" versus "all-or-nothing" firing (discussed in more detail in what follows). But they all accept the principles of parallel activation and conflict resolution.

Our extension of the Competition Model to morphological access has the same properties. In receptive language, an incoming stimulus simultaneously activates all of its associates; as information accumulates, the field of candidates is narrowed down until only one remains. In expressive language, an underlying meaning configuration simultaneously activates all associated forms (words, morphemes, suprasegmental targets); as the communicative plan takes shape and decisions are made, the field of possible forms narrows down until one (usually) well-formed possibility remains to complete the utterance.

Following Marslen-Wilson and Tyler (1980), we will use the term "cohort" here to refer to the pool of competitors that are activated in parallel and subsequently winnowed down during lexical retrieval – either in comprehension or production. However, we are using the term somewhat differently than it was intended by these authors, who define a cohort as the set of competitors activated by a word-initial phoneme. They also maintain that contextual information can affect spoken word recognition only after the cohort has been established purely on the basis of sensory information, in accord with the principle of *bottom-up priority*. There is certainly some evidence that the activation and subsequent selection of open-class words may work in this fashion. However, for closed-class words – particularly bound morphemes – the twin principles of word-initial activation and bottom-up priority may not apply. It is not always obvious where the "first" part of the sensory signal for a bound inflection is located. And the contextual determination of inflectional morphology may be so strong that the morpheme is necessarily identified before any sensory data is encountered. For example, Tyler and Marslen-Wilson (1986) provide evidence for contextual preselection of a suffix after the stem has been identified. In extending the cohort concept to grammatical morphology, we will be referring to a set of competing lexical forms that is activated by sensory information, by semantic/syntactic context, or by their conjoint effects. It is an empirical question whether this departure from "classical" cohort theory is warranted.

This approach has one particularly important implication for lexical access under damaged or noisy conditions, revolving around the issue of "cohort size." In a serial-search model, the size of the cohort of candidates plays an extremely important role in determining the amount of time needed to find a match: The larger the search space, the longer the search (e.g., the well-known phenomenon of Sternberg, 1966). As Marslen-Wilson and Tyler (1980) and Marslen-Wilson (1987) have shown, cohort size does *not* have a direct impact on search time in a parallel processing model, at least under normal processing conditions. To illustrate the point, imagine an artificial language that has 1000 words beginning with the string "STR." Half of these words continue with "O"; the other half continue with "A." In a parallel model, all 1000 candidates are active at the STR point; but by the time that vowel is processed, exactly half the candidates will have dropped out of the competition. Now imagine a language with only 10 words, all beginning with "STR"; half continue with "O" and the other half continue with "A." At the "STR" point, there are 10 candidates to choose from, but by the time the vowel is processed only 5 will remain. Regardless of whether the cohort has 1000 or 10 candidates, half the cohort is eliminated at exactly the same point. And by the end of the string, only one candidate will remain, regardless of the number of competitors available at the beginning. In other words, it is the "uniqueness structure" of the cohort that determines the amount of time needed to make a decision, that is, the amount of information that is necessary before a "decision point" is reached that eliminates all other candidates in parallel (Grosjean, 1980; Grosjean & Itzler, 1984; Marslen-Wilson, 1987).

However, the size of the cohort *will* have an impact if no unique candidate emerges when processing is complete. Natural languages have evolved to make sure that this rarely happens. However, under various kinds of "noise" conditions, when aspects of the stimulus are degraded, there may not be enough information to eliminate all the possible candidates. Then the possibility for error will be a function of the number of candidates that remain: If only two candidates remain, the probability of correct choice is 50%, if four candidates remain it is 25%, and so forth. The key point for aphasia is that receptive and expressive errors should be a function of both the size and similarity structure of a cohort of item candidates that are active when the error is made. The importance of this claim will hopefully become clearer shortly, when we discuss the set of item access properties.

Logogens and Morphogens as Processing Units.   Most parallel-processing models of word recognition incorporate some version of Morton's classic logogen model (Morton, 1970). A logogen is a kind of "demon" (after Selfridge, 1959), a pattern-detecting mechanism that looks for itself in the input and "cries out" when its name is called. Hence, this is a linguistic version of a concept that has considerable utility in many other aspects of perception and pattern recognition.

A "logogen," "word demon," or "word expert" (Small, 1980), is made up of (at least) two parts. The *form component* contains a specification of the physical pattern associated with a word (that is, a phonetic/articulatory configuration in spoken language; a graphemic configuration in written language). The *meaning component* contains a specification of the semantic/propositional structure associated with the "core" usage of a word. This component is generally considered to be the same for either the phonemic or the graphemic representation.

Each logogen is associated with a standard "resting weight" and a threshold that must be reached before the unit fires. Effects associated with the baseline frequency of a word are captured here by the absolute difference between resting weight and threshold. A logogen can be made to "fire" in two ways. Information can accumulate at the level of form, until the threshold is reached (that is, "bottom-up" processing). Or information can accumulate at the level of meaning, until the same threshold is reached (that is, "top-down" processing). This two-way activation captures a variety of well-known context effects in word recognition.

In the original version of the logogen model, units received activation but they did not facilitate or inhibit their neighbors. In the McClelland and Rumelhart model, individual units can "wake up" their associates and "shut down" their competitors. The strength of these facilitation and inhibition effects is proportional to the amount of activation going on in the individual unit – which brings us to a second revision of the original model. Morton's logogens fired on an all-or-nothing basis, when some decision criterion was reached. In the McClelland and Rumelhart model, units are activated – and begin to influence their neighbors – on the basis of only partial information. Hence, the probability that an item will "win" the competition is a function of (a) its initial resting weight, (b) its degree of inhibitory influence over other competitors, and (c) the *degree* of overlap between the logogen and the incoming information (at either the phonological/graphemic or semantic levels). Using these mechanisms, the authors can explain a native speaker's ability to deal productively with an input that has never been seen before, for example, to figure out how to pronounce a letter string like MAVE. When the novel input comes in, all partially overlapping competitors are activated (for example, MANE, MARE, CAVE, SAVE, and HAVE). The probability of a pronunciation rhyming with CAVE versus a pronunciation rhyming with HAVE in actual behavioral data can be simulated with extraordinary detail if this kind of a competition is going on. Taking a similar approach, Rumelhart and McClelland (1986) have also been able to simulate the overgeneralization errors produced by English children acquiring past tense morphology (for example, "bringed," "goed") – with no "rules" in the strict sense, simply a process of analogy based on partial activation of a large number of units in parallel. As we shall see later, the same approach may be very useful in predicting and explaining a variety of morphological errors produced by aphasic patients.

Bound and freestanding grammatical morphemes do not fit easily into the original formulation of the logogen model. Closed-class "morphogens" are not easily characterized in terms of a single phonetic form and a single well-specified meaning. Rather, at both the level of form and the level of function, grammatical morphemes are highly interdependent entities. They not only require information about *associates* who are likely to be active in the neighborhood; they must also have information about their *position* relative to those associates. An extended connectionist version of the logogen model can accommodate these "morphogens," thus accounting for both open- and closed-class items. The new logogen is more than a "two-headed animal". At both the form and the meaning levels, the unit is located within a network or correlation matrix of associated elements. Furthermore, this matrix contains positional information. For example, a past tense unit (if it is indeed a separate unit – see below) carries information indicating that it is supposed to occur at the end of a verb. And the verb, in turn, carries information indicating that it is often followed by "-ed." An important feature of this model is the fact that positional information is nondeterministic: A morpheme may *always* go in a particular position, or its positional privileges can be a matter of degree.

How does a unit "know" about position? McClelland and Rumelhart (1981) have provided a mechanism for capturing this kind of topological information in the visual modality. Individual words are built up out of "wickelfeatures," borrowed from Wickelgren's (1969) notion of context-sensitive phoneme units that carry information about their neighbors to the immediate left and right. For example, the /k/ sound in "CAT" would be made up of a "word-initial" symbol on the left and a symbol indicating the vowel to follow on the right. These context-sensitive wickelphones guarantee not only the phonemic "membership" of a word, but also the position of phonemes within the word. In fact, since all the wickelphones that make up a word contain information about their neighbors to the left and right, positional information is quite redundant.

Extending this concept to the morphological level, lexical items (both bound and free) may be stored with some equivalent of "wickelmorphs," that is, statistical information about the probability that larger segments will occur to the left and right. For our purposes, this kind of probabilistic information about the "neighborhood" guarantees that ordering will be *overdetermined*, by the sublexical units or "wickelphones" that comprise each item in the cohort, and by the "wickelmorph" correlations to the left and right of each word. A representational system with these properties could account, at least in part, for the fact that substitution or omission errors are common but positional violations are rare in the speech of aphasic patients.

Pinker and Prince (1988) have recently offered a serious critique of wickelfeature notation, as used by Rumelhart and McClelland in their simulation of morphological learning in English. Among other things, they note that such positional mechanisms may prove inadequate to account for complex syntactic structure (for example, Wh-extraction from embedded clauses, as in "Who did Mary say that Paul told her to go see?"). However, a number of alternatives have been offered that retain the context-sensitive properties of the original Rumelhart and McClelland model, in a form that avoids the criticisms raised by Pinker and Prince (e.g., Elman, 1988). The recursive properties of connectionist systems are still poorly understood, but they are known to be powerful enough to overcome many of the objections faced by the simple associationist theories of the 1950's and 60's. For grammatical morphology within and between simple phrases and clauses, a context-sensitive lexicalist model seems to work well (MacWhinney, 1989). This covers most of the territory that is relevant to morphological preservation and/or breakdown in aphasia. Above all, it may help to explain why positional information is resistant to brain damage (including knowledge about morpheme ordering within words, and the ordering of constituents within simple phrases and sentences).

However, if units contain information about their neighbors to the left and right, then the very definition of a "lexical unit" comes into question. In such a context-sensitive system, where does one unit leave off and another begin? In a sense, the notion of a single unit becomes a relative term, an emergent property of information that is in fact distributed across many different units of different size and complexity. This brings us to the issue of decomposition.

Morphological Decomposition.   Morphological decomposition is a major controversy within the lexical access literature. Is an inflected form, such as "walked", represented in the lexicon in the form of a root "walk" plus a morpheme "ed"? Or do we store inflected forms directly, so that there are separate representations in the lexicon for "walk," "walked," "walks," "walking," and so forth? There is no time here to go into the intricacies of experiments aimed at separating these two possibilities (e.g., Burani et al., 1984; Eling, 1985; Kintsch, 1974; Taft, 1979; Taft & Forster, 1975). However, within the kind of parallel processing model outlined here, with activations based on partial overlap between stimuli and representations, the issue essentially disappears.

First, in keeping with the "nondecomposition view" (Eling, 1985; Kintsch, 1974), separate representations for each inflected version of a lexical item are stored in the lexicon, each with its own probability of occurrence and corresponding resting weights. Bound morphemes are not "written in" as separate units, but are stored together with the context in which they occur. This approach has the advantage of accounting not only for segmentable combinations like "walk + ed," but also for morphological class relationships that do not decompose at all (for example, the relationship between "go" and "went").

Many of the phenomena that have been used to argue for decomposition and separate representations of bound morphemes can be accounted for in this model, by the mechanism of activation through partial overlap. When a word like "walked" comes in, each piece of the input activates demons that bear a partial relationship to the stimulus: for example, the "wa-" segment activates words like "wander" and "waffle"; the "-alk" component activates words like "talk" and "stalk": and the "-ed" component provides some activation to a vast array of words in the lexicon that end with "-ed," including the past tense forms of most regular verbs. Hence, the "-ed" unit can have an impact of its own, proportional to the number and strength of the representations of other items with "-ed." This can account for the fact that case suffixes and other inflections demonstrate frequency effects that are partially independent of the frequency of a particular root+suffix combination (e.g., Burani, Salmaso, & Caramazza, 1984; Taft, 1979; Taft & Forster, 1975; Stemberger & MacWhinney, 1986) as well as the finding that nonsense words with legal inflections can "prime" words with an associated inflection (for example, the difference between "wugs walk" versus "wugs walks" – see Katz, Lukatela, & McCann, 1983). It is also possible for us to predict and explain certain errors of morphological substitution in aphasia, without necessarily resorting to the theory that the "swapped" morphemes are independently represented and disrupted in the brain.

Item Access Properties and Their Predictions for Aphasia

The model that we have presented so far postulates a single, unified lexicon that includes content words, freestanding function words, and bound grammatical morphemes. Units are associated with baseline activation levels or strengths, and they can facilitate or inhibit their neighbors based on only partial information. Activation of these units can occur at the level of form, and at the level of meaning (accounting for both bottom-up and top-down effects). There is no morphological decomposition in the traditional sense, that is, separate representations for roots and inflections. Rather, all possible forms of each lexical item are stored; independent effects of particular root or suffix "pieces" emerge through a system in which partially overlapping representations are activated in parallel.

This brings us to a major limitation of most current processing models for aphasia research (including earlier versions of the Competition Model). Although logogenlike models of lexical access can make interesting predictions about the effects of "noisy" or degraded stimuli, to our knowledge none of the existing models provide mechanisms for describing the *selective* dissociations that we find in different forms of aphasia. To extend unified lexicalist models to account for double dissociations, we need a better characterization of the different kinds of cue cost factors that we have been forced to add to the Competition Model. Closed- and open-class items differ along a number of processing parameters that could explain the double dissociations reported in the aphasia literature.

Table 10.1 presents an idealization of the processing factors that impinge on lexical/morphological access. The same factors apply to all lexical items, both open- and closed-class (column 1 and column 2, respectively). However, there is a perfectly complementary distribution between columns 1 and 2 in the extent to which each processing factor is relevant to successful access. That is, they apply to a different *degree* for open- versus closed-class targets (or for open- vs. closed-class portions of a complex inflected word). Let us go through these factors one at a time, emphasizing their implications for similarities and differences between open- and closed-class items within different languages and patient groups.

Semantic Factors.   Open-class words usually have a rich set of seman-tic/imagistic associations that makes them easier to perceive and remember than closed-class words. This difference could account in part for the global

Table 10.1. *"Risk" and "protective" factors for open- and closed-class terms*

	Open	Closed
Phonological salience	+	−
Frequency	−	+
Semantic content	+	−
Assignability	+	−
Cohort size	−	+
Within-cohort confusability versus uniqueness	+	−
Positional predictability	−	+
Inter-item priming in context	+	−

Note: + = Promotes access,
− = Does not promote access

vulnerability of morphology in aphasia (see also Goodglass & Menn, 1985). But there is also variability within the two vocabulary types in the degree of semantic content associated with a given word: Prepositions have more content than many other closed-class items (which may in turn make them easier to retrieve – Friederici & Schoenle, 1980); abstract content words like "virtue" have less imagistic content than a concrete word like "dog" (which may account in part for the fact that most aphasics have a difficult time with abstract words – see Lesser, 1978). Semantic content is, then, one of the dimensions that yields a great deal of natural variation in the morphological systems of natural languages. For example, case systems also vary in their degree of "semantic transparency," a fact which may account for variations in vulnerability or strength of suffixes in different forms of aphasia (for example, the entirely regular and transparent system of Turkish versus the irregular and semantically opaque system of Serbo-Croatian).

This dimension also yields some possible predictions about patient group differences. Caramazza, Brownell, and Berndt (1978) report that posterior anomics may have difficulty in word retrieval because the semantic/conceptual fields surrounding a target item are disturbed. Anterior aphasics have more difficulty with the "sound image" of a word; the conceptual fields surrounding word meaning seem to be intact. This conclusion pertained only to content words, but it could be extended to some possible differences between these patient groups in the retrieval of grammatical morphology. For example, anterior patients may be more proficient in taking advantage of semantic/pragmatic context, showing larger differences in the relative disruption of morphological items with high versus low semantic content. And patients may also differ in the effect of task manipulations that emphasize processing of content (for example, comprehension of case suffixes) versus processing of form (for example, judgments of morphological well-formedness). In particular, we would expect anterior patients to have the advantage at tasks emphasizing the meaning or function of morphemes; posterior patients may do better – or at least not significantly worse – on tasks that emphasize form.

We also think it would be useful to obtain information from control groups who are known to have semantic/conceptual problems (e.g., Alzheimer's patients – see Albert & Obler, 1978; Appel, Kertesz, & Fisman, 1982; Bayles, 1982; Kempler, 1982; Schwartz, Marin, & Saffran, 1979), compared with controls who are known to have no semantic conceptual problems whatsoever (for example, neurologically intact deaf adults). With these extreme contrasts as background, we will be in a better position to evaluate the effect of variations in the degree of semantic support for morphological access in aphasic populations.

Phonological Salience.   By "salience" we are referring to a variety of factors that make a lexical/morphological item easy to perceive – as well as some factors that make the same item a difficult or easy "motor target." We have already found evidence to suggest that several aspects of phonological salience influence the likelihood that a morphological item will be accessed by an aphasic patient (for example, number of syllables, presence or absence of stress, presence or absence of a strong vowel). This provides support for at least some aspects of Kean's (1979) claim about the phonological basis of agrammatism (see also Goodglass, 1968).

In addition, crosslinguistic research with children has yielded some interesting dissociations between comprehension and production that warrant a thorough consideration in aphasia research. For example, some phonological factors which assist in the perception of a case suffix may actually hinder its production, and vice versa. A perceptually "strong" morpheme with many syllables may require a greater amount of articulatory "work." And a short, high-frequency morpheme that is easy to produce may actually be more difficult to hear.

This inquiry into the phonological aspects of morphological retrieval also leads to some plausible predictions about patient group differences. Within a given group, we would always expect "strong" or salient morphemes to be more resistant to loss than "weak" morphemes. However, the magnitude of the difference may not be the same for anterior and posterior aphasics. If anterior patients are particularly disrupted in the phonological aspects of processing, then they should show a more marked phonological effect than we find in posterior aphasics. Blumstein (1973) has reported that Broca's and Wernicke's aphasics tend to make the same kinds of phonological errors. However, more recent studies suggest that phonological factors may have a differential impact on the two patient groups, at least in receptive language processing.

For example, Milberg, Blumstein, and Dworetzky (1988) have examined the effects of phonological degradation on word-word priming, for normals compared with Broca's and Wernicke's aphasics. Given word pairs like "cat - dog," Milberg et al. created versions of the prime word that varied in degree of phonetic deviation from the original (for example, "cat" versus "gat" versus "wat", compared with an unrelated control word like "mop"). Normal listeners show a monotonic decrease in priming as a function of phonetic degradation (for example, cat > gat > wat > mop). Broca's aphasics show priming effects only with the "best" phonetic inputs (for example, cat > gat,wat,mop), whereas Wernicke's aphasics show equal priming effects for all primes except the unrelated control (cat,gat,wat > mop). It appears as though Broca's aphasics are *underprimed* and require very strong phonetic inputs, whereas Wernicke's aphasics are *over-primed* and create traffic-control problems that could account for their comprehension problems and their severe word-finding symptoms in expressive speech. Hence, a global difference in the size and timing of phonetic effects may help to produce qualitatively different symptom patterns (see also Kolk, 1985). In a crosslinguistic project we can examine such a broad range of phonological factors that equally interesting group differences could emerge, in both expressive and receptive language processing.

Frequency. Open- and closed-class items are markedly different in their relative frequencies. However, because closed-class morphology is so much higher in frequency, this factor should actually make those items *less* vulnerable in aphasia. So why are these the most likely items to be omitted?

Stemberger (1985a) has provided an interesting hypothesis in this regard, based on the idea that omission errors are really substitution errors, where the more frequent "zero form" is substituted for a less frequent morphologically marked form. He has extended this notion of "zero forms" from the level of the word to the level of the phrase. This is based on a very strong lexicalist claim, that essentially *all* grammatical forms are listed in the lexicon: words, morphemes, idioms that span several words, and various phrase structure types complete with nonterminal symbols (for example, an SVO template for simple active declarative sentences, or a DETERMINER + NOUN template for definite noun phrases).

In fact, the postulation of "clausogens" or phrase structure fragments, is not as radical or idiosyncratic as it may seem. For example, Lapointe (1985) has suggested a similar "phrase structure fragment" representation as an extension of Garrett's widely accepted model of speech production. The major difference is that Lapointe proposes a separate store for these phrase structure fragments, whereas Stemberger would list them together with other, smaller units in a single lexicon. Bock (1986) has shown that even phrasal structures can be "primed" in production. The probability that a normal speaker will use a dative-final or an object-final construction is a partial function of whether and how recently the speaker has heard that same phrase structure – even though the structural "prime" contained completely different lexical items. Bock suggests that phrase structure rules (expressed as "condition-action pairs") can have resting weights and activation levels that are similar in many important respects to individual lexical items.

Stemberger suggests that the omission of grammatical functors by aphasics actually involves substitution of an inappropriate but high-frequency phrase structure which does not contain the target morpheme for an appropriate but less frequent phrase structure which should have contained the target morpheme. For example, the high rate of article omission in English would occur because the patient has blended together a higher-frequency noun phrase structure that has no article (for example, a noun phrase headed by a pronoun) with a phrase structure that should have contained an article (for example, a noun phrase headed by a singular, definite noun). This interesting hypothesis should be tested against a broader range of languages – where the most frequent form is not always "zero marked". Something like Stemberger's model could be used to account for the fact that Broca's aphasics avoid stylistic word order variations in languages like Italian and Turkish. And it is compatible with our finding that English Broca's aphasics are far more likely than their German or Italian counterparts to omit the article before a noun.

A related issue involves frequency differences *within* grammatical morphology. Gordon and Caramazza (1982) have provided evidence suggesting that frequency effects are attenuated for both open- and closed-class items, when stimuli are restricted to the highest frequency range. Because most closed-class items come from this "flat" high-frequency range, we should expect frequency to play a rather limited role in morphological access. However, in research on aphasia in richly inflected languages, errors do tend to involve the substitution of a high-frequency form, such as nominative case, for a low-frequency form, such as the instrumental case.

A resolution of this apparent contradiction may come from some differences between expressive and receptive language processing. In research on normal memory processes, we know that frequency plays a larger role in *recognition* than it does in *recall* (Mandler, Goodman, & Wilks-Gibbs, 1982). In recall the best predictor of memory is not frequency, but "degree of elaboration," "meaningfulness," and/or "uniqueness" (which are sometimes negatively correlated with frequency – see below). In speech production, the speaker is engaged in a lexical retrieval process that has some of the properties of recall (see Bock, 1982). Hence, the uniqueness and/or meaningfulness of a word or morpheme may have a greater impact. In speech comprehension, and in all receptive language tasks (for example, lexical decision), the listener is engaged in a lexical retrieval process that has more in common with recognition. Hence, frequency effects may be somewhat smaller in production, with expressive language performance predicted primarily by the uniqueness of the target item, together with the amount of semantic activation or "priming" that the item has received.

Modality differences in the relative importance of frequency may be relevant to some of the differences observed among patient groups. If our analysis of frequency effects is correct, then we may find that frequency differences between grammatical morphemes play a larger role in expressive language disorders than they play in normal speech. As Mandler (1980) has pointed out, the distinction between recall and recognition per se is often too simple. Some recognition tasks involve a "recall check," a stage in which the subject carefully checks his memory for other possibilities before saying "yes" or "no" to a recognition item. Similarly, subjects may make use of recognition memory to check on the appropriateness of an item that presents itself for recall. This means that the relative contribution of frequency versus other item access factors will depend on the amount of time a subject spends on a given task. This point is underscored by several recent "on-line" studies of lexical access, showing that frequency effects occur very early in processing, whereas certain aspects of meaning or imagery have their effect further downstream (e.g., Marslen Wilson, 1987). From this point of view, we can make several predictions about the relative importance of frequency in fluent and nonfluent syndromes. Nonfluent patients, who carry out slow and deliberate processing, may be more affected by frequency in their expressive language because they subject their hesitant speech to more "recognition checks." All other things being equal, frequency and uniqueness will both make contributions to fluent speech. However, a hyperfluent patient (who "rushes into print") may substitute less frequent but more unique forms in expressive language. Hence, interactions between frequency and timing could contribute to qualitative differences between Broca's and Wernicke's aphasia.

Such hypotheses can be given a better test in richly inflected languages that permit at least a partial separation between frequency and the other semantic and perceptual properties of morphemes (for example, high- versus low-frequency case suffixes, and high- versus low-frequency allomorphs of a given case marker). For example, it might help to explain our finding that German Broca's aphasics make more substitutions of the nominative for other case forms, whereas German Wernicke's aphasics are more likely to substitute one low-frequency form for another.

Assignability, or Demands on Memory. As we mentioned earlier, morphological items vary along a dimension of local versus long-distance binding.

Local morphemes are those that can be bound quickly to the constituents that govern them, allowing the listener to make a rapid assignment of the meanings associated with that item (for example, case suffixes). Long-distance morphemes are those that can be bound to their constituents only after a certain amount of material has intervened, so that associated meanings cannot be assigned until a considerable amount of information is available (for example, subject–verb agreement).

Overall, the assignability dimension should have its biggest impact on closed-class morphology. There are very few discontinuous morphemes in the open class (if we exclude idioms, and a few root + particle combinations such as "look up" or "put down"). And given the referential/predicative functions played by content words, most of the "communicative work" an item must carry out can be completed quickly as soon as the word is identified. By contrast, most closed-class morphemes must be bound to a governing word or phrase, and sometimes to other morphemes further downstream in sentence processing. This means that closed-class morphemes make a heavier demand on short-term memory resources – which is problematic, given the fact that these items are low in imagery and other factors that make an item easy to keep in mind.

We would expect local morphology to be more resistant to brain damage. However, our results with children suggest that this effect may be restricted to receptive language processing (when the listener "doesn't know what's coming"). Hence, the assignability dimension permits another test of dissociations between perception and production in aphasia. We might expect to find more severe effects of long-distance assignment in posterior aphasics (a prediction which is suggested by the impaired but still relatively good performance on case by Serbo-Croatian anomics, compared with the seriously impaired performance on subject–verb agreement by a corresponding set of Italian anomics and Wernicke's aphasics).

Cohort Structure. The four factors reviewed so far (semantic content, phonological salience, frequency, and assignability) all refer to properties of an individual lexical unit. There are also a number of properties that have to do with the nature of the cohort in which a unit is embedded.

One of these properties is set size. By definition, the open class is an extremely large set, whereas the closed class is a small one. But across the course of sentence processing, the relevant cohort changes as a function of available information about form and meaning. For example, in the sentence "I take my coffee with cream and ...," the cohort of likely candidates has been narrowed down considerably (with a strong bias to nouns, and within nouns, to things that can go in coffee). Hence cohort size is a relative notion.

Nevertheless, it is often useful to talk about the "initial cohort" to which an item belongs. Within the closed class, comparable sets of morphemes do vary markedly in size from one language to another (for example, the number of articles available in prenominal position). In a processing system exposed to noisy data, the set of possible candidates is not always narrowed down to one – so that the possibilities for error are a function of set size.

In support of this notion, we have already shown that the size of the "article cohort" is related to the probability of article assignment errors in English, Italian, and German. This kind of outcome is compatible with a parallel processing model that has been subjected to some kind of internal "noise." In this regard, Nespoulous et al. (1984) have reported on a French Broca's aphasic who makes a large number of substitution errors in grammatical morphology. The patient's own introspective report suggests that something very much like a cohort effect in a parallel system underlies his difficulty:

I know how to build up my sentence but whenever I have to produce a grammatical word, even though I know perfectly well that it is a preposition or an article ... that I need, several of them come up in my mind and I never know for sure which one to produce.

Similarly, the size of the cohort will have an impact if for some reason the speaker/listener decides to make a decision before enough information is available, that is, before what Grosjean (Grosjean, 1980; Grosjean & Itzler, 1984) and Marslen-Wilson and Tyler (1980) and Marslen-Wilson (1987) call the "decision point" in a word. Normal speakers can be induced to make errors by manipulating their decision criteria. Aphasic speakers and listeners may make similar errors, not because of a voluntary decision to take an early guess, but because of some involuntary factor that destroys the temporal synchrony between processing and output (see also Kolk, 1985; Kolk & van Grunsven, 1985). It is entirely possible that the paraphasias and paragrammatisms of a posterior aphasic involve this kind of temporal disruption. By analyzing error types in terms of the cohort of available candidates (as we have done in the case of articles), we can make detailed and systematic predictions about the nature and extent of errors produced by both anterior and posterior aphasics.

Cohorts can also vary along a dimension of interitem confusability. Within a set of morphemes that are highly similar to one another in phonological structure, the likelihood of substitution error should be greater, in perception or production – particularly if the input is underdetermined in some way. This is related to the issue of phonological salience described above, except that the salience of an item is determined here with reference to the set of available competitors, rather than "absolute" factors that make an item more or less perceivable (for example, number of syllables). With regard to patient group differences, we predict that intraset confusability will play a particularly important role in the fluent aphasias. If these patients are rushing into word selection and interpretation without careful monitoring, they may be prone to assign items before the "decision point" is reached, so that the kinds of blends and substitutions that occur could be explained in terms of the structure of the competition pool that remains.

We may also find evidence to suggest that fluent patients are operating with a larger cohort, reflecting a predominance of interitem activation over interitem inhibition (see also Lecours & Lhermitte, 1969). If there are more items in the morphological cohort, we would expect more variety in the paragrammatisms that are ultimately produced by fluent patients, as compared with nonfluent aphasics in the same language. This is exactly what our analysis of German article errors suggests, that is, a broader variety of errors in Wernicke's aphasia.

Lexical and Morphosyntactic Context.   Both item effects (semantic content, phonological salience, frequency and assignability) and cohort effects (set size and intra-set confusability) derive from what we might call *paradigmatic* or *taxonomic* properties of a lexical target. In addition, the retrieval of any lexical item is also influenced by *syntagmatic* factors, that is, constraints imposed by the phrase, sentence, and discourse context leading up to lexical/morphological access.

First, the linguistic context provides *positional cues* that help to narrow down the cohort of lexical/morphological items that could occur in a given slot. For content words, these constraints are usually rather weak (e.g., Seidenberg & Tanenhaus, 1986). For example, a lead-in such as "John thought that he would..." provides information suggesting that a verb is likely to follow. Still, the set of possibilities that remains is so large that the listener has not gained much of an advantage. For grammatical morphemes, this kind of positional constraint is usually very strong, greatly narrowing down the set of possible forms that could follow. For example, at the end of a verb we would expect to find a verb suffix – which leaves us with a very small number of possibilities (particularly in English).

We have already described some context-sensitive features of "logogens" and "morphogens" that guarantee an overdetermination of ordering, within and between lexical items. Our crosslinguistic aphasia results to date suggest that violations of order (between major constituents, and/or between grammatical morphemes) are rare – if they exist at all. This is a strong conclusion, and one that warrants a further test against a larger corpus of aphasic speech. We also need to know more about the role of positional cues in receptive language processing, including tasks that focus on meaning (that is, comprehension) and tasks that focus on form (that is, well-formedness judgments). With regard to patient group differences, we suggest that positional cues are so pervasive and overdetermined that we will find few differences between aphasic syndromes in the role these factors play. However, as suggested by Bates et al. (1983), a fluent aphasic with severe word-finding difficulties may be forced to begin sentences on a "first come first served" basis, a factor which may reduce the utility of positional information in speech production.

A second kind of syntagmatic factor involves interitem correlations that are relatively independent of position. The garden-variety version of such "spreading activation" effects are those involved in semantic priming between content words (Swinney, 1979; Swinney & Taylor, 1971; Swinney et al., in press; McClelland & Rumelhart, 1981). If a word, such as "bug," has been mentioned at all in recent linguistic input, then normal and aphasic listeners are usually faster at processing a semantic associate, such as "spider." In closed-class morphology, where positional effects play such a massive role, this second kind of syntagmatic "priming" does not have a major impact. Nevertheless, we suggest that a form of interitem priming is operating in the application of agreement principles. For example, when Serbo-Croatian subjects see an adjective marked for nominative or accusative case (including a nonsense adjective), they will respond more rapidly to a noun that is marked in the same case (Katz et al., 1983). In general, then, closed-class morphemes can "prime" one another in a fashion that is similar to the priming that occurs among content words. We do not know, however, the extent to which these agreement-priming effects depend on the presence of positional constraints. For example, in the Serbo-Croatian experiment, the adjective prime and the noun target come in the canonical order for modifier and noun in that language. Would the priming work just as well, or at all, in the opposite direction?

We are now conducting a series of studies of morphological priming in normal speakers of richly inflected languages, within the framework of the Bates/MacWhinney crosslinguistic project. This will give us the information we need to investigate the role of positional and nonpositional morphosyntactic priming in aphasia. According to the standard interpretation of Broca's aphasia as a grammatical disorder, we might expect such priming effects to be attenuated in this population. However, our own results to date suggest that Broca's aphasics are actually better than Wernicke's aphasics at making use of convergence among grammatical cues – at least in receptive language processing. This finding is so surprising that it merits an extensive test.

Another kind of interitem priming occurs *between* open- and closed-class items. We have already discussed the strong influence of positional factors in the integration of content words and morphemes. Not only are positional violations rare in aphasia, but we also find very few cases of between-class substitution (for example, verb inflections placed illegally on a noun, and vice versa). This strongly suggests that patients are sensitive to the cooccurrence restrictions between a content word and the morphemes that they govern. We are also interested, however, in integration between content words and morphemes at a "deeper" semantic level. For example, preliminary data from Hungarian suggest that normal listeners are faster at making a lexical decision if the target noun carries a semantically probable suffix (for example, place names marked with a locative or tools marked with an instrumental). We would like to know whether this kind of speeded integration between lexical content and case morphology is preserved or indeed exaggerated in aphasic patients – and whether patient groups differ in the nature and extent of semantic/morphological integration.

To summarize, the processing differences observed to date between open- and closed-class items can be conceptualized in terms of "risk" and "protective" factors leading to the sparing or impairment of items in aphasia (see Table 10.1).

With regard to properties of the lexical/morphological item itself, the factors that have their greatest effect on retrieval of content words include *semantic content, phonological salience*, and *assignability*. The only item-level factor that provides an advantage for retrieval of grammatical morphemes is *frequency*.

With regard to properties of the cohort in which an item is embedded, *cohort size* provides some advantage for closed-class items. All other things being equal, there are fewer opportunities for error when the cohort of candidate items is small. However, *intraset confusability* provides an advantage for open-class items. This is related to the phonological salience issue, except that here we are talking about the salience of an item relative to its competitors in a given slot. Because closed-class items are generally quite limited in length, without variations in stress, they look and sound more similar to one another (although, as we shall see, there is some variation along this dimension between subclasses of morphemes).

Finally, with regard to properties of the context, content words are strongly affected by *interitem associations* or "priming." In the closed class, interitem priming effects tend to be limited to principles of agreement (for example, gender agreement across a noun phrase) and governance (for example, nouns activate the set of suffixes that they are most compatible with). However, closed-class items are very strongly influenced by *positional cues*, which have a rather meager influence on retrieval of content words.

In short, the various factors that constrain lexical retrieval have almost diametrically opposite effects on closed- versus open-class items. Given this distribution, dissociations between these two sets are not surprising – even if they are, as we maintain, both housed within a single, unified lexicon. We can see why closed-class morphemes should be at a disadvantage whenever the processor is subjected to stress or noise. We can also see why positional facts about morphological items are likely to be robust, whereas accessing of individual content items within a particular positional frame is frequently impaired.

This list of differences actually predicts more similarities than differences in the patterns of disruption we see in fluent and nonfluent aphasias. Indeed, our results to date suggest that the morphological errors produced by aphasic patients are quite similar. If we find qualitative differences between the major classes of aphasia, we expect that they will revolve primarily around (a) the differential contribution of phonological versus semantic/associative factors, (b) the importance of a given factor in expressive versus receptive language processing, and (c) the effects of timing and speed of activation on different item access principles, with overly fast and overly slow processing leading to different patterns of sparing and impairment.

Conclusion

The "same" syndrome can indeed look very different from one language to another. By investigating patterns of aphasia across natural languages, we will ultimately learn a great deal about the relationship between brain and language. By the same token, however, crosslinguistic research is itself enriched by the study of language breakdown in adults who were once fluent speakers of their native language. Data from aphasia can help us to find the seams and joints of the language processor, points of strength and weakness that are simply not evident under normal conditions.

Part IV. Formalization

11 The Acquisition of Cue–Category Mappings

Janet McDonald

Often we are called upon to make decisions or categorizations under conditions of less than complete or certain information. For example, when leaving the house in the morning we must decide whether to take an umbrella for the return trip later in the day. We may have several sources of information at hand – the forecast, the current weather, and typical weather for the season – but no one cue can tell us for sure if it will be raining several hours hence. In other words, the relationship between sources of information or "cues" and the categories they select is complex and often imperfect. Students of human decision making (Kahneman, Slovic, & Tversky, 1982) call this "judgment under uncertainty" and they have investigated many aspects of how people use incomplete and uncertain sources of information in making decisions.

The Competition Model of Bates and MacWhinney (1982, 1987, this volume), originally formulated for language processing, proves to be a general model of the decision processes made under such conditions of uncertainty. The model makes predictions about the order of cue acquisition and the strength of cue usage which have been well supported by a variety of studies discussed elsewhere in this volume. In this chapter, I will delineate a learning-on-error mechanism which yields the pattern of order of cue acquisition and strength of cue usage found in Competition Model studies. Evidence supporting the learning-on-error mechanism within the Competition Model is drawn from such diverse areas as linguistic role assignment, concept learning, and gender assignment in German.

Properties of Cue-Category Mappings

Although some categorizations can be made on the basis of a single attribute, many categorizations involve the integration of multiple cues. That is, the mapping between cues and categories is many-to-one, if not many-to-many. The forecast, the current weather, and the season all provide information about the afternoon's weather. GRE scores, undergraduate grades, and letters of recommendation are all cues to the potential success of a graduate school applicant.

One can describe the mappings of multiple cues to categories in terms of six major properties or parameters.

1. *Decision frequency.* To illustrate this first property, let us again consider the examples of decisions about the weather and about admitting students to graduate school.

375

Decisions about the weather are made quite frequently – perhaps several times a day. Decisions about admitting students to graduate school are made only once a year at the most. Because the graduate school decision is made so infrequently, we would expect that we would be relatively less expert at making that decision. In the area of language, one might well expect that, all other things being equal, we would be better at making decisions about how to form the plural of a noun than about how to form interrogative structures involving object raisings.

2. *Detectability*. Once a learner is confronted with a particular decision, he must begin to sample a variety of cues that can be used to predict the correct choice. However, in order to begin to track the correct cues, the learner must first be aware of those cues. If a cue is hard to detect, it may be some time before the learner begins to attend to it. For example, young children may be simply unaware of the way in which the barometer can be used to predict the weather. Children are most likely to attend to cues which relate directly to basic aspects of cognitive functioning of their daily life. Some potential cues may be more salient, or more computable than others, so they are detected early. Slobin (1973) has outlined some principles by which cue detection may occur in language acquisition and MacWhinney (1987, 1989, this volume) lists four particular cue types that are most relevant for learning the syntactic frames of words.

3. *Availability*. Although there may be multiple cues to a category, any particular cue may not be present or available in a particular instance (MacWhinney, Bates, & Kliegl, 1984). In trying to predict the need for an umbrella on any particular day, one may not have heard the weather forecast, or may, having recently moved to the area, have no information about the typical weather for the season. In accepting graduate students, letters of recommendation and transcripts may not have arrived by the application deadline. The availability of a cue is defined as the percentage of time that it is present over all exemplars.

4. *Reliability*. Even when a cue is present, it may not be reliable in indicating the correct categorization (MacWhinney et al., 1984). For example, even if the weather forecast for the day predicts all-day rain, it may in fact not rain in the afternoon. A high GRE score is not necessarily indicative of good graduate school material. The reliability of a cue for a particular classification is defined as the percentage of time the cue correctly indicates that classification on the cases that it is present. In the case of the weather, we may hear that the barometer is falling and decide to expect rain. If it always rains, then that cue is 100% reliable. If it only rains some portion of the time, we can conclude that the cue is only partially reliable.

5. *Validity*. The general utility of a cue for making decisions is a combination of the previous two concepts. The product of availability and reliability yields the validity of a cue, that is, the percentage of time that a cue is both present *and* indicates the correct categorization. When assessed over all exemplars, this concept is also referred to as overall validity. If only one cue is used to classify an exemplar, a cue that is high in overall validity will result in more correct classifications than a cue with lower overall validity. For example, if letters of recommendation are available for 80% of the students, and reliable predictors for 90%, they can be used to correctly admit students to graduate school 72% of the time. A cue that is available for 100% of the students but only 60% reliable, or one that is available for 60% of the students and 100% reliable, can only correctly admit students 60% of the time.

6. *Conflict Validity*. Because there are multiple cues to a category, it is often the case that more than one cue is available on any particular exemplar. These cues may agree with each other – an applicant for graduate school may have high GRE's, a good GPA, and good letters of recommendation. However, because cues do not always reliably indicate a classification, it is possible for cues to conflict with each

other. The sun may be shining during a usually rainy season. An applicant to graduate school may have promising GRE scores, but a low GPA. As is shown later, these conflict cases are crucial for determining cue usage in later stages of learning. Looking specifically at these conflict cases, we can evaluate the conflict validity of each cue that is, for conflict cases only, the percentage of time that a cue is both available and indicates the correct categorization.

The above six properties of cue–category mappings influence the order of cue acquisition and strength of cue usage in assigning an exemplar to a category. How early various categories are acquired should first depend on how categorization must be made. Within a categorization task, order in which cues are initially acquired should reflect, first, decision frequency, then detectability, then overall validity (the combination of availability and reliability), and, finally, conflict validity. Strength of cue usage should change from reflecting overall validities in the beginning learner, to reflecting conflict validities in the advanced learner. These predictions about order of acquisition and strength of usage have found strong empirical support from research on the acquisition of linguistic cues for role assignment. Less detectable cues are acquired later (MacWhinney, Pléh, & Bates, 1985); different cues will be acquired first in different languages because of crosslinguistic differences in overall cue validity and different cues will be dominant for adult speakers of different languages because of differences in conflict validity (Bates, MacWhinney, Caselli, Devescovi, Natale, & Venza, 1984; Frankel, Amir, Frenkel, & Arbel, 1980; Frankel & Arbel, 1981; Hakuta, 1982; Kail, this volume; MacWhinney et al., 1985; McDonald, 1986; Slobin, 1982; Slobin & Bever, 1982; Sokolov, 1988, this volume).

These predictions about order of cue acquisition and strength of cue usage are derivable from a learning-on-error mechanism within the Competition Model of Bates and MacWhinney (1982, 1987, this volume). The Competition Model provides an account of how multiple, sometimes inapplicable, unreliable, and conflicting cues are integrated in making decisions. According to this model, an activation strength proportional to its validity is associated with every cue–category mapping. When an exemplar is encountered, each cue that is present imparts its activation to the categorization that it favors. If cues agree, they send their activations to the same categorization and the strengths are added. If cues disagree, they impart their strengths to different categorizations. After the strengths have been distributed, the categorization that has accrued the most strength is chosen. The learning-on-error mechanism within this model details the process by which cues are acquired and strength is altered with continued exposure to the problem. Let us turn to how such a mechanism functions.

A prototypical learning-on-error mechanism is shown in Figure 11.1. According to this mechanism, learners categorize each new exemplar with their current cue strengths. This categorization is then compared to feedback available from the environment. Such feedback may occur in the form of comparisons

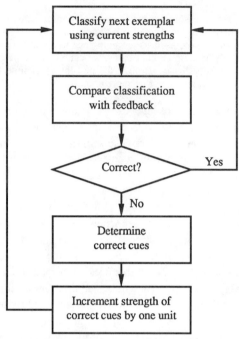

Figure 11.1. A mechanism for learning on error.

to external events, overt corrections, or from conflict internal to the learner (MacWhinney, 1978). If feedback indicates that the categorization is correct or if feedback is not available on a particular instance, cue strengths are not adjusted. However, if feedback indicates an incorrect categorization, the strengths of the cues that would have given a correct categorization are increased by a small amount, and these new cue weights are used for judging the next exemplar. Thus, cue weights are only adjusted on exemplars that are miscategorized.

Learners enter this mechanism with initial cue weights of zero. Having no information upon which to base categorization, learners will have to guess, causing a random subset of exemplars to be incorrectly classified. When feedback is present and indicates these misclassifications, the weights of the cues that would have yielded correct classification are increased. Obviously, such cues must first be detected before weights are increased. Cues that are more easily detected will thus be more likely to receive a boost.

With cues being strengthened over a random subset of all exemplars, the cue to get the most support will be the cue that correctly categorizes the largest number of all exemplars. This cue, by definition, is the one with the highest overall validity. After this first cue has increased in strength enough to overcome environmental noise, that is, after it is acquired, the set of exemplars incorrectly classified will no longer be a random subset of the whole. Rather, errors will only occur on exemplars for which the first cue is either not available, or where the first cue is unreliable. Cue weights will then be strengthened based on this more limited set of exemplars. The cue that indicates the correct categorization for the largest number of these remaining cases will be the next to be acquired. The pool of incorrectly classified exemplars again shrinks, and cue weights are adjusted on this new set. This acquisitional process continues until all relevant cues have gained enough strength to be significantly used. At this point, errors will only occur on exemplars where (1) the available cues conflict about the categorization and (2) the correct cue(s) currently has(have) a lower strength than the incorrect cue(s). Cue weight adjustment then occurs over this limited pool of exemplars until cues that correctly determine the categorization in these conflict situations increase in strength over the incorrect cues. At this point, cue strength should come to reflect the validity of cues on these conflict exemplars.

The learning-on-error mechanism predicts that the learner will first acquire detectable cues, and among these, acquire first the one highest in overall validity. As learning progresses, however, cue weights will continue to shift as long as conflict exemplars continue to be misclassified, until cue weights come to reflect these conflict validities. Note that this learning progression from overall validities to conflict validities allows the learner to correctly classify the largest number of exemplars at each point in learning. When the learner has acquired only one cue, the largest number of exemplars will be correctly classified when this single cue is highest in overall validity. When the learner has acquired all relevant cues, the largest number of exemplars will be correctly classified if the cue weights reflect the dominance relationship present in conflict cases. Nonconflict cases will continue to be correctly classified, while performance on conflict cases will improve.

Given any cue–category problem, it should be possible to predict the learning course from the detectability, overall validity, and conflict validity of the cues involved. Ignoring for now the issue of detectability, let us consider how overall validity and conflict validity may be calculated from a list of exemplars. Consider the problem of knowing whether it will rain in the afternoon based on the cues of the weather forecast, the morning weather, and typical weather for the season. Values for these cues, and the actual afternoon weather were noted for ten days (see Table 11.1). Over these ten exemplars, the forecast is heard on six of the days, for an availability of 60%. It is correct on five of the six days it is available, for a reliability of 83%. Overall validity of the forecast, the product of its availability and reliability, is therefore 50%. The morning weather is 100% available and 70% reliable, for an overall validity of 70%. The typical weather for the season is 100% available and 60% reliable, for an overall validity of 60%. Thus, by comparing a cue to the actual outcome over a pool of exemplars, overall validity is easily computed.

Table 11.1. *Cues to the afternoon weather*

Date	Afternoon forecast	Morning weather	Season's weather	Actual afternoon weather	
May 1	unknown	rain	rain	rain	
May 2	unknown	no rain	rain	no rain	*
May 3	rain	rain	rain	rain	
May 4	rain	no rain	rain	no rain	*
May 5	rain	rain	rain	rain	
May 6	unknown	rain	rain	rain	
May 7	no rain	rain	rain	no rain	*
May 8	no rain	rain	rain	no rain	*
May 9	unknown	rain	rain	rain	
May 10	rain	no rain	rain	rain	*

Note: Conflict cases marked by *.

In order to compute conflict validities, only those cases where two or more cues are in conflict are considered. In Table 11.1, the five conflict cases are marked by an asterisk. The forecast is known for 4 of these 5 cases, yielding a conflict availability of 80%. It is accurate on three of the four cases where it is known, for a conflict reliability of 75%. Its conflict validity, the product of availability and reliability on conflict cases, is 60%. Similarly, the current weather is 100% available and 40% reliable on the conflict cases, for a conflict validity of 40%. Finally, the typical weather for the season is 100% available and 20% reliable on conflict cases, for a conflict validity of 20%.

Note that computing validities over all exemplars and over conflict exemplars ranks the three cues differently. The morning weather is highest in overall validity, whereas the forecast is highest in conflict validity. Although cues need not be ranked differently by overall and conflict validity measures, they quite often are. When the measures do give different rankings, it means that the order of initial cue acquisition will not be identical to the strength of usage later in learning.

Thus, as shown above, if one has a list of cue values and actual outcomes, one can compute both overall and conflict validities. If such a list of exemplars is not available, or the number of exemplars is very large, one can also compute validities from estimates of the frequency with which various cue combinations and outcomes occur. Once overall validities and conflict validities have been computed, it is possible to predict the course of learning: Assuming equal detectability, the first cue acquired should be highest in overall validity, whereas final cue strength should reflect conflict validity. The remainder of this paper tests these predictions by comparing cue validities with cue acquisition and cue strength in three different domains: The development of linguistic role assignment in mono- and bilinguals, the course of concept learning, and the acquisition of German gender. In each case, the first cue acquired is that highest in overall validity, whereas strength of cue usage later in learning reflects conflict validities.

Role Assignment

The first area we will examine involves the use of cues to determine which noun in a sentence fills the basic grammatical roles of actor, patient, or recipient. We will focus particularly on the assignment of the actor role, that is, the role of the participant that performs the action of the verb. In English, this role is highly correlated with the linguistic roles of agent and grammatical subject, so that cues to agency and subjecthood also tend to be cues to actorhood. In English, cues to actorhood include word order (the noun before the verb tends to be the actor), noun-verb agreement (the noun that agrees with the verb in number tends to be the actor), noun animacy (an animate noun tends to be the actor), and case inflection (a pronoun in the nominative case tends to be the actor).

These cues map to the actor role in a many-to-one fashion, they vary in availability and reliability, and they can cooperate or compete with each other. Take, for example, the cue of noun animacy. This cue is not available in sentences like "The lightning struck the tree," since only inanimate nouns are present. It is not reliable in sentences like "The lightning struck the golfer," because the inanimate noun rather than the animate noun is the actor. It cooperates with the cue of preverbal word order in sentences such as "The woman hit the car" and conflicts with word order in sentences like "The car hit the woman."

Given equal detectability, the order of acquisition of the mappings between these cues and the actor role should depend on the overall validity of the cues – that is, the cue highest in overall validity should be the one first acquired by children. Thus, in simple comprehension tests such as the one used by Bates et al. (1984), the cue with the highest overall validity should be the first to be used significantly. Strength of adult cue usage, however, should follow the cue dominance relationship as reflected in conflict validities.

In order to test these predictions, McDonald (1986) examined cue validities and cue usage for the cues of word order, noun animacy, and case inflection for the actor role in both English and Dutch. These two languages have similar structures – they allow NVN sentences, do not explicitly mark animacy on nouns, and have case inflections only on pronouns. However, these languages have one crucial structural difference. Whereas English has very strict SVO interpretation of the NVN pattern, Dutch is more flexible – NVN sentences can be either SVO or OVS. The OVS interpretation is less frequent than the SVO, and occurs in questions (for example, *Wat zag zij?* = "What saw she?" = "What

Table 11.2. *Estimates of overall and conflict cue validities for English and Dutch NVN sentences*

	English		Dutch	
	Overall	Conflict	Overall	Conflict
SV(O) word order	95	100	35	48
Noun animacy	76	14	70	36
Case inflection	43	45	46	70

did she see?"), or reversed actives (for example, *De man zag zij* = "The man saw she" = "She saw the man"). When the OVS interpretation is desired, it is usually marked by other cues, such as noun animacy or case inflection. That is, in cases of conflict between SVO word order and other cues in Dutch, the other cues usually dominate. The opposite is the case in English – conflict with SVO word order is either not allowed (for example, conflict with case inflection yields ungrammatical sentences such as "The man saw she") or resolved in favor of the word order cue (for example, conflict with noun animacy does not change the SVO interpretation, as in sentences such as "The car hit the woman").

This difference in types of grammatical sentences allowed in English and Dutch causes the languages to have very different overall and conflict validities. The validity estimates are shown in Table 11.2. Overall validities were estimated from text counts from popular novels in English [*The Great Gatsby* (Fitzgerald, 1925) and *The Hotel New Hampshire* (Irving, 1982)] and Dutch [*Dagboek* (Hermans, 1976) and *Kopstukken* (Bomans, 1947)]. Because of a low incidence of occurrence of conflict sentences in the text counts, conflict validities were estimated from sentence frequency estimates made by native speakers of each language. The validity estimates in Table 11.2 show that in English, preverbal word order has both the highest overall validity, and the highest conflict validity. In Dutch, however, noun animacy has the highest overall validity, whereas case inflection has the highest conflict validity. Thus, in English, the first cue to be acquired should be preverbal word order, and this cue should be the strongest one in adult performance. In Dutch, the first cue acquired should be noun animacy, but adults should depend most strongly on case inflection.

The order of cue acquisition and strength of cue usage were assessed by examining the choice of actor by native English speakers (five-year-olds to adults) and native Dutch speakers (seven-year-olds to adults) on sentences such as those given in Table 11.3. These nine sentence types, all of the form noun-verb-noun, were created by crossing three levels of noun animacy and three levels of case inflection. The animacy cue could be neutral (N1 animate and N2 animate), or it could favor the first noun (N1 animate and N2 inanimate) or

Table 11.3. *NVN sentence stimuli*

Noun favored by animacy	Noun favored by case inflection		
	Neither	First	Second
Neither	"The farmer hit the artist"	"The judge called her"	"The father touched she"
First	"The runner stole the ball"	"She broke the tree"	"Him folded the string"
Second	"The tree spilled the father"	"The desk wrote her"	"The piano baked she"

the second noun (N1 inanimate and N2 animate). The case inflection cue could also be neutral (both N1 and N2 not marked for case), or favor the first noun (N1 nominative and N2 not marked, or N1 nominative and N2 accusative, or N1 not marked and N2 accusative) or the second noun (N1 accusative and N2 not marked, or N1 accusative and N2 nominative, or N1 not marked and N2 nominative). Word order was kept constant, and the effect of preverbal, first noun position was tested by noting if choice of this position differed from that expected by chance.

The choice of actor in each sentence was submitted to an ANOVA for each language-by-age group. Although the *F* values from these analyses indicate which cues were significantly used, the relative strength with which they were used, a more informative measure for our purposes, is given by the percentage of the variance that each cue accounted for. These percentages for each age group are graphed for English and Dutch in Figure 11.2. For English, the preverbal word order cue is strongly used, even by kindergartners, and its use remains strong across all age groups. This finding replicates the results of Bates et al. (1982, 1984). The use of the cues of animacy and case inflection in English is negligible, never accounting for more than 2% of the variance. Therefore, those lines are not plotted in Figure 11.2. The results for the English five-year-olds are the same as those given for the English seven-year-olds and are not included in Figure 11.2. In Dutch, strength of cue usage changes with age. Both word order and noun animacy are strong in the younger groups; however, adults most strongly use case inflection, followed by word order and very weak noun animacy.

The developmental pattern of cue acquisition and strength of cue usage supports the learning-on-error mechanism. The first cue acquired by native English speakers, word order, is the cue with the highest overall validity. Use of this single cue correctly assigns the actor role in nearly all English sentences other than passives and fragments such as " '...,' said he." (Passives may be treated as a special case because of the additional strong cues of the copular verb and the preposition "by," which may override or circumvent the usual word order cue use.) Because the word order cue yields correct interpretations for nearly all sentences, the other cues fail to gain significant strength. Even if an

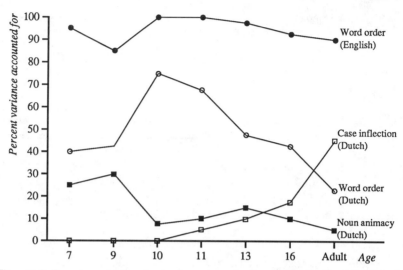

Figure 11.2. Percentage variation accounted across ages for three cues in Dutch and English.

error did somehow occur, use of the word order cue would most likely give the correct answer, even on conflict sentences, and, consequently, this cue would be strengthened.

Two cues have already been acquired by second and third grade native Dutch speakers. One of these cues, noun animacy, is the cue with highest overall validity for the Dutch actor role. The other cue, word order, can be used to correctly interpret 38% of the sentences in the text counts where the animacy cue is either unavailable or unreliable. In this regard, it is a better cue than case inflection, which only correctly interprets 17% of the sentences not handled by animacy. Although it is not possible to tell from the current data whether noun animacy or word order was acquired first, the fact that use of the noun animacy cue quickly declines, whereas word order continues to increase, suggests that the noun animacy cue may have been acquired first, and is on its way out, whereas word order may have been more recently acquired, and is taking over as the strong cue. Even when children use both the noun animacy and word order cues, they will continue to make errors in interpretation on conflict sentences involving the case inflection cue. Learning from these errors finally results in the acquisition of this cue around sixth grade. The case cue continues to increase in strength until it is able to correctly interpret conflict sentences containing the case inflection cue. For example, case inflection must be stronger than word order to correctly interpret sentences such as *De man zag zij* ("The man saw she" = "She saw the man"), and stronger than a combination of word order and noun animacy to correctly interpret sentences such as *Hem ramde de bus*, ("Him hit the bus" = The bus hit him).

As well as making predictions for cue acquisition and usage in monolingual speakers, the learning-on-error mechanism also makes predictions about cue strength in second language learners (Kilborn & Cooreman, 1987; McDonald, 1987a). The Competition Model (MacWhinney, 1987a) holds that second language learners transfer the cue strengths of their first language to the second language (Bates & MacWhinney, 1981). This transfer may result in correct processing of some sentences. However, use of these first language cue weights on second language sentences will cause errors on sentences containing cues with radically different conflict validities in the two languages. For example, consider a native speaker of English bringing English weights to the Dutch sentence *De man zag zij* ("The man saw she"). Since word order has a higher conflict validity than case inflection in English, the speaker would incorrectly assign the actor role to *de man*, rather than the correct *zij*. According to the learning-on-error mechanism, such errors would cause cue weights to be adjusted, increasing the strength of the correct cue(s). With increasing exposure to the second language, this cue weight adjustment mechanism will cause weights to gradually shift from first to second language conflict validities.

In order to test this extension of the learning-on-error mechanism to second language learners, English-Dutch and Dutch-English adult bilinguals were asked to assign the actor role in second language NVN sentences (McDonald, 1987a). These sentences, identical to the ones used in the monolingual experiment described above, contained word order, noun animacy, and case inflection cues (see Table 11.3). Recall that the cues highest in conflict validity are word order for English and case inflection for Dutch. If, as predicted, second language learners shift from first to second language cue weights, English-Dutch bilinguals interpreting Dutch sentences should gradually change their strongest cue from word order to case inflection, whereas Dutch-English bilinguals interpreting English sentences should do the opposite. In order to see the proposed shift in cue strengths, each bilingual group was divided into three subgroups, based on their amount of exposure to the second language, and their performance was compared to adult monolingual speakers of each language.

Figures 11.3 and 11.4 show the percentage of variance accounted for by each cue in the bilingual subgroups. These figures clearly show that, with increasing second language exposure, bilinguals neatly shift from using the strengths of their first language to using those of their second. English-Dutch bilinguals (Figure 11.3) decrease the strength of the word order cue and increase that of case inflection. Dutch-English bilinguals (Figure 11.4) do the opposite – increasing the strength of the word order cue, and decreasing that of case inflection. Noun animacy use stays fairly constant for all groups, as it is a weakly used cue in both languages. Thus, the predictions of the learning-on-error mechanism for bilinguals are borne out.

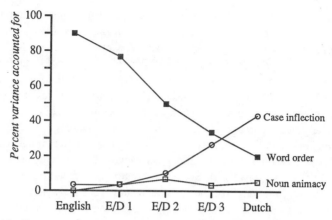

Figure 11.3. Percentage variance accounted for across English/Dutch bilingual subgroups with increasing Dutch exposure for three cues compared to native English and Dutch patterns.

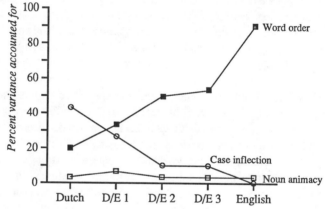

Figure 11.4. Percentage variance accounted for across Dutch/English bilingual subgroups with increasing English exposure for three cues compared to native Dutch and English patterns.

Concept Learning

The Competition Model properties of detectability, availability, reliability, over-all validity and conflict validity are formulated as general cognitive principles that could well apply to areas outside of linguistic decision making. In order to examine the extent to which these properties apply within the context of a standard nonlinguistic learning task, McDonald and MacWhinney (1987) constructed a concept formation task in which the variables of overall validity and conflict validity could be controlled. The task was designed to be analogous to the standard linguistic role assignment task. Rather than determine which of two nouns was the actor, subjects determined which of two geometric figures

Table 11.4. *Experimental Design*

		Cue 3		
		Absent	Agree Cue 1	Disagree Cue 1
Cue 2	**Absent**	*Cell 1* Cue 1 correct Cue 2 absent Cue 3 absent big black triangle small black triangle* frequency: 20	*Cell 2* Cue 1 correct Cue 2 absent Cue 3 correct small white triangle* big white square frequency: 20	*Cell 3* Cue 1 incorrect Cue 2 absent Cue 3 correct small white square big white triangle* frequency: 5
	Agree Cue 1	*Cell 4* Cue 1 correct Cue 2 correct Cue 3 absent big white square small black square* frequency: 20	*Cell 5* Cue 1 correct Cue 2 correct Cue 3 correct small black triangle* big white square frequency: 15	*Cell 6* Cue 1 correct Cue 2 correct Cue 3 incorrect small black square* big white triangle frequency: 5
	Disagree Cue 1	*Cell 7* Cue 1 incorrect Cue 2 correct Cue 3 absent big black triangle* small white triangle frequency: 5	*Cell 8* Cue 1 incorrect Cue 2 correct Cue 3 incorrect small white triangle big black square* frequency: 2	*Cell 9* Cue 1 incorrect Cue 2 correct Cue 3 correct big black triangle* small white square frequency: 8

Note: Cue 1 = size (small*, big). Cue 2 = color (black*, white).
Cue 3 = shape (triangle*, square). * = correct response.

was the "dominant" or correct one. The figures could contrast with each other on several dimensions and these contrasts, or cues, varied in availability and reliability, and could agree or disagree with each other.

The design of the stimulus space is shown in Table 11.4. Cue 1 was always present, and three levels of the other two cues – absent, agree with cue 1, and disagree with cue 1 – were crossed for a total of nine stimulus types. In cases of conflict, the correct figure was the one indicated by cue 2; if this cue was

Table 11.5. *Overall validities and conflict validities for concept learning problem*

	overall	conflict
cue 1	80	20
cue 2	55	80
cue 3	48	52

absent, it was the figure indicated by cue 3; if both cue 2 and cue 3 were absent, it was the figure indicated by cue 1. The correct figure in each cell is marked by an asterisk. In Table 11.4, cue 1 is filled in with size (small or large – the small figure tended to be correct), cue 2 with shading (black interior or white interior – the black interior tended to be correct), and cue 3 with shape (triangle or square – the triangle tended to be correct). However, in order to test for the effect of cue detectability on cue acquisition, the abstract design was completed in four different ways for different subject groups. The cues of size, shading, shape, and dottedness each took a turn as cue 1, cue 2, cue 3, and as an irrelevant cue. We first report results collapsed over these different subject groups to note the effect of overall and conflict validity. Later we will analyze the individual groups for the effect of cue detectability on cue acquisition.

Since subjects had had no exposure to the task prior to the experiment, it was possible to control the variables of overall validity and conflict validity by manipulating the frequency with which the various cells occurred in training. These frequencies, given in the last line in each cell in Table 11.4, were used to calculate the overall validity and conflict validity for each cue, which are shown in Table 11.5. Cue 1 has the highest overall validity, followed by nearly equal overall validities for cues 2 and 3. Cue 2 has the highest conflict validity, followed by cue 3, and, finally, by cue 1. Thus, cue 1 should be the first cue acquired, but cue 2 should be the strongest cue in later performance.

Subjects went through a series of eight training and eight test phases. During training, subjects were exposed to the exemplars with the frequencies indicated in Table 11.4. After indicating which figure they thought was correct in each trial, feedback about the correct figure was given. During testing, subjects were presented with one exemplar from each of the nine cells. The test phases consisted of blank trials (Levine, 1975) – that is, subjects received no feedback about the correctness of their answers.

The percentage of variance accounted for by each cue over the eight tests is shown in Table 11.6. As predicted, cue 1 was used strongly early in the experiment. By the third test, cue 2 had become the strongest, and continued to increase in strength with further exposure. One prediction about final strength of usage is not borne out – according to conflict validities, cue 3 should be stronger than cue 1. However, even at test 8, this is not reflected in the cue strengths. A

Table 11.6. *Percent total variance in response accounted for by each cue on each test*

Test	1	2	3	4	5	6	7	8
cue 1	28	20	17	12	10	11	10	10
cue 2	6	12	18	36	31	44	47	55
cue 3	10	4	8	7	10	8	3	2

very simple explanation of this is that even at the eighth test, subjects had not succeeded in completely solving the problem. A high error rate still exists in the cell where cues 1 and 3 compete in the absence of cue 2. With additional exposure to the problem the strength of cue 3 should increase relative to cue 1, resulting in a decrease in the errors made in this cell.

In order to discuss the effect of cue detectability on cue acquisition, we turn now to an analysis of the four subgroups of subjects who had different configurations of cues in the abstract design. The distribution of the cues over the design for the different subject groups is given below.

	Cue 1	Cue 2	Cue 3	Irrelevant cue
Group 1	size	shading	shape	dottedness
Group 2	dottedness	size	shading	shape
Group 3	shape	dottedness	size	shading
Group 4	shading	shape	dottedness	size

Previous research about cue salience has shown that for adults, shape is more salient than color (Brian & Goodenough, 1929). A study with children showed that shape dominated color, which in turn dominated size in hypothesis generation (Kagan & Lemkin, 1961). If color is considered to be a property of the interior of an object, the current experiment has two variations on color: shading (a black interior or white interior) and dottedness (a dot occurring in the interior of the object). Thus, if cue detectability or salience influences cue acquisition, one might predict that the shape cue would be acquired before shading or dottedness, which would be acquired before size.

Inspection of order of cue acquisition shows that all groups first acquire cue 1, the cue highest in overall validity. However, the order of acquisition of cue 2 and cue 3, cues with nearly equal overall validity (and nearly equal validity on those exemplars not correctly classified by cue 1), differed between the groups as would be predicted by cue detectability. Group 1 acquired cue 3 (shape) before cue 2 (shading); group 2 acquired cue 3 (shading) before cue 2 (size); group 3 acquired cue 2 (dottedness) before cue 3 (size), and group 4 acquired cue 2 (shape) before cue 3 (dottedness). Thus, two groups acquired cue 3 before cue 2, and two groups acquired cue 2 before cue 3, and this order of acquisition followed the salience hierarchy of shape over shading or dottedness over size.

These results indicate an effect of both overall validity and detectability on cue acquisition. In the current case, validity beat out detectability for the acquisition of the first cue – perhaps because this cue was much more valid than the others. However, when validities were close to equal, as they were for cue 2 and cue 3, the effect of detectability was clear. If larger differences in detectability were present in the cues, it is possible that detectability could overcome high validities in determining the order of cue acquisition.

Analysis of the performance of these subgroups also lends support to the claim that learning is occurring on error trials. Subjects in groups 1 and 2, who acquired cue 3 before cue 2, made more errors in the intermediate portion of the experiment than did subjects in groups 3 and 4, who acquired cue 2 before cue 3. However, these subjects who made more errors were more likely to achieve an error-free test trial at some point in the experiment than were subjects who acquired cue 2 before cue 3. In this way, the initial higher error rate of cue 3 before cue 2 subjects gave them more opportunity for weight revision, yielding an earlier mastery of the problem.

The Acquisition of German Gender

The third area in which I have examined the learning of cue–category relations is in the acquisition of cues determining the use of the German definite article. This is a highly complex linguistic problem that involves the integration of multiple cues for gender, number, and case. Of these classifications, the most difficult for native speakers and foreigners alike is the assignment of nouns to gender class. At first consideration, the gender system of German seems largely arbitrary. For example, why is "spoon" masculine *(der Löffel)*, "fork" feminine *(die Gabel)*, and "knife" neuter *(das Messer)*? However, recent work has shown that, although the German gender system is complex, it is not as arbitrary as it appears on first analysis. There is actually a large space of phonological, morphological, and semantic cues to German gender (Zubin & Köpcke 1981; 1983; Köpcke & Zubin, 1984). Some of these cues are shown in Table 11.7.

The cues that mark gender in German have the characteristics of cue–category mappings we have seen in the previous two examples – multiple cues, varying in availability and reliability, that sometimes agree and sometimes conflict. In fact, multiple cues is one of the most salient characteristics of the German gender classification system. For example, the endings -*e*, -*ung*, and -*ie* as well as natural feminine gender all map to feminine gender. These is no gender cue that is always available. For example, although the -*e* ending is highly indicative of feminine gender, this cue is not present on all feminine nouns. Gender cues vary in their reliability. Some cues are 100% reliable – for example, if a word has a diminutive ending (i.e., -*lein* or -*chen*), the noun is guaranteed to be of neuter gender. Other cues are less reliable – for example, although the presence

Table 11.7. *A selection of cues to gender*

	Associated gender	Example	Translation
Phonological cues			
s + consonant-	masculine	*der Schrank*	"closet"
-fricative + t	feminine	*die Nacht*	"night"
Morphological cues			
-el	masculine	*der Schlüssel*	"key"
-ling	masculine	*der Feigling*	"coward"
-e	feminine	*die Sonne*	"sun"
-ung	feminine	*die Zeitung*	"newspaper"
-lein	neuter	*das Fräulein*	"young woman"
-ment	neuter	*das Instrument*	"instrument"
Semantic cues			
Natural gender	masculine	*der Sohn*	"son"
Alcoholic beverages	masculine	*der Schnaps*	"schnapps"
Natural gender	feminine	*die Tochter*	"daughter"
Flowers	feminine	*die Tulpe*	"tulip"
Youth	neuter	*das Kind*	"child"
Metals	neuter	*das Gold*	"gold"

of the *-e* ending is highly likely to indicate a feminine noun, there exist both masculine words (for example, *der Junge*, "boy") and neuter words (for example, *das Ende*, "end") that contain this morpheme. Cues can cooperate with each other – for example, *der Schnaps*, "schnapps," begins with the phonological cue of *S* + consonant, which is indicative of masculine gender, and has the semantic cue of alcoholic beverage, also indicative of masculine gender. Cues can also compete – for example, *der Junge*, "the boy" has the *-e* morphological cue that strongly indicates feminine gender, but also has the semantic cue of natural masculine gender.

There is not a large amount of empirical data on cue acquisition and usage for German gender. Several studies have shown that adults and children do make use of phonetic and morphological cues to assign gender (Köpcke & Zubin, 1981; MacWhinney, 1978; Mills, 1986). Using nonce words, MacWhinney (1978) found that children between the ages of 4 and 6 were able to make use of the *-e* ending cue to feminine gender, as well as the *-erei* morpheme cue to feminine gender, and the *-chen* morpheme cue to neuter gender. Mills (1986) confirms that 3- to 6-year-old children also use the *-e* cue with real words. Using single syllable nonce words, Mills (1986) also reports that 7- to 8-year-old children were able to make significant use of word initial cues, all of which indicated masculine gender, but performed poorly with word final cues, all of which indicated feminine or neuter gender. Two possible explanations of these findings were offered – children could be more sensitive to word initial cues, that is, find them more detectable, or, since all test words used were monosyllabic, children may simply have used monosyllabicity as a cue to masculine gender. Therefore, they would perform well on words with other masculine gender cues, and poorly on words with feminine and neuter gender cues.

This empirical work on the acquisition of German gender provides some support for the claim that cue validity determines the order of cue acquisition. For example, the -e cue to feminine which appears to be among the earliest cues acquired, is a cue with high overall validity. Not only is it one of the most available cues to gender (approximately 15,000 words have this cue), but it has high reliability as well – Mills (1986, p. 33) reports that about 90% of these words are feminine. Similarly, the connection between monosyllabicity and the masculine gender is high in overall validity – numerous words are monosyllabic, and Köpcke and Zubin (1983) find that 64% of them are masculine.

Cue validity is also important in adult gender assignments. Mills (1986) reports that the strength with which adults used various cues for assigning genders to nonce words is influenced both by the number of words following the rule and the number of exceptions. However, there is little evidence about the role of conflict in adult cue usage in empirical work, since nonce words with conflicting cues have not been explored. Adults are able, however, to give correct genders to real words that contain conflicting cues. Thus, they have either adjusted cue strengths to allow the correct cues in conflict situations to dominate over incorrect cues, or they have learned these words by rote.

To provide a somewhat different test of the predictions of the Competition Model, Taraban, McDonald, and MacWhinney (in press) performed two computational simulations of the acquisitional process of German gender within a connectionist framework. The goals of this work were to (1) articulate the predictions of the Competition Model in computationally precise terms, (2) examine the match of these predictions to the empirical work on the acquisition of German gender, and (3) generate new predictions that could be tested in future empirical work.

Connectionist networks consist of large numbers of interconnected processing units which are themselves functionally simple. Information in the system is contained in the weights associated with each connection. A sample connectionist network for the solution of the German gender problem is shown in Figure 11.5. It consists of input units, which represent the various phonological, morphological, and semantic cues to gender, an internal layer, where the information from these cues is combined, and three output units, which represent the three genders. Each unit on each level is connected to each unit on the next level. Initially, the strengths associated with each connection are random. But with exposure to a training set, these strengths are adjusted according to a learning algorithm. The learning algorithm used in the current

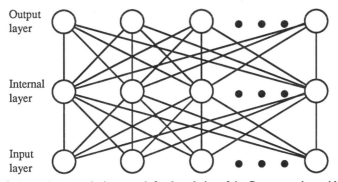

Figure 11.5. A sample connectionist network for the solution of the German gender problem.

simulation is the back propagation algorithm (Rumelhart, Hinton, & Williams, 1986). This algorithm reduces error in the network by comparing the obtained output of the network to the desired output, and adjusting weights to reduce this error.

The first simulation attempts to replicate the results of the empirical data by using elementary vocabulary in the training set. In order to approximate the type of input heard by a child, this training set consisted of 102 high-frequency spoken nouns, represented in proportion to their relative frequencies, for a total of 305 tokens. Each word was coded for the presence and absence of phonological, morphological, and semantic gender cues taken from Zubin and Köpcke (1981, 1983), Köpcke and Zubin (1984), and a German grammar book (Lederer, Schulz, & Griesbach, 1969), as well as cues for number and case. After repeated exposures to this training set, the network arrived at connection weights that successfully learned the correct definite article for each token. Using these weights, the network was then tested with novel words to examine the strengths of the various cues. The results of this test indicated that several cues had developed strong cue–category mappings. Among these were the mapping between -*e* and feminine gender, the mapping between natural gender cues and masculine or feminine gender, the mapping between a fricative + *t* ending and feminine gender, the mapping between the -*ung* ending and feminine gender, and the mapping between monosyllabicity and masculine gender.

The results of this first simulation show general agreement with the empirical data. Both the simulation and the data show a strong and early mapping of the -*e* cue to feminine gender, and both also find early use of the cue of monosyllabicity to masculine gender. There are also some differences in cue acquisition between the simulation and the empirical data. However, many of these can be explained by the limited number of words in the learning set given to the simulation. For example, although MacWhinney (1978) found good early command of the -*erei* cue, the network could not have acquired this cue since it was not contained in the learning set. In addition, there is no empirical data on the development of the usage of some of the cues, such as the fricative + *t* ending, or the -*ung* ending. Clearly, the simulation could be improved by using a larger learning set and encoding more cues, and the range of empirical data could be expanded by testing for the acquisition of more cues.

The first simulation shows that the acquisition of cues in a connectionist network seems to be affected by cue validity. The second simulation looks at this relationship more explicitly by examining the development of cue strength with increasing exposure to German vocabulary. In this case, the learning set consisted of 150 words, 75 of which came from examples provided by Zubin and Köpcke for their cues, and 75 of which came from an article in *Der Spiegel*, under the constraint that no two words were chosen that had exactly the same cues but different outputs associated with them. To simplify the problem, this simulation only encoded cues for gender. Learning occurred in the network by adjusting the strength of each connection after each exposure to the training set according to back propagation. With more and more exposures, the network mastered more and more of the training set.

If learning in this system is sensitive to validity constructs, the strengths of the connections between the input cues and the internal layer should reflect overall validity initially, and conflict validity later. (The effect of validity will only be directly evident in between these first two layers, as nonlinear combinations can occur on the next level.) Accordingly, connection weights at different points in learning were correlated to three different measures: overall validity of each cue for each gender within the learning set, the reliability of each cue within the set, and, as an approximation to conflict validities, β weights for each cue. These β weights were computed in a regression analysis over the learning set, using the cues as independent variables and the correct gender representation associated with a set of input cues as the dependent variable. These weights capture cooccurrence relationships among the cues, including both conflicting and cooperating relationships. (Because of the large number of cues in the set, it was difficult to compute conflict validities directly, so β weights were used.)

The correlation between connection strengths and these three measures is shown in Figure 11.6. In the early stages of learning, overall validity is the best predictor of connection strength. Later, cue reliability is briefly the best predictor, but in the last stages of learning, conflict and cooperation relations as reflected by the β weights are the best predictors of network weights. Thus, the simulation manifests a developmental pattern of cue acquisition and usage much like that found in human learners. Early acquisition is influenced by overall validity, and final cue strength is influenced by cue cooccurrence patterns, particularly conflict validity.

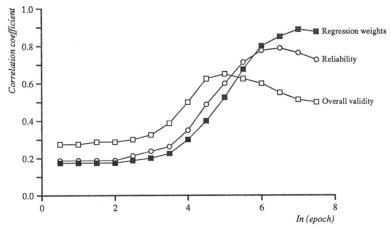

Figure 11.6. The correlation between connection strengths and three cue validity measures.

Discussion

The results of studies in three different areas of categorization support the predictions of the learning-on-error mechanism within the Competition Model. The first cue that learners acquire for classifying an exemplar is the cue highest in overall validity. The choice of this cue is sensible, as it will correctly categorize the largest number of exemplars possible with the use of only one cue. Later on in learning, cue strengths reflect cue dominance in conflict situations, thus allowing people to correctly classify not only nonconflict exemplars, but conflict exemplars as well.

The learning-on-error mechanism is especially important for cue adjustment later in learning. If, instead of learning on error, cue strengths were adjusted after each exemplar whether or not it was correctly classified, then cue weights would correspond to overall validity rather than conflict validity. Although use of these weights would still correctly classify nonconflict exemplars, conflict exemplars where the correct cue(s) had a lower overall validity than the incorrect cue(s) would always be incorrectly classified.

It should be pointed out that in order to make the predictions of the model clear, some sleight-of-hand has been worked in the claim that final cue usage should reflect conflict validity. Actually, the learning-on-error mechanism predicts that final cue strength should reflect cue validities on sentences still incorrectly classified after all relevant cues are acquired. Although these cases will certainly be conflict cases, not all conflict cases may still be incorrectly classified. Thus, it is possible that the pool of sentences over which validities determining final cue strength should be assessed is actually smaller than all conflict sentences.

The earliest versions of the Competition Model were formulated for categorization decisions made with cues that are combined in a linear fashion to define a category, rather than in some other way. Although many problems involve a linear cue–category relationship, others do not. For example, many of the concept learning problems studied in the past involved Boolean combinations of cues, such as exclusive ors and biconditionals. These types of problems are not solvable by combining cue strengths in a simple two-layer system (see MacWhinney, this volume). For example, if an exemplar is a member of a category when it is either red or square, but not both, there are no cue strengths that can be directly combined to correctly classify all types of exemplars. However, architectures such as those used in a connectionist framework can model nonlinear relations by assuming that the cue–category relation involves more than just an input and an output level. With such extensions, the Competition Model can be used to explain cue acquisition and usage for both linear and nonlinear categorization problems.

This paper has also clearly demonstrated the utility of the Competition Model outside the area of linguistic role assignment. The model is clearly applicable to other linguistic tasks, such as gender classification, and to nonlinguistic tasks, such as concept learning. In all these domains, we have seen that the learning-on-error mechanism provides us with a good account of the acquisition of cue–category mappings.

12 Maximum Likelihood Models for Sentence Processing

Janet McDonald and Brian MacWhinney

This chapter describes how maximum likelihood estimation (MLE) can be applied to the analysis of experimental data on linguistic role assignment. First, we outline a model of role assignment, the Competition Model (Bates & MacWhinney, 1982, 1987), and show how it may be actualized in a maximum likelihood model. We then compare MLE to the more conventional technique of analysis of variance (ANOVA), using crosslinguistic and developmental data to illustrate advantages and disadvantages. Unique aspects of the MLE technique are illustrated with bilingual, aphasic, and developmental data. Advantages and unique features of MLE include the direct estimation of strength of cue usage, goodness-of-fit statistics that allow the comparison of groups or individuals in an abstract cue space, the ability to analyze data from an individual subject, and the ability to predict performance from independently derived estimates of cue strength.

The Role Assignment Problem and the Competition Model

Assigning nouns to linguistic roles, such as actor or patient, is not a simple task. The mappings between cues that mark these roles and the roles themselves are many-to-many. That is, more than one cue can mark a particular role, and a particular cue can mark more than one role. In addition, cue–role mappings tend to be probabilistic rather than deterministic. That is, although a particular cue may usually indicate a particular role, it may not always be present, or it may not correctly assign the role. For example, consider the cue of noun animacy and the role of actor. Though an animate noun tends to be the actor in many cases (e.g., "The dog hits the ball"), the cue is not always present (e.g., "The ball hits the chair"), nor is it always correct (e.g., "The ball hits the dog"). Further, when more than one cue to a role is present in the same sentence, the cues can either agree or disagree with each other. For example, the cues of preverbal position and noun animacy agree in the sentence "The dog hits the ball," and disagree in "The ball hits the dog."

The Competition Model (Bates & MacWhinney, 1982, 1987) has been proposed as a model of the way cues are utilized in the role assignment process. According to this model, each cue has an associated strength, and these strengths combine when cues agree with each other, and compete when cues disagree. An

397

important tenet of the model is that the strength with which a cue is used should be proportional to its informational value, or *cue validity*. Cue validity, a concept taken from Brunswik (1956), has been defined by McDonald (1986, 1987a) as the product of cue availability (proportion of time the cue is present) and cue reliability (proportion of time when the cue is present that it indicates the correct interpretation). More simply stated, the validity of a cue is the proportion of time it is present and indicates the correct assignment. Cue validity therefore takes on values between 0 and 1 (or 0% and 100%), and can be estimated independently of performance on a role assignment task by counting how often a cue is correct over some sample of the language.

The results of the experiments we have conducted on role assignment support the connection between cue strength and cue validity hypothesized in the Competition Model. For example, it has been shown that, within a language, adult speakers use different cues with different degrees of strength, and that cue strength corresponds to validity. For example, adult speakers of English use pre-verbal position more strongly than noun animacy in determining the actor in a sentence; this word order cue is also the more valid cue in English (Bates, McNew, MacWhinney, Devescovi, & Smith, 1982; MacWhinney, Bates, & Kliegl, 1984). Other results show that, crosslinguistically, adult speakers of different languages use the same cues with different degrees of strength. This differential cue usage reflects differences in cue validity across languages. For example, when given a sentence in word order and noun animacy cues conflict, native English speakers follow word order, whereas native Italian speakers follow noun animacy. That is, in the sentence "The lasagna eats Giovanni," English speakers would choose "the lasagna" as the actor, whereas Italians would choose "Giovanni." This differential cue use is a result of different grammatical patterns in the two languages. English NVN sentences are nearly always SVO, resulting in high validity for this cue in English. Italian NVN sentences can be either SVO or OVS, depending on other factors, such as animacy or verb agreement, giving these cues higher validity than word order (Bates et al., 1982; MacWhinney et al., 1984).

Changes in cue strength during language acquisition have also been tied to cue validity. Developmental studies of role assignment show that the first cue acquired, or the first to emerge as statistically significant, is generally the one highest in validity over all sentences in the language. However, as more cues are acquired, cue strengths change and begin to mirror cue validity as assessed only over those sentences involving conflict between the cues (McDonald, 1986, this volume). Developmentally, speakers revise their cue strengths to follow the cue validities in sentences where they make interpretation errors. An additional cause for the change in cue strength over the course of acquisition may involve overcoming initial difficulties with detecting or using certain cues (MacWhinney, Pléh, & Bates, 1985).

Mechanisms that determine the ways in which cues combine are a central component of the Competition Model. Cues that agree with each other cooperate in supporting a role assignment; cues that disagree compete. A noun will be assigned to the actor role with a higher probability and more quickly, if it is supported by two cues, than if it is supported by only one of the cues. A noun will be assigned to the actor role with a lower probability, and more slowly if it is supported by one cue and opposed by another than if it is just supported by the first cue. In previous versions of the Competition Model, these mechanisms of cue combination have been described in qualitative terms. If these mechanisms could be specified quantitatively in a mathematical model, it would then be possible to apply the technique of maximum likelihood estimation to numerical analysis and prediction of role assignment data. Providing such a quantitative specification is the goal of this paper.

Maximum Likelihood Estimation

Maximum likelihood estimation is a technique which uses an iterative procedure in conjunction with a mathematical model in order to find values for the parameters in the model that jointly give the best fit to a set of data. The procedure yields a set of estimated parameters and goodness-of-fit statistics, the latter of which indicate the difference between the estimated model and the actual data.

One possible model of the cue combination process is shown below. This particular model is multiplicative and nonlinear. The model predicts the probability of choosing the first noun as actor based on the strengths with which cues favor the first and other nouns. Note that each cue favors each candidate for actorhood at some probability level between 0 and 1. In the multiplicative model, the cooperating cues reinforce each other by multiplying their strengths. This model has been used with success for other choice problems involving multiple cues (Massaro & Cohen, 1983; Massaro & Oden, 1980; Oden & Massaro, 1978).

$$\text{P(first noun choice)} = \frac{\prod_i S_{i1}}{\sum_j \left(\prod_i S_{ij} \right)} , \qquad (1)$$

where S_{ij} is the strength with which cue i favors noun candidate j, $i = 1$ to I, where I is the total number of cues available, and $j = 1$ to J, where J is the total number of candidates for the actor role.

The formula states that the probability that the first noun will be chosen as the actor in a sentence with I cues and J nouns is equal to the product of the I cue strengths that favor the first noun, divided by the product of the I cue strengths for each of the J noun candidates, summed over all J nouns.

It is possible to simplify this general multiplicative model for use with the current role assignment experiments due to the experimental paradigm used. In all experiments analyzed in this chapter, subjects were asked to choose the actor in sentences which contained only two nouns (e.g. "The dog the pencil chased"). Thus, the denominator of the above formula, which is summed over J nouns, will consist of only two terms, since only two nouns are candidates for the actor role. Therefore, the equation in (1) can be simplified as:

$$P(\text{first noun choice}) = \frac{\prod_i S_{i1}}{\prod_i S_{i1} + \prod_i S_{i2}}, \tag{2}$$

In addition, since the subjects had to pick one noun or the other as the actor, the strength with which a particular cue favors the first noun and the strength with which it favors the second noun should sum to 1. That is, the degree to which a particular cue favors one noun as the actor must be the additive complement of the degree to which it favors the other noun. For example, consider the cue of noun animacy in the sentence "The dog the pencil chased." It must favor "the dog" for actorhood at some strength, say .75. It would therefore favor the other noun, "the pencil" at the complementary strength of $(1 - .75)$, or .25. Because the two strengths of a cue sum to 1, we can substitute $(1 - S_{i1})$ for S_{i2} in equation (2), yielding:

$$P(\text{first noun choice}) = \frac{\prod_i S_{i1}}{\prod_i S_{i1} + \prod_i (1 - S_{i1})}, \tag{3}$$

As the model is given in (3), one parameter is needed to estimate each level of each cue. That is, if there were three levels of animacy in the experiment, three different animacy parameters would be estimated. One parameter, say S_{A1}, would be estimated for the cases where the first noun was animate and the second inanimate. In a sentence such as "The dog the eraser chased," S_{A1} would favor the first noun and $1 - S_{A1}$ would favor the second noun. A second parameter, say S_{A2}, would be estimated from cases where the first noun was inanimate and the second animate. For example, in "The eraser the dog chased" S_{A2} would favor the first noun and $1 - S_{A2}$ would favor the second noun. Finally, a third parameter, say S_{A3}, would be estimated from cases where both nouns were animate. In a sentence such as "The dog the camel chased," S_{A3} would favor the first noun and $1 - S_{A3}$ would favor the second noun.

However, one can also formulate alternative models with fewer parameters if one assumes that cues impart the same strength to a noun regardless of position. For example, if one assumes that having an animate noun in the first position will influence the assignment of the actor role to this noun by the same amount that having an animate noun in the second position will influence the assignment of the actor role to this noun, one can code all levels of the animacy cue with one parameter. This parameter, say S_A, would be entered into the equation differently depending on the level of the cue. When the first noun was animate, and the second inanimate, first noun preference would be given by S_A, and the second noun preference by $(1 - S_A)$. When the first noun was inanimate and the second animate, first noun preference would be given by $(1 - S_A)$ and second noun preference by S_A. When the cue was present on both the first and second noun, first noun preference would be given by $S_A \times (1 - S_A)$ and second noun preference by $(1 - S_A) \times S_A$. In this case, the influence of the animacy cue cancels out. Similar arguments allow one to reduce other cues such as case, verb agreement and stress to one parameter each. If cue strength interacts with position, however, this reduction could cause a loss of information.

Unlike symmetrical cues, different word order patterns (e.g., NVN, NNV, VNN) must each be estimated by a separate parameter. This is because the strength with which a first noun interpretation is preferred in one word order is not related to the strength of first noun choice in the other word orders. For example, in some languages the first noun interpretation is preferred for all word orders, whereas, in other languages, the first noun interpretation is preferred for some word orders, and the second noun for the other orders. Thus, although it is possible to reduce the number of parameters in the model for symmetrical cues, such reduction is not possible for unsymmetrical cues such as word order.

Parameters in the above reduced parameter multiplicative model were estimated for different data sets by using the STEPIT program of Chandler (1969), along with routines developed by Massaro and Cohen (1983). This program uses an iterative routine to obtain a fit that minimizes the squared deviations between the observed data points, and those predicted by the parameters. The parameter estimates are numbers between 0 and 1. In the reduced parameter multiplicative model, neutral cue use is given by a .5 value. This is the value that will cancel out in the numerator and denominator of the multiplicative equation, yielding no effect of the cue.

In addition to parameter estimates, the STEPIT procedure also provides goodness of fit statistics, the root mean squared deviation (or RMSD), and the correlation (or r^2), between the model's predictions and the data. When the procedure is allowed to set its own parameter weights, these statistics show how well the model is able to fit the data. If the parameters are fixed, the statistics indicate how well these parameters fit the data. The RMSD incorporates the distance between the predicted and actual data points; the correlation between the points indicates whether their ordering is correct, even if their absolute level is off. Thus, even if a model fits a data set poorly (has a high RMSD), it may actually have captured the correct ordering of cue strength (high correlation).

Below we explore the use of MLE on several data sets, including adult crosslinguistic data, developmental data, bilingual data, and aphasic data. We first compare the maximum likelihood estimation technique to the more conventional analysis of variance in order to point out the advantages and disadvantages of these methods on group data. Then we illustrate the advantages of MLE in modeling individual data and using theories to construct models that predict performance.

Adult Crosslinguistic Data

In order to compare the techniques of ANOVA and MLE, both types of analyses are performed on data from an experiment involving adult native English, French, and Italian speakers. The data come from a study of French by Kail (this volume) and a study of English and Italian by Bates et al. (1982). Thirty speakers of each language were asked to determine the actor in sentences involving the factors of word order, noun animacy and contrastive stress. Twenty-seven sentences, consisting of one verb and two nouns, were formed by crossing three levels of word order (NVN, VNN, and NNV), three levels of noun animacy (both nouns animate, first noun animate and second noun inanimate, first noun inanimate and second noun animate), and three levels of stress (neither noun stressed, first noun stressed, second noun stressed).

ANOVA Analysis

The data from this experiment were submitted to an ANOVA with language as a grouping variable, and word order, noun animacy, and contrastive stress as within-subject factors. Results of the analysis show significant main effects for language, $F(2,87) = 22.2$, $p < .001$, word order, $F(2,174) = 173.4$, $p < .001$, noun animacy, $F(2,174) = 155.1$, $p < .001$, and contrastive stress, $F(2,174) = 4.7$, $p < .05$. Language also significantly interacts with each within-subject factor (language by word order, $F(4,174) = 65.5$, $p < .001$, language by noun animacy, $F(4,174) = 17.8$, $p < .001$, language by contrastive stress, $F(4,174) = 5.0$, $p < .001$), indicating differences in the way each cue was used in each language.

In order to investigate differences in cue usage across languages, each language was individually submitted to an ANOVA. Relative cue strength in each language was computed by determining the percent of variance accounted for by each cue in each analysis (Keppel, 1982). The results of the analyses are shown in Table 12.1. All languages show significant effects of word order and animacy, and French and Italian also show a significant effect of contrastive stress. Crosslinguistic differences in cue usage are clearly shown in the percent variance accounted for. English relies most strongly on word order cues, whereas French and Italian rely strongly on noun animacy cues.

MLE analysis

This same data was also analyzed using the reduced parameter multiplicative model described earlier, in conjunction with the STEPIT program. Three word

Table 12.1. *Main effects in the ANOVAs on English, French, and Italian adults*

	d.f.	English		French		Italian	
		F	% variance	F	% variance	F	% variance
Word order	2,58	245.2‡	56	6.3†	1	26.9‡	4
Noun animacy	2,58	11.0‡	3	51.7‡	28	112.2‡	44
Stress	2,58	.5	1	6.7†	1	6.0†	1

Note: † p < .005. ‡ p < .001.

Table 12.2. *Parameter estimates for English, French, and Italian adults*

	NVN word order	VNN word order	NNV word order	Noun animacy	Contrastive stress
English	.9449	.0927	.1319	.7529	.4315
French	.6993	.5023	.6551	.8392	.5655
Italian	.8620	.4670	.7029	.9388	.3991

order parameters, as well as one parameter each for animacy and stress, were estimated. Parameter estimates for each language, shown in Table 12.2, reflect the same crosslinguistic differences in cue usage discovered with the ANOVA. That is, the most polarized (i.e., most deviant from the neutral point of .5) cue weights for English occur in the word order parameters, and for French and Italian in the animacy parameter. These parameter estimates also supply information about direction and relative strength of cue use that is not as readily available in the ANOVA format. For example, when the p values and percent variance in the ANOVA told us that word order was a very strong cue for English, this meant only that the amount of first noun choice varied significantly in the different word orders – only an examination of cell means and further analysis would indicate the strength of first noun preference for the various orders. The parameter estimates for English, however, clearly show that there is a very strong first noun preference for the NVN word order (weight is above .5), and strong second noun preferences for the VNN and NNV orders (weights are below .5). Similarly, the parameter estimates for French and Italian show there is a moderate first noun preference in the NVN and NNV word orders, whereas there is little or no preference in VNN sentences. The analyses summarized in Table 12.1 used five parameters. When stress was coded separately for the three word orders in a nine-parameter model, the RMSD for Italian adults was substantially lower (see Bates & MacWhinney, this volume).

In order to see how closely the cue usage of each language matched that of

Table 12.3. *Fit of English, French, and Italian models to each language group*

	English model		French model		Italian model	
	RMSD	r^2	RMSD	r^2	RMSD	r^2
English	.04	.99	.42	.12	.43	.18
French	.43	.11	.09	.90	.16	.81
Italian	.43	.19	.14	.88	.06	.97

the other languages, the parameter estimates for each language were used to fit the performance of the other languages. The resultant goodness-of-fit statistics, the RMSDs, and r^2s are given in Table 12.3. Each language has the lowest RMSD and highest correlation for its own parameter estimates. However, good fits are also obtained when the French model is fitted to the Italian data, and when the Italian model is fitted to the French data. Thus, we see that French and Italian are more similar to each other in processing terms than either of these languages is to English. In general, MLE can be used in this way to measure the relative distances between models for different languages, or different groups of speakers.

Comparing the results of the ANOVA and the MLE procedures, we note that both analyses yield information about strength of cue usage. This information is contained in the percent variance accounted for in the ANOVA, and in the parameter estimates in the MLE procedure. The analyses differ in that the ANOVA is able to provide information about the statistical significance of cue usage, whereas the MLE procedure provides goodness of fit statistics that are useful for determining a language's distance from others in an abstract cue usage space. Another application of this technique is given in the next example.

Developmental Crosslinguistic Data

In a developmental extension of the previous study, native speaking English, French, and Italian children were asked to determine the actor in sentences in which three levels of the cues of word order, noun animacy, and constrastive stress had been crossed (for an analysis of the English and Italian data, see Bates et al., 1984). There were forty subjects in each language, ten each at the ages of 2.5, 3.5, 4.5, and 5.5 years. Using the data, we illustrate again how the strength of cue usage gained from percent variance in the ANOVA and the parameter estimates in the MLE procedure agree with each other. In addition, we compare cue usage in the different language and age groups to each other by fitting each group's adult parameter estimates to the other groups, and comparing the resultant RMSDs and r^2s.

ANOVA Analysis

The results of an ANOVA performed on the whole data set with language and age as grouping factors, show significant main effects of age, $F(3,108) = 22.7$, $p < .001$, word order, $F(2,216) = 159.4$, $p < .001$, animacy, $F(2,216) = 53.8$, $p < .001$, and stress, $F(2,216) = 16.7$, $p < .001$. Significant interactions with language were obtained for each of the three cues: language × order, $F(4,216) = 13.6$, $p < .001$, language × animacy, $F(4,216) = 7.2$, $p < .001$, and language × stress, $F(4,216) = 3.2$, $p < .05$. Two of the cues were also used differently by different age groups. There were significant interactions for age × word order, $F(6,216) = 5.3$, $p < .001$, and age × stress, $F(6,216) = 2.4$, $p < .05$.

In order to illuminate crosslinguistic and developmental differences, separate analyses of each language and age group were performed. The results of these analyses, shown in Table 12.4, indicate that word order is significant for all groups but the Italian 2.5-year-olds, animacy is significant for all groups but the English 2.5-year-olds and the French 2.5- and 3.5-year-olds, and stress was significant only for English 4.5- and 5.5-year-olds, and French 2.5- and 3.5-year-olds. Turning to the more interesting statistic of the percent variance accounted for by each cue, we see that the percent variance accounted for by any cue for the younger speakers in each language tends to be very low – indicating that children are just beginning to use the cues. However, in the older groups, each language demonstrates its own developmental pattern. English speakers increase the strength of the word order cue; French speakers increase word order, and a bit later, noun animacy; Italian speakers increase noun animacy. In comparing the percent variance accounted for by these cues in this experiment to the adult data in the previous experiment, we see that English and Italian learners start to manifest the adult pattern early on, whereas French learners are acting somewhat differently than the adult French pattern. This pattern of later development in French may be tied to particular properties about the validities of these cues in French (see Kail, this volume; McDonald, this volume).

MLE Analysis

Table 12.5 gives the estimates derived from the five-parameter multiplicative model for each language and age group. These estimates correspond to the trends in the cue strength development derived from the variance figures in the ANOVAs. The younger subjects tend to have parameter estimates close to .5, indicating that cue use was not much different from neutral. The older subjects clearly show language specific cue strength development. English speakers show an increasing preference for the first noun in the NVN word order; by contrast, there is no real preference in the VNN and NNV word orders for children in this age range. The strong second noun preference in these latter

Table 12.4. *Main effects from ANOVAs for each language and age group*

	d.f.	Age 2.5		Age 3.5		Age 4.5		Age 5.5	
		F	% variance	F	% variance	F	% variance	F	% variance
English									
Word order	2,18	4.1*	3	26.4‡	18	29.8‡	31	19.1‡	34
Noun animacy	2,18	.2	1	3.3	6	16.6‡	7	4.3*	4
Stress	2,18	2.3	1	.9	0	3.8*	1	3.8*	1
French									
Word order	2,18	5.8*	6	17.4‡	16	24.7‡	22	31.6‡	32
Noun animacy	2,18	.1	0	.6	1	16.2‡	11	11.7‡	11
Stress	2,18	8.3†	4	8.4†	3	2.5	1	.6	0
Italian									
Word order	2,18	2.5	1	14.2‡	5	13.0‡	9	13.7‡	10
Noun animacy	2,18	5.0*	15	13.3‡	34	25.5‡	32	19.1‡	31
Stress	2,18	2.5	1	.1	0	.3	0	.2	0

Note: * p < .05. † p < .005. ‡ p < .001.

Table 12.5. *Parameter estimates for English, French, and Italian children*

	NVN word order	VNN word order	NNV word order	Noun animacy	Contrastive stress
English 2.5	.6372	.4974	.4610	.5225	.5315
English 3.5	.8436	.5288	.4830	.6339	.5220
English 4.5	.9490	.4203	.5496	.6501	.5818
English 5.5	.9759	.4509	.4511	.6488	.5639
French 2.5	.6163	.4114	.3979	.5097	.5988
French 3.5	.8135	.6089	.4226	.5759	.5873
French 4.5	.9400	.8724	.5060	.7581	.5500
French 5.5	.9818	.6766	.3955	.7571	.4571
Italian 2.5	.6051	.4736	.5380	.6980	.5280
Italian 3.5	.7717	.4532	.5726	.8299	.5008
Italian 4.5	.9235	.6787	.7062	.8183	.5179
Italian 5.5	.9457	.6766	.8124	.8649	.5064

orders exhibited by English-speaking adults has not yet emerged (see Bates & MacWhinney, this volume, and McDonald, this volume, for comments on late developments). French speakers develop a strong first noun preference in the NVN word order, a weaker first noun preference in the VNN order, and a weak second noun preference in the NNV order. A preference for the animate noun develops in the older children. Italian speakers develop a first noun preference

Table 12.6. *Fit of English, French, and Italian models to each language and age group*

	Adult models					
	English		French		Italian	
	RMSD	r^2	RMSD	r^2	RMSD	r^2
English 2.5	.34	.37	.28	.04	.36	.02
English 3.5	.31	.76	.23	.31	.29	.34
English 4.5	.32	.69	.28	.25	.32	.27
English 5.5	.28	.83	.30	.20	.33	.24
French 2.5	.33	.31	.31	.04	.39	.02
French 3.5	.35	.47	.29	.10	.36	.07
French 4.5	.45	.37	.31	.22	.34	.26
French 5.5	.35	.67	.29	.25	.31	.34
Italian 2.5	.38	.15	.15	.74	.22	.73
Italian 3.5	.38	.28	.12	.84	.14	.85
Italian 4.5	.44	.39	.19	.78	.22	.80
Italian 5.5	.46	.34	.20	.77	.22	.82

for all word orders, although it is strongest in the NVN order, and also develop a strong preference for the animate noun.

Using MLE, the performance of these young speakers of English, French, and Italian can be compared to adult performance in these languages by forcing the adult parameter estimates (Table 12.2) on to the child data. The goodness-of-fit statistics will indicate how closely each child group resembles each adult model. A low RMSD indicates good fit to the individual cells, whereas a high r^2 indicates a strong correlation in relative cell means. The RMSDs and r^2s for each group of children fit by each adult language model is given in Table 12.6. The data from the English-speaking children yield a poor absolute fit under all three adult models, receiving RMSDs in the .23–.36 range. However, the younger English speakers have fairly high r^2's under the adult English model, indicating that, although the absolute cell means are off, the relative cue strengths the English-speaking children are developing are appropriate to English. The data from the French children also receives poor absolute fit under all adult models, and the r^2's indicate a better relative fit to the adult English data than to the adult French data. This latter fact reflects the development of strong word order strengths in the young French speakers; the strength of these cues is not maintained by adults (see Chapter 1 and Kail, this volume, for an explanation of this developmental trend). Finally, the young Italians receive both reasonably low RMSDs and high r^2s under both the adult Italian and adult French models, indicating they are developing appropriate cue strengths, both relatively and absolutely, for their language.

This section has demonstrated a close agreement between the strength of a cue usage metric derived from ANOVA and that measured more directly and accurately by MLE. We turn now to some of the unique advantages of MLE. In the following sections we illustrate how MLE can be used with individual subjects, and how it can be used to compare actual performance to various estimations of cue strength.

Bilingual Data

In certain populations, important differences in individual performance may be obscured when data is collapsed into groups. This is especially true when subjects within a group do not display homogeneous behavior. One such special population in which the performance of individual subjects is of concern is the population of bilingual speakers. Previous research has shown that bilingual speakers may initially use first language strategies in interpreting the second language. With sufficient second language exposure, these speakers may shift to appropriate second language strategies (Bates & MacWhinney, 1981; Gass, 1987; Kilborn & Cooreman, 1987; McDonald, 1987b; Kilborn & Ito, this volume). Because individuals do vary in the extent to which they use first or second language processing strategies, it is desirable to be able to analyze the performance of individual bilinguals at various stages of second language acquisition. Using an MLE procedure allows us to compute parameter estimates for each individual subject, and to compare the performance of individuals to that of both first and second language control groups.

The data analyzed in this section come from a study on actor role assignment by German-English bilinguals (Kilborn, 1987). Subjects included 12 native English-speaking controls who performed the task in English, and 15 German-English bilinguals (native language German; second language English) who performed the task in both German (German control) and English (second language group). The stimuli were formed by crossing the cues of word order, noun animacy, and verb agreement as before, except that both animacy and agreement contained an additional level, one in which neither noun agreed with the cue (i.e., two inanimate nouns for the animacy cue, or two plural nouns and a singular verb, or vice versa for the agreement cue). This yielded a $3 \times 4 \times 4$ design. The subjects performed the task under two conditions – in one they listened to the sentences, in the other they read them. Performance in both versions tended to be similar, and since the previous studies reported here used auditory presentation, only the data from the auditory task are used here.

The current experimental design is larger than previous ones (i.e., a $3 \times 4 \times 4$ instead of a $3 \times 3 \times 3$). In the expanded design, the animacy factor included a level where neither noun was animate, and the agreement factor included a level where neither noun agreed with the verb. The number of sentences per cell heard by each subject in this experiment was over twice that of earlier experiments. This increase in the number of stimuli and the complete balancing of the cells of design were done in order to allow us to create MLE models for individual subjects' data that would have a low RMSD. This plan worked out and at least half of the models for individual control subjects had RMSDs less than .10.

With this new design we are still able to apply the reduced five-parameter model. Parameters are entered into the equations for the old conditions as before: When a cue favors only one noun, the parameter is entered for this noun, whereas 1 minus this parameter is entered for the other noun. When a cue favors both the first and second nouns (e.g., when both nouns are animate), the parameter and its complement are entered for both the first and second noun resulting in the cancellation of this parameter from this equation. Therefore, the cue actually has no influence on the decision. In the new condition, when a cue doesn't favor either noun (e.g., both noun inanimate), the parameter is not entered into the equation at all, again resulting in no effect of the cue on the decision. This application of the five-parameter model assumes that performance will be similar in cells where a particular cue either favors both nouns or neither noun as actor. This assumption is supported for the current experiment – if one examines the group means for these equivalent cells, they are indeed very similar (Kilborn, 1987). However, individual subjects may show some deviations from this pattern, and although we use the reduced model in our individual analyses below, some information is lost that would be retained in the full-parameter model. (See Kilborn, 1987, for analyses with the full-parameter model.)

The low RMSD values we attained for individual monolingual control subjects in these analyses address a potential criticism of the Competition Model. One could argue that the probabilistic cue interactions we find throughout the work discussed in this volume holds only on the level of group data and that individual subjects behave in a deterministic fashion. However, even on the level of the individual subject our MLE analyses show the same pattern of probabilistic cue interaction. It is not the case that some subjects show deterministic effects for word order with others showing deterministic effects for agreement or animacy. Instead the cue weights for individual subjects are slight variations on the overall pattern of probabilistic interactions. Indeed, it would have been strange to have found different types of monolingual subjects processing their native language in radically different ways.

MLE Group Analyses

We first performed group analyses of the data to see if the performance of the second language group as a whole did indeed lie between that of the two control groups. Table 12.7 gives the parameter estimates for the monolingual English

Table 12.7. *Parameter estimates for English control, German control, and German-English English performance*

	NVN word order	VNN word order	NNV word order	Noun animacy	Verb agreement
English control	.9474	.1328	.1649	.6027	.6004
German control	.6586	.5562	.6259	.6590	.8391
Second language English	.7378	.5125	.4015	.7465	.7385

Table 12.8. *Parameter estimates for English performance by individual German-English bilinguals*

Subj	Fluency	NVN word order	VNN word order	NNV word order	Noun animacy	Verb agreement	English RMSD	r^2	German RMSD	r^2
15	24.5	.9671	.9670	.9692	.9999	.9675	.62	.01	.41	.22
12	30.5	.6775	.4830	.6097	.9740	.7185	.49	.03	.32	.28
4	30.5	.8316	.7967	.8815	.9986	.9999	.57	.01	.25	.77
8	31.0	.9786	.9251	.9455	.9367	.9978	.56	.04	.23	.79
9	31.5	.8019	.6939	.5549	.9765	.9999	.54	.02	.23	.80
5	32.5	.8018	.7992	.7989	.9955	.4998	.57	.01	.41	.09
7	33.0	.4632	.5145	.6285	.9519	.9754	.54	.00	.24	.73
11	34.0	.9888	.5750	.7020	.6633	.9885	.47	.19	.24	.69
2	34.5	.9753	.6248	.0844	.5007	.4703	.32	.53	.45	.00
14	35.0	.5336	.4677	.4677	.8986	.5000	.45	.02	.34	.11
1	37.0	.9795	.0443	.0120	.7102	.7987	.12	.96	.51	.03
6	39.5	.9004	.9004	.9004	.9919	.9999	.61	.01	.29	.75
3	41.0	.9991	.9999	.0001	.9630	.9056	.50	.22	.53	.00
10	42.0	.9999	.0820	.0199	.5884	.6583	.13	.96	.54	.01
13	46.0	.2764	.0072	.0069	.5103	.7813	.41	.45	.54	.09

group (English control), the bilingual group in German (German control), and the bilingual group in English (second language English). As before, English speakers show a strong first noun preference in NVN sentences, a strong second noun preference in VNN and NNV sentences, and weak preferences for the animate noun and the noun that agrees with the verb. The German controls show a slight first noun preference for all word orders, a slight preference for the animate noun, and a stronger preference for the noun that agrees in number with the verb. The second language speakers of English show a pattern of cue strengths in between that of their first and second language control groups, with the exception of a stronger preference for the animate noun. Thus, the second language learners as a group appear to be moving from using first language weights to using more appropriate second language weights.

MLE Individual Subjects Analyses

The individual subjects in this experiment differed in their exposure to and ability in the second language. A composite "fluency index" for each individual was formed by combining years of second language exposure, both naturalistically and in school, and subjective self-ratings of speaking, reading, writing, and comprehension. Values of this fluency index are given in Table 12.8 for each subject. Also shown in Table 12.8 are the individual parameter estimates for each bilingual's English performance. An examination of the table shows different patterns of parameter estimates at different fluency levels. Less fluent subjects tend to have equal weights on all three word order cues, usually high weights, indicating a first noun preference for all orders. More fluent subjects have different weights in the different word orders, generally a high weight for the NVN order, indicating a correct first noun preference for these types of English sentences, and an extremely low weight on either or both the VNN and NNV orders, indicating a correct second noun preference for these types of sentences in English. (Recall that neutral cue use in the model is given by .5, therefore weights below .5 indicate a preference for the opposite noun.) The less fluent subjects also tend to have high verb agreement weights; the more fluent subjects tend to have more moderate weights. This indicates a lessening of the use of the verb agreement cue, as is appropriate in English.

Also included in Table 12.8 are the RMSDs and r^2s for each subject fit to both the English control and German control parameter estimates. Note that the less fluent subjects tend to have better fits to the German model (lower RMSDs and higher r^2s), whereas more fluent subjects tend to have better fits to the English model. Indeed, the fluency index correlates with these goodness-of-fit statistics. The fluency index correlates negatively with the RMSD of the English model, $r = -.50$, $p < .06$, and positively with the r^2, $r = .56$, $p < .05$, indicating a better fit (lower RMSD, and higher r^2) with increasing English fluency. The index also correlates positively with the RMSD of the German model, $r = .59$, $p < .05$, and negatively with the r^2, $r = -.38$, n.s., indicating a worse fit to the German model with increasing English fluency.

Kilborn (1987) also reports a significant correlation between achievement of nativelike performance on another second language processing task and RMSDs in the actor role assignment task. The other task consisted of detecting a target word in second language prose, a task that involves the integration of syntactic and semantic information. More nativelike performance on this task involved quick use of these types of information and resulted in more rapid detection of the targets. The fact that RMSD scores are not only correlated with a static measure of fluency (the fluency index), but also with nativelike performance on dynamic second language processing tasks supports the general utility of this goodness-of-fit statistic.

Aphasia Data

Another population of interest for MLE analysis is that of aphasics – people who have various problems with linguistic processing, usually due to some kind of trauma or injury to the brain. It is of particular interest to examine which aspects of linguistic processing are damaged in aphasics compared to control populations, and whether this damage is similar across different languages. Accordingly, in this section, we analyze data from Broca's aphasics in several languages, first comparing groups and individual aphasics to normal controls, and then comparing aphasic cue usage to several theoretical models of processing deficit.

The data used in this section comes from Bates, Friederici, and Wulfeck (1987b). An earlier analysis of these data was presented by Bates, McDonald, and MacWhinney (1986). Fifty-seven subjects participated in the experiment: eight native English-speaking Broca's aphasics, twelve college-aged English-speaking controls, seven native German-speaking Broca's aphasics, ten college-aged German controls, ten native Italian-speaking Broca's aphasics, and ten college-aged Italian controls. These subjects were asked to determine the actor in sentences formed by crossing three levels of word order (NVN, VNN, and NNV), three levels of noun animacy (both nouns animate, first noun animate and second noun inanimate, first noun inanimate and second noun animate), and three levels of verb agreement (both nouns agree, first agrees and second disagrees, first disagrees and second agrees). The English, German, and Italian vocabulary were basically translations of each other, with a few word substitutions made in German.

MLE Group Analysis

The data for subjects in each group were averaged and then fit to the reduced five-parameter model. The parameter estimates are given in Table 12.9. The English control group manifests a strong first noun preference in the NVN word order, and fairly strong second noun preferences in the other word orders, as well as showing a mild preference for the animate noun and a moderate preference for the noun that agrees with the verb. German controls show a strong first noun preference in all word orders, a mild preference for the animate noun and a strong preference for the noun that agrees with the verb. Italian controls show a strong first noun preference in the NVN word order, and more moderate first noun preferences in the other two orders, as well as strong preferences for the animate noun and the noun that agrees with the verb.

In general, the aphasic groups tend to have more neutral parameters than their native language control groups – that is, the parameters are closer to .5. Although the aphasics do differ from their control groups, some language-specific information is preserved in each group. English aphasics maintain

Table 12.9. *Parameter estimates for English, German, and Italian controls and aphasics*

	NVN word order	VNN word order	NNV word order	Noun animacy	Noun–verb agreement
English control	.9056	.1120	.2120	.6242	.7441
English Broca's	.9216	.2803	.5128	.6928	.5343
German control	.8605	.8806	.8786	.6224	.9436
German Broca's	.9382	.8181	.7563	.4998	.6206
Italian control	.9044	.7150	.6939	.8987	.9972
Italian Broca's	.6713	.5508	.4994	.6739	.7255

Table 12.10. *Fit of groups to control group models*

	English		German		Italian	
	RMSD	r^2	RMSD	r^2	RMSD	r^2
English Broca's	.24	.71	.44	.00	.46	.05
German Broca's	.50	.43	.31	.13	.47	.23
Italian Broca's	.33	.26	.26	.59	.26	.76

the strong first noun preference in NVN sentences, a damaged second noun preference in VNN sentences, and a slight preference for the animate noun. German aphasics maintain a general first noun preference and a damaged preference for the noun that agrees with the verb. Italian aphasics show damage to all their cues, but still manifest a first noun preference in NVN sentences, and moderate preferences for the animate noun and the noun that agrees with the verb. To see the extent of language-specific cue preservation, the parameter weights for each control group were forced onto the aphasic groups. The resultant goodness-of-fit statistics are given in Table 12.10. Although no RMSD is really low, each aphasic group finds its lowest RMSD under its own language control model. The best correlations are also given by the same language control, except for the German Broca's, who find a higher correlation under the English model because of their reduced use of the morphological noun–verb agreement cue. All in all, however, the results of the group analysis indicate language-specific information is largely preserved.

MLE Individual Subjects Analyses

Parameter estimates for individual aphasic subjects were also derived with the five-parameter model. Although the RMSD figures for these models are much higher than those for the subjects in Kilborn's bilingual study, part of the loss in RMSD power can be attributed to the fact that the aphasic subjects heard far fewer sentences than the Kilborn subjects. With fewer data points to estimate, it is more difficult to get a low RMSD for this group.

The weights for each subject are shown in Table 12.11. An examination of these cue weights shows that some strong cues are maintained by all or nearly all individual subjects. For example, the first noun preference in NVN word order in English is strongly evident in each English aphasic. Similarly, the general first noun preference for all word orders is evident in most German aphasics. Other cues show varying degrees of damage in the different individuals. For example, the strong noun–verb agreement cue in German is maintained by three individuals, neutralized in three individuals, and used in an opposite way by one individual. Similarly, the agreement cue in Italian is maintained by three individuals, and maintained at a weaker or neutral strength by the remaining seven subjects. Thus, we see a great deal of individual variability in the ability to maintain those language-specific cues such as agreement which are susceptible to damage in aphasics. It would be interesting to try to correlate the ability to maintain such susceptible cues with the severity of other aphasic symptoms.

To see how well individual subjects maintained language-specific information, the performance of individual aphasics was compared to each control group model by forcing the parameter estimates of each control group on each individual subject. The resultant RMSDs and r^2s are given in Table 12.12. Each English-speaking Broca's aphasic is best fit by the control English model with regard to both RMSD and r^2. Six of the seven German-speaking aphasics have the smallest RMSD under the German control model; in general, r^2s are low for this group, and the best correlation for an individual is spread over the control groups. Best fits to the individual Italian Broca's occur in each of the control groups; however, four out of ten RMSDs and six out of ten r^2s are best under the Italian model. The poor correlations of the German subjects and the poor fits of the Italian subjects to the Italian control model arise from differences in the degree of damage to the noun–verb agreement cue for individual subjects. Subjects that maintained the strength of this cue are generally better fit by native language controls; subjects who lose the strength of the cue may be better fit by other control groups. Thus, this analysis of individual aphasics shows that for the most part, language-specific information is preserved on an individual basis. Losses are most evident on the morphological cue of noun–verb agreement.

Theories of Aphasia

There are several theories about the kind of linguistic deficit suffered by an aphasic person. These include agrammatism, which should lead to the loss of all syntactic and morphological devices, and closed class damage, which should lead to loss or weakening of freestanding function words and bound grammatical

Table 12.11. *Parameter estimates for individual aphasic subjects*

	NVN word order	VNN word order	NNV word order	Noun animacy	Noun–verb agreement
English Broca's					
1	.9106	.0001	.5014	.6327	.4797
2	.9287	.3013	.5797	.8525	.5494
3	.9999	.1519	.3614	.8148	.7367
4	.9999	.1915	.9043	.9882	.9301
5	.8429	.3674	.3681	.7529	.4898
6	.8178	.4477	.4425	.5078	.3792
7	.8398	.3254	.3836	.6294	.5052
8	.9989	.1379	.7126	.7200	.7297
German Broca's					
1	.8372	.8796	.6322	.3310	.5849
2	.9983	.9788	.9948	.6143	.9901
3	.9999	.6111	.3889	.5000	.5000
4	.9617	.9617	.6093	.7598	.5200
5	.9999	.9897	.9902	.3745	.9901
6	.9993	.9872	.9999	.5001	.0614
7	.9999	.9954	.9999	.0314	.9686
Italian Broca's					
1	.8535	.4312	.5453	.7844	.6479
2	.8183	.7175	.5934	.9025	.7103
3	.8340	.4687	.3990	.8931	.6496
4	.3686	.3381	.5057	.7362	.6917
5	.8227	.0106	.1776	.9979	.9999
6	.6080	.5567	.4418	.4443	.5003
7	.9999	.9988	.6563	.7338	.9999
8	.7395	.8074	.5577	.3883	.4135
9	.9526	.9533	.5000	.9529	.9999
10	.5475	.3736	.4543	.5829	.6896

morphemes. With the use of the MLE procedure, and a modification to the weights of the various control groups, it is possible to test the predictions of these theories against the performance of individual aphasics. That is, we can selectively damage the different cues strengths of the normal model, and can see how well this mimics aphasic behavior by fitting patients with these new values.

Five different variants of the native language control group model were fit to each individual aphasic subject. These five models included *normal performance* with native language control weights unaltered, *agrammatism* with the animacy cue left intact and the agreement and word order cues set to neutral, *closed class loss* with animacy and word order intact and the agreement cue neutral, *closed class weakened* with animacy and word order intact and the agreement

Table 12.12. *Fit of individuals to control group models*

	English control		German control		Italian control	
	RMSD	r^2	RMSD	r^2	RMSD	r^2
English Broca's						
1	.31†	.50†	.59	.00	.60	.00
2	.43†	.27†	.53	.00	.55	.04
3	.31†	.59†	.54	.01	.54	.06
4	.44†	.40†	.46	.01	.50	.10
5	.35†	.31†	.52	.00	.52	.03
6	.41†	.14†	.52	.02	.58	.01
7	.34†	.34†	.50	.01	.53	.02
8	.36†	.47†	.52	.01	.53	.06
German Broca's						
1	.54	.03	.42†	.01	.50	.07†
2	.56	.04	.30†	.27†	.46	.23
3	.38†	.42†	.48	.01	.55	.00
4	.55	.06†	.42†	.01	.54	.02
5	.55	.20	.33†	.24†	.49	.23
6	.66	.02	.43†	.04	.62	.06†
7	.63	.06†	.41†	.02	.58	.04
Italian Broca's						
1	.39†	.26†	.43	.06	.46	.11
2	.48	.08	.43	.13	.43†	.23†
3	.45†	.14	.48	.10	.46	.17†
4	.45	.04	.48	.15	.44†	.23†
5	.47	.16	.39	.59	.27†	.72†
6	.47†	.01†	.49	.00	.53	.00
7	.49	.20	.24†	.67	.26	.73†
8	.52	.00	.44†	.02†	.55	.01
9	.51	.08	.28	.81	.14†	.91†
10	.41†	.10	.42	.26†	.44	.19

Note: † = best fit to the three models

cue halfway between normal and neutral, and *normalcy through noise* with all cues set halfway between normal and neutral. The goodness-of-fit statistics for each subject to each model are given in Table 12.13.

For the English aphasics the smallest RMSDs occur for the normal model, or the normal through noise model. The highest correlations occur for the normal and closed class models. Thus, English aphasics are preserving much language-specific information, with some general weakening of all cues, with agreement being the most susceptible. For the German aphasics the smallest RMSDs occur under the closed class models, and the best correlations, which tend not to be very good in any case, are distributed over many of the models. The German Broca's evidence a selective loss of the agreement cue. For the

Table 12.13. *Goodness-of-fit for each aphasic to theoretical models*

	Normal		Agrammatic		Closed class loss		Closed class weakened		Normalcy through noise	
	RMSD	r^2	RMSD	r^2	RMSD	r^2	RMSD	r^2	RMSD	r^2
English Broca's										
1	.31	.50	.43	.01	.28†	.59†	.29	.57	.34	.42
2	.43	.27	.41†	.27	.43	.29	.43	.30†	.41†	.27
3	.31†	.59	.43	.04	.32	.58	.31†	.60†	.34	.55
4	.44	.40†	.41†	.24	.46	.35	.45	.38	.41†	.39
5	.35	.31†	.34	.18	.36	.30	.36	.31†	.32†	.30
6	.41	.14	.36	.00	.39	.21†	.40	.18	.35†	.10
7	.34	.34	.36	.06	.33	.40†	.33	.38	.31†	.35
8	.36†	.47†	.44	.01	.38	.42	.37	.45	.36†	.42
German Broca's										
1	.42	.01	.44	.05†	.35	.05†	.34†	.00	.35	.02
2	.30	.27†	.42	.06	.28	.04	.25†	.23	.29	.23
3	.48	.01	.39	.00	.40	.02†	.40	.02†	.38†	.00
4	.42	.01	.42	.08†	.31†	.04	.31†	.05	.35	.04
5	.33	.24†	.47	.03	.27	.06	.25†	.09	.32	.16
6	.43	.04†	.49	.00	.17†	.00	.22	.03	.38	.03
7	.41	.02	.51	.05	.24†	.06†	.26	.00	.37	.02
Italian Broca's										
1	.46	.11	.33	.32	.31	.37	.30†	.40†	.31	.29
2	.43	.23	.32	.44	.30	.52	.28†	.59†	.31	.42
3	.46	.17	.32	.45	.33	.52	.32†	.56†	.35	.36
4	.44	.23	.36	.25	.43	.28	.39	.43†	.35†	.37
5	.27†	.72†	.48	.11	.51	.12	.43	.35	.35	.66
6	.53	.00	.50	.02†	.47	.00	.47	.00	.41†	.00
7	.26†	.73†	.54	.01	.45	.04	.38	.23	.31	.54
8	.55	.01	.51	.06†	.44	.04	.45	.03	.40†	.05
9	.14†	.91†	.52	.02	.51	.03	.42	.26	.31	.66
10	.44	.19	.44	.04	.47	.04	.43	.13	.35†	.24†

Note: † = best fit to the five models

Italian aphasics, the best RMSDs and correlations occur under the normal or normal with noise model, and the closed class weakened model. This indicates that these Italian aphasics preserve much language-specific information, and have either a weakening of the agreement cue, or a general weakening of all cues.

In general, individual aphasics in all languages appear to retain a great deal of language-specific information. Damage to cue strength usually occurs as a general weakening in all cues, or selective weakening of the agreement cues. The agrammatic model, where both word order and agreement cues are lost, is a bad model of the individual subject's performance.

Developmental Data and Cue Validity Estimates

In the introductory section of this chapter (see also McDonald, this volume), we mentioned that the Competition Model hypothesized a connection between cue strength and cue validity. This connection has been supported by a wide variety of empirical data. In addition, the model postulates a developmental shift from basing cue strength on overall cue validity (the validity of a cue over all sentence types in a language) to basing cue strength on conflict cue validity (the validity of a cue only on sentences involving conflicting cues). If one can get performance-independent estimates of overall validity and conflict validity, it would be possible to use them in the MLE procedure in order to predict performance. That is, performance could be predicted from distributional properties of each language. These predictions could then be compared to actual performance. This section examines the predictive power of MLE models in connection with cue validity estimates.

The data used in this section comes from an experiment in which native Dutch speakers were asked to determine the actor in simple Dutch NVN sentences containing cooperating and conflicting noun animacy and case inflection cues; word order was constant (McDonald, 1986). Subjects were 61 native Dutch speakers distributed over seven age groups: 7 second and third graders, 7 fourth graders, 7 fifth graders, 8 sixth graders, 11 seventh, eighth and ninth graders, 12 tenth, eleventh and twelfth graders, and 9 adults. The stimuli consisted of a full crossing of three levels of animacy (both nouns animate, first noun animate and second inanimate, and first noun inanimate and second noun animate) and three levels of case inflection (neither noun inflected, first noun favored, and second noun favored).

In order to predict performance by the younger speakers, estimates of the overall validities of the cues of SVO word order, noun animacy, and case inflection were derived from text counts; that is, over a corpus of Dutch sentences, the proportion of time each cue was both present and correctly indicated the actor was calculated. In order to predict adult performance, estimates of conflict validities for the three cues were calculated from estimates of the frequencies of various types of conflict sentences in Dutch. (Conflict validities were also directly calculated over the conflict sentences available in the corpus, but since these were limited in number, estimates of the relative frequencies of these types of sentences were gathered from native speakers and used to confirm the measure.) Estimates of both overall and conflict validity are shown in Table 12.14. Note that noun animacy has the highest overall validity, whereas case inflection has the highest conflict validity. Thus, we would expect noun animacy to be the first cue acquired, but case inflection to have the highest cue strength for adult speakers of Dutch.

In order to see if these measures of validity can predict performance, the

Table 12.14. *Estimates of overall and conflict validity in Dutch*

	Overall validity	Conflict validity
SVO word order	.35	.48
Noun animacy	.70	.36
Case inflection	.46	.70

Table 12.15. *Goodness-of-fit of overall and conflict validity models to various aged Dutch groups*

Multiplicative model with untransformed validities

	overall validity		conflict validity	
	RMSD	r^2	RMSD	r^2
Grades 2 and 3	.41	.78	.43	.16
Grade 4	.43	.74	.46	.24
Grade 5	.53	.48	.47	.04
Grade 6	.50	.43	.44	.00
Grades 7, 8, and 9	.44	.39	.40	.00
Grades 10, 11, and 12	.46	.20	.39	.07
Adults	.47	.01	.34	.34

Multiplicative model with transformed validities

	overall validity		conflict validity	
	RMSD	r^2	RMSD	r^2
Grades 2 & 3	.19	.86	.26	.23
Grade 4	.22	.71	.30	.13
Grade 5	.31	.78	.30	.36
Grade 6	.27	.91	.25	.64
Grades 7, 8, & 9	.20	.89	.19	.66
Grades 10, 11, & 12	.20	.78	.15	.83
Adults	.25	.47	.09	.96

parameters in the reduced multiplicative model were first fixed to overall validity values, and then to conflict validity values, and fit to the performance of all age groups. The goodness-of-fit statistics are shown in Table 12.15. Looking first at the r^2s, we see, as predicted, high values for the younger speakers with the overall validity values, and a higher value for the adults with conflict rather than overall validity. Thus, the performance of Dutch speakers with increasing age does reflect, relatively, a shift from overall to conflict validity weights. However, an examination of the RMSDs shows poor fits – indicating that the absolute levels of the parameters are off. That is, setting the parameters directly to the validity estimates does not give a good absolute fit.

However, the Competition Model only claims that cue strengths should reflect cue validities and does not claim identity between the two. Therefore, transforming the validities before putting them into the model may yield better fits. As a first attempt at this, validity values were transformed from the range 0 to 1 to the range .5 to 1. (Because validities were always calculated for the side of the cue that was more likely to be chosen as the actor – i.e., validities were calculated for noun animacy rather than noun inanimacy, this transformation moved values into the range that was positive in the multiplicative model. Recall that neutral cue use is indicated by .5 in this model.) The resultant fits for all age groups, when parameters are set to, first, the transformed overall validities and, then, the transformed conflict validities, are also shown in Table 12.15. The r^2s tell a similar, though better story than they did with the untransformed values – relative fit is better for the younger learners with the transformed overall validities; it is better for the older speakers with the transformed conflict validities. In addition, the absolute fits, as indicated by the RMSDs, are much improved, especially for the older speakers' fit with transformed conflict validities. RMSDs here certainly fall within an acceptable range for group fits.

In this section, we have shown how performance-independent estimates of parameters can be used to predict actual performance in conjunction with the MLE model. Consonant with the Competition Model, parameters reflecting cue validities give good fits to the data.

Conclusion

In this chapter we have used several different experiments on linguistic role assignment to illustrate the uses of the maximum likelihood procedure. We compared MLE to ANOVA, noting how the analyses confirmed and complemented one another. ANOVA has the advantage of detecting statistical significance in cue usage, and it is possible to derive a measure of the strength of cue usage from the percent variance accounted for by each cue. MLE, though not computing significance, gives direct estimates of relative cue strength, and provides goodness-of-fit statistics between the predicted and actual data. MLE requires the specification of a model of cue combination. Given such a model, both prediction of data and comparison between groups is possible in MLE, but not in ANOVA.

In addition, we noted two other types of comparisons that can be done via the MLE model. First, one can analyze the data of individual subjects. Our analyses showed that the probabilistic cue interactions stipulated by the Competition Model hold for individuals as well as groups. The individual MLE analyses are also useful for populations where variability in performance is large. Individual performance can be correlated to other metrics such as language fluency or amount of linguistic exposure, to detect systematic changes in cue strengths. Second, it is possible to use the MLE procedure to compare individual or group performance to theoretically derived models, whether they are parameters from a normal control group, selective alterations to control group parameters, or parameters set to independently derived measures such as cue validity.

A fundamental step in performing MLE analyses is the selection of an appropriate set of parameters. Most of the analyses in this chapter were carried out with the reduced parameter multiplicative model of cue combination. Other models do exist, such as the full-parameter multiplicative model or an additive model, as presented in McDonald (1987b). Each model has relative advantages and disadvantages, and only further work can tell us which one more accurately depicts the process. Current advantages of the reduced parameter multiplicative model are that it gives one rather than many values for symmetrical cues, and parameter estimates are easy to interpret. The full-parameter multiplicative model can get better fits than the reduced model, at the cost of having more parameters. If there are strong interactions between cues and position, that is, if cues do not act symmetrically, then the full-parameter model will give better fits. However, it is somewhat more difficult to interpret the meaning of the parameters estimated under the full model. The additive model has the advantage of operating on the same number of parameters as the reduced multiplicative, and parameters in the model seem to be directly compatible with independent cue validity estimates.

We have performed all our analyses using the STEPIT procedure of Chandler (1969), along with routines developed by Massaro and Cohen (1983). Another maximum likelihood estimation program of which we are aware is the VAR-BRUL procedure of Rousseau and Sankoff (1978). However, this program is somewhat less flexible than the STEPIT program, in that it does not allow one to specify a model of the cue combination process. Rather, the model is fixed and appears to be similar to the full-parameter multiplicative model.

In summary, we see the MLE technique as a useful technique, particularly for the linguistic role assignment problems discussed here. It complements the kind of information derived from an ANOVA, and has more theoretical depth, in that it requires a model of the cue combination process in order to work. Since the model chosen was one compatible with the tenets of the Competition Model, the analyses also help in exploring and supporting the claims of the model.

13   Competition and Connectionism

Brian MacWhinney

This last chapter will examine ways of using connectionist networks to formalize the Competition Model. The application of connectionist models to language acquisition and processing is a very new field and many of the current formulations are still rather crude. However there are many extremely promising aspects of connectionist work that map in quite well with the perspective developed within the Competition Model. Connectionist modeling allows us to formalize the principles of the Competition Model in a way that yields exact predictions for acquisition and processing. Just as the previous chapter exploited the formal techniques of mathematical modeling to predict data, this chapter uses connectionist networks to make explicit statements about how learning and processing should operate.

The paper divides essentially into three major parts. The first presents a fairly detailed set of findings from actual simulations of the acquisition of morphological systems in German and Hungarian. The second major section is far more speculative in nature, presenting a preliminary general characterization of ways of dealing with the acquisition of word meanings and ambiguity resolution in connectionist models. The third section examines ways in which our models of semantic processing can be helpful in understanding syntactic processing. Here we examine some problems that have been considered insurmountable for connectionist approaches (Pinker & Mehler, 1988) and present some concrete ways of overcoming these problems. The reader should be warned at the outset that, whereas the first sections are rich in empirical findings, the later sections are correspondingly rich in speculation.

Morphological learning in German

In order to make correct use of the definite article in German, the child has to learn a complex set of integrations involving the categories of gender, number, and case. Because of the complexities of these interactions, child language researchers such as Braine (1987), MacWhinney (1978), Maratsos and Chalkley (1980), and Pinker (1984) have viewed the acquisition of German declensions as an interesting challenge to language learning theory. This section presents a connectionist simulation that learns to correctly manipulate this system on the basis of simple input data. Before looking at the simulation itself, we need to go over the shape of the learning task confronting the German child.

422

The declensional paradigm in German is configured around three morphosyntactic dimensions.

1. *Number.* As in English, nouns and pronouns in German can vary in *number*, since they can be either singular or plural. For example, the word for "student" is *Student* and the plural form is *Studenten*. Changes in number are also marked on the article or other modifier, so that the singular form "the student" *der Student* becomes plural *die Studenten.*
2. *Case.* The second dimension along which nominals may vary is case. Both nouns and pronouns can be in either the nominative, the accusative, the genitive, or the dative case. For example, the nominative singular form of "student" is *der Student* and its accusative form is *den Student.* Typically, subjects are in the nominative, direct objects are in the accusative, and indirect objects are in the dative. The genitive is used primarily to mark possession. Prepositions can take either the accusative or the dative and sometimes the genitive. Typically, the dative is used when the verb is static and the accusative is used when the verb expresses motion.
3. *Gender.* The third dimension is gender. Nouns can be either masculine, feminine, or neuter. A male student is *der Student* and a female student is *die Studentin.* The choice of *der, die,* or *das* in the nominative reflects choice of one of the three genders for the noun. To some observers (Maratsos & Chalkley, 1980) the assignment of nouns to genders has seemed entirely arbitrary. To others, like Mugdan (1977), the assignment has seemed rule-governed, but exceedingly complex.

The noun itself is primarily marked only for the dimension of number. Gender is not marked on the noun and case is only marked on the noun for the genitive singular and the dative plural of certain nouns. The bulk of the work of marking gender, number, and case is done by the article or adjective that precedes the noun. Simplifying the situation quite a bit, we will focus on the way in which nominal marking is achieved by the selection of the correct form of the definite article. The reader should bear in mind that similar markings can be given by the indefinite article or by a variety of adjectives.

A complete cross of the categories of gender, number, and case would yield 24 possible cells for the full German declensional paradigm. Fortunately for the German child, gender distinctions for the definite article disappear in the plural, reducing the paradigm to 16 distinct cells. The complete paradigm for the German definite article is shown in Table 13.1. Although there are 16 cells in the paradigm, there are only six different forms of the definite article (*der, den, dem, des, die,* and *das*). Each form of the article occurs in at least two different cells of the paradigm, so that no form defines a unique combination of gender, number, and case. For example, the article *der* can mark the masculine nominative singular, the feminine genitive singular, the feminine dative singular, or the genitive plural.

Acquisition of this system can be viewed as a three-dimensional word-class formation problem (Levy, Schlesinger, & Braine, 1987). The three dimensions to be controlled are gender, number, and case. In production, control of this system involves correct selection of both an article and certain endings on the noun. In regard to gender, nouns must be placed into one of three classes. In

Table 13.1. *The German definite article*

| | Singular | | | Plural |
Case	Masculine	Feminine	Neuter	
nominative	der	die	das	die
genitive	des	der	des	der
dative	dem	der	dem	den
accusative	den	die	das	die

regard to number, the child must decide on semantic grounds whether a noun should be singular or plural. If it is to be plural, the child must choose from one of eight pluralization types. In regard to case, the various cues and configurations in the sentence must be grouped together so that they correctly select the case of the noun. In comprehension, the child's task is to use the form of the definite article and the ending on the noun as cues to the correct assignment of the noun to a particular gender, number, and case. Let us look in more detail at each of these three dimensions of this word-class formation problem.

Cues to gender assignment

The simplest way to solve the word-class formation problem for gender is for the learner to find a set of reliable cues that tells him when to assign a noun to a certain class. However, Maratsos and Chalkley (1980) have argued that German gender is so arbitrary that no set of cues would allow a child to assign a noun to its gender class. Why, for example, is "fork" feminine (*die Gabel*), "knife" neuter (*das Messer*), and "spoon" masculine (*der Löffel*)? In fact, recent work has shown that, while the German gender system is complex, it is not as arbitrary as it appears on first analysis. In a series of research reports, Klaus-Michael Köpcke and David Zubin (Zubin & Köpcke, 1981, 1986; Köpcke & Zubin, 1983, 1984; Köpcke, 1982) have conducted a broad survey of various types of German nouns and found that there is a large and powerful set of cues to German gender. Using these cues, Köpcke (1982) was able to correctly assign gender to 90% of the 1466 monosyllabic words listed in the first volume of the Duden (Grebe, 1973). The work of Köpcke and Zubin for German is parallel in many ways to that of Tucker, Lambert, and Rigault (1977) on the prediction of gender in French. Both research groups have found that there are indeed a large number of morphological and phonological cues predicting gender.

Most of the Köpcke–Zubin cues are phonological and morphological. The morphological cues tend to be fairly absolute. For example, if a word has a diminutive ending (i.e., *-lein* or *-chen*), the noun is guaranteed to be of neuter gender. The phonological cues are more probabilistic in nature. For example, although nouns that start with *sh-* followed by a consonant tend to be

Table 13.2. *Pluralization types*

Change	Singular	Plural	Translation
-e	Tag	Tage	days
-(e)n	Blume	Blumen	flowers
-er	Kind	Kinder	children
-s	Radio	Radios	radios
0	Zimmer	Zimmer	rooms
¨	Bruder	Brüder	brothers
¨-e	Hand	Hände	hands
¨-er	Mann	Männer	men

masculine, there are words, such as *die Stadt* and *das Spiel*, that violate this mapping. The use of phonological cues of this type will not guarantee a correct gender classification, but it will improve the chances of a correct classification. Umlauting in the singular tends to predict masculine gender, as do the endings *-el* and *-n*. The presence of a final fricative followed by the phoneme *-t* tends to predict feminine gender, and so on.

Cues to selection of a plural marker

Unlike the gender dimension, which has no single real-world correlate, the contrast between singular and plural number maps directly onto salient features of the external world. Whereas gender is marked only on the modifiers and never on the noun, number is marked most clearly on the noun itself. But this marking is not simple (Köpcke, 1988), since there are eight different ways to mark the plural. The actual choice of one of these eight forms is governed by a set of cues that are almost as complex as those governing gender assignment. For example, the plural of *die Flut* "flood" is *die Fluten*, the plural of *das Gut* "estate" is *die Güter* while the plural of *der Hut* "hat" is *die Hüte*. There are some regularities in the assignment of these plural morphemes to a word based on the suffixes and prefixes on the stem, the mutability of the stem vowel, and the gender and animacy of the noun (Köpcke, 1988). Table 13.2 illustrates the eight possible ways in which nouns may be pluralized.

Cues to case assignment

Like gender, case is marked primarily on the modifiers of the noun. Some nouns take the *-s* ending for the genitive singular and some take the *-n* ending for the dative plural, but often there is no information on the noun that indicates its case. Instead, case is mostly marked by the choice of one of the various forms of the articles or adjectives modifying the noun. Cues to case in German occur on the morphological, syntactic, and semantic level. Morphological cues include the *-(e)s* ending added to singular masculine and neuter words in the genitive case, and the -n ending added to plural nouns in the dative case. Other morphological and syntactic cues include accusative, dative, and genitive prepositions, subject-verb agreement, and word order. Semantic cues include verb meaning and semantic roles. Some cues to case are simple. For example, a word following the dative preposition *mit* is always in the dative case. Other cues are more complex. For example, some prepositions may take the accusative case or the dative case depending on whether the verb in the sentence is a verb of motion (e.g. *Ich lief unter die Brücke* "I ran underneath the-ACC bridge") or a static verb (e.g. *Ich stand unter der Brücke* "I stood under the-DAT bridge").

Empirical data on the learning of German declension

The two most comprehensive experimental studies of the learning of German declension are those done by MacWhinney (1978) and Mills (1986). The findings of these studies agree in large measure and also match well with non-experimental observations such as those of Park (1981) and the various other sources cited in MacWhinney (1978) and Mills (1986). Some of the most important findings of this literature are:

1. *Early acquisition of the nominative.* The empirical literature indicates that children first achieve correct mastery of the use of the nominative case. In particular, use of the nominative for the accusative is frequently reported (MacWhinney, 1978).
2. *Delayed acquisition of the genitive.* Of the four cases, it is the genitive that continues to cause problems for article marking. The dative plural is also a late difficult form, but this difficulty involves nominal marking rather than article selection.
3. *Children often omit the article.* Many of the cues to gender assignment are hard to detect and many are only imperfectly reliable. This forces the child to turn his attention to other ways of controlling gender categorization. One simple way of solving the problem is to omit the article. In fact, early on, omission of the article is very common and even later on, the article may be omitted when the child is in doubt about the correct gender assignment.
4. *Children often overgeneralize one gender.* Mills (1986) observed a tendency to overgeneralize the use of the feminine gender.
5. *Children make early use of the highly frequent -e cue.* Mills (1986) examined the role of some of the Köpcke-Zubin cues in the acquisition of German gender and found evidence for their use. MacWhinney (1978) conducted his work before the Köpcke-Zubin cues were available, but his experiment still included some of the cues. Both Mills (1986) and MacWhinney (1978) found early acquisition of the most highly available and reliable of the cues – the presence of final -e as a cue to feminine gender.
6. *Children make use of highly reliable cues.* MacWhinney (1978) also found that children between the ages of 4 and 6 were able to make correct use of the morphological marking -ei as a cue to feminine gender and -chen as a cue to neuter gender. Schneuwly (1978) reports similar findings. These data indicate that children are indeed sensitive to the various phonological and morphological cues to gender and that the stronger these cues are, the earlier they are used consistently by children. Tucker, Lambert, and Rigault (1977) report on a set of careful and detailed studies of cue use in predicting French gender which make it entirely clear that the higher the reliability of a cue the stronger its use by adult subjects.

7. *Children can use paradigmatic marking cues to infer word classes.* MacWhinney
   (1978) showed that 4-year-old children were able to make reliable use of the
   pronoun as a cue to the gender of nonce words. The experiment involved using
   the masculine form of the accusative personal pronoun "him" *ihn* to refer to a nonce
   word represented by a small toy. When the experimenter said, "I am picking him
   (*ihn*) up in my hand," children were able to successfully infer that the thing being
   picked up was masculine even though it was an object they had never seen before
   with a name they had never heard before.

The simulation

The simulations discussed in this article were based on earlier work by Taraban,
McDonald, and MacWhinney (in press) and MacWhinney, Leinbach, Taraban,
and McDonald (in press). In these simulations, the network is given a German
noun and is faced with the task of deciding which of the six forms of the definite
article to use with that noun. This task focuses on the use of morphology in
production, rather than comprehension. Later we will consider an architecture
that places comprehension and production into a clearer balance.

The simulation relies on the so called "back-propagation" architecture elaborated by Rumelhart, Hinton, and Williams (1986). One of our earlier sim-
lulations using this model is discussed by McDonald (this volume). Like
other connectionist models, our model consisted of a large number of densely
interconnected "units" or "nodes" operating in parallel. The model had three
layers of units: input units, output units, and intervening units, as can be seen
in Figure 13.1. The network's "knowledge" was contained in the strength of the
connections between the units in the network. Nodes in the network can receive
or send activation or both. Activation is sent across connections. Receiving
nodes update their activation as a function of the sum of their inputs. Each
input is the product of the activation of the sending node times the strength of
the connection.

The input layer encoded the presence or absence of cues associated with
a particular noun and its sentential context. Each node on the input layer
represented a single cue feature. If the cue was present for a particular noun, the
input node was fully activated, and if it was not present the node remained off.
The words, therefore, were represented as sets of cues. The activation of the
input layer produced activation on the internal layer(s), which in turn produced
activation on the output layer. Each of the six German definite articles was
represented by a unit on the output layer.

The beginning of a run of a simulation corresponded to the beginning of a
learning sequence. Initially, all the weights on the connections were assigned
small random weights. A training set for the simulation was then presented to
the network. The training set consisted of sets of cues for each word in the
list and the correct article for that set of cues. During the training phase, the

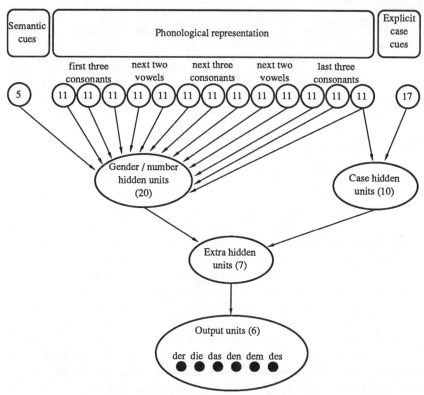

Figure 13.1. The connectionist network architecture used in the German declension acquisition simulation.

cues for each word were presented on the input layer and activated an output pattern. The activated output pattern was compared to the correct pattern and the difference between the two was used to compute an error measure. After a complete pass through all the words in the training set (an epoch), each weight in the network was individually strengthened or weakened so that during the next pass through the training set the activated patterns would be closer to the correct patterns – i.e., there would be less error. Each weight was changed according to the back propagation algorithm. The learning method was consistently applied to all the connections in the network, and there was no *ad hoc* intervention into the learning process.

The training set.   The training set consisted of 102 different nouns selected from a frequency count of a spoken German corpus of over 80,000 words (Wängler, 1963). From those nouns that had between 15 and 166 occurrences in the corpus, we selected a random sample of 102 nouns. The relative frequency of occurrence for these 102 nouns was preserved by entering each noun into the training set at one-tenth of the frequency with which it occurred in the Wängler corpus. Thus, a noun that occurred 80 times in the corpus occurred 8 times in the training set. Most nouns had only one (11 nouns), two (48 nouns), or three (23 nouns) occurrences; the remaining 20 nouns had from four to 17 occurrences. This yielded a total of 305 tokens in the training set.

Input units. The model relied on input units that came directly from a uniform coding of the actual phonological shape of input words. The design of the model is given in Figure 13.1. There were three types of input units: phonological, semantic, and case context units. The model used 143 phonological units to represent the full form of the noun in actual phonological features. These 143 units were distributed over 13 slots with 11 features in each slot. The 11 features were standard phonological distinctive features such as [+labial], [+coronal], [+voice], [+high], etc. Diphthongs and affricates were coded as pairs of phonemes. These features provided a unique 11-unit feature code for each German phoneme. The 13 slots were divided across these five positions:

1. up to three consonants in the initial consonant cluster,
2. up to two vowels in the post-initial vowel nucleus,
3. up to three consonants in the medial consonantal cluster,
4. up to two vowels in the pre-final vowel cluster, and
5. up to three consonants in the final consonantal cluster.

The last two syllables were coded for all words. In trisyllabic words, the first syllable was not coded. In the case of shorter words, some of the slots were sometimes left vacant. For example, if the word was a monosyllable, the medial cluster was left vacant and the pre-final and post-initial vowel nuclei were identical. All clusters were padded on the left. If there was only one consonant in a cluster it was coded in the final slot. If there was no final consonant, the final vowel was coded as being in the "pre-final" vowel slot.

In addition to the 143 phonological units, we used 5 semantic units to represent the properties of "natural male," "natural female," "young being," "superordinate," and "numeral." Only a few of the nouns had these units turned on. For example, the feature of real masculinity was on for *Sohn* "son" and the feature of "numeral" was on for *Hundert* "hundred." The particular semantic features chosen were those which figured most importantly in this particular word set.

Case Context Units. Each of the 305 tokens in the training set was presented in a case context. These contexts were represented by a set of 17 cues included in the input for each token: seven prepositions, seven word order configurations (NNV, NVN, VNN, NN, first noun, second noun, third noun), and three verb types (verb of motion, copular verb, and plural verb). In addition, the hidden units that connected to the case context units also connected to the final phoneme of the word, allowing them to detect the presence of the case endings -*s* for masculine and neuter nouns in the genitive and -*n* for plural nouns in the dative.

In the training corpus, particular nouns often appeared in quite different case contexts. Twenty case contexts were used, each of which was unique. There were eight nominative case contexts, five accusative case contexts, five dative case contexts, and two genitive case contexts. This distribution was chosen to approximate the frequencies with which these cases actually occur in German (41.6% nominative, 24.1% accusative, 24.9% dative, and 9.4% genitive) (Meier, 1967). The 20 contexts were then randomly assigned to noun tokens, with the restriction that the same context could not be repeated for the same noun. Given that the most frequent noun appeared with 17 tokens, as discussed above, no noun in the training set appeared in all 20 possible case contexts.

The 143 phonological units and the five semantic units all projected to a set of gender/number hidden units. The explicit case units and the phonological units for the final consonant of the stem all projected to a set of case hidden units. The phonological information was used to code the presence of noun-final markers for the genitive and dative plural. Both sets of hidden units projected to a third set of hidden units which then activated the six output units.

The network learned the input set completely by the end of 100 epochs of training.

Generalization across the paradigm

Although the speed and accuracy of this learning is impressive, one could argue that the network simply developed a complicated rote-like representation of the data presented to it without really acquiring anything that corresponds to rule-like behavior. In order to see if the network had learned something beyond the specific associations between combinations of cues and definite articles present in the training set, two different tests of generalization were made. The first test checked how well the network was able to apply the declensional paradigm. The test set consisted of the same 102 nouns used in the training set, but each noun was paired with the subset of case contexts it had not been paired with in the training set. That is, if a word had been paired with 17 of the 20 case contexts in the training set, it occurred with the remaining 3 contexts in this test. If a word had occurred with only one of the case contexts in the training set, it was paired with the remaining 19 case contexts in this test. This yielded a total of 1735 items for the generalization test. The test allowed us to see how well the network had learned the declensional paradigm and whether it could generalize the paradigm for particular nouns in case contexts in which the partlicular noun had not occurred in training.

This test set was given to the network after it had achieved 100% performance on the training set. The network was then run through a testing set. This was done five different times, always starting with the same single network that had just completed training. During testing, weights in the network were not altered. The results of this test were excellent. On the five generalization runs, the model had an average success rate of 94%. The chance level here would be 16%. This high level of performance provides strong evidence that the network was remarkably good at generalizing the overall paradigm to noun-case pairings that it was seeing for the first time.

Many of the errors that the network made were caused by ambiguities in the paradigm. For example, if a noun occurred in the training set in the nominative *die*, the accusative *die*, and the genitive *der*, but did not occur in the dative, neither a child nor the network could know whether the noun stem was a feminine singular or a plural, since the plural takes the same articles as the feminine singular in these three cases. The ambiguity is even more confounded, since one of the most frequent cues to feminine, final -*e* on the noun, is also a plural marker. When a noun with final -*e* was presented in the dative case in the test, the network most often assigned it the article *der* – i.e., the marker of a feminine singular noun in the dative. Thus, plural nouns, which should take the article *den* in the dative were sometimes assigned the incorrect article in the dative case in the generalization test. Another case of ambiguity in the training set occurred when a noun appeared in the dative case with *dem* and the genitive case with *des*, but did not occur in the nominative or accusative cases. In this situation it would be impossible to discriminate masculine singular from neuter singular nouns. Because of this overlap in the paradigm between masculine and neuter singular, the network often confused or conflated the two.

Generalization to new nouns

In order to test the ability of the network to generalize to new nouns, the next simulation used a much larger input set. This set used all the 2095 high-frequency German nouns in the Wängler corpus. From these, 199 nouns were picked out randomly and reserved for generalization testing. The remaining 1896 nouns constituted the training set. For this test we simplified the architecture of the system in various ways. We eliminated the five semantic cues. We also eliminated the dimensions of case and number from the simulation, using only the articles *der*, *die*, and *das* of the nominative. This simplified architecture allowed us to see more clearly the ability of the network to acquire cues for predicting gender. The results were exactly as expected. The simulation was able to predict the gender of new nouns with 70% accuracy. Since there are only three articles used in this simulation, chance is 33%. The nouns for which the simulation choose the wrong gender were generally ones which resembled patterns of another gender. We would not expect the model to achieve perfect or even near perfect performance in this task, since even native German speakers cannot achieve perfect accuracy in predicting the gender of new words. However, the strong performance of the model on this very large data set in this simplified architecture indicates that there are indeed many powerful cues to the prediction of German gender and that a connectionist network is a good tool for picking up these cues.

Late Learning

In order to look at late-learned items more carefully in the simulation with the smaller learning set, we stopped learning in 3 consecutive runs at a point at which about 15 words remained unlearned. The errors fell into two general categories: (1) weak learning for nouns in the genitive case and (2) errors associated with paradigm overlap. In half of the cases, the noun failed to activate an article. These will be referred to as cases of "omission" (or "misses"). These nouns were all in the genitive case. This case, as stated above, represented only 10% of the case contexts. The genitive case, therefore, was sparsely represented in the learning set, and the results here suggest a frequency effect for this case. Because the network is exposed to the genitive case relatively fewer times compared to other cases, it takes the network longer to learn these words. There may, in addition, be more specific difficulties associated with genitive cues, although we cannot comment on these at present.

The majority of the remaining errors involve paradigm overlap, either between feminine singulars and plurals, or between masculine and neuter singulars. As we noted earlier, the only difference between the articles that mark the feminine singular and those that mark the plural is in the dative. Given that singulars are more highly represented, there was a tendency to treat some instances of plurals as feminine singulars. Feminine plurals in the dative that were assigned the singular dative *der* on one or more of the test runs were *Leute, Fragen, Schuhe*, and *Minuten*. Instead of treating the dative plurals *Kinder* and *Männer* as feminine singulars, they were assigned masculine singular dative *dem*, consistent with their strong cue for masculine, which is the *-er* ending. Table 13.1 also shows that masculine and neuter singulars differ only in the nominative and accusative cases. Therefore, we might expect this overlap in the paradigm to cause some shifting between these genders, which it did: *Stück* and *Ding*, which are neuter, were twice treated as masculines, and *Hunger*, which is masculine, was twice treated as a neuter.

Comparison to the Developmental Literature

In order to examine the degree to which the performance of the network corresponds to early learning in the child, we ran a number of simulations to a point at which one-half of the total error at the beginning of a training

Table 13.3. *Percent errors in early learning in Simulation 1*

	Nominative	Accusative	Dative	Genitive
Percent errors	42	49	26	70
Percent omissions	34	44	9	40
incorrect *der*	2	0	13	18
incorrect *die*	4	4	0	0
incorrect *das*	2	1	0	0
incorrect *dem*	0	0	4	12

sequence was eliminated. At this point the network had an average error rate of 42% (range = 41–5%). Some of the results of these runs are given in Table 13.3. The numbers in Table 13.3 indicate the percentages of total usages that involved errors for particular case forms. These numbers do not sum to 100% across either rows or columns.

Let us look at the extent to which the simulation matched the six major phenomena noted in the developmental literature.

1. *Early acquisition of the nominative.* Table 13.3 shows the average proportion of tokens in each case that were errors for four consecutive tests of early learning. It appears that errors at this early stage are a function of the frequency of the case. The nominative case, which is most frequently represented in the training set, it shows the second lowest proportion of errors. This finding is in line with the predictions of the Competition Model.
2. *Delayed acquisition of the genitive.* The genitive case, which has the lowest frequency of occurrence both in real input and in the training set, is also the case which shows the highest proportion of errors. Here, again, the predictions of the Competition Model in regard to the role of frequency of occurrence are supported.
3. *Children often omit the article.* Mills (1986) reports that early on in acquisition, children tend to omit articles. The network also exhibited this behavior. On average, 73% of the errors made by the network were omissions – i.e., none of the articles reached the level of activation required to be considered "on." The proportion of the total error that involved omissions is presented by case in Table 13.3.
4. *Children often overgeneralize one gender.* Second, Mills (1986) reports that in the early stages of acquisition children tend to overgeneralize feminine articles. This tendency also occurs early on in the simulations. This is evident in the error patterns for articles, shown in Table 13.3. The majority of the errors follow the feminine singular paradigm (*die* in the nominative and accusative, *der* in the dative and genitive). Neither the masculine nor neuter paradigms fit the errors as well as the feminine paradigm does.
5. *Children make early use of the -e cue.* MacWhinney (1978) and Mills (1986) report that children acquire the connection between the -*e* ending and feminine gender early on in acquisition. The network is also quick to acquire this correspondence. All the feminine singular items containing the -*e* ending were consistently assigned feminine articles even at this early point in learning. In addition, the error rate for the masculine and neuter nouns that had the -*e* ending was 71%. Less than half of these errors were omissions; all of the remaining errors were consistent with the feminine singular paradigm.

6. *Children make use of highly reliable cues.* In a similar vein, we found no errors
    at all for words marked with highly reliable cues to gender such as *-chen* and -
    um. McDonald (this volume) shows how the performance of an earlier version of
    this model correlates well with cue reliability and conflict validity, as predicted by
    the Competition Model. A general finding of the Competition Model is that cue
    strengths depended on the *reliability* of a cue, both for morphological categories
    (MacWhinney, 1978) and syntactic categories (MacWhinney, Bates, & Kliegl, 1984;
    McDonald, 1986). There is also evidence that the relation between cue validity and
    cue strength changes during the course of acquisition, with initial stages dependent
    on cue availability and detectability and later stages on reliability (Sokolov, this
    volume), or on conflict cue validity (McDonald, 1986; McDonald & MacWhinney,
    1987).
7. *Children can use paradigmatic marking cues to infer word classes.* The ability of
    the model to generalize the paradigm to new cases for old words indicates that it
    was able to use the paradigmatic markings on the exemplars given to determine their
    gender. Although the model used no formal inferential logic, it was able to behave
    as if it were making this inference. This type of behavior of the model implements
    the notions of cooccurrence learning sketched out by Maratsos and Chalkley (1980)
    and discussed in Bates and MacWhinney (this volume). The important point here is
    that the same connectionist model is able to predict and control form classes on the
    basis of both cooccurrences and cues.

It is important for a model to match empirical data. However, it is even more
exciting when it makes predictions that have not yet been tested in empirical
research. Our simulations made a distinct set of predictions of this type. A
behavior that was exhibited by the model at all stages of learning before complete
mastery was the confusion of definite articles when there is substantial paradigm
overlap. This was especially serious for early learning. For example, every
feminine plural in the dative case was either omitted or, more frequently, was
assigned the feminine dative singular article *der*. This was true for *Leute*,
Fragen, and *Minuten*. As far as we know, there is not yet any child acquisition
data regarding this particular behavior. However, from the general analysis of
paradigm acquisition in Slavic outlined by Slobin (1973), one would expect
children to have problems with overlaps of this type. Given that this type of
paradigm overlap causes clear problems for the network, it would be revealing
to see if it also causes problems for German children.

Beyond mastering the problem of German definite article assignment, the
simulations presented here are in accord with more general patterns in the
empirical literature. As noted by McDonald (this volume), the strength of the
connection between a cue and a category changes during the learning process.
At first, cue strength follows overall cue validity; then it mirrors reliability,
and finally conflict validity. Similar shifts have been found in other cue-
category learning situations (McDonald, 1986; McDonald & MacWhinney, in
preparation; Sokolov, this volume).

The model went beyond generating a simple match to already known facts. It
also generated a number of predictions that can be tested in future developmental

research. It predicted strong difficulties with words like *Junge* and *Ende* that are exceptions to powerful cues. It predicted a confusion between *der* and *den* as markers of the dative plural. Finally, it also predicted fairly uniformly incorrect treatment of new nouns for which it has inferred the wrong gender. The ability of the model to generate clear new predictions for developmental research is an important strength and one not found in earlier accounts.

In terms of acquisitional theory, the model provides the first interesting alternative to the information-processing account of morphological learning presented first in MacWhinney (1978) and later in Pinker (1984). Within a single network the processes of rote, combination, analogy, and paradigm application are all expressed in terms of patterns of associations between cues. The ad hoc nature of the processes proposed in the earlier accounts is entirely eliminated. Whereas earlier research on morphological systems such as that of Tucker, Lambert, and Rigault (1977) or MacWhinney (1978) was forced to think of generalization in terms of rule use, we can now think about generalization in terms of cue acquisition. The model also allows us to merge the insights of the cooccurrence model of Maratsos and Chalkley (1980) with the cue-based learning emphasized in the Competition Model. Within a single network, we find prediction of form class on the basis of both cooccurrences and cues.

Toward a general model of morphological learning

The architecture used in the simulation we have been discussing is designed to model a very specific aspect of German language production. Given a noun and its case context, the simulation can activate the correct form of the definite article. This task corresponds to the part of the sentence production task that involves activation of the correct article. Given that the speaker knows what noun is to be used, given that the speaker knows whether that noun should be singular or plural, and given that the case context is clear, this network works to select the correct article. This system can solve only this limited problem in production and is of no use at all for comprehension.

Using a slightly different type of architecture, it is possible to simulate the processes of production and comprehension within a single network. To explore this possibility, we focused on the learning of nominal case marking in Hungarian. We chose a set of 92 Hungarian nouns, each having ten different declined forms. These ten different cases are what Hungarian grammarians call *ragok*. They include the accusative, the plural, the inessive, the dative, the benefactive, various possessive forms, and so on. Each inflected form is produced by combining a nominal stem with an affix. During the process of suffixation, both stem and suffix can undergo a variety of transformations that are described in detail in MacWhinney (1978, 1985). For example, when the stem *bokor* "bush" combines with the suffix *-ok*, the resultant form is *bokrok*.

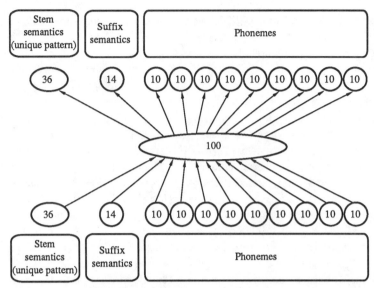

Figure 13.2. Network architecture for learning nominal case marking in Hungarian.

The actual shape of the suffix varies depending on the phonological shape of the stem. For example, the various possible forms of the plural suffix include *-k, -ok, -ak, -ek,* and *-ök.*

The goals of the simulation were threefold: (1) to be able to generate the phonetics of a declined form, given the semantics of the noun and the semantics of the desired declination (i.e., production), (2) to be able to generate the semantics of a noun and the semantics of its declination type, given the phonetics of its declined form (i.e., comprehension), and (3) to be able to improve performance on both of these tasks through training on the *other*. All of these goals were achieved with surprising success.

The structure of this network, as with the German simulation, was quite simple. Three layers of units were used: an input layer, an intermediate "processing" layer, and an output layer. Training was again carried out using the back propagation algorithm described above. In this simulation, however, both the input and output layers were used to represent the same thing: a semantics–phonetics pair that fully described the declined form af a noun (see Figure 13.2). The semantics of a declined form were represented by a random unique pattern specific to the noun, followed by a pattern across a set of 14 meaningful units which together expressed the meaning of a declination type. The phonetics of a declined form were simply represented as a string of the phonemes of that form, each phoneme being represented by a pattern across 10 feature units that together specified the desired phoneme.

Training was conducted in two modes. During comprehension training, the network was taught to generate a complete semantic and phonological description, given just the phonological form. The idea here is that children can often infer the meanings of words from context. They hear the word and can then check to see if what they thought the word might mean actually corresponds to what the context indicates. During production training, the network was taught to generate a complete semantic and phonological description of a declined form, given just the semantics of that form. One-third of the nouns were randomly selected to have one of their declined forms (randomly chosen) excluded from training (both comprehension and production). The ability to produce and comprehend these unseen forms was then tested once the network had learned to correctly produce and comprehend all of the forms it was trained with. The purpose of this test was to ensure that the network was actually using appropriate rules of comprehension and production, and not simply memorizing which output patterns went with each input pattern. The results indicated that the network had in fact learned some excellent rules for these tasks. When asked to comprehend the untaught forms, the resulting semantic descriptions of the forms were better than 99% correct in terms of the stem semantics and 100% correct in terms of the declination type semantics. When asked to produce the unseen forms, the resulting phoneme strings were 98.3% correct.

The network also demonstrated an interesting interplay between comprehension and production. The observation that the language learner is better prepared to produce a word if they have already learned to comprehend it was also captured by this network, as hoped. This was made possible by the "full-description" word representations that were used as output targets. These representations forced the network to learn not only how to produce semantics from phonology and phonology from semantics, but also to reproduce semantics from semantics and phonology from phonology. In doing so, each task generated middle-level representations that were useful to the other task. The comprehension task generated middle-level representations that were useful for producing phonological output (generally useful for performing production), and the production task-generated middle-level representations useful for producing semantic output (generally useful for performing comprehension). This meant that if the network had already learned one of these tasks, when attempting to learn the other it could exploit this previosly learned ability. This is apparently what the network did. Figure 13.3 shows the network's ability to remove error from its production performance over time, in each of two conditions. Clearly it is much more adept at learning the production task if it has already learned to comprehend the words it is trying to produce.

This architecture could also be applied to the German declination system, providing a much more robust consideration of the many processes involved there. Such a project, and a project involving the declination of English verbs into var-

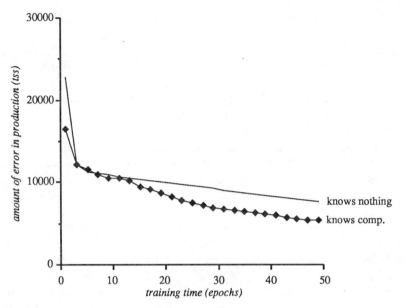

Figure 13.3. The network's ability to learn the production task.

ious tenses, are currently underway. These three projects will all use a uniform phonological architecture, a uniform network topology, and a uniform learning rule to model morphological learning in these three very different languages.

Connectionism and the processing of word meanings

Models of morphological processing are easier to develop than models of semantic processing. Morphology is a small, tightly defined domain for which empirical data are relatively easy to obtain. The development and processing of word meaning, on the other hand, is a much larger area without the same sharp data and tight definitions. Despite these practical differences, there are reasons to believe that the same connectionist concepts we have developed for the study of morphological development will also be useful in studying semantic learning and processing. I am not yet willing to declare that the same single connectionist net can handle both the processing of morphology and the processing of word meanings. Rather, what this section explores is ways in which a similar set of concepts can be applied to the problem of word meaning. It is somewhat early to attempt a full connectionist simulation of word learning, although interesting steps in this direction can be found in Kawamoto (1988) and St. John and McClelland (in press). At this point, it is more useful to sketch out the basic empirical facts that a connectionist model will be attempting to capture and to discuss the underlying logic of the competition between word meanings. There are three types of semantic competition that we will want to examine: lexical competition, polysemic competition, and attachment competition. Lexical competition arises during language production; polysemic competition arises during language comprehension. Attachment competition occurs during both production and comprehension. Let us begin by looking at lexical competition.

Lexical competition

The most basic type of semantic competition is lexical competition. This type of competition arises during production when we are trying to decide what word to use to refer to a particular object or activity. Consider a set of competing words like "cup," "mug," and "demitasse." In the Competition Model account, these three forms are seen as occupying neighboring parts of a multidimensional semantic topography. For simplicity, let us imagine that the crucial attributes distinguishing these three forms are size, thickness, and cylindricality. Figure 13.4 illustrates the core semantic territory for each of the three words on these three dimensions. For the adult, objects that fall within the core territories are clear cases of cups, mugs, and demitasses. Objects that fall outside the core will be attracted to one of the three neighboring semantic clusters depending on a feature-weighting algorithm. The closer they are to strong cues of a particular neighbor, the more likely they are to be pulled into the semantic influence of that neighbor. Thus the cue of cylindricality can be in competition with the cue of size for a smallish cylindrical object. Although most demitasses are not cylindrical and most mugs are, the size cue would probably win over the shape cue for most adults. As a result, we would tend to call a very small cup a demitasse, even if it is cylindrical.

Cues are sometimes not available when we need them to make distinctions between competing forms. For example, the attribute of heat-resistance might often be used to distinguish mugs from cups. However, we may not be able to judge whether a given drinking utensil is capable of holding hot liquids until we actually use it. Even if this cue is available, it still may not be entirely reliable, since many porcelain cups are as capable of holding hot liquids as are mugs.

The kind of competition occurring among "cup," "mug," and "demitasse" applies generally across lexical fields. One particularly interesting arena of competition is the one involving locative prepositions, such as "at," "on," and "near." These forms have been studied in some detail by Bennett (1975), Brugman (1983), Herskovits (1986), Langacker (1987), Talmy (1978), Miller and Johnson-Laird (1976) and many others. Harris (1988) presents an interesting connectionist treatment for the processing of the various senses of the word "over" based on the analysis in Brugman (1983).

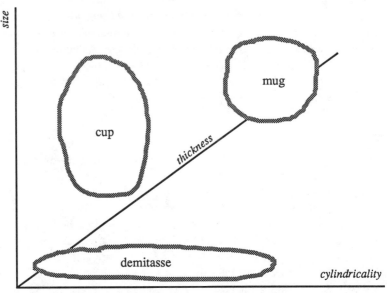

Figure 13.4. Competing words in a multidimensional semantic topography.

Often the competition between locative prepositions is influenced by semantic features of the noun. Consider the ways in which the preposition "at" competes with the prepositions "near" or "next to." If we say that "Frank is near his desk," we usually mean that he is not right "at" his desk. If Frank were right "at" his desk, we would say that he is "at his desk." When we choose one competing option over another, we are implicitly telling the listener that the option that did not win out was somehow less appropriate. Because of this, we need to think about characterizing the meanings of these words in terms of the contrasts or competitions in which they participate. In the case of "at" and "near" the contrast focuses on distance from the location. However, there are some locations for which "at" is not appropriate. For example, we would say that "the woman was near her grocery cart" rather than "the woman was at her grocery cart." It appears that "at" used in this way indicates a place where work or activity is conducted.

To take another example, consider the following sentences involving a competition between "in" and "at."

1. Marge is at the store.
2. Marge is in the store.
3. *Marge is at Paris.
4. Marge is in Paris.

In these sentences, the choice between "at" and "in" depends upon the speaker's interpretation of the object of the preposition. In the first sentence, the "store" is viewed as a small point location. In the second it is viewed as a full large building. In the third sentence, it is difficult to see the whole city of Paris as a single point, although this can be done by viewing "Marge" as a conquering general whose battle campaign had brought her to just outside the gates of the city of Paris. For smaller locations, "at" can be used to designate temporary position by a landmark that is treated as a point. However, once the landmark becomes large enough, it can no longer be treated as a point and "in" wins out even if the position is temporary. Sometimes the location is temporary because it is a position along a route. For example, the sentence "the restaurant is at the village" is a bit odd, but the sentence "there is a good restaurant at a village 6 miles from here" is perfectly fine (Herskovits, 1986). In this case, the point "at a village" is a temporary position along an itinerary. Yet another competition involving "at" is with the preposition "by." There are contrasts such as "house at the lake" and "house by the lake." Here again, "at" seems to indicate a certain temporariness of purpose or itinerary.

In the Competition Model, this matching of words to objects is determined by the feature-matching process discussed by McDonald and MacWhinney (this volume). Sometimes the features being matched relate only to the word itself, as in the example of the competition between "mug," "cup," and "demitasse." In other cases, as in the competition between "at" and "in," the features being weighted involve both the words themselves and other related words. The cue summation process involves summing the strengths of the cues favoring a particular candidate and dividing that number by the sum of all available cues. In a variant of this basic model, cue strengths are multiplied instead of added. In either case, the candidate with the highest cue strength is predicted to win in the competition. Cue summation models of this type are common in psychology. For example, Massaro (1987) presents a detailed account of the application of such cue integration models to various areas of perceptual processing.

The three-level connectionist networks we used for our work with morphology can also be used to study interactive effects in lexical competition. A network for this purpose would group together several competing nouns for a domain. A toy simulation could include only "mug," "cup," and "demitasse." Only those readings of these words that relate to drinking utensils would be involved in the model. For example, the reading of "mug" that relates to police practices would not be relevant. Going beyond the idea of a toy simulation, a more interesting simulation would include all the words referring to eating utensils. The input to the network would include perceptual and functional features of the type we have been discussing – features such as cylindricality, size, thickness, heat-resistance, and so on. The intervening or hidden units would detect nonlinear interactions between the cues. This type of network is easy to build. However, detailed coding of the features themselves is a laborious process and can only be handled reasonably for small domains. Lexical fields where connectionist simulations could make interesting contacts with current semantic theory include locative prepositions, transfer verbs, verbs of covering, reversible actions, and quantifiers.

Polysemic competition

So far, we have discussed the competition that occurs during production in our attempt to choose among totally different words. However, there is a level of semantic competition that occurs below the level of the word. This is the competition that occurs during comprehension when we have to select among alternative meanings or polysemes. When we hear a word such as "palm," we must decide whether to think of it as a tree or as a part of a hand. This competition between alternative meanings of the same word is an extremely pervasive aspect of human language. When a lexical item is detected, it automatically (Swinney, 1979) activates each of its polysemes. These polysemes are then placed into competition (Small, Cottrell, & Tanenhaus, 1988). The polyseme which is supported by the strongest cues wins. Like the competition between words, the competition between polysemes is determined by a process of cue strength summation. The notion of a multidimensional semantic topography is a useful way of understanding the way in which alternative meanings compete. This topography makes distinctions not just between words, but also within words. Consider a word like "ball." Looking in *Webster's Third*, we find three major entries for "ball." The first major entry is for a noun that describes round physical objects; the second is for a verb that involves formings things into balls; the third is for a noun describing a formal gathering for social dancing.

Within each of the major entries, we find a series of minor readings or polysemes. For example, the third entry for "ball" has one polyseme for "a formal gathering" and a second for "a good time." Or the first entry has polysemes for things like "odd ball," "a ball game," "a fast ball," "testes," or "keep the ball rolling," along with the basic meaning of "a round object."

Within a given minor polyseme, we can find further polysemy. For example, within the basic polyseme for the first entry of "ball," there are 15 minor polysemes. Various types of round objects which we call "balls" include: the ball of the foot, a baseball, the ball of the earth, an eyeball, a ball of fudge, and so on. Even within the minor polyseme for objects that we bounce or roll, there are a long list of types, including baseballs, footballs, golf balls, and so on. Nor does polysemy really end at this level. Within the interpretation of "ball" as "football," we can further distinguish specific object types such as "nerf football," "mini football," and "regulation football."

When we say the word "ball," we may be referring to any one of these many different polysemes at the various levels. It is the listener's job to try to decide which of the many competing options is the one which is currently intended. If the listener wants to understand the message at all, it is almost always important to pick out the correct major polyseme. If we hear that Cinderella "went to the ball," we would have a very strange idea of what happened if we thought of her as approaching a round object. If we hear "the baby threw the ball," we need to avoid thinking of a baby throwing a wad of hot candy or the bone in someone's foot. We certainly want to focus in on the reading of "round object for throwing or bouncing." However, within this general minor polyseme, it might not yet be possible to distinguish between a beach ball, a soccer ball, a volley ball, or a nerf ball. There may be no further information in the discourse or in the discourse context that could tell us which of these particular objects is being thrown by the baby. If there is further disambiguating information, we will attempt to use it. A series of studies by Anderson and Ortony (1975), Anderson and Pichert (1976), and Anderson, Reynolds, Schallert, and Goetz (1977) demonstrated the degree to which discourse context influences our final interpretation of lexical items. For example, in a sentence such as "The Coca-Cola poured all over the table, and then the container was empty," subjects tend to interpret "container" as a "bottle." However, in a sentence such as "The apples rolled all over the table, and then the container was empty," subjects tend to interpret "container" as "basket."

There are three major types of cues for resolving the competition between polysemes.

1. The first type of cues are those involved in interlexical spreading activation. Interlexical spreading activation effects are crucial in garden path sentences such as "The gardener emptied the pot of seeds and other debris, before he smoked it." At first the lexical associations with "gardener" and "seeds" strongly support the reading of "pot" as a container. However, the eventual appearance of the word "smoke" strongly tips the scales toward the reading of "pot" as marijuana. In a connectionist account of this processing, cues continue to enter into the competition up to the point where a final decision is rendered. If the secondary competitor is sufficiently weak, the competition may be shut down early on and an irreversible garden path can result.

2. The second type of cues used to resolve polysemic competitions are those deriving from the scene as a whole. In the sentence "The Coca-Cola poured all over the table, and then the container was empty" the cues for the interpretation of "container" as "bottle" derive not from particular words so much as from our interpretation of the scene as a whole. Of course, if we are comprehending this sentence in isolation, we must use the words to derive an interpretation of the scene. But it is the constructed scene and not the individual words, in such cases, that determine the resolution of ambiguity.

3. The third type of cues used to resolve polysemic competition are those that are concentrated in the particular words that are directly syntactically related to the polysemic word. In a sentence like "Bill met Tammy at the ball" the preposition "at" supports the "place" reading of "ball" which matches most readily with the "formal dance" interpretation.

Connectionist networks can be applied to the problem of processing polysemy. The simplest type of network would have all of the possible polysemes of a single word as output and all of the cues that are likely to be important in the polysemic processing as possible inputs. For example, one could build a network for the processing of the polysemes of the word "ball." In order to activate the reading of "ball" as a dance, the input could include features such as "music" or "costumes." These features would be turned only if there are words containing these features in the actual input. The inputs could activate intervening units that might be generally useful for collecting evidence regarding the concept "dance." Other intervening units would be more activated by meanings of "ball" that have to do with candy-making, and so on. There are four major problems with networks of this type.

1. Word-specific nets of this type would fail to capture the interrelatedness of the lexicon. Given the word "ball," the easiest way to activate the "golf ball" interpretation over the "basketball" interpretation and other competitors, is to activate the "golf" concept. However, if our networks only resolve competitions for single words, this interrelatedness is missed.
2. Isolated single-word networks also fail to capture general polysemic competitions such as metonymies, personifications, and the like. The same extensional logic that allows us to talk about "having a ball" can be used to talk about "having a spin." If the polysemes of "ball" and "spin" are processed in total separation, these effects cannot be captured.
3. Isolated single-word networks cannot, by themselves, resolve lexical competition of the type we discussed earlier for "cup," "mug," and "demitasse."
4. In reality, some words are more important than others in determining the polysemic competition. In particular, as we will see below, words tend to exert the greatest pressure on other words with which they have syntactic relations.

One straightforward way of dealing with these limitations is to build bigger nets. We can construct nets that model both the major lexical competitions for a given semantic domain and all of the polysemic competitions within that domain. Such nets could relate comprehension and production in the way we outlined for our simulations of Hungarian morphology. These richer nets would need to have more input features. For example, in the domain of "cup" and "mug," we would want to add to the cues of shape and function various cues to distinguish between "mug" as a drinking vessel and "mug" as a derogatory term for a person's visage. Of course, the cues for the latter polyseme of "mug" are really ones that are more relevant to the competition between "face," "mug," "visage," and "puss." Each of the first three problems mentioned above points out the need for constructing really large nets if we want to capture any of the interesting aspects of lexical processing. The fourth problem noted above points in yet another direction which we will explore in the next section.

Syntactic attachments and polysemic processing

The Competition Model account of syntactic relations is based upon the notion of "valence" presented by Tesnière (1959) and developed by Fillmore (1986). A valence relation holds between any two words or groups of words that are attached together into a syntactic construction. In more familiar terms, a valence relationship is simply a syntactic relation of a very particular type – one that holds between a single word as predicate and another single word as argument. In every valence relation, one word serves as the predicate and another word serves as its argument. For example, the word "another" has a valence for a count noun that will appear after it. The Competition Model sees the various possible fillers for these valence slots as competing for attachments. Each lexical item places specific requirements on the shape of the items to which it will attach. For example, the preposition "in" expects its object to be an enclosure. Thus, the phrase "in the store" induces us to view "store" as an enclosure, whereas the phrase "at the store" induces us to view the store as a locational point.

Languages differ markedly in the way they use grammatical cues to govern attachment competitions. Much of the work reported in this book has examined the way in which cues are used to determine the competiton between nouns for attachment to verbs. Indeed, the overwhelming majority of studies of syntactic processing within the Competition Model has focused specifically on the competition between nouns for the role of the subject of transitive verbs. As Bates and MacWhinney (this volume) have shown, the cue of preverbal positioning is the strongest cue in English to identification of the subject role. Given a sentence like "The eraser are chasing the boys," English-speaking subjects show a strong tendency to choose "the eraser" as the subject and, hence, the actor. This occurs despite the fact that the noun "boys" has the cues of verb agreement, animacy, and humanness all on its side. These three weak cues are just not enough to counterbalance the strength of the preverbal position cue in English. In Italian, however, the corresponding sentence is *la gomma cacciano i ragazzi* in which *la gomma* "the eraser" has support from the cue of preverbal positioning and *i ragazzi* "the boys" has support from the cues of agreement, animacy, and humanness. As Bates, MacWhinney, Caselli, Devescovi, Natale, and Venza (1984) have shown, agreement is a much stronger cue in Italian than it is in English. In Italian, the strongest cue is verb agreement and the second strongest cue is preverbal positioning. Thus Italians interpret this sentence as meaning "The boys are chasing the eraser."

How can a connectionist model account for this type of competition for syntactic attachment? It would be easy enough to construct a net for a particular sentence. The inputs to the net would be cues such as preverbal positioning, verb agreement, case marking, animacy, and so on. The output units would be the competing nouns. However, if this network is to be at all general, there must be some way of making it general across words. Unlike the morphological competition between *der*, *die*, and *das* or the lexical competition between "cup" and "mug," the cast of characters in these syntactic competitions is constantly changing. We could wire up a network to deal with the sentence "the dogs are chasing the cat," but we would want the same network to also deal with "the goats are chasing the balls." There are several attempts in the literature to deal with this problem. McClelland and Kawamoto (1986) and St. John and McClelland (in press) deal with the problem by setting up a fixed set of roles for each English verb. Rather than constructing valence relations between words, their model directly extracts a full sentence meaning from the input cues. Although such an approach is attractive in many ways, it is hard to see how it can be developed into a full model of sentence processing in general, since it requires detailed hand-coding of relations for a small set of verbs and nouns without reference to general semantic principles and provides no obvious mechanism for the combination of roles into larger units.

An alternative approach that fits in better with the Competition Model view of syntactic processing uses linear position as a way of identifying or keeping track of each competing noun. For example, in the sentence "the dogs are chasing the cat" the first noun phrase would be "the dogs" and the second would be "the cat." The net is designed specifically to resolve the competition between the *first noun* and the *second noun* for the role of subject of the verb. The cues that would be used include noun animacy, agreement, stress, and certain semantic features of the verb. Having set up the network in this way, it provides us with a faithful connectionist rendition of the basic syntactic claims of the Competition Model in regard to the competition between nouns for grammatical roles. The inclusion of certain semantic features of the verb is required to deal with evidence from Corrigan (1986, 1987) showing that a full consideration of the semantic features of the verb is important in understanding valence expectations (1986, 1987). But this is not the only reason to build in the semantics of the predicate into the same network that processes attachment competition. The other major reason for building semantics into these valence-processing networks is to deal with the phenomenon of pushy polysemy, which we will discuss later.

It is crucial to note that a network of the type being proposed requires some sort of external process to keep track of the position of the competing nouns. In an NVN language, such as English, this process can record position vis-à-vis the verb. One competing noun would be coded as "preverbal" and the other would be coded as "postverbal." Empirical research discussed by Bates and MacWhinney (this volume) has provided evidence for the psychological reality of the categories "preverbal" and "postverbal" in English. In languages with

NNV or VNN order, a better way of doing things would be to code the absolute position of the nouns. For example, in Hungarian, it would be best to track the "first noun" and the "second noun." Indeed, the evidence reviewed by Pléh (this volume) supports this analysis. Of course, not all syntactic competitions are between subjects and objects. For example, a processor that is dealing with the competition of nouns for the role of indirect object in English only needs to track the position of nouns that followed the verb. In this regard, it can act like a processor in a VNN language.

Anaphora as Polysemy

Some of the most extensive competitive polysemy occurs in the processing of anaphors. Anaphora pushes the use of cues to identify referents in a semantic topography to its logical limits. A single pronoun in English such as "it" or "that" could conceivably refer to virtually anything. However, given enough discourse, syntactic, and semantic cues, we are usually able to use anaphors to identify exactly the referent the speaker has in mind. Cues such as perspective maintenance, gender, number, implicit causality (Au, 1986; Caramazza, Grober, Garvey, & Yates, 1977), presence of a subordinating conjunction, and action readiness (MacWhinney, 1986) all operate to favor one interpretation of the anaphor over the other. Consider a sentence such as "The actress apologized to the costume men, because she was late." Here, the cues of gender, number, perspective maintenance and implicit causality all favor choosing "actress" as the antecedent of "she." However, often these cues compete. Consider these examples:

1. When it was copied, my file disappeared.
2. It disappeared, when my file was copied.

In the first sentence, the presence of the subordinating conjunction licenses a possible following reference for "it." This is not the only possible reading, however, since "it" could also refer to something discussed earlier or perhaps something that is obvious in the situation. In the second sentence, on the other hand, the referent must be something mentioned in earlier discourse, since "it" is a subject of a main clause and must be fully referential at the time of mention. MacWhinney (1984) discusses the many competing ways of interpreting anaphors and the ways in which cues help us decide between these competing readings.

The resolution of anaphoric polysemy takes place against a backdrop of real-time processing constraints. MacDonald and MacWhinney (in preparation) and McDonald and MacWhinney (1987) tracked the time course of the processing of anaphors against possible referents. Earlier work with anaphoric processing (Corbett & Chang, 1983; Leiman, 1982) had suggested that, during the process of identifying a pronoun with its antecedent the availability of the antecedent is increased or primed. MacDonald and MacWhinney (1988) tested this claim using a cross-modal probe recognition task to measure the speed with which subjects could judge whether a noun had already been mentioned in the sentence. For example, the subject may hear a sentence such as "John pushed Bill and he slipped on the rug." At various points before and after the pronoun "he" we presented either "John," "Bill," or "Frank" as test probes. The subject's task was to decide whether the noun has been mentioned. In both studies we found that subjects were consistently fastest in identifying the subject "John" as present. However, this real-time advantage for the perspective maintenance cue was either limited by or amplified by three other cues: gender matching, number, and implicit causality. In general, the strongest cues tended to lead to the greatest priming advantages for their referents.

A connectionist account of anaphoric processing can be constructed by extending the model for attachment processing sketched out earlier. In that model, arguments compete for attachment to their predicate. The identity of each noun is maintained by a processor that tags noun phrases with the positional features *first* and *second*. In anaphoric processing a similar technique can be used. The various candidates for attachment to anaphoric pronouns and other anaphoric devices can be given numerical labels such as *first* and *second*. These labels could either track their actual positional occurrence or possibly their position in a list of participants in working memory (Gernsbacher, 1987; Sanford & Garrod, 1981). Given this identification, the cues of gender match, number agreement, action readiness, verb features, and so on could be used to determine the winner of each competition.

Pushy polysemy

There is an important way in which polysemic competition is directly linked to syntactic competition. Consider the word "run." If we talk about "another run," as in "let's take another run," we are forcing the verb "run" to behave like a noun. If we talk about wanting "a deeper blue," we are forcing the adjective "blue" to behave like a noun. This use of syntactic combinations to push words into other part-of-speech categories is what we will call *pushy polysemy*. What is interesting about pushy polysemy is that it only works between words that are syntactically related through the type of valence relation we discussed earlier. In this example, it is the word "another" that is forcing the word "run" to behave like a noun.

Prepositions provide many good illustrations of the relations between polysemy and attachment. We noted above that the phrase "in the store" induces us to view "store" as an enclosure, whereas the phrase "at the store" induces us to view the store as a locational point. The preposition can also force the noun to assume a particular polysemic value. Consider these sentences:

1. I saw the dog in the car.
2. I saw the sun in the car.
3. I saw the dent in the car.

In the first example, the dog is inside the body of the car. In the second and third examples, the sun and the dent are located in the surface of the car.

Pushy polysemy can work in both directions at once. Consider the sentence "the trash can hit the fence." If we decide to select the nominal reading of "can," we lock in an adjectival reading for "trash." If we decide to select a verbal reading for "can," we lock in a nominal reading for "trash." Here the reciprocal nature of the constraint satisfaction system is fairly obvious, but when we look at minor polysemy, the effects become more subtle. Consider a sentence such as "John drives over the hill." In this case, the unmarked translative and punctative meaning of "drive" as "takes a one-time trip to a place" would usually force the word "over" to assume its reading of "path across a gap." It that case we can say that "drive" is pushing "over" into a marked place in its semantic topography. However, it is also possible to have "over" take on the sense of "position on the other side of a gap." In that case, the preposition "over" forces the verb "drive" to take on the meaning of a generic activity. In that reading, the whole event occurs in some habitual or generic way on the other side of the hill. In one case "drive" pushes "over" into a marked polysemic slot. In the other case "over" pushes "drive" into a marked polysemic slot. The least marked case is the one where the total amount of pushing is the least. In that sense, "over" appears to more easily assume either of these two meanings than does "drive."

Anaphoric processing can also involve pushy polysemy. Consider the following examples:

1. John put his arm into that of the Atlantic.
2. The curry was hot and so was the coffee.
3. The blade was nicked, but the knight pulled it anyway.

In these sentences, the words "that," "so," and "it" are initially interpreted as coreferent with an element in the first clause. We first think of the "arm" of the Atlantic as a human arm and of the "coffee" as "spicy," rather than "warm." Then, under the pressure of the other words in the second clause, we revise our interpretations and see the "arm" of the Atlantic as a body of water and the hotness of the coffee in terms of temperature instead of spiciness. In the third example, it is not the anaphoric pronoun "it" whose interpretation we revise, but that of the antecedent. We first think of the "blade" as a "razor," but then revise our thinking to view it as a "sword." As in the case of pushy polysemy involving arguments and predicates, these anaphoric relations could best be modeled within a network that determined the mutual constraints between attachments and polysemic competitions.

The reciprocal nature of pushy polysemy underscores the fact that polysemic processing and attachment processing must work together in the same network. Our network must have as outputs not only decisions about whether "trash" attaches to "can," but also about which polysemes of "trash" and "can" should win out. These decisions cannot be made independently. If we favor the adjectival reading of "trash," then we will want the nominal reading of "can." If we favor the nominal reading of "trash," we will want the verbal reading of "can." The full architecture we need to consider here is one in which there are a group of units that work to interrelate the part of the network that processes the polysemes of "trash" and the part of the network that processes the polysemes of "can." Overall, the network will attempt to find the best fit between the input cues, the default polysemes, and the hypothesized attachments.

Extensional pathways

Pushy polysemy is strong enough to overcome most of the standard categorizations of words into parts of speech and subclasses of the parts of speech. It can easily force a mass noun to assume a reading as a common noun. For example, often we are told that "sugar" is a mass noun and that phrases such as "another sugar" are ungrammatical (Gordon, 1985). From this we are to assume that the sentence "I'd like another sugar, please" is also ungrammatical. However, if we are asking for a small packet of sugar and using the contents of the packet to refer to the whole (metonymy), the extension is quite reasonable and even conventional. Or we may be working in a chemistry lab analyzing the reactions of various sugars such as fructose, sucrose, and glucose. Here we are using an extensional pathway that uses a word to refer to a member of a taxonomic class. One can say that only words like "sugar" can do this because of the special circumstances mentioned. However, even so unlikely a sentence as "I'd like another sand, please" can be interpreted in similar ways. Much like the interpretation of "another sugar" as referring to a packet of sugar, we might interpret "another sand" as referring to a bag of sand used either for construction or for sand-bagging a swollen river. Just as we could imagine a chemist working with various sugars, we could imagine a situation where geologists are describing the sand content of a new formation. They have used sieves to sort out the various types of sand in the formation and then placed these sands into jars. One of them asks the other for "another sand" for testing, meaning either another bottle of sand or another type of sand.

Proper nouns can also be converted into common nouns. Usually, we are told that a determiner such as "a" cannot precede a proper noun such as "Reagan." However, there is nothing wrong with a sentence such as "A wiser Reagan returned from Rejkjavik," if we are thinking of "Reagan" not just as a single man, but also as a man who can assume various states or values. Virtually any proper noun can be extended in this way. Another extensional path allows us to convert adjectives into nouns, as in the sentence "The green is nicer than the red." This type of conversion works best if we are able to conceive of the new deadjectival nouns as members of a collection or ensemble.

Prepositions seem to be particularly good at pushing their objects around. When the preposition "in" is combined with a noun that does not have a natural enclosure, that noun is forced into a polysemic reading that allows us to see it as an enclosure. For example, when we say that "the soldier is in the field," we conceptualize the field not as a flat surface, but as as extension with certain perimeters within which the soldier is located. When we say "the soldier parachuted onto the field" we see the field as a flat surface upon which one can alight. When we say that "the truck was in the road," we tend to see the road not as a line connecting two points, but as an expanse of asphalt. When we say "the truck was on the road," we see the road as a line or an extended surface. If we say that we see "the trout under the water," we are focusing on the part of the water that is between us and the trout. If we say that we see "the trout in the water," we are focusing on the entire body of water within which the trout is submerged. Another example is the use of the word "above" to refer to a one-story building whose base is higher up a hill than a six-story building below it. In this case, we say that the small building is "above" the large building even though the top of the large building is above the top of the small building. However, it is reasonable to use "above" to describe this relation, since there is no other single preposition to describe the relation and since we realize that our listener will not imagine that one building is actually suspended in space over the other. In general, the use of one preposition or another can force the noun into a particular polysemic pathway. This is the essence of "pushy polysemy."

PP attachment

A particularly well-studied type of role competition is the competition for prepositional phrase (PP) attachment. Consider the sentence, "The women discussed the dogs on the beach." We can interpret this sentence as saying that the dogs are on the beach or as saying that the women engaged in the discussion while on the beach. In the former case, the head of the prepositional phrase is the nominal. In the latter case, it is the verb.

There is a sizeable psycholinguistic literature investigating such sentences. Frazier and Fodor (1978) have used subjects' supposed preference for attachment of prepositional phrases to the verb as support for the Sausage Machine model of sentence processing. Oden (1978) has pointed out that a resolution of the competition between alternative parses requires the full real-world context described by the sentence. Ford, Bresnan, and Kaplan (1982) have shown how an LFG parser can handle attachment by following principles of local attachment and thematic control. The Competition Model approach to attachment is most similar to the approach of Ford, Bresnan, and Kaplan. It differs from that approach primarily in the importance it assigns to the preposition as an independent source of activation and in the emphasis it places on competition.

In the Competition Model, prepositions first attach to their heads yielding prepositional phrases. These prepositional phrases can then function in one of two ways. They can function as adverbs and attach to a verb or they can function as modifiers and attach to a noun. In a sentence such as "the women discussed the dogs on the beach" both possibilities exist. These two readings of the preposition are in competition. The final interpretation of the sentence depends on which reading wins out in the end.

Relative pronouns such as "who" or "which" can also show a competition between differing attachments. Relativizers first play a role in their own clause, serving as an argument of the verb. Then the whole relative clause can attach either to a noun, a verb, or an adjective. The head may be a nominal as in "Bill bumped the lamp which then fell onto the floor." The head may be an adjective as in "Tim was depressed, which is not a good thing to be." Or, the head may be a whole clause, as in "Mary criticized John, which surprised me."

Inheritance

There is an ongoing debate regarding the extent to which the syntactic attachment patterns of predicates can be predicted from their meaning. For example, some analysts claim that semantic features alone cannot predict whether verbs like "recommend" and "deliver" take double object constructions as in "*we delivered the library the book." Some propose that all verbs that possess certain features of transfer or delivery would inherit a similar set of syntactic properties on the basis of their semantic credentials. Pinker (1989) believes that the semantic features of verbs are indeed powerful enough to predict their valence descriptions. Inheritance seems to occur in many semantic domains. Verbs like "fill" that focus on the goal as the object generally place the material being transferred into a "with" phrase, as in "Paul filled the tub with water." On the other hand, substance movement verbs like "pour" that allow the material to serve as the object must then treat the goal in a locative phrase, as in "Paul poured the water into the tub." In some cases this predictability of roles from semantic cues (or what Pinker, 1989, calls "criteria") is exceptionless. In other cases, it runs up against specific lexical exceptions and preemptions from existing items.

Despite the force with which Pinker and Prince (1987) reject the connectionist approach to language learning, it is interesting to note that Pinker's analysis of cues to valence structure fits rather nicely into the Competition Model connectionist account. Pinker's emphasis on the use of semantic cues as ways of predicting formal patterns is close in spirit to that of the Competition Model. A network can be built that takes these features as inputs and uses them to predict case role structure. Adding the phonological features of the verbs to the network would allow it to encode the various stress patterns and derivational types that some linguists believe are important in generating valence descriptions. Finally, the connectionist network could also encode some idiosyncratic variation for high-frequency items. The same type of connectionist net that can achieve 70% prediction for the gender of new German nouns will probably do far better in using semantic and phonological features of English transitive verbs to predict their valence descriptions.

The Competition Model agrees with Pinker in its emphasis on the extent to which the child uses simple and direct cues whenever these are available. However, it also agrees with Maratsos in recognizing the child's ability to detect cooccurrences. Cooccurrence learning involves the "abduction" of semantic facts on the basis of formal regularities. For example, given a sentence such as "The man niffed the plate at the fence," the child can abduce some of the semantics of "niff" on the basis of its valence description. The child does this by attending to the underlying system of connections between semantics and verb frames. This system tells us that "niff" takes a subject and an object and that the action of the subject on the object is like that in "hit" and "slam."

The importance of a mechanism of this type has been stressed by MacWhinney (1978), Maratsos and Chalkley (1980), Bowerman (1982), and Schlesinger (1977). There is evidence that even very young children are able to infer the class of a word from cooccurrence data. For example, Katz, Baker, and Macnamara (1974) found that, beginning around 17 months, girls who were given a proper name for a doll learned this name better than girls who were given a common noun. In the proper noun frame, girls were told that the doll was called "Zav"; in the common noun frame they were told that the doll was "a zav." Thus, even at this early age, children seem to realize that names with articles are common nouns and names without articles are proper nouns. This ability to infer the semantics of words on the basis of cooccurrence continues to develop. By age 8, Werner and Kaplan (1950) were able to show in their classic "corplum" experiment that children could acquire many aspects of the semantics of abstract nouns from highly abstract sentence contexts.

The connectionist model of McClelland and Kawamoto (1986) does a good job of simulating this abductive learning. Words that behave formally like other words begin to be treated like those words. For example, in a sentence such as "the doll hit the ball" the simulation has a tendency to begin to attribute animacy to "the doll" on the basis of its status as the subject of "hit." In fact, this learning is not unproductive, because in both fantasy and fiction we often treat dolls as animate.

The eventual goal of this type of a connectionist analysis of verbs and case roles is to go from a set of semantic features to a set of valence descriptions. Such a system will allow for the emergence of generalities on the basis of semantic features, while still tolerating exceptions for high-frequency items (Stemberger & MacWhinney, 1986). Within the inheritance network that processes valence and polysemy, more detailed features of the predicate may activate more detailed features of the valence description. For example, if the predicate is "big," the feature [+measurable] is activated for the argument. Of course, we can treat virtually any object as measurable, but the point is that the presence of the word "big" would force us to focus on the size properties of its argument.

Making valence descriptions subject to semantic features of the predicate and its arguments has some further interesting consequences for extensional uses of verbs. For example, the first argument of the verb "polish" is usually an animate actor and the second argument is usually an inanimate object. However, when an inanimate occurs as the first argument in pre-predicate position, as in "this table polishes easily," its presence forces the verb to take on the features [+potential] and [+state] and to drop the feature [+activity]. This general change can apply to any action verb. We can say "this phone dials easily" or "this micro programs easily." We can produce and comprehend such forms without having had any prior experience with them, indicating that the valence descriptions involved cannot be frozen forms, but must arise from some general process. In fact, this general process is exactly what is captured by the valence description network.

Nouns have valence descriptions which simply require them to be the argument of other predicates. Thus, all nouns expect to be either the argument of some verb or preposition. However, common nouns have an additional expectation of being the first argument of a modifier with the feature [+delimiting], such as "another," "one," "a," or the plural suffix. Thus, we cannot say "I like dog" without treating "dog" as a mass noun. To treat it as a mass noun, we would have to think in terms of, say, "dog meat."

Clustering

The view of language processing that we have sketched out so far is well within the scope of the types of issues that can be dealt with by current connectionist models. Although many of these phenomena will require very large and complex models, there is little in what we have said so far that lies beyond the scope of connectionist processing. However, there is a fundamental issue which has been carefully concealed under the rug up to this point. This is the problem of the relation between polysemic processing and the formation of larger structural units. When the predicate "another" combines with the argument "beer," it forms a new structural unit which can then be further combined with additional predicates or which can be referred to anaphorically. We will refer to this new structural unit as a *cluster*. Clustering is the fundamental nonconnectionistic process that lies at the heart of the Competition Model approach to syntactic processing, as sketched out in MacWhinney (1987, 1989). Clustering takes an argument and a predicate, merges their semantic features, and outputs a new syntactic and semantic unit. Let us consider how clustering works to process a simple sentence, such as "the cat is on the mat." First, "cat" links with "the" to form a new cluster. Then "the cat" links with "is" to form a partially saturated verb. Then "on" links with "the mat" to form an adverbial phrase which then attaches to "is" and the processing is complete. The final clustered structure is:

$$((\text{the} \rightarrow \text{cat}) \leftarrow \text{sat} \rightarrow (\text{on} \rightarrow (\text{the} \rightarrow \text{mat}))).$$

This account of the processing of "the cat is on the mat" ignores any possible competitions for attachments and assumes that each lexical item assumes its default polysemic value. At various points in the left-to-right processing, there are often words that are not yet attached. The processor must be able to store these words temporarily. It must also be able to take the output of the polysemic processors and pass them on to new competitions. All that is really required here is the ability to keep track of lexical items and new clusters.

As a further example of how parsing works in the Competition Model, let us consider the processing of a sentence with a center-embedded relative clause such as "the dog the cat chased ate the bone." First, the unattached units "the dog" and "the cat" are built. The next item is "chased," which opens up argument roles for a subject and an object. The only real candidate for the subject role is "cat," which is in preverbal position and in the competition for this role. Then the processor encounters "ate," which opens up subject and object roles. There is no simple item in preverbal position, so "clustering" works to take all the material in preverbal position as a unit. To do this, "the dog" is taken as the head of a relative clause (RH) which places it in the role of the "described" and which inserts it as the object of "chase." Finally, the item "bone" receives support from the postverbal positioning cue and wins out with no competition for the role of object of the verb "ate."

The processor for the Competition Model takes the cue strengths estimated in these empirical studies and uses them to control role assignment. That processing can be handled connectionistically in the manner discussed earlier. In order for connectionist nets to handle syntax in a fully parallel fashion, they need to be able to deal with a large number of role competitions going on in parallel. For example, at the same time that "cat" is competing for the role of subject of "sit" there is also a competition for the role of the head of "on." Once the competition involving "on" settles down to a single noun, that cluster can then begin its attachment as an adjunct of the verb. These various decisions are cascaded so that, as soon as one competition is resolved, it then feeds into further higher clusterings. However, the principles governing the competitions remain the same.

If a given competition fails to yield up a reasonable clustering, then the whole process of sentence comprehension bogs down. The parser is driven by the attempt to instantiate the arguments of each predicate. A sentence parses successfully if all expectations are instantiated and no argument is left unattached. In a sentence such as "*John gave Bill the key Frank," the word "Frank" is extra material that does not attach to any other argument. In a sentence such as "*John put the plate," there is a missing argument, since it is not clear where John is putting the plate. Arguments need not always be instantiated immediately next to their predicates. The specific cues that the predicate is looking for are sometimes local, but they can also be for arguments that are distant, extraposed, or even anaphoric. In this regard, nonconfigurational languages like Warlpiri and variable word order languages like Hungarian receive a straightforward treatment in this type of processor, since the assignment of arguments to roles in these languages is primarily based on cues provided by grammatical markings, which are on an equal footing with word order cues within a connectionist network.

This system is designed to handle grammatical information as it enters the auditory buffer. In this sense, the system implements the principle of "immediacy of processing" espoused by Thibadeau, Just, and Carpenter (1982) and Marslen-Wilson and Tyler (1981). For example, each noun in a clause is a possible candidate for assignment to the role of subject. Cues serve to strengthen or weaken the candidacy of each noun for this role. For example, when parsing a sentence such as "the dogs are chasing the cat," the assignment of "dogs" as the subject is first promoted by its appearance as the initial noun. Then the fact that "are chasing" agrees with "dogs" in number further supports this assignment. Finally, when cat appears post-verbally, its candidacy as the object further supports the candidacy of "dogs" as the subject. Thus, at each point in the processing of the sentence, the strength of the candidacy of "dogs" is updated. The system tends to increase its "commitment" to a given attachment as cues supporting that attachment accumulate. To the degree that the language designs cues to permit ongoing updating, the need for backtracking is minimized. However, garden-pathing can occur when a competition between fragments is decided in the "wrong" way early on and the correct initial fragment can no longer be retrieved.

Conclusions

This paper has presented a mix of detailed findings from connectionist models of morphological processing with far more speculative claims about the design of a general connectionist system. Although connectionist accounts of language processing are extremely new, they offer a variety of advantages over earlier non-interactionist accounts. One major strength of connectionist approaches is the ability of networks to learn in a general way. The same basic mechanism of learning on error can be used to model the acquisition of declension in German or Hungarian, the development of lexical fields, and the learning of case role frames in English verbs of transfer. The other important property of connectionist networks is their ability to enforce mutual constraint satisfaction. In the area of sentence processing, this allows us to see how pushy polysemy interacts with attachment competition. Although current connectionist models require an external process to keep track of the identity of the competing lexical forms, it may be that future models will be able to express even control processes within a uniform connectionist architecture. From the viewpoint of the work we have reviewed in this book, what is most important about connectionism is the way in which it provides a powerful formal framework that correctly expresses the processing and learning claims of the Competition Model.

References

Ackerman, F. (1984). Verbal modifiers in Hungarian as argument-taking predicates: Complex verbs as predicate complexes in Hungarian. *Groninger Arbeiten zur germanistischen Linguistik*, 25:23–71.

Albert, M., & Obler, L. (1978). *The bilingual brain*. New York: Academic.

Ammon, M. S., & Slobin, D. I. (1979). A cross-linguistic study of the processing of causative sentences. *Cognition*, 7:3–17.

Amy, G., & Vion, N. (1976). Stratégies de traitement des phrases relatives: quelques considérations d'ordre génétique. *Bulletin de Psychologie*, Special issue on Semantic Memory:295–303.

Anderson, N. (1982). *Methods of information integration theory*. New York: Academic.

Anderson, R. (1984). *Second languages: a cross-linguistic perspective*. Rowley, MA: Newbury.

Angiolillo, C., & Goldin-Meadow, S. (1982). Experimental evidence for agent-patient categories in child language. *Journal of Child Language*, 9:627–43.

Ansell, B., & Flowers, C. (1982). Aphasic adults' use of heuristic and structural linguistic cues for analysis. *Brain and Language*, 16:61–72.

Antal, L. (1960). A magyar esetrendszer. *Nyelvtudományi ertekezések*, 16:1–146. Budapest: Akadémiai Kiadó.

Appel, J., Kertesz, A., & Fisman, M. (1982). A study of language functioning in Alzheimer patients. *Brain and Language*, 17:73–91.

Au, T. K. F. (1983). Chinese and English counterfactuals: The Sapir-Whorf hypothesis revisited. *Cognition*, 15:155–87.

Au, T. K. F. (1984). Counterfactuals: in reply to Alfred Bloom. *Cognition*, 17:289–302.

Badecker, W., & Caramazza, A. (1985). On considerations of method and theory governing the use of clinical categories in neurolinguistics and cognitive neuropsychology: the case against agrammatism. *Cognition*, 20:97–125.

Badry, F. (1982). The centrality of the root in Semitic lexical derivation. *Papers and Reports on Child Language Development*, 21:9–15.

Barkali, S. (1982). *The complete verb tables*. Jerusalem: Rubin Mass.

Bates, E. (1976). *Language and context: studies in the acquisition of pragmatics*. New York: Academic.

Bates, E. (1979). *The emergence of symbols*. New York: Academic.

Bates, E., Bretherton, I., & Snyder, L. (1988). *From first words to grammar: individual differences and dissociable mechanisms*. Cambridge, MA: Cambridge University Press.

Bates, E., Friederici, A., & Wulfeck, B. (1987a). Grammatical morphology in aphasia: evidence from three languages. *Cortex*, 23:545–574.

Bates, E., Friederici, A., & Wulfeck, B. (1987b). Sentence comprehension in aphasia: a cross-linguistic study. *Brain and Language*, 32:19–67.

Bates, E., Friederici, A., Wulfeck, B., & Juarez, L. (1988). On the preservation of word order in aphasia: cross-linguistic evidence. *Brain and Language*, 33:323–64.

Bates, E., Hamby, S., & Zurif, E. (1983). The effects of focal brain damage on pragmatic expression. *Canadian Journal of Psychology*, 37:59–84.

Bates, E., & MacWhinney, B. (1979). A functionalist approach to the acquisition of grammar. In Ochs, E. & Schieffelin, B. (eds.), *Developmental pragmatics*. New York: Academic.

Bates, E., & MacWhinney, B. (1981). Second language acquisition from a functionalist perspective: pragmatic, semantic and perceptual strategies. In Winitz, H. (ed.), *Annals of the New York Academy of Sciences conference on native and foreign language acquisition*. New York: New York Academy of Sciences.

Bates, E., & MacWhinney, B. (1982). Functionalist approaches to grammar. In Wanner, E., & Gleitman, L. (eds.), *Language acquisition: the state of the art*. New York: Cambridge University Press.

Bates, E., & MacWhinney, B. (1987). Competition, variation, and language learning. In MacWhinney, B. (ed.), *Mechanisms of language acquisition*. Hillsdale, NJ: Lawrence Erlbaum.

Bates, E., MacWhinney, B., Caselli, C., Devescovi, A., Natale, F., & Venza, V. (1984). A cross-linguistic study of the development of sentence interpretation strategies. *Child Development*, 55:341–54.

Bates, E., MacWhinney, B., & Smith, S. (1983). Pragmatics and syntax in psycholinguistic research. In Felix, S., & Wode, H. (eds.), *Child language at the crossroads*. Tübingen: Gunter Narr.

Bates, E., McDonald, J., & MacWhinney, B. (1986). A maximum likelihood procedure for the analysis of group and individual data in aphasia research. Paper presented at the Academy of Aphasia, Nashville, October, 1986.

Bates, E., McNew, S., MacWhinney, B., Devescovi, A., & Smith, S. (1982). Functional constraints on sentence processing: A cross-linguistic study. *Cognition*, 11:245–99.

Bates, E., & Wulfeck, B. (1989). Comparative aphasiology. *Aphasiology*, 3:111–42.

Bavin, E. (1989). Some lexical and morphological changes in Warlpiri. In Dorian, N. (ed.), *Investigating obsolescense: Studies in language contraction and death*. New York: Cambridge University Press.

Bavin, E. (to appear). The acquisition of Warlpiri. In Slobin, D. I. (ed.), *The corsslinguistic study of language acquisition, Volume 3*. Hillsdale, NJ: Erlbaum.

Bavin, E., & Shopen, T. (1985). Children's acquisition of Warlpiri: comprehension of transitive sentences. *Journal of Child Language*, 12:597–610.

Bavin, E., & Shopen, T. (1985b). Warlpiri children's development of narrative. *Berkeley Linguistics Society*, 11:1–13.

Bavin, E., & Shopen, T. (1987). Innovations and neutralizations in the Warlpiri pronominal system. *Journal of Linguistics*, 23:149–75.

Bayles, K. (1982). Language function in senile dementia. *Brain and Language*, 16:265–80.

Becker, A. (1984). Lokale Referenz in frühen Lernerstadien von italienischen Lernern des Deutschen. *Arbeitsbericht Arbeitsgruppe Heidelberg*, ESF-Project:62–77.

Behaghel, O. (1923–32). *Deutsche Syntax*. Heidelberg: Winter.

Behnstedt, P. (1973). *Formen und Strukturen des direkten Fragesatzes im Französischen*. Tübingen: Narr.

Beilin, H. (1975). *Studies in the cognitive basis of language development*. New York: Academic.

Berko-Gleason, J. (1958). The child's learning of English morphology. *Word*, 14:150–77.

Berlin, B., & Kay, P. (1969). *Basic color terms: their universality and evolution*. Berkeley: University of California Press.

Berman, R. (1978). *Modern Hebrew structure*. Tel Aviv: University Publishing Projects.

Berman, R. (1980). Child language as evidence for grammatical description: preschoolers' construal of transitivity in the verb system in Hebrew. *Linguistics*, 18:677–701.

Berman, R. (1982). Verb-pattern alternation: the interface of morphology, syntax, and semantics in Hebrew child language. *Journal of Child Language*, 9:169–92.

Berman, R. (1984). Cross-linguistic first language perspectives on second language acquisition research. In Anderson, R. (ed.), *Second languages: a cross-linguistic perspective*. Rowley, MA: Newbury.

Berman, R. (1985). The acquisition of Hebrew. In Slobin, D. I. (ed.), *The crosslinguistic study of language acquisition, Volume 1: the data*. Hillsdale, NJ: Erlbaum.

Berman, R., & Dromi, E. (1983). On marking time without aspect in child language. *Papers and Reports on Child Language Development*, 23.

Berman, R., & Sagai, Y. (1981). Word formation and innovation in young children. *Hebrew Computational Linguistics*, 18:32–62.

Berndt, R. S., & Caramazza, A. (1980). A redefinition of the syndrome of Broca's aphasia: implications for a neuropsychological model of language. *Applied Psycholinguistics*, 1:225–78.

Berwick, R. (1987). Parsability and learnability. In MacWhinney, B. (ed.), *Mechanisms of language acquisition*. Hillsdale, NJ: Erlbaum.

Berwick, R., & Weinberg, A. (1984). *The grammatical basis of linguistic performance*. Cambridge, MA: MIT Press.

Bever, T. (1970). The cognitive basis for linguistic structures. In Hayes, J. R. (ed.), *Cognition and the development of language*. New York: Wiley.

Bever, T. (1971). The nature of cerebral dominance in the speech behavior of the child and adult. In Huxley, T., & Ingram, E. (eds.), *Language acquisition: models and methods*. London: Academic.

Bickerton, D. (1984). The language bioprogram hypothesis. *The Behavioral and Brain Sciences*, 7:173–87.

Bierwisch, M. (1967). Some semantic universals of German. *Foundations of Language*, 3:1–36.

Black, M. (1980). Differential behavior of "function words" in agrammatic and normal production. Manuscript, Department of Linguistics, University College London, London, England.

Bloom, A. (1981). *The linguistic shaping of thought: a study in the impact of language on thinking in China and the West.* Hillsdale, NJ: Erlbaum.

Bloom, L. (1970). *Language development: form and function in emerging grammars.* Cambridge: MIT Press.

Bloom, L. (1974). Talking, understanding, and thinking. In Schiefelbusch, R., & Lloyd, L. (eds.), *Language perspectives: acquisition, retardation, and intervention.* Baltimore: University Park.

Bloom, L., Lightbown, P., & Hood, L. (1975). Structure and variation in child language. *Monographs for The Society for Research in Child Development*, 40.

Bloomfield, L. (1914). *An introduction to the study of language.* New York: Holt.

Blumenthal, A. L. (1970). *Language and psychology: historical aspects of psycholinguistics.* New York: Wiley.

Blumstein, S. (1973). Some phonological implications of aphasic speech. In Goodglass, H., & Blumstein, S. (eds.), *Psycholinguistics and aphasia.* Baltimore: Johns Hopkins University Press.

Bock, K. (1982). Toward a cognitive psychology of syntax: Information processing contributions to sentence processing. *Psychological Review*, 1–47.

Bock, K. (1986). Syntactic persistence in language production. *Cognitive Psychology*, 18:355–87.

Bolinger, D. (1986). *Intonation and its parts: melody in spoken English.* Stanford, CA: Stanford University Press.

Bolozky, S. (1978). Word formation strategies in the Hebrew verb system: denominative verbs. *Afroasiatic Linguistics*, 5:111–36.

Bolozky, S., & Saad, S. (1983). On active and non-active causativization verbs in Arabic and Hebrew. *Arabic Linguistics*, 10:71–80.

Bomans, G. (1947). *Kopstukken.* Amsterdam: Elsevier.

Borer, H. (1984). *Case studies in Semitic and Romance languages.* Dordrecht: Foris.

Bower, T. G. R. (1974). *Development in infancy.* San Francisco: Freeman.

Bowerman, M. (1973). Structural relationships in children's utterances: syntactic or semantic? In Moore, T. E. (ed.), *Cognitive development and the acquisition of language.* New York: Academic.

Bowerman, M. (1979). The acquisition of complex sentences. In Fletcher, P., & Garman, M. (eds.), *Language acquisition: studies in first language development.* New York: Cambridge University Press.

Bowerman, M. (1982). Reorganizational processes in lexical and syntactic development. In Wanner, E., & Gleitman, L. (eds.), *Language acquisition: the state of the art.* New York: Cambridge University Press.

Bowerman, M. (1983). How do children avoid constructing an overly general grammar in the absence of feedback about what is not a sentence? *Stanford Papers and Reports on Child Language Development*, 22:23–36.

Bowerman, M. (1985). What shapes children's grammars? In Slobin, D. (ed.), *The crosslinguistic study of language acquisition, Volume 2: theoretical issues*. Hillsdale, NJ: Erlbaum.

Bowerman, M. (1987). Commentary. In MacWhinney, B. (ed.), *Mechanisms of language acquisition*. Hillsdale, NJ: Erlbaum.

Bradley, D. C., Garrett, M. F., & Zurif, E. B. (1980). Syntactic deficits in Broca's aphasia. In Caplan, D. (ed.), *Biological studies of mental processes*. Cambridge, MA: MIT Press.

Bransford, J., Barclay, R., & Franks, J. (1972). Sentence memory: a constructive vs. interpretive approach. *Cognitive Psychology*, 3:193–209.

Bresnan, J. (1978). A realistic transformational grammar. In Halle, M., Bresnan, J., & Miller, G. (eds.), *Linguistic theory and psychological reality*. Cambridge, MA: MIT Press.

Bresnan, J. (ed.). (1982). *The mental representation of grammatical relations*. Cambridge, MA: The MIT Press.

Bresson, F. (1974). Remarks on genetic psycholinguistics: the acquisition of the article system in French. In *Current problems in psycholinguistics*. Paris: CNRS.

Bretherton, I., McNew, S., & Beeghly–Smith, M. (1981). Early person knowledge expressed in gestural and verbal communication: When do infants acquire a "theory of mind"? In Lamb, M., & Sherrod, L. (eds.), *Infant social cognition*. Hillsdale, NJ: Erlbaum.

Brian, C. R., & Goodenough, F. L. (1929). The relative potency of color and form perception at various ages. *Journal of Experimental Psychology*, 12:197–213.

Bronckart, J. P. (1983). La compréhension des structures à fonction casuelle. In Bronckart, J.-P., Kail, M., & Noizet, G. (eds.), *Psycholinguistique de l'enfant*. Paris: Delachaux et Niestlé.

Bronckart, J. P., Gennari, M., & de Weck, G. (1981). The comprehension of simple sentences: the representative perspective and the communication perspective. *International Journal of Psycholinguistics*, 8:5–29.

Bronckart, J. P., Kail, M., & Noizet, G. (1983). *Psycholinguistique de l'enfant*. Paris: Delachaux et Niestlé.

Brown, R. (1970). The first sentences of child and chimpanzee. In Brown, R. (ed.), *Selected papers by Roger Brown*. New York: Free Press.

Brown, R. (1973). *A first language: the early stages*. Cambridge, MA: Harvard University Press.

Brown, R., Cazden, C., & Bellugi, U. (1968). The child's grammar from I to III. In Hill, J. P. (ed.), *Minnesota symposia on child development*. Minneapolis: University of Minnesota Press.

Brunswik, E. (1956). *Perception and the representative design of psychology experiments*. Berkeley: University of California Press.

Budwig, N. (1989). The linguistic marking of agentivity and control in child language. *Journal of Child Language*, 16:251–262.

Burani, C., Salmaso, D., & Caramazza, A. (1984). Morphological structure and lexical access. *Visible Language*, 18:342–52.

Bybee, J. (1985). *Morphology: a study of the relation between meaning and form.* Amsterdam: John Benjamins.

Caplan, D. (1985). Syntactic and semantic structures in agrammatism. In Kean, M. L. (ed.), *Agrammatism.* New York: Academic.

Caramazza, A. (1986). On drawing inferences about the structure of normal cognitive systems from the analysis of patterns of impaired performance: the case for single-patient studies. *Brain and Cognition,* 5:41–66.

Caramazza, A., & Berndt, R. S. (1978). Semantic and syntactic processes in aphasia: a review of the literature. *Psychological Bulletin,* 85:898–918.

Caramazza, A., & Berndt, R. S. (1985). A multi-component deficit view of agrammatic Broca's aphasia. In Kean, M. L. (ed.), *Agrammatism.* New York: Academic.

Caramazza, A., Berndt, R. S., Basili, A. G., & Koller, J. J. (1981). Syntactic processing deficits in aphasia. *Cortex,* 17:333–48.

Caramazza, A., Brownell, H. H., & Berndt, R. (1978). Naming and conceptual deficits in aphasia. Paper presented at the Academy of Aphasia, Chicago.

Caramazza, A., & Zurif, E. B. (1976). Dissociation of algorithmic and heuristic processes in language comprehension: evidence from aphasia. *Brain and Language,* 3:572–82.

Carroll, M., & Dietrich, R. (1985). Observations on object reference in learner languages. *Linguistische Berichte,* 98:310–37.

Caselli, C., & Devescovi, A. (1989). The acquisition of cues to sentence meaning in Italian. Unpublished manuscript, CNR Rome.

Caselli, E., & Pizzuto, E. (1988). The development of grammatical morphology in Italian. Unpublished manuscript, CNR Rome.

Cedergren, H. J., & Sankoff, D. (1974). Performance as a statistical reflection of competence. *Language,* 50:333–55.

Chafe, W. (1970). *Meaning and the structure of language.* Chicago: University of Chicago Press.

Chafe, W. (1977). The recall and verbalization of past experience. In Cole, R. W. (ed.), *Current issues in linguistic theory.* Bloomington: Indiana University Press.

Chafe, W. (1981). *The pear stories.* Norwood, NJ: ABLEX.

Chandler, J. (1969). Subroutine STEPIT finds local minima of a smooth function of several parameters. *Behavioral Science,* 14:81–82.

Chapman, R. S., & Kohn, L. L. (1978). Comprehension strategies in two- and three-year-olds: animate agents or probable events? *Journal of Speech and Hearing Research,* 21:746–61.

Chapman, R. S., & Miller, J. F. (1975). Word order in early two- and three-word utterances: Does production precede comprehension? *Journal of Speech and Hearing Research,* 18:355–71.

Chien, Y., & Lust, B. (1985). The concepts of topic and subject in first language acquisition of Mandarin Chinese. *Child Development,* 56:1359–75.

Chomsky, N. (1957). *Syntactic structures.* The Hague: Mouton.

Chomsky, N. (1965). *Aspects of the theory of syntax.* Cambridge, MA: MIT Press.

Chomsky, N. (1975). *Reflections on language.* New York: Random House.

Chomsky, N. (1980). *Rules and representations.* New York: Columbia University Press.

Chomsky, N. (1982). *Lectures on government and binding.* New York: Foris.

Clancy, P. M. (1985). Acquisition of Japanese. In Slobin, D. I. (ed.), *The cross-linguistic study of language acquisition, Volume 1: the data.* Hillsdale, NJ: Erlbaum.

Clark, E. V. (1973). How children describe time and order. In Ferguson, C. A., & Slobin, D. I. (eds.), *Studies of child language development.* New York: Holt, Rinehart and Winston.

Clark, E. V. (1985). The acquisition of Romance with special reference to French. In Slobin, D. I. (ed.), *The crosslingusitic study of language acquisition, Volume 1: the data.* Hillsdale, N.J.: Erlbaum.

Clark, E. V., & Carpenter, K. L. (1989). The notion of source in language acquisition. *Language,* 65:1–30.

Clark, E. V., & Clark, H. H. (1979). When nouns surface as verbs. *Language,* 55:767–811.

Clark, H. H. (1965). Some structural properties of simple active and passive sentences. *Journal of Verbal Learning and Verbal Behavior,* 4:365–70.

Clark, H. H. (1966). The prediction of recall patterns in simple active sentences. *Journal of Verbal Learning and Verbal Behavior,* 5:99–106.

Clark, H. H (1973). Space, time, semantics, and the child. In Moore, T. E. (ed.), *Cognitive development and language acquisition.* New York: Academic.

Clark, H. H. (1978). Inferring what is meant. In Levelt, W., & Flores d'Arcais, G. (eds.), *Studies in the perception of language.* New York: Wiley.

Clark, H. H., Carpenter, P. A., & Just, M. A. (1973). On the meeting of semantics and perception. In Chase, W. G. (ed.), *Visual information processing.* New York: Academics Press.

Clark, H. H., & Clark, E. V. (1977). *Psychology and language: an introduction to psycholinguistics.* New York: Harcourt Brace Jovanovich.

Clark, H. H., & Haviland, S. E. (1977). Comprehension and the given-new contract. In Freedle, R.O. (ed.), *Discourse production and comprehension.* Norwood, NJ: Ablex.

Comrie, B. (1981). *Language universals and linguistic typology.* Oxford: Blackwell.

Cooper, W., & Ross, J. (1975). Word order. In Grossman, R., San, L., & Vance, T. (eds.), *Papers from the parasession on functionalism.* Chicago: Chicago Linguistic Society.

Corder, S.P. (1983). A role for the mother tongue. In Gass, S., & Selinker, L. (eds.), *Language transfer in language learning.* Rowley, MA: Newbury.

Crain, S., Shankweiler, D., & Tuller, B. (1984). Preservation of sensitivity of closed-class items in agrammatism. Presented at Academy of Aphasia 22nd Annual Meeting, Los Angeles.

Cromer, R. (1976). Developmental strategies for language. In Hamilton, V., & Vernon, M. (eds.), *The development of cognitive processes.* New York: Academic.

Cutler, A., Mehler, J., Norris, D., & Segui, J. (1986). The syllable's differing role in the segmentation of English and French. *Journal of Memory and Language,* 25:385–400.

Damasio, H. (1981). Cerebral localization of the aphasias. In Sarno, M. T. (ed.), *Acquired aphasia.* New York: Academic.

De Villiers, J. G., & De Villiers, P. A. (1974). Competence and performance in child language: Are children really competent to judge? *Journal of Child Language*, 1:11–22.

Delancey, S. (1980). *An interpretation of split ergativity and related patterns.* Bloomington: Indiana University Linguistics Club.

Dell, G. (1986). A spreading-activation theory of retrieval in sentence production. *Psychological Review*, 93:283–321.

Dewart, M. (1975). Children's preferences for animate and inanimate actor and object nouns. Unpublished manuscript, Medical Research Council, London, England.

Dezső, L. (1972). *Bevezetés a mondattani tipológiába.* Budapest: TIT Központja.

Dezső, L. (1982). *Studies in syntactic typology.* Budapest: Akadémiai Kiadó.

Dezső, L., & Szépe, Gy. (1974). Two problems of topic-comment. In Daneš, F. (ed.), *Papers on functional sentence perspective.* Prague: Academia.

Dietrich, R. (1984). Mit wenigen Wörtern. *Arbeitsbericht Arbeitsgruppe Heidelberg*, ESF-Project:78–99.

Dik, S. (1978). *Functional grammar.* Amsterdam: North Holland.

Dik, S. (1980). *Studies in functional grammar.* New York: Academic.

Downing, B. (1978). Relative clause structure. In Greenberg, J. (ed.), *Universals of human language, Vol 4: syntax.* Stanford University Press: Stanford, CA.

Driven, R., & Fried, V. (1987). *Functionalism in linguistics.* Amsterdam: Benjamins.

Dromi, E. (1979). More on the acquisition of locative prepositions: an analysis of Hebrew data. *Journal of Child Language*, 6:547–62.

Dromi, E., & Berman, R. (1986). Language-specific and language-general in developing syntax. *Journal of Child Language*, 13:371–87.

Dulay, H., & Burt, M. (1974). Natural sequences in child second language acquisition. *Language Learning*, 24:37–53.

Duranti, A., & Ochs, E. (1979). Left-dislocation in Italian conversation. In Givón, T. (ed.), *Discourse and syntax: syntax and semantics, volume 12.* New York: Academic.

É. Kiss, K. (1981a). Topic and focus: the basic operators of the Hungarian sentence. *Folia Linguistica*, 15:305–30.

É. Kiss, K. (1981b). Structural relations in Hungarian: a "free" word order language. *Linguistic Inquiry*, 12:185–213.

Elekfi, L. (1969). Kriterien der aktuellen Satzgliederung in ungarischen Kernsätzen. *Zeitschrift für Phonetik, Sprachwissenschaft und Kommunikationsforschung*, 22:335–51.

Eling, P. (1985). The production of morphologically complex words. Presented at the Royaumont Conference Center, Paris, France.

Elman, J. (1988). *Finding structure in time.* CRL Technical Reports, La Jolla: Center for Research on Language, University of California, San Diego.

Elman, J. L., & McClelland, J. L. (1984). Speech perception as a cognitive process: the interactive activation model. In Lass, N. (ed.), *Speech and language, vol. 10.* New York: Academic.

Emonds, J. (1975). A transformational analysis of French clitics without positive output constraints. *Linguistics Analysis*, 1:23–44.

Ertel, S. (1977). Where do subjects of sentences come from? In Rosenberg, S. (ed.), *Sentence production*. Hillsdale, NJ: Erlbaum.

Felix, S. (1984). Das Heranreifen der Universalgrammatik im Spracherwerb. *Linguistische Berichte*, 94:1–26.

Fernandez, O. (1985). Los clíticos como elementos intermedios entre la morfología y la sintaxis. Lecture at the University of Madrid.

Ferreiro, E., Othenin-Girard, C., Chipman, H., & Sinclair, H. (1976). How do children handle relative clauses? *Archives de Psychologie*, 44:229–66.

Fillmore, C. (1968). The case for case. In Bach, E., & Harms, R. (eds.), *Universals in linguistic theory*. New York: Holt, Rinehart and Winston.

Fillmore, C. (1977). The case for case reopened. In Cole, P., & Saddock, J. M. (eds.), *Grammatical relations*. New York: Academic.

Fillmore, C. (1987). *Fillmore's case grammer: a reader*. Heidlerberg: J. Groos.

Firbas, J. (1964). On defining the theme in functional sentence. *Travaux linguistiques de Prague*, 1:267–80.

Firbas, J. (1966). Non-thematic subjects in contemporary English. *Travaux linguistiques de Prague*, 2:239–256.

Firth, J. R. (1951). *Modes of meaning*. London. The English Association.

Fitzgerald, F. S. (1925). *The Great Gatsby*. New York: Scribner.

Flores d'Arcais, G. B. (1975). Some perceptual determinants of sentence construction. In Flores d'Arcais, G. B. (ed.), *Studies in perception*. Milan: Martello-Giunti.

Fodor, J. (1983). *Modularity of mind*. Cambridge, MA: MIT Press.

Fodor, J., & Pylyshyn, Z. (1988). Connectionism and cognitive architecture: a critical analysis. *Cognition*, 28:3–71.

Fodor, J. A., Bever, T. G., & Garrett, M. F. (1974). *The psychology of language*. New York: McGraw-Hill.

Foley, W., & Van Valin, R. (1984). *Functional syntax and universal grammar*. New York: Cambridge University Press.

Ford, M., Bresnan, J., & Kaplan, D. (1982). A competence-based theory of syntactic closure. In Bresnan, J., & Kaplan, R. (eds.), *The mental representation of grammatical relations*. Cambridge, MA: MIT Press.

Frankel, D. G., Amir, M., Frenkel, E., & Arbel, T. (1980). A developmental study of the role of word order in comprehending Hebrew. *Journal of Experimental Child Psychology*, 29:23–35.

Frankel, D. G., & Arbel, T. (1981). Developmental changes in assigning agent relations in Hebrew: the interaction between word order and structural cues. *Journal of Experimental Child Psychology*, 32:102–14.

Frankel, D. G., & Arbel, T. (1982). Probabilistic assignments of sentence relations on the basis of differentially weighted interpretive cues. *Journal of Psycholinguistic Research*, 11:447–64.

Fraser, C., Bellugi, U., & Brown, R. (1963). Control of grammar in imitation, comprehension and production. *Journal of Verbal Learning and Verbal Behavior*, 2:121–135.

Frazier, L. (1985). Syntactic complexity. In Dowty, D., Karttunen, L., & Zwicky, A. (eds.), *Natural language parsing*. New York: Cambridge University Press.

Frazier, L., Clifton, C., & Randall, J. (1983). Filling gaps: decision principles and structure in sentence comprehension. *Cognition*, 13:187–221.

Friederici, A. D. (in press). Autonomy and automaticity: accessing function words during sentence comprehension. In Denes, G., Semenza, C., Bisacchi, P., & Andreewsky, E. (eds.), *Perspectives in cognitive neuropsychology*. Hillsdale, NJ: Erlbaum.

Friederici, A. D., & Graetz, R. (1984). Processing passive sentences in aphasia: Deficits and strategies. Paper presented at the Seventh INS European Conference, Aachen, Federal Republic of Germany.

Friederici, A. D., & Schoenle, P. W. (1980). Computational dissociation of two vocabulary types: evidence from aphasia. *Neuropsychologia*, 18:11–20.

Friederici, A. D., Schoenle, P. W., & Goodglass, H. (1981). Mechanisms underlying writing and speech in aphasia. *Brain and Language*, 13:212–22.

Gaatone, D. (1976). Les pronoms conjoints dans la construction factive. *Revue de Linguistique Romane*, 40:165–182.

Gardner, H. (1983). *Frames of mind*. New York: Basic.

Garrett, M. (1980). Levels of processing in sentence production. In Butterworth, B. (ed.), *Language production, vol. 1, speech and talk*. New York/London: Academic.

Garrett, M. F. (1988). Processes in language production. In Newmeyer, F. J. (ed.), *Language: Psychological and biological aspects*. Cambridge: Cambridge University Press. Linguistics: The Cambridge Survey, Volume 3.

Gass, S. (1984). The empirical basis for the universal hypothesis in interlanguage studies. In Davies, A., Criper, C., & Howatt, A. (eds.), *Interlanguage*. Edinburgh: Edinburgh University Press.

Gass, S. (1987). The resolution of conflicts among competing systems: A bidirectional perspective. *Applied Psycholinguistics*, 8:329–50.

Gazdar, G., Klein, E., Pullum, G., & Sag, I. (1985). *Generalized phrase structure grammar*. Cambridge, MA: Harvard University Press.

Gee, J., & Savasir, I. (1985). On the use of will and gonna: toward a description of activity-types for child-language. *Discourse Processes*, 8:143–175.

Gergely, G. (1985). *Studies on the processing of Hungarian sentences*. Ph.D. thesis, Columbia University.

Giacobbe, J., & Cammarota, M.-A. (1986). Un modèle du rapport langue source/langue cible dans la construction du lexique. In Giaccomi, A., & Véronique, D. (eds.), *Acquisition d'une langue étrangère: Perspectives de recherche*. Aix-en-Provence: Presses Universitaires de Provence.

Gibson, E. J. (1969). *Principles of perceptual learning and development*. East Norwalk, CT: Appleton-Century-Crofts.

Gibson, J. J. (1966). *The senses considered as perceptual systems*. Boston: Houghton Mifflin.

Giuliani, V., Bates, E., O'Connell, B., & Pelliccia, M. (1987). Recognition memory for forms of reference: the effects of language and text type. *Discourse Processes*, 10:43–61.

Givón, T. (1979). *On understanding grammar*. New York: Academic.

Givón, T. (1984). *Syntax: a functional-typological introduction, Vol. 1*. Amsterdam: Benjamins.

Glanzer, M., & Ehrenreich, S. L. (1979). Structure and search of the internal lexicon. *Journal of Verbal Learning and Verbal Behavior*, 18:381–98.

Gleason, J. B., Goodglass, H., Green, E., Ackerman, N., & Hyde, M. R. (1975). The retrieval of syntax in Broca's aphasia. *Brain and Language*, 2:451–71.

Gleitman, L., & Wanner, E. (1982). Language acquisition: the state of the state of the art. In Wanner, E., & Gleitman, L. (eds.), *Language acquisition: the state of the art*. New York: Cambridge University Press.

Glushko, R. (1979). The organization and activation of orthographic knowledge in reading words aloud. *Journal of Experimental Psychology: Human Perception and Performance*, 5:674–91.

Goldin-Meadow, S. (1982). The resilience of recursion: a study of a communication system without a conventional language model. In Wanner, E., & Gleitman, L. (eds.), *Language acquisition: the state of the art*. New York: Cambridge University Press.

Goldman-Eisler, F. (1968). *Psycholinguistics: experiments in spontaneous speech*. New York: Academic.

Golinkoff, R., Hirsh-Pasek, K., Cauley, K, & Gordon, L. (1987). The eyes have it: lexical and syntactic comprehension in a new paradigm. *Journal of Child Language*, 14:23–46.

Goodglass, H. (1968). Studies on the grammar of aphasics. In Rosenberg, S., & Kaplin, J. (eds.), *Developments in applied psycholinguistics research*. New York: Macmillan.

Goodglass, H., Blumstein, S. E., Gleason, J. B., Hyde, M. R., Green, E., & Statlender, S. (1979). The effect of syntactic encoding on sentence comprehension in aphasia. *Brain and Language*, 7:201–9.

Goodglass, H., & Kaplan, E. (1983). *The assessment of aphasia and related disorders*. Philadelphia: Lea and Febiger.

Goodglass, H., & Menn, L. (1985). Is agrammatism a unitary phenomenon? In Kean, M. L. (ed.), *Agrammatism*. New York: Academic.

Gordon, B. (1983). Lexical access and lexical decision: mechanisms of frequency sensitivity. *Journal of Verbal Learning and Verbal Behavior*, 22:22–44.

Gordon, B., & Caramazza, A. (1982). Lexical decision for open- and closed-class words: failure to replicate differential frequency sensitivity. *Brain and Language*, 15:143–60.

Gould, S. (1983). *Hen's teeth and horse's toes*. New York: Norton.

Greenberg, J. H. (1974). *Language topology: a historical and analytic overview*. The Hague: Mouton.

Greenberg, J. H. (ed.). (1966). *Universals of language*. Cambridge, MA: MIT Press.

Grice, H. (1975). Logic and conversation. In Cole, P., & Morgan, J. L. (eds.), *Syntax and semantics: speech acts*. New York: Academic.

Grodzinsky, Y. (1982). Syntactic representations in agrammatism: Evidence from Hebrew. Paper presented at the Academy of Aphasia, Mohonk, NY.

Grosjean, F. (1980). Spoken word recognition processes and the gating paradigm. *Perception and Psychophysics*, 28:267–83.

Grosjean, F., & Itzler, J. (1984). Can semantic constraint reduce the role of word frequency during spoken-word recognition? *Bulletin of the Psychonomic Society*, 22:180–82.

Hakuta, K. (1982). Interaction between particles and word order in the comprehension and production of simple sentences in Japanese children. *Developmental Psychology*, 18:62–76.

Hale, K. (1973). Person marking in Warlpiri. In Anderson, A., & Kiparsky, P. (eds.), *A festschrift for Morris Halle*. New York: Cambridge University Press.

Hale, K. (1982). The essential features of Warlpiri main clauses. In Schwartz, S. (ed.), *Working papers of SIL-AAB*. Berrimah, N.T.: SIL-AAB.

Hale, K. (1983). Warlpiri and the grammar of non-configurational languages. *Natural Language and Linguistic Theory*, 1:5–47.

Halliday, M. (1966). Notes on transitivity and theme in English: part 1. *Journal of Linguistics*, 2:37–71.

Halliday, M. (1967). Notes on transitivity and theme in English: part 2. *Journal of Linguistics*, 3:177–274.

Halliday, M. (1968). Notes on transitivity and theme in English: part 3. *Journal of Linguistics*, 4:153–308.

Harrington, M. (1987). Processing transfer: language-specific strategies as a source of interlanguage variation. *Applied Psycholinguistics*, 8:351–78.

Harris, Z. S. (1951). *Structural linguistics*. Chicago: The University of Chicago Press.

Hawkins, J. A. (1980). Implication universals as predictors of word order change. *Language*, 55:618–48.

Hawkins, J. A. (1983). *Word order universals*. New York: Academic.

Heilman, K. M., & Scholes, R. J. (1976). The nature of comprehension errors in Broca's, conduction and Wernicke's aphasics. *Cortex*, 12:258–65.

Hermans, T. (1976). *Dagboek: Tussen mei en september*. Baarn: De Fontein.

Herskovits, A. (1986). *Language and spatial cognition*. New York: Cambridge.

Hirsh-Pasek, K., Kemler Nelson, D., Jusczyk, P., Cassidy, K., Druss, B., & Kennedy, L. (1987). Clauses are perceptual units for young infants. *Cognition*, 26:269–86.

Hoffmeister, R. (1978). The development of demonstrative pronouns, locatives, and personal pronouns in the acquisition of American Sign Language by deaf children of deaf parents. Ph.D. thesis, University of Minnesota.

Holland, A. L. (1985). Measuring aphasia treatment effects: case studies and group studies. Paper presented at Academy of Aphasia 23rd Annual Meeting, Los Angeles.

Hopper, P. J., & Thompson, S. A. (1980). Transitivity in grammar and discourse. *Language*, 56:251–99.

Hopper, P. J., & Thompson, S. A. (1984). The discourse basis for lexical categories in universal grammar. *Language*, 60:703–52.

Hornstein, N., & Lightfoot, D. (1981). *Explanations in linguistics: the logical problem of language acquisition.* London: Longmans.

Horvath, J. (1986). *Focus in the theory of grammar and the syntax of Hungarian.* Dordrecht: Foris Publications.

Huber, W., Poeck, K., Weniger, D., & Willmes, K. (1983). *Aachen Aphasia Battery.* Göttingen: Hogrefe.

Hull, C. (1943). *Principles of behavior.* East Norwalk, CT: Appleton-Century-Crofts.

Hupet, M., & Le Bouedec, B. (1975). Definiteness and voice in the interpretation of active and passive sentences. *Quarterly Journal of Experimental Psychology*, 27:323–30.

Hurtado, A. (1981). Le contrôle par les clitiques. *Revue Québecoise de Linguistique*, 11:9–67.

Hyams, N. (1986). *Language acquisition and the theory of parameters.* Dordrecht: Reidel.

Hyams, N. (1987). The setting of the null subject parameter: a reanalysis. Paper presented at the Boston University Child Language Forum.

Irving, J. (1982). *The Hotel New Hampshire.* New York: Pocket Books.

Jackendoff, R. (1983). *Semantics and cognition.* Cambridge, MA: MIT Press.

Jarovinskij, A. (1979). On the lexical competence of bilingual children. *International Journal of Psycholinguistics*, 15:43–57.

Jarvella, R., & Sinnott, J. (1972). Contextual constraints on noun distribution to some English verbs by children and adults. *Journal of Verbal Learning and Verbal Behavior*, 11:47–53.

Jespersen, O. (1924). *Philosophy of grammar.* London: Unwin.

Johnston, J., & Slobin, D. I. (1979). The development of locative expressions in English, Italian, Serbo-Croatian and Turkish. *Journal of Child Language*, 6:529–45.

Johnston, J. R. (1984). Acquisition of locative meanings: behind and in front of. *Journal of Child Language*, 11:407–22.

Kagan, J., & Lemkin, J. (1961). Form, color, and size in children's conceptual behavior. *Child Development*, 32:25–8.

Kahneman, D., Slovic, P., & Tversky, A. (eds.). (1982). *Judgment under uncertainty: Heuristics and biases.* Cambridge: Cambridge University Press.

Kail, M. (1975a). Etude génétique de la reproduction de phrases relatives: 1. reproduction immédiate. *L'Année psychologique*, 75:109–26.

Kail, M. (1975b). Etude génétique de la reproduction de phrases relatives: 2. reproduction différée. *L'Année psychologique*, 75:427–43.

Kail, M. (1983a). L'acquisition du langage repensée: les recherches interlangues. Partie I. Principales propositions théoriques. *L'Année psychologique*, 83:225–58.

Kail, M. (1983b). L'acquisition du langage repensée: les recherches interlangues. Partie II. Spécificités méthodologiques et recherches empiriques. *L'Année psychologique*, 83:561–96.

Kail, M. (1983c). Stratégie des fonctions parallelèles et coréférence des pronoms. In Bronckart, J. P., Kail, M., & Noizet, G. (eds.), *Psycholinguistique de l'enfant.* Paris: Delachaux et Niestlé.

Kail, M. (1986). Validité et coût des indices linguistiques dans la compréhension des phrases. *Bulletin de Psychologie, Special Issue on Judgment and Language*, 39:387–97.

Kail, M. (1987). The development of sentence interpretation strategies from a cross-linguistic perspective. In Pfaff, C. (ed.), *First and second language acquisition processes*. Rowley, MA: Newbury.

Kail, M., & Charvillat, A. (1985). Local and topological processing in sentence comprehension by French and Spanish children. Paper presented at ISSBD International Meeting in Tours.

Kail, M., & Charvillat, A. (1986). Linguistic cues in sentence processing in French from a cross-linguistic perspective. In Kurcz, I., Shugar, G. W., & Danks, J. H. (eds.), *Knowledge and language*. Amsterdam: North Holland.

Kail, M., & Charvillat, A. (1988). Local and topological processing in sentence comprehension by French and Spanish children. *Journal of Child Language*, 15:637–62.

Kail, M., & Segui, J. (1978). Developmental production of utterances from a series of lexemes. *Journal of Child Language*, 5:251–60.

Kail, M., & Weissenborn, J. (1984). A developmental cross-linguistic study of adversative connectives: French "mais" and German "aber/sondern." *Journal of Child Language*, 11:143–158.

Karmiloff-Smith, A. (1977). More about the same: children's understanding of post-articles. *Journal of Child Language*, 4:377–94.

Karmiloff-Smith, A. (1979). *A functional approach to child language: a study of determiners and reference*. New York: Cambridge University Press.

Karmiloff-Smith, A. (1981). The grammatical working of thematic structure in the development of language production. In Deutsch, W. (ed.), *The child's construction of language*. London: Academic.

Karmiloff-Smith, A. (1982). Language as a formal problem space. In Deutsch, W. (ed.), *Child language: beyond description*. New York: Springer-Verlag.

Karmiloff-Smith, A. (1984). Children's problem solving. In Lamb, M., Brown, A., & Rogoff, B. (eds.), *Advances in developmental psychology*. Hillsdale, NJ: Erlbaum.

Karmiloff-Smith, A. (1986). From meta-processes to conscious access: evidence from children's metalinguistic and repair data. *Cognition*, 23:95–147.

Karmiloff-Smith, A. & Planck, M. (1980). Psychological processes underlying pronominalization and non-pronominalization in children's connected discourse. In Kreiman, J., & Ojeda, A. (eds.), *Papers from the parasession on pronouns and anaphora*. Chicago: Chicago Linguistic Society.

Katz, L., Lukatela, G., & McCann, J. (1983). The autonomy of grammar and semantics. Paper delivered to the Psychonomic Society Meetings, San Diego.

Katz, N., Baker, E., & Macnamara, J. (1974). What's in a name? A study of how children learn common and proper names. *Child Development*, 45:469–73.

Kayne, R. (1972). Subject inversion in French interrogatives. In Casagrande, J., & Sacink, B. (eds.), *Generative studies in Romance languages*. Rowley, MA: Newbury.

Kean, M. L. (1979). Agrammatism: a phonological deficit? *Cognition*, 7:69–84.

Kean, M. L. (ed.). (1985). *Agrammatism*. New York: Academic.

Keenan, E. (1976). Towards a universal definition of "subject." In Li, C. (ed.), *Subject and topic*. New York: Academic.

Keenan, E., & Comrie, B. (1977). Noun phrase accessibility and universal grammar. *Linguistic Inquiry*, 1:63–99.

Keenan, E. L. (1978). Language variation and the logical structure of universal grammar. In Seiler, H. (ed.), *Language universals*. Tübingen: Narr.

Kempler, D. (1982). The relationship between linguistic and cognitive abilities: evidence from dementia. Unpublished doctoral dissertation, University of California, San Diego.

Kenesei, I. (1984). Word order in Hungarian complex sentences. *Linguistic Inquiry*, 15:328–42.

Keppel, G. (1982). *Design and analysis*. Englewood Cliffs, NJ: Prentice-Hall.

Keyser, S., & Roeper, T. (1984). On the middle and ergative constructions in English. *Linguistic Inquiry*, 15:381–416.

Kiefer, F. (1967). *On emphasis and word order in Hungarian*. Bloomington: Indiana University Press.

Kilborn, K. (1987). Sentence processing in a second language: seeking a performance definition of fluency. Ph.D. thesis, University of California, San Diego.

Kilborn, K., & Cooreman, A. (1987). Sentence interpretation strategies in adult Dutch-English bilinguals. *Applied Psycholinguistics*, 8:415–31.

Kintsch, W. (1974). *The representation of meaning in memory*. Hillsdale, NJ: Erlbaum.

Klein, W. (1983). Fünf Blicke in den Nebel. Unpublished manuscript, Nijmegen.

Klein, W. (1984). *Zweitspracherwerb*. Königstein: Athenäum. English translation: *Second language acquisition*. Cambridge: Cambridge University Press, 1986.

Klein, W., & Rieck, B. O. (1982). Der Erwerb der Personalpronomina im ungesteuerten Spracherwerb. In Klein, W., & Weissenborn, J. (eds.), *Zweitspracherwerb*. Göttingen: Vandenhoeck und Ruprecht.

Klein, W., & von Stechow, A. (1982). Intonation und Bedeutung von Fokus. *Arbeitspapier SFB 99 Linguistik*, 77.

Klein, W., & von Stutterheim, C. (1987). Quaestio und referentielle Bewegung in Erzählungen. *Linguistische Berichte*, 109:163–81.

Klima, E., & Bellugi, U. (1979). *The signs of language*. Cambridge, MA: Harvard University Press.

Kolk, H. (1985). Telegraphic speech and ellipsis. Presented at the Royaumont Conference Center, Paris, France.

Kolk, H., & van Grunsven, M. (1985). Agrammatism as a variable phenomenon. *Cognitive Neuropsychology*, 2:347–84.

Kolk, H., van Grunsven, M., & Guper, A. (1982). On parallelism in agrammatism: a case study. Unpublished manuscript.

Komlósy, A. (1985). Predicate complementation in Hungarian. In Kenesei, I. (ed.), *Approaches to Hungarian, Vol. 1*. Szeged: University of Szeged.

Köpcke, K.-M., & Zubin, D. (1981). Zur Frage der psychologischen Realität von genuszuweisenden Regeln zu den einsilbigen Nomen der deutschen Gegenwartssprache. Paper presented to the Linguistic Colloquium, University of Kiel, Federal Republic of Germany.

Köpcke, K.-M., & Zubin, D. (1983). Die kognitive Organisation der Genuszuweisung zu den einsilbigen Nomen der deutschen Gegenwartssprache. *Zeitschrift fur germanistische Linguistik,* 11:166–82.

Köpcke, K.-M., & Zubin, D. (1984). Sechs Prinzipien fur die Genuszuweisung im Deutschen: ein Beitrag zur natürlichen Klassifikation. *Linguistische Berichte,* 93:26–50.

Koster, J. (1975). Dutch as an SOV language. *Linguistic Analysis,* 1:111–36.

Krashen, S. (1978). Individual variation in the use of the Monitor. In Ritchie, W. (ed.), *Principles of second language learning.* New York: Academic.

Krashen, S. (1982). *Principles and practice in second language acquisition.* Elmsford, NY: Pergamon.

Kucera, H., & Francis, W. N. (1967). *Computational analysis of present-day American English.* Providence. RI: Brown University Press.

Kuno, S. (1973). *The structure of the Japanese language.* Cambridge, MA: MIT Press.

Kuno, S. (1986). *Functional syntax.* Chicago: University of Chicago Press.

Kutas, M., & Bates, E. (1988). Event-related potentials to grammatical and semantic anomalies in bilinguals. Unpublished manuscript, University of California, San Diego.

Kutas, M., & Hillyard, S. (1983). Event-related potentials to grammatical errors and semantic anomalies. *Memory and Cognition,* 11:539–50.

Labov, W. (1972). *Language in the inner city.* Philadelphia: University of Pennsylvania Press.

Labov, W. (1975). *What is a linguistic fact?* Ghent: Peter de Ridder.

Labov, W. (1986). Sources of inherent variation in the speech process. In Perkell, J., & Klatt, D. (eds.), *Invariance and variability in the speech process.* Hillsdale, NJ: Erlbaum.

Ladefoged, P. (1980). What are linguistic sounds made of? *Language,* 56:485–502.

Lakoff, G. (1987). *Women, fire, and dangerous things.* Chicago: University of Chicago Press.

Lakoff, G., & Johnson, M. (1980). *Metaphors we live by.* Chicago: University of Chicago Press.

Lancelot, C., & Arnault, A. (1969). *Grammaire générale et raisonnée.* Paris: Republications Paulet. Originally published in 1664.

Langacker, R. (1987). *Foundations of cognitive grammar.* Stanford, CA: Stanford University Press.

Lapointe, S. (1985). A theory of verb form use in the speech of agrammatic aphasics. *Brain and Language,* 24:100–55.

Laughren, M. (1977). Pronouns in Warlpiri and the category of number. Unpublished mss.

Lecours, A. R., & Lhermitte, F. (1969). Phonemic paraphasias: linguistic structures and tentative hypotheses. *Cortex,* 5:193–228.

Lederer, H., Schulz, D., & Griesbach, H. (1969). *Reference grammar of the German language.* New York: Scribner.

Lengyel, Zs. (1982). Az első és második (orosz) nyelv elsajátitásának alapvető pszicholingvinsztikai mechanizmusai. Ph.D. thesis, Szeged.

Lenneberg, E. H. (1967). *Biological foundations of language.* New York: Wiley.

Lesser, R. (1978). *Linguistic investigations of aphasia.* London: Arnold.

Levelt, W. J. M. (1981). The speaker's linearization problem. *Philological transactions of the Royal Society of London,* 295:305–15.

Levine, M. (1975). *A cognitive theory of learning.* Hillsdale, NJ: Erlbaum.

Levy, Y. (1983a). The acquisition of Hebrew plurals: the case of the missing gender category. *Journal of Child Language,* 10:107–21.

Levy, Y. (1983b). It's frogs all the way down. *Cognition,* 15:73–93.

Li, C. (ed.). (1975). *Word order and word order change.* Austin: University of Texas Press.

Li, C. (ed.). (1976). *Subject and topic.* New York: Academic.

Li, C. (ed.). (1977). *Mechanisms of syntactic change.* Austin: University of Texas Press.

Li, C. N., & Thompson, S. A. (1976). Subject and topic: a new typology for language. In Li, C. N. (ed.), *Subject and topic.* New York: Academic.

Lieberman, P. (1975). *On the origins of language: an introduction to the evolution of human speech.* New York: Macmillan.

Lightfoot, D. (1982). *The language lottery: toward a biology of grammars.* Cambridge, MA: MIT Press.

Linebarger, M., Schwartz, M., & Saffran, E. (1983). Sensitivity to grammatical structure in so-called agrammatic aphasics. *Cognition,* 13:361–92.

Loeb, D., & Leonard, L. (1988). Specific language impairment and parameter theory. *Clinical linguistics and phonetics,* 2:317–327.

Lotz, J. (1939). *Das Ungarische Sprachsystem.* Stockholm: Hungarian Institute.

Lust, B. (ed.). (1987). *Studies in the acquisition of anaphora: The data.* Amsterdam: Reidel.

MacDonald, M., & MacWhinney, B. (in preparation). Pronouns facilitate and inhibit nouns. Manuscript under review.

MacWhinney, B. (1975). Pragmatic patterns in child syntax. *Stanford Papers and Reports on Child Language Development,* 10:153–65.

MacWhinney, B. (1976). Hungarian research on the acquisition of morphology and syntax. *Journal of Child Language,* 3:397–410.

MacWhinney, B. (1977). Starting points. *Language,* 53:152–68.

MacWhinney, B. (1978). The acquisition of morphophonology. *Monographs of the Society for Research in Child Development,* 43:1.

MacWhinney, B. (1982). Basic syntactic processes. In Kuczaj, S. (ed.), *Language acquisition: vol. 1, syntax and semantics.* Hillsdale, NJ: Erlbaum.

MacWhinney, B. (1985). Hungarian language acquisition as an exemplification of a general model of grammatical development. In Slobin, D. I. (ed.), *The crosslingusitic study of language acquisition, Volume 2: theoretical issues.* Hillsdale, NJ: Erlbaum.

MacWhinney, B. (1987a). The Competition Model. In MacWhinney, B. (ed.), *Mechanisms of language acquisition.* Hillsdale, NJ: Erlbaum.

MacWhinney, B. (ed.). (1987b). *Mechanisms of language acquisition.* Hillsdale, NJ: Erlbaum.

MacWhinney, B. (1987c). Applying the competition model to bilingualism. *Applied Psycholinguistics*, 8:315–327.

MacWhinney, B. (1989a). Competition and lexical categorization. In Corrigan, R. (ed.), *Linguistic categorization.* Amsterdam: Benjamins.

MacWhinney, B. (1989b). The Competition Model and teachability. In Rice, M., & Schiefelbusch, R. (eds.), *The teachability of language.* Baltimore: Brookes-Cole.

MacWhinney, B., & Bates, E. (1978). Sentential devices for conveying givenness and newness: a cross-cultural developmental study. *Journal of Verbal Learning and Verbal Behavior*, 17:539–58.

MacWhinney, B., Bates, E., & Kliegl, R. (1984). Cue validity and sentence interpretation in English, German, and Italian. *Journal of Verbal Learning and Verbal Behavior*, 23:127–50.

MacWhinney, B., & Pléh, Cs. (1988). The processing of restrictive relative clauses in Hungarian. *Cognition*, 29:95–141.

MacWhinney, B., & Pléh, Cs. (in preparation). Real-time processing of competing grammatical cues: Agreement and case marking in Hungarian. Manuscript, Carnegie Mellon University.

MacWhinney, B., Pléh, Cs., & Bates, E. (1985). The development of sentence interpretation in Hungarian. *Cognitive Psychology*, 17:178–209.

MacWhinney, B., & Price, D. (1980). The development of the comprehension of topic-comment marking. In Ingram, D., Peng, C. C., & Dale, P. (eds.), *Proceedings of the First International Congress for the Study of Child Language.* Lanham, MD: University Press of America.

Mandler, G. (1980). Recognizing: the judgment of previous occurrence. *Psychological Review*, 87:252–71.

Mandler, G., Goodman, G., & Wilks-Gibbs, D. (1982). The word frequency paradox in recognition. *Memory and Cognition*, 10:33–42.

Maratsos, M. (1976). *The use of definite and indefinite reference in young children.* Cambridge: Cambridge University Press.

Maratsos, M. (1982). The child's construction of grammatical categories. In Wanner, E., & Gleitman, L. (eds.), *Language acquisition: the state of the art.* New York: Cambridge University Press.

Maratsos, M. (1988). The development of the English auxiliary. *Papers and Reports on Child Language Development*, 18.

Maratsos, M., & Chalkley, M. (1980). The internal language of children's syntax: The ontogenesis and representation of syntactic categories. In Nelson, K. (ed.), *Children's language: Volume 2.* New York: Gardner.

Marchman, V., Bates, E., Good, A., & Burkhardt, A. (1988). Functional constraints on the acquisition of the passive: toward a model of the competence to perform. Paper presented at the Annual Boston University Conference on Language Development. Boston, October 1988.

Marcus, M. (1980). *A theory of syntactic recognition for natural language.* Cambridge, Mass.: MIT Press.

Marr, D. (1982). *Vision: a computational investigation into the human representation and processing of visual information.* Cambridge MA: MIT Press.

Marslen-Wilson, W. (1975). Sentence perception as an interactive parallel process. *Science*, 189:226–7.

Marslen-Wilson, W. D. (1987). Functional parallelism in spoken word-recognition. *Cognition*, 25:71–102.

Marslen-Wilson, W. D., & Tyler, L. K. T. (1980). The temporal structure of spoken language understanding. *Cognition*, 8:1–71.

Massaro, D. (ed.). (1975). *Understanding language: An introduction-processing analysis of speech perception, reading, and psycholinguistics.* New York: Academic.

Massaro, D. (1987). *Speech perception by ear and eye.* Hillsdale, NJ: Erlbaum.

Massaro, D., & Oden, G. (1980). Evaluation and integration of acoustic features in speech perception. *Journal of the Acoustical Society*, 67:996–1013.

Massaro, D. W., & Cohen, M. M. (1983). Phonological context in speech perception. *Perception and Psychophysics*, 34:338–48.

Mathesius, V. (1939). O tak zvaném aktuálním cléneni véty. *Slovo a Slovesnost*, 5:171–4.

McClelland, J. (1979). On the time-relations of mental processes: an examination of systems of processes in cascade. *Psychological Review*, 86:287–330.

McClelland, J., & Kawamoto, A. (1986). Mechanisms of sentence processing: assigning role to constituents. In McClelland, J., & Rumelhart, D. (eds.), *Parallel distributed processing.* Cambridge, MA: MIT Press.

McClelland, J. L., & Rumelhart, D. E. (1981). An interactive activation model of context effects in letter perception. Part I. *Psychological Review*, 88:375–402.

McDonald, J. L. (1984). The mapping of semantic and syntactic processing cues by first and second language learners of English, Dutch, and German. Ph.D. thesis, Carnegie-Mellon University.

McDonald, J. L. (1986). The development of sentence comprehension strategies in English and Dutch. *Journal of Experimental Child Psychology*, 41:317–35.

McDonald, J. L. (1987a). Sentence interpretation in bilingual speakers of English and Dutch. *Applied Psycholinguistics*, 8:379–415.

McDonald, J. L. (1987b). Sentence interpretation processes: The influence of conflicting cues. *Journal of Memory and Language*, 26:100–17.

McDonald, J. L., & MacWhinney, B. (1987). Levels of learning: a microdevelopmental study of concept formation. Manuscript, Carnegie Mellon University.

Meier, R. (1987). Elicited imitation of verb agreement in American Sign Language: Iconically or morphologically determined? *Journal of Memory and Language*, 26:362–76.

Meisel, J. (1986). Word order and case marking in early child language. Evidence from simultaneous acquisition of two first languages: French and German. *Linguistics*, 24:123–85.

Miao, X. (1981). Word order and semantic strategies in Chinese sentence comprehension. *International Journal of Psycholinguistics*, 8:23–33.

Miceli, G., & Mazzucchi, A. (1985). The nature of speech production deficits in so-called agrammatic aphasia: evidence from two Italian patients. Paper prepared for the CLAS Project on Agrammatic Speech Production, directed by Lisa Menn and Harold Goodglass.

Miceli, G., Mazzucchi, A., Menn, L., & Goodglass, H. (1983). Contrasting cases of Italian agrammatic aphasia without comprehension disorder. *Brain and Language*, 19:65–97.

Milberg, W., Blumstein, S., & Dworetzky, B. (1988). Phonological processing and lexical access in aphasia. *Brain and Language*, 34:2.

Miller, G., & Johnson-Laird, P. (1976). *Language and perception*. Cambridge, MA: Harvard University Press.

Mills, A. E. (1986). *The acquisition of gender: a study of English and German*. Berlin: Springer-Verlag.

Minsky, M., & Papert, S. (1969). *Perceptrons*. Cambridge MA: MIT Press.

Moravcsik, E. (1978). On the marking of objects. In Greenberg, J. H. (ed.), *Universals of human language: Volume 4, syntax*. Stanford, CA: Stanford University Press.

Morgan, J., Meier, R., & Newport, E. (1987). Structural packaging in the input to language learning: contributions of prosodic and morphological marking of phrases to the acquisition of language. *Cognitive Psychology*, 19:498–550.

Morton, J. (1970). A functional model of human memory. In Norman, D. A. (ed.), *Models of human memory*. New York: Academic.

Naeser, M., Haas, G., Auerbach, S., Helm-Estabrooks, N., & Levine, H. (1984). Correlation between extent of lesion in Wernicke's area on CT scan and recovery of auditory language comprehension in Wernicke's aphasia. Paper presented at Academy of Aphasia 22nd Annual Meeting, Los Angeles.

Nespoulous, J. L., Dordain, M., Perron, C., Bub, D., Caplan, D., Mehler, J., & Lecours, A. R. (1984). Agrammatism in sentence production without comprehension deficits: Reduced availability of syntactic structures and/or of grammatical morphemes? A case study. Poster session presented at Academy of Aphasia 22nd Annual Meeting, Los Angeles.

Newell, A., & Simon, H. (1972). *Human problem solving*. Englewood Cliffs, NJ: Prentice-Hall.

Newmeyer, F. (1980). *Linguistic theory in America*. New York: Academic.

Newport, E., & Meier, R. (1985). Acquisition of American Sign Language. In Slobin, D. I. (ed.), *The crosslinguistic study of language acquisition, Volume 1: the data*. Hillsdale, NJ: Erlbaum.

Noizet, G. (1977). Les stratégies dans le traitement des phrases. *Cahiers de Psychologie*, 20:3–14.

Noizet, G., & Vion, M. (1983). Les stratégies de compréhension dans le traitement des relations fonctionnelles de base. In Bronckart, J. P., Kail, M., & Noizet, G. (eds.), *Psycholinguistique de l'enfant*. Paris: Delachaux et Niestlé.

Norman, D. (1981). Categorization of action slips. *Psychological Review*, 88:1–15.

Noyau, C. (1984). The development of means for temporality in French by adult Spanish speakers. In Extra, G., & Mittner, M. (eds.), *Studies in second language acquisition by adult immigrants*. Tilburg: Tilburg University Press.

Ochs, E. (1982). Ergativity and word order in Samoan child language. *Language*, 58:646–71.

Oden, G. K., & Massaro, D. W. (1978). Integration of featural information in speech perception. *Psychological Review*, 85:172–91.

Ornan, U. (1979). (In Hebrew) More on meaning: the Hebrew verb system. In *Shlomo Kodesh Jubilee Volume*. Jerusalem: Council on the Teaching of Hebrew.

Osgood, C., & Sebeok, T. A. (eds.). (1965). *Psycholinguistics: a survey of theory and research problems with a survey of psycholinguistic research, 1954–1964*. Bloomington, Indiana: Indiana University Press.

Osgood, C. E. (1971). Where do sentences come from? In Steinberg, D. D., & Jakobovits, L. A. (eds.), *Semantics: an interdisciplinary reader in philosophy, linguistics, and psychology*. Cambridge: Cambridge University Press.

Osgood, C. E. (1980). *Lectures on language performance*. New York: Springer-Verlag.

Osgood, C. E., & Bock, J. K. (1977). Salience and sentencing: some production principles. In Rosenberg, S. (ed.), *Sentence production: developments in research and theory*. Hillsdale, NJ: Erlbaum.

Osmán-Sági, J., & MacWhinney, B. (in preparation). Grammatical impairment in Hungarian.

Paivio, A. (1971). *Imagery and verbal processes*. New York: Holt, Rinehart, and Winston.

Paradis, M. (1987). *The assessment of bilingual aphasia*. Hillsdale, NJ: Erlbaum.

Peirce, C. (1932). *Language and context: collected papers*. Cambridge, MA: Harvard University Press.

Perdue, C. (1984a). A reply to Gass. In Davies, A., Criper, C., & Howatt, A. (eds.), *Interlanguage*. Edinburgh: Edinburgh University Press.

Perdue, C. (ed.). (1984b). *Second language acquisition by adult immigrants: a field manual*. Rowley, MA: Newbury.

Petitto, L. (1987). On the autonomy of language and gesture: evidence from the acquisition of personal pronouns in American Sign Language. *Cognition*, 27:1 52.

Piaget, J. (1970). *Structuralism*. New York: Basic. Originally published in 1958.

Piaget, J., Chomsky, N., & Piatelli-Palmarini, M. (1980). *Language and learning: the debate between Jean Piaget and Noam Chomsky*. Cambridge MA: Harvard University Press.

Pick, A. (1913). *Die agrammatischer Sprachstörungen*. Berlin: Springer-Verlag.

Pinker, S. (1981). On the acquisition of grammatical morphemes. *Journal of Child Language*, 8:477–84.

Pinker, S. (1982). A theory of the acquisition of lexical-interpretive grammars. In Bresnan, J. (ed.), *The mental representation of grammatical relations*. Cambridge, MA: MIT Press.

Pinker, S. (1984). *Language learnability and language development*. Cambridge, MA: Harvard University Press.

Pinker, S. (1987). The bootstrapping problem in language acquisition. In MacWhinney, B. (ed.), *Mechanisms of language acquisition*. Hillsdale, NJ: Erlbaum.

Pinker, S., & Prince, A. (1988). On language and connectionism: Analysis of a parallel distributed processing model of language acquisition. *Cognition*, 28:73–193.

Plas, R. (1981). Recent developments in French-language psycholinguistics. *French Language Psychology*, 2:125–43.

Pléh, Cs. (1981). The role of word order in the sentence interpretation of Hungarian children. *Folia Linguistica*, 15:331–43.

Pléh, Cs. (1982). Sentence interpretation strategies and dichotic asymmetries in Hungarian children between 3 and 6 years. In Sinz, R., & Rosenzweig, M. R. (eds.), *Psychophysiology 1980*. Amsterdam: Elsevier.

Pléh, Cs. (1983). Some semantic and pragmatic factors of anaphora interpretation in Hungarian. *Acta linguistica Academiae Scientiarum Hungaricae*, 33:201–11.

Pléh, Cs. (in preparation). Morphophonology and sentence understanding in Hungarian.

Pléh, Cs., Ackerman, F., & Komlósy, A. (1987). On the psycholinguistics of preverbal modifiers in Hungarian. *Folia Linguistica*, 21:5–27.

Pléh, Cs., Jarovinskij, A., & Balajan, A. (1987). Sentence comprehension in Hungarian-Russian bilingual and monolingual preschool children. *Journal of Child Language*, 14:587–603.

Pléh, Cs., & MacWhinney, B. (1985). Formai és szemantikai tényezők egyszerű magyar mondatok megértésében és a megértés fejlödésében. *Pszichológia*, 5:321–78.

Pléh, Cs., & MacWhinney, B. (1987). Formal and pragmatic factors of anaphora interpretation in Hungarian. *Acta Linguistica Academiae Scientiarum Hungariae*, 37.

Pléh, Cs., & Radics, K. (1978). Truncated sentence, pronominalization and the text. *Acta Linguistica Academiae Scientiarum Hungaricae*, 28:91–113.

Posner, M., & Keele, S. (1968). On the genesis of abstract ideas. *Journal of Experimental Psychology*, 77:353–63.

Pottier, B. (1968). L'emploi de la préposition "a" devant l'objet en Espagnol. *Bulletin de la Société Linguistique de Paris*, 53:83–95.

Pylyshyn, Z. (1978). What has language to do with perception? *Theoretical issues in natural language processing, 2*.

Pylyshyn, Z. (1984). *Computation and cognition: toward a foundation for cognitive science*. Cambridge, MA: MIT Press.

Réger, Z. (1978). Bilingual Gypsy children in Hungary: Explorations in 'natural' second language acquisition at an early age. *International Journal of Sociolinguistics*, 19:59–82.

Reis, M. (1982). Zum Subjektbegriff im Deutschen. In Abraham, W. (ed.), *Satzglieder im Deutschen*. Tübingen: Narr.

Rizzi, L. (1982). *Issues in Italian syntax*. New York: Foris.

Roeper, T. (1987). The acquisition of implicit arguments and the distinction between theory, process, and mechanism. In MacWhinney, B. (ed.), *Mechanisms of language acquisition*. Hillsdale, NJ: Erlbaum.

Roeper, T., & Williams, E. (1987). *Parameter setting*. Amsterdam: Reidel.

Rom, A., & Dgani, R. (1985). Acquiring case-marked pronouns in Hebrew. *Journal of Child Language*, 12:61–77.

Rosenblatt, F. (1959). Two theorems of statistical separability in the perceptron. In *Mechanisation of thought processes: proceedings of a symposium held at the National Physical Laboratory*. London: HM Stationery Office.

Rousseau, P., & Sankoff, D. (1978). Advances in variable rule methodology. In Sankoff, D. (ed.), *Linguistic variation: models and methods*. New York: Academic.

Rumelhart, D., Hinton, G., & Williams, R. (1986). Learning internal representations by error propagation. In Rumelhart, D., & McClelland, J. (eds.), *Parallel distributed processing: explorations in the microstructure of cognition*. Cambridge, MA: MIT Press.

Rumelhart, D., & McClelland, J. (1986). On learning the past tenses of English verbs. In McClelland, J. L., & Rumelhart, D. E. (eds.), *Parallel distributed processing: explorations in the microstructure of cognition*. Cambridge, MA: MIT Press.

Rumelhart, D., & McClelland, J. (1987). Learning the past tenses of English verbs: implicit rules or parallel distributed processes? In MacWhinney, B. (ed.), *Mechanisms of language acquisition*. Hillsdale, NJ: Erlbaum.

Rutherford, W. (ed.). (1984). *Language universals and second language acquisition*. Amsterdam: Benjamins.

Saffran, E. M., Schwartz, M. F., & Marin, O. S. M. (1980). The word order problem in agrammatism. II. Production. *Brain and Language*, 10:263–80.

Salasoo, A., & Pisoni, D. B. (1985). Interaction of knowledge sources in spoken word identification. *Journal of Memory and Language*, 24:210–31.

Sankoff, D. (ed.). (1978). *Linguistic variation: models and methods*. New York: Academic.

Sankoff, G. (1980). *The social life of language*. Philadelphia: University of Pennsylvania Press.

Sapir, E. (1921). *Language: An introduction to the study of speech*. New York: Harcourt Brace.

Schlesinger, I. M. (1974). Relational concepts underlying language. In Schiefelbusch, R. L., & Lloyd, L. I., (eds.), *Language perspectives – acquisition, retardation, and intervention*. Baltimore: University Park.

Schwartz, M., Marin, O., & Saffran, E. (1979). Dissociations of language function in dementia: a case study. *Brain and Language*, 7:277–306.

Schwartz, M., Saffran, E., & Marin, O. (1980). The word order problem in agrammatism. I. Comprehension. *Brain and Language*, 10:249–62.

Searle, J. R. (1970). *Speech acts: an essay in the philosophy of language*. Cambridge: Cambridge University Press.

Segui, J., & Chauvaut, N. (1974). Etude des stratégies de production d'énoncés à partir d'une suite de lexèmes. *L'Année psychologique*, 74:455–72.

Segui, J., & Kail, M. (1974). On the role of lexical features of verbs in sentence retention. In CNRS (ed.), *Current problems in psycholinguistics*. Paris: CNRS.

Seidenberg, M. S., & Tanenhaus, M. K. (1986). Modularity and lexical access. In Gopnik, I., & Gopnik, M. (eds.), *From models to modules*. Norwood, NJ: Ablex.

Selfridge, O. G. (1959). Pandemonium: A paradigm for learning. In *Symposium on the mechanization of thought processes*. London: HM Stationery Office.

Selinker, L. (1972). Interlanguage. *International Review of Applied Linguistics*, 10:209–31.

Selinker, L., Swain, M., & Dumas, G. (1975). The interlanguage hypothesis extended to children. *Language Learning*, 25:139–52.

Sheldon, A. (1974). On the role of parallel function in the acquisition of relative clauses in English. *Journal of Verbal Learning and Verbal Behavior*, 13:272–81.

Sheldon, A. (1978). The acquisition of relative clauses in French and English: implications for language learning universals. In Eckman, F. (ed.), *Current themes in linguistics, bilingualism, experimental linguistics, and language typologies*. New York: Wiley.

Silverstein, M. (1976a). Shifters, linguistic categories and cultural description. In Basso, K. H., & Selby, H. A. (eds.), *Meaning in anthropology*. Albuquerque: University of New Mexico Press.

Silverstein, M. (1976b). Hierarchy of features and ergativity. In Dixon, R. (ed.), *Grammatical categories in Australian languages*. Canberra: Australian Institute of Aboriginal Studies.

Sinclair, H., & Bronckart, J. (1972). SVO – a linguistic universal?: a study in developmental psycholinguistics. *Journal of Experimental Child Psychology*, 14:329–48.

Skinner, B. F. (1957). *Verbal behavior*. East Norwalk, CT: Appleton-Century-Crofts.

Slobin, D. I. (1963). Grammatical transformations in childhood and adulthood. Unpublished doctoral thesis, Harvard University.

Slobin, D. I. (1966). Grammatical transformations in childhood and adulthood. *Journal of Verbal Learning and Verbal Behavior*, 5:219–27.

Slobin, D. I. (1967). *A field manual for cross-cultural study of the acquisition of communicative competence*. Berkeley, CA: Language-Behavior Research Laboratory, University of California.

Slobin, D. I. (1968). Recall of full and truncated passive sentences in connected discourse. *Journal of Verbal Learning and Verbal Behavior*, 7:876–881.

Slobin, D. I. (1973). Cognitive prerequisites for the development of grammar. In Ferguson, C. A., & Slobin, D. I. (eds.), *Studies of child language development*. New York: Holt, Rinehart, and Winston.

Slobin, D. I. (1977). Language change in childhood and in history. In Macnamara, J. (ed.), *Language learning and thought*. New York: Academic.

Slobin, D. I. (1981). The origin of grammatical coding of events. In Deutsch, W. (ed.), *The child's construction of reality*. New York: Academic.

Slobin, D. I. (1982). Universal and particular in the acquisition of language. In Wanner, E., & Gleitman, L. R. (eds.), *Language acquisition: the state of the art*. New York: Cambridge University Press.

Slobin, D. I. (1985). Crosslinguistic evidence for the Language-Making Capacity. In Slobin, D. I. (ed.), *The crosslinguistic study of language acquisition, Volume 2: theoretical issues*. Hillsdale, NJ: Erlbaum.

Slobin, D. I., & Bever, T. G. (1982). Children use canonical sentence schemas: a cross-linguistic study of word order and inflections. *Cognition*, 12:229–65.

Small, S. (1980). Word expert parsing: a theory of distributed word-based natural language understanding. Ph.D. dissertation, Dept. of Computer Science, U. Maryland.

Small, S., Cottrell, G., & Tanenhaus, M. (eds.). (1989). *Lexical ambiguity resolution*. San Mateo: Morgan Kaufman.

Smith, S. (1985). Sentence interpretation in Serbo-Croatian children and adults. Unpublished manuscript, University of San Diego.

Smith, S., & Bates, E. (1987). Accessibility of case and gender contrasts for assignment of agent-object relations in Broca's aphasics and fluent anomics. *Brain and Language*, 30:8–32.

Smith, S., & Mimica, I. (1984). Agrammatism in a case-inflected language: comprehension of agent-object relations. *Brain and Language*, 13:274–90.

Sokolov, J. (1985). Free radicals not allowed: a lexicalist model of the acquisition of syntax. Unpublished Masters Thesis, Carnegie Mellon University.

Sokolov, J. L. (1988). Cue validity in Hebrew sentence comprehension. *Journal of Child Language*, 15:129–56.

Sperber, D., & Wilson, D. (1986). *Relevance: communication and cognition.* Cambridge, MA: Harvard University Press.

Sridhar, S. N. (1980). Cognitive determinants of linguistic structures: a cross-linguistic experimental study of sentence production. Ph.D. thesis, University of Illinois.

Sridhar, S. N. (1988). *Cognition and sentence production: a cross-linguistic study.* New York: Springer-Verlag.

St. John, M., & McClelland, J. (in press). Learning and applying contextual constraints in sentence comprehension. *Artificial Intelligence.*

Stemberger, J. (1985b). *The lexicon in a model of language production.* New York: Garland.

Stemberger, J., & MacWhinney, B. (1986). Frequency and the lexical storage of regularly inflected forms. *Memory and Cognition*, 14:17–26.

Stemberger, J. P. (1985a). Bound morpheme loss errors in normal and agrammatic speech: One mechanism or two? *Brain and Language*, 25:246–56.

Sternberg, S. (1966). High speed scanning in human memory. *Science*, 153:652–4.

Strohner, H., & Nelson, K. E. (1974). The young child's development of sentence comprehension: Influence of event probability, nonverbal context, syntactic form, and their strategies. *Child Development*, 45:567–76.

Swinney, D. (1979). Lexical access during sentence comprehension: (re) consideration of context effects. *Journal of Verbal Learning and Verbal Behavior*, 18:645–59.

Swinney, D., Zurif, E., & Nicol, J. (1989). The effects of focal brain damage on sentence processing: an examination of the neurological organization of a mental module. *Journal of Cognitive Neuroscience*, 1:25–37.

Swinney, D. A., & Taylor, O. L. (1971). Short-term memory recognition search in aphasics. *Journal of Speech and Hearing Research*, 14:578–88.

Szabolcsi, A. (1980). The possessive construction in Hungarian: a configurational category in a non-configurational language. *Acta Linguistica Academiae Scientiarum Hungaricae*, 31:261–89.

Taft, M. (1979). Recognition of affixed words and word frequency effects. *Memory and Cognition*, 7:263–72.

Taft, M., & Forster, K. (1975). Lexical storage and retrieval of prefixed words. *Journal of Verbal Learning and Verbal Behavior*, 14:630–47.

Talay, A., & Slobin, D. I. (in preparation). Grammatical impairment in Turkish.

Talmy, L. (1977). Rubber-sheet cognition in language. In Beach, W., Fox, S., & Philosoph, S. (eds.), *Papers from the thirteenth regional meeting.* Chicago: Chicago Linguistic Society.

Tanenhaus, M., Carlson, G., & Seidenberg, M. (1985). Do listeners compute linguistic representations? In Dowty, D., Kartunnen, L., & Zwicky, A. (eds.), *Natural language parsing.* New York: Cambridge University Press.

Tanenhaus, M., Leiman, J., & Seidenberg, M. (1979). Evidence for multiple stages in the processing of ambiguous words in syntactic contexts. *Journal of Verbal Learning and Verbal Behavior*, 18:427–40.

Tannen, D. (1986). *That's not what I meant!: How conversational style makes or breaks your relation with others.* New York: Morrow.

Tannenbaum, P., & Williams, F. (1968). Generation of active and passive sentences as a function of subject or object focus. *Journal of Verbal Learning and Verbal Behavior*, 7:246–50.

Taraban, R. M., McDonald, J. L., & MacWhinney, B. (in press). Category learning in a connectionist model: Learning to decline the German definite article. In Corrigan, R. (ed.), *Categorization.* Norwood, NJ: Ablex.

Thibadeau, R., Just, M., & Carpenter, P. (1982). A model of the time course and content of reading. *Cognitive Science*, 6:157–203.

Thompson, D. (1917). *On growth and form.* Cambridge: Cambridge University Press.

Tissot, R.J., Mounon, G., & Lhermitte, F. (1973). *L'agrammatisme.* Brussels: Dessart.

Tolman, E. (1922). A new formula for behaviorism. *Psychological Review*, 29:44–53.

Trévise, A. (1986). Quelques opérations de prédication et de thématisation dans l'interlangue d'une immigrante hispanophone en France. In Giaccomi, A., & Véronique, D. (eds.), *Acquisition d'une langue étrangère: perspectives de recherche.* Aix-en-Provence: Presses Universitaires de Provence.

Turner, E., & Rommetveit, R. (1967). The acquisition of sentence voice and reversibility. *Child Development*, 38:649–660.

Turner, E., & Rommetveit, R. (1967). Experimental manipulation of the production of active and passive voice in children. *Language and Speech*, 10:169–80.

Tyler, L. Spoken language comprehension in aphasia: A real-time processing perspective. Paper presented at Royaumont Conference Center, Paris, France.

Tyler, L., & Marlsen-Wilson, M. (1986). The effects of context on the recognition of polymorphic words. *Journal of Memory and Language*, 25:6:741–52.

Tzeng, O., & Chen, S. (in preparation). Grammatical impairment in Chinese.

Tzeng, O., & Hung, D. (1984). Psychological issues in reading Chinese characters. In Kao, H., & Hoosain, R. (eds.), *Neurological studies in processing Chinese languages.* Hong Kong: University of Hong Kong Press.

Vaid, J., & Chengappa, S. (1988). Assigning linguistic roles: sentence interpretation in normal and aphasic Kannada-English bilinguals. *Journal of Neurolinguistics*, 3:161–83.

Valian, V., & Coulson, C. (1988). Anchor points in language learning: the role of marker frequency. *Journal of Memory and Language*, 27:71–86.

Van Dijk, T., & Kintsch, W. (1983). *Strategies of discourse comprehension.* New York: Academic.

Van Petten, C., & Kutas, M. (1987). Ambiguous words in context: An event-related potential analysis of the time course of meaning activation. *Journal of Memory and Language*, 26:188–208.

Vennemann, T. (1974). Topics, subjects, and word order: from SXV to SVX via TVX. In Anderson, J. M., & Jones, C. (eds.), *Historical linguistics I: syntax, morphology, internal and comparative reconstruction.* Amsterdam: North Holland.

Véronique, D. (1985). Reference and discourse structure in the learning of French by adult Moroccans. Georgetown University.

Vion, M. (1980). La compréhension des phrases simples chez le jeune enfant. Une étude expérimentale. Ph.D. thesis, Université de Provence.

von Stechow, A. (1981). Topic, focus, and local reference. In Klein, W., & Levelt, W. (eds.), *Crossing the boundaries in linguistics*. Dordrecht: Reidel.

von Stockert, T. R., & Bader, L. (1976). Some relations of grammar and lexicon in aphasia. *Cortex*, 12:49–60.

von Stutterheim, C. (1986). *Temporalität in der Zweitsprache*. Berlin: De Gruyter.

Walden, Z. (1983). Children's construal of the root system in Hebrew. Ph.D. thesis, Harvard University.

Warren, R., & Warren, N. (1976). Dual semantic encoding of homographs and homophones embedded in context. *Memory and Cognition*, 4:586–92.

Warren, R. M., & Warren, R. P. (1970). Auditory illusions and confusions. *Scientific American*, 223:30–6.

Weissenborn, J., Kail, M., & Friederici, A. (in press). Language particular or language independent factors in acquisition? *First Language*, 10.

Weist, R. M. (1983). The word order myth. *Journal of Child Language*, 10:97–106.

Wenk, B., & Violand, F. (1982). Is French really syllable-timed? *Journal of Phonetics*, 10:193–216.

Whorf, B. (1967). *Language, thought, and reality*. Cambridge, MA: MIT Press. J. Carroll (ed.).

Wickelgren, W.A. (1969). Context-sensitive coding, associative memory, and serial order in (speech) behavior. *Psychological Review*, 76:1–15.

Wulfeck, B. (1987). Sensitivity to grammaticality in agrammatic aphasia: processing of word order and agreement violations. Ph.D. thesis, University of California, San Diego.

Wulfeck, B. (1988). Grammaticality judgments and sentence comprehension in agrammatic aphasia. *Journal of Speech and Hearing Research*, 31:72–81.

Wulfeck, B., Bates, E., MacWhinney, B., Opie, M., & Zurif, E. (in press). Pragmatics in aphasia: cross-linguistic evidence. *Language and Cognitive Processes*.

Wulfeck, B., Juarez, L., Bates, E., & Kilborn, K. (1986). Sentence interpretation in healthy and aphasic bilingual adults. In Vaid, J. (ed.), *Language processing in bilinguals: psycholinguistic and neuropsychological perspectives*. Hillsdale, NJ: Erlbaum.

Wundt, W. (1901). *Sprachgeschichte und Sprachpsychologie*. Leipzig: Engelmann.

Yehoshua, A. (1979). *Hama'ahev*. Tel Aviv: Schocken.

Zsilka, J. (1966). *A magyar mondatformák rendszere és az esetrendszer*. Budapest: Akadémiai Kiadó.

Zubin, D. A. (1977). The semantic basis of case alternation in German. In Fasold, R. W., & Shuy, R. W. (eds.), *Studies in language variation: semantics, syntax, phonology, pragmatics, social situations, ethnographic approaches*. Washington, D. C.: Georgetown University Press.

Zubin, D. A. (1979). Discourse function of morphology: the focus system in German. In Givón, T. (ed.), *Syntax and semantics: discourse and syntax*. New York: Academic.

Zubin, D. A., & Köpcke, K. M. (1981). Gender: a less than arbitrary grammatical category. In Hendrick, R., Masek, C., & Miller, M. F. (eds.), *Papers from the seventh regional meeting*. Chicago: Chicago Linguistic Society.

Zubin, D. A., & Köpcke, K. M. (1986). Gender and folk taxonomy: The indexical relation between grammatical and lexical categorization. In Craig, C. (ed.), *Noun classes and categorization*. Amsterdam: Benjamins.

Zurif, E. B., & Blumstein, S. E. (1978). Language and the brain. In Halle, M., Bresnan, J., & Miller, G. (eds.), *Linguistic theory and psychological reality*. Cambridge, MA: MIT Press.

Zurif, E. B., & Caramazza, A. (1976). Psycholinguistic structures in aphasia: studies in syntax and semantics. In Whitaker, H., & Whitaker, H. A. (eds.), *Studies in neurolinguistics, volume I*. New York: Academic.

Zurif, E. B., & Grodzinsky, Y. (1983). Sensitivity to grammatical structure in agrammatic aphasics: a reply to Linebarger, Schwartz, and Saffran. *Cognition*, 15:207–21.

Index

487